THE
LIFE AND
DEATH OF
DEMOCRACY

Also by John Keane

VIOLENCE AND DEMOCRACY

GLOBAL CIVIL SOCIETY?

WHATEVER HAPPENED TO DEMOCRACY?

VÁCLAV HAVEL: A POLITICAL TRAGEDY IN SIX ACTS

CIVIL SOCIETY: OLD IMAGES, NEW VISIONS

TOM PAINE: A POLITICAL LIFE

THE MEDIA AND DEMOCRACY

REFLECTIONS ON VIOLENCE

DEMOCRACY AND CIVIL SOCIETY

THE
LIFE AND
DEATH OF
DEMOCRACY

JOHN KEANE

W. W. NORTON & COMPANY

NEW YORK · LONDON

Copyright © 2009 by John Keane

First American Edition 2009

Excerpt from "Burnt Norton" in *Four Quartets* by T. S. Eliot © 1936 by
Harcourt, Inc. and renewed 1964 by T. S. Eliot, reprinted by permission of
Houghton Mifflin Harcourt Publishing Company. Excerpt from "Little Gidding"
in *Four Quartets* by T. S. Eliot © 1942 by T. S. Eliot and renewed 1970 by Esme
Valerie Eliot, reprinted by permission of Houghton Mifflin Harcourt Publishing
Company. Excerpts from T. S. Eliot, *The Complete Poems and Plays of T. S. Eliot*,
reproduced by kind permission of Houghton Mifflin Harcourt Publishing
Company / © T. S. Eliot Estate.

For information about permission to reproduce selections from this book,
write to Permissions, W. W. Norton & Company, Inc.,
500 Fifth Avenue, New York, NY 10110

For information about special discounts for bulk purchases, please contact
W. W. Norton Special Sales at specialsales@wwnorton.com or 800-233-4830

Manufacturing by RR Donnelley, Harrisonburg
Production manager: Julia Druskin

Library of Congress Cataloging-in-Publication Data

Keane, John, 1949–
The life and death of democracy / John Keane.—1st American ed.
p. cm.
Includes bibliographical references and index.
ISBN 978-0-393-05835-2 (hardcover)
1. Democracy—History. 2. World politics. I. Title.
JC421.K37 2009
321.8—dc22

2009010112

W. W. Norton & Company, Inc.
500 Fifth Avenue, New York, N.Y. 10110
www.wwnorton.com

W. W. Norton & Company Ltd.
Castle House, 75/76 Wells Street, London W1T 3QT

1 2 3 4 5 6 7 8 9 0

For Alice and George

CONTENTS

BAD MOONS, LITTLE DREAMS

Time present and time past
Are both perhaps present in time future
And time future contained in time past.

T. S. Eliot, 'Burnt Norton', *Four Quartets* (1936)

History is often said to be a catalogue of human sorrows, an unending story of bootlicking, a slaughterhouse of crimes. It is not always so. The mould of cruel servitude can be shattered, as happened 2600 years ago, when Greeks living on the south-eastern fringes of Europe laid claim to an invention that now ranks in historical importance with the wheel, the printing press, the steam engine and the cloning of stem cells. Born of resistance to tyranny, their claimed invention at first caused no great stir. Few spotted its novelty. Some condemned it for bringing chaos into the world. Nobody predicted its universal appeal. It seemed simply to be part of the great cycle of human affairs – yet one more example of power struggles among foes. The invention was soon to be seen differently. It was to magnetise millions and to arouse passions on a world scale, understandably so, since it required human beings to picture themselves afresh, to live as they had never before lived. The invention was a potent form of wishful thinking that is still with us today: the Greeks called it *dēmokratia*.

Wishful thinking – the longing to bend the present world into a different and better future – is often mocked, but the plain fact is that it is a regular feature of the human condition. Whenever we refer to the world around us in language, we habitually allude to things that are absent. We conjecture, we say things that miss the mark, or that express yearnings for things to be other than they are. We live by our illusions. The language through which we speak is an unending series of short little dreams, in the course of which we sometimes fashion new ways of saying things, using words that are remarkably apposite, and strangely inspiring to others. The feminine noun *dēmokratia* was one of those tiny terms that sprang from a little dream, with grand effect. It was to rouse many millions of people in all four corners of the world – and give them a hand in getting a grip on their world by changing it in ways so profound that they remain undervalued, or misunderstood. In contrast to things whose names immortalise their inventors – newtons, Hoovers, Rubik's Cubes for example – democracy has no known wordsmith. The roots of the family of terms that make up the language of democracy, and exactly where and when the word was first used, remain a mystery. Democracy carefully guards her secrets. Through the fog of the past only random clues appear, in the guise of wild-looking, ungroomed figures bearing suggestive names like Demonax of Mantinea, the bearded, robed, sandal-shod lawmaker who was summoned (around 550 BCE) by the women of the Oracle of Delphi to grant the people of Cyrene, a Greek-speaking farming town on the Libyan coast, the right to resist the tyranny of the limping, stuttering King Battus III, and the right to gather in their own assembly, to govern themselves, under their own laws.

Demonax may have been among the first public figures to describe himself as a friend of democracy, but we cannot be sure.[1] Not one of his writings or speeches or laws has survived. That makes him a fitting symbol of the way democracy carefully guards her own mysteries against those who think they know her every way. The subject of democracy is full of enigmas, confusions, things that are supposed to be true. It harbours not a few surprises, including the certainty – this book shows for the first time – that it was *not* a Greek invention. The belief that democracy is or could be a universal Western value, a gift of Europe to the world, dies hard. That is why one of the first matters to be straightened out in any present-minded history of democracy is what might be described as the Greek plagiarism of democracy. The claim put forward within most Greek plays, poems and philosophical tracts, that fifth century Athens wins the prize for creating both the idea and the practice of democracy, seemed plausible to contemporaries. It continues until this day to be repeated by most observers. But it is false.

The Life and Death of Democracy, the first attempt to write a life and times of democracy for well over a century, shows that the little word democracy is much older than classical Greek commentators made out. Its roots are in fact traceable to the Linear B script of the Mycenaean period, seven to ten centuries earlier, to the late Bronze Age civilisation (c. 1500–1200 BCE) that was centred on Mycenae and other urban settlements of the Peloponnese. It is unclear exactly how and when the Mycenaeans learned to use the two-syllable word *dāmos*, to refer to a group of powerless people who once held land in common, or three-syllable words like *damokoi*, meaning an official who acts on behalf of the *dāmos*. What is also unclear is whether these words, and the family of terms we use today when speaking about democracy, have origins further east, for instance in the ancient Sumerian references to the *dumu*, the 'inhabitants' or 'sons' or 'children' of a geographic place. But these uncertainties are tempered by another remarkable discovery by contemporary archaeologists: it turns out that the democratic practice of self-governing assemblies is also not a Greek innovation. The lamp of assembly-based democracy was first lit in the 'East', in lands that geographically correspond to contemporary Syria, Iraq and Iran. The custom of popular self-government was later transported eastwards, towards the Indian subcontinent, where sometime after 1500 BCE, in the early Vedic period, republics governed by assemblies became common. The custom also travelled westwards, first to Phoenician cities like Byblos and Sidon, then to Athens, where during the fifth century BCE it was claimed as something unique to the West, as a sign of its superiority over the 'barbarism' of the East.

Like gunpowder, print and other imports from afar, the arrival of popular assemblies and (later) the strange-sounding word *dēmokratia* in the region that today we call the West radically altered the course of history. It is even fair to say that it made history possible. For understood simply as people governing themselves, democracy implied something that continues to have a radical bite: it supposed that humans could invent and use institutions specially designed to allow them to decide for themselves, as equals, how they would live together on earth. The whole thing may seem rather straightforward to us, but think about it for a moment. The little dream that carried the big thought that mere mortals could organise themselves as equals into forums or assemblies, where they could pause to consider things, then decide on a course of action – democracy in this sense was a spine-tingling invention because it was in effect the first ever *human* form of government.

All government is of course 'human', in the simple sense that it is created, built up and operated by human beings. The exceptional thing about the type of government called democracy is that it demanded people see that nothing which is human is carved in stone, that everything is built on the shifting sands of time and place, and that therefore they would be wise to build and maintain ways of living together as equals, openly and flexibly. Democracy required that people see through talk of gods and nature and claims to privilege based on superiority of brain or blood. Democracy meant the denaturing of power. It implied that the most important political problem is how to prevent rule by the few, or by the rich or powerful who claim to be supermen. Democracy solved this old problem by standing up for a political order that ensured that the matter of who gets what, when and how should be permanently an open question. Democracy recognised that although people were not angels or gods or goddesses, they were at least good enough to prevent some humans from thinking they were. Democracy was to be government of the humble, by the humble, for the humble. It meant self-government among equals, the lawful rule of an assembly of people whose sovereign power to decide things was no longer to be given over to imaginary gods, the stentorian voices of tradition, to despots, to those in the know, or simply handed over to the everyday habit of laziness, unthinkingly allowing others to decide matters of importance.

Why should democracy in this sense still be of interest 2600 years later? Why bother writing or reading yet another history of the life and times of democracy? Such questions prompt a range of different answers, the first of which is the most straightforward. For those who relish the history of human inventions, *The Life and Death of Democracy* provides fresh details of the obscure origins of old institutions and ideals like government by public assembly, votes for women, the secret ballot, trial by jury, and parliamentary representation. Those curious about these and other institutions of what we now call democracy – political parties, compulsory voting, judicial review, referenda, electoral colleges, civil society and civil liberties such as press freedom – will find much to interest them here. So, too, will those with a sense of wonder about the changing, often hotly disputed meanings of democracy, or the origins of its key terms, or the best jokes at its expense, or the cacophony of conflicting reasons that have been given for why it is a good thing.

Every page of this book (and the brief thoughts on history and democracy at its end) tries to hammer home the point that forgetting, or remembering the wrong things, is dangerous for democracy, and that things that seem timeless are never so. Take one simple example that actually turns out to be rather complicated: the language of elections, whose vocabulary resembles a magpie's nest constructed from different terms with disparate origins. The word 'election' stems from the old Latin meaning 'to choose; to pick out (from among several possibilities)'. The group term for those who can so choose, the 'electorate', is much more recent; its first recorded usage dates only from 1879. Before then, the word that everybody used was 'electors'. Their general entitlement to vote is nowadays called the 'franchise', but that word (in thirteenth-century English) originally meant 'freedom, exemption from servitude or domination'. Talk of the franchise later came to refer to the legal immunity to prosecution, only then to evolve into several new meanings, including the act of granting a right or privilege, as when a sovereign monarch granted exemption from arrest, or an 'elective franchise' (the right to vote) or, as in today's use of the word, to describe a licence granted by a business to someone to sell or trade its products within a given area. Then there are words like 'voting', a term from Latin (*votum*) that first entered the English language during the sixteenth century to mean 'to wish, or to vow', then was transformed in Scotland around 1600 to mean what it means today: the act of expressing a choice in an election. The word 'poll' is also used to describe the act of casting a vote. In its old Dutch and Germanic origins (and in several surviving dialects) it meant 'head'. During the last years of the sixteenth century, a poll came to refer to the brand-new practice, during an election, of conducting an actual head count of supporters. The invention had its detractors: 'to poll' also meant to cut the hair or behead a person or animal. The poll was, however, designed to put an end to the old corrupt practice of elections being decided by those supporters who shouted loudest in favour of their own 'candidate'. That word in turn stems from the days of the Roman republic, where the Latin word *candidatus* meant 'clothed in white'. It referred to political men who tried to draw attention to themselves by dressing up in white togas as part of their bid to become members of the Senate.

It goes without saying that connotations of whiteness and purity are today not normally associated with candidates for election. Equally strange are the connotations of blackness of election words like 'ballot' – a word that comes to us from the Italian *ballotta*, the little ball that is secretly placed in an urn or box when voting, which was exactly the meaning that members of eighteenth-century gentlemen's clubs had in mind when they voted in secret to veto some proposal or other by placing a 'black ball' in a voting container, or 'ballot box'. 'Blackballing', meaning to reject or to vote against something or somebody, is an expression that we still sometimes associate with elections (as in the Citizens Alliance campaign against 'unfit' candidates in the National Assembly elections in Korea in 2000[2]), but the small example of black and white balls is telling of a much bigger point: that the families of terms that make up the languages through which people know and experience democracy today are not timeless. Whether in Japan, Nigeria, Canada or Ukraine, the languages of democracy are profoundly *historical*.

The Life and Death of Democracy tries to remind the reader that every turn of phrase, every custom and every institution of democracy as we know it is time-bound. Democracy is not the timeless fulfilment of our political destiny. It is not a way of doing politics that has always been with us, or that will be our companion for the rest of human history. This book sets out to raise awareness of the brittle contingency of democracy, at a time when there are signs of mounting disagreement about its meaning, its efficacy and its desirability. Of course, democracy commonly refers to a special type of political system in which the people or their representatives lawfully govern themselves, rather than being governed, say, by a military dictatorship, totalitarian party or monarch. In recent decades, democracy in this sense has enjoyed unprecedented popularity. Democracy has become one of those English words – along with computer and OK – familiar to millions of people around the world. Some pundits speak of a global victory for democracy, or claim that democracy is now a universal good. Yet what the word means, and whether and why democracy is to be preferred over its rivals, continues to be disputed. Opinions remain divided about whether existing democracies like the United States, Britain, India or Argentina live up to their democratic ideals. These ideals are also controversial. The most common disagreement, a dispute that this book tries to settle, is between the advocates of 'participatory' or 'direct' democracy, understood as the participation of all citizens in decisions that affect their lives, for instance by voting and accepting a majority verdict; and those who favour 'indirect' or 'representative' democracy, a method of governing in which people choose, through voting and the public expression of their opinions, representatives who then decide things on their behalf.

Assembly Democracy

The beginning of wisdom in such disputes is to see that democracy, like all other human inventions, has a history. Democratic values and institutions are never set in stone; even the meaning of democracy changes through time. This point is fundamental to *The Life and Death of Democracy*, which singles out three overlapping epochs in which democracy, considered both as a way of deciding things and as a whole way of life, has so far developed.

Its first historical phase saw the creation and diffusion of public assemblies. This period began around 2500 BCE, in the geographic area that is today commonly known as the Middle East. It stretched through classical Greece and Rome to include the world of early Islam before 950 CE; it came to an end with the spread of rural assemblies (called *tings*, *loegthingi* and *althingi*) to Iceland, the Faroe Islands and other offshore havens of what later came to be called Europe. Except for the bright moments associated with Scandinavia and classical Athens and republican Rome, this whole period is usually seen as a dark era of undemocratic degeneracy. 'With the fall of the [Roman] Republic,' says one respected commentator, typically, 'popular rule entirely disappeared in southern Europe. Except for the political systems of small, scattered tribes it vanished from the face of the earth for nearly a thousand years.'[3]

That perception, steeped in modern Western prejudice, is piteously false. The truth is that during the first phase of democracy the seeds of its basic institution – self-government through an assembly of equals – were scattered across many different soils and climes, ranging from the Indian subcontinent and the prosperous Phoenician empire to the western shores of provincial Europe. These popular assemblies took root, accompanied by various ancillary institutional rules and customs, like written constitutions, the payment of jurors and elected officials, the freedom to speak in public, voting machines, voting by lot and trial before elected or selected juries. There were efforts as well to stop bossy leaders in their tracks, using such methods as the mandatory election of kings, limited terms of office and – in an age as yet without political parties, or recall and impeachment procedures – the peaceful, if usually rowdy, ostracism of demagogues from the assembly, by majority vote.

Many of these procedures played a vital role in the famous city of Athens, where, through the course of the fifth century BCE, democracy came to mean the lawful rule of an assembly of adult male citizens. Women, slaves and foreigners were normally excluded. The rest gathered regularly, not far from the main public square, at a spot called the *pnyx*, for the purpose of discussing some matter or other, putting different opinions to the vote and deciding, often by a majority of raised hands, or by chunks of pottery or metal cast by hand into a pot, what was to be done. This first phase of democracy saw the earliest experiments in creating second chambers (called *damiorgoi* in some Greek citizen-states) and federated alliances or consortia of democratic governments coordinated through a joint assembly known as a *myrioi*, as happened among Greek-speaking Arcadians during the 360s BCE. This period also witnessed important efforts to create ways of being that would later be regarded as vital components of a democratic way of life. Many of these innovations happened in the Islamic world. They included a culture of printing and efforts to cultivate self-governing associations, such as endowment societies (called the *waqf*) and the mosque and, in the field of economic life, partnerships that were legally independent of rulers. Islam poured scorn on kingship, and triggered unending public disputes about the authority of rulers. Towards the end of this period, around 950 CE, its scholars even revived the old language of democracy. The world of early Islam emphasised as well the importance of shared virtues such as toleration and mutual respect among sceptics and believers in the sacred, and the duty of rulers to respect others' interpretations of life. During this phase Muslims' belief that human beings were bound to treat nature with compassionate regard, as if it was their equal, because both were divine creations, also surfaced. That imperative would later come to trouble all democracies.

Representative Democracy

From around the tenth century CE, democracy entered a second historical phase whose centre of gravity was the Atlantic region – the watery geographic triangle that stretched from the shores of Europe across to Baltimore and New York down to Caracas, Montevideo and Buenos Aires. This period opened with the military resistance to Islamic civilisation in the Iberian peninsula, which during the twelfth century CE triggered the invention of parliamentary assemblies. It ended on a sorry note, with the near-destruction worldwide of democratic institutions and ways of life by the storms of mechanised war, dictatorship and totalitarian rule that racked the first half of the twentieth century. In between, extraordinary things happened.

Shaped by forces as varied as the rebirth of towns, religious struggles within the Christian Church and revolutions in the Low Countries (1581), England (1644), Sweden (1720) and America

(1776), democracy came to be understood as *representative democracy*. This at least was the term that began to be used in France and England and the new American republic during the eighteenth century, for instance by constitution makers and influential political writers when referring to a new type of government with its roots in popular consent. Again, nobody knows who first spoke of 'representative democracy', though one political writer who broke new ground was a French nobleman who had been foreign minister under Louis XV, the Marquis d'Argenson. He was perhaps the first to tease out the new meaning of democracy as representation. 'False democracy soon collapses into anarchy', he wrote in a 1765 tract that reached the reading public posthumously. 'It is government of the multitude; such is a people in revolt, insolently scorning law and reason. Its tyrannical despotism is obvious from the violence of its movements and the uncertainty of its deliberations. In true democracy,' concluded d'Argenson, 'one acts through deputies, who are authorised by election; the mission of those elected by the people and the authority that such officials carry constitute the public power.'[4]

This was a brand-new way of thinking about democracy. It referred to a type of government in which people, acting as voters faced with a genuine choice between at least two alternatives, are free to elect others who then act in defence of their interests: that is, *represent* them by deciding matters on their behalf. Much ink and blood were to be spilled in defining what exactly representation meant, who was entitled to represent whom, and what had to be done when representatives snubbed those whom they were supposed to represent. But common to the second historical phase of democracy was the belief that good government was government by representatives. Thomas Paine's intriguing remark, 'Athens, by representation, would have surpassed her own democracy', provides a vital clue to the entirely novel case for representative democracy that was made forcefully by late eighteenth-century publicists, constitution makers and citizens. Often contrasted with monarchy, representative democracy was praised as a way of governing better by openly airing differences of opinion – not only among the represented themselves, but also between representatives and those whom they are supposed to represent. Representative government was praised as a way of freeing citizens from the fear of leaders to whom power is entrusted; the elected representative temporarily 'in office' was seen as a positive substitute for power personified in the body of unelected monarchs and tyrants. Representative government was hailed as an effective new method of apportioning blame for poor political performance – a new way of encouraging the rotation of leadership, guided by merit and humility. It was thought of as a new form of humble government, a way of creating space for dissenting political minorities and levelling competition for power, which in turn enabled elected representatives to test their political competence and leadership skills, in the presence of others equipped with the power to sack them. The earliest champions of representative democracy also offered a more pragmatic justification of representation. It was seen as the practical expression of a simple reality: that it wasn't feasible for all of the people to be involved all of the time, even if they were so inclined, in the business of government. Given that reality, the people must delegate the task of government to representatives who are chosen at regular elections. The job of these representatives is to monitor the spending of public money. Representatives make representations on behalf of their constituents to the government and its bureaucracy. Representatives debate issues and make laws. They decide who will govern and how – on behalf of the people.

As a way of naming and handling power, representative democracy was an unusual type of political system. It rested upon written constitutions, independent judiciaries and laws that guaranteed procedures that still play vital roles in the democracies of today: inventions like habeas corpus (prohibitions upon torture and imprisonment), periodic election of candidates to legislatures, limited-term holding of political offices, voting by secret ballot, referendum and recall, electoral colleges, competitive political parties, ombudsmen, civil society and civil liberties such as the right to assemble in public, and liberty of the press. Compared with the previous, assembly-based form, representative democracy greatly extended the geographic scale of institutions of self-government. As time passed, and despite its localised origins in towns, rural districts and large-scale imperial settings, representative democracy came to be housed mainly within territorial states protected by standing armies and equipped with powers to make and enforce laws and to extract taxes from their subject populations. These states were typically much bigger and more populous than the political units of ancient democracy. Most states of the Greek world of assembly democracy, Mantinea and Argos for instance, were no bigger than a few score square kilometres. Many modern representative democracies – including Canada (9.98 million square kilometres), the United States (9.63 million square kilometres), and the largest electoral constituency in the world, the vast rural division of Kalgoorlie in the federal state of Western Australia that comprises 82,000 voters scattered across an area of 2.3 million square kilometres – were incomparably larger.

The changes leading to the formation of representative democracy were neither inevitable nor politically uncontested. Representative democracy did not have to happen, but it did. It was born of numerous and different power conflicts, many of them bitterly fought in opposition to ruling groups, whether they were Church hierarchies, landowners, monarchs or imperial armies, often in the name of 'the people'. Exactly who 'the people' were was a vexed point that produced much mayhem. The age of representation witnessed not only a remarkable revival of the old language of democracy. The word itself was given new meanings that would have struck ancient observers either as oxymoronic or as plain nonsense. The second age of democracy saddled itself with new epithets. There was talk of 'aristocratic democracy' (that first happened in the Low Countries, at the end of the sixteenth century) and new references (beginning in the United States) to 'republican democracy'. Later came 'social democracy' and 'liberal democracy' and 'Christian democracy', even 'bourgeois democracy', 'workers' democracy' and 'socialist democracy'. These new terms corresponded to the many kinds of struggles by groups for equal access to governmental power that resulted, sometimes by design and sometimes by simple accident or unintended consequence, in institutions and ideals and ways of life that had no precedent. Written constitutions based on a formal separation of powers, periodic elections and competing parties and different electoral systems were new. So too was the invention of 'civil societies' founded on new social habits and customs – experiences as varied as dining in a public restaurant, playing sport or controlling one's temper by using polite language – and new associations that citizens used to keep an arm's length from government by using non-violent weapons like liberty of the printing press, publicly circulated petitions, and covenants and constitutional conventions called to draft new constitutions. Municipal government flourished in some quarters. A culture of citizenship rights and duties was born. Remarkably, this period also spawned – in the cooperative and workers' movements in the Atlantic region, for instance – the first talk of 'international democracy'.

The age of representation unleashed what the French writer and politician Alexis de Tocqueville famously called a 'great democratic revolution' in favour of political and social equality. Spreading from the Atlantic triangle, this revolution often suffered setbacks and reversals, especially in Europe, where it was mainly to collapse in the early decades of the twentieth century. The democratic revolution was fuelled by rowdy struggles and breathtaking acts, such as the public execution in England of King Charles I. Such events called into question the anti-democratic prejudices of those – the rich and powerful – who supposed that inequalities among people were 'natural'. New groups, like slaves, women and workers, won the franchise. The formal abolition of slavery marked off this period from the world of assembly democracy, which often rested on slavery. At least on paper, representation was eventually democratised, stretched to include all of the population, at least in those countries where it was attempted. But such stretching happened with great difficulty, and against great odds. Even then it was permanently on trial; in more than a few cases, the United States and Spanish American countries in the nineteenth and early twentieth centuries included, the definition of representation was actually narrowed by withdrawing the right to vote from certain groups, particularly black and poor and indigenous people. Not until the very end of this second phase – during the early decades of the twentieth century – did the right to vote for representatives come to be seen as a *universal* entitlement. That happened first for adult men and later – usually much later – for all adult women. But even then, as the experiences of totalitarianism and military dictatorship were to show, the opponents of democratic representation fought hard and with considerable success against its perceived inefficiencies, its fatal flaws and supposed evils. They demonstrated that democracy in any form was not inevitable – that it had no built-in historical guarantees.

Monitory Democracy

What is happening to democracy as we know and experience it today? Do the world's democracies have a rosy future? Are they suffering decline, or transformation into something that resembles 'post-democracy'? Does democracy remain a viable and desirable way of life? Or is it destined to join the dodo, the forests of Easter Island and our polar ice caps in the land of extinction?

What gives these questions such pique and prescience is the incompleteness of present-day democracies. They resemble an experiment whose final results have yet to be tabulated. When looking at where democracies around the world may be heading, *The Life and Death of Democracy* plays the role of time's advocate. It sets out to sharpen our sense that the history of democracy is still being made as the world's clocks tick, as each sunrise gives way to each new sunset. It does this by sketching, through the eyes of an imaginary historian writing fifty years from now, the ideas, characters, events and institutions that together have been powerfully shaping the fortunes of democracy for some decades. This story-telling technique involves looking back on our times from a point in a distant, fabled future. It calls on readers to imagine what a sober observer of our age will in future say about us. It is, of course, only one way of looking at present-day trends. But by making our own times feel a bit more distant from us, it offers the advantage of training our minds on things that we may not have seen. It challenges us to consider trends that may be genuinely new, or deeply threatening – and poorly understood, or wholly overlooked.

The technique of putting imaginary eyes in the back of our heads, so that we can look on our times half a century from now, prompts us to scrutinise differently the worldwide rebirth of democratic politics that took place immediately after World War Two. The grand renaissance was not the product of the 1974 carnation revolution in Portugal, or the 1989 velvet revolutions in central-eastern Europe, as is still commonly thought. It is a process much older than that, and it is by no means finished, even though it has already pushed democracy beyond familiar horizons, into unfamiliar territory. The most obvious development is that democracy has become a global force. For the first time in history, not only are the language and ideals and institutions of democracy becoming familiar to people living within most regions of the earth, regardless of their nationality, religion or civilisation. And not only is there new talk of 'global democracy', as well as references to democracy as a 'universal value' (to repeat the words of the Nobel prize-winning economist Amartya Sen). For the first time, racial and xenophobic prejudice has begun to be extracted from the ideals of democracy, such that many democrats around the world now find themselves embarrassed or angered by talk of 'backward', 'uncivilised' or 'naturally inferior' people – which is how they commonly talked well into the fateful decade of the 1930s.

The climate change in favour of democracy is certainly impressive. Since the end of World War Two, dictators everywhere have been battered by bad weather, the force of which can be measured by rereading the classic American novel *Democracy*, written in the late nineteenth century by Henry Adams. Its heroine, Madeleine Lee, finds herself fed up with the corrupting effects of power struggles, intrigues and general wheeling and dealing in Washington, DC. 'Democracy has shaken my nerves to pieces', she says, resigned, with a deep sigh. 'I want to go to Egypt.' Within the new era of democracy, under pressure from a great global democratic revolution, not even countries like Egypt are today safe havens for those afraid or sick of democracy. After devastating setbacks during the first half of the twentieth century – in 1941 there were only eleven democracies left on the face of the earth – democracy has bounced back from oblivion. It survived aerial bombing and threats of military invasion and economic and moral collapse in countries like Britain, the United States and New Zealand. Against amazing odds, it took root in India, where the world's first ever large-scale democracy was successfully created with the support of materially impoverished peoples of multiple faiths, many different languages and low rates of literacy. Democratic ideals and ways of life came to southern Africa and resurfaced in parts of Latin America and throughout central-eastern Europe. For the first time in its history, democracy became a global political language. Its dialects are now spoken on every continent, in countries as different as India, Egypt, Australia, Argentina and Kenya. Struggles for democracy have erupted in the least likely places. In the early years of the twenty-first century, there was a cedar revolution in Lebanon, a rose revolution in Georgia, an orange revolution in Ukraine. The spirits of democracy came alive in Japan and Mongolia, Taiwan and South Korea. They even stalked the halls and passageways of China, Burma and North Korea, and knocked loudly on their bolted doors.

The aggregate worldwide trends in favour of what loosely passes for democracy have been so striking that one influential report (produced by Freedom House) even speaks of the twentieth century as the Democratic Century. It points out that in 1900, monarchies and empires predominated. There were no states that allowed universal suffrage and multi-party elections; there were merely a few handfuls of 'restricted democracies', only twenty-five of them, accounting for just one-eighth of the world's population. By 1950, with the military defeat of Nazism, and with decolonisation and post-war reconstruction under way in Europe and Japan, there were twenty-two democracies. They were home to nearly a third of the world's population. By the end of the twentieth century, the report notes, 119 countries (out of a total of 192) could be described as 'electoral democracies', with eighty-five of them – 38 per cent of the world's inhabitants – enjoying forms of democracy 'respectful of basic human rights and the rule of law'. The report says that democracy is now within reach of the entire world. 'In a very real sense', runs the conclusion, 'the twentieth century has become the "Democratic Century".' It adds: 'A growing global human rights and democratic consciousness is reflected in the expansion of democratic practices and in the extension of the democratic franchise to all parts of the world and to all major civilizations and religions.'[5]

The conclusion of the report flirted with the art of seduction. It cleverly tapped the prevailing common-sense view that ordinary people, and not dictators supposing themselves to be extra-ordinary people, should rule; and by dressing up its definitions and concealing its methods, the report tried to prove that all the evidence now pointed to a global victory for representative democracy. *The Life and Death of Democracy* takes a radically different, more down-to-earth view of where democracy is heading. By putting things into a longer historical perspective, and by using different definitions and a more nuanced framework of interpretation, it proposes that present-day trends are quite different from, more contradictory and certainly much more interesting than has been supposed by far-fetched – and short-sighted – reports of the Freedom House kind.

So if glib exultations of its success are not in order, what is actually happening to democracy? It is true that during the past seventy years democracy, considered as both fact and ideal, has become more powerful and popular than at any moment since it began as a wishful thought in ancient Syria-Mesopotamia, Phoenicia and the cities of Mycenae and the Greek world. Contemporary democracies, led by the United States, have come to exert world power and world influence. The 'democracy club' (the alliance of democratic states first proposed by the former United States Secretary of State, Madeleine Albright[6]) has together put the name of democracy on the map, and on trial, in all four corners of the earth. The number of democratic states has more than doubled in a generation. During this third era of democracy, dictators, who seldom need pretexts, have everywhere dressed up in democratic clothes. Forced to bow to fashion, most of them – Hu Jintao, Vladimir Putin, Colonel Gaddafi and Lee Kuan Yew for instance – claimed to be democrats, all the while using the language of democracy to cover their tracks.[7] Meanwhile, following the collapse of communism, all the older democracies, including those like Germany that had once slipped into ruin, managed to keep out of trouble. That country in fact played an important role in the creation of the European Union, the world's leading experiment in regional integration, a new multi-layered political community that is itself committed, amidst much controversy among citizens and frequent confusion among policy makers about the appropriate rules and regulations, to the principle and practice of fashioning cross-border democratic structures, some of them without precedent in the history of democracy.

The European experiment with extending democracy across borders is a fitting symbol of another trend within the world of actually existing democracy. It is a most striking trend, in which the basic institutions and legitimating spirit of representative democracy have been undergoing major permutations for nearly a generation. In a striking departure from the normal way of seeing things, this book proposes that the era of representative democracy is passing away, that a new historical form of 'post-representative' democracy has been born, and is spreading throughout the world of democracy. One telling symptom of this historic change is the way democracy is nowadays defined and valued. Once seen as given by the grace of a deity, or by a God, or as founded on some other first principle, such as Man or History or Socialism or Truth – all detailed in the pages that follow – democracy is coming to be viewed much more pragmatically, as a handy and indispensable weapon for use against concentrations of unaccountable power, and their obnoxious effects. In the new era of democracy that is dawning, the word itself comes to have a new meaning: the public scrutiny and public control of decision makers, whether they operate in the field of state or interstate institutions, or within so-called non-governmental or civil society organisations, such as businesses, trade unions, sports associations and charities.

Other changes in the real world of democracy are happening as well. For some six decades now, assembly-based and representative mechanisms have been mixed and combined with new ways of publicly monitoring and controlling the exercise of power. In the new era of democracy, representative forms of government do not simply wither, or disappear. It is mistaken to think that they are heading for oblivion, for the old representative mechanisms that operate within the framework of territorial states often survive, and in some countries they even thrive, sometimes (as in Mongolia, Taiwan and South Africa) for the first time ever. There are also plenty of efforts to revitalise the standard institutions of representative government, for instance by fostering civic interest in the work of politicians, parties and parliaments, as has been attempted during the past two decades in the clean-up and public accountability and civic involvement schemes (known as *machizukuri*) in Japanese cities such as Yokohama and Kawasaki. But for a variety of reasons that are traceable to the devastating effects of World War Two, and that now include mounting public pressure to reduce corruption and foolish abuses of power, representative democracy is morphing into a type of democracy radically different to that our grandparents may have been lucky to know. For compelling reasons that will become apparent, *The Life and Death of Democracy* christens the emerging historical form of democracy with a strange-sounding name: 'monitory democracy'.

What is meant by 'monitory democracy'? Why the word 'monitory', with its connotations of warning of an impending danger, admonishing others to act in certain ways, or checking the content or quality of something? A vital clue in responding to these questions and understanding the changes that are under way is this fact: the years since 1945 have seen the invention of about a hundred different types of power-monitoring devices that never before existed within the world of democracy. These watchdog and guide-dog and barking-dog inventions are changing both the political geography and the political dynamics of many democracies, which no longer bear much resemblance to textbook models of representative democracy, which supposed that citizens' needs are best championed through elected parliamentary representatives chosen by political parties. From the perspective of this book, the emerging historical form of 'monitory' democracy is a 'post-Westminster' form of democracy in which power-monitoring and power-controlling devices have begun to extend sideways and downwards through the whole political order. They penetrate the corridors of government and occupy the nooks and crannies of civil society, and in so doing they greatly complicate, and sometimes wrong-foot, the lives of politicians, parties, legislatures and governments. These extra-parliamentary power-monitoring institutions include – to mention at random just a few – public integrity commissions, judicial activism, local courts, workplace tribunals, consensus conferences, parliaments for minorities, public interest litigation, citizens' juries, citizens' assemblies, independent public inquiries, think-tanks, experts' reports, participatory budgeting, vigils, 'blogging' and other novel forms of media scrutiny.

All these devices have the effect of potentially bringing greater humility to the established model of party-led representative government and politics. The same humbling effect is reinforced by the spread of monitory mechanisms underneath and beyond state borders. Forums, summits, regional parliaments and human rights watch organisations, as well as open methods of cross-border negotiation and coordination (OMCs) and peer review panels, of the kind practised respectively by the member states of the European Union and the Asia-Pacific Economic Cooperation, all begin to play a role in shaping and determining the agendas of government, at every level.

Experiments with spreading democracy through the institutions of civil society, into areas of life beneath and beyond the institutions of territorial states, are also much in evidence, so that organisations like the International Olympic Committee, whose membership is otherwise self-selecting, are governed by executive bodies that are subject to election by secret ballot, by a majority of votes cast, for limited terms of office. With the help of a new galaxy of communication media, including satellite television, mobile phones and the Internet, the public monitoring of international organisations of government is also growing. Bodies such as the World Trade Organization, the United Nations, and the Association of Southeast Asian Nations (ASEAN) find themselves under permanent or intermittent scrutiny by their own legal procedures, by outside bodies, and by public protests. In the age of monitory democracy, loud calls for 'global democracy' can be heard. And for the first time ever, there are even creative efforts to 'green' democracy. Time and money and energy are invested in building bio-monitoring institutions geared to the principle of public scrutiny of those who exercise power over our biosphere, which in effect is granted a virtual vote, a right to be represented in human affairs. There are growing numbers of examples of these experiments in 'democratising' our interactions with the world of nature, in whose affairs we act as if we are an outlaw species, with criminal tendencies. Independent monitoring bodies responsible for whole geographic regions and civic organisations sponsored by friends and protectors of the earth are cases in point. So, too, are newly established independent science and technology assessment bodies. An example is the Danish Board of Technology, a body rooted in much older Danish traditions of public enlightenment through networks of adult education (*folkeoplysnig*) but designed, in the new circumstances, to enable high-profile public consultation exercises, and to raise the level of parliamentary understanding of citizens' hopes and fears, in matters ranging from genetically modified food and stem cell research to nanotechnology and laboratory experimentation on animals.

Bad Moons

In contrast to those policy makers, activists and scholars who suppose that the fundamental choice facing contemporary democracies is that between accepting the terms of Westminster-style electoral democracy and the embrace of more participatory forms of 'deep' and 'direct' democracy – in effect, a choice between embracing the present or returning to the imagined spirit of Athenian democracy – *The Life and Death of Democracy* carves out a third possibility, one that has much contemporary history on its side, an option, the growth of 'monitory democracy', that needs to be recognised for what it is: a brand-new historical form of democracy. All the trends towards monitory democracy described later in this book illustrate the pertinent points: that what we mean by democracy changes through time; that democratic institutions and ways of thinking are never set in stone; and that exactly because they are the most power-sensitive polities ever known to humanity, democracies are capable of democratising themselves, for instance by inventing new ways of ensuring equal and open public access of citizens and their representatives to all sorts of institutions previously untouched by the hand of democracy.

Proof positive of the pertinence of these points is the unexpected coming of democracy to India. At a time when most democracies had been wiped from the face of the earth, the invention of democracy there proved that dictatorship and totalitarianism were not politically necessary, as many insisted at the time. Indian democracy shot other goats of prejudice. Awash with poverty of heartbreaking proportions, millions of Indian citizens rejected the view of their British masters that a country must first be deemed economically fit for democracy. They decided instead to become economically fit *through* democracy, so proving that the humble could inherit the earth, that the 'law' of the survival of the politically strongest and economically fittest was by no means absolute.

The change was of epochal importance. It extended the hand of democracy globally, to potentially billions of people who had one thing in common: they were not European. India defied the prevailing rule that democracy could take root only where there was a *dēmos* bound together by a common culture. India proved just the opposite. It showed that self-government was needed to protect a lively, loquacious society, one brimming with different languages and cultures, and therefore different definitions of the polity itself. The result was democracy with a real difference. The country soon invented and harnessed a wide range of new devices for publicly monitoring and checking the exercise of power. *Panchayat* self-government at the local level, the empowerment of women, the rise of regional anti-caste parties headed by iridescent figures like Mayawati, non-violent civil resistance (*satyagraha*) and compulsory quotas for minority groups are among the best known. Others include participatory budgeting, 'yellow card' reports, railway courts, student elections, fast-track courts known as *lok adalats*, water consultation schemes and public interest litigation.

It is hard to find a political language for speaking about the long-term significance of these inventions. Certainly Indian politics bears little resemblance to either textbook accounts of representative democracy or to the parliament-centred, Nehru-led Congress model of democracy, which after all supposed that citizens' needs were best championed through elected parliamentary representatives chosen by political parties. *The Life and Death of Democracy* shows that the sixty-year-old Asian democracy is not just the world's largest democracy – a convenient cliché – but also its most compound, turbulent and exciting prototype. Defined by various older and newer means of publicly monitoring and contesting power and representing citizens' interests, at all levels, it reinforces the conviction of this book that democracy can be improved by changing people's perceptions, and by humbling those who exercise power over others, and that the seeds of greater public accountability can be planted everywhere, from the bedroom and the boardroom to the battle-field.

But now it is time for the sceptic's question: how viable are all these different trends feeding the new age of monitory democracy? Can it survive either the mounting pressures on its institutions, or the efforts of its sceptics, critics and enemies to throw it into question, even to weaken or destroy outright its grip on the hearts and minds of many millions of people around the world?

The Life and Death of Democracy does not suppose that monitory democracy is leading us to paradise on earth. It pays attention to the way that trends in its favour are to a varying degree subject everywhere to counter-trends. It minces no words. It shows that democracy is nowadays plagued by market failures and social inequality. It is troubled by the visible decline of political party membership and, especially among young people and the disaffected poor, fluctuating turnout at elections and growing disrespect for 'politicians' and official 'politics', even boycotts and satirical campaigns against all parties and their candidates. Not for the first time in its history, but now with considerable venom, fun is understandably being poked into the face of democracy, as in this popular jibe from Japan: 'What's the best way to restore the public's faith in parties and governments?' asks a television chat-show presenter. 'The best way', answers a panellist, 'is first to let the political system collapse.' Whether and how democracies can adjust to the new world of campaign mega-advertising, organised lobbying, political 'spin' and corporate global media – the question of whether democracy might even disappear into the black holes of what in Italy and France are called 'videocracy' and 'telepopulism' – is proving equally challenging. Just as perplexing is the issue, felt strongly in countries as different as India, Taiwan and Indonesia, of whether and how democracies can come to terms with their own 'multicultural' foundations. The coming of an age of 'silver democracy', in which growing numbers of citizens live to ripe old ages in conditions of growing material and emotional insecurity, is likely to be just as daunting. Then there are the deep-seated trends that cut like knives into the bodies of democracies everywhere: trends for which there are no historical precedent and no easy solutions, like the rise of the United States, the world's first ever military empire that operates on a global scale and does what it does in the name of democracy, often in tension with Russia, China and the other authoritarian states that have no love or respect for democracy. Equally perilous trends include the spread of destructive uncivil wars; the step-by-step wrecking of this planet's biosphere; and the spread of new weapons systems with killing power many times greater than that of all democracies combined.

In paying careful attention to these difficulties within the current – unfinished – phase of democracy, this book tries to move beyond mere history, for the sake of history. It is no work of antiquarianism. It makes a spirited case for travelling backwards and forwards in time, for thinking differently about democracy, the better to grasp its past triumphs and failures, its current predicaments and its probable futures. The book supposes that democracy has no built-in historical guarantees; that its future is bound up with what has happened in the past, and with what is happening in the present; and that the history of democracy is therefore the business of everybody, not just of interest to antiquarians, or to professional historians. Among the big points developed within *The Life and Death of Democracy* is that the times are ripe for a comprehensive history, simply because democracies as we know them are sleepwalking their way into deep trouble. This book shows how democracies of the past have suffered and died under several bad moons. It shows as well that another bad moon is now rising over all democracies. Whether in the United States or Britain, Uruguay or Japan, democracies are confronted by problems for which there are no historical precedents, or current solutions. It follows from this approach that the continuation of democracy as a special way of life will require it to change – in response not only to new problems for which there are currently no solutions, but also to old irritants, like widening gaps between rich and poor, continuing discrimination against women, religious and nationalist intolerance, and political figures who give a bad name to democratic politics because they corrupt laws by helping themselves to greenbacks in brown envelopes.

The vexing thought that democracy as we now know it in all its geographic and historical variations might not survive indefinitely, that it could slit its own throat or quietly take its own life in an act of 'democide', even that it could be overpowered and killed off by outside forces that escape its attention, runs counter, of course, to much recent optimism about the global triumph of democracy. This book's strategy of challenging humbug is deliberately strident. For in weighing up the probable long-term effects of a wide range of deep-rooted problems, *The Life and Death of Democracy* gives voice to what growing numbers of people quietly think: that despite all the huffing and puffing, the so-called global triumph of democracy may well turn out to be a campfire on ice. The book explains why the great democratic renewal that first began in India now breeds worldwide anxieties about whether democracy itself can cope with its own problems, let alone its adversaries. In probing these anxieties, the book does not draw easy conclusions. It does not favour simple-minded partisanship. It most certainly stands on the side of democracy, with new arguments. But it is not apologetic for its illusions, follies and weaknesses. In supposing that the most obscure phase in the history of democracy is now, the book argues the need to rethink its fundamental features, including present-day trends and definitions of the term. With an even hand, and one eye constantly on the past, the book tries to expose the worrying lack of clarity about what democracy means today, and why, if they are lucky, future generations will enjoy its fruits and find it indispensable. The book also comes up with a new set of reasons for thinking that democracy is a superior method of government – a good way of life that in principle can be embraced and applied by our entire planet.

The whole approach owes a debt to the great nineteenth-century American poet and writer Walt Whitman. He famously noted that the history of democracy could not be written because democracy as he and others knew it was not yet properly built. Time proved him right. And so from the standpoint of the early twenty-first century, and the possible survival or destruction of a brand-new type of democracy, the same point can be put differently: we do not know what will become of monitory democracy because its fate has not yet been determined.

PART ONE

ASSEMBLY DEMOCRACY

Dēmokratia: a woman, crowning, shielding and sheltering old man Dēmos, the people. A detail from an Athenian law sculpted in marble, 336 BCE.

ATHENS

For by nature we all equally, both barbarians and Greeks, have an entirely similar origin: for it is fitting to fulfil the natural satisfactions which are necessary to all men: all have the ability to fulfil these in the same way, and in all this none of us is different either as barbarian or as Greek; for we all breathe into the air with mouth and nostrils . . .

From a fifth-century BCE papyrus fragment, On Truth, attributed to
Antiphon, Athenian orator and thinker

Where exactly did it begin?

Most people say: in the city of Athens, a long time ago.

That sounds convincing, as might be expected of a reply nourished by a founding myth with deep roots stretching back into the nineteenth century. Most people are today unaware of the legend, which tells how, once upon a time, in the tiny Mediterranean town of ancient Athens, a brand new way of governing was invented by its people. The glorious invention is said to have sprung from their bravery and genius, their good sense and willingness to fight. Calling it *dēmokratia*, by which they meant self-government among equals, the citizens of Athens celebrated its triumph in songs and seasonal feasts, in the dramas of stage and battlefield, in monthly assemblies and processions of proud citizens sporting garlands of flowers. So passionate were they about their democracy, the story goes, that the citizens of Athens defended it with all their might, even when knives rimmed their throats. And here the legend ends: it reaffirms how fortitude and genius earned Athens its reputation as the birthplace of democracy, as responsible for giving democracy wings, so setting it free to fly through doldrums and tempests, to deliver its gifts to posterity, to all four corners of the earth.

The founding myth is rarely stated so boldly, and it has a number of variants, certainly. But a striking thing about all of them, references to Athenian bravery and genius aside, is that they never much bother with how and why any of this happened in Athens. This has the effect of making things sound so straight-forward, which is a pity, because one trouble with the story of Athens as the glorious home of democracy is that it does not square with the messy realities from which its democracy actually sprang. Democracy was not the child of Athenian genius, military fortitude or simple good fortune. Its beginnings in that city rather illustrate an inconvenient truth: that except for a tiny handful of cases, democracy has never been built democratically. Historical records show that its invention does not happen overnight, and that it has causes and causers. It rarely springs from the clear-headed intentions and clean hands of people using democratic means. Accidents, good luck and unforeseen outcomes always play their part. It is usually bound up as well with farce, and with monkey business and violence. So it was 2600 years ago in the city of Athens, where democracy was born of a string of extraordinary events triggered by a botched murder.

Bloody Beginnings

The details are tricky, but put at their simplest they run something like this. During the middle years of the sixth century BCE, after several bungled attempts, a local Athenian aristocrat named Pisistratus seized power in Athens. Whether his tyranny was unjust remains disputed. There was the usual lavish consumption, cruelty against opponents, dishing-out of sinecures. Yet Pisistratus seems to have won local admiration for his efforts to improve communications by placing milestones between villages, and for his sponsorship of public building projects (including construction of the Acropolis, the Lyceum and temples in honour of Zeus and Apollo). Some people were impressed as well by his legal reforms, which included an instruction from Pisistratus himself that Athenian judges, for the sake of fairness, were to hold court in local settlements. As tyrannies went, the government of Pisistratus and his family was hardly comparable to the far more meddlesome and violent forms of modern dictatorship. So with hindsight the curious thing is that many Athenians found the concentration of government offices in the hands of one family exceptional – and utterly repugnant.

Why was this? Unlike other parts of the Greek-speaking world, Corinth for instance, Athenians had been spared tyranny, thanks in no small measure to their geographic and political isolation. They had kept to themselves. For long periods leading up to the invention of democracy, their city had resembled a frog sitting quietly on a rock overlooking its own pond. It had not needed to defend itself militarily or to submit or adapt to foreign rule. Athens had also refrained from joining the great rush of Greek cities to colonise the shores of the Mediterranean and the Black Sea from the middle of the eighth century; and in the next century, perhaps because an epidemic decimated its population around 700 BCE, Athens had wisely refused to get involved in the long and vicious war between the nearby cities of Eretria and Chalcis.

An attempt in the late seventh century to impose tyranny by Cylon, a former Olympic foot-race champion, was defeated by opponents who successfully mobilised the city's farmers against him. The victory was clever – Cylon fled for his life after being lured out of hiding with promises of his own safety – and the stunning success persuaded many local noble families that Athens was a city unusually blessed by its freedom from war and conquest. The nobility (called *aristoi*) and some of their subjects became convinced that theirs was a city where tyranny – rule by just one family or by one or two of its members – simply did not belong. That impression was bolstered by the vigorous reforms of a local leader named Solon, a noble who was born around 630 BCE. In a well-known poem, he likened human affairs to the sea and spoke of the calming effects of the effort to restore 'good order': 'It smooths what is rough, assuages the urge to overindulge, and cuts down presumption.'[1] He thought conservatively, in terms of returning Athens to an order that had been disturbed, for instance by Cylon's attempts to impose tyranny. On this basis, Solon freed mortgaged farms by decreeing the cancellation of all debts; declared an amnesty for all those Athenians who had fled to other parts of Greece to avoid those debts, or who had been sold illegally into slavery; established an elite legislative body called the Council of Four Hundred, so called because it comprised four hundred citizens drawn from the wealthier classes; introduced laws covering matters ranging from the placing of limits upon the purchase of land and lavish spending on funerals to widening the right to bring criminal charges before a citizens' jury in the courts; and required all Athenians to swear obedience to the laws.

The new regulations provoked stiff opposition among parts of the landowning class, but for a time even they could see the folly of attempting to foist a tyranny on to a polity the size of Attica, in which the town of Athens was located. Geographically speaking, Attica was among the largest polities of the Greek world. Protected by virtually impassable mountain ranges in the north and west and measuring some 2500 square kilometres (the size of modern-day Luxembourg), its edges could be reached from Athens only after a long summer day's journey on foot or by donkey. Such distances were unusual by ancient Greek standards; most other states in the region were traversable within a few hours. Size mattered in the Athenian case, and it did so by restraining the enthusiasm of the local aristocracy for concentrated political power, whose effectiveness they knew minimally demanded careful coordination across both time and space. Pressured by Solon's reforms, the wealthy families of Athens thus kept to themselves and their banquets, their love affairs, their sporting and hunting events – so bolstering the reputation of Athens as a safe haven for those who disliked the pestilence, war and rotten government caused by tyranny.

These certainties were jolted by the power grab by Pisistratus. His first stab at tyranny happened around 561 BCE (when he cleverly pretended to be under attack and called on his bodyguards to defend him in the city of Athens); he made two subsequent power grabs during the following two decades. The three coups, which had the backing of parts of the poor rural population, did more than wreck the reputation of Athens as a tyrant-free zone. When Pisistratus fell ill, and died of natural causes in 528/527 BCE, the regime controlled by his family faced a succession crisis. Like a delirious wild animal, it scratched and clawed itself to shreds. Ugly rivalries erupted between the sons who had inherited his power. Hipparchus and Hippias were their names, but their younger step-brother, Thessalus, was equally up to his ears in political mud. Contemporaries disagreed about the respective merits of these three inexperienced young aristocrats, who dressed in fine robes and wore their hair long and fastened with cicada-shaped golden pins; exactly who was causing trouble and who wanted what, when and how, remained unclear. The confusion confirmed the local belief that the foulest thing about tyranny was its vulnerability to murderous infighting. The people of Athens trembled, fearing the worst. But then, in the year 514 BCE, the revenge of the unexpected struck, with stupendous effect. Like an eagle, freedom swooped to earth, to inflict an unpleasant surprise on the courtly nest of feuding tyrants.

The tipping point had more than a touch of the absurd about it; at first, many contemporaries simply could not believe what had happened. During the Panathenaic festival, the spectacular carnival held once every four years in honour of the city's goddess Athena, one of the tyrants, Hipparchus, fell foul of a murder plot organised by disaffected young aristocrats. Fusing speed and secrecy, his assassins pounced. Wielding daggers concealed beneath their robes, they lunged at his heart, killing him instantly, in broad daylight, right in the main square of Athens. Their daring left bystanders voiceless; so, too, did its fickle effects. For, although the killers had been well acquainted with the tyrannical brothers, they bungled their murderous deed. They had evidently been after Hippias, in revenge (so they had thought) for his spiteful refusal to allow the sister of one of the assassins a place in the procession. But it transpired that the real culprit in the shadows was the young step-brother, Thessalus. His secret homoerotic crush on one of the assassins had recently met with rejection. That was why he had tried to extract revenge by ordering the girl's disqualification (and consequent public shaming) from the city's most important public festival.

Jilted homosexual desire was thus a conspirator in the plot, which backfired in yet another way, this time with historic consequences. While the assassins waited to pounce on the hated

Hippias, they panicked after spotting him from a distance, chatting with an accomplice. Fearing that their plot had been exposed, they lunged nervously with their daggers at Hipparchus, who was standing nearby. Better one dead tyrant than none at all, so they thought. Several contemporaries judged the botched assassination to be a personal vendetta for a multiple lovers' quarrel – the murdered tyrant was himself said to be in love with one of the assassins, who themselves were lovers – but whether or not the killing was part of a homosexual love quadrangle was soon of no consequence. The surviving tyrant Hippias, fearing that he would meet the cruel fate of his brother, dispensed rough justice on the spot. He ordered his guards to draw their swords against the assassins – whose names, Harmodius and Aristogeiton, soon became household names in Athens and beyond. Harmodius was hacked to pieces by the tyrant's soldiers; Aristogeiton was arrested, tortured and then condemned to a grisly death, along with several supporters.

The tyranny founded by Hippias and Thessalus enjoyed little legitimacy. So foul did it feel that a rival noble family, the Alcmaeonids, successfully plotted their overthrow around 510 BCE, after military intervention by the Spartans under Cleomenes had backfired by inciting yet more political violence, as well as a popular uprising that lasted for three full days and nights. The combination of power-grabbing above and a popular uprising from below proved contagious. For through the cracks within the elite of local wealthy families headed by the Alcmaeonids appeared the figure of Cleisthenes, a man who understood that tyranny founded on fear could never make for durable government. Like a sapling in search of sunlight, he introduced, in the years 508/507 BCE, a new constitution. The previously dispersed population of Athens and its surrounding countryside was integrated into ten 'tribes' and three new regional administrative units. A city-based army, rooted in these new structures and comprising non-elite, heavily armed foot soldiers called hoplites, was established for the first time. A governing body, the Council of Five Hundred, was set up, and official encouragement was given to an independent assembly based in Athens; in 506 BCE it passed its first decree. Each of these changes was designed both to cut the city's old family ties and to put an end to the violence and conspiracy of faction. But these reforms had another, more earth-shaking significance: they acknowledged the power of the powerless. Cleisthenes was the first Athenian ruler of the period to spot that large numbers of people could act in concert, that a *dēmos* could exercise initiative, take things into its own hands, without guidance or leadership by aristocrats. He drew from this a remarkable conclusion: that if from here on the Athenian polity was to survive it had to be based on the entirely new principle that the *dēmos* was entitled to govern itself.

That was no mean achievement, and it is why history should remember the aristocrat Cleisthenes as a political leader who was a proto-democrat. It is wrong to see him, as many people today still see him, as the Great Man who was responsible for 'founding' democracy in Athens. It is equally wrong to see democracy in Athens as the creation of a brave Dēmos that got tough when the going became rough. The blood-and-guts Athenian transition to democracy, like virtually all those that were to follow, was far messier and more protracted than Great Man or Dēmos explanations imply. Athenian democracy had many causes. It also had many causers. The assassins Harmodius and Aristogeiton played a vital part in the drama. So too did those unknown commoners who rose up and took things into their own hands against the Spartan invaders in 508/507 BCE and decisively crushed a plot by Isagoras, the arch-enemy of Cleisthenes, to set up an oligarchy backed by the Spartan forces. But Cleisthenes also played a vital role, for it was he who did the unthinkable: he was the political figure who extended political freedoms downwards, towards those previously excluded from citizenship, so providing much-needed direction and wider public appeal to the difficult process of unscrewing the lids of Athenian tyranny, this time by building a viable alternative to it.

Cleisthenes started with the middling ranks of farmers, artisans, merchants and other small propertied men – citizens with enough time on their hands to take an interest in public affairs. He certainly shared the reticence of his class about the poor and the powerless. Yet he saw that their enfranchisement – taking the *dēmos* into his arms and using them to ram through radical reforms – could be an effective weapon against blind, concentrated power. Proof of the power of his vision is found in the testimonies and inscriptions that have survived from this period. They show, for the first time in the city of Athens, that an assembly of citizens became an active and powerful authority. Sharing power with the Council of Five Hundred, its members included not only men of wealth who were called the 'five-hundred-bushel men' (so called because their land could annually produce five hundred bushels of liquid or dry produce); of great significance was the fact that the assembly also included struggling farmers and yokemen and other men of modest means. Their inclusion in government profoundly changed its form and meaning. These people of Athens now laid claim to a system of self-government founded on the principle that the populace were in charge – the principle that the '*dēmos* is kyrios', as Aristotle later put it.[2] Democracy had begun – with a little help from a botched murder whose spitefully libidinal motives were to have world-transforming political effects.

The Agora – and Its Deities

The story that the assassins triggered the downfall of a tyranny, whose downfall was in fact the consequence of a confused train of unexpected events, is still contentious. It is just possible that the supporters of Cleisthenes tried misleadingly to describe the assassins as restorers of an ancient ancestral order that had been interrupted by the tyranny of Pisistratus.[3] But fine points didn't much bother the citizens of Athens, who quickly showered their liberators with public honour. 'Truly a great light shone in Athens', was the dramatic way Simonides of Ceos, a lyric poet of the fifth century, described the effect of the assassination.[4] At symposia, conversation parties where wealthy men's tongues were loosened by luscious wine from the island of Chios, songs were crooned in praise of the two founding fathers, who were mentioned in a tough law (passed in 410 BCE) that sanctioned the killing with impunity of 'anyone [who] subverts the democracy at Athens or holds any office when the democracy has been subverted'.[5] The tyrannicides were meanwhile honoured, standing shoulder to muscled shoulder, ready for the kill, in an impressive bronze statue cast by the respected sculptor Antenor. It was to be stolen during a raid on Athens by Persian troops, but the

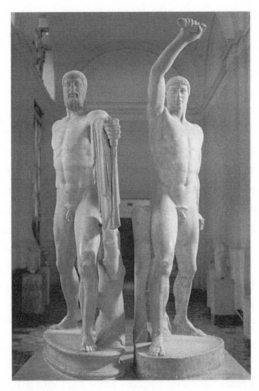

FIGURE 1: The young aristocrat tyrannicides Harmodius (right) and Aristogeiton; a Roman copy of the statue by Critius and Nesiotes, originally set up on the main square of Athens in 477–476 BCE. It was inspired by the original executed by the Athenian sculptor Antenor.

Athenians quickly commissioned a marble replacement, chiselled by local sculptors Critius and Nesiotes (Figure 1). Throughout the two and a half centuries in which Athenian democracy survived in one form or another – roughly from 508/507 to 260 BCE – both versions of the statue reportedly inspired collective memories of horror and pride: horror at the puddles of blood left behind by tyranny, but pride in its magnificent overthrow by brave citizens of the city.

It is hard to recapture these powerful feelings of pride and honour from another age, but one way of doing so is to understand why both statues were sited in the main square of Athens, a place locals called the *agora*. At the moment of birth of democracy, the population of the region called Attica stood at around 200,000 people. Athens itself was by far its largest city. It had a resident population of about thirty thousand men, slaves, women and children.

As democracy took root, that figure doubled. It was swelled by the tens of thousands of alien residents (called metics) and traders and travellers who annually entered its gates, passed through its winding and crooked streets, into the arms of a city that everyone considered special. The Athenians considered the agora the hub of their city, even the fulcrum of a state that soon became the most powerful in the Greek world. Set in the well-drained upper reaches of a valley dotted with poplars and plane trees, the four-sided agora was framed by clumps of white stone buildings topped with orange clay roofs (Figures 2 and 3). It measured just three hundred metres square, roughly the size of London's Trafalgar Square, but Athenians proudly embraced it as a grand space that was publicly owned, and publicly shared.

Here large numbers of people congregated freely, to take part in the many activities offered by a thriving city: parades, conversation, festivals, buying and selling, athletics contests, public trials and theatrical performances. The mix alone was enlivening; so, too, was the shared sense that flesh-and-blood mortals – men – had the means of governing themselves. Athenian citizens used their square for a variety of public purposes. They lingered, loitered, promenaded, chatted, gossiped, bickered, mused, joked. They met old friends and new, flirted (men with young boys; young men with flute girls), sometimes fell in love. The publicly shared space of the agora was not a place

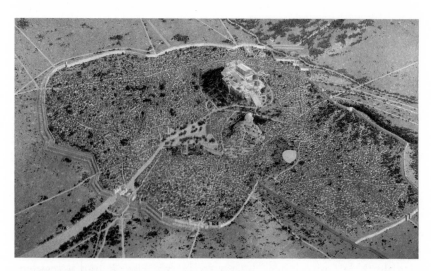

FIGURE 2: The walled city of classical Athens seen from the north-west, from a watercolour by Peter Connolly.

FIGURE 3: The Athenian agora, from a watercolour by Peter Connolly.

regulated by dead-serious communication through reasonable words (as has often been claimed by philosophers). It was much more a public space for fun and games, for the catharsis of competitions and festivals – a place for entertainment, as we would say today.

The Athenian democracy absorbed from its aristocrat opponents a strong will to 'perform glorious deeds and be the first among all', as Homer had famously said. Democracy was an energetic way of life marked by the urge to celebrate its achievements. The packed gravel street – it was called the Panathenaic Way – that passed diagonally through the agora was, for instance, wide enough to serve as a training ground for the cavalry. The great Panathenaic festival featured a splendid parade (depicted in a sculptured frieze now on display in the British Museum) that trailed along the same street, through the agora, on its way up towards a white-columned citadel, dedicated to the patron goddess Athena, and known locally as the Acropolis. During the first decades of democracy, the gravel street was also dotted with wooden grandstands that offered spectators a good view of parades and athletics events, including the breathtaking *apobates*, races in which the contestants, wearing full armour, jumped on and off chariots. The grandstands provided good views for the singing, dancing and plays performed before other citizens – until the early years of the fifth century, when the collapse of a stand during a performance injured many spectators and resulted in the transfer of these activities from the agora to the new Dionysos theatre, located just south of the Acropolis.

The point here is that Athenians helped fashion the rule that democracies require public spaces, open to all, where matters of common concern can be defined and lived by citizens who regard each other as equals. Like the later forums of imperial Rome, or the piazzas and squares of the cities of Europe that it foreshadowed, the agora was (in today's rather less elegant parlance) a civic centre. Reserved for public functions, it was physical and symbolic space combined and shared in common. The anti-democrats of Athens liked to complain that in the agora slaves and resident aliens, dogs, donkeys and horses behaved as if they were all equal. That gripe against uppity inferiors was understandable, for the democrats of Athens did indeed regard its agora as being owned collectively: not just by men of good blood or wealth, but as well by carpenters, farmers, ship owners, sailors, shoemakers, spice sellers and smiths. Many citizens saw democracy as a kind of government in which the people ruled as equals, thanks to their access to an agora that functioned as their second home, as a space in which citizens banded together and rescued themselves, collectively and individually, from the 'natural' ruin brought on by the passing of time, its progression towards death. By countering human frailty, the agora gave them a nest in the world, a sense of what Athenians called *aidós*: meaningful wellbeing and mutual respect. It was as if the agora infused citizens with a sense of reality, daily confirmed by the presence of others. That is presumably what the famous 'weeping philosopher' Heraclitus (c. 540–c. 480 BCE) meant by his aphorism that the world of the agora was one and common for those who were awake, whereas those who took no interest in its affairs in effect fell asleep, by turning their backs on one another.

Through their public encounters in the agora, Athenians liked to say, they could feel their own power, their ability to speak to each other, to act with and against their fellow citizens, in pursuit of commonly defined ends. The agora was their viagra. It was a vibrant place, buzzing day and night with busy people who identified proudly with the *dēmos*, with its rich and poor hands equally on the tillers of government. But archaeological evidence also confirms the strange and surprising point that many if not most citizens (it is hard to be sure about numbers) felt their agora to be watched over by gods and goddesses. In the twenty-first century many people think of democracy as a thoroughly 'secular', or this-worldly ideal. They say religion (like sex) is a 'private' matter, and think of government as properly separated from all sacred matters, except perhaps for the occasional use of hollow slogans, like 'in God we trust' (the motto that first appeared in the design of American banknotes and coins in 1864) or 'one nation under God' (the last two words of which were incorporated in the American Pledge of Allegiance only in 1954). It is thus little wonder that these same people find it difficult, or downright impossible, to imagine a non-secular democracy. Strange it may seem, but that is exactly how Athens should be described. It was not a secular city in any recognisably modern sense. It was not an irreligious democracy. Its entire ethos mixed together the sacred and the profane, to the point where talk of the separation of religion and politics would have made no sense to Athenians. Its democracy had room for dissenters, certainly. In the early 440s, the first Sophist, Protagoras of Abdera, told Athenians that man was the measure of all things, including the deities, who perhaps did not exist, except in men's minds. Others probably agreed, or silently pondered the same thought. But the reality was that Athenian democracy was widely seen through supernatural eyes. Those who accepted its terms were not in a position to take it or leave it, as and when they pleased. They had learned from an early age, in the religious cults and rituals practised within their own households, that life was anchored firmly in a polytheistic universe of gods and goddesses – in a community of deities who infused democracy with a strong sense of sacred standards for life on earth.

Citizens invested great hopes in deities. They also feared them. The public trial and execution of Socrates in 399 BCE for importing fake gods into the city, and for impiously corrupting its youth, confirmed to many that individuals who snubbed the deities would suffer harsh punishment. The priests and old men of the city loved to reinforce the same moral. They had a habit of reminding citizens who mingled in the agora (the story was taken originally from Homer) that at the entrance of the home of Zeus, the god of freedom, stood two large barrels, from which he dispensed ill to some newcomers, good to others, and to the rest a few ladles of good from one barrel and, from the other, a bit of ill. Tales like that put the whole city on edge. We may scoff at these deep feelings for the sacred. But, again, the reality was that many citizens of Athens thought of themselves as members of a community of worshippers who believed that deities like Zeus would punish them collectively if they or their leaders behaved unjustly; he and other deities were thought to enjoy the power to ruin democracy, for instance by bringing bad weather or failed harvests, or the death of oak trees, or the disappearance of fish from the nets of fishermen operating from the nearby port of Piraeus.

That was why the deities had to be feared and loved, respected and worshipped. The case of Zeus was spectacular proof of this. In the north-west corner of the agora, nestled beneath a hill topped by a large temple (the *hephaisteion*) that still survives today, stood an impressive colonnaded building, a civic temple known as the Stoa of Zeus Eleutherios. Built from marble and stone in the Doric style, with a red-brown terracotta-tiled roof, the temple's entrance was guarded by a large statue and altar of Zeus, his arms silently outstretched. The building was not exactly what it had been in pre-democratic times. But it is of more than passing interest that the old cult of praising Zeus was carried over by the democrats of Athens. Its popularity dated from the time of the liberation of Athens and the whole of mainland Greece from the clutches of the Persians, at the Battle of Plataia in 479 BCE. The building itself was a favourite among citizens, especially those who loved to promenade at sunset past its glorious structures, to linger on its elegant steps, or mingle amidst its tall columns and roomy insides. The interior of the temple was lavishly decorated, with glorious paintings of Democracy and the People done by a local artist named Euphanor. Exactly how he portrayed them remains a riddle. The paintings have not survived, yet what seems obvious is the intimate link they supposed between democracy and the sacred. Citizens who visited the temple to worship freedom in effect paid homage to a god that had supported them in their human struggle for democracy. Even the simple relics admired by today's tourists provide proof of the same democratic reverence for the sacred: chunks of Doric columns and cornices; a fine marble statue of the goddess Nike from the south corner of the south wing; samples of the shields of those – the many forgotten heroes – who died fighting for the democratic freedoms of Athens.

The Athenians' fear of gods and goddesses had a positive flipside, for it was widely believed that the deities put a spring in the step of mortals. They gave life guidance, meaning and protection. Put more precisely, the deities helped Athenians cope with the contingencies of life. Not only did they explain chance happenings and otherwise inexplicable events, like droughts and epidemics. The deities also proffered advice and issued instructions; and they spelled out the sanctions that would follow, as surely as day followed night, if citizens dared turn their noses up at their divine instructions. The deities could come to the rescue, especially in sticky situations, when solutions had to be found for problems. The deities helped define the vital issues. They gave credence to the practical decisions reached, so making those decisions more palatable to citizens who would otherwise have resisted them. Divination, approaching gods and goddesses, also reminded citizens of their mortality, and of their need for humility. The deities for that reason served as well as a brake on leaders who were too clever by half, or too headstrong to bother about others. Divination put power on a leash.

Then there was the striking resemblance between the respective methods of divination and democracy. The good thing about the deities is that they daily reminded the citizens of Athens of the need to practise the delicate arts of peacefully approaching others who might prove to be capricious or dangerous, negotiating with them and making decisions together, on the basis of trust and respect. There were many gods and goddesses, but there were no straightforward revelations, no sacred books and no official creeds. Besides, the deities were partisan types. They conspired together and took sides. But they were often malleable. There was room for playing noughts and crosses with them. They were open to persuasion; their opinions could be changed. So just as the deities had to be approached, consulted and their advice interpreted before decisions could be made, so democracy was a type of mortal government and way of life in which citizens felt moved to join together respectfully in public, to decide as equals how they should live together, in the face of uncertainty. The relationship between the deities and humans was unequal, of course; the gods and goddesses had the power to inconvenience, or to destroy human beings. But it was exactly that imbalance of power that made it mandatory for mortals living in the agora to mimic their relationship with the deities, in order better to please them.

How paradoxical things look when viewed from our times, but the classical reality was that Athenians regarded the divine and democracy not as enemies, but as close friends. They saw no contradiction between the infusion of their lives with religious sentiment and the fact that their agora was a peculiarly human invention that was worth preserving, through human effort. The very idea of a 'separation' of religion and politics, of distinguishing divine will and the 'secular' will of the people, was utterly foreign to the mentality of Athenians. Democracy for them required divination, and could not survive without it. That was why cults and sacrifices played such a vital part in its life; and why democratic Athens had its priests, chosen by lot, and why it was famous for spending more time and drachmas on festivals and theatre productions than any other city of the region. It was also why all of its subgroups, some of them advised by diviners and oracle interpreters, had their own festival calendars, there to make sure that the right sacrifices were performed at the right times during the year.

The consequence was that many Athenians in fact thought of their democracy as a system for establishing and enforcing the will of the deities, who in turn authorised the exercise of human powers. Many examples spring to mind. With the permission of the gods and goddesses, Athenian troops, after prayers and offerings, set out for battle, in search of victory, accompanied by diviners, or 'seers'. Both on and off the battlefield, whole armies consulted the deities, sacrificed animals to them, and inspected their guts for signs of what to do next. Livers were a particularly rich source of premonition. Before making public appearances – they were rare – the most famous citizen of Athens, the politician and military commander Pericles (c. 495–429 BCE), similarly prayed to the deities that he would not utter one word unbefitting of the subject under discussion. And whenever delegates from the city travelled to Delphi to seek advice from the oracle of Apollo – the god who was believed to be the interpreter of the wishes of other deities – they did so because they were convinced that important public matters had first to be negotiated with the gods and goddesses, and that good outcomes depended upon divine favour. This was all understandable because the deities were seen as wisdom's wellspring. They soothed the doubts of mortals. They calmed their fears and gave them courage and direction to act in worldly affairs. It was in this vein, reaching for his lyre, that the poet Pindar (518–438 BCE) found words to divine their favour. 'Come hither to the dance', he sang, 'and send us your glorious favour, Olympian gods, who in holy Athens approach the navel of the city, fragrant with incense, and the famous richly adorned Agora, to receive garlands of violets and songs gathered in the spring.'[6]

Heroines . . .

So the agora was a good place to frequent, to be seen in the company of others, in the presence of the deities. Citizens had their favourite spots. One of them was the small, ornate water fountain house on the south side of the agora. It was more than a source of pleasure on sweltering days. Fed by water passing through baked clay pipes that filled clattering pitchers from dawn until dusk, the fountain house (the surviving water jars marked with black figures suggest) was also a bustling social scene. It was frequented by crowds of young women and domestic servants taking advantage of one of the few sites outside the household where they could legitimately meet in public, to chat and gossip about matters in common.

Take note those who idealise the glorious democracy of the ancients: Athenian democracy was a deeply gendered affair. Many citizens supposed a sharp division between the public life of the agora and the privacy of the household, where women gave birth, their children brought up on stories and myths and (in the case of boys) taught to read and write, and where food was prepared and cleaning, repairing and other daily chores were done, with the help of domestic servants. The presumed gap between the private and the public enlivened another difference: the gulf between women and men. Some citizens noted that women had their own cults, passed freely through the streets and (especially if they were poor) sold their wares in public. But they drew from this the conclusion that democracy was having poisonous effects, simply because

women should neither be seen nor heard in the agora. 'So it is
seemly for a woman to remain at home and not be out of doors;
but for a man to stay inside instead of devoting himself to outdoor
pursuits is disgraceful', grumbled Xenophon (c. 427–355 BCE),
during a debate about household management.[7] It was the former
soldier's way of justifying women's absence from public affairs: it
boiled down to the view that the good citizen was a good man,
whereas the women and servants who ministered the necessaries of
life within the confines of the household were inferior 'by nature',
and so worthy of exclusion from public life.

The good citizen came equipped with a phallus, which prompts
the thought that there were deep connections between homosexuality and democracy in its Athenian form. Its democracy was a
phallocracy. Waited on hand and foot by their inferiors, men
bonded and ruled, as equals. They formed associations and spent a
great deal of time together in public. And they drew pleasure from
their efforts to preen young boys for public life. Yet it is worth
noting that not everyone accepted the view that the agora was a
man's world. It certainly was a space where men mingled, held
hands and kissed, where the bodily display of male affection and
love towards other men and boys was tied to the intensive pursuit
of physical beauty, the lust after pleasure, and the deep aversion to
growing old. But still, in spite of everything, women managed to
make their mark on the agora.

Any modern-day visitor to the public square would have been
struck by several paradoxes. One of them was that the very word
used by Athenians for nearly two centuries to describe their way of
life – *dēmokratia* – was itself a feminine noun with strongly feminine connotations. It takes some effort to imagine, let alone to
understand, a world whose spoken and written language contains
a word that was itself surrounded by a family of corresponding
nouns that are grammatically feminine (almost all of them formed
with the *ia* suffix, which is feminine). Think about it for a moment:
just as we describe a ship in feminine terms, imagine how our perceptions and feelings for such democratic institutions as press
freedom and periodic elections might be altered if we presupposed
that they embodied life-giving, 'feminine' qualities. Then try to
imagine how the feminisation of those institutions of necessity

meant that they had the firm backing of a deity – a goddess – blessed with the power of moulding men's hopes and fears. The personification of democracy was not simply a convenient intellectual exercise. Athenians routinely imagined their polity in feminine terms. That is why we need to jettison clichés about the 'male-dominated' democracy of Athens – or about how democracy hardened the male–female distinction that had previously been blurred by local aristocratic culture. Only when we do that can we grasp how democracy was habitually seen as a woman with divine qualities and, thus, a figure blessed with the power to give or take away life from her offspring – the people of Athens.

Given the female personification of democracy, we should not be surprised to learn that women played a vital role in the sacred life of Athens. Otherwise barred from law making and politics, women were full participants in both private rituals and religious festivals sponsored by the city. The rituals and festivals not only took them into public spaces otherwise reserved for men. They enabled them to act as priestesses – like the powerful women (the *pythia*) who communicated the will of Apollo to visitors at Delphi. Many men thought – and feared – that such women were more closely in touch with the divine than men themselves. There is evidence, too, that the goddess Dēmokratia was worshipped.[8] She attracted a cult following. Stone and wooden monuments to her stood within the agora. Her sanctuary is said to have been located somewhere in its north-west corner. If that's true, then (along the lines of the cult of Pity recorded by Pausanias[9]) there would have been a stone altar on which citizens, assisted by a priestess or priest, said prayers and offered public sacrifices, such as cakes, a loaf of bread, wine and honey, the slaughtering and burning of a cow, goat or spring lamb. The role of the priestess of democracy would have been especially powerful. Customarily appointed on an hereditary basis, from within a leading family of Athens, or nominated or chosen by lot, perhaps after consulting an oracle, her aim was to spread respect for the goddess, whose mysterious authority could not be profaned, except at the risk of punishment, which ranged from cold-shouldering and denigration to excommunication, even death. In return – the proud naming of a fleet of Attic ships after the goddess Dēmokratia is an example – the priestess would have helped protect democracy from bad outcomes. This is the gist of the most famous image from the period, a relief preserved today in the Stoa museum in Athens. Chiselled in white marble above an Athenian law against tyranny of 336 BCE, it shows Dēmokratia crowning, and thereby shielding and sheltering, an elderly bearded man who represents the *dēmos*, the people (Figure 4).

. . . and Middling Heroes

The deities blessed not only heroines, granting them powers of persuasion. There were lucky heroes as well. Not far from the fountain house, in the extreme south-west corner of the agora, was a favourite public haunt for male citizens. It was an eye-catching monument in the form of a line of statues known as the eponymous heroes (eponymous referred to the act of extending one's own name

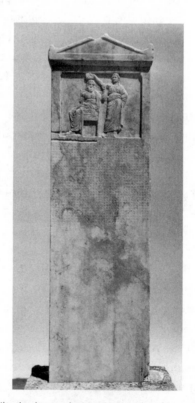

FIGURE 4: Athenian law against tyranny, sculpted in marble, 336 BCE.

custom by writing and memorising a long poem in favour of the military capture by Athens of the island of Salamis, then donned a small felt cap for disguise, entered the agora while pretending to be mad, and cheekily delivered his political poem before a large, appreciative crowd. In the era of democracy, speech making in the agora was strictly prohibited. Since it was widely thought that government and business, like olive oil and water, did not readily mix, the conclusion was that the conduct of politics was better located at a physical distance from the agora, at a nearby spot called the Pnyx.

Set on an elongated ridge and natural slope dotted with eucalyptus and olive groves, 400 metres uphill from the agora, the Pnyx is today a lonely spot, an ill-understood place left unfrequented by tourists in a hurry to scale and photograph the nearby Acropolis. Its sad neglect contrasts with the age of democracy, when it functioned as the place where the whole citizen body (the assembly, called the *ekklesia*) met to decide laws that governed how it would live together on earth. Since the time of Cleisthenes, when reportedly it

FIGURE 6: Speakers' platform, the Pnyx, with the Acropolis in the background, from the painting by Rudolph Müller, 1863.

had only ever met once, to handle minor matters like the selection and monitoring of magistrates, the assembly had developed long and sharp teeth. Its size was certainly impressive.

Aristotle once recommended that a city should be small enough for the voice of a herald to be heard by all its citizens, who should know one another, at least by sight, but Athens was most definitely not like that. Its active citizenry, comprising men aged twenty and over, numbered at least 6000. After several rebuildings – prompted by demands for citizenship from the sailors who powered Athens' growing dependence upon naval force – there was room in the Pnyx for just over double that number (Figure 6).

Stormy sessions and life-or-death issues attracted onlookers as well. Foreigners could have been forgiven for thinking that democracy required good weather. Especially in the summer months, business got under way early, shortly after the cool dawn breezes had vanished and the sun had just begun to paint the surrounding hills gold. Turnout was usually high, which was a tribute not to the weather, but to the intense feeling among citizens that citizenship mattered. High turnout was especially remarkable considering that some two-thirds of the citizens of the state of Attica lived outside Athens, and that therefore they had either to camp the night there or leave home during the night in order to reach the Pnyx by daybreak. Local stragglers were, meanwhile, dealt with by unorthodox means. In the days well before the invention of compulsory voting (first introduced in Belgium in 1892, Argentina in 1914 and Australia in 1924) or the nineteenth-century use of 'whipper-ins' in the Westminster parliament, Athenian slaves were used to round up citizens who tarried, or tried to play truant when the assembly was about to go into session. The method was as simple as it was colourful. Every exit from the agora was blocked, except the one that led up to the Pnyx. The ancient whips then armed themselves with long ropes made from twined reeds soaked with red paint, before trawling the public places, on the lookout for wayward citizens, who risked being scooped up like fish and fined – and having their clothes or bodies, perhaps even their faces, stained because they had lingered, or tried to shirk their duty.

Just how effectively red ropes rounded up red-faced shirkers is unknown. Evidence of actual attendance remains sparse, though one point is clear: when pressured by the need to be more inclusive, the Pnyx was rebuilt twice. Around 404/403 BCE, an artificial amphitheatre with excellent natural acoustics was carved from the local pink-grey granite rock. The speakers' platform was repositioned, so that listeners looked towards the sea and the speaker to the land, 'because they thought that naval supremacy had been the origin of democracy, and that tillers of the soil were less ill-disposed toward oligarchy'.[13] Later – perhaps sometime in the fourth century, though the evidence is patchy – the amphitheatre was again expanded, so that the Pnyx could hold up to 13,000 people. At no point did women, slaves or resident aliens win the entitlement to vote.

How did the assembly actually work? What were its functions? How effective was it? Considered as the bedrock of the whole polity, the assembly normally met for a day forty times a year, every ten days, or about four times per month in the Athenians' ten-month civil calendar, as well as on other special occasions. Its stated purpose was to debate and approve legislation. It also heard embassies from neighbouring political units, as well as dealing with such matters as food supply, the health of the population and the military defence of the city. Its deliberations were helped along by the recommendations and draft proposals put to it by a body called the Council of Five Hundred, whose on-duty members sat on wooden benches facing the assembly. Seating was egalitarian. All assembly business was face to face, and depended on the spoken word, commencing with the opening question from the presiding herald for that day: 'Citizens! Who has some useful suggestion for the *polis*?' So that citizens could better project their voices, speakers mounted a small platform (the *bema*), usually beginning their contribution with the words: 'Fellow citizens' or, simply, 'Citizens'. Debates and the resolutions that they produced were heard by messengers; warned not to fall asleep, their job was to pay attention to the business and, when required, to deliver important news to the rest of the city, on sandalled feet, or draped across a dawdling donkey.

Since government in Athens was considered a democracy, it was seen as a human – a thoroughly human – affair. References to the gods were frequent, and it was considered important always to have them onside. Sessions typically began with prayers to the ancestral gods and sacrifices of a lamb, or a piglet. The purification rituals were thought to empower the assembly, which is why its business was never passed on to oracles or soothsayers. They were regarded as private 'specialists' and their authority, or their predictions, could always be challenged, or ignored outright. Speakers took turns in taking the platform, and voting – deciding 'what seems best to the people', the Athenians' own words for 'decreed' – was by a show of hands held high in the air, or by pebbles dropped in urns. The decrees were written down on skin parchment or papyrus. They were then deposited in the city's archives, in the agora. All such records have been lost but, luckily, decrees sometimes stipulated that a copy be carved on stone, then displayed in the agora. The surviving fragments, like windows on to another world, reveal bits and pieces of assembly life. Some of them publicly praise the contributions of ordinary citizens. Many stone tablets record agreements and treaties with other powers, or honour citizens of other states for their support for Athens. 'With good fortune', one of them reads, 'it has seemed best to the People to praise Mikalion son of Philon of Alexandria and to crown him with a golden crown in accord with the law because of his virtue and good will toward the Athenians . . .'[14] Perhaps the most substantial and deservedly famous tablet is the so-called law against tyranny (Figure 4). Dating from 336 BCE, it records the fearful reaction in the assembly to the possibility that quislings – disloyal local men of wealth and influence – would collude with an outside enemy, most probably the Macedonian king, to hasten the overthrow of democracy and its replacement with a form of oligarchy. 'Be it resolved by the lawgivers', it begins. 'If anyone rises up against the People with a view to tyranny or join in establishing the tyranny or overthrow the People of the Athenians or the democracy in Athens, whoever kills him who does any of these things shall be blameless . . .' The law went on to detail plans for its own publicity. 'The secretary of the Council shall inscribe this law on two steles of stone and set one of them by the entrance into the Areopagus [near the Pnyx] . . . and the other in the Assembly. For the inscribing of the steles the treasurer of the People shall give twenty drachmas from the moneys expendable by the People according to decrees.'

FIGURE 7: The laughing democrat Democritus (c. 460–370 BCE), an engraving by William Blake, 1789.

Sessions at the Pnyx were often blustery. 'The city is full of freedom and unrestrained speech and there is licence within it for a man to do as he likes', complained an enemy of democracy, who went on to note that the echoes produced by the rock walls of the Pnyx 'redouble the din of the criticism and the praise'.[15] The complaint seems overdone. There is actually much evidence of citizens' self-discipline. They were acutely aware of the dangers of violent feuds (they called it *stasis*), and it is certain that within the assembly threatened or actual violence was not tolerated. Well-trained heralds as well as a detachment of archers and slaves were usually on hand, to enforce its rules and customs. Citizens, seated in the round on bare rock, some of them lying or propped up on soft cushions brought from home, expected others to respect the obligation to speak spontaneously, to trade in what they called frank speech (*parrhēsia*). There were jokes aimed at the rich and charges of disreputable private behaviour. There was talk of corruption; and signs of disquietude about a type of blind arrogance called *hybris*. Sessions were sprinkled with humour: some speakers, inspired by the pre-Socratic philosopher Democritus, who once visited the Pnyx,* practised the art of inducing laughter as a means of public persuasion. There were episodes of high jinks and self-mockery, and moments resembling the closing scene of a much-loved contemporary satire by Aristophanes (445–385 BCE), *Knights*, in which the figure of old man Dēmos is jabbed and jostled by a slave and a sausage seller.[16] But the assembly was often gripped by sobriety. There were constant reminders by speakers that to be a citizen meant being the 'equal and peer' of others. Many times each session was it said that a democracy was a special type of government that enabled each citizen to enjoy *isonomia* (equality before the law), the equal entitlement to speak and the freedom to 'rule and be ruled in turn'. That kind of talk was meant, and taken, literally. It even underpinned an odd and interesting device that anticipated the private member's bill in modern-day parliaments: the Athenians called it *ho boulemenos*, by which they meant that individual citizens were entitled in the assembly to

---

* Democritus, the laughing democrat (Figure 7), was born into a rich family from the city of Abdera, in a part of Thrace that had earlier been settled by Ionian refugees fleeing war in the region of Teos. He had used a handsome inheritance to indulge the curiosity natural to every young man to make the grand tour of the world. Democritus often boasted that he had travelled more widely than any other Greek, that he had spent five years in Egypt, studying mathematics with priests; and that he had travelled as well through Persia, Chaldaea, even through India and Ethiopia. After returning to the Greek lands, where he settled for a time in Athens, Democritus applied his cosmopolitan training to further study, with a master named Leucippus, and to teaching pupils of his own. Little more remains of his life, although it is said that he loved to laugh – he thought it the best remedy against human folly – and that he lived to a ripe age, helped along towards the end by a compulsion (based on his scientific interest in hot-cold, sweet-bitter qualities) to sip honey and inhale the steam oozing from the pores of piping-hot bread. It is known that Democritus was a skilled orator, and that during his life he wrote an imposing catalogue of books, on topics as varied as physics and astronomy, mathematics and grammar, coughing and fever. Most of his work has disappeared, but the surviving fragments prove that Democritus was a friend of democracy. His speeches were crammed with democratic sentiments. The good of the community must always be placed first, he liked to say. Private quarrels and the amassing of power are wrong. The well-run polity is the strongest protection against human greed and folly; if the polity is safe, all is safe, whereas if it is lost, all is lost. Democracy is the best form of polity because it ensures frank speech (*parrhēsia*). It gives a hard time to the foolish, and to the arrogant, who are often one and the same figure. According to Democritus, by protecting frank speech, democracy also ensures that the mistakes of men who hold office are remembered longer than their successes. Poverty under democracy, for that reason, is always preferable to so-called prosperity under tyranny, as freedom is to slavery. Yet poverty should be abhorrent to citizens. Voluntary generosity and mutual aid, together with the curbing of individual desires and ambitions, are vital for democracy to flourish. Equal sharing of power and property and speech does away with friction over 'mine' and 'thine'. The shared fish, he liked to say, has no bones.

inspectors of weights and measures, whose job was to protect buyers of goods in the marketplace. City magistrates, helped by slaves, tackled such tasks as maintaining public buildings, policing the streets and removing rubbish; they supervised theatre performances and oversaw the organisation of torch races and festivals, including the Panathenaic procession. Ambassadors were despatched abroad, to defend the interests of Athens. Jurors had to be assigned to courts and magistrates to offices. There were official messengers and magistrates of the armed forces. The point here is that we should not think of democracy in Athens as a simple, straightforward affair. The business of administration was often extraordinarily detailed. Cavalry riders were annually assessed and their damages (a lost horse in battle, for instance) were reimbursed; military officers in charge of frontier garrisons and patrolling borders were subject to inspections; according to official regulations, infantrymen were allocated state-owned armour, such as shields and spears. The field of taxation saw the same hands-on preoccupation with detail. Monies had to be collected from mines, alien residents and those leasing public lands; at the port of Piraeus, duties amounting to one-fiftieth of the goods imported or exported were imposed; and taxes (and fines for late payment) were carefully gathered from the sale of the skins of sacrificed animals.

Not only could citizens expect to be elected or allotted to service on a treasury committee or some other board dealing with some or other function. There was in addition a whole legal apparatus to service. Law making by debate and raised hands or pebbles in a pot was one thing. Quite another was the fair and efficient execution of the laws approved by the assembly. Each and every citizen was eligible for service to the Council of Five Hundred, whose job it was to prepare legislation for the assembly, and to help elect by lot the chief executive officers of the administration.[19] The Council also performed such essential functions as the inspection of ships and cavalry. It checked the qualifications of newly allotted officials and tried magistrates accused of wrongdoings. The Council also worked with public bodies responsible for such matters as the leasing of mines and the sale of property that had been confiscated.

Service as a juror within the various courts of law was also expected of all citizens. It was required by the democratic principle that all citizens were equal. In practice, service was confined to men aged thirty or over. Athenian democrats supposed that time ripened wisdom. Although the age limit was the same as for all other office holders, it was ten years greater than that required for participation in the assembly, which gave the role of juror more credibility and clout in the eyes of the agora than that of assemblyman. For men who had supposedly shaken off the rashness of youth, jury service was considered a privilege and a duty for which (by the late fifth century BCE) each of them was daily paid half a drachma, a bit less than a day's wage for a skilled workman. The pay was modest – hardly enough to warrant the claim of critics that the poor only messed around with politics to make money. The job demanded concentration and, because it carried with it considerable power to rectify injustices and to determine the future lives of fellow citizens, each juror was required to take an oath. But note: Athenian democracy was not based on anything like 'the rule of law', as we now call a type of government in which no power can be exercised except according to principles, procedures and constraints contained in laws that are designed to protect citizens, both from incursions by other citizens and from the officers of the state itself.

Athens was different. It had a system of jury courts called *dikasteria*. The word from which it derived (*dikastes*) meant both juror and judge. The combination of opposites here is significant, because this was a democracy without lawyers. No trained judges presided over its courts. Nobody gave legal direction to the jurors, or to the defendants. Even when they hired a speechwriter, litigants acted solely in their capacity as citizens. Each citizen was entitled to bring a public suit in matters that he reckoned affected the whole democratic order (the plaintiff was allowed up to three hours to speak before a jury, in accordance with the rule of *ho boulemenos*). The magistrates in charge of the courts were amateurs. Their one-year term of office, which they held once in a lifetime, involved only administrative functions, not matters of legal substance. Law was not seen as Law, as the special province of a privileged class of legal experts. Law was instead regarded simply as positive law, as rules made and applied by juror citizens themselves. They could not be censured or impeached, not even when they roared with laughter or shouted out their disapproval or disbelief of things said by litigants; and they were not held accountable to any other body for their decisions, which were final. Citizens decided for themselves what was right and wrong in each context. The ultimate expression of this rule was the introduction, in 416 BCE, of *graphe paranomon* ('indictment against measures contrary to the laws'). It made possible a challenge to any law proposed or passed by the assembly. The matter could be brought before a jury, which had the power to block or annul the law, and even to punish whoever had proposed the law in the first place. The whole procedure hinted at the supremacy of the courts, their outstripping of the powers of the assembly, as if they were destined to become an upper house, or a supreme court. The courts were not so destined, but writing several centuries later the widely read Greek historian and biographer Plutarch (c. 46–127 CE) had a point when he remarked that the popular courts in Athens had the ultimate say, the final word in many matters, such that they – and not the assembly – were in effect the final all-powerful voice of the *dēmos*.[20]

The preoccupation of the Athenian democracy with legal fairness should certainly be striking to our eyes. So, too, should its valiant efforts to avoid corruption and rigging of outcomes. The introduction of payment for public service – first for jury service around 462 BCE, then later for attendance at meetings of the assembly – is an example. It was designed to have 'purifying' effects on the democracy, though it is worth noting the curious irony that its champions – Pericles, following the advice of his teacher, Damon – derived their political scheme from a theory of music that supposed that changes of rhythm and tone directly affected the virtues of listeners, for instance by retuning their sense of self-restraint, courage and justice.[21] It was neither the first nor the last time in the history of democracy that an invention, in this case payment for public service, was valued by its inventors and users in radically different ways. The preoccupation with ensuring that government was uncorrupted, that democracy involved a show of clean hands, forced it to experiment as well with new methods of cultivating citizen participation in government, outside of the assembly. Juries, for instance, were unusually large and much rowdier by today's standards. For smaller suits (*dike*), the minimum jury size was 201 members; that number was increased to 401 if a sum of over 1000 drachmas was in dispute. For larger public suits (*graphe*), it was not uncommon to find courts of 1000, or 2000, even (on special occasions) 2500 jurors. On at least one occasion – the *graphe paranomon* mentioned already – all 6000 members of the juror pool were summoned to court.

To avoid corruption, which would displease the deities, the selection process was intricate, even a bit tedious – and, for the sake of political equality, surprisingly mechanised. There was a nifty allotment machine called a *kleroterion* that was used in Athens to allocate individual citizens immediately before a court sat, on a basis that was said to be fair both to them and the accused. This is how the clever device worked. Eligibility for jury service was open to all citizens who had passed a test. It certified such points as who their parents and grandparents were, whether they had performed their military duties and paid their taxes, and if they showed respect towards the deities. Jury membership was decided only on the trial day – in order to minimise blackmailing and corruption.

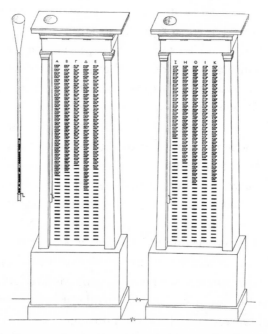

FIGURE 9: A pair of juror selection machines, known in Athens as *kleroteria*, fourth century BCE.

Each and every citizen-juror was in possession of a wooden or bronze ticket, on which was inscribed both his name and the number of the jury section to which he belonged (there were ten such sections: one for each tribe). At daybreak, he went to his tribe's local *kleroterion*, a tall, rectangular slab of stone about the size of a grown man, and about half a foot thick. Chiselled into its front side was a curious grid of deep, thin slots, into one of which the citizen deposited his own named and numbered ticket. After the tickets of all those wanting to do jury service that day had been so deposited, an official pulled a few of them out in random order from the *kleroterion*.

The selected sample of nametags was then ferried by officials to the two main law courts located in the south-western corner of the agora, the Heliaia (dating from the sixth century) and the Square Peristyle (originally built in the fifth century). There, officials reloaded the bronze or wooden tags, one by one, into the vertical slots of the agora's two principal *kleroteria* (Figure 9). The tags of each available juror were lined up from top to bottom, in ten vertical columns, each one reserved for a particular tribe. The magistrate in charge of the day's cases, after deciding how many jurors would be needed, then set the justice machine to work. He randomly filled the funnel on the left-hand side of the *kleroterion* with as many little black and white balls as there were tickets in the shortest column. The magistrate automatically excluded tickets below that shortest column, then slowly turned a handle at the bottom of the funnel, letting drop one ball at a time. The first ball to drop determined the fate of the first row, across all the columns: if it was a white ball then all the names in that first row became jurors for the day. A black ball resulted in their dismissal from service that day. The magistrate repeated the ball-dropping exercise for each other row; and so the fate of each juror was randomly decided.

It is not known where or when or who invented this clever machine. It was a small symbol of the big preoccupation of the Athenians with what they called legal 'equality'. That concern stood alongside the resolute conviction that all citizens – as citizens – should be treated as indistinguishable, that in matters of law they had the same or similar qualities, so enjoying what Aristotle called 'numerical equality'.[22] The *kleroterion* was not just a micro-processor of individual fates. It embodied the hope that the equality of equals could become more than just a wish – that even-handed treatment or fairness among citizens was an enforceable rule, and that a polity based on the self-government of equals was possible.

Behind that conviction stood a suspicion: that others might cheat and so tear the fabric of trust and interdependence that helped bind the democratic community together. There are lots of examples, from the small to the large, of how this suspicion was mobilised. Consider the water clock used in courts of law. The principle of equal treatment was considered vital for a fair trial. Since litigants put their own case through an exchange of speeches, both plaintiffs and defendants were allocated the same amounts of time to present their respective claims – helped along by an early form of clock called a *klepsydra*. It was a clay vessel that was filled to the brim with water by a slave, who then at the beginning of a speech removed a plug from the tiny bronze tube in its base. When the vessel had drained into an adjacent pot, the time allotted ended – about six minutes per speech was allowed in cases involving minor offences or smaller claims (less than 5000 drachmas). All speech making then ceased. Exceptions were allowed – the time spent tabling documents and the testimony of witnesses was not counted – but the point of time limits was to settle legal disputes within a single day, and to do so by means of a fair-handed treatment of the disputants.

The opposition to cheating and the concern for fairness were also evident in the unusual secret balloting method employed by the public juries. Jurors used a one-man, one-vote arrangement to produce their collective verdict. After hearing the case, each juror was handed two small ballots cast from bronze. Both were inscribed with the words 'public vote'. One had a solid axle, and was used for acquittal; the axle of the other ballot, used for guilty, was pierced (Figure 10). When the time came to declare his verdict, the juror, clasping in each hand a ballot, each gripped by his thumb and forefinger so as to conceal from others his voting intention, cast one ballot into a container for valid votes, the other into one for discards. So the fate of the accused was decided – secretly, in public, by fair means.

FIGURE 10: Jurors' ballots and a sample ticket of a citizen named Demophanes, Athens, fourth century BCE.

Dēmokratia . . .

Among the juicy paradoxes of Athenian democracy is that its quest for machine-like precision through the use of bronze axles, water clocks, ballot machines and carefully executed lots, all under the watchful eyes of the deities, had the combined effect of injecting a strong element of unpredictability into its political life. The use of special public investigations into alleged cases of treason and bribery and the reliance of the assembly upon open debate and quirkier rules like ostracism had similar effects.

Although the democrats of Athens did not put things this way, their democracy resembled an experiment in puncturing common-sense perceptions of the world. Democracy skewered talk of stern necessity through the heart. It highlighted the contingency of things, events, institutions, people and their beliefs. The originality of democracy lay in its direct challenge to habitual ways of seeing the world, to thoughtless regard for power and ways of governing people, to living life as if everything was inevitable, or 'natural'. Some matters, such as respect for the deities and belief in the necessity of slavery, largely escaped challenge, however much ambivalence they bred. It is also true, when seen in retrospect, that the democracy ultimately clung to a picture of the world that supposed that it would always remain the same, subject to the power of deities and to what Athenians liked to call 'nature'. So, for instance, the awareness that people and institutions are creatures of time, and that hopes and expectations at odds with the present could be put into practice in the future, never won the day among Athenians. Even the oft-quoted remark in Sophocles' *Ajax* about the transience of things presupposed that everything in the world comes full circle, back to the beginning.[23] And yet – the qualification is difficult to overstate – Athenian democracy still managed to trigger a process of radical questioning of who gets what, when and how in the world. It pulled the rug from under the high and mighty. In doing this, democracy ensured that matters of justice were no longer seen as untouchable givens. Monarchy, tyranny and oligarchy were rejected; those who tried to defend them as 'natural', as the way of the world, were greeted with puzzled disbelief, with strong counter-arguments, with satire and belly laughs. Democracy prepared the ground for rejecting the so-called necessity of governing others. It was a brand-new form of open-ended government, one that fuelled public deliberation and rowdy controversy among equals, often to the point where political outcomes were surprises, or nail-biting cliffhangers.

It is easy to see why. Athenian democracy lacked – and as a way of life actively opposed – a clearly defined dominant ideology or political Truth that could answer all its questions and solve each and every problem it encountered. The democracy encouraged scepticism about power and authority. It stimulated the sense that life was open-ended, constantly shaped by the judgements of citizens. This was the fundamental point made forcefully by the movement of rhetoricians and teachers known, from the middle of the fifth century, as Sophists (from *sophos*, 'one who is wise'). Larger-than-life figures like Callicles and Gorgias and Protagoras encapsulated the new democratic spirit. They liked to insist on the distinction between unchangeable 'nature' (what they called *physis*) and worldly things that are contingent, such as customs, institutions and ways of thinking. The distinction was encapsulated by Protagoras (c. 481–c. 411 BCE) in his famous remark that 'human beings are the measure of all things: of things which are, that they are, and of things which are not, that they are not'.[24] This distinction between nature and convention had a real bite. It fuelled the efforts of the Sophists to tease and mock the powerful, for instance by heckling them in the assembly, or by farting loudly when they made an appearance in the agora.

The same vital point about the contingency of human affairs springs from many of the thousand or so plays that were written and produced by Athenian playwrights and watched by citizens during the annual three-day festivals held during the fifth century. These tragedies and comedies underscored how the institutions, customs and decisions of the political order seemed permanently adjustable, as if it were a malleable system of opposites that included truth and deception, war and peace, chaos and order, life and death. Consider for a moment the way in which the otherwise untouchable subject of slavery was poked and prodded in the surviving bits and pieces and whole plays of Euripides. Individual slaves are shown to have qualities, such as intelligence, loyalty and bravery, that are equal or superior to those displayed by free men. The institution of slavery is seen to degrade those who do not deserve such injustice. In the play *Alexandros*, a slave named Paris manages to win his case for competing against free men in heroic games held at Troy. And in the *Ion* a loyal slave, who is willing to risk his life for his mistress, speaks for the view that all men originally had the same appearance, and that the fluke of being born into the ranks of the nobility, or of the citizenry, or into slavery, does not in itself guarantee good moral qualities. 'One thing alone brings shame to the slaves, the name,' says the slave, expressing democratic sentiments. 'Apart from all of that, a slave is no worse than freemen in anything, if he is good.'[25]

The democracy mirrored these sentiments. It changed the shared mental infrastructure of Athenians. It reminded them of the frailty of human endeavours. Democracy stimulated public awareness of the difficulties of making political decisions, and of the ubiquity of perplexity – what the locals called *aporia*. Not knowing today what tomorrow's laws or legal judgements would be, citizens stood permanently on the edge. It was as if they lived their lives in the subjunctive tense: who received what, when and how today, or the day after, depended very much upon what was decided by the assembly, or by the courts of law. Often enough, outcomes were the resultant of different judgements by competing institutions: as in the famous case of Antiphon, the exile who was arrested for illegal entry at the port of Piraeus, let off by the assembly then charged again and subsequently convicted by the Areopagus; or as in several recorded cases where that august court ruled that it could not decide, so handing down the case to a public jury that had to wrestle with the fates of a man charged with privately selling meat from a public sacrifice, a defendant accused of robbing the captain of a ferryboat, and a citizen who had tried to make a fortune out of pocketing the five-drachma-per-citizen public subsidies for attending the theatre. In each case, despite whatever comforts the deities provided, democracy meant unpredictability. In contrast to tyrannies and oligarchies, in which subjects knew minimally their place in the world, democracy nurtured the sense that the lives of its citizens dangled on ten thousand strings – that they were acting parts in a play whose script was always being written, and rewritten, with an ending that was by definition unknown.

. . . and Her Enemies

The popularisation of the brand-new word *dēmokratia* reinforced this deep self-consciousness of the uncertainty of things. What did this word mean to Athenians? From where did it come? Why did its enemies snarl whenever it passed their lips?

We do not know straightforwardly how to answer these questions, but it is safe to say that daily life in Athens was from the time of Cleisthenes peppered by references not only to the presumed bearer of sovereign power, the *dēmos*, but also to *dēmokratia* as a new method of government, as a precious experiment in the art of empowering the powerless and treating all citizens as equals. Imagine for a moment that an inquisitive stranger, recently arrived in Athens, approaches a group of bronzed, wild-bearded citizens dressed in white robes and rough-cut leather sandals, milling at the entrance to the Pnyx, waiting in the cool, pine-scented air for the day's business to get under way. The visitor's question reveals that he is a foreigner. 'What is to take place here, on this hill? Who is ruler [*tyrannos*] of this city?' he asks. One of our band of citizens replies, softly: 'Your question is wrong, stranger. Do not seek a *tyrannos* here. This city is free and ruled by no one man. The *dēmos* reigns, taking turns annually. We do not give supremacy to the rich; the poor man has an equal share in it.'

Sometime towards the end of the sixth century, speech of this kind became common currency, both inside and outside the assembly. Thanks to the work of Harmodius and Aristogeiton, the popular revolt against Spartan troops and the reforms introduced by Cleisthenes, talk of the *dēmos* and democracy tingled the senses of Athenians, confirming that their new form of government, the self-government of equals, was special. Prudence is advisable when piecing together the evidence, if only because among the many intriguing things about the whole subject of democracy is its puzzling origins as a political language. For some time, the mystery has been cloaked in a scholarly consensus that the word *dēmokratia* was a belated invention of the mid-fifth century BCE; and that the new term wasn't widely used until the end of that century. This orthodoxy supposes that the democracy was not initially called by its proper name – and was not so called for more than a half-century.[26]

The consensus is ill founded. It should be rejected. Well before the mid-fifth century BCE, *dēmokratia* – meaning, literally, 'a form of government or rule (*kratos*) by the people (*dēmos*)' – was in fact the word used by the Athenian supporters of their new polity. The archaeological records are telling. Among the tiny clues is the case of an Athenian citizen named Dēmokrates (otherwise known as the father of Lysis, the young boy described by the philosopher Plato) whose gravestone, unearthed only during the past generation, shows that he was born around 470 BCE. The name Dēmokrates shared the same roots as *dēmokratia* and, literally translated, meant 'a person who rules the dēmos'. The proper inference from this bit of evidence is that his naming (by his father, as was the custom, to please the deities) required that the term was already in circulation, that it was a venerated name for newborn male citizens, and therefore had been so since at least the early sixth century.[27]

A spicier reason for giving up on the old orthodoxy, as new archaeological evidence shows, is that the word *dēmos*, from which the more abstract noun *dēmokratia* derives, is much older than the sixth century BCE. Its earliest known meanings in ancient Greek – strange to modern ears – are 'country' and 'land'. The widespread reference to *demes* (a small geographic and political district) before and during the age of democracy carries that sense.[28] Digging more deeply – histories of democracy have until now never attempted this – it is probable that the classical Greek word *dēmos* had its immediate roots in the ancient civilisation we call Mycenaean, after its principal city, Mycenae. It is unclear why the Mycenaean world that flourished for several centuries from the middle of the second millennium BCE suddenly collapsed, leaving behind a rich store of archaeological treasures. The surviving fragments include traces of a strange pictographic language called Linear B, among whose several hundred pictographs appears the little two-syllable word *dāmos* (or *dāmo*):

What did this Linear B word mean? Nobody knew until the Linear B code was cracked in the early 1950s, enabling us to see for the first time that it was used as a (probably feminine) noun to denote a group of people who were landholders, a village community that was entitled to allocate and protect holdings of land. In a feudal system of land tenure marked by a clutch of villages not yet centralised into towns, the Mycenaean *dāmos* was contrasted with both the temples and the palace administration and organised army of the monarch.[29] The *dāmos* did not govern. Yet the word was personified and had deep political connotations. Especially in matters of land, she had the ability to speak for herself, as when inscriptions say: 'but the *dāmos* says that she . . .'.[30] Some members of the *dāmos* (in the settlement of Pylos, for instance) sat on a council that was responsible for allotting and subsequently administering the leases of 'communal plots' of land *paro dāmōi* ('from the community'). These councillors were variously called *dāmokoro* (an overseer of a village) and *opidamijo* (accountable men of a village). The councillors were entrusted with the job of defending the *dāmos* against the claims of outsiders, as when a priestess from a vegetation cult tried on behalf of a goddess to claim land currently occupied by tenants.[31] The *dāmos* (through its council) protested loudly to the palace, which duly recorded the complaint; whether it reaffirmed, through the *dāmos*, the tenants'

vested entitlements to the land it occupied and worked is not known.

There is a point to this digression into the remote past, because although Mycenaean civilisation seems far distant from Athenian democracy, there is mounting evidence from inscriptions and other artefacts that reveals an exciting link: this ancient civilisation, itself connected to peoples further to the east, bequeathed to the Athenians a family of terms that contained a vital word that both described and defended the powers of a potentially active group within the body politic. It is unknown how the term *dāmos* was passed on, and to what extent it experienced mutations, but one fascinating change is clear. Around 1200 BCE, the meaning of *dāmos* underwent an inversion that was itself bound up with the convulsions that marked the end of the Mycenaean period. Many of the *dāmos* lost their property. Yet – don't miss the deep irony – despite their political defeat by the rise of new kingship and property patterns, they continued to be called the *dāmos*. The old word not only changed meaning. It changed political sides. As it underwent a transmutation from a pictographic language to five little letters in the vernacular of Greek, it came to have the new connotations of 'without land', 'the people of the countryside who are poor'. In other words, the word *dāmos* referred to a body of people who were without property and therefore not in the ranks of the superior class of wealthy landowners (the *gaiadamos* they continued to be called at Sparta) that now exercised political power – over the *dāmos*.

This remarkable change smoothed the way for another: the replacement of the old word *dāmos*, with its negative meaning of a downtrodden people without property or power, by the more positive-sounding word *dēmos*, which came to mean a body of people that was potentially fit to govern. The status of the word *dēmos* changed from that of a lowly mob worthy only of being beaten with a stick – the image articulated by the warrior Odysseus in the *Iliad* – to that of a potential ruling class. The upshot was that by the middle of the fifth century, in the city of Athens, the derivative word *dēmos* appeared in inscriptions (few of which otherwise survived before this period) and in literary prose (although such prose written between c. 460 and 430 has been completely lost).

Antiphon used it in his orations, where at one point in *For the Choregus* there is talk of the custom of making offerings to Dēmokratia. The earliest historian Herodotus speaks of her. So did the first Athenian political pamphleteer, Pseudo-Xenophon, who laid into democracy repeatedly. Although, for metrical reasons, the word *dēmokratia* doesn't appear in the oldest surviving poetry and lyrics, it does appear in the oldest surviving comedy, the *Acharnians* by Aristophanes, a ribald diatribe against the miseries of war first performed in the year 425 BCE. There is also an important passage on the subject of democracy in *The Suppliants*, a tragedy by Aeschylus. First performed around 463 BCE, and a great favourite of Athenian audiences, it reports a public meeting at which 'the air bristled with hands, right hands held high, a full vote, democracy turning decision into law'. Set in a mythical time past, the tragedy tells of a group of sisters, cousins of an African ruler named Aegyptus, who arrive with their father at the Greek city of Argos, claiming that they have escaped rape and forced marriage. Pelasgus, the King of Argos, is confronted with a choice: between satisfying the deities by honouring the sacred law of hospitality (and ensuring protection of the suppliants) and exposing his polity to the wrath and military might of Aegyptus. The king chooses prudently. The suppliants are granted asylum.

So with the help of the past, the Athenian *dēmos* took over an old descriptor and breathed new life into its body. It might be too slick to say that Athens democratised the old Mycenaean word *dāmos*, but its act of reinterpretation towards the end of the sixth century was bold and imaginative. It demonstrated just how much Athens was robustly aware of its own contours, its foibles and successes – its utter originality when compared to other ways of governing the world of human affairs, past and present. The invention and use of the word *dēmokratia* to express this originality naturally caused a grand stir. Yet its growing popularity in Athens during the years marked by tyrannicide, popular revolt and political reform also produced an almighty backlash, as might have been expected. This was after all a time when politics was still dominated by aristocrats locked in competition with themselves, and with their opponents. What this self-styled class of aristocrats had in common was their deep disgust for democracy. Volumes of vituperation against it poured from their quills. They hated the word. They despised everything for which it stood. Whenever they heard talk of *dēmokratia*, it confirmed to them that the whole of Athens had taken a wrong turn, foolishly placed itself in the hands of a self-interested sectional group. This so-called *dēmos* was to be loathed and feared. It was poor and property-less, ignorant and excitable. Worst of all, it was driven by a wolfish hunger for political power.

The depth of this frontal attack on democracy should not be missed. For many Athenian aristocrats, democracy was not just an unhinged polity, a type of government racked and ruined by the exercise of selfish sectional power over others. They pointed out that the word *dēmokratia* had negative connotations buried deep within it – connotations of manipulation, trickery and violence. That was why they were sure that much was at stake whenever it was used – and why it had to be given a bad name.

To understand their train of thinking, consider for a moment the verb *kratein*. Nowadays it is usually translated (through the Latin *regulare*: to control, to exercise sway over somebody or something) as 'to rule' or 'to govern', but its original connotations are in fact much harsher, tougher, even brutal. Strange it may seem to us, but when Athenians used the verb they spoke the language of military manoeuvring and military conquest. *Kratein* means to be master of, to conquer, to lord over, to possess (in modern Greek the same verb means to keep, or to hold), to be the stronger, to prevail or get the upper hand over somebody, or something. The story of the origins of the world and the birth of the deities told by the Greek poet Hesiod in his *Theogony* uses the word in this way: the personified figure of Kratos is seen as the no-nonsense, loyal agent of the much-feared Zeus. The noun *kratos*, from which the compound *dēmokratia* was formed, referred to might, strength, triumphant power and victory over others, especially through the application of force. The now obsolete verb *dēmokrateo* brimmed with all of these connotations: it meant to grasp power, or to exercise control over others.

Seen from a twenty-first-century vantage point, these are indeed strange connotations, exactly because for many Athenians, and most certainly for its enemies, the word *dēmokratia* had the *opposite* meaning it has today. When we employ the word, we use it positively, to mean non-violent inclusiveness, power-sharing based on compromise and fairness, equality based upon the legally guaranteed respect for others' dignity. For its Athenian critics, in striking contrast, *dēmokratia* was a menace. They agreed that it was a unique form of rule – a calamitous form of rule in which the *dēmos* acts foolishly in pursuit of its own selfish interests. That is why they hated it. When the enemies of democracy spoke of *dēmokratia*, they wanted to point out that the *dēmos* was a particular group whose particular interests were not identical with everyone's interests. The fact that democracy was a woman reinforced the point. For in a *dēmokratia*, the *dēmos* holds *kratos*, which was their way of saying that, just like a woman, it is prone to act forcefully, to get its own particular way by using cunning and violence, against itself, but especially against others.

The opponents of democracy saw proof of the semantics in the world around them. They had long memories for incidents of the kind that had shocked Athenians when they heard news of the fate of the sixth-century city of Miletus (located on what is today the coast of Turkey). There, a disaffected *dēmos* hounded the local wealthy families from power, seized their cattle and used them to trample their children to death. Some of the ruling class managed to fight their way back into the city, rounded up the ringleaders, including their children, smothered them with tar, then set them on fire. Violent shenanigans triggered by appetites for power were very much on the mind of the Athenian philosopher Plato (c. 427–c. 347 BCE) when he remarked that democracy was a two-faced form of government, 'according to whether the masses rule over the owners of property by force or by consent'.[32] He considered democracy to be a gimcrack invention that corroded good government by pandering to the ignorant poor. He likened democracy to a ship manned by sapheads who refuse to believe that there is any such craft as navigation – sailors who treat helmsmen as useless stargazers. Switching metaphors, Plato even called it *theatrocracy*: comparing the assembly to rowdy theatregoers, he insisted that the presumption of democrats, that commoners are qualified to talk about everything, in defiance of immutable laws, leads to the reign of posturing, the rhetorical seduction of the powerless, and lawlessness among the powerful. The unknown Old Oligarch had much the same thing in mind when dressing down *dēmokratia* as the rule of the lowest and most misguided section of the population, the *dēmos*, who sometimes strive to govern by making common cause with sections of the aristocracy.[33] When this happens, he said, the people are ruled in their own name. Used in this way, *dēmokratia* still referred to a form of sectional rule based on force. But its emphasis underwent a subtle shift, towards something like empowerment *through* the people. In other words, *dēmokratia* is a form of government in which the people are ruled while seeming to rule.

Faced with such spirited attacks, the democrats of Athens chose to button their sun-dried lips and keep their bearded heads down – or so it has often been said. 'The philosophers attacked democracy', wrote one of the great twentieth-century experts on Athens, 'the committed democrats responded by ignoring them, by going about the business of government and politics in a democratic way, without writing treatises on the subject.'[34] That is a valuable way of seeing things, if only because it reminds us that, from the time of its birth, Athenian philosophy was largely an anti-democratic affair, something like an allergic reaction against the feelings for equality nurtured by democracy. Yet to see the missing reflections on democracy by Athenian democrats as due largely to their tactical silence is to squander a more fundamental point. It is this: the silence of Athenian democrats about their democracy enabled black ink to be squirted into its face by its octopoid enemies. Their efforts to silence democrats by polluting their reputation was the first recorded example in the history of democracy of how its enemies tried to take everything – by robbing their opponents of their own precious language.

Since the friends of Athenian democracy either mistrusted or never used writing as an instrument of public expression, the field of recorded history was left wide open to its opponents. That is why Athens produced no great theorist of democracy. It is also why virtually all the written commentaries on Athenian democracy were hostile to its novelty, especially to the way it stirred up public resistance by the poor to the rule of the rich. The attacks on democracy sprang from the minds of intellectuals who found the *dēmos* disgusting; these were men who indulged aristocratic sympathies, and who wanted to turn back the water clocks. In a city that both valued participation in public life and condemned aristocratic leisure, these were men, from the viewpoint of democrats, who not only clenched a fist in their minds whenever they spoke and wrote about democracy. These were quite literally men who were 'inactive', even 'useless'.

The democrats had a point. Writing in philosophical ways about democracy required wealth, leisure and distance from political life. That is why democrats were so opposed to the *aristoi* – and to their writing and thinking about democracy. The democrats' reaction was credible, but they were to pay heavily for their unwritten opposition. Firm believers in their own originality, convinced that they had a goddess on their side, the democrats underestimated the risk of their own obliteration, which is what nearly happened. In matters of memory, they put themselves at the mercy of a class that not merely dreamed of crushing underfoot the ugly beetle of Athenian democracy. The nobles were a class of amnesiacs that had something far more sinister in mind: they wanted nobody to record for posterity what democrats themselves had to say.

Hubris

The dirty tactics used against the language of Athenian democracy by its opponents were twice rewarded towards the end of the fifth century. During the Peloponnesian War, two coups briefly interrupted democratic government. Both interludes were named after the number of conspirators that had grabbed the reins of power: the Four Hundred in 411 BCE, and the Thirty, in 404 BCE. The limited numbers revealed the principal motive behind each of them: to reduce the size of the electorate by linking citizenship to property qualifications. Rearguard actions by men of property were to be repeated many times in the history of democracy, but in these two cases the attempt by Athenian oligarchs to overturn rule by the people produced rogue governments. Even Plato, the arch-opponent of democracy, writing in his *Seventh Epistle*, conceded that the government of the Thirty was such a disgrace that it made the democracy that came before it look rather appealing. We could say that there was a bigger point here, since the whole attack on democracy confirmed the rule that when it comes to politics – the inescapable process of determining who gets what, when and how – everybody should watch their backs. Politics produces losers, especially when some grow greedy for power over others – or so many Athenians thought. They were convinced that the gods and goddesses would heap destruction or 'nemesis' on kings, tyrants and great lords who chased after the world, blindly gambled with their power, sometimes risking everything for the sake of gain. Hubris (*hybris*) was their name for such gluttony. Ruin was said to be its penalty. Cupidity – the lust after money, fame, possessions or power – was stupidity.

This prompted some troubling questions: would the deities turn a blind eye to the meteoric rise to power of a city like Athens? Was there possibly a link between hubris and democracy?

The first Athenians to reflect upon the subject did so with a boldness that still resonates today. For these orators, poets, playwrights and thinkers, the ambitious striving for more than one's fair share of power, such that it seriously assaults the honour of others – hubris – is a chronic feature of political life. There are times and places when mortals forget their own mortality. When that happens, they so succumb to high spirits and misuses of their energy that they extract pleasure from causing harm to others, not for the sake of revenge but essentially because the harm that is inflicted seems to prove the inferiority of the victim. Hubris – a word possibly imported from the east, from the Hittite *huwap*, said to mean 'harm', 'maltreat' or 'outrage' – is cause and effect of a superiority complex. Acting as if they were gods, or bent on competing with the gods, those hungry for power over others typically violate the dignity of their foes. It turns them into victims of the desire for superiority. It causes them shame. That sense of hurt in the presence of others fans the coals of individual and collective anger, which burst easily into the flames of revenge. And so the misadventures of unbridled power invariably bring bad outcomes to ruler and ruled alike. The young and rich tend to fall into the trap of hubris, noted Aristotle: when they ill-treat others, they feel as though their own superiority is the greater. Hubris is the progeny of high position, the playwright Euripedes (480–406 BCE) explained in a famous passage in *The Suppliant Women*, where it is also said that the conqueror 'is like a poor man who has just become rich: he commits hubris, and his hubris causes him to be ruined in his turn'. Along similar lines, citizen Pericles was prompted to say that he feared before everything else that the proud democracy of Athens would make arrogant mistakes, such as acting cruelly against enemy cities, just for the hell of it.

The conviction that hubris harboured disaster, the effects of which are felt whenever power is exercised arrogantly, seemed obvious to Athenian democrats who raised their hands in protest against tyranny and oligarchy. But the point potentially applied to military campaigns conducted in the name of democracy. The case of Athens serves, in this history of democracy, as the opening example of the general rule that no democracy is an island unto itself. From its sixth-century beginnings, the whole experiment with democracy took place in a geopolitical laboratory of rivalry among states and empires set on using violence against their neighbours. Throughout most of the sixth-century BCE, before the age of democracy, Athens had been lucky. Involved in less than a dozen military campaigns, all of them for limited goals, it had been just one among many of the region's mountainous island micro-polities, without a substantial army or navy. But just two years after the constitutional reforms instituted by Cleisthenes had begun to whittle down the power of the old aristocracy, setting Athens on a course towards democratic rule, trouble began. The states of Boeotia and Chalcis, the traditional enemies of Athens, launched a simultaneous attack. Both suffered defeat in a single day. Many observers were impressed. Athens was to win yet more admiration for its support for Ionian Greeks in their ill-fated revolt against Persia – whose army commanded by Darius was roundly defeated in 490 BCE, on the plain of Marathon, by nine thousand Athenian troops, helped by a small contingent from Plataia.

Democracy's stunning victory against the great empire of the East fuelled many Athenians' mistrust of barbarians (*barbaroi*: a word which to them meant simply 'foreigners', non-Greeks who spoke incomprehensible languages). The triumph of the Athenian David over the Persian Goliath was consolidated (in 480/479 BCE) by further successes, notably in the sea battle of Salamis. Such military gains began to tip the balance of power throughout the whole region, in favour of Athens. But that in turn raised the stakes. By piling up victories, the democracy was steadily drawn into a protracted struggle, mainly against Sparta, for hegemony over the Greek world. In the wake of the triumph over the Persians, there began, during the 480s, thanks to a windfall of silver, a vigorous expansion of the navy. Two hundred warships were constructed. Resources were poured into building vast fortifications to protect the city, including its port of Piraeus. Then came the first efforts to assume leadership of a confederacy of several hundred Greek states, called the Delian League. Vowing 'to have the same friends and enemies', its military aim was the liberation from Persian control of the Greek island states and cities of Asia Minor (modern Turkey). Step by step, state by state, battle by battle, Athens turned herself into an imperial power – into what the Athenians called an *arkhē*.

By 450 BCE, Athens had no fewer than 160 subject states around its imperial fingers. How did it happen? The growth of empire was, of course, nurtured by the geographical fact that she found herself almost at exactly the centre of a vast region stretching from the southern Balkan peninsula across the entire Aegean. But the feeling that Athens was the centre of the universe of Greek-speaking peoples was rooted in more than geography. There was a strong sense among Athenians that they were greatly superior to the tough, but politically disorganised Thracian and Scythian peoples living to the north-east of the Greek world. Athenians also thought of themselves as several cuts above Asiatic peoples, who were mostly ruled by the Persian empire. These 'barbarian' peoples to the east were widely supposed to be uncourageous and less bellicose, partly due to their climatic conditions, whose seasons were more uniform and equable, without the sudden changes in temperature that the Athenians supposed toughened their own wills and stirred up their own passions. The flaccidity of the Asians was also traced to their peculiar customs, laws and political institutions – especially to the fact that these peoples were mostly ruled by monarchs, who had managed through time to ruin their subjects by turning them into creatures too weak-willed to put up a fight for their own good.

These dogmas sprouted wings after the stunning Athenian victories in the great Persian Wars (490–480 BCE); the subsequent extension of Athenian sea power to the Aegean and the coast of Asia Minor, areas once ruled by Persia, had the same effect. The upshot was immense pride among the Athenians. They regarded their democracy as a source of strength to act on the wide world around them. By the middle of the fifth century BCE, 'power' and the striving for its accumulation stood at the centre of the experiences and expectations of the Athenians. Power politics and imperialism were seen as typically Athenian, and as typically democratic. The reputation of Athens as a 'busybody' constantly striving for power over others became synonymous with democracy itself. Democracy encouraged citizens to think of themselves as lords paramount, as rulers of the world as they knew it. Strong traces of pride in their democratic achievements are much in evidence, for instance in Thucydides' famous account of the funeral oration delivered by Pericles at the beginning of the Peloponnesian War. 'For this land of ours, in which the same people have never ceased to dwell in an unbroken line of successive generations, they by their valour transmitted to our times a free state [and] the empire we now possess', Pericles reportedly said. 'We live under a form of government which does not emulate the institutions of our neighbours; on the contrary, we are ourselves a model which some follow, rather than the imitators of other peoples . . . [O]ur government is called a democracy, because its administration is in the hands, not of the few, but of the many . . . And our city is so great that all the products of all the earth flow in upon us . . . We are also superior to our opponents in our system of training for warfare . . . Wealth we employ rather as an opportunity for action than as a subject for boasting . . . For we alone regard the man who takes no part in public affairs, not as one who minds his own business, but as good for nothing; and we Athenians decide public questions for ourselves or at least endeavour to arrive at a sound understanding of them, in the belief that it is not debate that is a hindrance to action, but rather not to be instructed by debate before the time comes for action . . . In short', concluded Pericles, 'I say that our city as a whole is the School of Hellas.'[35]

Talk of Athens as teacher and master of the whole Greek world burned as dried dung in the fires of empire. It did so by fostering belief in the citizenly virtue of military prowess – and by twinning *dēmokratia* and military success. It was a simple but lethal concoction. Imperial power necessitated the mobilisation of troops, who in return expected a share of government. At the beginning, the backbone of the Athenian army had been self-funded. The wealthier citizens served in the cavalry, mounted in their own saddles, on their own horses. The subsequent reliance on the hoplite battle as a principal method of waging war kick-started a new dynamic. Backed up by horsemen and archers, usually on a flat field, infantry marched against infantry; the winner on the field took all and, as a rule, the entire war came to an end. This new form of tournament fighting had democratic consequences, for the growth of a light-armed infantry made up of poorer hoplites made their case for inclusion in the polity irrefutable. But as the Athenian navy grew in power and influence democracy's logic of inclusion meant as well that the poorest citizens, the *thetes* who formed the bulk of navy crews, pressed for full equality with their fellow citizens. The sea and democracy seemed to be twins too. 'The steersman, the boatswain, the lieutenant, the look-out man at the prow, the shipwright – these are the people who confer power on the city far rather than her heavy infantry and men of birth and quality', noted one observer.[36]

Among the ironies of the bungled murder of Hipparchus was the way it triggered political reforms that required the free males of the whole of Attica to register as citizens in their *demes* and tribes, thus effectively putting in place the city's first ever, standardised system of mass mobilisation. Given the size and population of Attica – twenty times larger than the average Greek polity – organised call-up, initially of hoplites, gave democratic Athens a huge military edge on its potential rivals. But the deadly connection between democracy and empire ran deeper. Despite mounting death tolls, battle success provided good cheer for some Athenians. The spirit of war seemed to fill a vacuum; it shielded them against the chronic uncertainty for which democracy itself was partly responsible. Its citizens, of course, toughened their resolve, and generally succoured their lives, by many different means: poetry and singing, theatre and sports, cult feasts and politics at the Pnyx, brothels and symposia with plenty of drink and penetration of guests. But compared with all these life-giving rituals, the near-permanent mobilisation for war had a special potency. War and rumours of war put a spring into the steps of the *dēmos*, as the comic dramatist Aristophanes (c. 446–388 BCE) pointed out forcefully when joking that his fellow citizens would launch a fleet of 300 warships if their Spartan enemies dared to steal even a puppy.[37] War made everyone equal in the struggle to escape the clutches of death. It encouraged painful toil that produced honour. It confirmed men's sense of manly excellence (the Athenians spoke of *aretē*). War blessed life with unshakeable meaning. It parenthesised the pessimistic thought that men were like leaves in the wind, the mere shadows of shadows, meant only for the moment, like a passing day.

Fighting against enemies made men feel that they were valuable citizens. It also brought wealth to their pockets. Democracy profited from empire. The consolidation of imperial power tempted the Athenians to centralise their control over key legal cases, in effect to bring them from the periphery to Athens. That move created more work for the citizens of Athens, more opportunities for them to earn income and to participate in its legal machinery, which consequently grew in size and importance within the overall structures of the democracy. The physical size of the principal civil court of Athens (it was located in the south-west corner of the agora) reflected this; a large, square structure whose roof was partly open to the sky, it was certainly big enough to serve as a meeting place for between one and two thousand jurors. Empire also brought wealth and revenues to the democracy, partly to pay for its machinery of government and to employ vast numbers of ordinary Athenian males as soldiers. Save for a small number of states that chose to keep their nominal independence by providing ships that sailed in the Athenian fleets, all cities of the empire were required (by the early 440s) to pay an annual tribute; they were required as well to fork out duties on exports and imports that passed through the hub port of Piraeus.

The extent to which the wealth generated by empire was vital for the survival of democracy remains disputed. But there is little doubt that one of the most potent effects of empire – before it began to slip away during the fourth century – was to expand the power of military forces in the day-to-day functioning of the polity. More money from the public budget was spent on war and preparations for war than on any other activity. Imperial revenues were used to revolutionise the standard methods of war. The Athenians were good democrats. They were also good fighters. They experimented with siege warfare and tactical retreat. They trained their hoplites and naval crews for weeks and sometimes months, and perfected the art of using their ships as high-speed, offensive weapons. Huge numbers of ships and fighters were moved around the whole of the eastern Mediterranean for campaigns that sometimes lasted months or, when sieges were employed, up to a few years; even during peacetime, dozens of ships on practice and guard missions spent several months a year cruising the seas.

The democracy, already enjoying among friends and enemies alike a reputation for restlessness, hatched and executed new plans for fighting simultaneously on several fronts. During the fifth century, Athens found itself at war on average two out of every three years; never once did it enjoy more than a decade of peace. Especially with the introduction of pay for military service in the 450s, war came to dominate the everyday lives of Athenians, their visual arts, the proceedings of their assembly. Citizenship and military service grew indistinguishable; the spirit and institutions of democracy felt deeply 'martial'. At the outbreak of the Peloponnesian War, for instance, nearly a third of Athenian citizens were hoplites. When young men turned eighteen, they had to register as a citizen within their *deme*. Following the approval of their registration by the Council, some of them were inducted into military service, along with other conscripts from their tribe. These young servicemen learned how to fight in full armour; they became skilled in the use of the bow, the javelin and catapult. They were taught such arts by older men (usually over forty) who had been elected by their tribe to act as trainers, or mentors, of the young recruits. The young conscripts were in service for two years, after which they were entitled to have their names inscribed on stone columns that were prominently displayed within the agora. That rite of passage prepared them for a lifetime of vigilance. They remained on call for the next forty years; in a trice, in a military emergency, they could be instructed to report for active service with several days' provisions in hand.

The End of Democracy

When looking back on these times, it seems obvious that the dalliance of democracy and armed force proved fatal for Athens. During the zenith of empire in the fifth century, it led to restrictions upon political freedoms at home. Empire bred demagoguery. It gave undue prominence to elected military leaders like Cimon and Pericles, who (unusually) were entitled to hold office for several successive terms. These men of the battlefield were entitled by custom to interrupt assembly proceedings, to introduce their own business. That meant that their enormous power to determine the city's fate, unchecked by parties, laws or customs, depended mainly on their skilful rhetorical massaging of the body of citizens gathered in the assembly. Surrounded by advisers, Pericles carefully cultivated his charisma by likening himself to Athens' courier ship, the *Salaminia*: enjoying office for a quarter of a century (from 454 to 429 BCE), he appeared before the assembly only when pressing public matters required urgent treatment. Thucydides and others understandably complained that when he did appear in public, before the assembly for instance, he spoke and acted like an arrogant monarch. 'Hatred and unpopularity have become the lot of all who have aspired to rule others', Pericles said to mourners gathered to honour dead soldiers. But he added, defiantly: 'Remember, too, that if your country has the greatest name in all the world, it is because she has never bent before disaster; because she has expended more life and effort in war than any other city, and has won for herself a power greater than any hitherto known . . . it will be remembered that we held rule over more Hellenes than any other Hellenic state, that we carried out the greatest wars against their united or separate powers, and inhabited a city unrivalled by any other in its resources or magnitude.'

The great leader's words dripped with the poison of hubris. They spelled out not just the death of soldiers and civilians. They pointed to the beginning of the end of the Athenian experiment with democracy. Its decline was protracted, certainly. Setbacks were camouflaged by victories. Whether it could or should have behaved differently, for instance abandoning the quest for empire by forming partnership alliances based upon give-and-take compromise, remains a moot point. Yet there is no doubt that the growing militarisation of political life in support of empire began to turn Athens into its own worst enemy – into a source of envy and jealousy among the states within and beyond its empire. At home, it unleashed a malignant force that the Athenians called delusion (*ate* was their word for it). The stench of death bred political hallucinations, of the kind manifested in their declining interest in compromise, and in their habit of seeing glory in the fall of cities, and in the misfortune of other peoples. Especially during the fifth century, appeals to a fictive common ancestry also grew ever louder. Such appeals took their cue from a restrictive law of citizenship (passed in 451 BCE) that tried to make it impossible for resident aliens (metics) and foreigners to become Athenian citizens. The city had previously allowed a citizen to marry and father children with either an Athenian or a foreign-born woman. After the passage of the law, foreign women were ineligible for marriage, while children born illegitimately from foreign women were ineligible for citizenship.

The effect of limiting citizenship to those born from two native Athenians was to clamp down on women, who, after all, had within them the power to grant both sexual pleasure and children to men, hence the power to violate distinctions between insiders and outsiders, Athenians and barbarians, free persons and slaves, legitimate citizens and bastards. The limitation of citizenship was also a warning to free men to pay attention to their city by strengthening their feelings for descent, bloodline and nativity. All this was not yet racism or nationalism, as we have known it in modern times. Athenians did not think of themselves as either a 'race' or as a 'nation'. But, thanks to the constant pressures of war, they found themselves caught up in a drive towards internal 'purification' that was fuelled by fear of enemies. Suspicion was directed against those suspected of being born of impure eggs and careless sperm. The first outlines of what in modern times would be called witch-hunting became evident, for instance in the abuse hurled publicly at the bad boy of fifth-century Athenian democracy, Alcibiades, who was said to have fathered a son with a Melian slave woman, so breeding an enemy of democracy. On several occasions, along the same lines, every available citizen was compulsorily drafted into the navy or army to fight against a neighbouring city; and laws were passed by the assembly to enable citizenship to be stripped from those found guilty of desertion or draft-dodging.

That was not the end of the story. The deadly dalliance of democracy and armed force had wider, geopolitical implications. The democracy obviously carried within it the seeds of expansion by anti-democratic means. 'Wherever you go, there will you be a *polis*' was the old watchword of Greek colonisation from the time of the westwards expansion, during the eighth century BCE, towards Sicily and southern Italy. At first, Athenians refused the impulse to expand. Temptation soon ruled. Democracy became synonymous with the continuous emigration and interaction of Athenian settlers, from far distant Marseilles and down the Spanish coast in the west, to the Crimea and the eastern end of the Black Sea, in the north-east. The spread of Athenian power, especially during the first half of the fifth century, usually went hand in hand with the creation and nurturing of democratic ways of life. New architectural forms and public space sprang up. A new form of government, run by citizens for citizens, was installed. So, too, were legal systems that followed the rule that nobody was to be above the laws, and that laws must apply equally to everybody.

These inventions undoubtedly proved attractive to others; in various parts of the burgeoning empire, citizens downtrodden by their local nobility or suffering from *stasis* sometimes welcomed Athenian intervention in their local affairs. A model example was the rebuilding in 444/443 BCE of the ancient city of Sybaris, which received an influx of settlers, a new layout and a brand-new democratic constitution. The trouble was that democracy did not spring naturally from the depths of the Aegean, or the region's soil, or from the souls of its peoples. Athens discovered that democracy promotion was difficult. Democratic lawgivers found that their subjects were sometimes far from law-abiding. Democratic laws might therefore have to be imposed, perhaps by cunning or, if necessary, by means of violence. But if that were to happen, Athenian democracy would then find it hard to 'place things in the middle', as their citizens liked to put it. Athens would come face to face with an ugly possibility: in the name of democracy, and for the sake of holding or expanding its own position, it might be forced to set up garrison colonies, to plunder whole cities, even to heap cruelty on those who tried to stand in its way.

Precisely this happened, in 416/415 BCE, during the expedition launched by Athens against the Aegean island of Melos. A prosperous Spartan colony located directly to the south of Athens, Melos had claimed that it was militarily neutral in the region's conflicts. A decade earlier, the island had successfully repelled an invasion by the Athenians, whose generals this time tried diplomacy, rather than force. Their envoys were received within the city, but their request to address the full body of assembled citizens was refused. So negotiations with the Melian authorities were held in private. Trained in the rough and tumble of assembly life, the Athenians were tough bargainers. They insisted there could be no discussion of the rights and wrongs of the situation. They said the sole matter to be analysed was the imbalance of power between the two states. Melos was told that it had to submit – or suffer disaster – but the Melians stood their ground, mainly by trying to persuade the Athenians that it would serve their interests better if they allowed Melos to remain neutral. The Athenian negotiators firmly rejected that argument. Then they burst into laughter. A quarrel about the importance of honour followed. The Athenians then withdrew.

After returning home, the Athenian negotiators were informed that the Melians refused to budge. No surrender under any circumstances was their position. So the Athenian generals declared war. For several months, Melos was cordoned off from the outside world. The siege had terrible effects. Starvation followed by discord and treachery resulted in the unconditional surrender of the Melians. The Athenian democrats wasted no time in pulling apart the local polity. They executed all captured men of military age and sold the women and children into slavery, leaving infants and the elderly to the mercy of wolves. Five hundred citizen-settlers were soon shipped to Melos. The island became a colony of Athens. The rule of democracy was sealed, in cruelty and blood.

What were the lessons of the campaign against Melos? For a start, it showed that democracy could be good at war, and could inflict terrible violence upon its neighbours. The campaign proved as well that violence was a double-edged sword for the Athenian democracy. It could be charged with double standards – and with acts of military reprisal. The heroic survival of the Athenian democracy against its Spartan and Persian enemies had a flip side: by arming to protect itself, by stirring up trouble (as Athens did in Macedonia from the early 360s BCE) and acting as if it had been born into the world to give no rest either to itself or to others, it encouraged its rivals to seek, and to win, the ultimate prize: forcing Athens on to its knees, and drowning it in its own deep pools of blood.

During the last quarter of the fourth century BCE, exactly that came to pass. Pressured by hubris at home and military defeats abroad, Athens was forced to give way to the well-armed kingdom of Macedon. The spectacular rise to power of Philip II in 359 BCE signalled the beginning of the end for democracy. If Harmodius and Aristogeiton were the first heroes of democracy, Philip II of Macedon was its ultimate villain. Within his recently discovered vaulted tomb at Aegeae is a spotted marble fresco depicting a bearded king hunting on horseback. Fixing one eye on his prey – Philip lost the sight of his right eye in battle – he bears down on a lion, poised for the kill. Philip indeed enjoyed a wide reputation as a brilliant soldier of aristocratic descent; it was convenient that he happened as well to be an absolute ruler of a large population. None of his smaller or less bellicose neighbours managed to stand up to him. Striking first in one direction, then in the other, making peace with one enemy as a prelude to annihilating the next, between 359 and 339 BCE he ruthlessly extended Macedonian control south to central Greece and eastwards, towards the Sea of Marmara.

The Athenians went on high alert. So terrified were they that at one point political business at the Pnyx was paralysed by morbid silence.[38] The Athenian troops meanwhile tried several times to stop the one-eyed king in his cavalry tracks. But when they despatched troops to protect Byzantium (Istanbul), Philip out-manoeuvred them by suddenly marching down on to the Greek lands, towards Athens.

For nearly two centuries, several times the Athenian democracy had escaped mortal wounding, but now its time was up. It is true that its defeat was to take nearly eighty years. There was plenty of high-spirited resistance from the Athenians, for instance through the themes, rhetorical conventions and plot devices of popular comedies written and staged by poets and playwrights like Menander (342–291 BCE); and, of course, the archaeological ruins and political vision of Athens were to live on, as a little dream. Helped by posterity, the city would be remembered, in all four corners of the earth, as an experiment that had defied prevailing political customs. It had cultivated institutions – public juries, free public discussion, voting by lot, or through a show of hands, or pebbles in a pot – that enabled not just men of good blood and wealth, but humble carpenters, farmers, sailors and shoemakers to make their own laws. It had shown how the powerless could win the power to reprimand their leaders, and to govern themselves, as political equals. But whatever else the city of Athens had stood for was about to be damaged badly, by a string of events that are now landmarks of a great but tragic history.

In 338 BCE, backed by a gigantic army of 32,000 men, Philip II crushed the democrats and their allies at the Battle of Chaeronea, in Boeotia, to the north-west of Athens. The battle was reportedly protracted and vicious. More than a thousand Athenians fell in battle; at least two thousand were taken prisoner. The rout by slaughter allowed Philip militarily to subjugate the whole of the Peloponnese, and to establish Macedonian garrisons at many key points. The hundreds of polities of the Greek lands were reorganised into a league under his control – the so-called League of Corinth – after which a general peace was proclaimed, in preparation for an all-out attack on Persia. Despite the assassination of Philip by one of his trusted bodyguards, at the annual Macedonian sunrise festival in 336 BCE, the Athenian empire was forced to get down on its knees. But despite the setback at Chaeronea, its assembly struck back. It passed several emergency measures, including one championed by the orator Hyperides, to provide for the call-up of every able-bodied man, to defend the city against the Macedonian invasion that now seemed imminent. That political move caused eyebrows to be raised, since by including up to 150,000 slaves and alien residents it effectively extended citizenship to all adult males. Decisions were taken as well to stockpile armour, weapons and gold, and to fortify the city and the navy. Many democrats compared the coming contest with the Macedonians to the famed Persian Wars of the previous century – and hoped that the city would taste ultimate victory.

The Macedonians reacted cautiously, as if they knew how to lull the democracy into complacency, in order better to kill its spirit. The tactic worked. When the expected Macedonian invasion didn't materialise, Hyperides was put on trial, and convicted, for proposing an illegal measure. The Macedonians, meanwhile, tightened the foreign-policy noose around the neck of the Athenians, who in 322 BCE suffered another catastrophic military defeat during the Greek-led rebellion against Macedonian rule, known as the Lamian War. Athens was forced this time to pay a much higher price. As part of the peace settlement that followed, Macedonian troops led by Antipater stormed the agora and promptly replaced the democratic government with an oligarchy. Somewhere between 12,000 and 22,000 Athenian citizens were disfranchised. Some were packed off to remote Thrace. Quite a few democratic leaders, among them Hyperides and Demosthenes, either suicided or were executed.

The remaining supporters of democracy licked their wounds, hoping against hope that their democracy would survive the seesaw of sordid fortunes. When Antipater fell ill and died in 319 BCE, democracy did indeed return briefly to the city, but only until Antipater's scheming eldest son, Cassander, installed Demetrius of Phaleron as direct governor of Athens. He ruled the city for a decade, after which local democrats fought back, did deals with the Macedonians, played along with their boasts about liberating other Greek cities from oligarchy, only to suffer once again the imposition of oligarchy. Such was the power of their lingering spirit of resistance that in 287 BCE, against tremendous odds, the Athenians managed yet again to claw back their structures of self-government, this time for some twenty-five years. But the Macedonians would have nothing of it. In the year 260 BCE, Antigonus Gonatas, the son of Demetrius, ordered his troops to recapture the city. Its democrats were crushed, this time for good.

Gradually, painfully, a democracy had suffered its first death.

WEST BY EAST

'Where shall I begin, please your Majesty?' he asked. 'Begin at the beginning,' the King said, very gravely, 'and go on till you come to the end; then stop.'

Lewis Carroll, *Alice's Adventures in Wonderland* (1865)

The step-by-step pillaging of Athenian democracy, the scattering of its remains in the cities and countryside by the marauding troops of the Macedonian empire, had the effect among writers of deadening interest in the whole subject of *dēmokratia*. It slid slowly into obscurity. Democracy became little more than a fribble, an odd fossil in the curiosity shop of Greek antiquity.

The job of forgetting Athens started during the Roman republic that lasted nearly five centuries. Historians and political writers either dismissed it as a legally disordered state undeserving of serious examination, or (as with Cicero) condemned the ingratitude of its *dēmos* towards their leaders. During the early years of the Roman Empire, which is customarily thought to have begun during the first century CE, figures like the historian Pompeius Trogus and the writer and rhetorician Valerius Maximus (whose father had served as secretary and interpreter for Julius Caesar) remained unimpressed by Athens; conscious that Rome had slipped and degenerated since the glorious days of its republic, they nevertheless comforted themselves with the thought that Romans still towered above the world, that they were morally and politically superior to the Greeks. The proof of Rome's superiority was the decline and death of democracy.

By the time the Roman Empire had mutated into the Byzantine world that mixed together Roman legal traditions with elements of Greek and Christian culture and prepared the way for what is now called the Middle Ages – a term that we shall soon see makes no sense in the history of democracy – most people seemed to have forgotten the subject entirely. Among those who still thought about matters of power and the sharing of power, the overthrow of Greek democracy by military conquest and monarchy nurtured an interest in the need for written, mixed constitutions. Constitutions were seen as devices for countering what a statesman and historian from Megalopolis called Polybius (201–120 BCE) called 'hubris and arrogance'. When political men fall prey to their charms, so the thinking ran, the constitution comes to the rescue. It does so by stopping one part of the polity, an army or a faction of the landowning aristocracy for instance, from seizing power by enabling another part to stand in its way. Rarely did this kind of defence of written constitutions cross-refer to the old Greek ideal of democracy, though at least one commentator, a publicist and travelling scholar from a wealthy, Greek-speaking Jewish family named Philo of Alexandria (c. 15 BCE–50 CE), explicitly did so. Philo's work and life – he was no cloistered bookworm – were part of the great cultural scene in Alexandria, at this time the largest and easily the most vibrant city in the Mediterranean world. The system of self-government called democracy is about equality under the law (isotēs), Philo liked to say. But he stressed as well that that did not mean democracy is rule of the people, something he viewed with disapproval. Democracy meant – note the parallels here with what the word democracy has come to mean today – legally sanctioned alternation in the exercise of power, such that one group temporarily rules others, so that through time each group or person receives in turn their fair share of power.

Philo's meditations on democracy, including his rejection of popular rule, were born of conditions of post-democracy: although in his part of the world the language of dēmokratia was practically extinct, many surviving reports show just how often, in the region's city plazas, amphitheatres and racetracks, a lively dēmos continued to shout, bargain or riot its way to success, often in opposition to top-down rule. There were sometimes bizarre moments of great consequence, as in Jerusalem (Mark 15: 8ff; Matthew 27: 15ff), where during Passover a 'crowd began their demands as they usually did' for the release of a prisoner, a man accused of murder. The local governor named Pilate at first refused the assembly's demand; he proposed instead to release a man named Jesus, but the people grew upset. 'They shouted back, "Crucify him!"' The governor, 'in his desire to satisfy them', caved in. Lung power prevailed. The man accused of murder was released; Jesus was led away by soldiers, flogged and crucified. Such outcomes confirmed Philo's suspicion that rule by the people always suffered from agonising contradictions, but the truth was that his view did not much matter. As the Romans and then Byzantines tightened their grip on the whole region that is today the eastern Mediterranean, the flesh-and-blood power of the *dēmos* lost contact with the ideals of *dēmokratia*. Memories of Athens by and large disappeared. It would be more accurate to say that Athens was disappeared. It fell prey to the forces of amnesia, a pawn in the hands of opponents who were sometimes so convinced of its obsolescence that they thought it expedient to forget even what they knew about it. At best – the thought is sobering when measured against the global popularity of democracy in our times – tiny memories of its grand achievements were kept alive in the parchment manuscripts of scholars who read the works of figures such as Polybius and Philo, but who were mainly preoccupied with larger matters of law and philosophy, and later Christianity.

Little changed with the fourteenth-century Renaissance rediscovery of ancient Greek and Roman culture and political institutions. Many who took an interest in the classical world, political commentators like Giannotti and Guicciardini for instance, preferred armed republics because they thought them to be better than democracy at maintaining law and order, and promoting good government. The rest, fearing outbreaks of popular rebellion, urged the taming of the plebs through 'mixed constitutions', such as those of Sparta or Rome. For all of these observers, the little dream of democracy was more like a nightmare, as was explained by the most famous and influential contemporary political writer, Niccolò Machiavelli (1469–1527) (Figure 11). This is how he put it: for one reason or another, the rule of princes (monarchy) sooner or later degenerates into tyranny. Tyranny is then replaced by the rule of an aristocracy that tends towards oligarchy. Popular struggles bent on overthrowing rule by the few clear the path to democracy, but any polity founded on the rule of the sovereign people quickly degenerates into anarchy – into licence that fuels the fires of political decadence. This favours the rise of monarchy, government by a prince, so triggering the infernal cycle of monarchy, tyranny, oligarchy and licentious disorder.[1]

Machiavelli captured the anti-democratic tempo of the times. Well into the sixteenth century, all writers were lukewarm about or downright hostile towards the Athenian experiment. They presumed that the origins of democracy could be forgotten with impunity, and they did so by parroting the classical critiques, especially by branding Athenian democracy a misguided political formula for disorder, contempt for law and foolish injustice to wise

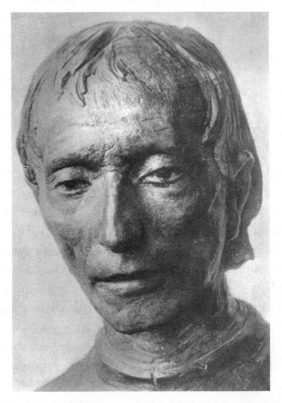

FIGURE 11: Terracotta bust of Niccolò Machiavelli, by an unknown sixteenth-century master.

figures like Socrates. Exactly that negative message leaped from the pages of Jean Bodin's *Six Bookes of a Commonwealth* (1576), a work that was translated into many languages and enjoyed much popularity throughout Europe. 'If we shall believe Plato,' ran the first English translation of 1606, 'wee shall find that he hath blamed a Popular estate, tearming it, A Faire where every thing is to bee sold. We have the like opinion of Aristotle, saying, That neither Popular nor Aristocraticall estate is good, using the authorities of Homer ... And the Orator Maximus Tirius holds, That a democraty is pernicious, blaming for this cause the estate of the Athenians, Syracusians, Carthagineans and Ephesians: for it is impossible (saith Seneca) that he shall please the people, that honours virtue.' Such testimonies, selectively drawn from the past, convinced Bodin that democracy was worth forgetting, that the very idea of self-governing assemblies deserved nothing more than contempt. 'How can a multitude, that is to say, a Beast with many heads, without iugement, or reason, give any good councel?' he asked. The answer was easy: 'To ask councel of a Multitude (as they did in oldtimes in Popular Commonweals) is to seek for wisdome of a mad man.'[2]

This kind of prejudice against Athens persisted well into modern times. There were a few charitable figures, but mostly contempt or indifference condemned Athenian democracy to the prisons of mental and political life. Far into the eighteenth century, on the subject of democracy, political figures and thinkers within the Atlantic region found more to condemn than to praise. The first dictionaries in France and England treated democracy with a cool hand; like an epitaph, the word referred to a dead form of polity that had flourished for a brief time in Athens, only to succumb to its inherent flaws. 'It would be a happy thing if popular government could conserve the love of virtue, the execution of laws, morals and frugality,' commented Monsieur de Jaucourt in his entry on 'Democracy' in the greatest French encyclopaedia of the eighteenth century. Pointing to the experience of Athens, he went on to conclude that 'it is the fate of this government to become almost infallibly the prey of the ambition of certain citizens or of strangers and so to exchange precious liberty for the greatest servitude'.[3] Dr Samuel Johnson's *Dictionary of the English Language*

(1755) handed over the task of defining the word 'democratical' to the well-fed English Anglican author Sir Thomas Browne (1605–82). He had not a kind word for the 'Democratical enemies of truth'. They played on the instincts of 'the People', a body of halfwits who 'live and die in their absurdities; passing their days in perverted apprehensions, and conceptions of the World, derogatory unto God, and the wisdom of the Creation'.[4]

Amen. During the same generation, on the far shores of the Atlantic, virtually all of the American revolutionaries adopted a similar standpoint, with passion and purpose. All the evidence goes against the popular view that they were the 'founding fathers' of democracy in their country, or that they were the founders of modern liberal democracy, as has been claimed by Francis Fukuyama.[5] The American revolutionaries were in fact Romans rather than Athenians. Favouring a mixed republican constitution modelled on republican Rome, they consistently saw themselves as avoiding the folly and trickery bound up with the spent ideal of democracy. At the convention that assembled behind locked doors and closed windows in the red-brick Pennsylvania State House in Philadelphia for four exhaustive months of constitution making, from mid-May to mid-September 1787, speaker after speaker, day after day, distanced himself from the whole idea of democracy.

Let us eavesdrop on the morning and afternoon sessions of Thursday 31 May.[6] After agreeing the need for a new national legislature made up of two chambers, the delegates fell openly into disagreement about whether or not the 'lower' house, later to be called the House of Representatives, should be based on popular election. Mr Roger Sherman from New Haven, Connecticut, said he favoured a scheme based on the appointment of members by the existing state legislatures. He was opposed to 'election by the people' because they always 'want [lack] information and are constantly liable to be misled'. In full agreement, Mr Elbridge Thomas Gerry from Massachusetts – famously remembered for later voting against the constitution because it did not contain a Bill of Rights, and for his part in introducing the word gerrymandering into the language of democracy – sprang to his feet. 'The evils we experience flow from the excess of democracy', he said. 'The people do not want virtue, but are the dupes of pretended patriots.' He went on to express his concerns about the grave dangers of 'the levelling spirit'.

Forced on to the back foot, the advocates of some or other form of popular election bounced back. What is striking is that not one of them defended democracy by name. Mr George Mason from Virginia said that the country needed a 'grand depositary of the democratic principle of Government', like the House of Commons in Britain, but he quickly confessed to his fellow delegates that recent events in the newly independent country had shown it to be 'too democratic'. Mr James Wilson from Pennsylvania backed him up. 'No government could long subsist without the confidence of the people', he said, quickly adding that that was why 'republican Government', and not democracy, was now required. Choosing his moment carefully, Mr James Madison from Virginia then took the floor. The man who elsewhere famously remarked that democracy was 'a vile form of government' told the convention that day that he agreed that 'popular election of one branch of the National Legislature' was essential in a scheme of 'free Government'. He cleverly went on to say that he thought the second chamber of the legislature, plus the executive and the judiciary, should be set up on an appointed basis. He described himself as a friend of 'the policy of refining the popular appointments by successive filtrations', only then to conclude that the new form of government under discussion 'should rest on the solid foundation of the people'. Talk of 'filtering' and 'refining' popular pressures seemed to settle the matter. The motion to establish a popularly elected first branch of a new national legislature was carried. Delaware and Connecticut delegates were divided, and those from New Jersey and South Carolina raised their voices for 'no'. But the delegates from Massachusetts, New York, Pennsylvania, Virginia, North Carolina and Georgia voted in favour. The Roman 'ayes' had it. Dinner was then served.

The Banker

By the last quarter of the eighteenth century, things looked bleak for democracy. Its rejection and disappearance as an ideal provide a salutary warning that the spirit, language and institutions of democracy enjoy no privileged historical status – that in matters of democracy the dead are never safe in the hands of the living. The resuscitation of democracy, as we are about to see, happened with difficulty and against tremendous odds, but by the early nineteenth century there were signs that the victim was still breathing. The Athenian revival was a hands-on work of political and intellectual labour, above all by several European historians.[7] Jean Victor Duruy (1811–94), who helped Napoleon III prepare his biography of Julius Caesar and went on to become minister of education in France, published a three-volume illustrated history of ancient Greece. The Lübeck-born German historian Ernst Curtius (1814–96), who had conducted archaeological fieldwork in Greece and later became court tutor to Prince Frederick William (after-wards Emperor Frederick III), published an earlier multi-volume history of Greece. But of greatest importance was the sympathetic account of ancient Greece by a middle-class Englishman, a banker, utilitarian thinker, university governor, parliamentarian, husband and self-styled democrat named George Grote (1794–1871).

His hugely influential *History of Greece*, published in a dozen volumes between 1846 and 1856, passionately defended Athenian democracy against the heavy weight of neglect and criticism that had nearly buried it alive.[8] It is curious that Grote (Figure 12), a no-nonsense man of facts who was the son of a Puritan mother and a Bremen merchant and banker, never visited Athens. His father had prevented him from attending university, instead grooming him for the banking trade. That left Grote with no alternative, in his spare time, but to morph into a model *honnête homme*, a self-educated, middle-class man of letters. No nineteenth-century playboy, Grote was a hardworking chap who resembled a figure from a novel by Charles Dickens: perhaps Charles Darnay in *A Tale of Two Cities*, an honest man of good breeding who was staunchly opposed to the snobbishness and cruelty of the aristoc-racy. Grote was gripped by a desire for self-improvement. He had a considerable appetite for reading, and at one point during the 1820s he helped convene a discussion circle that met twice weekly before business hours, in a back room of the bank co-owned by his father and later inherited by him, in Threadneedle Street, in the heart of London's financial district.

FIGURE 12: George Grote, a pen-and-ink sketch by Sir George Scharf, 1861.

Figures like Grote convinced nineteenth-century critics such as Karl Marx that democracy was just a bourgeois plot – in this case, one to ensure that bankers could protect their assets from wolfish governments. Grote did not see things this way. He thought of himself as a barrister caught up in a lengthy trial in defence of the Greeks, and especially the Athenians, against the injustice they had suffered for nearly two millennia. Helped along by a great deal of patient reading, and by his use of the method of 'cautious conjectures, founded upon the earliest verifiable facts', he managed to defend Athens as nobody before had done. Grote pleaded not guilty to the charges levelled at his client, the city of Athens. For him, its whole experience with democracy was a rich and vibrant example of how to prevent the misery produced by concentrations of power. Athens was not just an object of antiquarian interest. It was a precious ally from the past, an inspiring example of a system that, 'while ensuring to the mass of freemen a degree of protection elsewhere unknown, acted as a stimulus to the creative impulses of genius, and left the superior minds sufficiently unshackled to soar above religious and political routine, to overshoot their own age, and to become the teachers of posterity'.

Grote's views rested on the presumption – shared with his friends Jeremy Bentham and James and John Stuart Mill – that oligarchies always behave badly. Men are selfish, Grote thought, but this was no cause for despair. There is a remedy for their egoism: granting the franchise and education to the many, so as to ensure the maximum happiness of the greatest number. Grote's train of reasoning was crafted to remind his readers of just how much Athenian democrats hated the tyrant who 'subverts the customs of the country: violates women: puts men to death without trial' (Grote here repeated the words given to Otanes by Herodotus). The emphasis placed by Grote on the merits of ostracism as a check upon political ambition was also consistent with this view. So was its corollary: that compared with all other forms of government, including the aristocracy that ruled Britain in his day, responsible democratic government was easily superior. The same thought backed his rejection of Plato's critique of democracy. Grote admired Plato's use of inquisitive dialogue to sharpen the critical faculties and to criticise received ideas, including theological beliefs. But he disliked Plato's dogmatic attacks on the Sophists. Grote found in the conversational techniques of figures like Protagoras a defence of such principles as toleration of diversity, the autonomy of mind of individuals, and the public entitlement to express dissent in the company of King Nomos. All these principles had been born and nurtured in the Athenian *polis*, Grote insisted. They now needed to be revived; the nineteenth-century European struggles for democracy against oligarchy had to be encouraged, by way of a return to the birthplace of democracy.

Grote's work was monumental. It changed everything. Despite some ups and downs, thanks to his bold efforts the belief that Athenian democracy is an indispensable ally of modern times came alive, and has remained very much alive ever since. The hand of Grote seems to be everywhere. Read any short work or watch any television programme on the subject, in any language. Athens is the original home of Western civilisation, it is said, or quietly presumed. To that great city can be traced not only the origins of what we now call the modern world – like the development of coinage and the market economy – but the very principles of what it means to be human. Athens gave us the philosophies of Socrates, Plato and Aristotle: the Great Generation at Athens, as the great Anglo-Austrian philosopher Karl Popper called them.[9] It blessed us with figures like Aeschylus, Thucydides and Demosthenes. It gave us history, the theatre, classical sculpture and other arts. It also gave us politics in its most special form: democratic government.

Slowly, but surely, the belief that it all started in Athens became an intellectual orthodoxy, a political mantra that nowadays usefully doubles as a marketing ploy. The Greek government's campaign to host the 2004 Olympics in Athens successfully relied upon this point. Travel agencies around the world also tirelessly promote the city in this way. The brochures usually contain a pithy paragraph that runs something like this: 'Capital of Greece, cradle of democracy, birthplace of Western Civilisation – Athens is a vibrant city where old and new join hands. The majestic Parthenon rises above the city, its ancient glory still visible in the timeworn stone, and the National Archaeological Museum holds countless treasures from Athens' Golden Age.' Pity the pithiness, one might add, for in various circles such commercialisation of democracy has yielded spoonfuls of disbelief and pinches of cynicism. Athenian democracy has understandably become easy prey for word-jugglers and jesters. Hence the old jokes with a new twist. 'This is now the finest country in the world,' said an employee to his colleague in an office cafeteria in downtown Athens, on the eve of the Olympic Games. 'Much less corruption in government, no puppet dictators, none of your soldiers in the streets; palace revolutions and street violence are a thing of the past. This is a democracy. Equal chances for everyone. We Athenians gave it to the world . . .' 'Democracy?' snaps his workmate. 'Everyone talks about it, but what the hell does it mean?' 'I'll tell you,' replies the first man confidently. 'It's like this. You're going home late at night after a hard day at the office. You've missed your bus, it's pouring with rain, and you're soaked to the skin. The boss pulls up in his Mercedes. He offers to take you to his house, where he lets you dry your clothes in front of a big log fire. He gives you a big meal and even offers you a glass of his special brandy. Since it's still raining he invites you to stay the night. That's democracy!' 'But did that ever happen to you?' came the scoffing reply. 'No . . .,' stammered the first man, 'but it once happened to my sister.'

Counterpoints

What are we to think of the claim that Athenian democracy was the starting point of the Palaeozoic era, the geological degree zero when the hard-shell animal of democratic ideals and institutions first began to appear on earth? Don't the archaeological sources seem very much to favour this view? They do – and to see why they do is the beginning of wisdom in matters of democracy.

The political pre-eminence of Athens as a dominant power in the region inevitably placed it centre stage in the dramas of ancient Greek history. As the grand imperial city, it made history as well as attracted those who helped record its history. Many figures associated with the accomplishments of Greek history of this period were native Athenians; or they were immigrants drawn from all over the Mediterranean by the magnetic dynamism of the city. Athens was made famous by orators and statesmen, philosophers and playwrights, poets and historians – by men who are still known to us as Thucydides, Praxiteles, Socrates, Aeschylus and Demosthenes. All of them spent time in its agora, tracked the decisions of its assembly and courts, and together they left behind a rich stock of literary sources. These documents were supplemented by the extensive and permanent record-keeping habits of the Athenian democracy. Perhaps more than any other contemporary polity of the Greek region, Athens carved its history in stone and fired clay: more than 7500 inscriptions (treaties, laws, shopping lists, dedications, building accounts, honorary decrees, boundary stones, votes, statue bases) have been excavated in the agora alone. Large investments of money, time and archaeological labour, especially by the American School of Classical Studies at Athens, dating from the 1930s, have subsequently confirmed its pre-eminence. The whole effect has been to produce 'facts' that feed the view not only that Athens was special, but that Athens was of world-historical importance: that it was the cradle of Western civilisation, the *polis* at the eastern end of the Mediterranean where democracy was invented, the place from where its ideals and institutions spread to other Greek *poleis* from the time of the fifth century BCE.

And yet here we meet a counterpoint – the moment when the first leap of imagination is required to see the history of democracy with fresh eyes. Put simply, the art of self-government by assemblies of people who regard each other as equals was *not* an invention of the Athenians. We have learned already that the word *dēmokratia* was much older than the Athenian democracy. Of greater significance is the mounting evidence that, among the Greek-speaking city-states scattered throughout the Mediterranean, democratic assemblies flourished quite separately from Athens, and well before the last decade of the sixth century BCE, when the citizens of that city could legitimately claim that it was becoming a democracy.

The usual warnings about reliable sources apply with a vengeance to these old democracies: time has ravaged the evidence and in any case few of the jumbled fragments that survive have been blessed with the intense efforts at archaeological resuscitation applied to Athens itself. Matters have been made worse by the sloppy organisation of under-funded museums, and by the private pilfering of the gems in their collections. Yet traces of reliable evidence still remain – even if in badly neglected condition. Examples include a reference to 'the *dēmos*' on a block of reddish volcanic rock, found in southern Chios and dated 575–550 BCE; and a small block of grey schist from the temple of Apollo Delphinius at Dreros, dated 650–600 BCE, which is of huge interest, not only because it may be the oldest surviving Greek law, but because it mentions a body called 'the *damioi*' that was involved in deciding matters of common concern to the city (Figure 13).

FIGURE 13: The oldest surviving Greek law on stone, from the temple of Apollo Delphinius at Dreros, 650–600 BCE. It reads: 'The city has thus decided; when a man has been a *kosmos*, the same man shall not be a *kosmos* again for ten years. If he does act as a *kosmos*, whatever judgements he gives, he shall owe double, and he shall lose his rights to office, as long as he lives, and whatever he does as *kosmos* shall be nothing. The swearers shall be the *kosmos* and the *damioi* and the twenty of the city.'

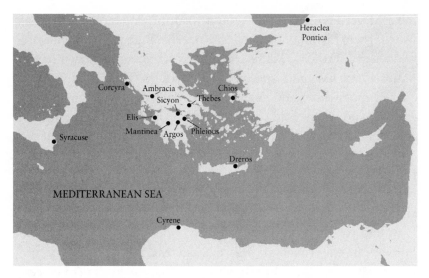

FIGURE 14: Location of some ancient Greek democracies, several founded during the sixth century BCE.

There were altogether some two hundred Greek citizen-states like that of Dreros and Chios. Up to half of them – including Ambracia (in north-western Greece) down to Cyrene (on the Libyan coast) to as far eastwards as Heraclea Pontica, on the southern coast of the Black Sea (Figure 14) – had a taste of democracy at one time or another. The details of these early *dēmokratiai*, as contemporaries called them, may initially seem a bit tedious, but their cumulative effect on our understanding of the history of democracy is powerful, and important to absorb. Patience is required; the rewards are rich.

The surviving evidence is not altogether good news for democrats. It often describes in painful detail the destruction of democratic institutions, either by military conquest, or by conspiracies of the rich, or by single-minded tyrants, or by all three, in some combination or sequence. Each case provides yet another reminder of the utter contingency of democracy – of the ease with which it can be blown away, like a leaf in the autumn winds.

Some of the oldest remaining evidence of this fragility of democracy comes from the far-eastern Greek colony of Heraclea Pontica, situated at the mouth of the River Lycus, on the coast of Asia Minor, well inside the Black Sea. Following the military subjugation of the

local Mariandynian population, a form of democracy was established there around 560 BCE – nearly a generation before it
happened in Athens. There is evidence of extensive citizen participation in the assembly and on the jury courts. There were annually
elected magistrates, or *boule*, of the kind that later appeared in
Athens, and whose job it was to draft proposals for acceptance or
rejection by the assembly; and there was a college or board of officials called *damiourgoi*, who were in effect an executive authority
that was helped in its work of promoting the welfare of the city by
officers or magistrate overseers known as *aisumnetai*. Within the
city of Heraclea Pontica there was a custom that stipulated that all
laws had to be based on decisions of 'the *boule* and the people'.
How deep the roots of that custom ran is uncertain, if only
because, shortly after the city was founded, the local *dēmos* seems
to have been seduced by demagogues, who pressed hard for the
expropriation of the property of the rich upper class of notables
called *gnorimoi*. Members of that dispossessed class scampered for
their lives, into exile, only to return, heavily armed, to overthrow
the democracy by force.

Elsewhere in the world of Greek citizen-states, democracy enjoyed
a long and happier life. There were more than a few success stories,
some of them again predating Athens, sometimes by more than a
generation. These democracies are important because they teach us
to begin thinking about the wide variety of ways in which democracy can be built; they also alert us to the amazing diversity of species
of assembly democracy. Consider the prosperous island state of
Chios, located just five miles off the coast of Asia Minor, where
around 575–550 BCE a freestanding stone displayed in a public place
commanded officials, magistrates known as demarchs (*demarchos*),
to observe the *rhetras* (laws? decrees? agreements?) of 'the *dēmos*',
or otherwise face fines. The early maritime democracy here seems
to have been unusually dependent upon a large slave-labour population, most of whom were probably linked to the large-scale cultivation
of vines, the production of wine for export and overseas trading of
other commodities. Rich landowners wielded considerable political
clout, and it is probable that they tried to enforce their will on a council of magistrates, a body that the islanders called the *boule demosie* –
which is why the stone tablet on public display daily reminded the

aristocracy to behave themselves, to remember that the final say in public matters belonged to the *dēmos*.

That democratic rule also applied in the rather different case of Cyrene, a Greek colony centred on a spring located in a lush valley in the uplands of what is today coastal Libya. Famous for its exported crops of silphium, a medicinal herb, Cyrene suffered a disastrous political crisis following its military defeat at the hands of the Libyans, in 555–550 BCE. The military defeat prompted the overthrow of its monarchy. The Cyrenian monarch, King Arcesilaus II, was murdered. His stammering son Battus found it impossible to govern with any coherence or authority. So the Cyrenians sent a delegation to the Delphic oracle, to ask for advice. It delivered sad news for monarchy. The deities told Battus that the best way to cure his stammer was to seek a kingship in Libya (wise advice, many thought); the rest of Cyrene was counselled to bring in a mediator (called a *katartister*), who appeared in the form of our bearded friend, the suitably named Demonax. He was a well-known and respected citizen from nearby Mantinea, and the surviving evidence suggests that he wasted no time in stripping the monarchy of most of its powers – certain lands and priesthoods were exempted – and reorganising its old administrative districts. The poorest inhabitants who lived on the fringes of the state's territory (and possibly Hellenised Libyan settlers as well) were granted citizenship; and the bulk of governmental powers were turned over to a *dēmos* made up of people previously excluded from government.

Among the oldest and most fascinating cases of Greek democracy is the Corinthian-founded citizen-state of Ambracia. The colony itself was established sometime between 650 and 625 BCE, a few miles inland from the sea, on the bend of a navigable river, in the midst of a fertile wooded plain. Within that promising setting, self-government by a popular assembly dates to around 580 BCE, a full generation before the assembly in Athens went on record to issue its first decree. True to the rule that democracies are rarely founded democratically, the assembly-based democracy of Ambracia was born of plots and an uprising against the harsh rule of Periander (the nephew of the Corinthian tyrant of the same name). He apparently aroused widespread indignation after rumours circulated, during a heavy drinking session, that he had rudely asked his young male lover whether he had yet fallen pregnant. The indignation caused by that remark in a society tolerant of male homosexuality is barely understandable to us. So serious was the insult that it seems to have hatched a plot by Periander's jilted lover to overthrow the ruler, using violence. It was a trial run for the Harmodius and Aristogeiton affair a generation later in Athens. In this case, the violent plot against Periander gave courage to others. It galvanised a coalition of the local *dēmos* and his enemies, presumably the upper class of disaffected property holders. According to Aristotle, 'the *dēmos* joined with the tyrant Periander's enemies to throw him out and then took over the constitution itself'.[10] The property qualification for public office had never been very high in Ambracia. It was now effectively abolished. The poorest ranks of men entered government, to act as its principal source of authority.

The Ambracian model was to be widely replicated throughout the Greek world. Within a few years of the tyrannicide that helped trigger events that led to the birth of democracy in Athens, similar experiments were launched not only in Chios, Cyrene and Heraclea, but also in wealthy and politically important communities, such as the gulf state of Argos, in the Peloponnese, and in the beautiful and prosperous city of Syracuse (in Sicily), where democracy was born around 491 BCE with an uprising against the ruling landowners (the *hoi gamoroi*). The trend there towards popular power sharing was triggered by the surprise military defeat of Syracusean forces at the River Helorus – so satisfying the rule of thumb that military loss frequently destroys the authority of oligarchs, thereby paving the way for democratic experiments. The uprising against the rich aristocracy seems to have enjoyed the unswerving support of the local trading class, who for some time had been complaining that far too much wealth from trade remained in the hands of the landowners. The rebellion was backed as well by the local *dēmos* and (unusually) the slaves of the colony, known locally as the *kyllikyrioi*, whose ancestry may have belonged to those who were natives of the island.

Most of the other Greek cities in Sicily later followed suit; tyrannical, oligarchical and monarchical rule, the three main alternatives of the period, suffered widespread defeat there during the fifth century. By the 460s BCE, popular self-government had come to a number of cities in southern Italy, to the sickle-shaped Ionian island city of Corcyra, and to the Peloponnesian mainland. From one of its states, Elis, comes an intriguing inscription, the conclusion of a lengthy law dating probably from the early years of the fifth century BCE. It shows that in Elis written laws could be superseded not by a court judgement (*dika*), but only by means of a public enactment that had the consent of a body called the 'whole people assembled' (*damos plethyon*). According to some observers, neighbouring Mantinea had for some time been a vibrant farming democracy governed by a class of small property owners called the *dēmos ho georgikos* – a social group that was the backbone of the best and oldest kind of democracy, in the opinion of Aristotle.

Meanwhile, in a third Peloponnesian state named Argos, *dēmokratia* came in fits and starts – as it did in many other city-states – commencing with the end of the Temenid monarchy in the mid-sixth century. If one account is to be believed, the *dēmos* of Argos grew angry after military setbacks had prompted the giving away of large tracts of land by the king, who saved his own skin by going into exile. A constitutionally elected council of *damiourgoi* then ran the state – until its devastating military defeat at the hands of the Spartan armies, at the Battle of Sepea (c. 494 BCE). Losses were estimated at 6000 men. So great were they that the shortage of adult men on the island enabled the takeover of government by a newly self-created *dēmos* made up of freed slaves (called *douloi* and *oiketai*), plus a large number of previously unenfranchised inhabitants from the surrounding countryside, including people known as *gymnetes*, those who are 'naked' or 'without clothes'.

'Ancestral Democracy'

The whole trend towards democracy was contagious, and was boosted by the outbreak of war in the Peloponnese between Athens and Sparta (431–404 BCE). On the coasts and islands of the Aegean, many members of the vast military coalition under the command of Athens were already, or soon became, governed by democratic rules. Democracy promotion was the deliberate policy of the Athenians, who for the sake of empire building lent a hand to democratic factions wherever they could, in contrast to the Spartan taste for well-ordered oligarchies.

It wasn't all plain sailing for democracy; there were difficulties, for instance during the Peloponnesian War, when the military victory of Sparta resulted in a brief period of autocracy in Athens. Early in 411 BCE (as we have seen) there was a coup led by oligarchs. With the composition of those assembling at the Pnyx distorted by the absence of many poor citizens on naval duty, and with the will of many remaining citizens weakened by conspirators brandishing the swords of fear and propaganda, the Athenian assembly voted itself out of existence. The military victory of Sparta, meanwhile, led to the overthrow of democracy among many of its allies. The return of tyranny in Syracuse around the same time threatened an end to the experiment in self-government throughout the whole region. War was bad for democracy. But whether or not it proved fatal depended in every case on the action of citizens. That was certainly true of Athens, where, thanks to a brief flurry of street fighting, and the growing unpopularity of the ruling Council of Four Hundred, its citizens managed to shake off oligarchy, and to restore democracy.

The resistance in Athens was unexceptional; many citizen-states in the Aegean clung desperately to their own democracies. On the mainland, the Argives followed the pattern; so did Sicyon, Phleious and Thebes. A remarkable cluster of citizen-states in Arcadia, in the Peloponnese, did so as well, and for more than a century. Founded in 370 BCE, the Arcadian League, as it was known, was designed to bring peace to a region that had previously been dominated by Spartan power. The League had its roots in the fifth century. It resembled a small and simplified version of today's European Union, in that it tried to achieve something never before attempted: a two-tiered confederacy bound by the rules of democratic negotiation and compromise. It maintained a standing army based at its newly founded capital, Megalopolis. The Arcadians invented a coordinating council known (as in Athens) as the *boule* and manned at any one time by fifty officials, called *damiourgoi*. Remarkably, the League also established a regional assembly called the *myrioi*, or 'ten thousand'. It is uncertain whether that name should be taken literally, so that the actual size of the assembly was restricted to the middling class of hoplite property holders, and to those above them. It is just possible that the name *myrioi* had the more figurative meaning of 'a very large number' of citizens, perhaps even all free adult males – so making it the first ever recorded experiment in cross-border democracy.

The Arcadian League was to run aground on the reefs of wider regional struggles for power led by shifty alliances under the thumbs of Athens, Sparta and Thebes. The League suffered invasion and, at one point (in 362 BCE), it split apart. Differences were patched up, and the League in fact survived as long as did the democracy of Athens, probably until the 230s. It is significant that it did so, for a vital reason. The whole Arcadian experiment in protecting democratic states on a regional basis by democratically negotiating their integration rested on a working principle that remains as rock-solid today as it did then. Stated simply, the principle is that in order to survive and flourish, democracies must tame the political and military pressures on their borders. Perhaps in this context we might speak of an Arcadian Law: the viability of any democracy is inversely proportional to the quantity of outside ('geopolitical') threats to its existence.

The Arcadian Law had a gloomy corollary: a warning that democracy could kill itself off by misusing its military power on its neighbours. The Arcadian experiment was a brave effort to deal with the grave danger posed by Athens for the plurality of democracies of the region – to prevent the Athenian empire from gobbling up democracies in the name of democracy. The Arcadian League experiment showed that democracies had a strong self-interest in banding together, peacefully, to ensure their survival through politics, so as to avoid their massacre through rivalry, expansion and armed conflict.

That is not all. There are more lessons to be learned from Arcadia and other early Greek experiments with democracy – more reasons why the tight grip of Athens on our democratic imagination needs to be broken. One lesson is that the ancient Greek world knew no single type of democracy, that outside of Athens there flourished a wide range of different assembly democracies and – most probably – different understandings of what democracy was all about. In the Greek world, democracy was not a single or fixed form: although the assembly was its core institution, it resembled an odyssey, in which different mental imaginings and various practical experiments were par for the course.

There is another lesson: the great number, variety and tenacity of Greek democracies heap a mountain of doubt on the old prejudice that democracy was a localised and serendipitous phenomenon, a spur-of-the-moment creation of single inventors, of mischievous or heroic figures like Aristogeiton and Harmodius, or founding fathers like Solon and Cleisthenes. The prevalence of democracies of different shapes and sizes, some of them much older than Athens, rather suggests the existence throughout the region of invented *traditions* of democratic behaviour that favoured equality, respect for the laws and self-government through assemblies – traditions that had to be acknowledged for tactical reasons by otherwise hostile figures like Alexander the Great, King of Macedonia and world conqueror until his assassination in 323 BCE, who reportedly sometimes did all he could to overthrow oligarchies and establish assemblies among the Greek city-states he freed from the clutches of Persian control.

Empire building demanded respect for local habits, of the kind that Isocrates (436–338 BCE), a rhetorician who lived through nearly a century of democracy in the region, called 'ancestral democracy'. In his political pamphlet *Areopagiticus* (perhaps written in 358 and 352 BCE), he grumbled that 'sitting in our shops, we criticize the current situation, and complain that we've never had a worse government under the democracy, but in our actions and thoughts we are fonder of it than of the democracy left by our ancestors'. Isocrates proposed a remedy: democrats should remember their ancestors. 'The only means of averting future dangers and escaping from current evils', he concluded, 'is the willingness to restore the democracy which Solon, who was the most democratic ruler, established by legislation, and Cleisthenes, who expelled the tyrants and returned the people to power, originally founded.'[11]

Let us set aside tricky questions about the veracity of Isocrates' claims, especially his backdating of the origins of democracy and (for his times) commonplace attribution of hero status to Solon. Striking is his deep self-consciousness of the need for *a history of democracy*. Such awareness of what today we call tradition, of the material threads of language and life that bind the living to the dead, whether or not they know or like it, was not a product of 'Greek genius'. *Dēmokratia* was, rather, the resultant of a variety of overlapping forces and events that together combined for a time – in spite of everything – to spread self-government by assembly as a way of life throughout the wider Greek world of city-states.

What background forces promoted the birth of assembly democracies within the world of the Greeks? Figuring out the patterns of forces within the kaleidoscope of poorly recorded events is not easy, but of critical importance was the strange powerlessness of the rich oligarchies of the region. These were small city-states whose enemies of democracy – compared with dictators and totalitarians of modern times – enjoyed very limited means of control over their subject populations. States commanded by monarchs, aristocrats and tyrants certainly landed considerable body blows on their victims. But that serves merely to indicate that in politics violence is not everything, that although people could be made to do things at the point of a sword or spear, those who subsequently ruled over them could not rely upon weapons alone. Violence was not capable of winning what the Greeks of this period called *egemonia*, the consent of the governed.

What should be surprising to modern eyes is just how easily the region's oligarchs crumbled under the pressure of plots, violent disturbances and military catastrophes. These local oligarchies were permanently vulnerable to what contemporaries called *stasis*, a very broad and much-feared term used to describe the factional squabbling, outright sedition, open civil war, bloodshed and mass exile that was endemic in a geopolitical system of independent city-states that lacked any coordinating centre and, hence, constantly violated the geographical isolation and political autonomy of states by sucking them into a vortex of bitter rivalries. These were states whose power at home was also vulnerable to the fires of rumour that periodically raged through the populace. The oligarch's means of surveillance were often sporadic; that made undemocratic regimes vulnerable as well to conspiracies, plots and attempted coups.

The arts of tyrannical rule were not made easier by the popular belief in gods and goddesses. Those who ruled supposed that beings more powerful – judges of motive, character and action – always looked over their shoulder. That was why rulers were forced to see, ultimately, that there were occasions when they had no choice but to obey the instructions and decrees issued by the much more powerful forces of the sacred powers. The will of the deities could be disobeyed, but in that case the gods and goddesses and the people would likely conspire to bring ruin to the tyrant – or so many Greeks thought. Some would-be rulers even believed that *dēmokratia* had the deities on their side, as Herodotus made clear in a gripping account of the first moves made by a leader named Maiandrios to establish popular self-government on the island of Samos, in 522 BCE.

In memory of Polycrates, from whom he claimed to have received the licence to govern the island, Maiandrios built 'an altar to Zeus the Liberator', then summoned citizens to the assembly, where he began his speech: 'As you know, Polycrates' sceptre and power have been entrusted to me, and I can now rule over you.' The crowd hushed, Maiandrios paused, then continued: 'In so far as I am able, I will however avoid doing the things I criticize others for doing. I did not like the way Polycrates was the master of people who were, after all, no different from himself, and I would not condone such behaviour from anyone else either. Anyway, Polycrates has met his fate. For my part, I put power in the hands of the people, and proclaim to you equality.'[12]

The case of Samos showed that although the sacred could not guarantee democracy, it could irritate and frighten tyrants, even tie their hands in knots, at least for a time. The dependence of Greek rulers upon naval power had further restraining effects. Causal links between the sea and democracy have often been alleged, most famously perhaps by the twentieth-century English writer George Orwell (1903–50), who stirringly contrasted land-based tyranny and the 'loose maritime democracy' of the English.[13] The contrast, just like the boundaries between land and sea, is by no means watertight, but there is some evidence that a few secrets of the early Greek democracies are to be found in the Mediterranean foam. Quite a few of these states were indeed 'maritime democracies', in which the commoners who rowed the ships and the officers who commanded them often struck fear into the hearts of oligarchs. These men of the sea were used to the vagaries of the unexpected. They knew how to cope with contingency. Tides and storms had put them to the test. They had been toughened by the wider world, and had learned to respect its harsh and unpredictable realities. They respected and feared the gods. And their characters were marked by the good sense that came from earthly doubt. Trusting only in themselves and in their citizen-state – outsiders were those who lived in the next citizen-state, along the coast or down the valley – they were most probably not believers in sublime notions, like the feeble appeal to Hellenic patriotism. These maritime people with maritime qualities knew the meaning of collective self-discipline in the face of hardship. That was why they disliked hubris and slavery. It was also why they looked unkindly on the arrogant petulance of oligarchs like Smindyrides of Sybaris, a political giant who regularly travelled with a kitchen of a thousand staff and loved to complain constantly that his nightly bed of roses gave him blisters (it was probably the DNA or the diet, or the drunken sex).[14]

Aristotle hinted at the importance of these maritime qualities when discussing the role of fishermen in the establishment of *dēmokratia* in the little Sicilian state of Taras after 473 BCE,[15] but the point can be broadened. The sea and the harbours of the region were rich not only with fishermen, ferrymen and naval crews, but also with thousands of commodities that circulated through markets that brought prosperity to the cities and countryside alike. Taras was a case in point. Famous in the region for their bronze industry, and for their wool, oil, wine, fish and other natural products, the people of Taras believed that tyrants too easily meddled with trade and commerce. Oligarchy was for them a barrier to prosperity. Hence the unpopularity of anything less than democracy by assembly among those who brought wealth to the people: not only fishermen and ferrymen, but also the producers and merchants, and their labouring dependants.

Ancient Eastern Assemblies

Enough has been said about the need for a more measured assessment of Athens – to see with fresh eyes that democracy was not its monopoly, and that other Greeks invented and practised it, sometimes with great purpose and effect. A sceptic bent on causing trouble might intervene at this point, to pose a few perplexing questions: 'That's all very well', she might say. 'But doesn't the humbling of Athens in our understanding of democracy's past simply reinforce the point that the Greeks as a whole gave us our birthright? Surely Grote and other nineteenth-century figures were right? The old story basically remains true. Two thousand six hundred years ago, democracy indeed sprang from the genius of Greeks living in the eastern Mediterranean. Doesn't that reinforce the conclusion that democracy is a gift of all Greeks to the whole world?'

These are excellent questions that prompt another epiphany, a counterpoint that requires a leap of imagination to see democracy with fresh eyes. For the fact is that the story of Athens or the wider Greek world as the birthplace of democracy is more than just a story. It has served as a founding myth – an unchallenged dogma that purports to show that the neighbouring peoples of 'the East' were slow on the uptake in matters of democracy. Thanks to this dogma, they have been seen as unfit for democracy, as so awkward in its presence that they only managed much later, and then with great clumsiness and often without success, to cultivate and harvest the crops of democracy that were first planted with such great finesse by the more civilised peoples of 'the West'.

The Dogma of Western Democracy – let us call it – has been expressed in various ways, and has a long pedigree. It was a concoction of the Greeks themselves; later it resonated through literature, painting, theatre, not to mention the worlds of trade and commerce, politics and diplomacy and international relations. Scholars, some of them leading figures in their fields, have reinforced its presumptions, especially the image of the 'Eastern' world as a place where political despotisms of one kind or another flourished. In the ancient world of the East – writes an eminent contemporary scholar of Greek democracy – politics did not exist. There was only government by antechamber. Courtiers exercised some influence, as did royal advisers. Citizens as such did not exist. Only kings ruled.[16] An influential early twentieth-century survey of modern democracies by James Bryce put the same point, with a degree of spite. 'When the curtain rises on that Eastern world in which civilization first appeared,' wrote Viscount Bryce, 'kingship is found existing in all considerable states, and chieftainship in tribes not yet developed into states. This condition lasted on everywhere in Asia with no legal limitations on the monarch until Japan framed her present Constitution in 1890. Selfish or sluggish rulers were accepted as part of the order of nature, and when, now and then, under a strong despot like Saladin or Akbar, there was better justice, or under a prudent despot less risk of foreign invasion, these brighter intervals were remembered as the peasant remembers an exceptionally good harvest. The monarch was more or less restrained by custom and by the fear of provoking general discontent', admits Bryce, for whom the exceptions to Eastern despotism proved the rule that this was hostile territory for democracy. 'Insurrections due to some special act of tyranny or some outrage on religious feeling occasionally overthrow a sovereign or even a dynasty, but no one thought of changing the form of government . . .'[17]

We need here to be frank with ourselves. For such thinking betrays a deluded arrogance that arouses the suspicion that democracy – the ideal that today places a high value upon openness to doubt – has for a long time harboured Western or Orientalist prejudices that are themselves anti-democratic, if only because they have the effect of erecting a rock-solid high wall between peoples who in fact share overlapping histories. The corollary, that the history of democracy is itself in need of democratisation – that it needs to be bombarded with new evidence, novel opinions, fresh thinking – is beginning to dawn on some scholars. They have seen that Greeks would not have become Greeks without contacts with peoples to the east. They point out that the remoulding of the Greek-speaking people who originally lived around the Aegean Sea into Greeks, as we now know them from history, began to happen during the eighth century BCE. That period was defined by jolting bursts of mental and institutional restructuring that used tools drawn from the East. Alphabetic writing – a new medium that in principle could be learned and used by everyone, for a variety of purposes – is cited as an example. So, too, is the importation of Eastern words and concepts (*hubris* is an example we have already come across). New forms of knowledge (such as astronomy) and old myths that were told to explain the world in fresh ways were important parts of the mutual interdependence, which was shaped as well by the importation of new techniques of production and their attendant rising standards of living and available luxuries.

The odd thing about the rising scholarly awareness of the 'Eastern' qualities of the Greeks is that the patterns of interdependence seem never to extend to political institutions. There is certainly growing agreement that 'Greeks' during the time of the democracies that lasted from the sixth to the third centuries BCE did not become Greeks all by themselves. It is agreed that in spiritual and cultural terms they were partly oriental, that they were peoples with mongrel identities. There is also some awareness that the Greek-speaking peoples most certainly did not think of their home-land as the birthplace of European civilisation, as was supposed by the prejudices that sprang up in the age of George Grote, who him-self was well aware of the fact that in the imaginings of Greek mythology 'Europa' was the daughter of Agenor, the king of the city-state of Tyre, on the coast of what is today Lebanon. Granted these and other 'oriental' qualities of the Greeks, the really odd thing is that the patterns of interdependence are never supposed by historians and other scholars to have extended to democratic ways of being, despite the accumulation in our time of much breathtaking evidence to the contrary.

Byblos

Consider this tiny first example: from an ancient source, a rare papyrus scroll miraculously preserved in the desert sands of Egypt, comes the strange story of the misfortunes of a diplomat from the city of Thebes, named Wen-Amon (Figure 15). He had travelled by ship around 1100 BCE to the thriving Phoenician port of Byblos, seven hundred kilometres to the east of Athens. There, Wen-Amon was to purchase from local Byblos merchants fine-quality timber hewn from the cedar forests of the nearby mountains. The business was commercially important, but straightforward: with the permission of the local prince, the trimmed cedar would be loaded by slaves on to a ship, freighted across the east end of the Mediterranean sea, unloaded in the kingdom of Thebes, then transformed by the best local craftsmen into a river barge, to be used in the sacred fleet of the Egyptian ruler Rameses XI (1100–1070 BCE), in honour of Amon, the god of fertility and patron of pharaohs.

FIGURE 15: Papyrus fragment of the report of Wen-Amon, discovered in 1890 at al-Hibah, Egypt, and subsequently purchased a year later in Cairo by the Russian Egyptologist Vladimir Goleniščev.

Things went reasonably well, as planned, or so for a time it seemed. Despite a protracted wrangle about payment, and delays caused by winter snow, the fine-quality timber was eventually hauled by a team of 300 oxen and loaded on to the ship anchored in the harbour of Byblos. But hours before setting sail, the deities turned fickle. Poor Wen-Amon and his crew found themselves surrounded by a hostile fleet of eleven ships manned by the neighbouring Theker people. Upset by his trade, they demanded his arrest by the local authorities. A large crowd gathered around the crescent-shaped harbour of Byblos. It puffed with excitement. Violence charged the Mediterranean air. A message was sped by runner to the local prince of Byblos, Zakar-Ba'al, calling upon him to resolve the crisis. Confusion reigned. Wen-Amon and his crew feared for their lives.

The prince arrived at the harbour. He seemed calm, and announced that he would provide the envoy and his crew with several flagons of wine, a sheep for roasting and a songstress to cheer them up. The prince informed Wen-Amon that he wanted to take measure of the dispute and to consider his options overnight. 'When morning came', reads the rare document, 'he [Zakar-Ba'al] had his *mw-'dwt* summoned, and he stood in their midst, and he said to the Theker: "Why have ye come?"'[18]

The document goes on to record that Wen-Amon and his men were escorted safely beyond the harbour, where strong winds filled their sails, giving them a porpoise start on the Theker pirates. The rest of what happened at Byblos remains unclear, which doesn't much matter here because the details are uninteresting by comparison with the strange little word – *mw-'dwt* – that appears in the text. Some archaeologists either leave this masculine noun in transcript form –

– or they translate it (misleadingly) as 'bodyguard'. It is actually an old Semitic word for 'assembly' or 'council' (*mô'ēd* in Hebrew), and it is used in biblical passages, such as the reference to those who are 'famous in the congregation', the 'men of renown' who gather in 'the assembly' (Numbers 16: 2). The same word crops up in Exodus 27: 21, where Moses commands the Israelites to fetch oil made from hand-crushed olives: 'Aaron and his sons shall arrange for [the lamps to burn] from evening until morning in God's presence, in the assembly tent.'

But what does any of this have to do with the history of democracy, it might be asked. One answer might be that Wen-Amon's tale is significant because it reveals clues to the existence of a functioning form of self-government a full five hundred years before the Athenian experiment with democracy. At the time of Wen-Amon's expedition, Byblos – later called Gebal and today known as Jbail in the republic of Lebanon – was a small but thriving maritime city-state. Its reputation ran high in the ancient world of the Mediterranean not only for its wood and paper – some treasured words like book, bible and bibliography are named after it – but also for its system of government by 'assembly'. It even gets a mention in the Bible, where the region is described as a zone of free trade and commerce. 'Thy borders are in the midst of the seas' runs a well-known passage, which mentions as well not only the prized wheat, honey, oil and balm from the Land of Israel and fine-quality ship masts hewed from the ancient cedars of Lebanon, but also an assembly comprising 'the elders of Gebal and her wise men' (Ezekiel 27: 9).

Primitive Democracy?

There is a bigger, more unsettling point here. Our plot is about to thicken. For the shreds and shards of surviving evidence of the existence of assemblies in Phoenician cities like Byblos have been given greater credence during the past generation by evidence that the Phoenicians practised government by assembly much more widely than has previously been thought. The Phoenician peoples who initially lived in the Levant, a geographical region that today includes Israel, the West Bank and Gaza, Lebanon and Syria, had roots stretching back to the third millennium BCE. It wasn't until around 1100 BCE, the time of Wen-Amon's expedition, that they managed to wriggle out from under Assyrian and Babylonian dominance, to become a major political and cultural force in the whole region. They were traders and sailors, who managed to establish colonies across much of the Mediterranean and North Africa, as far west as today's Spain. They were renowned for promoting assemblies, especially councils comprising traders and wealthy merchants whose reputations had been built from their extensive commercial networks stretching from Mesopotamia to the western Mediterranean. These councils exercised formidable power over monarchs everywhere. There is plenty of evidence, of the Byblos kind, that at the highest levels of power kings were forced to consult these assemblies of free male citizens. A seventh-century BCE treaty signed by the kings of Assyria and Phoenicia suggests that an assembly of wealthy Phoenician elders even governed as a 'counter power', alongside their king. And within the outlying remote Phoenician colonies that were established across the seas and coastlines of North Africa and the Mediterranean, including the world of the emergent Greek-speaking peoples, there is plenty of evidence that the Phoenicians promoted three-tiered forms of government – featuring a supervisory body of magistrates, a senate that made legislative proposals and a sovereign people's assembly – that were remarkably sophisticated for their time.

It is easy to see that the Phoenicians were ultimately responsible for introducing the culture of government by assemblies into the Greek world. Less obvious is the way in which the Phoenicians' taste for assemblies had been acquired by their sustained contact with peoples who lived further to the east, in the vast river basins etched from the desert hills and mountains of Syria-Mesopotamia by the Tigris and Euphrates and their tributaries.

Around 3000 BCE, this was a world of far-flung tribal affiliations based on tent-dwelling settled peoples and nomadic shepherds who moved their flocks of goats and sheep seasonally, across fairly long distances, up and down and through the fertile and well-watered steppes and country plains. There is not much surviving evidence of how these country peoples lived, though it is clear that they had a rich vocabulary to describe 'assemblies', and that they insisted on

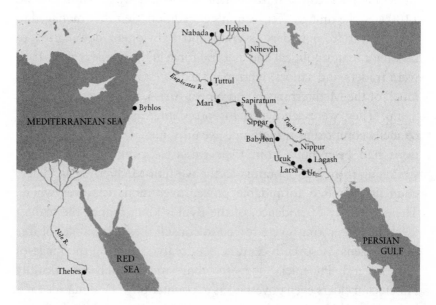

FIGURE 16: Principal ancient cities of the region of Syria-Mesopotamia, c. 3200–1000 BCE.

their indispensability in defining and resolving disputes. Even more plentiful evidence of assemblies comes from the cities that sprang up in this region, for the first time anywhere on earth (Figure 16).

Dating from around 3200 BCE, Syrian-Mesopotamian cities like Larsa, Mari, Nabada, Nippur, Tuttul, Ur, Babylon and Uruk today mostly resemble windswept heaps of motionless grey-brown earth. In their heyday, their imposing temples, often built on massive stone terraces or gigantic artificial mountains of sun-dried bricks, the famous *ziqqurats*, took away the breath of those who saw them for the first time. These early cities lived off dramatic local increases in agricultural production and surplus food. They fostered the development of specialised artisan and administrative skills, including the use by scribes of the rectangular-ended stylus to produce wedge-shaped cuneiform writing; they served as well as conduits of long-distance trade in raw materials, such as copper and silver.

The cities varied in size from 40 to around 400 hectares; typically situated at the centre of an irrigated zone, where land was valuable, they felt crowded in a way that the earth had never known. Like modern-day Venice, they were subdivided by canals that provided fresh running water and shaped the movements of town residents on streets that ran parallel, and at right angles. Cluttered mud-brick housing ensured that high officials and humble fishermen lived side by side; and the hub of city life was often the 'quay', the busy harbour run by guilds of merchants. Selling products like butter and beans, honey and beer, woollen cloth and leather, the merchants operated at arm's length from both the palaces and the temples, which (to please the gods) were usually erected on a high platform, being visible for many kilometres around.

These features of rural and urban life shaped every feature of the world of Syria-Mesopotamia, including its patterns of government. Permanent tensions – in the form of political processes that decided who got what, when and how – developed around matters such as landownership and trade, and especially around the institution of kingship. Kings are conventionally thought to have dominated this region during these centuries. This convention needs a kick in the pants. Kings, in fact, were neither almighty nor omnipresent – despite whatever those with Western prejudices have said.

It is true that the old image of Eastern Despotism correctly pinpoints the wide range of important functions performed by kings, who were prone to be meddlesome, and who took pleasure in extracting duties from their subjects. Around the palace, rulers like Hammurabi (king of the first dynasty of Babylon, 1792–1750 BCE) fiddled with the lives of their courtiers and other dependants. In policy matters, they were endowed with considerable powers. Likened most often to shepherds of flocks, they were supposed to appease the gods who had inspired or appointed them. Kings were meant to lead and to protect their people during times of war. During times of peace, they had to guarantee the welfare of the population, for instance by ensuring the fertility of the land by building and developing networks of irrigation canals. In return for these and other services, kings often demanded that their subjects pay taxes. Or they insisted that they should contribute their labour directly to agricultural projects; or get involved in fighting wars for the court. Or so it has often been said.

The powers of monarchs were indeed considerable, but those who divine from the surviving evidence the hard and fast conclusion that ancient Syria-Mesopotamia was run by despotic kings tell much less than half the story – and an ideologically prejudiced one at that. For a start, the human figure of the king of a city was hemmed in from all directions by the visible presence and power of the temple of the city god. The king was in effect supposed to be the subject of the deity. An example: when, after thirty years as ruler of the small city-state of Babylon, Hammurabi managed to pacify all of southern Mesopotamia, his military success was widely understood as a victory for Marduk, the city god of Babylon, who was said to have been chosen by the assembly of leading gods to administer the empire, with the assistance of his human steward, Hammurabi. Another example: in the city of Mari, an entire temple was dedicated to the frightening god of storms, Dagon, while the goddess Eštar was regularly honoured and 'consulted' in festivals and sacred rites that sanctioned not just the blessing of the king and his court, but also encouraged the active participation of the whole population. Just one more example: in the Mesopotamian city of Lagash, the main temple belonged to a god by the name of Ningirsu, who had at his disposal a large staff of divine and human servants, including doorkeepers, goatherds, brewers and armourers. The temple was by far the largest landowner; its patronage extended far and wide, including substantial numbers of sharecroppers and serfs.

Such arrangements connected with the sacred served to keep kings in check, making them more humble than they might otherwise have been. But archaeological evidence shows as well that the power and authority of kings – at least 2000 years before the Athenian experiment with democracy – were effectively restrained by popular pressure from below, commonly through networks or chains of procedures or institutions called 'assemblies' (in the vernacular, they were called *ukkin* in Sumerian and *pŭhrum* in Akkadian). Treading the tracks of the Danish scholar Thorkild Jacobsen (Figure 17), some observers have even detected a flourishing 'primitive democracy' throughout Syria-Mesopotamia, especially in early second-millennium Babylonia and Assyria.*

* Thorkild Peter Rudolph Jacobsen (1904–93) came from his native Denmark in 1928 to join a team working on the *Assyrian Dictionary* at the Oriental Institute in Chicago; such were the times that the young immigrant recorded how he spent his first nights staying in a downtown hotel with the gunfire of Prohibition-era gangs audible in the background. Jacobsen survived the ganglands and remained with the Institute for almost three and a half decades. There he held a variety of posts ranging from research assistant and archaeologist to member of the editorial board and later Director of the *Assyrian Dictionary*, and Director of the Oriental Institute (1946–50). Jacobsen was driven by an intensely personal vision of scholarship and had a reputation for standing up for what he thought to be the right principles. Some colleagues found him prickly, and the tensions that resulted led to successive resignations, early retirement from the University of Chicago – and to the production of some of his most interesting later work in the fields of Sumerian religion and literature. In 1962 he accepted a visiting professorship at Harvard, which became permanent the next year. He retired in 1974, but continued in active research, delivering his final address, as President of the American Oriental Society, less than two weeks before his death. By then, Jacobsen had earned a reputation as one of the world's foremost scholars on the ancient Near East. His work encompassed a variety of fields – archaeology, history, literature, religion and grammar – to each of which he made seminal contributions. Responsible for reopening the excavations at Nippur after they had been abandoned, half a century before, by the University of Pennsylvania, Jacobsen's work was sometimes minutely detailed; examples include his critical edition of the Sumerian King List (published in 1939 and still the definitive edition), and his study of the textile industry at Ur. With Seton Lloyd he discovered, surveyed and published evidence of a seventh-century BCE Assyrian aqueduct constructed by Sennacherib to provide Nineveh with water. Jacobsen is remembered as well for his creative reconstructions of early Sumerian religion and translations of Sumerian poetry and commentaries on the intricacies of the Sumerian verbal system. He pioneered new research methods, such as his introduction of the archaeological surface survey to southern Iraq. He also made path-breaking contributions to the interpretation of early Mesopotamian political history using literary as well as documentary sources. His classic contributions are Thorkild Jacobsen, 'Primitive Democracy in Ancient Mesopotamia', *Journal of Near Eastern Studies*, 2 (1943), pp. 159–72, and 'Early Political Development in Mesopotamia', *Zeitschrift für Assyriologie*, 52 (1957), pp. 91–140.

FIGURE 17: Thorkild Jacobsen taking notes during the clearance of a large residential quarter at Tell Asmar, Iraq, in 1931–2.

Jacobsen liked to say that the region resembled a political 'commonwealth' owned and governed by gods, who possessed executive organs for exerting outward pressure and enforcing law and order and justice internally – with the help of humans, all of whose undertakings, great or small, originated in assemblies of citizens. But is there any substance to this radical talk of a Syrian-Mesopotamian world of 'primitive democracy'? Much speaks against the whole idea. The implied teleology lurking within the word 'primitive', the inference that this was the first of its kind, a prototype of what was to follow, begs tough questions about the historical connections between the assemblies of the Greek and Mesopotamian worlds. It also supposes – wrongly, as we shall see in the next part of this book – that in spite of all the differences there is an unbroken evolutionary chain that links assembly-based democracy and modern representative democracy, as if the vastly different peoples of Lagash, Mari and Babylon were brothers and sisters of James Madison, Winston Churchill and Jawaharlal Nehru. The free use of the term 'primitive democracy', like that of 'proto-democracy' (developed around the same time by the Polish-American anthropologist Bronislaw Malinowski), also risks falling into the trap of calling too many societies 'democratic' just because they lack centralised institutions and accumulated monopolies of power, or because they prohibit centres of violent oppression, blatantly illegal or camouflaged, against which people have no redress or appeal.

Matters are not helped by the anachronistic use of the word with Linear B origins, 'democracy'. Nowhere was it used during this period, although – remarkably – there is possibly a semantic link between the family of terms that include *deme*, *dēmos* and *damu* and a distant cousin in the ancient Sumerian language, the word DUMU, 'son'. Its plural means 'sons' or 'children', and when identified by a geographic location refers (like the Linear B word *dāmos*) to inhabitants of that place who have family ties and common interests. And then there is the least obvious but most consequential objection: by calling the political and legal institutions of the Syria-Mesopotamians 'primitive' and 'democratic' there is a great danger of overlooking or understating their *strange originality*.

Those who have spoken of primitive democracy obviously did not intend such oversight, but nonetheless that has been the unfortunate effect. It is true that those in favour of including these 'primitive democracies' in the history of democracy have made an important move, intellectually and politically speaking. The ancient assemblies of Syria-Mesopotamia are indeed the fossils present in the ruins of Athens and other Greek democracies, and the assemblies of the Phoenician world. These much older assemblies of Syria-Mesopotamia teach us fundamentally to rethink the origins of democracy. They demand that we prepare ourselves for a shock: they invite us to see that democracy of the Greek kind had eastern roots and that therefore in a very real sense today's democracies are indebted to the first experiments in self-government by assembly of 'Eastern' peoples traditionally written off as incapable of democracy in any sense. *Ex oriente lux*: the lamp of assembly-based democracy was first lit in the East.

Anu

The remaining trouble with talk of 'primitive democracy' is that the use of the word 'primitive' to describe these eastern roots has the unintended effect of writing off something that is as fascinating as it is puzzling: that assemblies were inspired by myths.

A mental revolution is required to see that assemblies were commonplace throughout the region that has come to be called the Near East, or West Asia. Until quite recently, it hasn't seemed that way. One key reason why so little is known about these assemblies is that their existence seemed utterly improbable in a world ruled by myths – an overgoverned world (as Marx famously put it) that shackled 'the human mind within the smallest possible compass, making it the unresisting tool of superstition, enslaving it beneath traditional rules and depriving it of all grandeur and historical energies'.[19] Had Marx had the opportunity to learn some Sumerian (in 1853 it was still a 'dead' language awaiting decipherment) and consulted the sources, he might have seen things rather differently. The first assemblies were born of a world defined by powerful myths invented around the middle of the fourth millennium BCE. These myths were not mere stories that somehow served to blind their believers to the 'reality' of things. They were not 'true' or 'false', 'right' or 'wrong'. They instead provided mental categories that shaped, structured and energised people's lives, gave them significance and provided them with a map that located their position in space and time.

To the people of the Syria-Mesopotamian region – as for Greeks 2000 years later – the cosmos was a conflict-ridden universe pushed and pulled by powerful forces with personalities of their own. These deities had to be feared. Thanks to them, the world was racked by cracking thunderstorms, and by torrential rains that suddenly halted all travel by transforming firm ground into mud. The local rivers sometimes rose unpredictably, fitfully smashing barriers and inundating crops. Scorching winds smothered humans in suffocating dust. Such natural events were seen as the doing of a god or goddess, and the same applied to everything else in the universe: mountains, valleys, stones, stars, plants, animals and humans themselves.

The whole world was in motion, and it was this animated existence that – remarkably – resulted in order. Syrian-Mesopotamians believed that the deities had emerged from the watery chaos of primeval time. They had won an important victory over the powers of chaos and had subsequently worked hard to bring energy and movement into the world and, on that basis, to create order through dynamic integration. The resulting balance was the outcome of negotiations that took place in 'assemblies' – gatherings that overcame inactivity and speechlessness by wielding the power to issue commands that decided the great coming events, otherwise known as destiny.

Whatever is thought of the veracity or attractiveness of mythical reasoning of this kind, the fact is that it was widely believed, and that it had empowering implications for the people of Syria-Mesopotamia, who otherwise thought of themselves as puny creatures caught up in a world ruled by forces that were regarded with considerable dread. There were reckoned to be some fifty gods and goddesses, but the important shots were called within their assemblies by an inner circle of seven, the most influential of whom was Anu, the god of the sky. A rider of great storms, wondrously regal and tremendously powerful, his name was both the everyday word for 'sky' and a reminder of his role (as local myth had it) as convenor of 'the ordained assembly of the great gods'. By today's democratic standards, the rule of the big seven resembled some kind of oligarchy that lorded over a world in which democracy was neither a word nor nothing so much as a creature void of form.

But pause for a moment to consider the intriguing belief of Syrian-Mesopotamians that the personality of the gods is flexible, in that they meld with the character of other gods, and with the human world more generally, so infusing others with some measure of their own qualities. Consider Nin-tu, 'the mother of the gods' and (an inscription states) the 'mother of all children'. Stone carvings showed her as a woman suckling a child; embryos surround her and children peep out at the world from under her dress. It was thought possible for all women to achieve partial identity with her, and so to conceive by sharing in her procreative powers. Note the way that the goddess is not an abstract and distant entity, but rather a 'Thou' who confers equality and confirms equality among equals. Note too the understanding that women and men need to take care in Nin-tu's presence, for she has the power to deny evildoers offspring, even to put a stop to all births in the land. Her power is so great that from time to time she takes her seat with Anu and Enlil in the assembly of the gods. There, in the ruling body of the universe, she becomes Ninmah, the 'queen of the gods', the 'queen of kings and lords', the woman who determines fates by making 'decisions concerning (all) heaven and earth'.[20]

It was this very possibility of merging with the powerful gods that gave human beings courage to pick themselves up, to stand erect and shift for themselves in the world. As in Athens, so in Syria-Mesopotamia: getting a god was a means of self-empowerment. That is why letters were frequently written to the gods, and why cult festivals that featured wailing processions in search of a god that had gone missing always aroused great popular interest. That is also why in every dwelling there was a small shrine for a personal god, who was daily worshipped and presented with offerings, in order (note the logic of mythical thinking) that the dwellers might join hands with their gods to become like them. It followed that since humans were created especially for the benefit of the gods, and perforce were required to serve those gods, the act of mimicking their self-governing methods was supposed to have the same effect: to absorb some qualities of their gods by emulating their capacity for assembly and speech and making decisions, normally through negotiation and compromise based on discussion.

The Syrian-Mesopotamians called this skill 'asking one another'. Their view of the world, unlike ours, did not analyse matter according to whether it was living or dead, animate or inanimate. Nor did people think in terms of different 'levels' of reality: the distinction between a god 'up there' in the heavens and people 'down here' on earth was not meaningful. The peoples of Syria-Mesopotamia instead supposed that they lived within a cosmos that was alive, dynamically integrated, subject constantly to the push-pull of forces, among which the wills displayed and exerted in assemblies were vital sources of cosmic order. There is insufficient evidence to back the description (of Jacobsen) of the Mesopotamian polity as a great 'commonwealth' founded upon a 'general assembly of all citizens'. The exaggeration nevertheless foregrounds the vital point made well by Aristotle: that human beings 'imagine not only the forms of the gods but their ways of life to be like their own'.[21] That shrewd observation certainly applied to Syria-Mesopotamia, where the custom of gathering together to decide things had pagan and polytheistic roots. When men of various occupations and standing gathered together to consider some or other matter – men who believed that the ear, not the brain, was the seat of intelligence – they thought of themselves as participating in the wider world of the gods, as suppliants of their favours, as active contributors to the soothing integration of a world otherwise prone to disorder and chaos.

Deep Christian and modern prejudice against myths of this kind has ensured that the ancient assemblies of the Syria-Mesopotamia lands have gone unrecognised in previous histories of democracy. Something else has played a part in this ignorance: the political economy of literacy. It was in this region that writing was invented, at first serving to facilitate the ever more complicated accounting that had become so vital for the expansion of local cities and temple economies. The surviving evidence shows that while writing enabled the birth of a significant literature in Syria-Mesopotamia, literacy was limited in scope. And writing was used primarily for the recording of trade and commerce, and especially for the administration of public institutions, like temples and palaces. That fact, combined with the restriction of literacy and record keeping to governmental institutions and wealthier individuals and families, had the long-term effect of rendering the assemblies mostly invisible to the eyes of posterity. The effect has been reinforced, paradoxically, by the strength of these assemblies: exactly because centralised bureaucracies like the palace monopolised the process of economic and administrative record keeping, the decentralised politics that took place in the assemblies went unrecorded – or so the sporadic surviving evidence implies.

If those archaeological traces look faint then that is due not to the absence or weakness of assemblies, but rather because of the Dogma of Western Democracy, the vagaries of record keeping and literacy, the tyranny of time, the luck and skill of excavation and, most recently, the pity of war in the region. The fact that the old Sumerian and Akkadian words for assembly, *ukkin* and *pŭhrum*, refer (as in English) to both an informal gathering of people and a governing body has made archaeological work that much more difficult. The skimpy evidence is, however, not a measure of either the political impotence or the historical irrelevance of these assemblies. Documents that describe their operation in detail may be seriously in short supply, but some stunning examples have nevertheless survived.

Some of them show that assemblies were not just an urban phenomenon. During the second millennium, for instance, there is evidence from north-west Mesopotamia that tent-dwelling pastoralists regularly gathered to thrash out matters of common concern.[22] The West Semitic noun used for these gatherings – *rihsum* – applied to talks between different groupings of pastoralists, such as the Yaminites and the Zalmaqum. 'Zalmaqum and the Yaminites have met', reads one document, 'and they have engaged in talks [*rihsum*]. The object of their talks is alliance.' Sometimes these gatherings seem to have been initiated by outside authorities, including the king of Mari, Zimri-Lim (1775–1761 BCE). 'Go chase down the Hana [pastoral tribes]', runs one of his written instructions, 'and engage in talks [*rihsum*], so that the Hana may assemble and [at] the raising[?] of the torch, all the Hana may come as one man to my assistance.' The instruction suggests that popular involvement in such *rihsum* may sometimes have been broad, perhaps even including women and children. Willingness of participants to travel seems to have been common, but the evidence suggests that there was nothing like a fixed meeting place where talks were regularly held.

Mobile gatherings where words were exchanged and agreements struck were one kind of assembly. Another sort comprised city gatherings for the purpose of hearing disputes and making legal judgements. From the sacred city of Nippur, one of the oldest Babylonian settlements on the Euphrates and the place where Enlil is supposed to have created humanity – it is today a gigantic desert ruin located 100 miles south of Baghdad – survives a record of a trial for homicide from the early second millennium. It details the murder by three men of Lu-Inanna, the son of a local priest, and the subsequent cover-up of the deed by the victim's wife. 'Their case was taken to ... King Ur-Ninurta [who] ordered that their case should be decided by the assembly of Nippur.' The record shows that the assembly of commoners (the word used was *muškēnum*) – men with professions such as bird catching, gardening, potting and the military – debated the case thoroughly, then found all four accomplices guilty. 'In the assembly of Nippur', it records, 'Nanna-sig, son of Lu-Sin, Ku-Enlila, son of Ku-Nanna, the barber, Enlil-ennam, slave of Adda-kalla, the gardener, and Nin-dada, daughter of Lu-Ninurta, wife of Lu-Inanna, were given up to be killed. Verdict of the assembly of Nippur.'[23]

There is evidence that assemblies like that in Nippur during the second millennium were quite often more than popular courts of civil law – that their mandate included the power to tread on the toes of monarchs. Hints to this effect are found in a surviving letter from an assembly of Babylon, addressed jointly to the king of Babylonia, Shamash-shuma-ukin, and to his brother, the Assyrian king Assurbanipal. The assembly's letter reminds them of the Babylonian king's earlier guarantee that 'whoever enters Babylon is assured permanent protection' and that 'even a dog which enters it will not be killed'. It goes on to request that both kings grant the right of protection to all of Babylon's residents, even those of foreign origin.[24] The petition resonated with the well-known proverb that whatever is given in submission becomes a medium of defiance. The petition echoed a political text called *The Advice to a Prince*, a clay tablet recovered from the world's oldest library at Nineveh. Written around the end of the second millennium, it warned monarchs that the gods and goddesses would not look kindly upon acts of meddling with the freedoms of city and country life. If a greedy prince 'takes silver of the citizens of Babylon and adds it to his own coffers, [or] if he hears a lawsuit involving men of Babylon but treats it frivolously, Marduk, lord of heaven and earth, will set his foes upon him [and] will give his property and wealth to his enemy'. Similar penalties were listed for such wrongdoings as the failure to heed advice, the improper conviction or unjust imprisonment of citizens, or attempts to force them to work in the fields or temples. The political text reminded princes, present and future, that the assemblies of Babylon, Nippur and Sippar had each established – with divine help – their own immunity from despotic or arbitrary rule. 'Anu, Enlil, and Ea, the great gods who dwell in heaven and earth, in their assembly affirmed the freedom of those people from such obligations.'[25]

We need to be wary of the overexcitement bred by stumbling upon sources of this kind. A critic of this whole foray into the world of ancient assemblies might say: 'All very well. But from the point of view of princes, assemblies were mighty useful, surely? They were valuable sources of information – listening devices for princes otherwise deafened by distance from their subjects. And didn't assemblies also provide a channel for mobilising support in favour of policies that had been pre-decided by princes – so giving these policies at least a fighting chance of being successfully adopted?'

The questions are pertinent. Assemblies were indeed vital channels of communication between governors and governed in small communities where rulers found it virtually impossible to avoid mixing daily with those over whom they exercised power. But to put things in this one-sided way, as the Dogmatists of Western Democracy like to do, is at best to tell merely half the story, so perpetuating a whopping untruth. For exactly like the Greek polities that followed over a millennium later, the ancient assemblies of Syria-Mesopotamia were also venues in which public learning and suspicion of power and the arts of what would later be called politics – making judgements in public about who gets what, when and how – were cultivated.

It is quite probable that the older gatherings of Syria-Mesopotamia were more plentiful, mobile and dispersed, that is, much less centralised than the city-state assemblies of the Greek world to come. Fixed assemblies of the Greek kind, with readily definable constituents living within a given territory, were unusual. This difference is not surprising, given the ubiquity, energy and strongly ethical character of the Syrian-Mesopotamian deities. The gods and goddesses who served as role models for the human assemblies were not capricious deities acting merely in the pursuit of their own desires, their orgiastic rites. These were deities actively preoccupied with the proper ordering of the universe, down to the tiniest details. Meeting in their own assemblies in no fixed place, they warned against arrogance, lawlessness and cruelty and counselled moral deliberation, penitential prayer and jurisprudence. The surviving evidence suggests that the 'ethical polytheism'[26] of the world of Syria-Mesopotamia may have incited the proliferation of human assemblies and deliberations wherever and whenever they were deemed necessary. This would explain why assemblies seem to have been taken so seriously, why they had such a protean and 'homeless' character, why they had a long arm, in the sense that they touched and shaped various people's lives in a wide variety of settings, and why they seem to have had a 'nested' or 'modular' distribution within the countryside and cities in which they flourished.

We do not know whether future fresh evidence is just around the corner, but there is already an abundance of details, coming from the countryside as well as the villages and cities, of popular gatherings in the fields of law and in matters ranging from disputes over water and land to questions of taxation and public safety. There is also plenty of evidence that popular assemblies were based within the leading temple of cities. Temples were not just places for the worship of deities; especially during the first millennium, they served as well as spaces of deliberation and buffers against arbitrary exercises of governmental power. That was true, too, of the local assemblies of cities, which were normally subdivided administratively into quarters, each of which had its residents' assembly that doubled as a court of law in which disputes among residents were publicly heard and resolved.

The ancient assemblies of Syria-Mesopotamia were remarkably polymorphous, and that ensured that they were not just organs dominated by local monarchs, who sometimes convened them, or by the temple, or by rich and powerful imperial rulers. But how inclusive were these assemblies? How did they operate? Did they have methods of moderating the lust for power of ambitious participants? Were votes taken? Was majority rule (as a few surviving documents suggest) the order of the day? We can't be certain.

What is clear is that the assemblies that sprang up in the territory bound together by the Tigris and the Euphrates and their tributaries were a force to be reckoned with. We know that they were not 'secular' institutions (the distinction between the sacred and the profane wasn't meaningful to the peoples of the region, as it wasn't for the Greeks or the Phoenicians), and that they were sometimes racked by controversy, as suggested by a surviving prayer to the gods by an inhabitant of the old Assyrian trading colony at Kanish, in Anatolia. 'Do not abandon me, my lord, to the assembly where there are many who wish me ill', runs the prayer. 'Do not let me come to harm in the assembly.'[27] There is also impressive evidence, cited already in the homicide trial in Nippur, that at least some of the ancient assemblies of Syria-Mesopotamia were more genuinely popular than that of Athens. Whether women were regularly included – the evidence either way is thin on the ground – seems doubtful. Slaves and children normally had no voice in these assemblies. But potters, gardeners, bird-catchers, and soldiers in the service of the local temple were among the 'commoners' who sat in assemblies. They did so alongside assemblies convened by particular crafts or professions, such as merchants. There is even some interesting evidence, from exactly the same time when Athenian democracy was flourishing, that suggests the existence of self-governing associations of foreigners, like the assemblies of Egyptian and other immigrants in fifth-century Babylonia. Such assemblies never happened in Athens. There is as well a record of a domestic slave attending a meeting of an assembly in Kanish. From the Old Babylonian period (c. 1700 BCE) evidence survives of an assembly attended by all the residents – men and women of every background and occupation – of an outpost town on the Euphrates called Haradum, whose mayor, Habasanu, was publicly accused of embezzling taxpayers' funds. And from the archives of the city of Mari, seat of a modest kingdom on the valley of the Euphrates just inside Syria's current border with Iraq, comes a clay tablet with wedge-shaped cuneiform writing that records a public dispute over the legal status of palace land in Sapiratum, a town just downstream from Mari. Conducted in the presence of the local king Zimri-Lim, with the whole town of Sapiratum and forty-three of their spokesmen present, the gathering heard details of how the land had been claimed by an independent person. It is recorded that the assembled town had voted against the claim, that it had reaffirmed royal ownership of the property, and that it had sworn an oath before the king.[28]

Any thought that the assemblies of Syria-Mesopotamia were genuinely popular – examples of 'democracy' in the making – is scotched by evidence that some of them were dominated by the so-called 'elders of the city' mentioned already in the case of Byblos.

At least that is the clue provided by the famous Sumerian literary story of Gilgamesh and Agga. Composed probably in the late third millennium BCE, it tells of the siege of Uruk (the city where Gilgamesh was king) by troops from the city of Kish. With his back to the wall, Gilgamesh, the supposed demi-god of superhuman strength, humbly turns for advice to two assemblies: the 'men of the city' or 'able-bodied men' (*guruš* in Sumerian), and the 'elders of the city' (*ab.ba* in Sumerian; *šibūtum* in Akkadian). Exactly what kind of relationship existed between these 'elders' and the rest is unclear, but the distinction itself reveals that the world of ancient assemblies was no egalitarian paradise – that it contained tall hierarchies based (perhaps) on criteria such as age, or on gender, wealth or professional status.

The Syrian-Mesopotamian Legacy

Whatever became of these ancient assemblies that flourished as long ago as two millennia BCE? Did they just fizzle out, like a flat-bottomed cotton wool cloud that dissolves without trace into a hot summer sky?

The most influential answer given today runs as follows: through time, with the growth of empires in the region, the popular assemblies weakened, or were strangled to death by the growth of centralised power backed by force of arms. This answer puts us on the spot, but even allowing for the fickleness of the surviving sources, the evidence in fact points towards a quite different conclusion: throughout the region, popular assemblies not only survived but in some places grew *stronger*, exactly because long-distance empires of the Babylonian or Assyrian type could only function effectively when they 'outsourced' their power by developing 'contractual' agreements and cultivating good working relations with the pastoral tribes and cities that dotted their territorial domain.[29]

The positive connection between empires and self-government – a tricky one to which we shall return several times – is suggested in an intriguing Old Assyrian letter from the early second millennium. It records a demand from the city of Assur, an instruction that the

colony must now disburse funds to enable the building of new fortifications.[30] The letter illustrates the manner in which 'the
assembly' is typically used within Old Assyrian correspondence as
a synonym for 'the city'. That (as Thorkild Jakobsen once claimed)
the assemblies were routinely blessed with the power to appoint
and revoke monarchs may or may not turn out to be true, but one
trend seems certain: these assemblies persisted for at least two millennia, which is to say, like the Phoenician and Greek assemblies
that came after them, they formed a *political tradition* that was neither easily revoked nor snubbed.

Although the evidence on the ground remains thin, we can say
with some certainty that the ancient self-governing assemblies
of Syria-Mesopotamia were contagious. What does this mean?
Geographically speaking, it means that assemblies spread towards
the east, for instance into what is today the Indian subcontinent,
where sometime after 1500 BCE, in the early Vedic period, republics
governed by assemblies became common.[31] Thanks to the river trade
and caravan routes that filtered through Syrian-Mesopotamian
cities like Mari, Tuttul and Nabada, the custom of assembly-based
discussions also migrated westwards, towards the Mediterranean
coasts that came to be controlled by the Phoenician 'peoples of the
sea', as well as towards peoples – our Greek cousins – who cheekily
claimed for themselves the honour of inventing assemblies by giving
them a new name: democracy.

The impertinence was usually denied as such by Greek contemporaries, though there is one remarkable exception. It is an account
of the military expedition of the Persian Mardonios through the
eastern Mediterranean in the spring months of 492 BCE, and it
strikingly corroborates our story of the Eastern origins of assembly
democracy.

Backed by a huge army and massive naval force, Mardonios,
recently married to Artozostra, daughter of King Darius, swept down
the Asian coast through the Greek cities of Ionia, heading towards
Eretria and Athens. The expedition was ultimately scuppered by bad
weather, but everywhere he went in Ionia Mardonios tried to win
local support by deposing every despot he could get his hands on. In
their place, he established government by popular assembly. He managed as a result to win the favour of local oligarchs, including even

the Persian nobleman Otanes, whose praise for self-government through assemblies was fulsome.

At the time, the political sympathy of Otanes for Mardonios was thought by more than a few Greeks to be 'a great marvel'.[32] Most were surprised; many regarded the whole episode as incredible. That is why it was recorded and why, since it is something of a Greek–Persian dialogue about the importance of publicly account-able government, it is worth repeating here in full. 'To me', Otanes began, 'it seems best that no single one of us should henceforth be ruler, for that is neither pleasant nor profitable.' The Persian noble-man paused, then took a breath before putting his point using the example of his fellow Persian Cambyses II, the drunken criminal ruler who was thought to have been punished by madness after slaughtering a sacred animal. 'Ye saw the insolent temper of Cambyses, to what lengths it went . . . and how should the rule of one alone be a well-ordered thing, seeing that the monarch may do what he desires without rendering any account of his acts? Even the best of all men, if he were placed in this position, would be caused by it to change from his wonted disposition: for insolence is engen-dered in him by the good things which he possesses, and envy is implanted in man from the beginning; and having these two things, he has all vice: for he does many deeds of reckless wrong, partly moved by insolence proceeding from satiety, and partly by envy. And yet a despot at least ought to have been free from envy, seeing that he has all manner of good things. He is however naturally in just the opposite temper towards his subjects; for he grudges to the nobles that they should survive and live, but delights in the basest of the citizens, and he is more ready than any other man to receive calumnies. Then of all things he is the most inconsistent; for if you express admiration of him moderately, he is offended that no very great court is paid to him, whereas if you pay court to him extrav-agantly, he is offended with you for being a flatterer. And the most important matter of all is that which I am about to say: – he dis-turbs the customs handed down from our fathers, he is a ravisher of women, and he puts men to death without trial.'

Otanes the nobleman then moved to propose his remedy for des-potism. 'The rule of the many on the other hand has first a name attaching to it which is the fairest of all names, that is to say

"Equality" [*isonomia*]', he said. 'Next, the multitude does none of those things which the monarch does: offices of state are exercised by lot, and the magistrates are compelled to render account of their action: and finally all matters of deliberation are referred to the public assembly. I therefore give as my opinion that we let monarchy go and increase the power of the people; for in the people is contained everything.'

The Desert Orphan

The power of the people, in whom is 'contained everything': such exultant words, prompted by a Persian noble, should raise eyebrows because they jolt us into seeing just how communicable was the *Eastern* custom of publicly controlling power by submitting important decisions to popular assemblies. Customs are, of course, not 'natural' and have no historical guarantees. That is why new questions easily come before us, caps in hand: what happened to the art of self-government by public assembly after the disappearance of the Hellenic democracies of the eastern Mediterranean region? Did assemblies go underground, or disappear without trace? Was the work of putting new flesh on the old bones of self-governing assemblies left to Christian Europe, as all previous histories of democracy have surmised?

Persuasive answers to these questions are difficult to summarise without deference to bland generalities, but careful replies are needed, if only to complete our picture of the early history of assembly democracy. To do this we must question just one more prejudice: the dogma that supposes that the tragic collapse of Athens and other Greek democracies following the military triumph of the Macedonian, Roman and Byzantine empires produced a political graveyard. According to this dogma, democracy died, and was then forgotten, for a long time. Popular rule 'vanished from the face of the earth for a thousand years', only to be revived, like an extinct species that miraculously reappeared after a cataclysmic ice age, in the cities of northern Italy around 1100 CE.[33]

Like all prejudices, the story that democracy vanished for a millennium contains grains of truth. Democratic institutions and ways of life and thinking in the Hellenic world were badly damaged by Macedonian rule; they did indeed suffer under the impact of the Roman Empire, and its subsequent collapse and mutation into Byzantine rule. Everywhere in the region, the centralised states that succeeded the democracies of Greece were mainly monarchies, ruling over extensive webs of smaller city-states, some of them garrison cities.

Until the end of the first century BCE, but only for a time, the Roman republic was something of an exception to this anti-democratic trend. While it is undeniable that the power wielded by consuls and praetors, proconsuls and pro-praetors was oligarchic, they depended heavily on popular opinions expressed in public meetings (*contiones*) filtered through the Senate, whose hand exercised considerable counter-powers, for instance in the matter of how the provinces were best governed.[34] Magistrates of the republic regularly summoned assemblies of male citizens to the Forum, where they were asked to convict or acquit defendants, to authorise laws, or to decide among candidates for public office. In practice, given the geographic size of the republic (it was six hundred kilometres from Rhegium (Reggio) to Rome), most citizens never once exercised their right to vote. Those who did gather to hear speeches for or against propositions were typically offered only a 'yes' or a 'no' vote; the right to speak was normally granted only to officeholders and ex-officeholders; and, through time, assemblies were increasingly fractured by trials of strength and violence among rivals for power. Empire soon sapped the energies of the remaining mechanisms of public control. The government based in Rome degenerated into an imperial oligarchy deeply hostile to the principles and practice of democratic self-government. So despite apparent continuities, such as competition for public offices, the democratic spirit of the subordinate cities dried up. The cities of the Roman Empire lost control over their military and foreign affairs; and in local affairs they found themselves hemmed in by the growth of a stratum of courtiers, functionaries and 'friends' of power, men equipped with the means of collecting taxes, commanding garrisons and generally restricting the administrative autonomy of city life. Institutions like the Assembly, the People's Court and the Council of Five Hundred disappeared. Their traces remained within the obituaries to democracy found in various political treatises, certainly; but in general power rituals centred on cults, games and the gymnasium flourished. So, too, did the *courteoisie*, or functionaries of the ruling power: called parasites and flatterers by their opponents, they gorged themselves on gifts of land and cash, fine clothing and uniforms, the work of servants, and privileged access to the levers of power. All this had the effect of pushing the arts of democratic government beyond the horizons of memory for nearly a thousand years – or so it has been said.

Things were not in fact what they now seem. The dogma of democracy's disappearance from the world is a fraud, an unsound bias vulnerable to lots of contrary evidence that brings us to perhaps the biggest surprise so far in the early history of democracy: to the vital contributions of Islam to enlivening, and geographically expanding, the old principle that human beings are capable of gathering in assemblies and governing themselves as equals.

Democracy as we know it is not simply the single-minded invention of Athenians, or Greeks, or the Phoenicians, or the ancient Syrian-Mesopotamians. The early history of assembly-based democracy instead resembles a vast Euphrates fed by many different streams of influence. The connections between its deltas and upstream sources are complicated – so much more complicated than previous accounts have supposed that it is better to say that democratic ideals and institutions were born, and first nurtured, within the quadrangle of territory bounded by the cities of Athens and Rome in the west, and Babylon and Mecca in the east.

Mecca? The desert city revered by Muslims, the holiest place in the Islamic world? Its inclusion within the history of democracy seems preposterous, but to ignore the supporting evidence is to pander to the prejudice that democracy is purely a Western – ultimately Greek – invention. We are about to discover that the world of Islam, during its first four 'golden' centuries, not only kept alive the regional traditions of assemblies that had their roots in ancient Syria-Mesopotamia. Muslims also invented a variety of brand-new mechanisms for publicly monitoring and sharing power among peoples who considered each other as equals. And of great political importance is the fact that early Islam served as a covered bridge that enabled the peoples of the world to pass from the ancient forms of assembly-based democracy to the world of representative government. Quite simply, none of this has been registered in previous accounts of the history of democracy, all of which have suffered what is best described as a motivated ignorance of Islam. 'Of all the religions of the world', thundered Sir Thomas Erskine May (1815–86) in one of the last attempts to write a history of democracy in Europe, 'none have been more opposed to freedom than that of Mohammed.' He added: 'The followers of the Prophet were pitiless conquerors, and the new faith . . . was theocratic: absolute rulers were an essential part of its polity: its immutable laws were prescribed by the Koran.'[35]

May's views were not extreme by contemporary standards, but their practical implications were profoundly anti-democratic. Muslim peoples were written out of the story of democracy, for reasons that were made clear by the nineteenth-century French politician and writer Alexis de Tocqueville, otherwise famous for his rich defence of democracy in the young republic of the United States. Tocqueville minced no words. He had no doubt that in America the spirit of Christianity had fertilised the growth of a bustling society and solid democratic institutions. By contrast, the Muslim faith had from the outset infected its believers with the linked diseases of materialism and fatalism. So decadent was Islam that 'the great violence of conquest' perpetrated by European colonisers in countries like Algeria was as necessary and justified as the 'smaller acts of violence' that would be needed to maintain such colonies. Tocqueville considered that 'there have been few religions in the world as deadly to men as that of Mohammed' and he was sure that it was 'the principal cause of the decadence so visible today in the Muslim world'. Democracy was impossible in Muslim societies. The only alternative was a two-tier political order: a top layer governed by men who lived democratically by the principles of Christian civilisation, and a bottom layer of institutions inhabited by natives left to wallow in the backward laws and customs of the Qur'an.[36]

The biased arrogance buried in such thinking should today be repugnant. It needs to be rejected. So does the flipside view that the world of Islam has nothing to do with the tainted Western devil of democracy. A fresh start must be made, initially by cutting a path

back to the beginning of the seventh century CE, to a region of the
Arabian desert blanketed with crescent-shaped dunes and spotted
with palm-fringed oases and teeming market towns. It was in these
parched lands, populated by wandering tribes of Arab pagans and
Jewish and Christian traders and travellers, that a new world religion was proclaimed. Its founder was an orphaned resident of
Mecca. He was known locally as al-Amin ('the trustworthy'), a
man born of the tribe of traders known as the Quraish and later
revered as the Prophet Muhammed. Near the age of forty, during
one of his retreats to a cave on nearby Mount Hira, Abu-l-Qasim
Muhammed ibn Abd-Allah, when meditating, repeatedly heard
voices and tinkling sounds and saw visions. They came to him 'like
the breaking of the dawn'. They summoned him to worship the
God who had created the world – Allah, whom ordinary Arabs
already honoured, but without granting Him exclusive cult status.

In the year 622 CE, after the death of his first wife Khadija, and
under pain of persecution from both the leading families of the
Quraish and the divided town of Mecca, Muhammed was forced
into exile, to the oasis of Medina, together with his band of faithful. It so happened that in power terms the oasis was up for grabs:
its population of feuding tribes of pagan Arabs nearly outnumbered the local Jewish settlers, and there was no tradition of stable
government. Muhammed and his supporters filled the vacuum. The
desert orphan quickly developed a reputation as a fair-minded but
disciplined man of power. He became spiritual leader, rule-maker,
lawgiver, supreme judge, even a budding commander-in-chief who
took advantage of the significant geopolitical fact that the whole
region of western Arabia stood safely on the margins of two great
warring and plague-ridden empires, those of the Byzantines and the
Persian Sassanids.

From inside this political vacuum, helped along by zeal, cunning
and camel power, the political community of Islam was born.
Following his spectacular success at the Battle of Badir (624 CE), the
Prophet later returned in triumph to Mecca, where his recitations
(the Qur'an) were completed. Recorded in all their beauty in the
language of Arabic, they contained rules concerning the ordinances
of religion, such as prayer, fasting, almsgiving and pilgrimage. The
text also included strictures on civil and criminal matters, the laws

of succession and inheritance, and the importance of non-violent power-sharing between rulers and ruled, who are considered as equals.

It is true that early Islam quickly became mixed up with dubious older customs, such as the willingness to fight for what was right, even to use military violence to build an empire, in defence of its own religious community. Considered as a body of believers, Islam also harboured deep ambiguities that subsequently raised tough questions about its commitment to equality. Its earliest views on the role of women are a case in point. While the first Muslims were strongly opposed to the victimisation of women, as can be seen in their forthright opposition to female infanticide and the disinheritance of women in matters of property, these same Muslims were not always clear about the extent to which women were the equals of men. It is important to note these ambiguities. But equally vital is the need to see how Islam nurtured a vibrant culture of non-violent power-sharing between rulers and ruled – and how it spread this sensibility into geographic areas previously untouched, or touched lightly, by assembly democracy.

To understand the proto-democratic instincts of the early Muslim communities is to see that democracy often comes camouflaged, that democratic inventions happen under other names.[37] Let us pause for a moment, to look at the evidence with a new eye.

The Qur'an rejected the idea of a chosen people. It emphasised instead a strong sense of common human destiny. The monotheistic belief in Allah as Creator implied a universal ethic. It required that human life be measured by standards larger than group pride, blood-feuding honour and other tribal standards; the quest for goodness implied living up to the God-given standards set for the whole world. The universalism of Islam naturally implied the need to rid the world of superstition and idolatry, of the kind that had played a vital role in the Greek democracies and assemblies of Syria-Mesopotamia. The belief in Allah as Creator was seen to demand moral purity and responsibility of all individuals for their own actions. Although the Qur'an made no attempt to lay down a comprehensive system of morals – it never pretended to be a know-all ideology – its emphasis on responsibility implied the need for people to apply rules of justice to their own social behaviour, as well as the need for a just political system that would curb the licence of the strong and extend generosity to the weak.

The curb on licence extended – unusually – to the earth's biosphere, as we now call it. Like the respect for the deities of Greek democracy and Syrian-Mesopotamian assemblies, but in sharp contrast to the anthropocentrism of early Christianity, the spirit of Islam displayed a powerful sense of respect for the transcendent world of nature in which human beings and other creatures dwell. 'Praise be to Allah, Who created the heavens And the earth, And made the Darkness And the Light' (S. 6.1), runs a well-known Qur'an passage. Similar sentiments leap from the pages of the remarkable, much-loved fable called *The Animals' Lawsuit Against Humanity*.[38] Written by a group of tenth-century Sufi Muslims from near Basra, it features an assembly in which eloquent envoys of all members of the animal kingdom – from bees to horses – come before the respected Spirit King to complain of their dreadful treatment at the hands of humankind, who in turn deftly defend themselves by arguing their counter-points with equal eloquence. The implication of this text was clear: believers should not regard themselves as separate from and superior to nature. They are forbidden to use it contemptuously, as if it were their plaything. Human beings are instructed to act humbly in the presence of a vast universe that cannot be grasped fully by the human mind, let alone the human hand. In matters of government, the early Islamic believers stressed, not only humans but also the world of nature enjoyed certain entitlements, including the public right to be heard, or at least treated with respect by others. Compassion towards nature is service to God. Muhammed repeatedly forbade cruelty to animals. 'A good deed done to a beast', records one well-known saying of the Prophet, 'is as good as doing good to a human being; while an act of cruelty to a beast is as bad as an act of cruelty to a human being.' The Qur'an explains that such benevolence flows directly from God: 'There is not an animal (That lives) on the earth, Nor a being that flies On its wings, but (forms Part of) communities like you' (S. 6.38).

These were egalitarian or democratic sentiments in all but name, but Muslims were remarkably inventive as well in the business of human institutions. Within a century of the Prophet's death (632 CE), the call of the muezzin from the minaret – 'There is no god except God and Muhammed is the Apostle of God' – echoed in lands as far afield as Spain and China and the Indian subcontinent. By the third and fourth Islamic centuries (the ninth and tenth centuries CE), a world empire dominated by Muslims had been built under a canopy of different governments, erected in different spots. Following the death of Muhammed, the tricky problem of succession was temporarily solved by the appointment as caliph of Abu Bakr al-Siddiq, who had been the leader of public prayers during Muhammed's last illness. Abu Bakr was the first of four caliphs (known to Sunni Muslims as the Rashidun, or 'Rightly Guided' Caliphs (632–661 CE)), three of whom were assassinated. The empire was thereafter shaped and reshaped by a succession of Damascus-based caliphs, known as the Umayyads (661–750 CE). Then came the mainly Baghdad-centred Abbasids, so named after their first caliph, Abu'l-'Abbas al-Saffah (749–54 CE).

Those who enjoy delicious ironies will find plenty to feast on in all this. Not only were the early caliphs typically appointed by an inner clique, and without the consent of those whom they tried to govern, but there was also the odd fact that the new world religion of Islam, the militant champion of humility and power-sharing, resulted in the birth of the earth's first aspiring global empire. Just as ironic was another fact: that Islam, a way of life that quickly spread across several continents, its champions using means that included negotiation, religious conversion, handouts of gifts of land and resources, and (when all that failed) force of arms, had the long-term effect of laying the foundations of *social* institutions that functioned as effective brakes upon concentrations of governmental power.

The growth of a swathe of social institutions that Muslim and other scholars later called 'civil society' (*jamaa'i madani*) was unknown to Greeks, Phoenicians and the peoples of Syria-Mesopotamia. The lands that curved from Spain and Gibraltar around through North Africa and stretched eastwards to the Middle East and Persia, then all the way to the Indian Ocean, were seen by Muslim traders, clerics and scholars as the centre of gravity of the human world, as can be seen (when visiting the Bibliothèque Nationale in Paris) in the famous map prepared in

1154 CE by Muhammed al-Idrisi, the Arab cartographer of the court of King Roger of Sicily: with south at the top, it places the Arabian peninsula at the top centre, with the diminutive European lands – spelled Urūba – placed on the right.

The early Muslim view of Islam as the fulcrum of the world – in reality it was divided by a rich fare of conflicting trends – had economic foundations. Islam was the religion of traders with urban connections, not a religion of peasants or (as was commonly supposed in the nineteenth century) lonely desert dwellers conscious of their own insignificance. The sprawling civil society of Muslims resembled a modern-day bazaar writ large: a covered kaleidoscope of differently sized rooms, twisting alleys, steps leading to obscure places, people and goods in motion, to all four corners of the earth. The simile of the bazaar is apt, for among the basic institutions of this society was a long-distance economy sustained by credit systems and a common currency, the so-called Abbasid gold dinar. The huge economy spawned by Islam was dotted with cities, including new-founded urban centres like Basra and Kufra in Iraq and Fustat (later Cairo) in Egypt. These cities served as intersections within vast highways of production and trade and the consumption of commodities. From India and China, by ships fitted with lateen sails and iron compasses, Muslim merchants brought pepper and other spices, fine cloth, porcelain and precious stones. Atop the backs of camels well organised into caravans, produce was imported and re-exported: furs from northern countries, Spanish silk, gold from West Africa, metals and olive oil from the Maghrib.

Innovations spread fast, generally westwards, from China and India through Persia into the Mediterranean basin. New methods of crop rotation and large-scale irrigation, including the water well from Syria and the underground canal from Persia, bore gifts of watermelons, apricots, sugar cane, cotton, rice, oranges and lemons. For its time, the Islamic economy was unrivalled in its ability to foster state-of-the-art technical inventions, like paper from China. Baghdad, the main capital of the Abbasids, was famous for its paper mills and shops selling big sheets of fine-quality paper, which enabled the development of Arabic numerals, map-making and the impressive calligraphic copies of the Qur'an. Paper made from rags proved to be a revolutionary medium. Light, durable and cheap to produce – remember that each parchment copy of the 641-leaf Gutenberg Bible required the skins of three hundred sheep – paper made possible government and administration at a distance. And it enabled the growth of reading publics, the spread of scientific knowledge and the development of a pioneering system of contract laws.

The civil society of the early Muslim period was impressive. Distinguished by its pioneering development of private and civil laws that covered the protection of trade and property, its pre-dominant form was called 'the partnership'. Economic partnerships bore no resemblance to the later European employer–worker relationship (which was later regarded by many Muslims as a form of slavery) and they certainly did not spawn the rise of class differences between owners and non-owners of property. In Muslim social life, property, production, trade and consumption were deeply embedded in other social institutions, such as households and neighbourhood and religious bodies. The upshot was that those involved in business, women and men alike, regarded each other as 'owners', regardless of whether or not they contributed capital or labour to the partnership. The resulting social ties were typically multiple, fluid and dynamic. Their effect, from the point of view of a history of democracy, was twofold. They blocked the emergence of large-scale trading and manufacturing firms – market capitalism – of the kind that first developed nearly a millennium later, in Europe's Low Countries. They also prevented the rise of European-style absolutist regimes skilled at the art of sticking their fingers into others' economic business.

Seen in this way, Erskine May's allegation that in the world of Islam 'absolute rulers were an essential part of its polity: its immutable laws were prescribed by the Koran' is utterly unfounded. The 'Oriental' despotic state about which he and others fantasised and which they feared was a much later development – and one very much caused by foreign conquest and Western colonisation, whose effect, in most cases, was to maim or destroy the vibrant foundation of social partnerships on which the Islamic empire rested. Business partnerships were among the key props of Islam's civil society, but it had others, including the *waqf*. This was an endowment society, a non-governmental institution based on the principle that the living had a duty to the future, that they were obliged to prevent unfair accumulations of property and riches by ensuring that the whole community, especially its least powerful members, were provided with access to land and various kinds of benefits, all for the purpose of ensuring that they did not lose their dignity before others, and in the eyes of God.

Established for the purpose of collecting and providing endowments by Muslim governors and rich nobles to the whole community, *waqf* institutions were more than guarantors of minimum standards of living for all. As sources of social bonding and social differentiation, they also served as barriers designed to keep tabs on rulers, to stop them becoming despots. Many Muslim legal scholars laid great emphasis on the precedent set by a man who later (634–44 CE) became caliph: Umar ibn Abd al-Khattab, who after the military conquest of the Jewish town of Khaibar in 628 CE, acquired a strip of valuable land (perhaps a palm garden). He approached the Prophet for advice about what to do with the property, and was told: 'Retain the thing itself and devote its fruits to pious purposes.'

The widely practised principle of *waqf* supposed that the right of private ownership could be disconnected from its exercise; it was thought that private property should be harnessed for good social purposes by creating a legally binding duty to provide endowments, which were of two kinds. Wealthy individuals made grants in perpetuity to particular groups of people, for example to their children or grandchildren (self-endowment was strictly prohibited); or they made grants to the poor, for instance by allowing them to graze animals for their milk and wool, or to harvest the fruit from trees. Endowments were also made in perpetuity for public or religious purposes. Resources were given over to the construction, staffing and upkeep of hospitals, caravanserais (inns where tired travellers could spend the night), public libraries, bridges, stables, waterworks and warehouses. Support was given as well to mosques, schools, gardens, farms and cemeteries, and to businesses ranging from bakeries and baths to paper works and sugar presses. The famed Al-Azhar University in Cairo, founded in 972 CE, was financed by revenues accrued from *waqf* properties.

What is most interesting about these social arrangements is that they enabled people to resist vigorously attempts by rulers and government officials to confiscate or control the *waqf*. It mattered that the administration of the *waqf* was normally in the hands of a supervisor (called a *nazir, kaiyim* or *mutawalli*), who received a salary for carrying out certain caretaker duties. Payment of a salary to a local custodian was just one of many different methods of protecting endowments from the twin blights of embezzlement and abuse of power. *Waqf* institutions could, of course, malfunction as elaborate patronage systems that nailed down the power imbalances between the endower and the endowed. That was why *waqf* inscriptions were normally posted on the premises to remind publics of the founding aims of the endowment, which was inalienable; and why endowments were commonly subject to detailed legal contracts. Founders themselves were bound by various controls. The subdivision of the endowment into a number of smaller parts (so ensuring that several administrators could check and balance both the endower and each other) was commonly practised. So, too, was the public supervision of the endowment by either a local commission that included prominent local citizens or (as in Córdoba under the Umayyads) a self-governing regional board.

The endowment societies were bolstered in their social duties by Sufi brotherhoods (*turuq*). By the eleventh century, these brotherhoods had moved from the fringes of social life to become mainstream organisations within the civil society of Islam. The Sufis trained disciples and carried religious sentiments from the cities into the surrounding countryside; they operated large-scale, horizontally self-organised networks that often stretched vast distances. The Sufi mystics tried to live lives of contemplation, self-perfection and spiritual harmony with God. They rarely withdrew permanently from society; they enjoyed remarkably close ties with a wide range of occupations. Everywhere they were renowned for their humility, their suspicion of power and their simple ways of living – and for their ability to address the common people in the vernacular. There are many recorded cases in which they took the side of underdogs, in defence of their grievances and claims for greater justice. Stories within stories and meanings within meanings were among their favourite weapons. One day, according to a famous contemporary Sufi tale, a young man named Si'Djeha was strolling on the outskirts of his town when he came upon an Islamic judge (*qadi*) snoring under a tree, burning off his last wine-drinking bout. So deeply sunk in drunken slumber was the judge that Si'Djeha managed to remove his fine new woollen cloak without waking his victim. When the judge stirred and realised that he had been robbed of his costly cloak, he sent his assistants looking for it. Before long, the men spotted it on Si'Djeha's back and dragged him into the town court. 'How did you come to possess so fine a cloak?' demanded the judge. 'I saw an unbeliever grossly drunk with the stink of wine, lying asleep under a tree,' replied the young man. 'So I spat on the infidel's beard and took his cloak. But if your honour should claim the cloak then it is only just that you should have it back.' 'I have never seen this cloak before in my life,' hissed the judge. 'Now be off with you, and take the cloak along with you.'

The Mosque

At the heart of the civil society that stretched from the Atlantic to the Indian Ocean lay the new architectural form called the *masdjid* (hence the English word 'mosque', taken from the Spanish *mesquite*). The mosque was not exclusively a place for communal prayer; resembling a combination of the agora and the Pnyx of Athenian democracy, it functioned much more as a public space used by assemblies of the whole local community to conduct their public business, with a buzz.

The mosque was a powerful carrier of the spirit of assembly democracy. Access was universal. Young and old, rich and poor, men and women were equally welcome, though (in the case of women) subject sometimes to certain restrictions: women were not meant to be perfumed, or menstruating; they should assemble separately from men; and they should leave the mosque before their menfolk. Also welcome were the People of the Book – Jews and Christians of all sects and tendencies, although sometimes (as in Hebron) they had to make a payment upon entry. Bans on peoples of different cultural background and language were frowned upon.

The community of Muslims called the *umma* knew nothing of the later European habit of cultivating nations and nation building and national boundaries – or discriminating against people supposed to be inferior because of the colour of their skin.

Most mosques were small, and informally run. Built of local materials and reflecting local tastes and traditions, they functioned as houses of prayer flanked by various rooms and buildings. There were hostels to provide shelter for travellers or pilgrims; courts where justice was handed down by a local judge; and hospital facilities for the sick. In the early period of Islam, mosques were also places where the local society mingled, for a variety of purposes. Perfumed by incense, lit with lamps and lanterns in the evenings, partly to assist those people who wanted to read, partly to prevent crime, mosques were places where people liked to pass time. Summer nights were spent there because people found them safe – nocturnal vigils were commonplace in early Islam – as well as pleasantly cool. Mosques were usually equipped with a drinking fountain; there were washing arrangements and even a nearby watering point for animals.

Mosques were also sites of sadness, and fear. In Persia, it was the custom for families of the deceased to receive visits of condolence for three days after the death of loved ones. In times of trouble, during severe droughts or nasty plagues for instance, people went to the mosque to pray, or simply to be with one another. Mosques were equally places of celebration. During the nights of the month of Ramadan, mosques hosted festivals, as they did as well on other occasions, such as the New Year, new moon and in the middle of the month. The entire mosque on these occasions was illuminated; there was eating and drinking, women singers performed, and people clustered around speechmakers to listen to their stories and 'discourses' (*kasas*) on various subjects.

The early mosques were also markets. Contracts were signed and oaths taken, hawkers peddled their wares, women sold thread, and fresh and prepared food – including wine – were sold there. Business seems to have been conducted even in the great mosques of Damascus and Aleppo, Jerusalem and Medina, Qayrawan and Córdoba, the Muslim capital of Spain. These largest and most loved sacred houses of the empire were considered special. They were places where body oil, perfume and best clothes were worn for the Friday service. Polite manners were expected. Sandals were removed and spitting was prohibited (at least in certain directions and spots). The design of these great mosques was remarkably similar. Each had a minaret from which the muezzin called the community to prayer at the appointed times. The open courtyards of the mosque adjoined a covered area that provided space for long lines of worshippers, guided by a prayer leader (*imam*), to assemble and face in the direction of Mecca. Each mosque contained a niche (*mihrab*) that marked the wall towards which worshippers faced; nearby stood the pulpit (*minbar*) from where on Fridays during the noon prayer the sermon was preached – and matters of public concern were often raised.

The mosque was more than lodgings, a shelter for the afflicted, a market square, a meeting point, a nook for prayer and quiet reflection. It also had a political function. It was to the empire of Islam what the assembly was to the world of Greek democracy. The custom of combining the political with the social and the sacred in the mosque had older, pre-Islamic roots: the very word for the Friday address (*khutbah*) was derived from the Arab tribal practice of an orator or judge speaking from a place of authority. In the mosque at Medina, the Prophet, seated upon the pulpit, made political statements, conducted government business and received ambassadors from far and wide. The principle was consolidated during Muhammed's last illness, when Abu Bakr was invited to lead the public in worship. That established a precedent that was followed to the letter by provincial and local urban governors, one of whose first public functions upon appointment was to say a few words and to lead prayers at the head of the assembly of local believers. During this 'golden age' of Islam, the caliphs themselves nurtured the same custom. It was from the pulpit in Medina that Caliph Umar (634–44 CE) appealed for volunteers after announcing to the assembled congregation that things were going badly for the Muslim armies in Persia. It was from the pulpit, too, that Caliph Uthman (644–56 CE) delivered a speech defending himself against public criticisms of his methods of administration.

Appeals to justice were commonly made in the mosque, but not in the name of kinship, or (as in modern Europe) 'nations', 'estates' or 'states'. Justice, instead, took its cue from the whole community of faithful, the *umma*. Resembling the function of the Greek *dēmos*, this community of living Muslims was the last word on earth. Simultaneously religious and social and political, it was guided in practice by the sacred laws, the *shari'a*. These rules and regulations derived in principle from the Qur'an and *hadith*; in practice, they emerged through the work of its interpreters, the specialists in law or jurists (*fuqaha*), also known as the *ulama*. The vital role of judges and interpreters of law (*mufti*), played out through various independent legal institutions, such as courts and schools of law (*madhahib*), was unique to Islam and its quest to ensure that the laws of the political community belonged to the whole community.

Obey Every Ruler?

This equality rule had a practical corollary: in principle, early Islam accorded no special legitimacy to its political governors. Their job was to govern by ensuring the observance of the laws, and by respecting their autonomy, so guaranteeing the plurality of connected social freedoms that one great Islamic thinker liked to call 'the union of all the societies in the inhabitable world'.[39]

This was the theory. The trouble in practice, especially the more Islam became synonymous with a vast polity stretching from India and the borders of China in the east, to the shores of the Atlantic and North Africa in the west, was that the greatness of empire, and the power and riches it brought to its Muslim rulers, tempted them into believing that God stood by their side. Beginning with Umar, who succeeded Abu Bakr in 634 and called himself 'Khalifah of the Khalifah of the Apostle of God' as well as 'Commander of the Faithful', Muslim rulers demonstrated that they saw themselves as divine. They were prepared to risk everything by embracing the role of an earthly ruler who was supposed to be divinely guided and therefore capable of keeping Islam in touch with its original perfection, if need be by the fist of military force.

The vainglorious appeal to the spiritual superiority of temporal power whipped up much dissension among Muslims. There were moments of great strife, and it is not accidental that three of the first four caliphs were either murdered or assassinated (uncertainty surrounds the first caliph, Abu Bakr, who was said either to have died of natural causes, or to have been poisoned). There were plenty of Muslims who happily supported rule by the descendants of the Prophet, but that deference seemed strange to many contemporaries. In effect, it meant appealing to the Medina model of personal autocracy invented and practised in that city by Muhammed. Medina still gets much praise today, but the truth is that it had little to do with assembly-based democracy. Government rotated around the charismatic figure of Muhammed, who played the role of supreme arbiter in all negotiations and disputes. Administration was patriarchal and rudimentary; protection was supplied by a bevy of military believers; and the public treasury was kept filled by voluntary gifts and levies extracted from tribes in the region.

The obligation of prayer and the acceptance of Muhammed as Prophet were in effect compulsory. This model of government promised government by mutual agreement, even the peaceful self-government of Muslims, but beginning with the Medina community first established by negotiation, spiritual conversion and armed struggle, the empire of Islam undoubtedly carried within it the seeds of hubris. Its promise of self-government was vulnerable to the counter-claim that all earthly authority is by divine appointment – and that, since responsibility ultimately rests with God, the duty of subjects is to be lickspittles, to obey even unjust rulers, whose wicked deeds would one day be divinely punished, just as rulers who are righteous would one day be divinely rewarded. The accumulated stock of stories and sayings of the Prophet, the *hadith*, contained plenty of encouragement for rulers to treat their subjects in this way, as mere subjects. 'When God wishes good for a people', runs one of them, 'He sets over them the forbearing and wise, and places their goods in the hands of generous rulers; but when God wishes evil for a people, He sets over them the witless and base and entrusts their goods to avaricious rulers.'[40]

While the authenticity of such advice is difficult to confirm, there is no doubt that some of the early Muslim caliphs acted as if they could do no wrong, exactly because they had divinity on their side.

While Abu Bakr is said to have protested against being addressed as Caliph of Allah, there were plenty of later rulers, especially during the 500-year reign of the Abbasids, who thought of themselves in this way, essentially because they claimed descent from Abbas, the uncle of the Prophet. Mansur (754–75) proclaimed himself as the power (*sultan*) of God upon His earth. Mutawakkil (847–61) seems to have taken no offence when a captured rebel addressed him as the caliph who resembled a rope stretched between God and His creatures. Similes of that kind evidently went to the heads of many caliphs during the first few centuries of the Islamic era. Thinking of themselves as holy men saddled with the God-given task of running an empire, they busied themselves with flaunting their own splendour and – following much older Byzantine and Persian traditions – keeping their distance from their subjects by barricading themselves in splendid palaces.

Festival by festival, prayer by prayer, the religion of Islam slowly found itself mixed up with the methods and rituals of imperial power. Its rulers invested much time and money in setting up systems of regular administration by subdividing it into various offices, called *diwans*, paid for by new systems of taxation of land and produce, imports and exports; the wealthy were also targeted and poll taxes were applied to non-Muslims. Then there were the palaces decorated with magnificent gardens and parks, treasures from around the world, splendid dining and fine tableware, exotic birds and elephants caparisoned in peacock-silk brocade. Dressed in exquisite jewellery and fine clothes embroidered in pure gold, expecting (in the case of the Abbasids) their subjects always to kiss the ground on which they set foot, the caliphs indulged themselves in elaborate court ceremonies, waited on hand and foot by chamberlains and eunuchs, pages and servants. Various government officials handled the rest, beginning with a chief adviser called a *wazir*, but including as well teams of spies and informants to keep the caliph abreast of what was happening in the regions. Then there were the well-armed soldiers drawn up in serried ranks – and the sinister figure of the executioner, standing by the side of the caliph, eager to dispense summary justice, clutching a leather towel to catch the blood of the ruler's least favourite subjects.

The presumption, bloated by hubris, that concentrated power was sanctioned by God bred widespread discomfort and loud protests from contemporary Muslim scholars, theologians and citizens – as might have been expected of a region shaped by robust traditions of assembly-based government. The recent Muslim joke that when God dispensed envy on earth He gave 2 per cent to human beings and the rest to politicians and clergymen reminds us that early Islam never straightforwardly whetted people's insatiable appetites for power. By the standards of the time, as scholars and pundits otherwise hostile to Islam today concede, the society of Muslims that flourished during its first four fertile centuries was unusually sensitive to the problem of how to make power publicly accountable.[41] With reference to the caliphate, many pointed out that only someone who is dead or absent can have a successor, and that God, of course, could never be supposed to be in either of these conditions. Various groups known as Kharijis maintained that in Islam only virtue – not proximity to Muhammed – counted. They thought that only clean-living, pious Muslims were entitled to rule, which implied either that rulers who went astray should be opposed, or that pious Muslims should try to create their own virtuous political community, perhaps in a distant place.

A different version of the same line of political thinking cropped up among those who insisted that caliphs, like all other Muslims, were obliged to submit to the ordinances of the *shari'a*, the laws of Islam guarded by the *ulama*. That objection fuelled several major civil rebellions against the Umayyad rulers – in the 740s, for instance. Such resistance made clear that there was no room in early Islam for the distinction that arose in the Christian world of Europe between canon law and the law of the state. Islam rolled law, government and politics into one packet. All law was seen to be of divine origin, and so even the caliph himself was duty-bound to abide by the limits on earthly power that it specified. Rulers could indeed portray themselves as authorities in matters of law, but such presumption regularly ruffled the robes of the *ulama*, who were fond of pointing out that they were the only authoritative exponents of laws – and that political power grabbing, along with the spiritual opportunism that underlay it, were contrary to the Islamic way of life. The same point was put forcefully by the

eighth-century poet Sudayf, in an outburst against the seizure of
power by the Abbasids. 'By God', he reportedly wrote, 'our booty,
which was shared, has become a perquisite of the rich; our leadership, which was consultative, has become arbitrary; our
succession, which was by the choice of the community, is now by
inheritance . . .'[42]

Milk and Cream

The rock-ribbed political emotions exhaled through these words
help explain why, from the seventh century onwards, there were
forthright calls among Muslims for the open election of rulers.
Loud trumpet blasts were plentiful, but easily the most sonorous
was produced by the first Muslim to speak of democracy, Abu
Nasr al-Farabi (c. 870–950).[43]

Ranked today among the greatest Islamic philosophers, he left
no autobiography and details of his life are now scarce, except for
the traces that pop up in odd places, like the 200-tenge banknote of
contemporary Kazakhstan and the Malek Library in Tehran (Figures
18 and 19). It seems that al-Farabi was born in Turkestan and that
he later studied Arabic, Greek and other subjects in Baghdad, the
seat of the Abbasid caliphs; it has been claimed that most of his
books were written there while he laboured by day in a vineyard,
and that he read and wrote in the evening, by the light of the lamps
of the night watchmen in the adjoining gardens. It was said that he

FIGURE 18: Abu Nasr al-Farabi, as imagined by the Kazakhstan authorities on their country's
200-tenge banknote.

was no admirer of the caliphate and lived an ascetic life on a diet of water mixed with sweet basil juice, and lambs' hearts; that he always wore a brown Sufi tunic; and that visitors marvelled at both his intellect and his knack of mastering languages (some claimed he spoke more than seventy). He liked to wander in the desert and he travelled widely – to Damascus, Egypt, Haran and Aleppo, where he settled when he was an old man and famous writer to join the literary circle sponsored by the Hamdanid ruler, Sayf al-Dawla. We cannot be certain about any of these details. Even the circumstances of al-Farabi's death remain unclear. Some accounts portray him dying naturally in Damascus. At least one report maintains that he met his end at the hands of a mugger on the rocky road from Damascus to Ascalon.

If that report is true, then the irony shrouding his death is rather painful: al-Farabi was a great champion of a new form of government that secured people's freedom and happiness (what he called *sa'ada*). He was thoroughly familiar with the Greek experiment with *dēmokratia*, although in some parts of his work, which was written in a simple style for an Arabic-reading Muslim public, he regarded the ideal with ambivalence. Al-Farabi worried, as Plato's *Republic* before him had worried, that democracy (he used the

FIGURE 19: Title page of Abu Nasr al-Farabi's *Principles of the Opinions of the Citizens of the Perfect Polity* (Mabadi Ara Ahl al-Madina al-Fadila), from a rare copy dating from the eleventh century CE and today preserved in the Malek Library, Tehran.

words *al-madina al-jamaiyya*) rather overstated the virtue of what he called 'absolute freedom'. Democracy for that reason might degenerate into a free-for-all because the people would devote themselves to self-interested pleasure-seeking.

The interesting thing is that al-Farabi was even less impressed by other forms of earthly government, which he analysed into different forms of 'city' (a word meaning political community, and most definitely not a territorial state in our modern sense). Most of these degenerate polities (he no doubt had in mind the caliphate of the Abbasids) were seen by him to be misguided, in the sense that they frustrated or denied outright human beings' divinely given capacity to choose freely how they could live happily on earth. He especially disliked decadent polities that catered merely to men's animal needs; cities based on meanness, the belief that property, wealth and money-making are the only things that count in life; and cities driven by the pursuit of recognition, honour and power, based on the right of the stronger. He called these degenerate polities 'ignorant cities'; hence his attraction to democracy, which he thought the least ignorant of all polities. True, it could never reach perfection, but it was extremely unusual because its members were acutely aware that democracy differed from other types of polities – a self-awareness that sprang from democracy's unique stress on frank speech and self-government through open public assembly.

Al-Farabi liked these qualities. They danced to the tune of his conviction that humans were in no way subject to divine predestination, and that since they were equipped with the divinely given capacity for free deliberation they could contribute very substantially to their own perfection, understood as the desire to cooperate for the sake of happiness. Democracy unleashed this human capacity. It ensured that 'democratic people have many aims'.

There were times, al-Farabi admitted, when democracies led to excessive polarisation among differing aims and conflicting opinions. Democracies were especially vulnerable to war, the threat or possibility of which tends to subdivide the people into two hostile groups: those in favour of peace and those who 'maintain that the good consists in ruling by force, to be attained in two ways, by straight attack and by ... cheating, fraud and treachery, ruse, hypocrisy, deceit and leading people astray'. Democratic freedom for al-Farabi was a double-edged dagger. It could bring out the worst in people, but it could also produce virtuous citizens. Democracy might even be seen as a step in the direction of a perfect government. 'In the "democratic" polity', he wrote, 'all sorts of desires and ways of behaviour come together. Therefore it is not impossible that in the course of time excellent men should grow up in it, and that wise men, orators and poets should happen to exist in it . . . Thus it would become possible to gather from it parts for the Perfect Polity. This is one of the good things which arise in this polity.' Al-Farabi was no straightforward fan of numerical equality. He favoured the freedom and happiness of all God's creatures on earth and thought that this in turn required political leadership by good men of active intellect, good judgement and strong physique, leaders who were good orators, lovers of learning and truth and who stood above the materialism of this world. A few men of virtue should govern. The trouble, al-Farabi noted, is that all polities except one block the emergence of virtuous leadership. That was the singular advantage of democracy: it enabled the cream freely to rise to the surface of the milk.

Consultation

In the early Islamic world, that way of thinking creatively in favour of democratic freedom and happiness prompted nervous replies that exposed muddles in the way early Muslims handled questions of political authority.

Consider the comments of Basra-born Abu al-Hasan al-Mawardi, who until his death (in 1058) at the ripe age of eighty-six was considered a leading contemporary jurist. He reacted to the crumbling Abbasid dynasty by proposing that the office of Caliph or Imam should in principle be elected, not appointed. All adult men, at least those who were capable of pious reasoning and mature judgement, should take part. Knowing that almost every caliph had been nominated by his successor, Mawardi took a step back from this initial bold recommendation. He observed that the authorities were not agreed as to the number of electors required for an election to be considered valid; and he noted the practical

difficulty of securing unanimous agreement among all duly qualified Muslims in every part of Muslim civil society. So Mawardi
went on to cite the election of Abu Bakr as evidence that those
present at the death of the former leader of the community were
sufficiently representative of the whole body of Muslims. That
slipshod conclusion prompted an obvious query: was there a minimum number of spokespeople of this large and diverse political
community? Mawardi was not sure how to answer. In the election
of Abu Bakr, it was five. Before his death, Umar appointed an electoral college of six. Mawardi admitted that some contemporaries
were of the opinion that succession resembled a marriage contract,
so that three persons would be sufficient: one to draw up and sign
the contract in the presence of two witnesses (note the missing
bride); and to make matters worse, Mawardi confessed, still others
said that successors could be decided by a single voice. How then
could the problem be solved? Mawardi's conclusion must have
been music to the ears of some rulers: safe in the knowledge that
his choice would be representative of the opinions of the whole
community of Muslims, each caliph was entitled to appoint his
own successor!

Faced with that kind of intellectual bedlam, there is little wonder
that power craving in the early Muslim world was confronted with
not only words but a rich fare of inventions designed to guarantee
that governors kept their promises, and observed their duties. Chief
among these inventions was *mashwara* (sometimes called
mashura): the custom according to which all earthly laws made by
governors gained legitimacy only insofar as they were openly discussed and negotiated beforehand in public with advisers, who
could be variously defined.

The practice of open consultation was thought by some Muslims
(correctly) to have been inherited from pre-Islamic times, for
instance from the old Arabian practice of consultation among the
elders of tribes. The art of consultation was clearly indebted to the
even older traditions established by the Syrian-Mesopotamians and
the Phoenicians. Muslims liked as well to recall at least two passages in the Qur'an (S.3. 153–9; 42. 36–8) that specified a duty of
consultation upon decision makers. The dangers of arbitrary personal rule (*istibdād* was the bad-sounding Arabic word) and the

merits of negotiated agreements were also frequently mentioned in the *hadith*.

It is unclear just how inclusive the earliest Muslim forms of consultation were. There was the severely restricted precedent set by the caliph Umar, who on his deathbed appointed a committee to choose freely a successor from among its members. Consultation here meant little more than rulers deciding who should rule, at the expense of others. That is why members of the so-called *ulama* were notoriously vocal on their own behalf when confronted with governors who wanted to take matters into their own hands. These spokesmen – they seem always to have been men – thought of themselves as experts in matters of scripture, law and political wisdom. They were sure that the whole community of believers needed protection – and they were confident that they were the proper guardians of the correct way of living on earth.

The reasoning of the *ulama* rested upon the generous (or was it foolish?) presumption that men of piety would always have the best interests of the whole political community at their fingertips – that they could do little or no wrong. For some Muslims of the early period the presumption was quite unacceptable. They squirmed, then banged on about the need for permanent and wider consultation. A prime example was the loose but influential associations of believers known as the Mu'tazilites, who emerged during the 720s in and around the cities of Basra and Baghdad, and later flourished in Iran, well into the eleventh century CE. The Mu'tazilites reminded their fellow Muslims that kingship was forbidden, and they generally peddled the view that political leadership must be based on merit, otherwise it would result in social disturbance and civil war, which would split the community of Muslims, without guaranteeing better outcomes. Many insisted that merit had no connection with tribal or ethnic affiliation; office should be open to Arabs and non-Arabs alike. There were even Mu'tazilites who insisted that non-Arab imams were much to be preferred because they would display greater independence of judgement, and because (lacking the backing of a majority tribe) they would be easier to oust, in the event that they acted arrogantly. The Mu'tazilites were certain that Muslims permanently preserved the right to depose their leaders, if need be through the sword. Some of them went much further, by denying the need for imams. A prominent figure named Abu Bakr al-Asamm (he died in 816/817) pointed out that imams, unlike prayer and pilgrimage, were merely human conventions. They had a nasty habit of turning into kings, or pseudo-kings (like the reigning Abbasids of his time), and in any case the community of Muslims had become too large and complex to be governed by just one of them. Sensing (correctly) that the Abbasid caliphate was fated to suffer implosion, he recommended that it would be better, at any one time, to have multiple governors within the empire, just as Muhammed had supposed when appointing various imams in Arabia to maintain order, collect taxes and teach people respect for the laws. Without using anything like the term, al-Asamm came close to recommending something like a decentralised federation of governors who would be subject to the wishes of those whom they governed. Al-Asamm did not say how to coordinate this multiplicity of governors, but he was sure that in each case popular assemblies were mandatory. They were the only fair and open way of handling and dispensing questions of ultimate justice, in the shape of punishments (called *hudūd*), such as lashings, amputation and the death penalty. Government based on the assembly of large numbers of people was also the only way of preventing self-interested biases and dangerous conspiracies.

Meshwerets

Looking back on this period, Mu'tazilites like al-Asamm foreshadowed the later recommendations of a young religious scholar named Ibn Taymiyya (1263–1328), who tried to push the principle of consultation to its levelling limits. His conclusion was striking: citing classical sources, he emphasised that governors should consult not only with their own military and administrative officials, or with the *ulama*. Governors, he said, should also consult with assembled spokesmen of the general population. Taymiyya was here voicing a principle whose roots stretched back to the earlier worlds of Syria-Mesopotamia, Phoenicia and the Greek democracies; without knowing it, he was also strongly anticipating things to come in the history of democracy.

Although he was to suffer several periods of imprisonment for his efforts, Taymiyya's way of thinking about power helped inspire the consultative assemblies that for a long time flourished in the world of Islam, most powerfully in the Ottoman Empire that lasted from the beginning of the thirteenth century until 1922. From their inception, Ottoman governments, it was widely believed, were established upon the basis of negotiated agreement. According to at least one version, the Ketkhudas and the Beys of that region assembled to hold a *mashwara* (the Ottoman word was *meshweret*). After much discussion, they agreed to elect a new leader, renowned for his distinctive jet-black hair and arms so long that he could touch his knees with his hands when standing upright: a young man nicknamed the 'bone breaker', Othman Bey, or Osman I.

Apocryphal or not, the foundational story resonated with the widespread use, especially from the fifteenth century onwards, of consultative assemblies throughout the Ottoman Empire, which at its zenith spanned three continents. The rules of open deliberation were practised in many institutions, normally without the ruling sultan being present. There are plenty of records of *meshwerets* held in the city of Istanbul to discuss and to resolve a wide range of local problems, as and when they arose. Military commanders often resorted to consultation in the field. Government at the highest levels of the empire was conducted according to the same procedure: presided over in earlier times by the sultan, in later times by the Grand Vizier, a body with a prescribed membership called the high council (*diwan-i humayun*) that met at regular intervals, at fixed times, to review the condition of the empire, to address its problems as they emerged, and to find solutions. Towards the end of the eighteenth century, with the Ottoman Empire feeling the pressure of rising great powers, Russia included, such meetings grew in frequency. A major historical turning point was reached in May 1789, a few weeks before the outbreak of the French Revolution, when Sultan Selim III, at the start of his reign, convened a consultative assembly of leading officials to discuss the main problems of the empire, and how they could be remedied by that body, which had become a parliament in all but name.

Here we are getting much too far ahead of ourselves. The sobering fact is that by the tenth century, Islam's aspirations to win political acceptance as a universal way of life were checkmated, frustrated by the break-up of the unified caliphate, and by the formation of rival caliphates in Spain, Egypt and Persia. By the time of the caliph Muqtadir (908–32 CE), the authority of the Abbasid rulers extended not much beyond the precincts of Baghdad. Muqtadir himself became the plaything of his own undisciplined Turkish troops, who took offence at his reign marked by drunken extravagance and killed him in a skirmish. His corpse was left to rot where it fell. His head was stuck upon a spear: as a sign to all with eyes to see that vainglory would not be tolerated. That was perhaps why, just two years later, his brother Qahir, who tried to rule through the use of terror, was deposed. His eyes were put out with red-hot needles. He was imprisoned for eleven years and was last seen begging for alms in a mosque.

Urūba

Gruesome moments like these bloodied the green flag of Islam, but this should not stop us from seeing the ways in which Muslims effectively built a political bridge that linked the ancient assemblies of Syria-Mesopotamia, Phoenicia and Greece with the coming world of representative democracy.

Beneath the ugly canopy of power struggles and military strife, the social landscape of Islam proved resilient. Its civil society based on partnerships lived on. Linking lands and peoples from the Indian Ocean to the Mediterranean basin, the empire of Muslims created a single trading system driven by path-breaking changes in agriculture and crafts that enabled great cities to flourish. Although Jewish, Christian and other faith communities continued to play a prominent role, a large part of the imperial population came to identify with the religion of Islam. The Arabic language served as its medium – as well as a dynamic source of integration of an astonishing variety of local cultural traditions and common artistic forms, including distinctively Islamic buildings, poetry and books, new clothing fashions suited to the seasons, and inventions like algebra, the abacus and woodblock printing.

Islam did something else as well. The geographic spread of *waqf* institutions, Sufi networks and other means of holding those who governed publicly accountable to the political community was to have radical – utterly surprising – effects on the region that Muslims called Urūba. On its soil Islam planted the seeds of non-governmental organisations that administered their own affairs, at arm's length from both organised religion and governmental power. An important example is the *madrasa*. These colleges of religious study served as a model for the first European universities that were born in areas, such as southern Italy, where the influence of Islam was great and cross-fertilisation of institutions more easily took place. Among the defining features of the new universities was their explicit commitment to self-government, a principled reliance upon bodies that were variously called elected councils, syndics, congregations. In the centuries to come, when transplanted into other institutions, these bodies inspired by Islam were to play a decisive, at times revolutionary, role in reshaping the political contours of the European region.

Islam played a fundamental role in the renaissance and redefinition of democracy in another, less obvious but more long-lasting way. By demonstrating, across great swathes of territory, that it could organise dynamic political communities that frowned on extreme disparities of wealth and power, Islam proved to be an attractive way of life, one that was capable of making real gains, certainly at the expense of other types of economy, society and government that seemed backward.

The European talk of 'Oriental despotism' that flourished in modern times – such chatter was in reality always a ruse for European conquest – has blinded us to this genuine appeal of early Islamic ways of being. Medieval Christians on the front lines of contact with Muslim traders and invaders well understood this magnetism. It put them on the spot. Sometimes the gracious living of Muslims convinced their opponents to change their ways, by defecting into the arms of Islam, as happened in cities like Córdoba and Granada, whose Christians were so profoundly transformed by Muslim culture, in everything except their religion, that they were known as Mozarabs, or 'Arabisers'. At other times, the charms of Islam steeled the determination of Christians to build new lines of military defence and new means of political resistance, in the hope that the power of Muslims could be rolled back permanently, or crushed outright under hoof and sword and cross.

We are about to see that this life-and-death dynamic of cooperation, confrontation and resistance had many strange and ironic consequences. Easily the most remarkable was the birth, on the front line of European opposition to Islam, of a new institution never before seen on the face of the earth: a parliament of representatives of diverse social interests. The newcomer was a gift of Islam to the modern world, and it was to force a fundamental redefinition of democracy. It appeared suddenly during the twelfth century, at a moment when Christian communities in the northern reaches of the Iberian peninsula realised that they were trapped in the jaws of a crisis that might swallow them whole. That sudden realisation, among dominant groups like the nobility and the Church and urban traders, made them pull together, suspend their rivalries, agree to disagree, and come, side by side, to the negotiating table. Acutely conscious of their political weakness, they invented a new way of banding together to reach agreement by mutual consent.

The result was of great historical consequence. For the institution that was born on Iberian soil of mixed Muslim–Christian parentage bore more than a passing resemblance, in all but name, to the much older Islamic custom of consultation and the defining principle buried within it: the principle that government is only ever legitimate when it has been sanctioned by the active consent of the representatives chosen by the governed themselves.

PART TWO

REPRESENTATIVE DEMOCRACY

A late sixteenth-century drawing by Cesare Ripa (?–1622), the author of a highly influential book of emblems and virtues, showing democracy as a roughly dressed peasant woman clutching a pomegranate, a symbol of the unity of the people, and a handful of (presumably cunning and poisonous) snakes.

ON REPRESENTATIVE GOVERNMENT

To be a king is one thing,
To be a tyrant another.

Manegold of Lautenbach (*Liber ad Gebehardum*, 1085–6? CE)

The Mystery of Things

If a humble citizen acquainted with the assemblies of old Babylon and Nippur suddenly returned from the land of the dead, to hear the stories of early democracy so far told here, how might she react? Would she feel pride in the way these assemblies of Syria-Mesopotamia spread eastwards and westwards, helped along by the efforts of Phoenicians, Greeks, Jews and Muslims? Would she be astonished by their ability to survive – for a time – against overwhelming odds? Or would our ancestor smile at the utter implausibility of an earthly way of life marked by such cluttered, conflicting origins?

We do not know, of course, but the last question is especially interesting, if only because it puts its finger on the way democracy – assembly-based self-government – had beginnings that defy simple descriptions. In the first of its three historical lives, democracy owed its invention to disparate forces. It was fed by popular beliefs in God and the power of gods, by the growth of trade and commerce among towns, and the collapse of governments defeated in war. It was equally the child of tactical manoeuvres by figures like Cleisthenes and Demonax, botched crimes of passion, women who whispered the advice proffered by oracles, plus the brave resistance of sailors, soldiers and slaves fed up with tyrants. That's how it was: no clear-cut laws of motion, no regular patterns, just higgledy-piggledy breakthroughs and setbacks bound together by continuous struggles of people to control publicly the exercise of power through the use of assemblies.

Exactly the same clutter marked the redefinition of democracy at the beginning of the second millennium, when its centre of gravity moved towards medieval Europe. Much ink and paper were to be devoured by efforts to grasp how it happened, but not a single pen would succeed. That should not be surprising, if only because there are no evident patterns or 'laws' of historical development of 'modern' democracy, which is perhaps as it should be, given that the various democratic ways of dwelling on earth have in common their attachment to uncertainty, openness and surprise. The recent scholarly fashion – it is really an old habit that began with Aristotle – of trying to pin down the patterns inherent in the 'transition' towards and 'consolidation' of democracy, as if such statistical and comparative knowledge could then be applied rigorously anywhere to build or to refine democratic institutions, overlooks the simple point that democracy as a way of life is always born, nurtured or destroyed in particular contexts. That means that democracy is a form of human action shaped by institutional circumstances; and that surprise and democracy are twins. 'And take upon's the mystery of things' – the words spoken so wistfully by King Lear to Cordelia in Shakespeare's *King Lear*[1] – certainly applies to democracy. Its birth and survival, as well as its mutation and death, defy the gravity of universal laws. Whether democratic institutions survive or thrive, and in which form, depends in every case on indeterminacies: on the unpredictable dynamics of particular settings, on careful calculations, spur-of-the-moment decisions and – never to be underestimated – the fickle power of unforeseen consequences.

Representative Government?

We could say that democracy dwells in a house of contingency. Its proof of residence is well illustrated by the chain of events that triggered a second stage in the history of democracy: a wholly unexpected round of inventions that invested the word 'democracy' with a brand-new meaning.

It is difficult to date the change with precision, as we shall see. Roughly speaking, from about the tenth century CE the old Greek practice of *dēmokratia*, the self-government of equals by means of assemblies that had their roots in the Phoenician *mw-'dwt* and the Babylonian *pŭhrum*, underwent a slow but fundamental redefinition. The mutation was the work of many hands. Monarchs, monks, shepherds, statesmen, aristocrats, artisans, republicans, clergymen, money makers, city dwellers, farmers, soldiers, publishers, God-fearing religious dissidents all played a role. The consequent change that came over democracy was not simply an expression of 'the rise of the bourgeoisie', or of 'liberalism', as was commonly thought during the nineteenth and early twentieth centuries. The new democracy was a bastard. Its creation was unintended. Its survival was at no point in time guaranteed. It was not inevitable. Step by step, with many twists and turns, slowly but never surely, a miracle nevertheless happened. Democracy came to be defined as *representative democracy*.

This at least was the term that began to be used – belatedly – towards the end of the eighteenth century, for instance by constitution makers and political writers when referring to a new type of government, with its roots in popular consent. Nobody knows who first spoke of 'representative democracy'. The oxymoron seems to have been born of Anglo-French-American parentage. One political writer who broke new ground was an eighteenth-century Frenchman, a modestly wealthy member of the Bordeaux aristocracy who had had a generous taste of parliamentary experience as the deputy president of the Bordeaux *parlement*. Charles-Louis de Secondat, Baron de Montesquieu (1689–1755) was his name. His seminal book *The Spirit of the Laws* (*L'Esprit des lois* (1748)) spoke, unusually, positively of republican government and democracy,

Rome and Athens, in the same breath. Probably without knowing that what he was saying radically violated conventional ways of thinking about the subject, he went on to point out that in a democracy 'the people, in whom the supreme power resides, ought to have the management of everything within their reach'. He added: 'that which exceeds their abilities must be conducted by their ministers'.[2]

Ministers? What did it mean to entrust the people's business to them? The French nobleman, foreign minister under Louis XV, the Marquis d'Argenson (1694–1757), was well placed to answer such questions. He was perhaps the first person ever to tease out both the meaning of the word 'ministers' and the new definition of democracy as representation that it implied (Figure 20). D'Argenson did so by distinguishing between 'false' and 'true' democracy. 'False democracy', he said, 'soon collapses into anarchy. It is government of the multitude; such is a people in revolt, insolently scorning law and reason. Its tyrannical despotism is obvious from the violence of its movements and the uncertainty of its deliberations. In true democracy, one acts through deputies, who are authorised by election; the mission of those elected by the

FIGURE 20: René-Louis de Voyer de Paulmy, Marquis d'Argenson, from an eighteenth-century engraving.

people and the authority that such officials carry constitute the public power.'[3]

Others soon set about popularising the links between democracy and representation, and their observations travelled – fast. On the other side of the Atlantic, James Madison, who avoided the word democracy as if it were leprous, nevertheless counted himself among those who saw the novelty of the American political experiment in 'the delegation of the government . . . to a small number of citizens elected by the rest'.[4] Alexander Hamilton (c. 1756–1804) was perhaps the first American to nudge the words representation and democracy together, even at one point using the brand-new phrase 'representative democracy', evidently without knowing what he was saying. It is strange to think that some of the most precious terms in the history of democracy were invented as if in a dream, but so it was with Hamilton and the new phrase – representative democracy. He was normally hostile to popular rule, which he regularly called democracy and condemned as a formula for 'tyranny' and 'deformity' led by 'an ungovernable mob'. Yet on one occasion, shortly after the Declaration of Independence, he seemed to be in the grip of hallucinations that led him to deny that 'instability is inherent in the nature of popular governments'. Such governments, he said, could be 'happy, regular and durable' if they took the form of 'representative democracy, where the right of election is well secured and regulated and the exercise of the legislature, executive, and judiciary authorities is vested in select persons, chosen really and not nominally by the people'.[5] A more clear-headed rendition of the same point was soon to be put forward by a fellow Scot, James Wilson (1742–98), an erudite Presbyterian lawyer who also helped draft the 1787 Constitution. He noted that the new federal Constitution of the American republic was unusual in two respects: it recognised that 'representation is made necessary only because it is impossible for the people to act collectively', in consequence of which the new republic was 'purely democratical', since 'all authority of every kind is derived by representation from the people and the democratic principle is carried into every part of the government'.[6]

These were brand-new ways of thinking about democracy, by which was meant a type of government in which people, understood

as voters faced with a genuine choice between at least two alternatives, are free to elect others who then act in defence of their
interests, that is, *represent* them by deciding matters on their behalf.
Much ink and blood was to be spilled in defining what exactly representation meant, who was entitled to represent whom and what
had to be done when representatives snubbed those whom they were
supposed to represent. But what was common to this period, which
lasted for a thousand years, roughly from the tenth until the middle
of the twentieth century, was the belief that good government was
government by representatives. In a striking analogy drawn from
geometry, the biggest-selling author of the eighteenth century, the
Englishman Thomas Paine (1737–1809), thundered in favour of
'representation ingrafted upon democracy' as a new type of government that admitted its own divisions – in contrast to monarchy, and
its outdated belief in a unified body politic, and in contradistinction
to the 'simple democracy' of ancient Athens, whose *dēmos* was
under constant pressure to strike agreement with itself.[7] This is what
Paine intended by his intriguing remark that 'Athens, by representation, would have outrivalled her own democracy'. He meant to say
that democracy in representative form rejected the presumption that
disagreement was undemocratic, that ideally its body politic should
be indivisible. 'A nation is not a body', Paine explained, 'the figure of
which is to be represented by the human body; but is like a body
contained within a circle, having a common centre, in which every
radius meets; and that centre is formed by representation.'

That was quite a complex thought. It was used by Paine to justify ridding the world of hereditary stupidity. Representative
government exposed the fallacy that sperm was a carrier of good
government. It was a type of polity that encouraged the public
airing of different interests and opinions, as well as their handling
and resolution through leadership guided by merit. Representative
government was praised as a way of freeing citizens from the fear
of leaders to whom power was entrusted; the elected representative
temporarily 'in office' was seen as a positive substitute for power
personified in the body of unelected monarchs and tyrants.
Representative government was hailed as an effective new method
of apportioning blame for poor political performance – a new way
of encouraging the rotation of leadership, guided by merit and

humility. It was thought of as a new form of humble government, a way of creating space for dissenting political minorities and levelling competition for power, which in turn enabled elected representatives to test their political competence and leadership skills, in the presence of others equipped with the power to sack them. If they failed, they were removed. The rotation of leaders was, hence, a means of peacefully controlling the exercise of power by means of competition for power. 'The representative system', Paine explained to his American readers, 'is fatal to ambition.' Paine also offered a more pragmatic justification of the new form of government. It was seen simply as the practical expression of a simple reality: that it wasn't feasible for all of the people to be involved all of the time, even if they were so inclined, in the business of government. Given that reality, so the argument ran, the people must delegate the task of government to representatives who were chosen at regular elections. The job of these representatives was to monitor the expenditure of public money. Representatives made representations on behalf of their constituents to the government and its bureaucracy. Representatives debated issues and made laws. They decided who would govern and how – on behalf of the people. 'In its original state', Paine concluded, 'simple Democracy was no other than the commonhall of the ancients. As these democracies increased in population, and the territory extended, the simple democratical form became unwieldy and impracticable.' The remedy for complexity was representative democracy. 'By engrafting representation upon democracy, we arrive at a system of government capable of embracing and confederating all the various interests and every extent of territory and population.'

These sentiments expressed an epochal change in the meaning and institutions of democracy, a change that has often been hailed, without much more than a cursory mention of how or why it happened. Representative democracy had a history, and a complex one at that. Its roots ran deep into the 'classical' era of assembly-based democracy, which should serve as a reminder that the boundaries between the first and second phases of democracy are not physically 'real', but instead products of the writer's imaginary reworking of the raw materials of that so-called reality. The old train of assembly-based democracy did not simply terminate at one historical station, where passengers alighted, then boarded the brand-new train of representative democracy. There were no such clear-cut moments and physically discrete points of rupture. And yet the change that came over democracy was nonetheless striking, and, in retrospect, unmistakable. Sometimes quick, usually slow, the metamorphosis took almost a millennium to mature. It first happened in the European region, where it was typically unplanned and messy, even when consciously intended. And exactly because of its ad hoc construction, the change resulted in many different concrete forms of representative democracy. The point is that the book of representative democracy lacked a consistent plot. There were many loose pages, bits and pieces, random paragraphs, a few completed but mostly unfinished outlines of possible themes. But amidst all the clutter there was one common theme that lives on today: the remarkable invention of the principle and practice of representative institutions.

As a way of naming and handling power, representative democracy was certainly something new under the sun. It was an unusual species of political system, a whole way of life defined by written constitutions, independent judiciaries and laws that guaranteed such procedures as periodic election of candidates to legislatures, limited-term holding of political offices, voting by secret ballot, competitive political parties, the right to assemble in public and liberty of the press. Compared with the previous, assembly-based form, representative democracy greatly extended the geographic scale of institutions of self-government, and more successfully so than the world of Islam had managed to do. As time passed, and despite its localised origins in towns, rural districts and large-scale imperial settings, representative democracy came to be 'housed' mainly within territorially defined states backed up by standing armies and law-making and taxation powers. These states were qualitatively bigger and more populous than the political units of the first phase of democracy. Most states of the Greek world of assembly democracy, Mantinea and Argos, for instance, were no bigger than a few score square kilometres. Many polities in the age of representative democracy were incomparably larger. What would Demonax, Aristotle and others have thought of the largest representative democracies, such as Canada (9.98 million square kilometres) and the United States (9.63 million square kilometres)? And just how astonished would they have been to hear stories of the mobile polling teams using planes and four-wheel-drive vehicles to deliver ballot papers and ballot boxes to the 82,000 electors living in remote towns, hospitals, nursing homes and prisons in the largest electoral constituency in the world, the vast rural division of Kalgoorlie in the federal state of Western Australia, a division that comprises an area of 2.3 million square kilometres stretching from Kalumburu in the north, on the Timor Sea, to Exmouth on the Indian Ocean, down to the suitably named Esperance on the Southern Ocean.

It is safe to say that the champions of government by assembly would indeed have been dumbfounded by the scale and complexion of representative democracy. They might have been astonished even more by the fact that the transformations were neither inevitable nor politically uncontested, despite what others have said in the past. 'Ever since the birth of modern societies', the nineteenth-century French liberal author and politician François Guizot (1787–1874) told a Paris audience during a famous course of public lectures on the subject, 'their condition has been such, that in their institution, in their aspirations, and in the course of their history, the representative form of government . . . has constantly loomed more or less distinctly in the distance, as the port at which they must at length arrive, in spite of the storms which scatter them, and the obstacles which confront and oppose their entrance.'[8] Only nineteenth-century believers in progress could have thought so optimistically about the origins and development of representative government. For the truth is that its appearance was bitterly contested, subject to unforeseen consequences and constant setbacks. It was also dogged incessantly by its failure to solve problems of its own making, such as the exclusion of the poor and women from the structures of government.

Representative democracy was in fact the child of bitter power conflicts, many of them fought in opposition to ruling princes, churchmen, landowners or imperial monarchies, often in the name of 'the people'. Struggles in support of 'the people' produced great strife during the second age of democracy. It witnessed the birth of neologisms, like 'aristocratic democracy' (that first happened in the Low Countries at the end of the sixteenth century) and new references (in the United States) to 'republican democracy'. Later came 'liberal democracy' and 'social democracy' and 'Christian democracy', even 'bourgeois democracy', 'socialist democracy' and 'workers' democracy'. These new terms fuelled many different struggles by groups for equal access to governmental power that then resulted, sometimes by simple accident or unintended consequence, in institutions that had no precedent. Trial by jury, written constitutions based on a formal separation of powers, parliaments, periodic elections and parties were among the most important inventions. So too was the creation (following the rather different Muslim precedents) of European-style 'civil societies'. These were founded on markets and social customs – experiences as varied as reading a novel, dining in a public restaurant, or using polite language – as well as on new civil associations that enabled citizens to keep an arm's length from government, for instance by using non-violent weapons like the uncensored printing press, publicly circulated petitions, and covenants and constitutional conventions called to draw up brand-new constitutions.

The struggles for representative democracy filled these centuries of the second millennium with growing excitement, and sometimes much pandemonium. With a whiff of empowerment permanently in the air, this period unleashed what Alexis de Tocqueville (1805–59) famously called a 'great democratic revolution' in favour of political and social equality. Sending shock waves outwards from the Atlantic region, this revolution often suffered setbacks and reversals, especially in Europe, where in the early decades of the twentieth century, as we shall see, it was to collapse into a swamp filled with political predators. The democratic revolution in favour of representation was fuelled by rowdy struggles and breathtaking acts, like the uprisings of artisans in the Low Countries and the public execution in England of King Charles I. Such events threw into question the anti-democratic prejudices of those – the rich and powerful – who supposed that inequalities among people were 'natural'. New groups, like slaves, women and workers, won the franchise. At least on paper, representation was eventually democratised, stretched to include all of the population. But such stretching, which often reached breaking point, happened with great difficulty, and against terrible odds. Representative democracy was permanently on trial; in more than a few cases, the United States in the nineteenth and early twentieth centuries included, the reigning definition of representation was actually narrowed by withdrawing the right to vote from certain groups, particularly black and poor people.

Not until the very end of this long historical period – during the early decades of the twentieth century – did the right of people to vote for their representatives come to be seen as a *universal* entitlement. That happened first for adult men and later – usually much later – for all adult women. But even then, as the experiences of totalitarianism and military dictatorship showed, the opponents of democratic representation fought tooth and claw, and with considerable success, against its perceived inefficiencies, its fatal flaws and supposed evils. They demonstrated, with word and pen, sword and musket, tank and fighter plane, that representative democracy was not inevitable – that it had no built-in historical guarantees.

Alfonso IX

But first let's go back in time, to the years of the twelfth century, to the extraordinary moment of birth of one of the core components of what would later be called representative democracy. The institution had no precedent. It was a new type of governing body, a place for making decisions by representatives of various social interests, drawn from a wide geographic radius. It was called the *cortes*, or parliament.

Where was it born? Contrary to some old-fashioned, devoutly British accounts, which think of Big Ben as timeless, and suppose, arrogantly, that parliamentary institutions were 'incomparably the greatest gift of the English people to the civilization of the world',[9] parliaments were in fact an invention of what is today northern Spain, in Europe, that little patch of earth that stretches from the Mediterranean basin to the Arctic Circle. The invention came more than a millennium after the Greek experiments with self-government and pre-dated by six hundred years the arrival of representative democracy as it was to be understood (say) during the French Revolution. Slow it may have been in coming. Yet the invention was among Europe's first gifts to the new world of representative democracy. With just a touch of exaggeration, it could even be said that Muslims were responsible for parliaments, inasmuch as they were spawned by power struggles among Christians bent on the military conquest of the lands of Islam.

The first parliament was born of despair. Sometime around 1000 CE, many Christian communities living in the northern parts of the Iberian peninsula grew convinced that their days were numbered. The dangers seemed obvious. The seventh century had seen the followers of the Prophet Muhammed conquer Syria, Palestine, Egypt and the North African coast. During the eighth century, Muslims advanced to the gates of Constantinople and, after conquering Spain, entered southern France. The ninth century saw the sack of Rome and the occupation of Sicily and the coasts and foothills of southern Italy by Saracen forces. Fears that Christianity might lose its way in the world were compounded by the loss of Jerusalem, and by the sense that the world of Christianity was fraying at its African and Asian edges. Nestorian and Jacobite churches were cut off by the Saracens' occupation of much of Asia Minor – and then of Persia. The Church in Abyssinia was similarly quarantined, while in Syria, Egypt and elsewhere tens of thousands of Christians felt squeezed by the combined forces of what they saw as discriminatory taxation and contemptuous toleration by Islamic rulers.

So the stage was set for a Christian revival, in military form. The mood was moulded in 1095 by the bellicose address of Pope Urban II (1088–99), before a large crowd gathered at Clermont, a French town today famous for the chain of extinct volcanoes surrounding it. The text of the speech itself has not survived, but his various chroniclers concur that Urban attributed the impending disaster facing Christianity to God's punishment for human wickedness – and that he called upon his hearers to recover grace by fighting for the cross, in the name of Europe. What exactly was required to 'go forward in happiness and in confidence to attack the enemies of God'[10] was left to the good judgement of Christian-minded princes.

FIGURE 21: Crusader Alfonso IX of the kingdom of León.

Among them was King Alfonso IX of León (1188–1230), a young but shrewd ruler who was to become a star political player in the bitter struggle to snatch the fields and towns from the Muslims of northern Iberia (Figure 21).

The details of what happened are worth recalling. Even though the evidence is fragmentary and sometimes contradictory, it shows clearly enough that Alfonso IX had been dogged by personal problems prior to mounting the throne. His early years had been complicated by terrible fits of epilepsy, earning him the nickname of 'the dribbler' (*baboso*). Being the first son of Fernando II by a marriage that the Pope had refused to sanction, Alfonso found himself confronted by a powerful stepmother (Urraca López de Haro) who coveted the throne for her own son. Fearing assassination, Alfonso fled to Portugal. There he shortly learned some wholly unexpected news: not only that his father had died, but that the Archbishop of Santiago, some prominent León nobles and his cousin, the Castilian King Alfonso VIII, were all backing his bid for the throne, in order to stop the outbreak of a local civil war.

So, at the ripe age of seventeen, Alfonso IX wore the crown of a kingdom whose problems quickly catapulted him into the real world of grown-up politics. His kingdom was under intense military pressure, not only from neighbouring kingdoms, but also from the Moorish armies that had first begun conquering swathes of land four hundred years earlier. Repeated invasions by Muslim armies threatened to sap the entire fiscal base of the kingdom. The old custom according to which Muslim governors contributed money to the Christian kings of the region, a custom known locally as *parias*, had collapsed. New taxes had been imposed on the Church and towns, but these proved highly unpopular. Petitions began to pour in to the new king's officials.

Alfonso IX caught everybody by surprise. He took the dramatic decision to fight his way out of a tight corner by reconquering territory that he and many of his subjects considered rightfully Christian. It was a risky move, but one that later yielded vital military victories, in the reconquests of Cáceres (1227) and Mérida and Badajoz (1230), that led in turn to the retaking of Seville. At the time, Alfonso's decision to fight seemed politically dangerous, even foolhardy. Strapped for cash and men, he slapped taxes on all Christians. In the era before the slogan 'no taxation without representation' had been invented, he also set about enlisting support outside his court. The prince's aim was to take the lead in defending and expanding his kingdom, even if that meant gambling with the monarchy by making compromises that might have the effect of diluting his kingly powers. Alfonso IX naturally turned to the local nobility, to the warrior aristocrats who were committed in their bones to the preservation of their lands, and seemed always hungry for more. They were convinced that monarchs had the Christian duty to wage unending war against Muslim infidels; and they were sure that war, and success in war, was not only a commandment of Pope Urban II, but also necessary for nurturing their own status, as well as bolstering the machinery of government by good Christian princes.

Both Alfonso IX and the local nobility agreed that the reconquest required political deals to be struck, minimally by waging war in tandem. But that meant winning over the bishops of the Church, the estate that saw itself as the guardian of souls, and the spiritual protector of God's lands. Launching war also meant covering costs. Permanent warfare against the Moors had somehow to be paid for. With the whole region permanently under siege, and strategically vital towns like León now resembling walled fortresses, Alfonso IX decided to appeal for their solidarity. He turned to their spokesmen. These citizens – contemporary documents referred to them as *cives* or *boni homines* – were 'good men' with a reputation for leadership that stemmed from their prior election as officers of the town councils called *fueros* and, quite possibly, from their family connections with parts of the lower nobility. These good citizens were well placed to deliver to the king townsmen who were trained to arms. They could also contribute large chunks of money. But, once again, the principle of mutual compromise had to apply: with the backing of the warrior nobility and the Church, Alfonso XI offered to provide protection for the besieged towns of his realm in return for their provision of soldiers and cash.

So from within this princely triangle formed by the nobles, bishops and urban citizens, the modern practice of parliamentary representation was born. It was in the walled, former Roman town of León, in March 1188 – a full generation before King John's Magna Carta of 1215 – that Alfonso IX convened the first ever *cortes*, as contemporaries soon christened it, using the local term for both a city council and the city where a king resides.[11]

FIGURE 22: Cloisters of San Isidoro, the place where the first *cortes* met in León, northern Spain, in 1188 CE.

Delegates from all three of the region's estates – the nobility, Church and towns – met there, within the yellow and red-grey sandstone cloisters of the magnificently modest church of San Isidoro (Figure 22). The place name suited the occasion, for St Isidore was the good Bishop of Seville who was famous for his maxim that only he who governs and acts well is a true king. Confirmation that Alfonso IX tried to live up to this maxim was later chiselled into the walls of the church, in the form of an inscription signed by the young king himself. It reads: 'A LOS COMIENZOS DE MI REINADO, CUANDO POR PRIMERA VEZ CELEBRE CORTES EN LEON, DENTRO DE SAN ISIDORO ALFONSO IX REY DE LEON 1188'.

The announcement, that at the beginning of his reign the young king for the first time consecrated the *cortes* inside the church of San Isidoro, rather understated what went on there. In the name of custom – the first decree discussed and agreed by those present in the church was to respect the customs of the realm – the assembly kicked hard against old habits. Called to discuss and agree constitutional matters, it was the first recorded gathering of all three estates (the interests of the towns had hitherto been ignored in meetings convened by the monarchs of the region). The León assembly was not the usual gathering of courtly sycophants. It was most definitely not an occasion when the monarch waved the flags of courtly pomp to impress his subjects, a solemn court ritual of the kind that had been staged a few months earlier, in the neighbouring city of Carrión. At that encounter, the governors (*maiores*) of forty-eight cities from the kingdom of Castile, together with members of the Church and nobility, had been summoned by King Alfonso IX; they were required to witness and swear acceptance of the marriage of Conrad of Swabia, the son of the Emperor Frederick Barbarossa, to the Infanta Berenguela. Those attending that assembly had been instructed, on bended knee, to consent to an important clause in the contract, which specified that the government of the kingdom would in the future be devolved to the princess, her husband and their successors.

The *cortes* convened in San Isidoro was altogether different. Set against the backdrop of war, the talks had an air of urgency and grievance about them (Figure 23). Written protests had evidently

FIGURE 23: Representatives (known as *procuradores*) at the León *cortes* of 1188.

poured in beforehand from each of the chosen estates of the kingdom. The surviving evidence suggests that the teenage king had been forced by this subterranean pressure to act, and to be seen to be acting, especially in the face of a developing alliance between the local nobility and men of the towns. Little wonder then that the meeting that took place in the cloisters of San Isidoro produced up to fifteen decrees (the authenticity of several is disputed) that together amounted to something like a constitutional charter.

The king promised that from here on he would consult and accept the advice of the bishops, nobles and 'good men' of the towns in matters of war and peace, pacts and treaties. The bishops of the Church, until now forbidden to take oaths of allegiance to temporal power, joined the knights and town citizens in promising the king that they would also work for peace and justice. The participants together agreed that property and security of residence were inviolable. They accepted that judicial proceedings and the laws they produced would be respected; and that the king's realm would be guided wherever possible by the general laws inherited from earlier times (the so-called Book, or *Liber Iudicorum*, from the time of the Visigoths). And it was agreed by the participants that there would be future assemblies of the king and the three estates.

Both the substance and method of agreement heralded a new way of governing. It was based on the path-breaking principle that who got what, when and how could be best decided by talk, by cunning manoeuvres, peaceful threats and artful compromises – by politics. Although committed to open discussion, the first ever *cortes* was not an assembly of citizens of the Syrian-Mesopotamian, Phoenician, Greek or Islamic kind. It was also not a western version of the *meshawara* that developed during the Ottoman Empire. It was instead the brainchild of a self-interested Christian monarch bent on building up his realm, the creation of a political animal who saw that effective government required the creation of a new mechanism for resolving disputes and striking bargains among interested parties who felt they had a common interest in reaching compromise, so avoiding internecine violence.

Details of what happened at the subsequent assemblies called by Alfonso IX, for instance at Benavente in 1202, in the presence of Queen Berenguela and their son Don Ferdinand, remain sketchy. But in retrospect it is hard to overstate the originality of the *cortes* first convened in 1188. It clearly broke with the old custom of meeting to reaffirm fealty to a sovereign's will. The *cortes* supposed, with a good measure of self-awareness among those who were present, that its guarantees of fair play could foster political deals among conflicting interests without resorting to the use of naked force. In striking contrast, say, to the presumption in Athens that democracy required an undivided sense of political community, the *cortes* rested on the opposite premise, on the likelihood of competing and potentially conflicting interests, and the desirability of peaceful compromise among them. The *cortes* supposed that the chances of reaching workable agreements were improved by limiting the numbers of decision makers, some of whom were required to travel great distances. It supposed as well that governments could govern at a distance from their subjects without losing their trust and consent, exactly because those involved in making decisions had the power to snap at the heels of the monarch, to defend their respective interests in the presence of the king. Fairly soon, they would locally be called *representatives* (*procuradores*).

The Spread of Parliaments

What are the origins of this language of representation associated with the *cortes*? We do not know. There is an outside chance that locals who spoke of representation had drunk from the streams of Islamic political thinking that ran through the northern hills of the Iberian peninsula. Local Muslims were certainly familiar with the business practice of employing a legal representative (*wākil*) in a nearby town or a faraway land. The *wākil* was usually a religious judge, a man chosen by a merchant to act in his stead, for instance to take care of his lawsuits, supervise the warehousing and sale of his merchandise, and to act as the merchant's banker and post-master. It is unclear whether or not the representatives who gathered around young Alfonso IX had been influenced by this Muslim custom of representation, understood as the practice of empowering someone to work on behalf of another, to define and protect their interests. What we do know is that the word of self-description used by the members of the first *cortes* hailed from the Latin *procurator*. It referred to a man who does or carries out something on behalf of another, with his consent. It is likely (as a little-known eighteenth-century dictionary reminds us[12]) that the old Latin word was first given a new lease of life in towns like León, where the term *procurador* had several meanings. It referred to someone authorised to appear before a court to defend another in a lawsuit or dispute. It was used as well to speak of an official (known as the *procurador general*) who took care of the property and wellbeing of the city. And the word referred to an outside person (called a *procurador de pobres*) who was involved in the affairs of the poor, in whose lives he had no direct material interest.

The stretching of the elastic word *procurador* to cover the case of a city official nominated to defend the interests of a town against the monarch, in the *cortes*, was historically significant. Just as poignant was the way the word was applied to *all* the *cortes* delegates. That semantic generosity fitted well the expanding geography of political power during this period. Thanks to the invention of the *cortes*, the scope of self-government was greatly stretched, as happened for the first time in 1250, when the *cortes* of

León voted to replicate itself by forming a second, upper-level *cortes* to monitor the neighbouring kingdoms of León and Castile, recently merged under Saint Ferdinand (1230–52).

Encouraged by military victories over the Moors, the León assembly managed to survive for several hundred years. Long-distance government subject to the consent of parliament worked. Indeed, by the end of the fourteenth century, with the adjoining kingdoms of León and Castile now united, the kingdom's represen-tatives enjoyed considerable powers. Their right of gathering and presenting petitions, and their insistence that the agreements struck by the parliament were legally binding, became customary, even if at the price of strife. The *cortes* was the site of intense bargaining about definitions of the welfare of the realm. Money was often the key cause of friction. There were constant reaffirmations by the rep-resentatives that kings were forbidden from levying extraordinary taxes without the explicit consent of all the estates. Before the end of the fourteenth century, there were times when the *cortes* report-edly demanded an audit of the court's expenditure. On at least one occasion, it demanded a rebate on taxes that had already been paid.

Blessed with powers like that, it is little wonder that the *cortes* proved contagious. For the next two centuries, as the military campaign to reconquer Muslim lands gathered pace, the new León style of governing was copied in neighbouring kingdoms. Records show that at the concluding session (called a *solio*) of every *cortes* of Catalonia, the king had to swear to abide by all the enacted laws before he was granted the *donativo*, or tax. To ensure that he stuck to his word, a six-member body known as the *diputación general* acted, from the end of the fourteenth century, as a watch-dog between sessions. There were moments when the parliaments of the region took advantage of the fact that the monarch was either incompetent or a minor, sometimes to the point where it seemed that the monarch was a functionary appointed by the dif-ferent estates. There was no norm, for the actual powers exercised by these early parliaments that had spread from León and Castile throughout the Iberian peninsula varied considerably. In some areas, and at certain times, the young parliaments were immensely effective. 'Our Lord the King, with the consent of the Cortes, establishes and ordains ['El señor Rey de voluntad de la Corte estatuesce y ordena']', read the preamble of Aragonese laws, so revealing a parliament with razor-sharp teeth. There, the *cortes* ratified treaties and debated questions of war and peace. It sometimes appointed ambassadors. It exercised control over the naturalisation of strangers coming in to the kingdom. New or extraordinary taxes could not be levied without its prior approval, and its consent was required as well for proposed changes in either their rate or their manner of collection. The *cortes* nominated a committee, the *diputación permanente*, that had the job of monitoring the administration of public funds and ensuring that the laws were observed equally by the Crown and its subjects. The *cortes* of Aragon – as the preamble to its laws emphasised – even enjoyed for a time the power to investigate allegations of breaches of the law by the monarch or his officials, and to call for justice in cases of wrongdoing. Similar powers were enjoyed by the representatives of the *cortes* of Valencia, which watched over the laws of the realm and the powers of the estates during periods when the parliament was not in session.

The degree to which the various social groups did successfully press home their powers to advise, to persuade and (if necessary) to handcuff the courts varied. Things very much depended on the local balance of forces, and on the negotiating rules that the parliaments managed to put in place. In the kingdom of León and Castile, freedom of speech in the *cortes* and freedom from arrest during its sessions were customary. Towns like Barcelona tried to maximise the independence of their representatives by paying their wages, and their travel and accommodation costs. Much effort was put into backing the principle of regular sessions and keeping a close eye on the courts. Juan I, Fernando IV and other monarchs – anticipating by more than half a millennium the nineteenth-century English Chartist demand for annual parliaments – summoned parliaments every twelve months.

In other cases, the principle of regular supervision had to be fought for, as in the *cortes* of Catalonia, where in 1283 Pedro III issued a constitution that stipulated annual assemblies of nobles, townsmen and clergy, unless 'urgent necessity' stood in the way; and as in Aragon, whose *cortes* (from the year 1307) met every two years and, in between sessions, employed a watchdog, a powerful official called the *justicia de Aragón*, whose job it was to safeguard the rights of the assembly. In the realm of Valencia, the *cortes* used another, potentially radical weapon to ensure that every move of the monarch was watched, at all times. This parliament insisted on the right of each estate to meet during periods when it was not in session, in order to keep tabs on the Crown. Then there were attempts by the estates, for instance in the kingdom of León and Castile, to box in monarchs by issuing carefully worded instructions to its representatives. The idea in each and every case was to rein in reigning monarchs. The principle was clear, the practice firm: those who govern must reckon with the possibility that representatives need to refer back to those whom they represent, so drawing out proceedings that might well result in the axing of unpopular measures, or their amendment.

Talk Shops?

The representative assemblies inspired by young King Alfonso IX impacted deeply upon political life in all of the Spanish kingdoms. They were to play a vital role throughout the lands of Europe as well. During the thirteenth century, parliaments spread from León and Castile to Aragon, Catalonia, Valencia and Navarre, as well as Sicily and Portugal, England and Ireland, and the states of Austria and Brandenburg. During the next two centuries, parliaments developed in the large majority of German principalities, in Scotland, Denmark, Sweden, France, the Netherlands, Poland and Hungary. Nearly all of these original parliaments survived until the seventeenth and early eighteenth centuries; despite the growth of absolutist states, which wiped out the assemblies of Aragon, Catalonia and Valencia, many continued to function until the outbreak of the French Revolution in 1789. A few (the Navarrese *cortes*, the Swedish *Riksdag* and the Hungarian *Diet*) lasted into the nineteenth century. The powerful Estates of the Duchy of Mecklenburg survived intact until 1918.

The durability of these parliaments naturally raises questions about their relationship with later modern representative democracies. What exactly was the connection?

Medieval and modern parliamentary assemblies are clearly separate links in the same historical chain, which is why it is tempting to suppose that democracy sprang up with parliaments, as if they were twins. That is not so. Parliamentary assemblies did indeed eventually become rich synonyms for democracy but, as we are just beginning to see, parliamentary democracy in fact had deep and tangled roots. Its parliamentary component first sprang up in the European region, but this happened long before either the word or the egalitarian thrust of democracy had come on the scene. It is simply anachronistic to say that parliaments are a specifically modern, or a 'liberal' or 'democratic' invention. None of these older parliaments were based explicitly on principles or procedures that could remotely be described as 'liberal' or democratic. The noun 'democracy' in any case was still a dirty morpheme, as the illustration in Nicolas Oresme's famous fourteenth-century French translation of Aristotle's *Politics* shows. On its right (good) side stand monarchy, aristocracy and timocracy (a type of government whose propertied rulers are motivated by a strong sense of honour). On its left (bad) side stand tyranny, oligarchy and democracy. Democracy itself is symbolised by commoners and soldiers, and by a half-dead victim slumped in a pillory (Figure 24).

This much is clear – the early parliaments were not clothed in the language of democracy – but here we hit upon a subtlety, a point

FIGURE 24: Democracy: an example of bad government, in Nicolas Oresme's fourteenth-century French translation of Aristotle's *Politics*.

made earlier about how democratic institutions have often taken root under other names. The parliamentary saplings that first sprang from the soil of the Spanish kingdoms later turned into the giant trees of representative government, as they appeared in political eco-systems otherwise as different as the United States, Germany, Uruguay and New Zealand. Parliamentary government supposed that 'government' and 'society' are not unified entities. It further supposed that society itself is divided, that it contains a diversity of interests in need of representation before government. These founding principles – utterly foreign to the Greek assembly democracies – germinated wherever and whenever monarchs, claiming to represent the unity of their kingdoms, encountered opposition from their estates – the nobility, clergy and townsmen – who claimed to represent better the diverse non-governmental interests which in their opinion deserved recognition and perforce had every right to be woven into the tapestry of a more just political order.

Within this zone of high tension between monarchs and estates, the early parliaments often wielded great influence. It is mistaken to see them as pushovers before power, mere gossip parlours or talk shops (a favourite epithet of all later critics of assemblies). Parliaments like the *cortes* of Aragon – by the end of the fourteenth century the most powerful and most talked about – clearly differed from earlier consultative bodies like the German *Hoftage* or English *witanegemots*. Historical records show that these ancient bodies had mainly operated as loosely organised forums summoned by the monarch whenever she or he needed advice, or wanted to publicise special events, such as dynastic marriages, international treaties and new judicial and legislative measures. The first representative parliaments also differed from the gatherings of residents at Thingvellir in Iceland.[13] In contrast to these old consultative bodies, which they succeeded, the first parliaments met more often, and regularly. And they were born with teeth. They were not just means of consultation or acclamation; they also made binding decisions. Parliamentary privilege certainly strengthened their hand, as in the early fourteenth-century Castilian *cortes*, whose members enjoyed complete freedom from arrest and seizure of their property during their travel to and from, and during, parliamentary sessions. By standing as well on ancient customs and rights, a tactic that was not unknown to nineteenth-, twentieth- and twenty-first-century assemblies, the earliest European assemblies raised common grievances about a very wide range of matters, from the conduct of war, relations with Muslims and Jews and the environmental damage caused by the monarch's animals, through to forcible military recruitment, the appointment of ambassadors, standards of weights and measures, and the back-breaking labour and general exploitation of the peasantry.

The early parliaments had one eye on taxes. They often seemed unafraid of making themselves a nuisance when monarchs tried to decide things arbitrarily, without regard for their subjects' wishes. Monarchs could rarely claim a grant (sometimes called a *servicio*) or impose taxes without their consent. Parliaments often collected taxes through their own agents and treasuries; prescribed how they should be spent; and even demanded audits of the king's budget. Parliaments wielded considerable powers of initiating financial legislation, for instance, in the form of bills that became statutes upon receiving royal assent. They investigated alleged financial injustices and illegal acts committed by monarchs or their officers. They enforced the principle that grants of supply be made conditional upon the monarch's redress of grievances. These parliamentary powers of taxation were reinforced, especially in periods of crisis, by the exercise of such prerogatives as the conduct of foreign policy, the settlement of succession to the throne, the guarantee of treaties, partitions and settlements, and the appointment of the monarch's advisers and ministers. In this and other ways, parliaments served more than the particular interests of the dominant estates. They opposed arbitrary, arcane and violent rule; acted as a counterweight to petty tyranny and absolute government; and positively nurtured the spirit of 'liberty' and constitutional government commonly associated with later forms of representative government.

And Democracy?

Friends and fans of representative government need to be aware that these early European parliaments paved no highroads to democracy. The bitter truth is that Whiggish accounts of mettlesome, refractory parliamentarians struggling in dark times to establish a parliamentary opposition, which subsequently undermined absolutist monarchies and set nineteenth-century nation-states in the Low Countries and Britain on the well-lit road to full parliamentary democracy, are downright misleading, in several respects.

Why? The most obvious fact is that, despite all their hard-won powers, the first European parliaments found their field of vision constantly blinkered by self-interested monarchs who dominated their proceedings. Looked at more cynically, from the hard-nosed standpoint of state-builders, these parliaments often served as political instruments for regularising money supply by consent, and for making laws binding upon the representatives who formulated these laws. And despite all the deep continuities between democratic parliaments and their late medieval and early modern predecessors, important differences divided them. The earliest parliaments convened less regularly and their members usually varied from session to session. When they did meet – as the image of Emperor Charles V in a session of the Diet in Augsburg in 1530 shows – they very often did so according to the whim or will of the monarch, or subject to the cunning, skill and veto power of the nobility and clergy (Figure 25).

The life of representatives wasn't easy. Monarchs skilfully exploited bitter disagreements about what it took to be a representative, and

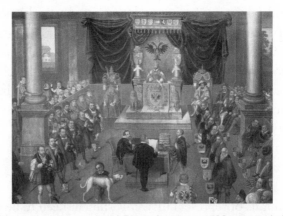

FIGURE 25: Charles V presiding over the Diet in Augsburg, 1530, surrounded by representatives of the Catholic Church (seated to the king's right) and (seated to the left) the Protestant congregations.

there were times when representatives literally came to blows over two conflicting definitions of representation. Were they mere servants and mouthpieces of their constituents, who thus needed to keep them on a short, strong leash? Was it therefore desirable, as the Castilian *cortes* supposed, that every city should provide its own representatives with a set of carefully worded, binding instructions that were called *poderes*? Was it best practice to give representatives a grilling when they returned from a session of parliament, as frequently happened in the Catalonian town of Barcelona, which used a permanent standing committee, called the Commission of the Twenty-Four (*Vintiquatrena de Cort*), to keep tabs on the public and private lives of its representatives? Or were representatives to be treated instead as free-spirited guardians of the whole political community? Were they sometimes obliged to say no to their constituents, to stand above the fray and to work selflessly for the higher political good, for instance by reaching an absolutely unanimous consensus on each and every important measure? For the sake of improving life in the kingdom did unanimity sometimes require – in defiance of the ancient Spanish proverb that politeness begets politeness (*cortesias engendran cortesias*) – the physical ejection of recalcitrant representatives from parliament, kicking and shouting? How sensible was the alternative method used by the *cortes* of Aragon, which elected officers to vet representatives by putting them through a test, known as the *habilitación*, designed to guarantee their commitment to unanimity? Was it true (as the local joke had it) that the passage of every law in Aragon was nothing short of a divine miracle?

Monarchs spotted that there was no easy answer to these tough questions. Especially when caught in sticky jam, kings and queens tried as well to act as if the assemblies were their own councils, summoned to solve their problems with the help of representatives of their own choosing. Monarchs quite often won out. Between the thirteenth and the sixteenth centuries, when the *cortes* of the various kingdoms of Spain were at the height of their powers, the time and place of assembly meetings were normally decided by the Crown. If perchance the king was ill or forced to be absent from an assembly, then his own representatives conducted business on the basis that the right to summon an assembly was an inalienable royal prerogative. That royalist view of assemblies was reflected in the customary procedures that guided their business. After presenting their credentials, representatives were forced to sit through a speech from the throne, in which the purposes of the assembly were set forth. Representatives were usually allowed to make formal replies. They could present their petitions, gather within their own estates for further deliberation, and engage the king in quiet debate. But there was often no final round-up session in the presence of the king, who might see himself as under no God-given compulsion to act on the requests and demands of representatives. At best, they could expect to receive at some unspecified time a copy of a document called a *cuadernos* – a list of all the petitions that had been presented to the assembly, together with the king's replies.

Monarchs played politics with assemblies in other ways. Making the representatives constantly vulnerable to dis-invitation was a favourite ploy. It was quite exceptional for monarchs to summon the same prelates or the same nobles or *procuradores* from the same towns; to do so, as every even slightly cunning monarch spotted, would have introduced an element of self-government from below. That would have jeopardised the very principle of monarchy. For that reason the clergy was typically represented by archbishops and bishops chosen by the monarch, on an ad hoc basis; while custom and courtesy certainly dictated that important figures, like the Bishop of Toledo and higher clergy resident at the court, be invited, even they had no unquestionable right to attend. The same story can be told about the dukes, marquises, counts, viscounts, *caballeros*, *hidalgos* and *escuderos* of the nobility, whose individual members thought themselves entitled in principle to attend, although whether they did so in practice often depended on the pleasure of the king. Such biases were reinforced by the kings' insistence that attendance was absolutely compulsory for officers of the Crown, including subject-kings, a tactic that defined non-attendance as treason and therefore amounted to 'stacking' assemblies in favour of the Crown.

Such biases in favour of kings made a mockery of the whole process of representation, however it was understood. Parliamentarians who considered themselves formally equal to one another in status, and who thought their authority as members of parliament stemmed from their efforts to represent the entire realm, were made to look silly. The fairy-tale representativeness of these early parliaments was compounded by the fact that the voices of peasants were nowhere to be heard; that women – except for the occasional noblewoman of the highest rank – were systematically excluded; and that the earliest parliaments rarely defended their positions through political theories with sharp teeth, along the lines that Montesquieu, François Guizot, John Stuart Mill and others would later develop, during the eighteenth and nineteenth centuries. The early parliaments preferred to look back over their shoulders to ancient customs and privileges, which they doggedly refused to modify. It was as if they misunderstood their own novelty, or that they failed to realise their own potential. And despite the fact that bodies like the *cortes* of the Spanish kingdoms of Aragon and Catalonia planted the life-giving seeds of at least two notions of representation, in practice they suffered from several life-threatening ailments that they failed – to their cost – ultimately to heal.

Put simply, the *cortes* of the Spanish kingdoms never became *democratic* institutions, even in the minimal sense that the estates and the monarch were equal debating and deciding partners. The Crown managed not only to retain certain prerogatives, including the basic power to decide when to summon 'their' parliaments. Almost everywhere, thanks to its foot-dragging and resort to loans and imposts and alternative means of supply, the monarchy effectively resisted efforts to tie taxes and the redress of grievances into a tight knot; the right of petitioning was rarely translated for any time into the right to make laws backed by the right to refuse taxation. Not only was there no systematic victory for the principle of no taxation without representation. There were often unequal taxation powers, as in the first parliaments of León and Castile, which found themselves compromised by the fact that the nobles and the clergy were normally exempt from taxation, the burden of which consequently was borne by the *hombres buenos* of the towns. In money matters, their representatives consequently had to fight the Crown alone, potentially isolated and constantly vulnerable to defeat.

Matters were worsened by the refusal of monarchs to relinquish their broad definition of what counted as 'appropriate' taxation. Certain taxes like the tax upon sales, known as the *alcabala*, were not considered 'extraordinary', though that is how they were widely perceived throughout the realm, and especially in the towns. The isolation of the *hombres buenos* in money matters was refracted through the interest-based squabbles among all the estates. The solidarity of their representatives – obviously – was imperative if the hands of the monarch were to be tied. Yet this was not yet the era of disciplined parties operating like machines on an agreed parliamentary assembly line. There were times – the *cortes* convened in 1188 by King Alfonso IX was an example – when the nobility, clergy and townsmen seemed to form a united front. But things seldom went so smoothly, sometimes because power-hungry monarchs stirred up trouble, in order to divide and rule from above. There were disputes over the basic meanings of representation. The estates often failed to see eye to eye. Rivers of mutual envy and hostility often swamped the nobility, clergy and townsmen, sometimes to the point where kings must have privately cackled at the riotous disorder that sprang from jealously guarded provincialisms. Particular estates sometimes even quarrelled badly with themselves, with tragic-comic consequences. One example: in 1645, a late-night session of the *cortes* of Valencia was interrupted by a noble who complained of fatigue and demanded his right to go to bed. His right was suspended after a crusty and irritable baron rose before the assembly to demand that 'that idiot be thrown into the street', which is what then promptly happened, amidst uproar.[14] On more than one occasion, the divisions within estates proved utterly self-destructive, as happened in the two-and-a-quarter-century (1348–1570) struggle for supremacy between the towns of Burgos and Toledo, whose representatives several times had physically to be restrained by the king's men. One year's session (1506) of the Castilian *cortes* was even suspended after the representatives of the two towns 'all arose and shouted at one another so loud that not a word could be understood'.[15]

Nature and Representation

Amidst all the scrambling and shouting that marked the long history of struggles for parliamentary representation, it is important not to lose track of one vital fact: that parliaments were not always the prime cog within the machinery of dynamic institutions that later came to be called representative democracy.

The invention of parliaments in Europe was of fundamental historical importance, certainly. They were indeed destined to become prime symbols of democracy, but during the long – ten centuries long – transition towards representative democracy, parliaments were not always at the epicentre of things. Many times the decisive action took place elsewhere. Untold numbers of otherwise unconnected events, characters, movements and organisations joined hands in creating the institutions of representative democracy, often without having that intended consequence. Regional assemblies, independent judiciaries, territorially defined states, Church councils, petitions and covenants – as we shall see shortly – proved to be decisive inventions. Representative institutions were shaped as well by non-European forces after being transplanted across the oceans, say, to the colonies of North America and the Caribbean, Australia and New Zealand. The overall picture is decidedly messy, but there is still one general point that cannot be overstated: representative democracy only happened because parliaments were outflanked by political and social forces that gave them hefty nudges, pushed and elbowed them, from outside and from below, so forcing these parliaments to accept the universal entitlement of 'the people', women included, to elect their own representatives.

Parliaments as we now know them were typically the product of extra-parliamentary forces. These pressures eventually conspired to infuse representation with the principle of political equality, but they cannot be described in terms of the heroic struggle for emancipation of some body called 'the People'. That way of thinking about the emergence of democracy in Europe is plain wrong. It so simplifies matters that it loses contact with all the fascinating fusion of forces that dragged Europe towards much more democratic forms of representative government, sometimes with stunning success.

One surprising impetus was nature itself, which sometimes conspired to democratise the patterns of representative government. It did so by supporting peoples of the countryside in their struggles to govern themselves with the help of local intermediaries, despite whatever parliaments elsewhere decided. In the half-frozen, short-summer farmlands of Scandinavia, for instance, many communities developed representative forums called *tings*.* These were law-making and law-enforcement bodies that conducted their business in public, usually at some natural feature, such as a large rock outcrop, a lake, a clearing or meadow, or a great tree. Ancient burial grounds and cult stones were also favourite sites. In the remote area of Norway known as Gulen, at the mouth of the breathtaking Sognefjord, an open-air *gula-thing* was regularly convened during summer months at a sacred place marked off by staves and ropes. Membership of the forum was restricted to thirty-six sworn representatives, known as *laugrettomen* ('law-amendment men'), who were required to gather and take their seats while the sun was still in the east, to refrain from eating and drinking and, in cases of disputed judgements, to abide by the rulings of a self-appointed Lögmann, or Law-man, who reputedly knew the laws by heart. Perhaps the best-known representative forums were those that appeared from around 930 CE in Iceland, an island anciently divided into thirty-six (later thirty-nine) provinces, three of which formed a *ting*, or judicial district, in which a twelve-man body appointed by magistrates, the *varthing*, the court for that district, was annually held. Judgements issued by any *ting* could be appealed at the highest court held at the island's mid-summer assembly, called the *al-thing*, or *alþing*. Held in the south-western corner of the island, at a rugged place marked by a fault line called Tingvellir ('the ground for tings'), this tribunal of last resort initially comprised forty-eight jurors, twelve appointed from each quarter of the island, again by magistrates (called *goðar*), big men whose power stemmed from their ownership of land, their ability to assemble local farmers as fighters, and their capacity to provide protection in petty quarrels, for instance over thefts of livestock or accusations of witchcraft.

Farming communities in southern Germany invented similar networks of representative forums for making laws and resolving local

---

* The word for these representative assemblies comes from the Old Norse and Icelandic: *þing*. The term lives on today in the official names of the region's legislatures, such as the Danish *Folketing*, the Faroe Islands' *Løgting* and the Norwegian *Storting*. The word makes its presence felt as well within the English 'thing', meaning 'object', a word that is an end link within a chain of connotations stretching from 'assembly' to 'court' to 'case' to 'business' to 'purpose' to 'object'.

FIGURE 26: A session of the Water Tribunal (*El Tribunal de las Aguas*) in Valencia, from a painting by Bernardo Ferrándiz Bádenes, 1865.

problems, if need be by badgering the higher Crown authorities. In the Iberian peninsula, for instance in the *huerta* of the river valleys of drought-prone Murcia and Catalonia, farmers developed crop irrigation systems that were maintained by organisations – water tribunals – that had their own legal jurisdiction and were monitored by the farmers themselves, through meetings of the kind that are still held today in the north porch of the cathedral of Valencia (Figure 26).

In neighbouring Castile, an association of cattle owners (known as the Honrado Concejo de la Mesta) was recognised in 1273 by King Alfonso X (Figure 27). He granted the owners the right to graze their prized merino sheep freely along prescribed drove roads, some of which stretched hundreds of kilometres from high mountain summer pastures to winter pastures on the plains. The twice-yearly mustering of huge herds required the construction of an elaborate system of bridges, drinking troughs and resting points. It required as well huts and hermitages, counting places (*contaderos*), shearing stations and wool laundries – all of which had to be kept in good working order. That was the job of the shepherds, who formed themselves into a Castilian association and governed themselves through mobile assemblies; these councils of representatives (locals called them *mestas*) met two or three times a year, in different locations, according to the season. These

FIGURE 27: Coat of arms of the medieval association of cattle owners in Castile, the Honrado Concejo de la Mesta.

councils dealt with such matters as the price of wool, the identification of stray animals and the condition of the pastures and facilities. Transhumance bred politics by representation. The association, guided by the councils of representatives, levied its own taxes on its members. The revenues were used to pay the Crown's officials, who kept a close eye on the shepherds' privileges. A portion of the taxes was paid directly to the Castilian monarchs, which obliged them to negotiate directly with the association over pressing wider issues, such as the shepherds' exemption from wider military service, rights of pasturing and threats to the safety of humans and animals and pastures posed by the ongoing war against the Moors.

In each of these schemes, it was as if the world of nature itself had political rights – that it was blessed with a voice that prompted local people to take care of nature by finding ways of representing it and governing themselves. To speak as if nature favoured political inclusion is, of course, only a way of speaking, but it serves to pinpoint the manner in which shepherds and farmers were deeply mindful that their labours would be in vain without heeding nature's powers – and without getting others to do the same. The common European custom of peasants bringing animals, plants and vegetables into local courts for the purpose of settling ownership disputes was driven by that same kind of logic. So, too, were the powerful water boards or water trusts (known as *waterschappen* or *hoogheemraadschappen*) that sprang up in the low-lying parts of the North Sea coast, during the twelfth century.

Subject to periodic flooding, villagers tried to protect themselves and their fields by raising dykes and digging drainage canals. The reclamation and protection schemes involved much hard work, as did their subsequent upkeep. Banding together as equals, villagers (probably male heads of household) handled the schemes at first through self-governing associations that elected a water board. Each landowner was entitled to one vote. The trustees they elected were charged with the upkeep and management of the dykes under the leadership of an elected 'dyke count' (a position that has survived to this day in the Netherlands). Later, during the thirteenth century, these local boards held hands and linked arms to form regional water boards charged with the responsibility of supervising the large-scale schemes for protecting men, women, children, animals and crops against the sea and its mood swings. Regional princes sometimes tried to interfere, but that was exceptional.

The interesting thing is that the water boards enjoyed substantial rights, including the power of their representatives to levy taxes, to operate courts of justice and to enforce the laws. In some coastal areas, particularly in Friesland, Holland and Utrecht, the land sagged so badly, well below sea level, that the water boards were transformed into complex organisations staffed with officials experienced in the arts formerly monopolised by the right hand of Moses. They wielded great power and correspondingly political battles for control of their resources were common. As in the Spanish kingdoms, questions about the work of representatives and the meaning of representation surfaced. In Zeeland, Flanders and elsewhere, there were complaints about the way poor decisions of some water boards increased flooding by the sea. Water board representatives were sometimes accused of selfishness. And there were calls for the stricter observance of the principles of proportional sharing of benefits and burdens by everyone, including wealthy property holders who tried to manipulate the boards to serve their own propertied interests.

Sanctuaries of Freedom

These examples show that rural Europe deserves a proper place in the history of efforts to popularise the principles and practice of representative government. Yet although representative mechanisms flourished in many parts of pastoral Europe, their power was hampered not only by internal rifts, but also by the harsh facts of country life. History was against rural self-government. It was to suffer from limited accumulations of capital, restricted access to wider markets and the constant vulnerability of country people to outside interference, especially by well-equipped armies that with ease could physically overwhelm thinly populated farmlands. For these and other reasons now to be explored, it turned out that towns were much more hospitable towards experiments with new methods of representative government.

The pattern was evident within the flourishing frontier towns of northern Spain, including León, which enjoyed a vigorous form of self-government, but the trend was far more widespread. From the time of the eleventh century, especially in northern Italy, the European region witnessed a great urban revival. It came to be symbolised by bustling towns like Bruges and Genoa, Nuremberg and London, Antwerp and Barcelona. Never mind how it happened (the prime cause was rapid population growth in the countryside and the advent of a surplus and footloose labour force triggered by the outbreak of peace and intensive cultivation of the land). The important thing to note is that in terms of the history of representative democracy the influence of these and other European cities was out of all proportion to their numbers of inhabitants. Around the year 1500 – census data is unreliable, and far from comprehensive – only one-tenth of Europe's population lived in towns, most of which were tiny by today's standards. There were only three or four cities with populations of more than 100,000 – Naples was the largest – and only about 500 cities with more than 5000 inhabitants, most of them shadowed constantly by death caused by harvest crises or epidemic diseases.

Despite their limited numbers and small populations, cities functioned as laboratories of power. They were places where experiments were conducted in matters as diverse as architecture and theatre, scientific invention and family life, and the production and consumption of new market commodities. Cities were also places where much energy was expended in creating new forms of self-government. The freedoms they brought no doubt had to be fought for. The bitter and protracted struggles of the Lombardy towns against the emperor Frederick Barbarossa during the twelfth century soon became legendary. So too did early town leaders like Cola di Rienzi (c. 1313–54), the subject of a famous opera by Richard Wagner. The Roman-born son of a tavern keeper, Rienzi was a rabble-rouser who taught himself stories of the glories of ancient Rome. He trained as a notary, and dedicated his short life to rebuilding the independent power and reputation of his native city, which he managed for a time to do by playing off popes and princes against each other. In May 1347, he declared himself tribune of the sovereign Roman people, some of whom eventually ganged up against his bombast and cruelty, first by attempting to burn down his capitol, then by capturing him as he tried to escape in plebeian garb, after which he was stood before a huge crowd and his body cut to pieces by a thousand daggers.

Every European town seemed to have its own (usually milder than Rienzi) champion. The local freedoms won by their 'good men' citizens normally depended upon the backing of princes and kings and (in the case of a town like Nuremberg) the Holy Roman Emperor, who granted the cities charters in return for various benefits, including favourable tax arrangements. Cities were often given permission to protect themselves by walls punctuated by gates and watchtowers; some cities even had elaborate systems of fortifications, with bastions and outer works. Hemmed in by a dense jungle of estates, churches and monarchies, cities resembled armed strongholds, and that – ironically – enabled them to become sanctuaries of freedom from arbitrary exercises of power.

How exactly did this happen? The very short answer is that European towns were the first places in the world where large-scale forms of market exchange blossomed. Towns nurtured market interactions in strange combinations of proximity and distance, new money-driven networks and encounters among many different actors, within specific times and places. They carved up old communities into a thousand pieces, and they did so by activating new modes of money-fuelled mobility, long-distance trade and other types of market-driven social interaction. The combined effect was to link together the quite different Europes of (say) the Mediterranean, the Atlantic and the Baltic regions. Although the distribution of European towns was highly uneven, with the weakest patterns of urbanisation in Russia and the strongest in the Low Countries, they were typically linked to each other in networks, or archipelagos stretching across vast distances. In opposition to feudal lords and princes, cities had an interest in mutual cooperation. Barcelona was a leading example. During the thirteenth century, it cultivated long-distance networks that stretched through the western Mediterranean, with settlements in Sicily, Sardinia and the Balearics. It had consulates as well in Oran, Tunis and Bougie. The collective body known as the German Hansa did much the same thing. Springing from an alliance of trade associations in the area around Lübeck, Westphalia, Saxony and Prussia, it was first formed in 1356 to protect the trading interests of merchant citizens. Backed by a network of commercial courts, it later

FIGURE 28: Hamburg, 1497: a session of a commercial court of the Hansa, a German trading network that operated in the regions around the North Sea and the Baltic.

grew into a powerful league of almost two hundred towns stretching from Novgorod through the coast of Scandinavia to the Low Countries (Figure 28).

Wherever these urban archipelagos thrived, they acted like magnets that attracted strangers fascinated by their well-lit hustle and bustle, their higher wages, and their real or imagined freedom from a hostile political order dominated by feudal lords, bishops and nobles. Cities attracted outlaws, who swore oaths, *coniurationes* ('swearing together'), in which they confirmed that they would stand tall with their own townspeople; after taking an oath, they acquired freedom under the town's laws after living there peacefully for a year and a day. Law-making and adjudication powers were vital to free towns, which supervised their own affairs in ways that laid the foundations for independent judiciaries, which were to play a vital role in all representative governments.

Within the towns that arose out of the European countryside, disputes were typically handled by magistrates with sharp teeth and tongues that talked of the importance of the public weal (they used Latin phrases like *utilitas publica* and *bonum commune*). During the twelfth and thirteenth centuries, the towns of northern and central Italy experimented with new methods of ensuring that their magistrates kept open minds as well. They did so by employing an independent judicial officer (called a *podestà*), a legal representative who was brought in from the outside for a six-month period, required to swear an oath on the town's statutes and regulations, and asked to assess the performance of the local magistrates. Some towns, thirteenth-century Bologna for instance, set up committees of legal scholars saddled with the job of making sense of the maze of accumulated laws deposited in the town's eighty-five statute books. Many cities grew jealous of their legal power to define who was a citizen (citizenship was usually acquired by birth, marriage, merit or by paying a fee). Cities organised the swearing-in ceremonies for new citizens, who were expected to cultivate a sense of civic belonging and duty towards others – in return for the enjoyment of civic privileges, including the right to be put on trial only in one's own city.

Meanwhile, cities developed laws that strictly prohibited feudal customs of rough justice and retaliatory violence. Chivalry was adjudged no friend of urban freedom. 'If anyone pursues a fleeing enemy to the vicinity of a town', ran a proclamation for Rhenish Franconia issued by the emperor Frederick Barbarossa in 1179, 'then he must throw away his lance and his weapons at the town gate. In the town he will be required to declare under oath that he came into the town not of his own will, but by the strength of his horse, otherwise he will be held to be a peacebreaker.'[16] Around the same time, Ghent and other towns in Flanders banned acts of violence. They adopted strict laws, backed by harsh penalties, prohibiting the general bearing or public display of swords and other weapons by all citizens except merchants in transit, judicial officers or town residents about to travel out of the fortified city. Some towns even moved to ban cruel punishments. With the permission of the count of Flanders, the citizens of Ypres replaced trial by combat and ordeal by ducking and hot irons with orderly trials, in which plaintiffs were entitled to draw upon five honest witnesses under oath.

City Republics

The flight from arbitrary laws, violence and serfdom added to the feeling that towns were unusual clumps of people engaged in a multitude of legally permitted tasks, living in houses close together, often joined wall to wall with buildings like churches, chapels, city halls, granaries, warehouses, hospitals and almshouses. The towns resembled some new kind of tension-producing engine. They seemed to recharge life by adding motion to its elements. It felt as if town-dwellers were perpetually on the move. They travelled regularly to and fro among built-up areas and regularly spent only part of their lives there. During harvest times, for instance, artisans and others typically abandoned their trades and houses for work in distant fields. The constant rumble of wheeled carriages, the weekly or daily markets, and plentiful trades added to the sense of motion through space. Town-dwellers bumped into water carriers, floor polishers, sawyers, porters and chair carriers. They rubbed shoulders with pedlars, rabbit-skin merchants, wigmakers, barbers, cobblers, domestic servants. They encountered a floating population of paupers, thieves and unskilled labourers, who lived in small rented quarters and supported themselves by performing the menial tasks – carrying, digging, transporting and animal tending – that abounded in a pre-mechanised society. All these occupations, together with ethnic and religious minorities, came across members of the better sort: merchants, some of them very rich, masters, mercenaries, engineers, ships' captains, doctors, professors, painters, architects, all of whom knew what it meant to travel through time and space.

The winding, twisting layout of towns added to their dynamic feel. Medieval and early modern Europe was one of only two civilisations – the other was Islam – that fashioned large towns with an irregular maze of streets. What was different about towns in Europe was their enjoyment of much greater freedom from a clutter of ruling political authorities. The world of Islam, we have seen, was the inventor of institutions of civil society – symbolised by the mosque and the *waqf* and the economic partnership – under the imperial rule of caliphs. Within the European region, civil society institutions also sprang up, but there they were principally the children of city life and its markets. Local merchants, traders, craft guilds, manufacturers and bankers formed the powerful backbone of a long-distance money economy capable of dictating or co-deciding the terms and conditions on which princes, popes, bishops and monarchs ruled. Seen in this way, urban markets were the cuckoo's egg laid in the little nests of the medieval towns. These nests were woven from a complex variety of non-governmental institutions, such as households, religious sects and guilds. Self-organised guilds were especially important sources of the new freedoms. The guilds achieved much more than protecting their members' livelihoods. Their principal purpose was to control the production and exchange of commodities. Guilds regulated the way apprentices became journeymen and journeymen became masters. They prevented the manufacture of goods by non-member craftsmen and merchants in the surrounding countryside, or within the city itself. Yet the guilds also nurtured the arts of self-government. What these unions aimed at was not the 'high politics' of a share in government – the great matters of the whole realm – but the protection of their members' interests, by acting as a self-governing body that elected or appointed their own representatives. Like other non-governmental 'societies' rooted in market structures, the guilds helped to nurture something new: unfettered social space within which concentrated political power could be checked, criticised and generally held at arm's length from citizens who no longer considered themselves the property of others.

Seen as a vital move in the twists and turns that led to the invention of representative democracy, towns were remarkable because they prompted fresh political thinking about city life, and its connections with the wider world. The political style known as republicanism was unquestionably its most potent product. It was a visionary mode of politics; it hatched a new language that celebrated free city-states and pondered how they could best be preserved in a world bristling with armed enemies. Republicanism found some inspiration in idealised versions of the small Greek citizen-states; but it took sides especially with the presumed virtues of the Roman republic. Republican language was hostile to monarchy, which it usually equated with tyranny; and friendly towards free cities run by citizens who refused to be subject to arbitrary exercises of power. But republicanism was anti-democratic, minimally in the sense that it peddled the hackneyed image of democracy as mere fun for the riffraff. Yet such were the times that republicans curiously championed arrangements that later became vital conditions of representative democracy. The state (Machiavelli was among the first republicans to speak of *lo stato*) was one of these institutions. Through a bold leap of political imagination, the republicanism that first sprang up in the medieval towns of northern Italy helped shape the image of the state as a type of institution that was separate from both the ruler and the ruled, an anonymous body that consequently functioned as the supreme political authority that guarded over a defined territory and its inhabitants. This territorial state was later to become the power container of representative democracy, so it is to republicanism that democracy owes a linguistic and political debt. It is ironic that Machiavelli, against his anti-democratic intentions, turned out to be one of the pioneering republican thinkers to make the mental leap so vital for the invention of representative democracy. Like later democrats, he spoke, for instance, of politically dangerous moments when not only 'the state has need of its citizens', but those in charge must fend off conspirators and overawe enemies by mobilising 'the majesty of the state'.[17]

There were other sweet affinities between the two bitter foes. Since republicans knew well that such an arrangement of impersonal power could easily degenerate into tyranny or oligarchy, they called for checks and safeguards on the state. They usually rejected monarchy because they were convinced that government was in principle the common business of its citizens. Republicans not only saw the importance of written constitutions and representative assemblies – some favoured annual parliaments – but envisaged as well a variety of other institutions that would so diffuse power that citizens could rule and be ruled in turn, through their representatives.

Republicans disagreed about which other institutions should be given priority. Some favoured limited-term government and fair trials by citizens' juries. Others thought mainly in terms of military prowess and glory, and not a few were adamant that a citizens' militia, rather than a standing army, was an indispensable condition of the freedom of cities. In the context, the differences seemed less important than the overall agreement among virtually all republicans that the cultivation of a spirit of citizenship was of primary political importance. Free cities needed citizens who were free: public-spirited individuals who thought of themselves as equal members of a political community that protected their entitlements and secured their obligations to their fellow citizens.

The People?

Many republicans liked to talk of citizens and 'the people' without so much as a pause between the two words. The two were commonly understood as synonyms, and this naturally raises the Greek question of what republicans meant by 'the people'. Who exactly were they?

The question is easily dealt with, for, to put matters bluntly, the fatal flaw within early republicanism lay in its elitism. With few exceptions, it had no time or patience for the vast majority of the population – women and those without property – except in their capacity as quiet complainants (Figure 29), or as chattels of courageous, public-spirited men distinguished by their patriotic willingness to tame their private interests in property for the common good, if necessary by taking up arms in defence of the state. When republicans referred to 'the people', as they grew ever more accustomed to doing, they usually meant men like themselves – citizens who were soldiers, councillors, property owners and fathers rolled into one. Republicans continued to speak that way well into the eighteenth century. Listen to the words later used by the great American republican John Adams. The queue of adjectives he formed when analysing 'the people' was normally reserved by his fellow New Englanders for when they spoke of God: 'all intelligence, all power, all force, all authority', he wrote, 'originally, inherently, necessarily, inseparably, and inalienably resides in the people'.[18] That way of speaking, suitably distilled for public consumption, was to reappear as 'We, the People', the first three words

FIGURE 29: A letter box for anonymous complaints against usurers and smugglers, Verona town hall.

of the American federal Constitution adopted in Philadelphia in mid-September 1787.

The forgotten democratic language of the people was reinvented by the republicanism that first came to life in the cities of northern Spain and northern Italy. Here was yet another honeyed irony. By going on about 'the people', early republicans helped unwittingly to breathe new life into the dead language of the *dāmos* and the *dēmos*, which is to say that republicanism secretly colluded in later efforts to resuscitate the lifeless language of democracy, to give it self-assurance in entirely different historical circumstances. In another way, republican thinking had the unintended effect of nudging the European world towards representative democracy. Since its talk of 'the people' was two-faced – 'the people' excluded most flesh-and-blood people – early republicanism stood on the wrong side of popular power and the principle of universal equality. It was to pay for this mistake, for it stirred up political trouble about who exactly was entitled to own the mechanisms of government. And so, unwittingly, it prompted reactions – rebuttals, rebellions, revolutions – that paved the way for the democratisation of citizenship.

Its elitism was not by chance. Early republicanism was an ideology whose language reflected the oligarchic power relations of the emergent towns. Far from being havens of equality, they were dominated visibly by social elites, normally comprising merchants and professionals, notably lawyers. Large cities, such as Nuremberg and Venice, even had a higher stratum of patrician families, whose members were no longer active in trade but lived off their investments and fancied themselves as aristocrats. It is easy to spot exceptions to this trend. Bustling Barcelona was among them. In 1387–8, it was granted the right to govern itself by King Juan I. The city went on to wield considerable power against monarchs – so much so that there were times when the kingdom of Catalonia (of which Barcelona was effectively the capital city) resembled an elected monarchy. Its seat of royal power was often made to feel the sharp teeth of the city's elected representatives (called *síndicos*), who governed through a body called the Council of One Hundred. Its method of public election, at dusk or dawn in the main square of the city, was by a show of hands of the majority of the assembled male heads of households.

Barcelona was not typical, however. The general rule was that European cities were initially not havens of open democratic government; they became so, if at all, very late in their history. From their beginnings in the eleventh century, typically, cities were governed by a single council, which held a monopoly of executive, legislative and judicial power. Cities like Venice, which (among republicans) had a much-admired, complex system of interlocking councils, with a leader (*doge*) and a senate, were rare. City mayors sometimes rotated in and out of office, but council members generally served for life. Occasionally, councillors were elected and sometimes a certain number of seats were reserved for particular constituencies, such as guilds and neighbourhoods. But in most cases, when a seat on a council became vacant through death or retirement, the sitting councillors themselves decided the replacement. Research on the social background of these urban councils shows that the end result was usually the same: council members were typically among the wealthiest inhabitants of the city.

The new towns strengthened the hand of town-based market wealth at the expense of status based on pedigree. Market wealth also changed the composition of the councils. Whereas the earliest councils were typically composed of merchants, proprietors and wealthy craftsmen, by 1550 rentiers and lawyers came to occupy council seats in the town hall. In some Protestant cities they were joined by clergymen, who sat with council members on consistories that defined and enforced policies about marriage arrangements and personal conduct. Virtually all councils were male preserves. City women from notable families could inherit and sometimes own property and engage in certain forms of economic enterprise, but normally they were excluded both from decision making in the guilds and from membership of any of the governing councils. The net effect of all these factors ensured that the urban councils resembled plutocracies – highly conservative institutions run by men from a few notable families who prided themselves on their honesty and civic uprightness.

Buckler and Friend

The tremendous power wielded by these urbane plutocrats did not make them invulnerable. Kings and princes constantly tried to poke their noses into the affairs of municipal government, for instance by installing their own officials or extracting new taxes. From the time of the eleventh century, urban leaders had struggled to assert their autonomy from state rulers. But by the sixteenth and seventeenth centuries, on the seesaws of power, the growing fiscal and military resources of these rulers served as weapons in the struggle to rein in the local urban bodies. A few cities, such as the free towns of the Holy Roman Empire, vigorously resisted. Some cities, Venice and Florence among them, took advantage of the weakness of their local monarchs to turn themselves into armed states whose ruling elites called themselves republicans. Elsewhere, urban oligarchs often saw the advantages of cooperation with princely governments, sometimes to the point where the two groups were fused into a single urban oligarchy comprising households run by wealthy men who had no special feelings of responsibility for those they ruled.

But things did not always run smoothly for city oligarchs. Since municipal governments never had professional police at their disposal, instead employing a few constables or beadles, they normally depended upon the cooperation of civic militias and neighbourhood watches organised by citizens themselves. The threat of an armed citizenry that expected to be treated decently, with public respect, often functioned as a major drag on arbitrary power. Most magistrates and councillors feared a crowd of citizens in the marketplace, armed with torches, bucklers, poles, guns and knives. Oligarchs knew in their guts that they could govern effectively only by heeding the interests of the rest of the city's householders. In an era still without periodic elections, striking a balance proved difficult. There were times when excessive taxes or unwelcome policies caused uprisings. Council members were given a serious fright; or they were actually thrown from office, in the name of established customs and the principle of resisting arbitrary government.

A sign of rowdy things to come was the armed uprising in 1254 led by the coppersmiths of the town of Dinant, in the Meuse Valley of Belgium. They proclaimed their right to govern their own affairs and decorated themselves with a bell and a seal. The town was besieged and the rebellion was soon crushed with an iron fist that bore a different seal: that of the 'greater folk' of town merchants, soldiers of the local nobility and the bishop of nearby Liège. Sporadic uprisings of the region's weavers, metalsmiths and assorted urban craftsmen persisted, for half a century. They culminated in the dramatic events that have come to be known as the Matins of Bruges. On 17 May 1302, under cover of night, Pieter de Coninc, an obscure weaver from Bruges, led an uprising of Flemish wool workers disgruntled by the interference of the French monarchy with their trade, and by their subsequent loss of control over supplies of sheep's wool from England. The guildsmen seized the town church and rang its bells. They filled the streets with cries of *schild en friend!* ('buckler and friend') and *des gildens friend* ('friend of the guilds') in support of Coninc. Knowing that such Flemish phrases were tongue twisters for the French king's troops garrisoned in the town, the rebels began to comb its streets, in search of their opponents. They turned on the French king's soldiers, the aldermen and their local patrician allies; many of them were massacred before order was temporarily restored. A few months later, at the Battle of Golden Spurs, the king's troops were again routed.[19]

For the next several centuries, revolts of the 'lesser folk' of European towns erupted regularly. Commoners tried to keep alive memories of resistance – and of its violent repression – so that something like traditions of urban revolt sprang up in various parts of Europe. The inhabitants of many towns usually paid heavily for their habits; and their resistance was normally spasmodic, and very often in vain. To say this is not to put the urban resisters in the same camp as Robin Hood's outlaws, rural secret societies, peasant millenarians and other groups that clung to the landscape of Europe, then to condemn them all as historical misfits and failures because they did not conform to some or other well-composed scheme of interpretation, influenced, for instance, by Marxism. That way of condemning as 'primitive' or 'archaic' commoners who socially resisted power should be shown the door within any history of democracy. It does not belong because it condescends. It also ignores the fundamental point that these rebellions typically paralysed themselves because they lacked their own political language. The revolts were just that: provoked by random happenings and motivated by yearnings to cling to established customs by teaching others a lesson, not by dreams of changing the rules by which great matters of government were decided. Not surprisingly, these urban and rural rebellions failed to bring about long-term changes in favour of the poor and the downtrodden. Something more than plebeian revolt – or representative parliaments convened by monarchs, rural pressures and urban republicanism – was needed to push Europe towards representative democracy. Urban revolts, Robin Hood banditry, rural secret societies and peasant millenarianism were one thing; building institutions that acknowledged the rights of 'the people' to elect their own representatives was quite another.

Democracy and the Cross

In mapping the many pathways that led to representative democracy, we have so far seen the importance of the invention of parliaments, and the influence of representative bodies that sprang from both countryside and town. We have looked as well at the pivotal significance of the republican defence of civic belonging within territorial states, and at the disappointing early efforts by commoners to add a human voice to the principle that 'the people' ought to govern themselves. All these pathways bring us to another crossroads, and another surprise. For the critical force that gave impetus and direction to the different and conflicting trends we have so far examined was inspired by images of suffering and death of one man on a rocky, windswept hill called Golgotha, one thousand years before. Modern representative democracy, as it would come to be called, had the spirit of medieval Christianity written all over its institutions. Without Jesus, there would have been no representative government, or representative democracy, if by that is meant what many of its Christian progenitors meant: a new way of handling political power based on a lengthy list of practical principles, such as the right to resist tyranny; the civil right to petition for good government; a free press; popular elections; limited terms of office; and the abolition of monarchy, if need be by public execution.

The Christian genealogy of modern representative democracy is today not a fashionable topic, certainly not as it was a generation ago, when democracy as such was forced down on its knees. But never mind fashion, because the subject of religion is unavoidable in any fair-minded account of democracy during its second historical phase. It is naturally a controversial matter. With good reason, Christians of this period are accused of stoking the fires of bigotry and violence, conquest and subordination. But that is only half the story, which remains poorly understood, beginning with the vital role played by the Christian churches in spreading the practice of office holding – a practice of fundamental importance in the emergence of the representative form of democracy.

Today we take for granted the custom of someone being appointed to an office for a defined purpose, often for a specified period of time. We shouldn't, because the custom is a delicate one, with old and tangled roots. They stretch back to such institutions as the Babylonian courtier and priest, the elected magistrate of the Athenian *polis* and the muezzin of the Islamic world. The Roman Empire similarly created and nurtured offices that were linked to administrative units, some strongly defined by territory, and by a distinct hierarchy of official competencies and functions. In the centuries that followed the break-up of the Roman Empire and its mutation into Byzantine rule, the Christian Church based in Rome both preserved and greatly developed these practices. It did so to the point where the principle of holding office for a time, for the purpose of serving a higher cause, was to take root in many other kinds of secular organisations, including government itself.

How did the Church make this happen? A vital clue is provided by the fact that it was the only medieval institution fuelled by universal aspirations to control the whole European region. Held together by attachments to God, law, property, the Latin language and, of course, the yearning for power over others, it was a sprawling organisation whose coordination depended upon, and expanded, many Roman imperial structures. There are plenty of examples. During the fourth century CE, when it began building its own power structures, the Church set up its capital in Rome, the former imperial capital. It created administrative bases in the old provincial capitals, called *civitates*, from where the hands of bishops reached out to touch and cure souls. It also replicated the hierarchical divisions, created by the Emperor Diocletian in 292 CE, of prefectures, dioceses and provinces, each governed by officers responsible for carrying out certain predefined tasks. Then it added its own version of offices and officers. The so-called curia was an important case in point. These were high-ranking administrators and jurists who thought of themselves as men of God responsible for assisting the papacy and bishops of dioceses. Notaries, deacons, court advocates, judges and other members of the curia held well-defined ecclesiastical posts. They were expected to perform their well-defined duties – and to measure themselves against well-defined role models, like the medieval Church's favourite, the former shepherd King David of ancient Israel (2 Samuel 7: 12–16), who was said to have shown Christians how to live, how to repent and how to depend upon God during times of adversity.

Because of its canonisation of figures like David – paradoxically – the Church stood at right angles to purely personalised views of power. It rejected, for instance, the personification of leadership by Muslims who accepted the rule of the caliphate. The Church was also opposed to the kind of rule by personal deals, table talk and servants that was common among the Germanic and Slavic peoples and the equestrian tribes that conquered parts of the Balkans and central Europe. Church views of office holding implied an entirely different – a much more 'depersonalised' or 'disembodied' – understanding of how power should be exercised. Individuals who held office within the sprawling structures of the Church were supposed to abide by its norms and its laws. Inspired by the precedents set by the Bible and Roman law, the Church was the great upholder of legal codes and legal ways of doing things. Long before modern Western states copied their ways, popes ruled through Church laws and, during the eleventh to thirteenth centuries, they spearheaded a drive to draw together and systematise the jumble of published canons and decrees. The Church expected its servants to accept its jurisdiction, and to abide by its laws, down to the tiniest details. That meant that all office holders – cardinals and jurists, notaries and provosts, monks and friars – were expected to hold their office and perform its duties within the bounds of Church law. Individuals who held office were supposed to have a well-defined sum of qualifications that enabled them, on the basis of the well-defined duties of the post, to exercise power. In doing just that, they were subject to the rule that if and when they fell below the level of stated qualifications, or exceeded or violated their duties, they could and should be dismissed.

The appointment to a legally defined office always entailed defined rewards. Although the Church preached the virtues of poverty and the importance of giving, it guaranteed its lower office holders gifts, rents and prebends, or simple means of subsistence. Holders of higher office were normally entitled to the fruits of a chunk of land and the feudal rights attached to it. The income or support so received – it was called a beneficium – was not seen as a gift. To take up an office was to gain material security, on condition of the faithful performance of a specific set of tasks. The point was that office holding carried with it certain expectations and obligations. That in turn meant that an office resembled a depersonalised or 'disembodied' role; it was not identical with its holder. Jobs and persons who did jobs were not the same. To hold an office was not to 'own' that office – not even when the office was held for life. On the contrary, office holding was a contingent matter because it implied the ongoing possibility, subject to certain procedures, of removal from office. The removal rule, let us call it, was a basic ingredient of what later came to be called bureaucracy. Yet it had equally strong affinities with the theory and practice of modern representative democracy. Think for a moment of elected city mayors, or members of parliament who are elected for a fixed term of office, or presidents or prime ministers who are forced to resign. Each one of these political roles rests upon the old Christian presumption that office holders are not synonymous with their office, that they do not privately 'own' their position, that every holder of political office, from the most humble to the most powerful, is in the post only for a specified time – such that (to paraphrase a song by Bob Dylan) in a representative democracy even presidents of the most powerful democracy on the face of the earth are periodically forced to stand naked before their citizens, and the whole world.[20]

Juries

Within medieval Christianity, even Supreme Pontiffs were sometimes forced to stand naked before their flock. Thanks to the custom of defining offices separately from persons, the Church inadvertently posed for itself a political question that would similarly trouble all representative democracies: what mechanisms could the Church legitimately (threaten to) use to ensure that those who held spiritual or political office did not fall into the bad habit of abusing their power by treating their office as if it were their own?

One answer was to point a finger at governments who meddled with Church affairs. The custom of trial by jury was born of finger pointing. The participation of citizen representatives in juries in public courts of law in democracies such as Canada and the United States is today seen as a vital way of checking arbitrary exercises of power by governments. Juries are said to introduce a strongly egalitarian element of unpredictability into legal proceedings ('riding a ship into a storm' was the way former French justice minister Robert Badinter once described jury trials). Jury service is also seen to foster citizens' direct involvement in government; improve their understanding of legal complexities; and widen their horizons by cultivating their sense of personal responsibility for the quality of life in society at large. Among the many ironies in the history of representative democracy is that jury service in this sense is a bequest passed on to us from the spiritual struggles of medieval Christianity against earthly monarchs. Juries comprising representatives were something new: quite unlike the Athenian or *ting* courts, or the capital trials coordinated by lay judges in front of juries (*commitias*) composed of hundreds or thousands of citizens in the Roman republic, the forensic body known as the jury was not the court itself. Trial by jury was a substitute for trial by acclamation of an assembly, or by battle, wounding or death by duel. It supposed that juries did not determine questions of law, and that there was a strict separation between the roles of jury and judge. Jurors comprised a body of men who were selected by lot, and who temporarily represented the wider community, usually the district or county within which the trial was held. The jury neither predetermined the law nor decided the sentence that followed the delivery of its verdict. As a sworn tribunal of lay representatives, the jury was charged with a narrower brief: to weigh evidence and to divine from hearsay and conflicting testimonies the truth of disputed facts.

Among the first genuine trials by jury for which full records survive is one that happened in England: the red-hot dispute over the title to pastoral lands in the county of Kent between Gundulf, the Bishop of Hrof, and Pichot, one of the king's sheriffs, during the reign of William I of England (1066–87). It seems that the king tried initially to end the dispute by convening a special court, to conduct a head count of all the notables who mattered in Kent. Under the thumb of a sheriff, they swore on oath that the land indeed belonged to the Crown. Gundulf protested, so loudly that Otho, the good Bishop of Bayeux who had presided over the court, instructed the notables to select twelve of their number to reconsider their decision.* The portly men with impressive names – Edward of Chippenham, Leofwine and Harold of Exninge, Eadric of Giselham, Ordmer of Berlingham, Wulfwine of Landwade, and six others – retired for a short time to consider their verdict, which remained unchanged. The matter seemed settled, until an honest monk named Grim decided to pay a visit to Bishop Gundulf. Brave Grim informed him that he had for some time been the bailiff who had collected rents and services from the disputed land, on behalf of the Church. So Bishop Gundulf went back to Otho, who agreed to summon Grim as well as one member of the jury, who instantly

---

* The origins of the rule of a dozen jurors are unclear, but there is evidence that in England and its colonies the rule was widely interpreted through Christian eyes. See, for example, the work attributed to Lord Somers, *A Guide to English Juries* (London, 1682), pp. 10–11: 'In analogy of late [the jury] is reduced to the number of twelve like as the Prophets were twelve, to foretell the Truth; the Apostles twelve, to Preach the Truth; the Discoverers twelve, sent into Canaan to seek and report the Truth; and the Stones twelve, that the Heavenly Hierusalem is Built on: and as the Judges were twelve anciently to Try and Determine matters of Law, and always when there is any waging Law, there must be Twelve to Swear in it.'

fell to the ground and confessed (such was the sway of religious morality and fear of retribution) to having perjured himself. After interviewing a second jury member, who similarly confessed to perjury in quick time, Otho ordered that the twelve men of the jury, together with all the other notables of Kent who had sworn that the land belonged to the king, should convene in London before a special barons' court, over which he presided. The court confirmed by a big majority that the jury had indeed committed perjury, and that the disputed land belonged rightfully to the Church. There were two handfuls of dissenting notables from Kent who rattled their swords and continued to say that the king owned the land. So the good Bishop Otho called their bluff by instructing them to clear their reputations by submitting themselves to the ordeal of hot irons. They backed down. Each was fined £300, payable to the king. With that outcome, the case affirmed the basic principles that juries would later follow in more democratic times: that juries are not the property of government; that jurors, considered as 'peers of the accused' and lacking a legal education, generally do not determine questions of law; so that juries are responsible for listening to a dispute, evaluating the evidence presented, deciding on 'the facts' and reaching a verdict, in accordance with the existing rules of law and the jury instructions issued by the judge.

A Humble Monk

The Church tactic of blaming degeneracy of the spirit on the temptations of earthly power can be seen as well in the protracted struggles that unfolded, from 1075 to 1122, between the popes and the German kings Henry IV and Henry V. The battles, now known as the investiture conflict, illustrated another way in which the Church formulated new questions about the power of those who held political office. At the heart of the boisterous and bitter conflict was the vexed relationship between the roles of emperor and Pope. When on any matter of importance push came to shove, should the Pope kneel before the emperor? Or was it the emperor's knee that should instead bend?

Pope Gregory VII (1073–85) was certain that a successor of

Peter would never stray from the rocky path of righteousness, in either the spiritual or secular realm. He was convinced of the primacy of popes over emperors, kings and princes. He matched his self-assurance with enthusiasm, so that in 1075, after toughening Church rulings on matters like simony and marriage of the clergy, he dealt with Church opponents of reform by rounding on both the emperor and the Church rank and file. Gregory announced that upon the death of a bishop or abbot, the power of appointing a successor would be exercised hereafter by the Pope. Henry IV reacted angrily. Under no circumstances could he or any future emperor accept a change of the old custom according to which they, the earthly powers, conferred on bishops and abbots the ring and staff with the words: *accipe ecclesiam* (accept this Church).

Much was at stake. For well over a century, bishops had been gaining power in their role as princes of the empire, as privileged feudal lords over great stretches of territory, as props of imperial power, as potential threats to the power and authority of the Pope. Not surprisingly, the respective positions hardened. Henry IV defiantly carried on appointing bishops in the lands of Germany and Italy. Gregory retaliated. At a Lenten Synod in Rome in 1076, in a prayer to Peter, the Prince of the Apostles, he delivered judgement of the emperor: 'I depose him from the government of the whole Kingdom of Germany and Italy, release all Christians from their oath of allegiance, forbid him to be obeyed as king . . . and as thy successor bind him with the fetters of anathema.'

There followed an extraordinary chain of events, beginning with the emperor's seeming repentance. In the depths of winter, he journeyed into the foothills of the Apennines, to the castle of Canossa, at whose entrance he spent three days and nights, barefoot, dressed in the rags of a penitent, before kneeling before Gregory, to beg forgiveness and freedom from excommunication. Granted exoneration, cunning Henry was free once more to scheme, but German supporters of the Pope retaliated by appointing a new king, Rudolf of Rheinfelden. Henry threatened to set up an antipope, which prompted Gregory, at the Lenten Synod of 1080, to excommunicate him for the second time. That prompted his bishop supporters at the next synod to rally behind the emperor, to depose the Pope and to elect as antipope Guibert, Archbishop of Ravenna, who came to call himself

Clement III. With the gap between Church and Emperor King growing wider, Henry went for broke. He launched four major military assaults on the city of Rome, which he captured in its entirety, in 1084.

His recrowning as emperor by the antipope in the spring of that year had all the elements of a latter-day tabloid farce. Among contemporaries it certainly furrowed brows and raised eyebrows. Remarkably, it prompted a flurry of writings that were widely circulated, on hand-copied parchment, especially on days when local markets or courts were being held. Usually short and sharp, they served not only to reinforce the drama sparked by the protracted rifts over investiture between Church and empire. In matters of power, the writings also tabled fundamental differences of principle – and streams of dissent that fed the upper tributaries of modern representative forms of government.

The most remarkable development was the savage row sparked by supporters of the emperor who insisted, in the most militant language, that monarchy was God's gift to the world. Some believers drew from this the worrying conclusion that to Him alone was any king responsible, while the Church, if it wanted to retain its purity of spirit, had no business in matters of government. As the totality of the faithful, bonded together in one society by the Word of God and the spirit of love and peace, the Church was entitled to bear only the spiritual sword. It was forbidden to muck with temporal power. Influential royalist arguments of this kind flooded the Christian scene, as can be seen in the anonymous pamphlet *Liber de unitate ecclesiae*, a work that appears to have been written by Lampert or some other monk from the eighth-century abbey of Hersfeld in Hessen, in central Germany.

The royalist reasoning of such works caused twitching in the Church. Some men of God called for compromise. Gregory himself commissioned Cardinal Deusdedit and Anselm, Bishop of Lucca, to compile collections of canons, in support of the Church's role in earthly affairs. The most radical replies to the emperor came from deep down within the Church – from the monastic orders that formed its grass roots. That was no coincidence, since the monasteries were spaces wherein men and women, living frugally as charitable equals by the grace of God, were able to ponder right ways of living. They were often unusually sensitive to matters of governance and

obedience. They knew well the standard advice given to superiors –
'Let him admonish the unruly, cheer the fainthearted, support the
weak, and be patient toward all' (1 Thessalonians 5: 14) – though
exactly what should be done when superiors like abbots and abbesses
transgressed the limits of their authority remained unclear. Monks
and nuns were familiar with the admonition of St Augustine to all
who held positions of power. 'The superior', he had said, 'must not
think himself fortunate in his exercise of authority but in his role as
one serving you in love. In your eyes he shall hold the first place
among you by the dignity of his office, but in fear before God he shall
be as the least among you.'[21] The message was forceful; it rang loudly
through the villages and fields of a feudal order wherein many people
believed that the relation of lord and tenant was contractual, and that
breaches of contract by a lord justified the withdrawal of allegiance
by tenants. But the message begged a barbed question: what on earth
should be done if a superior succumbed to the temptation to love and
serve only himself? Pray for him? Call on him to lift up his heart and
not seek after what is vain and earthly? Beg him to reunite himself
with the common life?

FIGURE 30: The humble monk Manegold of Lautenbach with Bishop Gebhard of Salzburg,
to whom he addressed his eleventh-century *Liber ad Gebehardum*.

The thunderous reply of a modest monk named Manegold of Lautenbach was that rebellion against tyrants is obedience to God (Figure 30). Working at night by candlelight from a secret refuge on the edge of the Black Forest, near his own small monastery that had been wrecked by soldiers commanded by the Holy Roman Emperor Henry IV, Manegold stood firmly behind Gregory VII. He worried that calumnies against the Pope were being 'echoed in the streets, shouted in the market place, and even gossiped about by women at their spinning'. So he crafted a reply to Gregory's critics, in the form of a polemical parchment letter to Bishop Gebhard of Salzburg. Later named *Liber ad Gebehardum* (1085–6?), it is not an easy read. Weighed down by adjectives, quotations from Scripture, papal decrees and the insistence that Henry IV was doomed to hell, it nevertheless proposed a view of kingship that was utterly original for its time. Manegold put to good use Church talk of office and office holding. 'As bishop, priest, deacon are names not of virtues but of offices,' he wrote, 'so king, earl, duke are names of offices and ranks, not of nature or of virtues.' If kings were mere office holders, and not given by 'nature' or by God, then they could certainly be thrown from office if they strayed from their duties, as Henry IV had done. Jesus had shown the way forward in such situations. 'For he who bade all to obey the powers, chose rather to die than yield to Nero, thus teaching us by his example that when we cannot obey God and the secular power, we should obey God rather than men.' Gregory VII was treading the same path. He was similarly blessed with the authority to release subjects from their dependence upon an earthly ruler. Manegold was no democrat, but so comfortable was he with the old Roman language of 'the people' that he went on to liken cruel tyrants to a disobedient swineherd who steals his master's pigs and perforce deserves to be sacked by his master. Giving the simile a Christian shake and twist, Manegold was clear that 'to be a king is one thing, to be a tyrant another'. The implication was equally clear: 'If the king ceases to govern the kingdom, and begins to act as a tyrant, to destroy justice, to overthrow peace, and to break his faith, the man who has taken the oath is free from it, and the people are entitled to depose the king and set up another, inasmuch as he has broken the principle upon which their mutual obligation depended.'[22]

Councils

The precept that bullies and tyrants should be ousted from office was to become a fundamental principle of representative government. Manegold powerfully put the point by using fabulously florid language, which was to flourish at many moments within the Church – to the point where its whole edifice would be shaken and cracked by spiritual tremors caused by Christians who not only flung that language back in the face of the Church, but did so by organising themselves into bodies that they called councils.

Church councils may not be everybody's cup of tea today, but not to be ignored is the way they powerfully nurtured the spirit of self-government within the early Christian world (Figure 31). Their historical significance is hard to overstate. Like the representative assemblies that sprang up in parallel elsewhere in the countryside and towns and princely courts, they helped encourage Europeans away from the world of ancient assemblies towards the new world of representative government. 'Council', as well as the originally synonymous 'synod' (from Latin *concilium* and Greek *synodos*, both meaning assembly), were words that referred to gatherings of Church representatives for the purpose of discussing matters of faith and order, reaching decisions, and issuing decrees. Attended by bishops, as well as some abbots, priests, deacons and members of the lay nobility, councils were in effect special assemblies through which the Church governed itself in spiritual and earthly matters. There were so many different types – imperial synods, provincial synods, patriarchal synods, plenary synods – that the medieval Church came to resemble a honeycomb of councils. Some, provincial synods for instance, were convened locally and had mainly local effects. Others, imperial or ecumenical synods, had major effects throughout the whole Christian world. All of them were supposed to enjoy equal theological status and significance. The new term 'conciliarity' (or 'synodality' or 'sobornicity', the Slavic equivalent) captured this multi-layered complexity. It referred to the constant inner need of the Church to demonstrate its organic unity and visible presence in the world by coming together in periodic or regular assemblies to pray, to confer and to make decisions and issue binding decrees.

FIGURE 31: A meeting of the representatives of the General Council of the Church, c. 1350.

It is most interesting – and quite consistent with our earlier revelations about the Eastern origins and traditions of self-governing assemblies – that the first regional councils were convened in Asia Minor, and as early as the second half of the second century CE. It was as if the Church had absorbed these old traditions through the local soil, through osmosis. What is certain is that when the earliest Church representatives used the word *synodos* they were aware of its close connection with the biblical term *ekklesia*, and that it had roots in Jewish religious practices in the time of Jesus.[23] But by practising conciliation on a large scale, the early Christian Church in effect functioned as a bridge that led from the world of ancient assemblies to the modern world of representation. Its nurturing of assemblies of representatives usually sprang from local efforts to broker deals in the face of tensions and splits. Councils were in effect political remedies for the violence lurking within the kind of conflicts that were triggered in Phrygia (in today's Turkey) by Christian sects like the Montanists, a band of ascetic proselytes led by Montanus and two female prophets, Maximillia and Prisca, who thought of themselves as oracles of the Holy Spirit and preached that Judgement Day was just around the corner.

Synods spread westwards, for instance to Carthage in North Africa, where they became well established during the third century, soon extending to Spain and Gaul. Convened to handle controversies over such matters as the persecution of Christians, rights of baptism and what attitude believers should take towards those who had fallen away from the Church, the councils were at first congregational gatherings. They sometimes featured dramatic performances from lay martyrs, prophets and confessors. Only gradually, for reasons that are not altogether clear, did the power to set agendas pass into the hands of bishops, who considered themselves successors of the apostles. These bishops liked to cite Acts 15: 6: 'And the apostles and elders came together for to consider of this matter . . .' They believed themselves entitled to claim scriptural authority for their decisions, whose unanimity was guaranteed by the Holy Spirit. It is significant for our story that they also insisted that synods were the supreme authority in the Church – certainly higher than individual congregations and individual bishops, including even the Bishop of Rome.

It is again interesting to note that these councils of bishops developed most quickly in the East, where they attained sovereign ecumenical status, thanks to the efforts of the early fourth-century Roman emperor Constantine, the new convert to Christianity who conquered Byzantium and renamed it 'Nova Roma', or Constantinoupolis. Constantine was convinced of the strategic importance of effectively linking together Church and empire. Church unity would promote that of empire, he thought. That is why he did something that nobody did during the early centuries of Islam. In the spring of 325 CE, he convened the first ever imperial synod, in Nicaea, in what is today the Turkish city of İznik (Figure 32). Held in the imperial palace there, with the emperor in attendance, the council was attended by at least 250 bishops, who had travelled from as far as Dijon and Córdoba in the west, Egrisi in the north (near the contested border of present-day Russia and Abkhazia) and Damascus, Jerusalem and Alexandria to the south.

FIGURE 32: Delegates attending the first ecumenical council in Nicaea, 325 CE.

The Council of Nicaea was something new. Not only was it the first ecumenical council charged with deciding matters for the whole of the Christian world but it was also the first time that Church and empire collaborated for the purpose of crafting a common governing strategy. The formula proved infectious, and a further six ecumenical councils were convened, all of them in the East: at Constantinople I (381); Ephesus (431); Chalcedon (451); Constantinople II (553); Constantinople III (680–81); and Nicaea II (787). These councils were in effect dalliances between spiritual and temporal power. They would bring great troubles to both parties in the centuries to come, as we shall soon see; they would have the unintended effect of hastening the arrival of representative democracy. But no one saw that at the time. Until well into the ninth century, when a great schism led to the excommunication of the Byzantine patriarch Photius, ecumenical councils were regularly summoned by the Roman or Byzantine emperors and met under their protection, and their direction. Thereafter, with the Church based in Rome and master of its own house, emperors and princes regularly struck alliances with bishops and popes, the combined effect of which was to transform council decisions of the Church into laws that were promulgated either by the empire, or by more local governing authorities.

Constance

The council that gathered at Nicaea was to spawn a movement, later called conciliarism, which forced the Church to vent its own disagreements and to find ways of resolving them without bloodshed. The belief in councils as a God-given device buried presumptions of Christian unity. Like the first parliament convened by young King Alfonso IX, councils actually codified divisions, and they did so by sowing the seeds of politics within the Church, through the medium of council representation. Council representatives quickly raised a political question that would eventually split the Church right down the middle, for ever. There were actually two questions: who was entitled to govern this sprawling body of believers? And which means were they entitled to use?

The questions were central during the richly conflicted – some said terminally torn – General Council that got under way in November 1414 in the imperial city of Constance in Swabia. The Council of Constance resembled a modern political party conference riven by faction, but desperately wearing a mask of unity, all the while standing before an audience – in this case, a European audience of Christian elites – tearing at each other's throats. Preparations took twelve nervous months. Prime credit for setting up the Council went to Sigismund of Luxembourg, the King of Hungary. His razor-sharp instinct for compromise through clever scheming sprang from the experience of watching his elder brother, the drunkard Wenceslas of Bohemia, make a mess and muddle of the Empire, then pay for it by being given the big boot by the Rome-based body of Church cardinals known as the Electors. With the backing of Sigismund, some six hundred men of the Church gathered to discuss ways of patching up the huge Schism that had befallen it. The councillors knew well that a Church split by the existence of no fewer than three popes – Pope John XXIII, Gregory XII, Benedict XIII – each of whom claimed exclusive title to the

Head of the Church, was unsustainable. The only question was: how could the worldly trinity be combined into one?

As if to close ranks, the Council revealed its theologically conservative mood at the outset by turning on Jan Hus, the dissident scholar and preacher from Bohemia who had been guaranteed safe passage to Constance by Sigismund personally (Figure 33). The trick played on Hus was cruel; he was figuratively murdered at the table of the lavish banquet to which he had been invited. He was thrown into prison, then, after a lengthy interrogation, condemned for reading too much of John Wyclif and accepting his heresy that the true Church consisted of those predestined to salvation. Hus confessed to drawing the conclusion that much of the existing Church order was unwarranted by Scripture, and that the Council itself therefore had no legitimacy. Not Church orders but the Word of God should rule. For this heresy, Hus was found guilty. He refused to repent. Condemned to death by order of Sigismund, he ended his life bravely, at the burning stake, on 6 July 1415. His ashes were then tossed into the Rhine.

FIGURE 33: The death at the stake of Jan Hus, the Bohemian reformer, from a Hussite prayer book, 1563.

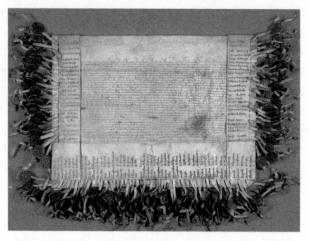

FIGURE 34: Protest petition signed by a hundred Bohemian and Moravian noblemen against the burning of Jan Hus, October 1415.

The written protest against victor's justice by a hundred Bohemian and Moravian noblemen three months later (Figure 34) was something new under the sun. Acting against the grain was hereafter to be dubbed 'Bohemian', while petitioning power in public, for the sake of justice, was to become an option for groups of dissenters of all persuasions. The petition would often be used as a political tool during the age of representative democracy. The Council, mostly by default, meanwhile contributed other political tools for keeping tabs on power. Seen from our times, easily the most dangerous device was the successful attempt at Constance to defend the principle and practice of government by representatives who are elected 'from below', by the governed. The principle earlier established in León, that a governor could summon 'from above' representatives of the social order, was one thing. To turn that practice on its head, as happened in Constance, was quite another matter, with radically different and far-reaching implications. The change sprang from the desire to tackle a basic problem: whether or not the General Council was blessed with the power to appoint, or to recall, or, less politely, sink a big boot into the backside of a pope.

The good men of God wrestled with the matter from November 1414 until April 1418. Time and again – note the parallel with the rows over the caliphate in early Islam – discussions came back to the question of sovereignty in the Church. There was general acceptance of the visible Church, the need for its unity and the institution of the papacy. Yet there were no fewer than three popes, and at least two had to be deposed. The devils born of their rivalry and greedy claims upon power had to be cast out. Church precedent and canon law were of little or no help because they stood on the side of papal absolutism, which was manifestly part of the problem. The situation of Christians felt exceptional. It was as if the Church had to start again.

Something more, something new was needed. That line of thinking was strong among not a few of the Constance delegates, especially those familiar with figures whose reform proposals were in the air. Their names are now part of Church history: figures such as Dietrich of Niem, who spoke of the universal Church but knew that unbridled papal rule was the source of many abuses and much corruption; Pierre d'Ailly, the Bishop of Cambrai, who wanted the Church to be governed by a succession of General Councils; and, standing between them, Jean Gerson, Chancellor of the University of Paris, a man convinced that the General Council should champion reform, but who still thought of papal rule as indispensable, so long as it was corrigible and made accountable to the members of the Church.

Some delegates thought that corrigible papacy was oxymoronic, but in the end a version of Gerson's views was to win out, even though papal authority had to pay a considerable price for the concession. During April 1415, the General Council issued a decree affirming that it held its power, on trust, from Christ, and that even popes were obliged to obey its rulings. Pope John XXIII, who had fled into exile, was tracked down in Freiburg-im-Breisgau and flung into prison, to await trial. On 29 May 1415, he was deposed. That left two remaining popes. Gregory XII caved in without a fight. Benedict XIII was then outflanked by Sigismund, who managed to win support for the General Council from among most of the third Pope's followers. With its hands at last free, the Council began to act like a latter-day constitutional convention.

Delegates agreed to elect a Pope, but on condition that several decrees be generally accepted. Two such canons stand out. The

Sacrosancta declared in tough language that the Council itself derived its power directly from Christ and that its authority was therefore primary, even in the face of opposition or objections from the See of Rome. That principle implied something radical. It insisted that the powers exercised by the Supreme Pontiff were held on trust, for the benefit of the Church, and that any abuse of these powers meant that they could be forfeited. The Pope was the minister, not the sovereign, of the Church. His government rested upon the consent of the governed.

The second canon – cast in an agricultural metaphor and called the *Frequens* – drew the practical conclusion that the Council was no one-off affair. 'A frequent celebration of general councils is an especial means for cultivating the field of the Lord and effecting the destruction of briars, thorns, and thistles, to wit, heresies, errors, and schism, and of bringing forth a most abundant harvest.'[24] The *Frequens* (adopted on 9 October 1417) laid down strict procedural rules designed to prevent papal tyranny. It called for continuous monitoring of its power through timetabled councils. The first was to be convened after five years; and the second after another seven years. Subsequent assemblies would be convened at intervals of ten years. The *Frequens* further specified that no pope could alter the location of the next Council meeting without the prior consent of a two-thirds majority of each of its blocs of members, who comprised cardinals plus representatives of the French, Spanish, German, English and Italian 'nations', each of which was treated as a voting unit. The *Frequens* added, for good measure, that while a Supreme Pontiff could never lengthen his term of office, he could, when facing 'emergencies', shorten the gap between Council meetings, so long as two-thirds of the cardinals of the Holy Roman Church agreed, and on the condition that he give written notice to Council delegates twelve months in advance of the next meeting.

In the Beginning Was the Word . . .

It requires little imagination to see that the Constance resolutions bore more than a faint resemblance to a modern system of representative government, one based on the consent of a majority of the governed, whose views were aggregated by an electoral system that made room for party competition. The strong analogy extended further, to include the principle that those who governed should always remain under the watchful eye of an interested public of spectators. During the four-year life of the Council, huge crowds of Christians and other witnesses flocked to Constance in order to see with their own eyes and hear with their own ears what was going on. Cardinals, patriarchs, archbishops, bishops, abbots, provosts and doctors (mostly of theology) came from all over Europe. Some 5000 monks and friars showed up. Many European sovereigns and princes popped in; so too did the ambassadors of the kings of France, England, Scotland, Denmark, Poland, Naples, and the Spanish kingdoms, all guests of the emperor. Towards the end of the Council, the Greek emperor, Michael Palaeologus, made an appearance, accompanied by nineteen Greek bishops. But the Council was not just an elite affair. The humble were there in force. There were fakirs (religious ascetics who lived solely on alms) and merchants and mountebanks selling their goods and services. Somewhere between 50,000 and 100,000 outsiders spent a few days, weeks or longer exercising their curiosity.

The whole thing was quite a show, but, for all their contemporary significance in healing the Schism, the resolutions passed by the Council served to mask disagreements about the future of the Church. The rifts ran so deep that, for a while, the newly elected Pope Martin V could sleep soundly in his grand bed, with little to fear from a powerless and deeply split Council, which soon dissolved into scores of local concerns. The General Council was wound up on 22 April 1418. Thereafter, the papacy drifted back into its old ways – haunted by the ghost of Jan Hus.

The radical changes that came next surprised everybody; they followed the rule that in matters of democracy radical innovations are sometimes born of conservative intentions. The extended upheaval in the world of Christianity, associated with Hus and other dissenters, and now known as the Reformation, certainly had that quality about it. Hus himself was no avowed radical. The conciliarist opponents of the papacy were also conservatives. Their opposition to its unbridled powers was anchored in the conviction that they were true protectors of the faith. Dissenting groups who later bore names like the Zwinglians, Calvinists and Anabaptists reasoned in the same way. They railed against the papacy, but they did so from within a world in which they agreed with their opponents that the Almighty God had an overwhelming presence in everyday life – and that this was a world in which all dissent from religious orthodoxy should be routinely punished.

Catholic supporters of the papacy were often accused by their opponents of bigotry, of deep intolerance of heterodoxy. Understandably so, since characters like Paul IV, a fierce pope who loved the Index of Prohibited Books, were indeed bigots. Yet popes had no monopoly on bigotry. The historical fact is that both the Protestant Reformation and the Catholic Counter-Reformation lived in the same universe of discourse. They had in common a dogmatic yearning to bring Christianity to the urban and rural populations of Europe. Their eyes burned with the desire to make the Ten Commandments a matter of individual habit, with the help of zealous moralising and, if that failed, red-hot irons, swords and crossbows.

The dissenters themselves were no angels. If there were such a thing as an instrument that measured bigotry, it would show that the arrogant self-assurance of the religious dissenters often soared way above that of their Catholic opponents. Martin Luther, the man who for a time held the honour of being the Christian most feared and hated by the powers spiritual and temporal of Europe, struck back at papal authority with swift, bold strokes that matched the vicious assaults he launched on his opponents. Luther's conscience was enthralled by the conviction that the Bible was the Word of God. It was for him the only true foundation of the faith of the Church. But his single-minded concentration on the Word sometimes had foul effects. Luther was no democrat, ancient or modern. At one point, in a pamphlet called *Against the Robbing and Murdering Hordes of Peasants* (1525), he railed against rebellious peasants, recommending that their ears be 'unbuttoned with musket balls till their heads jump off their shoulders'. His friend Calvin, who consistently refused to sanction resistance to legal rulers and mostly believed tyrants were God's instruments, was equally fanatical on most matters. He approved of the torture and execution of men and women accused of spreading the plague in

Geneva in 1545. He also castigated anything he regarded as a breach of morality, whether that was adultery, or playing skittles, or the mixing of sexes at sermons. Erasmus, condemned by Luther as an eel whom only Christ could catch, regarded women as fools. John Knox, who was convinced, in Jesus' words, that he had indeed been born again, firmly agreed.

None of this bigotry should be surprising, for the thinking of the Protestant dissenters came from deep within the very tradition they denounced. The Reformation was not a novelty in its own eyes. That is why, from the point of view of a history of democracy, the revolutionary events triggered by the Reformation conservatives of the sixteenth century seem wonderfully unexpected. The grand irony of the Reformation is that its dogmatism – in retrospect, it resembled a kind of religious Bolshevism – unintentionally gave birth to living traditions of civil and political liberty that all citizens could enjoy. There was, in other words, another face of the Reformation. In the name of shoring up the old order, figures like Hus, Luther, Knox and their disciples had the combined long-term effect of fostering the growth of several customs that later came to be seen as basic prerequisites of modern, representative democracy.

Covenants

Among the weightiest inventions of Christian dissidents was the art of campaigning publicly for a cause, in order to win over many thousands of supporters, so that the power of numbers might persuade a government to change its mind, or to mend its ways. The events kick-started by Protestant Calvinists in the lowlands and highlands of Scotland during the sixteenth century certainly had this effect. They pointed the way to a form of civil disobedience that would become commonplace in the era of representative democracy.

This is how it happened: in their efforts to make their country safe from papal authority and idolatrous Catholic habits, the local Calvinists agitated in support of 'godly bands' or 'covenants'. Putting it simply, these were written professions of faith that were considered binding on the faithful. The first recorded example was the Duns Covenant, an anti-Catholic band signed in 1556 by five lords. Prompted by John Knox's return to Scotland from exile on the Continent, the covenant took its cue from the Bible, where the word appears no fewer than three hundred times. For many covenanters, as they were soon called, the act of placing an inky quill on a parchment was a stroke of empowerment. Following a ritual described in the Old Testament, some believers even signed with their own blood. Whether black or red, the signature felt to them as if it were an act of direct communication with their God.

A covenant was verification of true faith. It was a solemn contract between the individual and God. It had to be signed freely, after an inner struggle with one's own conscience. The covenant could be confirmed before the pulpit, in the company of friends, or when standing silently in the graveyard of the local kirk (church), alone in the company of God. But wherever and however the contract was made or renewed, one thing was clear. The covenant was not merely a human act, but a divine gift given by the grace of God. His grace was based on goodwill and benevolence towards humanity. It called upon individuals to reciprocate, to give thanks by banding together with others. Grace heals and elevates. It is the sign of the (potentially) elect. It is an unmerited offer of assistance to those sinners otherwise condemned to death. It gives individuals a helping hand in atoning for their sins and seeking everlasting life, through the Lord Jesus Christ.

Grace? Representation? Democracy? How did it happen that a basic custom of representative democracy – the defence of civil society through peaceful mobilisation and organised political campaigning by movements, organisations and political parties – originated from such pious thinking? Surely apocalyptic faith in the possibility of deliverance to another, higher world had nothing to do with representation or democracy of any kind? Wasn't it more probable that local material conditions in Scotland played the primary role in nurturing the mobilisation of God-worshipping civilians?

Local factors certainly go some way in explaining the invention of civilian resistance to government. The poverty of the Scottish lands, the anxieties generated locally by the outbreak of the Thirty Years War (in 1618) and the fact that King Charles I had put cold fears in the hearts of many of his subjects by marrying (in 1625) a French Catholic, Henrietta Maria, certainly played their role. But still it was religion – the militant religious instincts of many kirk worshippers, some of them nobles but many of them humble folk – that proved to be the most vital catalyst in the invention of civil resistance.

The case of covenants in Scotland demonstrated yet again, within the history of democracy, that the raw, blind, passionate conviction that God is the source of all things human could spark the level-headed demand of mortals to rein in earthly rulers who saw themselves as divine. We have seen already that some basic institutions of both assembly democracy and representative government were twins of the belief in the power of transcendent forces. Mesopotamian assemblies took their cue from Anu and Enlil and other gods and goddesses; Greek democracies were nourished by the belief that the deities watched over them carefully; while Muslim institutions – the mosque, the endowment societies, economic partnerships – were self-evidently manifestations of a loving and benevolent God. Early Christians followed suit. In the name of God, they popularised the practice of responsibly holding office for limited terms. They had a hand in cultivating such things as the reliance on councils of representatives, the practice of petitioning, and the insistence that states run by monarchs need to be kept constantly on their toes – held publicly accountable for their actions – by their subjects.

The covenanters of Scotland radicalised these principles. In that country, the religious rhetoric born of the Reformation motivated tens of thousands of people to do things that were astonishing for their times. The starting point of the covenanters was their unshakeable belief that the spiritual matters of the kirk were not to be tampered with by temporal authorities of any kind, including monarchs. It was a point similar to that made by Manegold of Lautenbach, but now the argument was quite different, and definitely tougher. Just like the people of Israel, so the covenanters reasoned, the beleaguered people of Scotland had entered into an existential covenant with God. The contract was sacrosanct; nobody was entitled to break or interfere with it. Power lay ultimately in the hands of God – not in the clutches of mere mortal men.

Dozens of times in the course of half a century, bellowed with the oxygen of these principles of spiritual independence, fervent Scots banded together, scouring the town streets and country estates in search of faithful believers who would pledge their support for the covenant of faith. The banding usually took place during periods marked by an upsurge of fears of a Catholic takeover of Scotland. Not surprisingly, tens of thousands signed. Some did so several times, simply because they believed passionately that covenants were in need of constant renewal. The most important of these bands proved to be the 1581 King's Confession (sometimes known as the Negative Confession). It was drafted with the help of a religious dissident from Aberdeenshire named John Craig (1512?–1600), minister to King James VI, a colleague and friend of John Knox, and a former Dominican monk who, two decades before, had narrowly escaped execution and burning at the stake after a riotous crowd in Rome had burst open the gates of the papal prison in which he had been incarcerated. Craig's influence on the document was strong. So, too, was its language – which nevertheless didn't deter King James VI and his household from putting their signatures to it (hence the name King's Confession). The Confession openly denounced the Pope and laid into the doctrines of the church based in Rome. It called upon Scots to rally against falsehood, in support of their own true religion. It saw itself as a foundational text – as a guide for the living, as well as a gift of God's grace to the coming generations of faithful.

So strong was the tradition of spiritual banding that during the 1630s, when numerous troubles descended on the Scots, covenanters sprang once again into action, in defence of a new National Covenant. Led by men from the kirks and their representatives in higher-level district assemblies (called presbyteries), the covenanters were characters gripped by the feeling that the world might end in apocalypse, at any moment. Biblicist, self-righteous and so deeply dogmatic that it is today hard to imagine their aplomb, they believed themselves (as one preacher said typically to his parishioners in 1638) members of a spiritually privileged nation. It was as if they were 'the children of Izrael' who 'ask the way to Zion' by joining themselves 'to the Lord in a perpetual covenant that schal

FIGURE 35: Signing the anti-papist National Covenant, covenanters, men and women alike, assembled before Greyfriars kirk, Edinburgh, 28 February 1638, painting by Sir William Allan.

not be forgotten'.[25] Such talk may have been hot air, but there was enough of it to keep aloft a year-long campaign of fasts, prayers, sermons and public signings, of the kind that happened in the churchyard of Greyfriars kirk, the first church built in Edinburgh after the Reformation (Figure 35).

Passed by the Assembly, the highest governing body of representatives drawn from the local churches and presbyteries of Scotland, the text of the National Covenant played on the prevailing anti-Catholic mood. Signed by 60,000 people, it condemned 'all contrary religion and doctrine; but chiefly all kind of Papistry in general and particular'.[26] Recycling the earlier King's Confession, 'a confession of the true Christian faith', the National Covenant reminded covenanters of the parliamentary laws that had been passed in Scotland in favour of 'liberty & freedom' of the 'true Church of God'. A remarkable thing about the covenant was the priority it gave to government and law. By favouring parliamentary statutes rather than Church ordinances, politics rather than spirituality, the uniquely Scottish brand of Protestantism plumped for the unity of government and Church, protected by a sovereign monarch – the appeal to a good Christian prince was a standard trope of all petitions of this period – a ruler whose power was subject to the withdrawal of the consent of the governed, if need be through organised campaigns of civil resistance.

Perhaps the most radical thing about the National Covenant was the way it questioned the orthodox view that obedience to government was natural. The point was well summarised in the year 1638, in a sermon preached by Alexander Henderson in support of the Covenant, at a Glasgow meeting of its supporters. Obedience to power, whether ecclesiastical or governmental, was not in the nature of things, stated Henderson. Deference was not automatic; it had to be earned. It followed from this that if those who governed displayed their 'calling from God' and obeyed the laws based on that calling, they should be regarded as both lawful and legitimate. But, concluded Henderson, if those who exercise power showed signs of contrariness then 'we owe them no obedience'. The political principle was clear. It would soon scare tyrants and fuel more than a few political revolutions: 'whenever men begin to go out of line, forget their own subordination, then those that are under them become no way subject to them, because they go out of the right order'.[27]

By hinting at the possibility of civil disobedience, the covenanters not only threw down a heavy gauntlet to Charles I, reminding him that parliamentary statutes were important, and that his tendency to govern without parliamentary support was unacceptable, even a violation of 'true religion'. The covenanters upended the old canon that rulers should determine the religion of their states; they spotted that religion and tyranny could hold hands, that faith and force could be confused, with evil effects. The covenanters were sure that religion was safer in the hands of society. That is why they swore to defend each other – to support 'every one of us of another, in the same cause' – if the royal prerogative was misused in civil matters. That implied a threat of collective action. Such action was not old-fashioned mob rule, but organised civil disobedience that rested in turn upon a new vision of power: of the power of the powerless, of strength in disciplined solidarity, of a covenanted nation that included *all* the Scottish people, not just the nobility, gentry, town oligarchs and clergy.

'So the last shall be first, and the first last' (Matthew 20: 16)

were words not far from the lips of the dissidents, who were prepared to stick up for the most humble sinners in the cause of
putting the world to rights. Aside from those 'hereticks and enemies to the true worship of God', membership of the covenanted
nation was in principle open to everybody, men and women, rich
and poor, so long as they were willing to hold the hand of God by
using their own hand to sign the covenant. The National Covenant
breathed fresh life into the ancient Roman law maxim which stated
that what concerns all must be approved by all. The campaign for
the Covenant stood up for the principle that 'whatsoever shall be
done to the least of us for that cause, shall be taken as done to us
all in general, and to every one of us in particular'. In a word, it stood
for spiritual and political *equality*. It was an early seventeenth-
century equivalent of what would later be called the universal
franchise.

Liberty of the Press

Measured by the European standards of the times, all this was
heady stuff. It raised an equally lofty question: how exactly did
religious conservatives like the Lutherans, Calvinists and Scots
Presbyterians manage to make such radical marks on the face of
the world?

A strong explanation is that most (not all) of the Protestant radicals with conservative minds were urban men. They took refuge in
towns like Nuremberg and Magdeburg, within whose walls they
added religious zeal to the efforts already under way to establish
something like a counter-power to the crumbling feudal order.
These towns resembled places of siege, and it is little wonder that
they functioned as levers that were used by the Protestants to turn
the Christian world upside down. This they did by raising basic
questions about who was entitled to get what, when and how on
earth. The questions that were asked spread fast and wide, thanks
to the Protestants' use of a new printing technique that hailed originally from China. It was entirely coincidental that the launch of the
printing press by Johannes Gutenberg in 1456 – the year in which
the first Bible was printed using movable metal type – happened in

the same generation as the first signs of religious ferment and resistance to the papacy. The coincidence was much more than serendipitous. It proved explosive. Like phosphorus exposed to oxygen, the mixing of movable type and religious dissent produced spectacular amounts of political light and heat.

The social effects of harnessing printing technology were dramatic. Thanks to the labours of type founders and typesetters, correctors, translators, copy editors, illustrators, indexers and others, the art of printing made it possible for the first time to publish hundreds, even thousands and tens of thousands of copies of texts that were alike and could be distributed over a wide geographic radius (Figure 36). That breakthrough in turn enabled the birth of the figure of 'the author' – a literate creature who created books with a quill and who therefore differed from scribes, compilers and commentators, who mainly reproduced or repeated the words of others. Some authors – Luther, Calvin, Knox – were to become famous figures skilled at riding high on the crest of the waves created by printers who used the printing press to run off thousands

FIGURE 36: A printing press, from a mid-sixteenth-century woodcut.

of ever cheaper editions written in the vernacular. A few of those who won celebrity status even had books written about their private lives. Martin Luther was among the first modern public figures to become a victim of mudslinging in print. Calvin soon came in for a plastering. He was the subject of a scurrilous but entertaining biography in 1577 by Jerome Bolsec, who described his victim as a bigoted, tedious, malicious, bloodthirsty, frustrated homosexual who indulged himself sexually with any female he could get his hands on.[28] The experience of reading, and listening to someone reading aloud, meanwhile, seemed to have intoxicating effects. With every swallow, books and bookish opinions acted as if they were a magic elixir. Readers of different books no longer had to be wandering scholars. Cross-referencing of texts became commonplace. And there were the first signs of a flourishing culture of comparing different texts and their viewpoints – and even the first publishing scandals, like that whipped up in 1631 by the misprinting of the Seventh Commandment ('Thou shalt commit adultery') in one thousand copies of the 'Wicked Bible', published for King Charles I by the Englishman Robert Barker.

That typographic scandal reminds us just how mistaken it is to suppose that the spreading culture of printing and reading automatically fostered secular ways of seeing the world. Within the first century of printing there was certainly plenty of scientific material on what happens on earth, and in the heavens. But bibles, catechisms and religious tracts on how to get from earth to heaven more often filled whole bookshelves, to the exclusion of other reading matter. The Protestant activists were the prime movers of this trend. It was not only that they were prolific writers and publishers. It was as if they wanted to baptise the whole world in their own rivers of words. They certainly put the quest for universal literacy – a deep precondition of representative democracy – on the spiritual and political agenda.

Luther himself set the pace. For thirty years he published on average a book every two weeks. It is hard to know exactly who his readers and listeners were, but what is certain is that membership of the Commonwealth of Publishers and Readers was an elite affair. While the printing press certainly had one clear democratising effect – precious documents like the Bible were removed from locked vaults and chests and reproduced for all to see, to read, and to hear – few could read and lucky were the people who had texts read aloud to them. That was why many dissenters felt there was an urgent need to sow the seeds of literacy – and why their efforts led to clashes with new censors, either within the Church or within government, and often from within both.

The frictions quickly sparked awareness among writers, publishers and readers alike that the new-found freedoms linked to the printing press could be choked to death by Church and government, as well as by mercenary printers, who would jump at the chance of taking the shillings offered to them by bishops and kings. A famous contemporary example, one that worried more than a few Protestants, was that of the Antwerp printer Christopher Plantin. He made a great deal of money by joining forces with the King of Spain, Philip II, to supply Spanish priests with some 15,000 copies of a sixteenth-century breviary. Such patronage helped spread the ways of the Church, but it simultaneously threatened the freedoms that the printing press potentially offered, or so claimed the earliest defenders of what soon came to be called 'liberty of the press'.

The fight for press freedom happened for the first time in the world in the northern and western regions of Europe, including Ireland and the British Isles, from where it spread to the American colonies and Upper Canada. It is another grand irony in the history of democracy that liberty of the press, a cherished cornerstone of modern power-sharing government and politics, was invented and championed by deeply religious men, for whom the word 'democracy' was strange, and certainly repugnant. For these pious men, the printing press was a technical means of shoring up obedience to God by spreading the Word through the world. That at least was the point made by a great discourse in favour of freedom of expression, publishing and reading: a tract with a nose for classical Athens called *Areopagitica*, written by the English Protestant man of letters who later had a hand in a major state secrets scandal, John Milton (Figure 37).[29]

The grandiloquent tone of Milton's poetic plea for liberty of the press – 'for the entire human race against the foes of liberty', as he later put it – was defiant. Written in Aldersgate, a stone's throw

FIGURE 37: The English poet and author of the tract *Areopagitica*, John Milton (1608–74).

from his childhood neighbourhood of Bread Street, in the over-crowded, rubbish-littered streets of London, *Areopagitica* was fuelled by a strong sense of urgency. 'The people', he asserted, 'should be disputing, reasoning, reading, inventing, discours-ing ... [about] things not before discoursed or written of.' *Areopagitica* knew well the subject it was addressing. It tried to kill two birds with one stone. It was a spirited reply to the church-man Herbert Palmer, who had delivered a hostile sermon against Milton's views on divorce before parliament a few months before. *Areopagitica* brimmed with fierce contempt for established churches, formal ceremonies, religious tithes and priests – the 'glutton Friers' he called them. It also blasted a petition to the House of Commons Committee on Printing by the Stationers' Company, which had recently named Milton as a violator of print-ing regulations and had urged the government to tighten up the laws. Against the whole practice of licensing and pre-publication censorship of books, the tract melded Milton's mixture of com-mitments: to contemporary republican ideas, his scholarly interest in ancient Greece and Rome, and his passionate belief in freedom of agency, conscience, responsibility and other virtues of Christian individualism, manifested as the doctrine of the 'inner light', the belief that God lives within the elect. Published without a licence in November 1644, priced fourpence, bearing no traces of the name of its publisher, who otherwise might have been harassed or arrested, *Areopagitica* contained a frontispiece featuring a quotation from Euripides' *The Suppliant Women*. It announced the theme and thrust of the tract: 'This is true Liberty when free born men / Having to advise the public may speak free, / Which he who can, and will, deserv's high praise, / Who neither can nor will, may hold his peace; / What can be juster in a State than this?'

Many commentators subsequently thought Milton's unlicensed tract on press freedom to be the first and greatest such tract of modern times, in any language. That is probably an inflated prejudice of posterity. The first edition did not sell out, and it was not reprinted until the end of the seventeenth century. Yet the tract was undoubtedly among the earliest and most enduring interpretations of the political significance of the printing press. Milton's arguments were partly pragmatic. He noted that efforts to padlock the cheap, light and portable printing press were as ineffective as the foolish actions of the 'gallant man who thought to pound up the crows by shutting his Parkgate'. The sarcasm was backed by deep repugnance at press censorship because, according to Milton, it stifles the exercise of individuals' freedom to think for themselves. It weakens their capacity for exercising discretion – and for choosing to live a Christian life.

Milton's cup of open defiance of censorship brimmed with his Protestant belief that a free press would allow the love of God and the 'free and knowing spirit' to flourish. Milton was sure that God had loaned individuals reason and, hence, the ability to read and to choose, according to the inner light of conscience, between Good and Evil. The keys to the press had passed from paradise to earth, with the instruction that God trusts men and women to use their reason, which must not be cloistered. That means that the virtue of individuals has to be nurtured and tested continually by engaging conflicting opinions and contrary experiences. Christian virtue is not the child of innocence. Good and Evil are twins: 'it is not possible for man to sever the wheat from the tares, the good fish from

the other frie; that must be the Angels Ministry at the end of mortall things'. Good can be known only through familiarity with Evil,
which functions to exercise the Good. Blasphemy and ungodly libel
live together in the house of Truth. Hence, the toleration of different and conflicting opinions is a basic condition of individual
discretion and the possibility of virtue: 'that which purifies us is
triall', wrote Milton, 'and triall is by what is contrary'.

Toleration was a tricky principle, as Milton freely acknowledged. In the fight for virtue, toleration of the intolerant would be
self-defeating, which meant that the published works of popish
bigots should be prohibited. Milton was not in favour of full freedom of the press. During this period, nobody was. While he did not
think that governments were entitled to act as if they could substitute for the inner light, certain books could so arouse the social
world that that light could be extinguished. That in his view was
probably true of opinions of 'the Turk' and undoubtedly true of
'popery', which was 'a priestly despotism under the cloak of religion', which 'extirpates all religious and civil supremacies'. Popery
in effect functioned as a potential Spanish or French fifth column in
England. So Milton insisted that the books of popish bigots should
be expurgated. He was adamant that in the fight for virtue, toleration of the intolerant – as well as toleration of the lascivious
ignorance of the commoners – would be self-defeating. He reserved
the law of subsequent punishment for any abuse or licentiousness
of the press. A future polity would need to suppress its suppressors.
It should 'have a vigilant eye on how Bookes demeane themselves,
as well as men' and 'thereafter to confine, imprison, and do
sharpest justice on them as malefactors'.

Although not in favour of the lifting of all state restrictions,
Milton nevertheless drew the conclusion that heavy-handed controls on the press were evil. Rhetorically speaking, it was a brilliant
argument. Knowledge of Good and Evil, he said, is neither a cen-
sorable matter nor a commodity on which duty is payable.
Censorship treats individuals like wicked children. It lowers the
dignity of a nation. Government censorship demonstrates no faith
in the capacity of Christians to resist false doctrines – and to win.
Censorship rests on blindness, on the myopic failure to see that
when Truth and Falsehood engage in 'a free and open encounter',

Truth will always win out. Worst of all, censorship steals God's gift of reason to man. It is a form of homicide: 'who kills a Man kills a reasonable creature, Gods image; but hee who destroyes a good Booke, kills reason it selfe, kills the Image of God, as it were in the eye [that is, as reflected directly in the human mind]'.

Uprising in the Low Countries

Tough reasoning. Sharp words. They sounded a trumpet blast calling on others to muster behind a new form of government that rested upon the publicly expressed opinions and consent of the governed. Milton called it a 'Commonwealth'. Powerfully and persuasively, at least for those who could read and write English, Milton's prose tract *Areopagitica* in effect assembled the various silver threads of representative government, then tied them together with the golden bow of liberty of the press. He favoured republican government through parliamentary assemblies. Given the large territorial scale of 'national' governments like that of England, he saw the need for the mechanism of representation, including in local government and in the churches. Milton was confident that the printing press could be used to ensure that representatives did not step out of line, or that if they did fall in with the demons of Falsehood their deceits and false pride could be exposed in print, for a reading public who had opinions about how they wished to be governed. In terms of a vision of representative democracy, considered as a bunch of complementary institutions held together by the golden bow of press liberty, there was only one thing missing: the diamond word, democracy.

The missing sparkle had in fact already been added several decades before, just across the Channel from England, by likeminded Protestants caught up in a stupendous struggle for representative government against an arrogant imperial monarchy dubbed 'Spanish slavery'. With little pomp and circumstance, the first ever modern European transition to representative government in the name of democracy happened halfway through 1581, in the Low Countries of Europe. On 26 July of that year, a representative assembly called the States General of the United

Provinces met in The Hague. The delegates – well-heeled Protestant citizen-deputies from towns in the provinces of Brabant, Gelderland, Flanders, Holland, Zeeland, Utrecht, Overijssel and Friesland – spoke a political language whose vocabulary resembled a dictionary filled with all the different origins of representative government that we have so far traced. The deputies noted in a written declaration that 'the people were not created by God for the sake of the prince, and only to submit to his commands, whether pious or impious, right or wrong, and to serve him and his slaves'. They listed terrible tales of violated oaths, of repeated perfidies, of cruel wars, of extortions, banishments, executions, martyrdoms and massacres. Such crimes were against the will of God, the drafters insisted, and that is why relations with Philip II, King of Spain and Count of Holland and Zeeland, had broken down irretrievably. After 'despairing of all means of reconciliation and left without any other remedies and help', the drafters wrote, they had reached the conclusion that they must declare themselves a republic, free of the King of Spain. The declaration of independence had been made 'in conformity with the law of nature and for the protection of our own rights and those of our fellow countrymen, of the privileges, traditional customs and liberties of the fatherland, the life and honour of our wives, children and descendants'.[30]

The supporters of what came to be called the Act of Abjuration meant business, in more ways than one. Throughout the territory in which the rebellion was taking place (Figure 38), Philip's seal was smashed, his coat of arms torn down from buildings. His name was forbidden on any public document, and a new oath was administered to all persons in public office and employment. The Act itself did not mention the word democracy, but some of its supporters certainly did, on the basis of their acquired taste for urban self-government. Their resistance to monarchy and embrace of parliamentary rule had deep roots. It sprang from four facts: that during this so-called 'beautiful sixteenth century', the Low Countries became the most urbanised in the world; that this region was the most commercially developed in the whole of Europe; that the Netherlands had for nearly two centuries seen the steady growth of a centralised state in royal hands; and that this region enjoyed old traditions of self-government, rooted

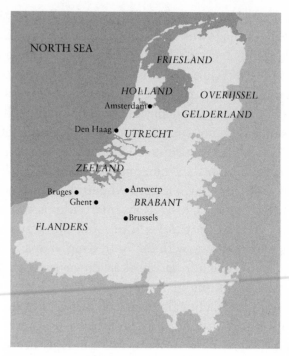

FIGURE 38: The provinces and principal towns of the Low Countries, around the time of their declaration of independence, known as the Act of Abjuration (1581).

within the waterways and the towns, and blessed with Christian zest. The confluence of these factors triggered a revolution; it was to be copied on many future occasions, and its effects were to be felt for a long time, in various parts of the globe.

Why exactly did this revolution happen? Revolutions are by definition magical, unpredictable affairs, but the marked degree of urbanisation of the Low Countries was undoubtedly critical, and certainly impressive to travellers who passed through the area during this period. On the eve of the Low Countries rebellion, around three million people lived in the region; two-thirds of them dwelled in the core provinces of Holland, Brabant and Flanders. They had thriving agricultural economies, but almost half of their overall population lived in towns, some of them sizeable. At the time of the overthrow of the Spanish monarchy, Antwerp, with a population of 90,000, was the financial and trading centre of Europe. Brussels, the second-largest city, had around 50,000 inhabitants;

and about 25,000 people lived in Amsterdam, which was becoming the new hub of the Baltic grain trade.

Not everyone profited – market competition always produces losers – but one thing was clear: the urban elites enjoyed both great prosperity and the political power that came with their control over the governing institutions of their towns. These elites thought of themselves as God-fearing citizens, as men of property who were 'nobles', as gentlemen who stood a metre above the rest of the population. They were burghers who were used to taking things into their own hands. They believed firmly in the benefits of commerce, banking and trade. Many of them supposed that people, by nature, were vain, that they yearned to distinguish themselves from others, but they drew from this the conclusion that the old feudal system of building up a retinue of retainers was no solution to the problem of vanity. It was far better that people invested their energies in work, property and the accumulation of wealth; possessing money was clearly preferable to possessing people. For that reason, they were skilled at protecting their assets through local government, where they had enjoyed a long track record in determining the composition of such posts as the town burgomaster and town magistrate, the justice-dispensing courts of aldermen, as well as the town councils that were chartered to handle important matters of money, justice and administration.

The political empowerment of the urban bourgeoisie – in class terms, that is what they should be called – was helped along, paradoxically, by the drive to unify the Low Countries through the building of a centralised state apparatus. The process proved to be fickle. It started in the late fourteenth century and fed upon the same power-sharing strategy used by rulers otherwise as different as Cleisthenes and Alfonso IX: the region's ruling dynasty was forced to secure its power by acquiring territory, brokering cooperation and arbitrating disputes among its various political units. True to his name, Philip the Bold, the Duke of Burgundy, first took over Artois and Flanders (in 1384), then seized control of Limburg and Brabant. In 1430, his grandson Philip the Good effected a working union among these political units; and three years later Philip completed the unification of the core provinces of the Low

Countries by appointing himself Count of Zeeland, Holland and Hainaut. Together with his son Charles the Bold, he set about building up centralised, territorially demarcated institutions that started to resemble what the early republicans had begun to call 'the state'.

The job of joining up previously scattered governments, and of crafting core judicial and financial institutions, was vulnerable both to outside interference and to inside resistance. On the foreign front, the Duchy of Burgundy, headed by Charles the Bold, was militarily defeated in 1477 by the French king, at the Battle of Nancy. The conquest surprised many by arousing patriotic sentiments within the Burgundian kingdom – against the new French rulers. Dozens of towns and some provincial privileges came alive, and sprang into action by recognising Mary of Burgundy as her father's legitimate successor, and threatening to use arms against the French monarchy. But Mary thrust a sword at the opposition by marrying Maximilian of Austria. The Habsburg and Burgundy dynasties merged – and the whole deal was consolidated by the surprise marriage of Mary's son, Philip the Fair, to Juana of Castile. Through a simple twist of fate, she soon became Queen of Castile. So, thanks to the politics of royal seductions and suits, the Low Countries became part of Spain. When Charles V, Philip's son, became both King of Spain and Holy Roman Emperor, he moved to complete the unification of the Low Countries by snapping up regions like Friesland, Utrecht, Overijssel and (in 1543) Gelderland. Six years later, the emperor decided something that he would later deeply regret: he moved to establish the administrative independence of the Netherlands as a province 'one and inseparable'.

Although many participants in the reforms didn't yet realise it, the drawn-out business of marriage, inheritance, integration and 'top-down' administrative reform became a school where the arts of power-sharing assemblies would be learned 'from below'. The subterranean efforts of local God-fearing burghers to create and defend their assemblies culminated in the 'Union of Utrecht' in 1579 – an impressive confederal alliance forged by representatives of the states of Holland, Zeeland, Utrecht, Gelderland, Zutphen, Overijssel and Groningen to protect their common liberties, including the right of Protestants to enjoy religious toleration.

The confederation was something new. It was a gamble in building representative government within a defined territory. The experiment chose as its symbol a ship on the high seas without sails or oars, accompanied by the words *incertum quo fata ferant* ('We know not whither the fates shall bear us'). The choice was prudent, if only because considerable political uncertainty flowed from the fact that the government of Philip II, who had succeeded his father Charles V in 1555, was strictly speaking neither an absolutist regime nor an open system of representative government. Philip II instead operated a political system of favours. It was a form of government by patronage that was targeted especially at the local burghers. Their support was considered vital both for cultivating a sense of patriotic conscience and for 'buckling' the clutter of governing arrangements into something resembling a coherent polity.

So Philip II played the risky game of divide and rule from above. Some of the richest bourgeois 'nobles' in particular were consequently showered with offices. They were handed provincial governorships, with handsome sums of money, wrapped in titles bearing such pompous names as Knight of the Order of the Golden Fleece (set up in 1430 by Philip the Good). The whole system of patronage proved self-contradictory, mainly because the monarchy, in recognising its subjects and designating some of them (the noble burghers) as fair-haired favourites, in effect gave them an active say in its affairs. Hence the proliferation under Philip II of scores of negotiated regulations and procedures that in practice began to function as an implicit constitution – as a brake on the sovereign's claim to be chief legislator and supreme judge. Government tended to become conciliary, or what the locals called a *chose publique*. The monarch was advised on 'the great and principal affairs of state' by bodies with names like the Collateral Council (originally created by Charles V in 1531) and the Council of State, a body specialising in matters of domestic order and foreign affairs. The regulation of law and public administration in general was put into the hands of several Councils of Justice. Meanwhile, other tasks of preparing and implementing legislation were assigned to the Privy

Council, a body that also granted patents, privileges and acts of grace, as well as served as a public court of final appeal in certain policy disputes.

For Love of Money

Government through conciliation tried to imagine itself as both the master and servant of the noble burghers, on whose support it depended heavily. It was certainly a delicate balancing act, yet the rulers of the Low Countries had no alternative but to succeed, which they tried to do by wrapping their power in ceremonial pomp. Easily the most dramatic example of their courtly spin was the public oath called the Joyous Entry of Brabant. The ceremony dated from the middle of the fourteenth century. Called *la joyeuse entrée* because it was first proclaimed during the state entry into Brussels of the new Duke of Brabant, Wenceslaus of Luxembourg, accompanied by his new wife Johanna, the ceremony exercised a powerful grip upon the political imagination of the region. Murals, paintings and other decorations were conspicuously placed in the city halls of towns like Ghent and Bruges. Crowds gathered and allusions were made to biblical allegories. It was a custom that mattered, in that every Duke of Brabant – including Philip II, who made his fateful 'entry' in 1549 – was expected to take a solemn oath in public that he or she would abide by laws that guaranteed the inhabitants protection against corrupt and arbitrary rule. The articles of the Joyous Entry guaranteed equality before the law. They acknowledged the duty of rulers to restrict central power and to work for the good and foster the participation of all the inhabitants of the Low Countries in the government of its provinces. The Joyous Entry also specified the need to hold governments publicly accountable – with the flip-side principle that in certain circumstances the subjects of the kingdom had the right to disobey imprudent rulers.

Disobedience implied obedience, which is why nobody had imagined that these principles of the Joyous Entry could be used to justify the abolition of monarchy. But that is exactly what happened in the summer of 1581. The burgher rebels demonstrated that the pomp of monarchy could not be used to camouflage a cardinal question: who would bear the burden of the taxes needed to run the royalist government of Philip II?

During the course of the sixteenth century, especially in Zeeland and Holland, the wealthy noble burghers learned to flex their political muscles when answering this question. They already in effect enjoyed the final say in municipal affairs, including the power to submit to the monarch short lists of candidates for posts such as town magistrate. The noble burghers jealously guarded those rights – and concluded that they could only protect them by projecting their power 'upwards', from the towns on to the highest tiers of government. There, at the summits of power, they pressed home the principle that their opinions should be taken seriously, and that their consent was required in such diverse matters as the declaration of war and the levying of taxes. It is a curious irony that the Burgundian monarchy, building on the pioneering efforts of Philip the Good, had encouraged these demands by combining the regional assemblies into a quasi-federal parliament called the States General. Its powers (first defined in what has come to be called the 1477 Grand Privilege) included the authority to block declarations of war, and the freedom to 'discuss the matters, well-being and profit of our common countries'. The Grand Privilege went further than affirming the principle of liberty of discussion and parliament's power to have a say in matters of armies and wars. It also mentioned the right to approve new taxes, the demands for which the monarchy had shunted towards the States General parliament.

So the principle of no taxation without representation of the governed – one implicit in the earliest *cortes* of northern Spain and basic to all later representative democracies – was put on the bargaining table. The matter of taxation quickly grew to be a thorn in the backside of the noble burghers. During the sixteenth century, with the centralisation of government, the monarchy's demands for increased revenues grew to the point where the burghers and their representatives began to zip up their purses – in the name of democracy. Just how unusual was this association of money and democracy can be seen in the fact that, before the sixteenth century, money and democracy, like oil and water, had normally been regarded as non-mixing, self-repelling elements. At least, many ancient Greek and Roman friends and observers of democracy thought so. 'It is money that sacks cities', wrote Sophocles, 'and drives men forth from hearth and home; warps and seduces native innocence, and breeds a habit of dishonesty.'[31] 'He who first called money the sinews of affairs seems to have said this with special reference to war', added Plutarch.[32] Diogenes was no kinder: 'The love of money is the mother-city of all evils.'[33] In each case, money was seen to breed much more than money. It was supposed to drive its lovers to crave power over others, thereby ruining the spirit of self-government.

It was in the sixteenth-century cities of the Low Countries that the received equation between money and democracy was fundamentally altered, for the first time. Instead of regarding money as democracy's foe, it was said to breed democracy, a word that for the first time in modern Europe came to be seen as a valuable political ideal, as a good thing. It was an extraordinary – one could say alchemical – transformation. Triggered by bitter public controversies over taxation, it deserves a brief explanation.

For many city-dwellers in the Low Countries, particularly prosperous traders and merchants, it was a truism that all standing governments, whatever their shape or form, needed to raise resources so that they could function as governments. These citizens probably knew little about the history of taxation, beginning with ancient tribal governments, like that of the early Israelites, which were unfamiliar with the practice of taxation. These early governments indulged themselves on the spoils of conquest. Land, grain, animals, precious metals, slaves and other goods were snapped up, disbursed among the conquerors, sometimes stored up in anticipation of leaner times to come. Conquest naturally provided opportunities for tribal chiefs to monopolise the allocation of plunder and so to turn themselves into monarchs, rulers who could legitimately extract gifts and other material contributions from their subjects.

That historic mutation of ancient tribal governments into ancient monarchies was a bitterly contested process. It proved to be pregnant with unintended consequences, as the birth of assemblies in the classical world proved. Those ancient assemblies often developed allergies to leaders hell-bent on extracting resources from their subjects. The Athenian democracy was no exception. It relied ever more heavily on infantry for self-protection and expansion, but what was interesting about its adventure with government by assembly was the way its citizens refused the indignity of being taxed. Their contract with government was not a fiscal relationship. It was different. Its growing need for men bearing arms was satisfied by compulsory enlistment, in return for which these same subjects demanded active involvement, as citizens, in shaping their government; the decision-taking warriors insisted that they were decision-making citizens. The contract was lived to the letter by poor commoners, especially those men whose job it was to row the warships. These sailors, known as *nautikos ochlos*, wielded great power in the assembly of citizens exactly because it was from their ranks that the navy was heavily recruited.

As the Athenian empire expanded, successive assemblies groped their way towards the development of methods of public borrowing. Public borrowing was used by the young Roman republic, which by the third century BCE bore a public debt that approximated half the value of its annual production. That debt burden was partly eased by imperial expansion – until intolerable fiscal pressures burst the shell of the whole Roman Empire. Contrary to received opinion, its collapse was not due primarily to external factors, such as poor leadership and the numerical superiority of its 'barbarian' enemies. The source of its destruction instead lay in the gradual disappearance of commerce, the decline of cities and the growth of a barter economy – and the consequent undermining of the fiscal resources so vital for a type of imperial state bent on politically administering a vast geographic region.

In matters of self-government and taxation, the constellation of tiny republics that sprang up in northern Spain and northern Italy during the late Middle Ages represented the beginning of a genuine innovation. In northern Italy, as we have seen, almost every town of 10,000 inhabitants or more – Venice, Genoa and Florence among them – experimented with a form of republican self-government. The local merchants and moneyed men who ruled those urban enclaves were vehemently opposed to the surrounding feudal system that survived into the fourteenth century, and within whose bosom the new cities had been born. They disliked its relationships of deference, its cultivation of personal bonds of mutual loyalty among warrior chiefs and their handpicked companions in adventure, honour and matters of leadership. These merchants objected as well to the feudal custom of *commendatio*, according to which superior lords granted rights to land and its population of slaves, serfs and freemen to dependent vassals who received protection at the cost of submission, or outright subjection to the lords' power of disbursing such rights. These entitlements, or so-called *beneficium* (later called *fevum*, then *feudum*, and hence 'fief'), were thought of as an exploitative power relationship. They dubbed it *seigneurie*, by which they meant a cramping and unjust system in which lords granted certain entitlements to their socially inferior vassals, in return for rendering to the lord the services he required, including the provision of mounted warriors capable of performing on the battlefield.

The merchants of the northern Italian cities so despised these customs that they were driven to create an entirely different relationship with government. Since their control of money, property, trade and commerce effectively enabled them to control their own city-states, they were strongly inclined to regard the business of government as the government of business. This led them to kick-start a revolution in the arts of statecraft, especially in matters of public finance. A new contract that was anti-feudal both in intention and in effect was struck. They thought of themselves as citizen-creditors. Seeking to avoid the burdens of direct taxation in money or kind, all the while recognising that government had to be paid for, they experimented with the principle of lending governments their own money. Various ingenious schemes were devised. Paper notes were issued. Dowry funds and pension funds were developed. There were experiments with repayable taxes and saleable loans.

The trouble was that these Italian republics squandered their resources in futile wars against each other, so the initiative in refining and extending the contours of what might be called the creditor state was taken by various cities in the prosperous Low Countries. It is estimated that in the aftermath of the rebellion against Philip II, two-thirds of urban households – 65,000 out of a total of 100,000 – were public creditors. These citizen-creditors, who liked

FIGURE 39: An impression of the exchange in Amsterdam, painted after 1688 by Job Berckheyde.

to mill and mingle in the courtyards of exchanges (Figure 39), learned through time to pressure their provincial parliamentary assemblies to craft new methods of taxation that rested upon a new political bargain. Here it was: the subjects of these cities would pay their taxes on the condition that such monies were repaid with interest, and that the creditors be recognised as *citizens*. The resulting equation supposed that trust could be put in money only if and when money was put in trust. But trust required that governments prove they could be trusted with their creditors' money. Financial trust presupposed political trust. Trust was seen as a gossamer-thin substance stretching between government and its subjects. It needed constantly to be renewed and that could only happen, so the reasoning ran, when subjects kept their eyes and ears open, doubted what their governments said and did, and demanded of them openness and propriety.

Seen in this way, all political power was a trust exercised for defining and protecting the general good of the population. Representatives must therefore be permanently accountable to the

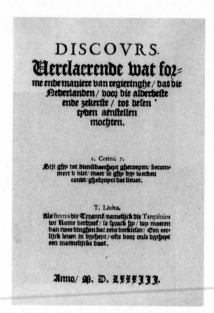

FIGURE 40: The *Discours* (1583), a Dutch pamphlet whose unknown author was perhaps the first to defend democracy as a desirable type of government based on popularly elected representatives.

people from whom it ultimately springs. This at least was the line of reasoning employed in an anonymous pamphlet written in Dutch and published in 1583. It was called *Discours verclaerende wat forme ende maniere van regieringhe hat die Nederlanden voor die alderbeste ende zekerste tot desen tyden aenstellen mochten* (Figure 40). It was just one of scores of pamphlets and books sparked by the decision of the States General of the United Provinces to declare null and void the authority of Philip II. Yet this particular twenty-four-page pamphlet was special. It attempted, probably for the first time anywhere in the modern world of representative government, to use the word democracy positively, for explicitly political purposes.

We do not know the identity of the author of the *Discours*. Once again – recall Demonax, or spare a moment's silence for the unknown inventor of the word *dēmokratia* – here is one more case where democracy has hidden away her secrets, for ever. The anonymous *Discours* was more than likely written for an audience of politically aware citizen-creditors. It recommended democracy as a type of elected representative government that could ensure the rule of the 'best members of the nobility and the wisest burghers'. Democracy was seen as a way of governing guided by strict laws. That is why the author launched a sizzling attack on monarchy, which it equated (with figures in mind like Philip II and the Duke of Anjou, who had just led a military attack on the town of Antwerp) with the absolute rule of one person. Monarchy had to be abolished, partly because historical experience showed that it always tended to degenerate into tyranny. Monarchy was also condemned as incompatible with human beings' God-given natural condition, that of living together in freedom. 'In the beginning of the world', noted the author, human beings had enjoyed this natural condition of liberty. For the sake of fostering 'chastity, virtue and justice' subsequent generations chose 'by godly inspiration' to elect 'regents' and 'governors'. These early governments had no earthly or divine entitlements, except those granted them freely by their electors. The monarchies that had sprung up subsequently had overstepped the mark.

Another form of government, aristocracy, had shown itself to be less prone to degenerate into tyranny. Defined as the rule of nobles bearing titles that they had acquired, either through inheritance from virtuous parents or through their own contributions to justice within their country, aristocracy was admirable, argued the author of the *Discours*. Yet the reign of monarchy in the Low Countries had corrupted parts of the local nobility. Virtuous nobles were now in short supply. That fact, combined with the oppression of citizens implicit in aristocracy in its pure form, meant that the newly emancipated country should not strive after government by aristocrats. The Low Countries now needed a healthy dose of democracy – note the elliptical but wonderfully innovative reasoning – in order to create the best form of government, which was a mixture of aristocracy and democracy. By giving support to democracy – defined as 'an honest, well-appointed bourgeois government [*borgerlijcke regieringhe*]' – aristocratic virtue could be reinvented. That would in turn enable the creation of a government of 'the best members of the nobility and the wisest burghers', a government in which 'the most competent and able inhabitants and citizens are elected to the government by their fellow citizens on certain conditions and for a specified period of office'.

In speaking of such matters as offices, elections and citizens, the pamphlet nodded in the direction of virtually all of the medieval and modern inventions that made up the early history of representative government: inventions such as parliaments, republican states, office holding, councils, public petitions, covenants and liberty of the press. Interestingly, the pamphlet also poached from a figure named Polybius, the Greek historian of the second century BCE who had been taken political prisoner by the Roman armies, had witnessed their military defeat of Corinth (in 146 BCE), and had subsequently gone into seclusion to write a forty-volume work called *Histories*, only a small part of which survived into the sixteenth century. Polybius had taught that the truest and happiest republic was one in which three forms of government – monarchy, aristocracy and democracy – were effectively combined into one. It is unclear what the author of the *Discours* actually thought of Polybius; or whether he or she reckoned that the ideals of aristocracy could survive the pressures of democracy towards levelling; or whether democracy itself would be corrupted by the cultivation of respect for aristocratic values. Those problems, as we shall see, would trouble many later thinkers. In the circumstances, the issue of whether aristocratic democracy was an impossible oxymoron didn't much matter. For what was genuinely mind-stretching about the treatise was the way its 'recombinant' quality – marshalling arguments for political independence by drawing upon the ideals of theology, natural liberty and aristocracy – resulted in a fundamental transformation of the meaning of the little word 'democracy' (it used the Dutch *democratie*).

Not only was democracy, in contrast to many Athenian commentators, seen as a good form of polity. The ideal itself was modernised: it was seen to be applicable not only to towns like Amsterdam (whose population in 1566 was 30,000 inhabitants), but also to polities that were qualitatively larger in territory and population than any of the classical Greek city-states. Democracy tinged with aristocracy had been achieved in the republics of Switzerland, the author noted. Democracy could now be achieved in the Low Countries, on a scale larger than ever before attempted. The author pleaded for determined political effort. A standing territorial army would need to be established. Citizens now needed 'to open our eyes and to use our own hands and people for our liberation and protection'. The treatise modernised the word democracy in still another way. Since it could be applied to large-scale government, which was seen as essential for the successful functioning of more local forms of government, citizens would not always govern directly through city-council forums. While the phrase 'representative government' does not appear in the treatise, the idea of it is certainly there. Under aristocratic democracy, citizens retain the 'power and liberty' to elect those who are to govern them, locally or from a distance. They also retain the right periodically to get rid of those who govern them, wherever they are positioned in the tiered structures of power, especially if they display incompetence, or arrogance. Democracy meant the readiness 'to put out of office again those who have been found to be inefficient in government, or who have conducted themselves in a way unbecoming to office; and to refill them as they should be'.

A Crowned Republic

The astonishing case for democracy put by this tiny pamphlet had a downside. It pointed unwittingly to the way the revolution of the Low Countries against 'Spanish slavery' was saddled with a contradiction. Simply put, the struggle to establish 'democratic' self-government was led by a God-fearing Protestant bourgeoisie which thought of itself as an 'aristocracy'. No less contradictory was the remarkable transition towards a proto-democratic form of representative government that took place in central Europe, more or less around the same time, within the kingdom of Poland-Lithuania. There, it was not townsmen or burgesses, but blue-blooded aristocrats of Catholic persuasion who managed to outflank monarchy, by stealth, in the name of what they later called 'aristocratic democracy' (*demokracja szlachecka*).

The case of Poland proves that the language of democracy was promiscuous.* It showed as well that there was nothing essentially 'liberal' or 'bourgeois' about parliamentary assemblies, and that they could be the work of a class of landowning nobility bent on expanding their grip on the whole society. During the sixteenth century, the monarchy in that country was effectively sidelined, along with bourgeois interests, as can be seen in the clutch of laws passed in the parliament (called the *Sejm*) between 1496 and 1541. The peasantry were confined to the soil, denied access to royal courts, and instead subjected to the decisions of seigneurial courts. All but a few towns lost their right of representation in the parliament – even then they had no voting rights – and most came to be directly administered by nobles. By the last years of the sixteenth century, deputies from both the Church and the towns disappeared from the *Sejm*. From 1573 onwards, the king was directly elected at a gathering of the whole nobility and forced to swear that he would faithfully abide by the terms and conditions of his contract with the nobility.

How did the aristocracy manage to humble monarchy in this way? Geography – the flat plains of the region, and especially the absence of rugged mountain ranges – certainly helped the formation of a unified kingdom, beginning with the military conquests of

---

* An example of this promiscuity is the remarkable book that ended up on Pope Paul IV's dreaded List of Forbidden Books, *Commentariorum de republica emendanda libri quinque* (Commentary on Reforming the Republic, in Five Books). Written by Andrzej Frycz Modrzewski (1503–72), the country's greatest sixteenth-century theologian and political commentator, it defended the need for political reforms in the Polish-Lithuanian republic by mentioning the importance of 'democracy', which Modrzewski defined as a 'polity governed by the majority of the people', a special type of republic in which 'governmental posts are distributed through a fair election based on the common good'. Published between 1551 and 1554, Modrzewski's work was among the first modern publications to speak positively of democracy and republics in the same breath. It caused a minor sensation, for several good reasons. It proposed that monarchs were not 'God-given authority', and that instead they should be subject to periodic election by all adult men (Modrzewski thought that women, following Eve's bad example, bring nothing but 'mischief in public affairs'). He called on the Polish nobility to share its power more equally with other social ranks; proposed that the Church should conduct masses in Polish, instead of Latin, and that it should allow priests to marry; and he insisted that the education of (boy) children should hereafter be the responsibility of government, not the Church. Following the banning order applied by Pope Paul IV, the *Commentariorum* was rapidly translated from Latin into Spanish, Italian, German and French. A third, full-version Latin edition, revised by Modrzewski himself, was published in Basel in 1559. The above quotations are from the Polish edition, *O poprawie Rzeczpospolitej* (Warsaw, 1953), pp. 99, 121, 133.

Boleslav the Mighty (992–1025). Although the kings of the realm came to regard its land and people as their family estate, to be divided among their sons, the administrative control of such vast territory in practice forced them to do what the monarchies of León and Castile first did. They solicited local support, and so made their power dependent upon the consent of others. Initially they did this by offering land and privileges to local magnates, who morphed into knights and officials powerful enough to obstruct the workings of the court. By the twelfth and thirteenth centuries, something like a class of greater nobles (the *szlachta*) had formed. To speak of it as a class is perhaps a bit misleading, for at the beginning it lacked an integrated geographical vision. Power was exercised locally, over local populations, usually through provincial assemblies, dominated by local ecclesiastics and noble families.

The rivalries generated by the de-concentration of power nearly wrecked the realm, not least because many peasants, enjoying a measure of prosperity triggered by demands for Polish cereals elsewhere in Europe, grew uppity. With their social and political power besieged, the *szlachta* rallied by turning towards the lesser nobility. By the early fourteenth century, nobles both rich and poor joined forces. Comprising nearly 10 per cent of the population (elsewhere in Europe the figure was usually less than 2 per cent), they began to refer to themselves as a privileged 'noble community' bound together by common aims and common privileges. They wriggled out of taxation duties. Following the reunification of Poland in 1320 under Vladislav I, they gradually forced the hand of the court, beginning with the famous Pact of Koszyce. It gave the nobility virtually everything they wanted. It solved the political problem of taxation by declaring them exonerated from it, in perpetuity. The Pact guaranteed them an exclusive monopoly on the offices disbursed by the monarchy. But the nobility's greatest moment of triumph came when Ludwig the Great died, leaving behind his heiress, Hedwig, who was forced by the nobility to wed Jagiello, the Grand Duke of Lithuania. At a stroke, the Polish *szlachta* secured the union of Poland and Lithuania and established a most basic entitlement: the right to appoint the monarch!

Many nobles agreed that the right to clip the wings of monarchs required a territorial parliament. The central Diet, or *Sejm*, served as the shears; it was the chamber in which the nobility spoke its mind, to announce the shocking truth for monarchists all over Europe that the Polish polity was a crowned republic. From the time of the accession of Jagiello (Vladislav II), the deputies of the *Sejm* flexed their muscles at least once a year, and sometimes twice, usually during a six-week period. Dominated by nobility or officials of noble birth (such as bishops and high dignitaries, including governors of castles, or castellans), the chamber laid down the laws of the realm. From the year 1454, each king had to be elected, through a ceremony called the *pacta conventa*. He was forced to agree that there could be no new taxes or levies of the army without the consent of the local parliaments, or dietines, dominated by the nobility. Successive kings tried to play off the dietines with the *Sejm*, but the tactic backfired. By the last decade of the fifteenth century, the *Sejm* had been turned into a two-chamber forum. Its Senate, presided over by the king, was dominated by noble voices in the shape of high state dignitaries, bishops, castellans and a mere handful of townsmen. The new Chamber of Deputies, formed in 1493, a year after Columbus sailed for North America, comprised representatives of the dietines.

So by means of a form of representative government guided by a bicameral parliament, the nobility came to institutionalise its differences in order better to exercise a stranglehold over any monarch who tried to act as if he or she were a true monarch. In the process, the members of the bicameral chamber guarded their own social flanks, especially by tightening the political screws on the remaining few representatives of the towns. This was no triangular parliament, in the style of León. There were no urban *boni homines*, and nobility and churchmen were effectively rolled into one; from these groups, membership of the *Sejm* was limited to dignitaries from the capital cities of Kracow and Vilna, and just a few other towns. Their voting powers were soon suspended, so that they became mere observers, with no voting rights. Then in 1496 the *Sejm* struck a final blow against the townsmen by legislating away their right to acquire and own land – thereby ensuring that outside the towns all property and all local political power was in the hands of the nobility. The famous 1505 constitution, *Nihil Novi*, capped the total victory of the nobility over the monarchy. It did so by instituting something of a condominium comprising the Senate, the Chamber of Deputies and the king. That in turn enabled the nobility to dictate the terms and conditions of government, including such institutions as the supreme court of justice, which in 1578 was removed from royal hands and renamed the Tribunal of the Crown, elected annually by the nobility itself.

The crowned parliamentary republic dominated by the nobility survived well into the eighteenth century. The elections of kings by the whole of the assembled nobility (suggests a famous painting of the installation of the last King of Poland-Lithuania, Stanisław August Poniatowski, Figure 41) were splendid affairs that made it clear that the powers of the Crown were utterly dependent upon the given consent of their electors. It was a topsy-turvy world of 'aristocratic democracy' – the term began to be used sometime during the seventeenth century – in which kings were subjects and nobles were

FIGURE 41: Aristocratic democracy: a scene from the public election and coronation of Stanisław August Poniatowski, Warsaw, November 1764, from a painting by Bernardo Belotto (1770).

sovereigns. So powerful were the men of good breeding that from the second half of the sixteenth century they had thought and talked of themselves as a pure 'noble nation', one that was cleansed of the muck of monarchs, and peasants and burgesses as well. In effect (as Jean-Jacques Rousseau noted) Poland was composed of three orders: the nobles, who were everything; the burghers, who were nothing; and the peasants, who were less than nothing.[34]

The noble nation certainly thought of itself as a self-governing nation. So jealous of their powers were the nobility that from 1699 the principle of unanimity – the right of any noble to veto any legislation – began to be applied to all decisions taken by the *Sejm*. Some contemporary observers praised the practice of this *liberum veto* (as it was called), but the bitter truth is that its revolt against the principles of representative government was a Pyrrhic victory. The fantasy that Poles were Greeks soon began to have implosive consequences. The *Sejm*, already enjoying a near-monopoly of power, began to quash sentences imposed by the Tribunal of the Crown, so transforming itself into a legislature with combined judicial powers. The *Sejm*'s use of the right of veto became systematic, so that between 1652 and 1764 it disbanded fifty-three times without passing any legislation at all. Drift and stagnation resulted. Tensions between magnates and the lower nobility worsened. The resulting power struggles between rich and poor nobility spread to the local dietines, where the biggest landholders, like the Czartoryskis and the Patockis, usually held sway.

In the face of what Rousseau described as 'democratic tumult', the Polish crowned republic began to implode. In the name of the king, local magnates raised troops and taxes to protect their own interests; threatening military force, some of them even declared confederacies in opposition both to the monarchy and to other magnates. Political power became concentrated in the chateaux of the richest magnates. The monarchy was paralysed. Any attempts at reform, as when Augustus II tried in 1719 to initiate constitutional changes with the support of Hanover and Austria, against Russia, were checkmated. So it was little wonder that foreign powers, the well-armed monarchies of Prussia and Russia in particular, began to rub their hands together in contemplation of the spoils, especially when violent infighting erupted. For seventy years after 1648, Poland drifted into permanent war, pauperisation and plague. The population declined by a third. Towns suffered utter disrepair. Living conditions were so bad there that most artisans were forced into agriculture, whose outputs and exports of grain declined dramatically.

The whole experiment in recreating the world of Greek assemblies in central Europe came unstuck; and with the surprise First Partition in 1772 the whole country stumbled towards dismemberment. It was reduced (as Rousseau put it in April of that fateful year) to 'a depopulated, devastated and oppressed region, defenceless against her aggressors and at the height of her misfortunes and anarchy'. Wearing a brave face, the magnates tried – unsuccessfully – to forestall further damage by centralising power in the form of a powerful permanent executive council of thirty-six members, chosen by the *Sejm*, to advise the king and to steer the institutions of government. The effort to manage the political crisis failed. Following the great irony of the May 1791 bloodless revolution, which saw the king and local patriots persuade the *Sejm* to accept hereditary monarchy, a national legislature stripped of the veto, and the renunciation of noble privilege, Poland was to suffer partition twice. The Polish experiment in aristocratic democracy was over – along with Poland, which disappeared off the maps of Europe for the next century and a half.

The King's Cabinet

Quite a few lessons were to be learned from the death of aristocratic democracy in Poland, not least of which was the folly of its disapproval of leadership and its willingness to believe that representative mechanisms could be dispensed with when governing a large republic containing serious social divisions. But in retrospect, when judged in terms of the mature ideals of representative democracy, the fundamental weakness of the Polish adventure had to do with the fake democratic qualities of its aristocratic democracy. Its degree of legitimacy in the eyes of the population of the country is unknown, though that should not stop us asking a tough question that others would soon ask: what kind of so-called democracy was this that reduced everybody to pawns in the power games of the aristocracy backed by a monarch?

It took an upheaval more radical than those in the Netherlands and Poland to pose this kind of question to millions of people. Something drastic was needed: something like the thunk of a king's plump head on a scaffold, in full view of a breathless public.

Exactly that bloody end to monarchy was foreshadowed in the English revolutionary events that erupted a generation after the rebellion in the Low Countries. The English drama had many causes and causers. It produced many surprises, but here was among the biggest: a publishing extravaganza that clawed at the heart of the whole system of sovereign power. During his defeat at the Battle of Naseby (on 14 June 1645) by Parliament's crack cavalry regiment, called the Ironsides or New Model Army, King Charles I suffered the added misfortune of having a trunk filled with his personal possessions confiscated by the victorious rebels on the parliamentary side. Various letters tucked away in his baggage were of particular interest to his enemies. So in early July 1645 – thanks to several printing presses using movable type of the kind first applied by Johann Gutenberg to produce a printed bible – they arranged for the publication of *The Kings Cabinet Opened* .[35]

An almighty rumpus in print instantly followed. Never before had the secrets of a monarch been treated so disdainfully – or so publicly. With the whole country sliding into civil war, the highest matters of state were revealed to all who could read, or could be read to, or who could pluck fruit from the grapevine of gossip. The letters (said the radicals) revealed the king's and queen's intentions 'to bring Forraigne Forces, a Forraigne Prince with an Army into this Kingdom'. The letters mentioned the king's stated intention 'to put a short period to this perpetuall Parliament'. Such words (continued the radicals) and his general sympathies for 'Papists' were clear proof that the shortest king in the history of the country, the monarch who was still unable to walk or talk at the age of three, now had ambitious plans. He allegedly aimed 'to overthrow the Law of the Land by Power'. He wanted as well 'to repeale the Lawes and Statutes of this Realme by Force and Armes . . . to repeale all the Statutes of this Kingdome against

Papists'. It was good for the cause of liberty 'that things are now discovered and brought to light, that have been so long hid in darkenesse'.

The king's supporters were furious. Contradicting themselves by repeating verbatim the revelations and putting their own objections into print, they denounced 'the Rebels of this Age' for having seized 'such ignoble Trophees' and so 'prostituted those chast and holy Papers, to the base adulteries of all common Eyes'. The whole act was treachery. It was a direct violation of the 'sacred person' of the king and the 'happy Government' called monarchy. 'They will not let him *loath* a Rebel', the critics complained, in astonishment. 'They will not let him use his *Sword* . . . they will not let him use his *Pen*, but they will expose him for it.'[36]

It seemed not to occur to the royalist defenders of secrecy that by using the printing press to combat the printing press they had walked right into the trap cunningly set by their enemies. They succeeded in fuelling a publishing frenzy – with fatal consequences for the institution of monarchy. Two summers after his military defeat at Naseby, the king fled from his power base in Oxford. He gave himself up to the Scottish army, which promptly sold him for a handsome sum of money to the Parliament at Westminster. The king instantly refused its conditions for returning to the throne. His intransigence stirred up disagreements among the supporters of Parliament. Sections of the New Model Army, whose core support and leadership were Protestant radicals who favoured humbling the king, and who knew how to do just that by fighting in formation on horseback, grew restive. The king was arrested and held at Hampton Court Palace; fearing that he would be murdered, he managed to escape his captors and fled to the Isle of Wight, whose governor placed him under house arrest at Carisbrooke Castle. Ever scheming, ever duplicitous, the king then tried to do a deal with Scots royalists, who pledged to place him back on the throne if he promised to make Presbyterianism the official religion of both kingdoms.

That deal triggered rage in parliamentary circles. At an army prayer meeting in May 1648, it was noted by some soldiers that they had a God-given duty to 'call Charles Stuart, that man of blood, to an account, for that blood he had shed, and mischief he had done, to his utmost, against the Lord's cause and people in these poor nations'. Note the reference to 'people' and the self-conviction of the radicals that God and Righteousness were on their side. The subsequent refusal of the king and his opponents to talk prompted another round of bitter fighting throughout the country, with the New Model Army commanded by Cromwell on the side of Parliament – against the king and his Scottish support-ers, whose invasion of England was stopped dead in its tracks, at the Battle of Preston, in mid-August 1648.

Now firmly in control, the army began to purge parliament of its Presbyterian sympathisers and moderates. The remaining Rump Parliament, as it came to be called, appointed a parliamentary com-mission for the purpose of negotiating with the king, and restoring him 'to a condition of safety, honour and freedom'. That would be on the condition that he agreed to regular biennial parliaments that exercised control over the army, paid outstanding remuneration and approved the appointment of the principal ministers of state. The king refused to vote for his own humbling. So, twelve days before Christmas 1648, negotiations with the king were broken off. With great difficulty, and the outright opposition of the House of Lords, parliament tried to cobble together a special court to bring charges against the king. It managed to do this, so that on Saturday 20 January 1649 the newly formed High Court of Justice assem-bled to try the king, who was unaware of the claims about to be put before him.

Dressed in a black gown, the Solicitor-General John Cook, a barrister of Gray's Inn, rose to read the accusation. The king was charged with 'high treason and high misdemeanours . . . in the name of the commons of England'.[37] The king tried to interrupt, but Cook persisted, contending that the king had been 'trusted with a limited power to govern by and according to the laws of the land and not otherwise', and that instead he had 'traitorously and maliciously levied war against the present Parliament and the people therein represented'. The charge concluded that the king was 'A Tyrant, traitor and murderer and a public and implacable Enemy to the Commonwealth of England'.

The subsequent altercations between Cook and the king revealed two fundamentally opposed definitions of sovereignty. Cook called on the accused to respond before the court to the charges. He did so, without his usual stammer, by denying the authority of the court. The power of parliament may have grown out of barrels of gunpowder, but it could never be a source of right. 'I would know by what power I am called hither', he snapped. 'I would know by what authority, I mean lawful. There are many unlawful authorities in the world, thieves and robbers by the highway.' He paused, then issued a threat. 'Remember I am your king, your lawful king, and what sins you bring upon your heads, and the judgment of God upon this land; think well upon it, I say . . .'

No believer in the presumption of innocence, Cook insisted that the king should answer the charges 'in the name of the people, of which you are elected King'. The accused erupted. 'England was never an elected Kingdom, but a hereditary Kingdom, for near these thousand years', he spluttered. 'I do stand more for the liberty of my people, than any here that come to be my pretended judges . . . I do not come here as submitting to the Court . . . Let me see a legal warrant authorised . . . by the constitution of the Kingdom and I will answer.'

That reply, heckled by soldiers in the court shouting 'Justice! Justice!', earned the king the ultimate verdict. During the morning of Tuesday 30 January, the House of Commons passed emergency legislation declaring itself – as the parliament of the representatives of the people – the ultimate source of authority, and making it an offence to proclaim a new king. As the Commons went about its business, the king was escorted on foot from the Palace of St James, through the adjoining park, towards Whitehall, guarded by a regiment of foot soldiers, their colours flying and drums beating. The king was made to wait several hours in a small room. He took the Sacrament and around noon nibbled some bread and drank a glass of claret.

Then came his last engagement. Like a marked tree surrounded by a forest of woodsmen wielding muskets, the king was shuffled through the Banqueting Hall, with its ceiling painted by Peter Paul Rubens, out to Whitehall Gate, near to which there had been erected a gigantic scaffold draped in black cloth with an axe and block laid out in its middle. Thousands of spectators surged forwards. The king, his surgeon, a bishop and several officers, including Colonel Hacker, the masked executioner, slowly mounted the scaffold.

The crowd hushed. The king seemed calm. Reportedly dressed in two shirts to prevent the cold January weather from causing him to shiver, which might have prompted onlookers to think that he shook with fear, or weakness, the king was heard to utter some confused sentences. 'I think it is my duty to God first and to my country for to clear myself both as an honest man and a good King, and a good Christian', said the king, who still stood firm in the view that he was by Divine Right. 'A national synod freely called, freely debating among themselves, must settle this, when that every opinion is freely and clearly heard', he said, with a clear understanding of the history of Church councils. 'I am the Martyr of the People', he continued, sounding momentarily as if he were on the side of the Protestant radicals, only to return to his original thought: 'For the people. And Truly I desire their Liberty and Freedom as much as any Body whomsoever. But I must tell you. That their Liberty and Freedom, consists in having of Government.' He added: 'A subject and a sovereign are clean different things.'[38]

Words were about to morph into the silence of violence. The king, always in command, turned to Colonel Hacker and instructed him to take care with the axe, so that he would not inflict undue pain. He then asked for his nightcap, under which his long, curled hair was tucked with the help of the executioner. 'I have a good Cause, and a gracious God on my side', said the king, steadying himself. 'I go from a corruptible, to an incorruptible Crown; where no disturbance can be, no disturbance in the World.' With those words, the king moved towards the block.

He stared at it for some seconds, then said to the executioner: 'You must set it fast.'

Executioner: 'It is fast Sir.'

King: 'It might have been a little higher.'

Executioner: 'It can be no higher Sir.'

King (stretching out his hands): 'When I put out my hands this way, then . . .'

After two or three words to himself, the king stooped, kneeled on the platform, then put his head on the block. The executioner re-tucked the king's hair under his nightcap.

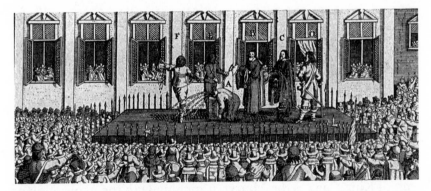

FIGURE 42: The public execution of King Charles I at Whitehall, London, 30 January 1649, from an etching by an unknown contemporary artist.

King (thinking that the executioner was about to strike): 'Stay for the sign.'

Executioner: 'Yes, I will, and it please Your Majesty.'

Several seconds later, the king stretched out his hands, the breathless crowd gasped, and down came the axe, clamping its victim to the block. With one clean stroke, a fountain of blood surged across the platform (Figure 42). As the body was lifted gently into a coffin, then draped with black velvet, the executioner clawed at the severed head and in silence, for several minutes, raised it high in the air, so that all who had eyes could see that the time of kings and queens was no more.

The Poorest Man Hath as True a Title and Just Right . . .

Politically speaking, things were never again to be the same in England, or in the rest of Europe. Like all revolutionary events, the king's execution produced shock waves that triggered perverse effects, certainly. During the Commonwealth period, which lasted from 1649 until 1660, the execution turned the English parliament into a handpicked Barebones Parliament and put England for a time under the thumb of Cromwell's military dictatorship (and were it not for loud protests in the army, Lord Protector Cromwell would have accepted the crown as king). Great violence was heaped upon the Irish. Scotland was conquered and the bullish policy of commercial expansion through naval power led to a war with the Dutch, who had monopolised the carrying trade of the world during the first half of the seventeenth century, and to war against the Spanish. The abolition of feudal tenures and the establishment of an absolute right of property against government made possible the social misery and political conflict generated by the wholesale enclosures and expropriations of the next 150 years. And although it is true that monarchy began to feel cheaper, as if it had been merely an office whose duties were written in the king's blood, the public execution of Charles I had the effect of creating a cult of King Charles the Martyr, beginning with the publication of his supposed meditations during his final months. Rivers of rumour began to cut through the body of the new republic. Prodigies flourished in the popular press. It was revealed that Oliver Cromwell had ordered the king's head to be sewn back on his body. It was said that a huge whale had beached at Dover within the same hour of the king's execution, that a blazing star had fallen that night over Whitehall, and that next morning a commoner who swore that the king deserved to die had had both his eyes pecked out by a murder of black crows.

It is true that martyrdom sustained the royalist cause and prepared the way for the restoration of monarchy (in 1660) and its sanctification by the Anglican Church. It is true that Charles II came back, pretending that he had been king by divine hereditary right ever since his father's head had been held high over a Whitehall crowd; and it is also undeniable that, to this day, wreaths of remembrance are laid on the anniversary of the king's death at his statue, which faces down Whitehall to the site of his beheading. But despite all the setbacks and degradations, and the unfair gains made by a rising propertied middle class and a gentry that dominated local government, the fundamental change that came over England was the permanent humbling of the Crown and its Church, in favour of the visible appearance of the common man and common woman on the stage of political history.

An anonymous Flemish-language pamphlet had complained loudly about the way in which the earlier rebellion in the Low Countries had so stirred up discussion among 'uneducated weavers and furriers' that even commoners in Leiden and Ghent had put democracy on their agenda.[39] The English events did that, but in much more radical fashion. The executioner's sharp axe sliced deeply into the social fabric of England, and for a time legitimated some new voices: the cries of the downtrodden to be treated with dignity, with respect, seen as rightfully privileged, even. Monarchy was declared to be 'unnecessary, burdensome, and dangerous' and abolished in the name of 'the liberty, safety and public interest of the people'. And that old category 'the people' came alive, with fresh spirit and new meaning. Especially in southern and eastern England, and within the New Model Army, which for a time governed itself using its own elected representatives, the struggle to defeat the monarchy enlisted the support of plain-clothed commoners who had political ideas of their own. 'We had a thing here called a Committee', recorded a gentleman from the Isle of Wight, 'which overruled Deputy-Lieutenants and also Justices of the Peace, and of this we had brave men: Ringwood of Newport, the pedlar: Maynard, the apothecary: Matthews, the baker: Wavell and Legge, farmers; and poor Baxter of Hurst Castle. These ruled the whole Island, and did whatsoever they thought good in their own eyes.'[40]

The execution of Charles I was the dramatic ending of a long phase in the history of representative government. Not only did it give a public voice to pedlars, bakers, apothecaries, farmers and simple servants, it signalled the fact that the spectre of political equality – of democracy – would hereafter haunt representative government. The fact that the king was buried at Windsor rather than Westminster Abbey because of fears of public disorder pointed to a future that nobody had envisaged – certainly not the God-fearing radicals, some of whom even liked to preach equality by citing Galatians 3: 28 ('there is not here Jew or Greek, there is not here servant nor freeman, there is not here male and female, for all ye are one in Christ Jesus'). The failed English revolution succeeded in putting a sting in the tail of this old Christian principle. Though Colonel Hacker probably did not think in this way, he managed to execute two monarchs on that cold winter's afternoon at Whitehall: the physical body of the king, of course, but as well a symbolic killing of deference. From that day forward, and not only in England, symbolic regicide, carried out in public, with or without masked executioners, promised that humble folk who had been subjects of a Crown were transformed into citizens with straightened spines, who lived in a country, as Albert Camus later famously put it in *The Rebel*, in which the throne of sovereign power forever remained empty. The beheading of the king put an end to the practice of sitting on thrones. It put to death a form of government and a whole way of life in which the monarch ruled alone, like God, over a visible and actual body politic, itself understood as an extension of the earthly sovereign's body. Monarchy had been more than one individual's claim to rule, for example by Divine Right. It was also a justification of a certain kind of political order, one that could only be ruled by one sovereign individual. The oft-repeated phrase of the contemporary French bishop Bossuet (1627–1704) that 'the State is in the person of the prince' highlighted that point. The body politic required a particular kind of leadership, a leader who was God's deputy, a peacemaker, a lord of everything, a sole knower of the mysteries of the State, a father who protected and lovingly disciplined his childlike subjects.

The public trial and execution of Charles I proved fatal to this type of regime. Assassins and court murderers could strike down monarchs in private, but putting a king on trial and executing him before an open-mouthed public killed two bodies, that of the king and that of the God-given body politic. Government was hereafter open in principle to all and sundry and – more radically – power relations were consequently seen not as divine, or as symbolically linked to an individual of royal birth. Matters to do with who got what, when and how were to be seen as contingent: as up for grabs, as depending upon human judgements and actions, preferably by a government of elected representatives enjoying the support of all its citizens.

THE AMERICAN CENTURY

Thunder on! Stride on! Democracy. Strike with vengeful strokes.

Walt Whitman, Drum-Taps – Rise O Days From
Your Fathomless Deep (no. 3)

The blade that cut short the reign of Charles I fortified Europe's reputation as the home country of representative government, the birthplace of such basic practices as office holding, parliaments, liberty of the press and government by consent of people living within territorial states. Towards the end of the eighteenth century, without warning, the action suddenly swung westwards, away from Europe, across the Atlantic Ocean, towards bustling towns like Boston, Charleston and Philadelphia. The swing of the compass made the United States of America the new centre of gravity of democracy in the world. It also spawned the proud local belief that the upheaval of 1776 was the first modern democratic revolution.

The political dramas staged much earlier in the Low Countries and in Protestant England suggest that things were more complicated, but let us first allow the other side to speak. There is a venerable American custom of supposing that a sprint for democracy began with the musket shots of 1776, the moment when local colonists, previously thinking of themselves as loyal British subjects, bravely declared their independence from the white-sailed navy and red-coated army of the mother country. The resulting Philadelphia model of self-government, so runs the reasoning, envisaged a federation that placed the hands of the American people firmly on the levers of governmental power. The new federation was the natural outgrowth of such 'cardinal tenets of American colonial democracy' as a passion for 'local self-government and repugnance to social and political aristocracy'.[1] During the brief decade of Confederation, the story continues, lax government at both the central and state levels, combined with the temperamental conservatism of the framers of the Constitution of 1787, produced a 'marked anti-democratic reaction'. That was eventually reversed, in the early 1790s, by the formation of the Democratic-Republican Party led by Thomas Jefferson, in opposition to the Federalists, dominated by Alexander Hamilton. In 1801, following the first ever, bloodless, transfer of governmental power from one party to another, democrats led by Jefferson gained full control of the American government, save the judiciary. Jefferson's inaugural address of that year is seen as a full-blooded statement of democratic principles that today are taken for granted, or universally accepted, as the basic principles of the institutions of American government. Jefferson stood up for 'democracy', against aristocracy. He defended (so the story runs) the 'rights of man', the widening of political opportunities and the levelling of social ranks. 'I believe this . . . the strongest government on earth', he said in his stirring inaugural presidential address, before listing the 'blessings' enjoyed by the new republic: 'Kindly separated by nature and a wide ocean from the exterminating havoc of one quarter of the globe; too high-minded to endure the degradations of the others; possessing a chosen country, with room enough for our descendants to the thousandth and thousandth generation; entertaining a due sense of our equal right to the use of our own faculties, to the acquisitions of our own industry, to honor and confidence from our fellow citizens, resulting not from birth, but from our actions and their sense of them; enlightened by a benign religion, professed, indeed, and practiced in various forms, yet all of them inculcating honesty, truth, temperance, gratitude, and the love of man. . .with all these blessings', Jefferson asked, 'what more is necessary to make us a happy and prosperous people?'[2]

The Chrysalis and the Butterfly

The story that American democracy was founded in the glory of 1776 is today still widely repeated by Americans, at public meetings, within school curricula, by journalists, and on government websites. The trouble is that it badly understates how the American commitment to the devolution of popular power tilled the ground in which a pro-slavery politics watered by the doctrine of states' rights produced the crops that fed the furies of civil war. As we are about to see, the inspiring history of representative democracy in America is no simple tale of blissful progress. Politically speaking, its triumph was never guaranteed; it was always more fraught and fragile than the textbook story supposes. But the really odd thing about the story of the glory of 1776 is its silence about a simple fact: that the republican gentlemen who championed the Philadelphia model of government, regardless of their political views on a wide range of issues, were not keen on democracy in any sense.

There is no doubt about the historical originality of the Philadelphia model of republican government. The world had never before seen what James Madison famously called a 'compound republic': a two-tier, federated system of state power that was designed to dispense with the trappings of monarchy by striking a balance of power between the president, Congress and the Supreme Court, a republic that privileged the rule of law and periodic elections and so enabled citizens to nurture respect for their civil and political liberties – on a continental basis. When seen with the wisdom of hindsight, this constitutional republic called the United States of America was a remarkable innovation with great democratic potential, but to say that just serves to heighten the irony that the whole edifice was built in the name of putting a stop to democracy. Some members of the revolutionary elite opposed 'democracy', using words so brash that many today would find them embarrassing. An example was the way the influential politician from Boston George Cabot (1752–1823) openly sided with his fellow revolutionaries by denouncing (in italics) democracy as *the government of the worst*.[3]

Most local politicians preferred milder words in normal fonts, but they, too, shared the thought that democracy meant Athens, a type of small-scale government that was prone to breakdowns because it rested upon the potentially vicious fickleness of the great unwashed. Even radicals like Thomas Paine, not yet a declared friend of democracy, spoke the same language as his conservative opponents. In his daredevil *Common Sense*, the biggest-selling pamphlet of the revolutionary period, the first ever published call for independence whose prose, priced two shillings, set important parts of America on fire, Paine warned that republics could easily succumb to populist tyranny. He pointed to the case of the seventeenth-century fisherman-turned-tyrant Tommaso Aniello, otherwise known as Masaniello, who had first stirred up the inhabitants of Naples in the marketplace, appealing to their basest passions, employing demagogic speeches, then led them into revolt against their Spanish conquerors. 'If we omit it now', warned Paine, 'some Masan[i]ello may hereafter arise, who, laying hold of popular disquietudes, may collect together the desperate and the discontented, and by assuming to themselves the powers of government, finally sweep away the liberties of the continent like a deluge.'[4]

Paine's sentiments were not exceptional. Madison, the principal author of the Constitution who doubled as a Virginia slave owner and tobacco planter, made exactly the same point when attacking those ancient 'theoretic politicians' who once upon a time favoured 'democracy'. Terms like 'democrat' and 'democracy' were used and understood by him as unsuited to his times, hence as mudslinging terms. Democracy meant a form of small-scale government by a majority of uncouth commoners, a species of class rule in which the interests of the many and 'the confusion of the multitude' swallowed up the higher concerns of the few. Democracy should be feared. 'Democracies', he concluded in a newspaper article written under the Roman allonym 'Publius', and later known as Federalist 10, 'have ever been spectacles of turbulence and contention; have ever been found incompatible with personal security or the rights of property; and have in general been as short in their lives as they have been violent in their deaths.' Hostile to representation, democracy was incapable of producing political leaders 'who possess the most attractive merit and the most diffusive and established characters'. Practised on a small scale, democracy blinkered people's horizons, so that it produced leaders and citizens 'too little fit to comprehend and pursue great and national objects'.[5] Had Madison known about the Dutch republican sympathy for 'democracy' two hundred years earlier, or had he acquainted himself with the latest French talk of 'representative democracy', he might well have regarded his own views about 'democracy' in ironic terms, held them at arm's length, enabling him to foresee that the new institutions prepared by the Revolution were capable of giving birth to an entirely new species of democracy. But Madison never saw things this way.

We should not be surprised that he did not, if only because his unironic defence of republicanism against 'democracy' was part of the reigning orthodoxy of his times. That helps to explain some oddly elitist features of the revolutionaries' behaviour, beginning with the strict rules of secrecy they followed in drafting and approving the 1787 Constitution, behind locked doors at the Pennsylvania State House. Their elitism was camouflaged by singing the praises of 'the people'. Like a hymn to an absent deity called upon to work wonders, the state builders worshipped 'the people', an imagined figure that was both present and absent. All sorts of proposals were justified in its name. 'The people at large, who will know, will see, will feel the effects of them', said Pennsylvania's Gouverneur Morris (1752–1816) in defence of the principle of an elected executive that could in practice stand up to haughty legislatures. John Dickinson (1732–1808), the former President of Delaware, agreed. 'The people will know the most eminent characters of their own States', he argued, 'and the people of different States will feel an emulation in selecting those of which they will have the greatest reason to be proud.' Most other revolutionaries gestured towards 'the people' and sometimes even invoked what the slave owner George Mason (1725–92) of Virginia grandly called 'the genius of the people'.[6]

In the minds of gentlemen like Mason, Dickinson and Morris, the genius of 'the people' was utterly unpredictable, and full of paradoxical opinions, which helps explain why 'the people' were thought by them to favour or disfavour so many different and contradictory positions. The ornery delegate from Massachusetts,

Elbridge Gerry, told the Constitutional Convention that 'the people of New England will never give up the point of annual elections' (they soon did). Connecticut's Oliver Ellsworth (1745–1807), a lawyer and great champion of the new term 'United States', meanwhile insisted that 'the local genius of the people' was incompatible with a continental standing army. Gouverneur Morris replied by asking, in the name of the people, and on behalf of the people's protection, 'who can judge so well of the discharge of military duties for the protection and security of the people, as the people themselves who are to be protected and secured?'

More than two centuries later, we can see more clearly that the effusive references to 'the people' were serious word games within serious power games aimed at resolving hard questions about how the new republic was to govern itself. The popularity of 'the people' as the imagined source of sovereign power was pregnant with democratic possibilities, if by democracy is simply meant the self-government of the people. But the interesting and less obvious point is the way in which most of the revolutionaries defended 'the people' against the perceived vices of democracy. 'We the people' begins the famous first line of the Constitution, but almost everything embodied in that document was intended to hold 'the people' at bay, and to keep its supposed 'genius' or wisdom in reserve. 'We the people' meant 'We the elected and distinguished representatives of the people'. The people were seen to need firm rule. Most of the Philadelphia revolutionaries dismissed them in the language of Plato. The people were said to be too ignorant for their own good. Giving them the right to choose their own president, observed George Mason, would resemble 'a trial [test] of colours to a blind man'. The delegate who doubled as Mayor of New Haven, Roger Sherman (1721–93), the man whom Thomas Jefferson praised for never having said a foolish thing in his life, also favoured an indirectly elected president, as well as a House of Representatives elected by the state legislatures, because he considered that the people 'will never be sufficiently informed of characters' because they are 'constantly liable to be misled'.

Democracy was thus seen as the rule of the ignorant. Republics, by contrast, were thought to be best when governed by men of knowledge who kept the passions out of politics. Concerns about the hot-blooded ignorance of 'the people' – the flip side of their worship – led the revolutionaries to perform mental gymnastics, sometimes with breathtaking skill. Two interesting examples can be given. One is James Madison's recourse to the argument that only men of wisdom could decide the fundaments of government because 'the People' is a neurotic personality incapable of knowing itself. In a speech to the Constitutional Convention, he insisted that 'if the opinions of the people were to be our guide, it would be difficult to say what course we ought to take'. He continued, in a forceful manner: 'No member of the Convention could say what the opinions of his Constituents were at this time; much less could he say what they would think if possessed of the information and lights possessed by the members here; and still less what would be their way of thinking six or twelve months hence.' Madison's conclusion befitted a republican gentleman: 'We ought to consider what was right and necessary in itself.'

Gouverneur Morris's swift-footed, oft-repeated comments on the difficulties of breaking the links between democracy and oligarchy is a second case in point. The rich should be prevented from running government, he said, because they indulge the bad habit of whipping up the enthusiasm of the rest. Both the people and the rich needed to be controlled. 'We should remember that the people never act from reason alone', he warned fellow delegates at the Federal Convention. Like children, the people needed restraint, for their own good. Since the 'Rich will take advantage of their passions and make these the instruments for oppressing them', government run by republican gentlemen was vital, indeed necessary.

So one man's delight in 'the people' was evidently another's horror. For all its talk of liberty, Morris's reasoning found itself holding hands with institutions and practices that later came to have a distinctly oligarchic feel. He was not the only one. Virtually all leaders of the revolution thought in terms of the tricky political problem of how to go beyond a polity run by a monarch and a rump parliament, by building a republican form of government that kept its source of sovereignty – 'the people' – at arm's length from the levers of governmental power. This sympathetic mistrust of the people helps explain the deep anomalies within the state-building process. No united body named 'the people' called for a convention to decide post-colonial America's fate. It was in fact the work of a tiny minority of activists deliberating in their name. Those who drew up the Constitution at the Federal Convention that began in Philadelphia on Friday 25 May 1787 were delegates sent by twelve of the thirteen member states of the new polity (for reasons of principled opposition to federation, no delegates travelled from Rhode Island). They deliberated in strict secrecy. It was agreed that the Convention proceedings could not be 'printed, published, or communicated without leave', a point that James Madison raised in a letter to Thomas Jefferson in Paris a week after the Convention opened by reiterating that not 'even a confidential communication' about the issues and votes was allowed by the Convention's own rules.

Various alibis were given for secrecy. Some (like George Mason) pointed out that delegates were free agents and therefore entitled to change their opinions, which would not (or be less likely to) happen if written and publicly available records were kept. Others worried that the enemies of the Convention would take advantage of freely circulating accounts of the constitutional deliberations. Republican freedom required iron discipline. There were as well deeper prejudices against popular involvement in state making, especially the fear of 'passions most unfriendly to order and concord', as James Madison and Alexander Hamilton warned in a newspaper article that later came to be called Federalist 49.[7] Expressing hostility towards a defeated proposal to include within the new federal Constitution provision for a constitutional convention, the invention of Scottish Calvinists, the two revolutionaries reaffirmed their faith in the mantra that 'the people are the only legitimate fountain of power'. But periodic appeals to them would cheapen the reputation of government, while frequent appeals, for instance through annual elections, would be worse, they said. Such appeals would imply defects in government, so depriving it 'of that veneration which time bestows on every thing, and without which perhaps the wisest and freest governments would not possess the requisite stability'. Hamilton and Madison warned as well that 'the people' normally comprised a 'diversity of opinions on great national questions'. If they were frequently consulted, they would only speak in tongues. The 'spirit of party' would rack the young republic. With that discord would surely come 'the danger of disturbing the public tranquillity by interesting too strongly the public passions'.

The combined effect of these various arguments was to bolt down the conclusion that 'the people' would have their turn to be informed and to speak out later, during the ratification process that was to follow. That is why the constitution makers ordered the Pennsylvania State House, where they were meeting, to be guarded by sentries; and why they agreed that debates would not be officially recorded; that the official journal would show only formal motions and roll-call votes tabulated by state; and that the proceedings were to be locked away until such time as the new Constitution was ratified. Naturally, the press had to be kept well clear of the tough business of writing a constitution for four million people. George Washington, military leader turned presiding officer, angrily chided one of the delegates for absentmindedly dropping his notes on the floor of the State House. 'I must entreat Gentlemen to be more careful, lest our transactions get into the News Papers, and disturb the public repose by premature speculations', he said. James Madison, whose own notes were not published until after his death in 1840, was equally adamant that tight-lipped prudence was necessary because the press would otherwise spread divisive rumours. 'No Constitution', he later said, 'would ever have been adopted by the Convention if the debates had been public.'[8]

The rule of confidentiality fed a political culture of deference towards men of property, knowledge and civic virtue. Some of them, of course, were owners of slaves. George Washington, a Virginia plantation proprietor and lifelong slave-holder, was among those republican gentlemen who regarded themselves as spokesmen of men who were better dressed, better educated, better fed and taller than most commoners, whose manners, speech and reasoning were as rough as the skin on their grubby hands. Washington was no democrat, and wasted no words when summing up the case for deference: 'The very idea of the power and the right of the people to establish government presupposes the duty of every individual to obey the established government.'[9] This was the anthem of a political culture that came down hard on political parties. It was mistrustful or antagonistic towards 'factions' and 'party spirit' and organised civic associations in general. It feared what Madison variously called the 'rage of party', the 'violence of faction' and 'the superior force of an interested and overbearing majority'. It was even a political culture that harboured worries that the new republic would be weakened by disloyalty, or undermined by substantial social differences, for instance among the plantation owners of the Carolinas and Virginia, Dutch settlers along the Hudson, the Puritans of New England and German-speaking shopkeepers of Philadelphia. All these anxieties fed the politically triumphant 'spirit of 1776'. They help to explain why the form of government the revolutionaries built was premised on checking the growth of civil society, and filtering out popular pressures, if need be through the exercise of supreme judicial authority, backed by the threatened use of armed force.

In the name of the compound republic and its 'people', the revolutionary gentlemen of 1776 were prepared to get tough and play rough, against flesh-and-blood opponents, as they demonstrated in the events leading up to the subsequently famous ruling of the young and untested Supreme Court, known as *Marbury v. Madison*.[10] The case is particularly interesting, because it demonstrated both their power to pull strings – and their dependence on the vagaries of the institutions they had created, especially when they fell into open dispute.

For over a year before the case was heard, during the month of February 1803, an ugly showdown had loomed between Chief Justice Marshall and President Jefferson over the appointment of William Marbury as Justice of the Peace in the District of Columbia. Many observers feared the worst. Marbury was a prosperous financier gentleman from Maryland. He had been appointed to the judiciary, along with a clutch of other anti-Jefferson circuit judges and justices of the peace, by the outgoing president, John Adams, just two days before his departure from office. Comics quickly dubbed the last-minute appointees the 'Midnight Judges'. Jefferson was not pleased. So he instructed his Attorney General, Levi Lincoln, and his new Secretary of State, James Madison, to stop the patrimony and deny the appointment of Marbury, and of several others, who promptly petitioned the Court to reverse the presidential decision.

After examining the case for nearly two weeks, the Court rendered a unanimous (4–0) decision. Chief Justice Marshall, who wrote the searing opinion, stated that Marbury indeed had a right to petition the Court. That followed from the fact that the government of the United States was 'a government of laws and not of men'. He agreed with Marbury that by blocking his and other appointments of the so-called Midnight Judges, Jefferson had been wrong, and had violated 'a vested legal right'. But many republican gentlemen were about to be shocked, and taught a lesson, for Marshall surprised everyone by turning the legal tables on both Jefferson and poor Marbury, who never received his judgeship. Marshall's opinion landed a blow against all those who thought they could grab power in the name of 'the people'. Marshall reiterated that the popularly elected Congress did not have the power or the authority to modify the original jurisdiction of the Supreme Court. In plain American English, that meant that if a law passed by Congress – a law such as the 1801 Judiciary Act, passed by supporters of President Adams to enable him hurriedly to make the new appointments to the judiciary – was in conflict with the Constitution, then the Supreme Court was bound to abide by the Constitution. At a stroke of his clever quill, Marshall declared both parties in violation of the fundamental laws of the republic. 'To what purpose are powers limited, and to what purpose is that limitation committed to writing', he asked, 'if these limits may, at any time, be passed [exceeded] by those intended to be restrained?' The question was in fact an answer that pointed to a singular conclusion: if two laws conflicted with each other, the Court must decide which law applies. It must do so by upholding the Constitution before the 'laws of the United States'. When push came to shove, the Court was entitled, and had a 'judicial duty', to reaffirm the principle of judicial review – no matter what the government of the day said, or did, in the name of 'the people'.

Moonshine Men

Some loud-mouthed opponents of Jefferson's presidency did not see things in this way. One newspaper article even tried to say that the Court's decision had shown that 'Mr Jefferson, the idol of democracy, the friend of the people, had trampled upon the charter of their liberties.'[11] But the cold truth was that the opinion of Marshall was as much a blow to the efforts of republican gentlemen to stack the federal judiciary with their own men as it was to presidents claiming to represent 'the people'. *Marbury v. Madison* did not for the first time spell out the principle of judicial review, as has often been said; that principle, at least as it pertained to the laws of the member states, was already invested in the Supreme Court. What was new about *Marbury v. Madison* was the way it shored up the federal judiciary against factional fights and undue politicisation, at least for a time. It showed as well that the institutions of the new compound republic were amendable, from above, for instance through principled assertions of the independence of the federal judiciary from the executive.

Seen from below, along and up the noses of the common settlers of the United States, *Marbury v. Madison* left untouched the republican prejudice against democracy. For several decades after 1776, republicans of all description, including gentlemen as different in their political views as George Washington and James Madison, saw no contradiction between their favouritism of white men of property – men just like themselves – and their profoundly mistrustful, sometimes contemptuous respect for 'the people', whom they otherwise praised as the foundation stone of the republic. But contradictory and unsustainable their position was, as became clear during 1794, in the first big popularity test among the lower orders of the new federated republic: a dispute that centred on an organised revolt called the Whiskey Rebellion.

By the early 1790s, the American republic resembled a chrysalis, out of which the butterfly of representative democracy (and the wasp of empire) soon emerged. The catalyst that burst the chrysalis was public disaffection. In both the seaboard cities and the rural hinterlands of the republic, tens of thousands of citizens had grown disgruntled at the direction in which they felt the country to be heading, led by Federalist politicians like George Washington and Alexander Hamilton. Several scores of 'societies' or clubs sprang into action, to voice their concerns about the palpable strengthening of the federal government and the way its powers were being used and abused by the Federalists, especially to favour the well-connected and the wealthy. Among the first to appear (in April

1793) was the German Republican Society in Philadelphia. Its printed appeal to fellow citizens is worth repeating. 'In a Republican government', it said, 'the spirit of liberty, like every virtue of the mind, is to be kept alive only by constant action' by citizens. It went on to say that it was now 'high time they should step forward, declare themselves independent of other influence, and think for themselves'.[12] Calling themselves citizens, the members of such societies were men – women seemed not to exist – who were ordinary farmers, tradesmen, doctors, booksellers, churchmen and some self-made men of wealth and learning. Many thought of themselves as men of 'middling' rank who simply wanted things to be better for themselves, and for their families. Despite their considerable social differences, they commonly reasoned that periodic elections were not enough to prevent the drift away from the egalitarian spirit of 1776, and towards what many called 'aristocracy' and 'monarchy'. So their members organised public meetings, published memorials and petitions, and held street parades, very often in support of their own legal registration, which often proved difficult. The protracted battle in the town of New York of the General Society of Mechanics and Tradesmen to win local registration – which they finally managed to do in 1792 – was a case in point. One of their supporters pointedly asked why moneyed interests like the banks could so easily win registration, when master mechanics and journeymen had to wait. Another supporter, calling himself a 'Friend to Equal Rights', protested just as loudly. 'Those who assume the airs of "the well born"', he wrote, 'should be made to know that the *mechanics* of the city have *equal rights* to the merchants, and that they are as important a set of men as any in the community.'[13]

His words were the carrier of a new spirit of democracy, which was exactly the term first used openly by the good citizens of the German Republican Society in Philadelphia. The metamorphosis was a great moment in the history of democracy, an epiphany that was all the more remarkable because it came as a gift from the French. By early April 1793, shortly after the German Republicans had formed their society, details of the public execution of the French king Louis XVI had begun arriving on British packets. The news spread like a brush fire. It was fanned by the excitement sparked by the arrival of the new French minister to the United States, 'Citizen' Edmond-Charles Genêt. Whatever was subsequently said about him – many Americans found him a bombastic and duplicitous player of unsavoury ambassadorial games – he was the one who personally spearheaded a drive to rename the existing societies as supporters of 'democracy'.[14] Just imagine the palpable sense of sudden change, the glee prompted by the thought that things would never again be the same, when at the end of May 1793 the first group to do this, an umbrella organisation called the Sons of Liberty, a body that included the German Republican Society and other bilingual German Philadelphian citizens, proudly renamed itself the Democratic Society shortly after meeting the French ambassador, who was on a visit to their city.

Suddenly, within months, Democratic Societies and Democratic-Republican Societies sprang up, mostly along the eastern seaboard. It was a great victory for democracy – at least in name. The substance soon followed. It was provided by the commitment of the Democratic-Republican societies to the defence of the right of public assembly, and their right to differ publicly from the governors of the day, to say things that they did not want to hear or could not understand. Such rights had not been written into the Constitution; the anomaly stoked the fires of resentment within the societies, convincing many of their supporters that the United States was now in danger of tumbling backwards, into an 'aristocratical' abyss lorded over by proto-monarchs like George Washington. For these citizens, banded together in societies, talk of 'aristocratic democracy' – first heard in the Low Countries – was pure double Dutch. These citizens preferred instead to describe themselves using two old enemy words – republican democrats – that were now friends. Hence the singular sensitivity of these republican democrats to political arrogance – and their support for rebels willing to take on the Federalist government. Hence the societies' outright rejection of the old republican platitudes about 'factions' and 'factious spirit' – and hence the knowing smiles and riotous laughter triggered by the worn-out warnings, by James Madison and other gentlemen, that the republic was endangered by the 'mischiefs of faction' and 'spectacles of turbulence and contention'.

Civil society was about to speak, and in a loud democratic voice. The biggest outcry was undoubtedly sparked by alcohol, and specifically by the decision of Congress, backed by Treasury secretary Alexander Hamilton, to force whiskey and other spirit producers to register their stills and to pay an excise tax on the alcohol they produced. The reaction was virtually instant, as if the decision stung the tongue tips of tipplers. Public tempers flared. Moonshine men grew red in the face, and calls mounted for civil disobedience against the law.

At stake among the whiskey producers, who liked to distil their product from the surplus grain they produced, was not only an independent source of income that was vital for their survival within small commodity markets. The new law doubled their sense of exclusion from the polity. Many complained that large distillers often had to pay only half as much tax as small cash-poor distillers, who were supposed to pay in cash to a federal revenue officer based in their county. There were just as many complaints about the new form of tyranny that made them feel that they had been reduced to mere taxpayers, to subjects who were at the whim and mercy of federal tax collectors and federal court prosecutors. That is why the moonshine men picked up pitchforks and sharpened sticks, tarring brushes and guns. In the summer of 1794, in south-west Pennsylvania, federal troops scattered after protesters fired shots and burned to the ground the house and barn of the hated district tax inspector, John Neville. Seven thousand demonstrators marched through the streets of Pittsburgh. Mail deliveries were robbed. Protesters interrupted court proceedings. Tax collectors were assaulted, in one case by a group of farmers who dressed up as women, pounced on their victim, cropped his hair and coated him with tar and feathers, before riding off with his horse.

The young republic had never before witnessed organised resistance on this scale, which underscores one of the oddest features of the Whiskey Rebellion – the fact that many of the country rebels themselves professed belief in the prevailing consensus that deference towards a government of elected representatives was a basic principle of a republic. It was another of those moments in the history of democracy when actors did not quite know what they were doing – when they were in fact helping to give birth to representative democracy, as their offspring would know and cherish it. Under orders from George Washington, who publicly attacked the country rebels as an upstart mass of 'self created societies' who were operating 'under the Shade of Night' to 'destroy the government of this Country',[15] a 13,000-strong militia force moved in. It was an army as big as that which had operated against the whole of the British occupying forces. The government meant business, but the rebels cleverly scattered, and only twenty of them were arrested and put on trial in Philadelphia, charged with high treason. Two were convicted, sentenced to death by hanging, only to be pardoned by Washington, on the grounds that one was 'insane', and the other a 'simpleton'. That ended the rebellion, but the damage to an ordered republic run by elected gentlemen was palpable, and permanent.

The Whiskey Rebellion proved to be the quick beginning of the slow death of undemocratic republicanism. The rebels not merely publicly repudiated the principle of parliamentary sovereignty by practising civil disobedience against unjust laws. A special feature of the rebellion was the way various Democratic-Republican societies – formed in support of the French minister and the French Revolution he represented – rallied to the side of the rebels, some of whom were members of these clubs and who, following the fashion set in the seaboard towns and cities, proudly called themselves 'democrats'. The consequence was that the language of democracy, newly arrived from France and spoken as a gesture of solidarity with all citizens who felt dismay with the Federalist government, came to take up permanent residence within the American polity. In contrast to previous disputes within the young republic, Tom Paine's sharp, shattering attack on Silas Deane, for instance,[16] the Rebellion gave a whole new meaning to talk of 'the people'. They were no longer simply a wooden idol carved by the hands of constitution makers. They instead became flesh-and-blood citizens operating on the fringes of government, and potentially its opponents. The Whiskey Rebellion was civil dissent marching under the flag of 'democracy'. It promised the democratisation of the American republic, as the minutes of a public meeting organised by the Democratic Society of Pennsylvania spotted. 'The enemies of

Liberty and Equality have never ceased to traduce us – even certain influential and public characters have ventured to publicly condemn all political societies', its members complained. They knew what had to be done: 'If the laws of our Country are the echo of the sentiments of the people is it not of importance that those sentiments should be generally known? How can they be better understood than by a free discussion, publication and communication of them by means of political societies?'[17]

Sedition

The American dissidents of the early 1790s had a point. Men of the middling ranks who found themselves attracted to 'democratical' politics, their initiatives painted the graffito 'd' word all over the walls of the new republic. In its name, they challenged the whole spectrum of the Philadelphian republican spirit of 1776, forced it to open up to popular pressures 'from below', so accepting that the body politic contained legitimate divisions. During the course of the 1790s, it was thanks to their efforts, despite the prevailing hostility to 'faction', that America witnessed the birth of competitive political parties.

The primary division at first centred on two bitterly contested visions of the future republic. On one side of the new party divide were those who supported the strengthening of central government, the reorganisation of the agrarian order, and commercial expansion (the so-called Federalists who included men like George Washington and Alexander Hamilton). On the other side stood those, the so-called Republicans or Democratic-Republicans or Anti-Federalists, who were suspicious of both centralising government and the unrestrained accumulation of private wealth by means of unrestrained markets, essentially because they feared that governments and markets would combine to destroy the foundations of the republic.

In practice, the divisions between Federalists and Anti-Federalists or Democratic-Republicans were not always clear-cut. Although their principal differences were soon symbolised respectively by the figures of Alexander Hamilton and Thomas Jefferson, the loose clusters did not at first operate as named 'parties', with formal membership, or printed platforms. In states such as Pennsylvania, for instance, printed tickets listing candidates were illegal. Only handwritten ballots were accepted, which is one important reason why, at this delicate point in time, the young republic did not drift towards civil war.

Thomas Jefferson famously swore that if he were allowed to go to heaven accompanied by a party he would rather choose against paradise. He also insisted publicly that he was neither a Federalist nor an Anti-Federalist. And yet he and his friend James Madison secretly set about (in 1790) cultivating newspaper support for their views. It was a bold move against the prevailing consensus, a giant step in the direction of institutionalising party politics, in the sense that we now know it. At the time, the anti-party consensus was serviced by presumptions that propertied gentlemen should rule, and that legislatures were the people themselves in a state of refinement. The anti-party consensus was also lubricated by fears that an end to military conflict (with the old enemy, Britain) and the appearance of peace would bring to the surface, as Madison put it in the Federalist Number 49, 'the passions most unfriendly to order and concord'. That is why the emerging conflict between the Federalist and Republican-Democratic tendencies was so highly charged with accusations and counter-accusations of conspiracy and sedition.

The passage through Congress of loosely worded legislation designed to restrain aliens and ban sedition, during the year 1798, was thought by many Federalists to be a weapon necessary for the protection of the republic, especially because at that very moment it was waging an undeclared naval war with France. Behaving like gentlemen with a taste for power, their legislation tightened up naturalisation procedures; alien residents now had to wait fourteen (rather than five) years before becoming citizens. A system of registration and surveillance of all foreign nationals was established, and the legislation empowered the president to deport any alien considered to be a threat to what Alexander Hamilton pompously called 'national unanimity'. The legislation also banned all statements, both written and unwritten, that could be construed as bringing Congress or the president 'into contempt or disrepute'. Such breaches of public disorder were now punishable by up to five thousand dollars in fines and five years of prison.

The legislation stirred up enormous trouble. Behind the scenes, Hamilton and others began to push hard for calling in the army to quash what they considered to be a conspiracy to overthrow the Federalist government. Jefferson himself appealed for calm. Patience was required, he told a friend: 'we shall see the reign of witches pass over, their spells dissolve, and the people recovering their true sight, restore their government to it's [sic] true *principles*'.[18] But many citizens, who now thought of themselves as 'democrats', and on his side, grew alarmed at the prospects of the outlawing of opposition to the federal government. The fires were stoked by Washington's widely reported complaint to James McHenry, the Secretary of War, 'that you could as soon scrub the blackamoor [black-skinned person[19]] white, as to change the principles of a profest Democrat; and that he will leave nothing unattempted to overturn the Government of this Country'. Public controversy about the independent role of newspapers, voluntary associations and proto-parties grew more fractious, to the point where the federal election of 1800 became an almighty battle between the supporters and opponents of the legislation, of whose annulment Thomas Jefferson declared himself in favour.

His election turned out to be a cliffhanger. It was one of those moments of sublime uncertainty and visceral surprise for which representative democracy would later become famous. Thanks to yet another silence written into the Constitution, it turned out that although Jefferson and Aaron Burr, his declared running mate, had won enough votes to be elected, their appointment could not be confirmed by the election. This was because the Constitution called for the electors in each state to cast two ballots, one for their presidential choice, and one for the vice-presidency. The framers had intended that the person with the most ballots would be the president, and the runner-up the vice-president. But by the time of the 1800 election, political parties had become a fact of political life. And so it happened that voters opposed to the Federalist government of John Adams cast two ballots, one for Jefferson and one for Aaron Burr. Since the ballots were not designated 'president' and 'vice-president', the vote produced a tie between the two men: seventy-three votes each.*

As specified in the Constitution, the drama relocated to the House of Representatives, which was controlled by the Federalists, who were loath to cast their votes for Jefferson. The representatives were required to vote as states. It was one state, one vote, and, since there were sixteen states, an absolute majority – nine votes – was required for victory. There was much monkey business, and state representatives behaved in fickle ways, with most Federalist-dominated states initially voting for Burr, and all Democratic-Republican states voting for Jefferson. Vermont and Maryland cast blank ballots, thus denying Jefferson an absolute majority, by one vote. Paralysis loomed. So for seven continuous days, in an effort to break the deadlock, the House of Representatives voted thirty-five different times. Such was the mounting sense of crisis that Alexander Hamilton decided to play president maker. He said he supported Jefferson because he was 'by far not so dangerous a man' as Aaron Burr, who never forgave Hamilton for his betrayal, killing him in a private duel three years later. Finally, on Tuesday 17 February, with threats of blank ballots and disloyalty still in the air, the House voted for the thirty-sixth time. Jefferson was declared winner, with an overall majority of ten votes.

---

* For those people who are today convinced that American elections have degenerated into pure dirt and grime, it is sobering to remember how exactly this figure was achieved. Of the sixteen states of the republic, a clear majority of ten decided their candidate for president and vice-president exclusively through a vote of their state legislators. There was no involvement of 'the people'. These states included Georgia, Massachusetts, New Hampshire and Pennsylvania, whose representatives actually voted to abolish their state's existing provision for a popular vote in the matter, and to grant themselves as representatives the exclusive power to make the choice. The minority six states (Kentucky, Maryland, North Carolina, Rhode Island, Virginia and Tennessee) that did allow popular voting had widely varying property-based restrictions on male suffrage. In no state was there universal male suffrage. There was also no overall attachment by the states to simultaneous voting for the sake of fairness. Since each state was entitled to choose its own method and day of election, voting lasted from April until October 1800. With the Federalists and Democratic-Republicans tied 65–65, the South Carolina legislature, the last to deliberate, was in the lucky position of knowing that it would cast the winning votes, which it did by giving all of its votes to the Democratic-Republicans, so ensuring them a preliminary victory. Measured as electoral votes, the result was: Thomas Jefferson 73; Aaron Burr 73; John Adams 65; Charles Cotesworth Pinckney 65; and John Jay 1. The fun and games then began in Congress.

His knife-edge victory was much more than what spiritless political scientists today call a 'realigning election'. It was both a watershed in American politics and a crucial turning point in the democratisation of the modern mind, for in the history of representative democracy it represented the first ever handover of governmental power from one elected party to another elected party, without violent upheaval.

The change left locals gasping for air. Many old-fashioned European observers expected the United States to plunge into civil war, as the theory and practice of both monarchy and republicanism, with their hostility to 'faction' and 'party', had supposed it would. And it was widely anticipated at home that in his 1801 inaugural address, delivered to an invited audience seated in the new Senate Chamber of the partially constructed Capitol building, the triumphant Jefferson would stir things up. But here was a new president who in fact did the opposite. Magnanimity ruled. He held out a long and leafy olive branch to his opponents. In a remarkable paean to representative democracy, understood as a way of living peacefully with opponents for whom one has no particular love or liking, he defended the vision of a government and a civil society that were bold enough to give full play to differing principles and interests. Jefferson warned his audience that his own defective judgement was bound to produce mistakes. 'I ask your indulgence for my own errors', he said, 'which will never be intentional, and your support against the errors of others.' He went on to single out the 'sacred principle' that 'though the will of the majority is in all cases to prevail . . . the minority possess their equal rights, which equal law must protect'. He reminded his listeners that 'every difference of opinion is not a difference of principle', and neatly recalled, using different words, the motto on the great Seal of the United States: E pluribus unum ('From many, one'). 'We are all Republicans', he even claimed at one point, 'we are all Federalists.'[20]

The call for an agreement to disagree was original, and remarkably clever. Only by turning enemies into opponents and allowing people full freedom to differ could a republican democracy thrive. Here was a new precedent, something unknown to the world of assembly democracy, for in effect Jefferson was saying that political parties, no matter how bitter the electoral fight, would hereafter be expected to honour the results of elections. If they were ousted from power, they would have to accept defeat gracefully. Then they would have to wait for another chance at office, at the next poll.

Jacksonian Democracy

So began a new episode in the history of the American polity, a period defined by the spectacular electoral triumph (in 1828) of Andrew Jackson, a wealthy slave-owning cotton cropper; a tough politician who was proud of the scars on his body inflicted by his refusal as a young man to clean the boots of a British officer; a man of the people who magnified the idealised self-image of millions of Americans committed to individual enterprise and local self-determination; a military-toughened political fighter who had a gut dislike of bankers, speculators and other moneyed men, and who quickly became the most forceful president since Washington, thanks in no small measure to his use of new governing techniques, such as vetoes and pocket vetoes (the refusal to sign bills during the last ten days of a congressional session) and a Kitchen Cabinet of informal unelected advisers who could be trusted, or sacked, at will. The period that stretched from roughly 1800 through the breathtaking election of Jackson to the mid-1850s would ultimately bring the republic to the edge of civil war, but it also witnessed a number of inventions that would later set the agenda for all representative democracies. Machine-like, well-oiled political parties; the birth of national party conventions; the rowdy fun and games and paper rocks of popular elections; a flourishing civil society that fostered self-consciously democratic forms of art and literature, as well as a powerful anti-slavery movement that helped large numbers of women find their public voice for the first time: so profound were these innovations that quite a few contemporary observers, some of them with an eye on fifth-century Athens, claimed that the nineteenth century was a century of democracy, with America acting as its driving force. The seventh edition of the *Encyclopaedia Britannica* noted in 1842 that the government of the United States was among 'the best and wisest in the world' and currently 'the most perfect example of democracy'. The observation was not wrong, though the reasoning was suspect, and certainly too brief.

Especially after the War of 1812, the years of the nineteenth century were indeed to be America's when it came to the expansion and revaluation of representative democracy. While people on other continents (as we shall see) would make important contributions, the new republic of the United States impressively demonstrated that representative government could be democratised and its seeds sown so widely that crops of democratic rights and duties could be harvested, for the first time in the modern world, on a continental scale, by growing numbers of people. The effect was to reinforce the sense among many observers that both geography and history had come between Europe and America; while America was in its origins an offshoot of Europe dominated by European peoples, representative democracy in the New World was seen to have made an epochal difference. The past was Europe. America was the sharp cutting edge of the modern. Europe was the old; the new was the death of the old. America was the great escape, the grand adventure. 'Sail, sail thy best, ship of Democracy ... Earth's *résumé* entire floats on thy keel', wrote the period's greatest poet, Walt Whitman (1819–92), in a prayer that dramatised his and many other Americans' love for the potential of their own country (Figure 43).[21]

FIGURE 43: A defiant Walt Whitman, July 1854, from a steel engraving by Samuel Hollyer based on the original (now lost) daguerreotype by Gabriel Harrison.

Its mission was to throw off the shackles of a cramping past bound by inequality, war, snobbery and other evils. America – democratic, looking with optimism towards the future, not sullenly at the past – implied the repudiation of Europe.

Quite a few political inventions altered the landscape of American politics during this period. Of great consequence was the birth of party competition for voters' support. The roots of such competition extended back in time, to the other side of the Atlantic. There, early modern party systems developed slowly, against great political odds, and despite widespread hostility to their allegedly factious and seditious effects. Their birth dated only from the early years of the eighteenth century. Their growth, exemplified by the small parties that took shape in the House of Commons in England during the long reign of George III, was linked with the resistance to despotism and the growth of representative government. At first they assumed, as Edmund Burke put it, the form of 'honorable connections' of gentlemen whose role was to criticise, restrain or support ministers of state in the name of dominant class power groups of the young civil society. Until the early nineteenth century, these fledgling parties comprised loosely organised groupings of the parliamentary representatives of the aristocratic and bourgeois classes. Positioned exclusively in the legislature, they neither engaged in open electoral competition nor solicited members outside the chamber. Nor did they discipline themselves by means of party rules and regulations.

The rise of open party competition in the United States changed all this, but progress towards its acceptance was slow. Well after the peaceful handover of the presidency to Jefferson, official hostility towards would-be party representatives, described by Gouverneur Morris as 'brawlers, who make popularity their trade',[22] remained strong. The fears generated by the build-up to the War of 1812 against the British served to stifle divisions as political figures across the spectrum appealed for unity under the flag. Self-deprecation and disdain for party politics flourished, and to a degree that is almost unimaginable today. Service within the state legislatures was widely seen to be corrupting of character, while most legislators complained of loss of privacy. Things were perceived to be no better in the capital, Washington. It felt both geographically and emotionally distant from most citizens, and its famed ramshackle buildings, mud and mosquitoes seemed to breed self-contempt among politicians. Thick skins were needed for the job, John Quincy Adams (the son of President John Adams) famously warned, because politicians were targets of 'perpetual and malignant watchfulness' that had only one malignant aim: to savage them by means of 'public obloquy or public ridicule'.[23]

The remark captured a perennial refrain that survives even today within American politics: that politics is not exactly a legitimate vocation because politicians and their parties are rogues who should never be trusted fully. With hindsight, the anti-party sentiment was essential for the growth of representative government, in which the systematic reliance upon elected representatives was premised upon their periodic and regular removal from office. Representative government was thought of as humble government, as a new way of creating public space for dissenting minorities and open competition for power, which in turn enabled elected representatives to test their political competence and leadership skills, in the presence of electors armed with the power, on election day, to throw paper rocks. That was the whole point of periodic elections: if elected representatives were always saints then elections would simply lose their point.

One thing that is interesting about America during the first half of the nineteenth century is the way that scepticism about party politics combined dialectically with active support for its methods. Public meetings held to discuss and to pass resolutions, and to express support for candidates, spread fast through the young republic. The fashion swept up even those Federalists who had previously opposed the trend; having failed to stem the tide of party politics, they chose to launch their boats. Parties organised town committees, whose work included luring the undecided by hosting clambakes, barbecues and fish fries and personally visiting prospective voters on the eve of elections. Party committees were organised as well at the county, district and state levels where, in anticipation of the later system of primary elections, legislative candidates were chosen using the old Scottish principle of conventions, now applied in secular form, often on an annual basis. Stump orators called 'spellbinders', travelling from town to town and let loose on assemblies of curious voters, then did their job, backed by what in the 1840s party men called 'the Chinese business': marching clubs, orchestras, flag-raising ceremonies, fireworks, chowder parties, winter balls, summer excursions, street-corner hand shaking, cavalcades of uniformed party supporters riding on horseback, sporting party buttons.

These inventions breathed new meaning into an old English word that once meant a deliberative assembly, or council: party campaigners and candidates set about wooing supporters through meetings called hustings (a name derived from the Old Norse: *hústhing*: household assembly held by a leader; from *hús* (house) and *ting* (assembly, parliament)). One effect of the hustings was to stretch the cycle of election campaigning. Federalists meanwhile cultivated the practice of serving up lavish helpings of cherry pie in memory of George Washington on his birthday (22 February). All parties seized on Independence Day (4 July), which had not been regularly celebrated during the 1790s, as the country's prime holiday. Americans were reminded of their duties to take an interest in public affairs, and to vote, and not surprisingly the hustings had another effect: it widened the circles of potential voters. Growing demands for extending the franchise ensured that by 1824 every state of the republic had granted the vote to virtually all white male adults (that did not happen until 1867 in Britain). The American republic had shrugged off the old monarchist and republican fear of factions. It gave birth, for the first time anywhere in the world, to full-time parties and full-time politicians.

Martin Van Buren, who served as the eighth president of the republic, between 1837 and 1841, was a prominent symbol of this change. Bright red hair, standing only five feet and a couple of inches, always impeccably dressed in a long-tailed coat and matching ruffles, he was the first American president to have been born on American soil, of non-British parents, in the small town of Kinderhook, New York (Figure 44). Those who knew him liked to say that he was the first true American president. The son of a Dutch tavern keeper and small farmer, he was also the first of a breed of full-time politicians who had no ties with the military campaigns and constitution writing of the gentleman republicans. After studying law, he fell into the thickets of New York state

FIGURE 44: 'The Little Magician', Martin Van Buren: salted paper portrait by the New York photographer Mathew B. Brady, who disguises his subject's small size by recalling (in 1855) his former prominence as an American president.

politics, becoming a member of the state Senate in 1812. Political survival quickly became his vocation. He lived for politics. He cut his political teeth as a leading organiser of the 'Bucktail' Republicans, a ginger group made up of shrewd party men who worked for greater organisational discipline within their faction-ridden, personality-dominated state party. These suave, well-dressed men knew that there was no 'iron law' of oligarchy within political parties, and that whatever coherence and leadership they enjoyed had to be worked for, by party workers. Dubbed the 'Albany Regency', their apparatus became famous, and notorious, as the prototypical political machine, using caucuses and patronage to control its ranks by rewarding loyalty and votes with political promotion.

In the wider American political scene, the group was a force to be reckoned with. It affiliated with the national Democratic Party led by Andrew Jackson, and backed his successful bid for the presidency in 1828. The new president promptly rewarded Van Buren by appointing him Secretary of State, which he used as a ladder to the vice-presidency. The reward was a mark of respect for the way Van Buren had skilfully cultivated a support system of Democratic

Party activists who distributed handbills and party tickets to houses, and organised horses and carriages to whisk supporters from home to polling place; once Jackson had been elected, Van Buren also helped dish out federal jobs for the party faithful, a new 'spoils system' that he claimed was perfectly 'democratic' because it proved that ordinary American citizens could become administrators, and that there was no need for a permanent class of parasitic civil servants.

The 'Little Magician' was one of his nicknames. Van Buren campaigned with gusto. Convinced that organisation was the secret of victory, he was blessed with the knack of cultivating party enthusiasts, like the 'Hurra Boys', who honoured Andrew Jackson's nickname 'Old Hickory' by handing out tough, heavy hickory sticks at campaign rallies organised by the Democratic Party. Van Buren, who sometimes followed suit by using the name of 'Old Kinderhook', loved the rough and tumble of public meetings. Quite generous with his opponents, he could play dirty when necessary. He was certainly not averse to contacting journalists behind the scenes, to convince them to write positive pieces about the Democratic Party. He cherished the virtues of hard work, patience, and laughter and solidarity with equals. He was not especially charismatic, and not an outstanding orator. That did not harm his political career, because he was far more the party operator using thoroughly modern methods based on the thoroughly modern belief that political parties were vital for representative democracy. He was convinced that parties resembled power machines. They served as good means of fastening different groups of citizens to the governing institutions of their republic; in that way, parties made those same institutions more publicly accountable for their actions to the representatives organised by parties. Party conventions – as opposed to backroom caucuses in legislatures – also gave people a say in the business of choosing leaders and making policies. But the inverse was also true: party machines could manipulate conventions and better empower governments to get on with the business of governing, to get things done that might otherwise cause great strife, or that might never otherwise happen. If they failed in that aim, then their electoral supporters would reject them. Governing parties would then humble themselves, by resigning, so allowing their opponents to operate their own power machine, for a time.

Van Buren was to have his share of ups and downs in the splintery world of American party machine politics, at its highest levels. His rapid rise to the presidency, following his unanimous nomination at the Democratic convention in Baltimore in May 1835, and his victory in the next year's elections, gave him a taste of his own medicine, which he drank with grace. By now balding, but sporting bright red mutton chops, he announced his intention 'to follow in the footsteps of his illustrious predecessor'. But things went rather badly for Van Buren, who learned from first-hand experience that representative democracy was deeply dependent upon regional security arrangements, and upon the fickle dynamics of market economies. During his presidency, British-Canadian government forces actually crossed over on to American soil, triggering a wave of anti-British sentiment. Far more serious was the government and Democratic Party wrangling triggered by an economic crisis that bit American society badly during Van Buren's first year of office. Quickly ridiculed as Martin Van Ruin, he failed to win a second term of office. Yet his peaceful defeat in 1841 by General William Henry Harrison, the Whig candidate, bequeathed both a large and a small legacy to the world of representative democracy.

The big gift was the replicable model of the tightly disciplined political party, hungry for governmental power. The small gift took the form of two little words that would later enjoy global popularity. During their 1840 bid for re-election, Van Buren's supporters found themselves up against snappy tactics used by William Henry Harrison and his Whig party machine. They hurled sarcastic abuse at Van Buren, who was dubbed not only the 'Little Magician' and 'Martin Van Ruin', but less salubrious names, like 'King Martin the First' and (reminding voters of his remaining red hair and cunning) 'the Kinderhook Fox'. The supporters of Harrison came up with 'Tippecanoe' for their candidate, a reminder of the place, in a wooded area a few miles north of Lafayette, Indiana, where he had commanded a military victory over Native Americans, who subsequently lost their grip on the fertile mid-Western lands they had roamed for several thousands of years. Harrison's running mate was John Tyler, so the whole Whig campaign was easily oiled by a slogan that doubled as a short and simple ditty: 'Tippecanoe and Tyler too!' With their backs to the electoral wall, Van Buren's campaign workers invented a good reply. Drawing upon the old Choctaw word 'okeh', they came up with the idea that the image of 'Old Kinderhook' could be improved by setting up the Democratic 'O.K. Club'. Those two letters, meaning that Van Buren was all right or 'oll korrect' by the Democrats, quickly spread across the country, later to become a slang term used by people in virtually every society on earth to express approval of somebody, or something.

Civil Society

That was some victory for the Choctaw, and for representative democracy. But the special importance of this period, something that marked a radical break with the world of assembly democracy, Islam included, was the way that early nineteenth-century American party activists and supporters supposed that the body politic was irrevocably split, and that the division between governmental and non-governmental institutions was on balance a good thing, if only because freedom required the imposition of checks upon the daily misadventures of governments and government officials.

Think of it this way. The new political parties were engaged in an odd but necessary, richly conflicted but useful exercise. Their job was to break up the polity into its constituent parts, to protect and nurture its subdivision through efforts to bind (some) citizens to government, and to do so by protecting them against arbitrary interference, thus providing them with leverage over its institutions and policies. The whole principle of open party competition supposed that citizens themselves had different interests and preoccupations, and that periodically they needed to combine themselves into meaningful 'aggregates'. Parties required and supposed (to speak in the language of the day) a 'civilised society' comprising independent 'societies' – large numbers of them, even.

By mid-century, millions of Americans, ignoring Washington's strictures against self-created societies, actively participated in clubs and voluntary organisations of many different kinds. These associations were nurseries where the etiquette of democratic self-organisation was learned. Taking a leaf from the book written by the founders of the republic, these organisations wrote their own bylaws and constitutions, and elected their own officers, according to the rules of representative democracy. Sometimes they created state-wide organisations that held annual conventions to decide matters of strategy, goals and leadership. Volunteer fire companies sprang up in cities and towns, for instance. Banks owned and run by citizens were chartered by states to service clients who previously depended for credit on the personal generosity or whims of individual merchants.

For those who could read, independent points of view and stories were put into circulation, despite political opposition and barriers of money and geography, by hundreds of printers, bookshops and newspapers, like the *Poughkeepsie Journal* and the *Boston Weekly Advertiser* (founded in 1811 by James Cutler, for readers who could not afford daily newspapers). Artisans of every description, whether coopers, tailors, hatters, bakers, masons, printers, shipwrights or butchers, formed themselves into voluntary associations. By the 1830s, working men had followed suit; some of them saw the need to shed their old shell of deference and form their own political parties. There were even federation-wide civil associations. Mimicking the path-breaking tactics of much earlier bodies like the Cincinnati, a pro-Federalist society of ex-army officers that had agitated to raise funds in support of the widows and children of those killed during the Revolutionary War, these federal associations defended the principle of freedom of civil association. They paid more than lip service to such values as the right of petition, which they understood as a form of voting between elections, to social decency and justice, and to solidarity of citizens across state borders, on a continental scale. Their activities implied a form of 'federalism from below', as was evident in the huge growth during this period of middle-class temperance organisations. The biggest of these was undoubtedly the American Temperance Society, which by 1835 claimed more than 8000 auxiliaries and 1.5 million members, about one-fifth of the free adult population of the republic.

The temperance societies mostly had their roots and power base in the New England Puritan tradition, but their style and message had continental effects. Not only were their efforts decisive in the formation of the Whig Party by Henry Clay and others in 1832; they worked as well to build new institutions, like schools and Sunday Schools, libraries, bible societies, colleges, orphanages and asylums. They also spread the good news of the gospel through charity work for the deaf and petitioning in the taverns. They publicly grilled candidates of the leading parties and despatched missionaries to the 'frontier' communities of such states as Ohio and Vermont. The core activists were evidently middle-class and backward-looking in their concerns about the moral degradation of the republic. Yet the most striking and thoroughly ironic fact is that they proved to be the driving force behind the acceptance of non-governmental bodies that was central to the protracted religious upsurge that swept America during this period: the so-called Second Great Awakening.

While this Christianisation did more to reinforce the religious instincts of the society than anything before or possibly since, it had profoundly democratic effects within the emergent civil society and its churches. Within the non-governmental sphere of civil associations, rebel Baptists, Mormons, Methodists and others offered common people, especially the poor, compelling visions of individual self-respect, public organisation and collective confidence. Preachers within America's churches reciprocated by offering what they thought commoners wanted. They gave them down-to-earth doctrines, unpretentious leaders, singable music and local churches in local hands. Some observers trembled at the 'enthusiasm' with which the standard Christian tenets were preached from the pulpit, yet the fact remained that the Second Great Awakening, like the earthquake of Methodism in Britain a generation earlier, rocked the foundations of the established structures of religious authority. Worship came to be associated instinctively with ordinary folk, rather than the clergy as a separate order of men. That exaltation of the vernacular in word and song called into question doctrinal orthodoxy. It brought frowns to the faces of respectable churchmen, especially when they heard news of figures like Lorenzo Dow, the highly intelligent, fellow-travelling Methodist who travelled

FIGURE 45: Lorenzo Dow and the 'Jerking Exercise'.

more miles, preached to more people and consistently attracted larger
audiences to camp meetings than any other preacher of the period
(Figure 45).

Dow's career provides an interesting example of the eccentric
ways in which egalitarian virtues were nurtured in the young democratic republic. In 1804, Dow set the pace for fellow believers by
barnstorming through the country, speaking at between five hundred and eight hundred meetings, often beginning his sermons with
quotations from his fellow deist Tom Paine. Dow poured scorn on
inequalities of wealth. He railed variously at tyranny, at priestcraft,
and at the professions of law and medicine. Most who encountered
'Crazy Lorenzo Dow', as his critics called him, agreed that he was
the most astonishing preacher they had ever heard. He talked the
rights of man and looked like John the Baptist. For him democracy
did not mean 'I am as good as you are'. It meant instead something
like: 'You are as good as I am.' This made Dow a popular figure

among commoners, but his magnetism had as much to do with his roguish clothes, weather-beaten face, long reddish Jesus beard, hair parted down the middle like a woman's, flashing eyes, crude gestures and rasping voice. His sermons were spellbinding theatrical performances. He often made dramatic last-minute public appearances at venues arranged months earlier. He told hilarious jokes, smashed chairs on the floor for effect, moved his listeners to tears, even divining them into states of religious ecstasy, neck-dislocating spasms known as 'the jerking exercise'. Often picking on well-known sinners and alleged murderers and thieves in the audience, Dow refused to kowtow to any established church structure, least of all to the Methodist authorities, which held back from openly curtailing his movements, for fear of inflating his great popularity. The whole point for him was that religion was for the people, who had the right to assemble publicly to express themselves as people, regardless of what politicians, parties and judges said, or whether they tried to frustrate their wishes by having them arrested.

The Aristocrat

The slow fermentation of democratic spirit within significant sections of the American population was palpable. The ethos of equality with liberty guaranteed by elections was inscribed in their simple body language, tobacco-chewing habits and easy manners, their bold dreams and high expectations, their self-consciously democratic art and literature – for instance, Walt Whitman's *Leaves of Grass* (1855), a celebration of the potential boundlessness of the American experiment with democracy and of the power of the poet to rupture conventional language, and the greatest of all nineteenth-century American novels, Hermann Melville's *Moby-Dick* (1851), a tale that warned against the hubris and self-destruction that awaits all those who act as if the world contains no boundaries, rules or moral limits.

The growth of an open, experimental society, a political order that was defined by daringly egalitarian instincts, was noted by many observers, among them the young French aristocrat, Alexis de Tocqueville (1805–59). In 1831, for nine short months, the twenty-six-year-old Tocqueville travelled through the United States, to make up his own mind about representative democracy. He went almost everywhere. Like a determined tourist, he rode on steamboats (one of which sunk), sampled the local cuisine and stayed in log cabins. He found time for research and for rest, and for conversation, despite his imperfect English, with useful or prominent Americans, among them John Quincy Adams, Andrew Jackson and Daniel Webster. Setting out from New York, he travelled upstate to Buffalo, then through the frontier, as it was then called, to Michigan and Wisconsin. He sojourned two weeks in Canada, from where he descended to Boston, Philadelphia and Baltimore. Next he went west, to Pittsburgh and Cincinatti; then south to Nashville, Memphis and New Orleans; then north through the south-eastern states to the capital, Washington; and at last back to New York, where he returned by packet to Le Havre, France.

At the beginning of his journey, in New York, where he resided from 11 May for some six weeks, Tocqueville was openly hesitant about this bustling market society whose system of representative government was still in its infancy. 'Everything I see fails to excite my enthusiasm', he wrote in his journal, 'because I attribute more to the nature of things than to human will.' He was still seemingly under the influence of the political false starts of his native France. But Tocqueville, the slightly built son of a count from Normandy – the Château de Tocqueville still stands, within sight of the harbour of Cherbourg – was soon to change his mind. Sometime during his stay in Boston (7 September–3 October 1831), Tocqueville became a convert of the American way of life. He began to talk of 'a great democratic revolution'[24] now sweeping the world from its American heartlands. He became convinced that 'the time was coming' when representative democracy would triumph in Europe, as it was doing in America. The future was America. It was therefore imperative to understand its strengths and weaknesses, he thought. On 12 January 1832, just before boarding his packet for France, he sketched plans to bring to the French public a work about democracy in America. 'If royalists could see the internal functioning of this well-ordered republic', he wrote, 'the deep respect its people profess for their acquired rights, the power of those rights over crowds, the religion of law, the real and effective liberty people enjoy, the true rule of the majority, the easy and natural way things proceed, they would realise that they apply a single name to diverse forms of government which have nothing in common. Our republicans would feel that what we have called the Republic was never more than an unclassifiable monster . . . covered in blood and mud, clothed in the rages of antiquity's quarrels.'

Tocqueville proceeded with his plans. The two-volume *De la démocratie en Amérique* (1835–40) that resulted is still regarded, justifiably, as one of the great books on the subject, as a classic, in part because at a crucial moment in the democratic experiment in America he put his finger on several sources of its dynamism. Tocqueville was certainly impressed by its 'civil society' (what he called *société civile*). He found the new republic brimming with many different forms of civil association, and he pondered their importance for consolidating democracy. Tocqueville likened these associations to schools of public spirit, permanently open to all, within which citizens become acquainted with others, learn their rights and duties as equals, and press home their concerns, sometimes in opposition to government, so preventing the tyranny of minorities by majorities through the ballot box. He noted that these civil associations were small-scale affairs, and yet, within their confines, individual citizens regularly 'socialise' themselves by raising their concerns beyond their selfish, tetchy, narrowly private goals. Through their participation in civil associations, they come to feel that they are *citizens*. They draw the conclusion that in order to obtain others' support, they must often lend them their cooperation, as equals.

Tocqueville's descriptions of America are interesting in many ways, especially because they show, at a poignant moment in the nineteenth century, just how some people's thinking about representative democracy had become self-conscious of its novelty. Tocqueville called upon his readers to understand representative democracy as a brand-new type of self-government defined not just by elections, parties and government by representatives, but also by the extensive use of civil society institutions that prevent political despotism by placing a limit, in the name of equality, upon the scope and power of government itself. Tocqueville also pointed out that these civil associations had radical social implications. The 'great democratic revolution' that was under way in America showed that it was the enemy of assumed privileges in all spheres of life. American society was democratic, not aristocratic. Proof of this lay in the way representative democracy was undermining various inequalities inherited from old Europe, showing that they were neither necessary nor desirable. Further proof was provided by a trend that was even more remarkable: the spreading passion for the equalisation of power, property and status among people, who come to feel that current inequalities are purely contingent, and so potentially alterable by human action itself.

Tocqueville was fascinated by this trend towards equalisation. In the realm of law and government, he noted, everything tends to dispute and uncertainty. The grip of sentimental tradition, absolute morality and religious faith in the power of the divine weakens. Growing numbers of Americans consequently look upon the power of politicians and governments with a jealous eye. They are prone to suspect or curse those who wield it, and thereby they are impatient with arbitrary rule. Government and its laws gradually lose their divinity. They come to be regarded as simply expedient for this or that purpose, and as properly based on the voluntary consent of citizens endowed with equal civil and political rights. The spell of absolute monarchy is forever broken. Political rights are extended gradually from the lucky privileged few to those who once suffered discrimination; and government policies and laws are subject constantly to public grumbling, legal challenges and alteration.

Thanks to representative democracy, something similar happens in the field of social life, or so Tocqueville proposed. The American democracy is subject to a permanent 'social revolution'. Himself a self-confessed sentimental believer in the old patriarchal principle that 'the sources of a . . . woman's happiness are in the home of her husband', Tocqueville nevertheless pointed to a profound change in the relationship between the sexes in American society. Representative democracy gradually destroys or modifies 'that great inequality of man and woman, which has appeared hitherto to be rooted eternally in nature'. The more general point he wanted to make is that under democratic conditions people's definitions of social life as 'natural' are progressively replaced by self-consciously chosen arrangements that favour equality. Democracy speeds up the 'de-naturing' of social life. It becomes subject to something like a permanent democratisation. This is how: if certain social groups defend their privileges, of property or income, for instance, then pressure grows for extending those privileges to other social groups. 'And why not?' the protagonists of equality ask, adding in the same breath: 'Why should the privileged be treated as if they were different, or better?' After each new practical concession to the principle of equality, new demands from those who are socially excluded force yet further concessions from the privileged. Eventually the point is reached where the social privileges enjoyed by a few are redistributed, in the form of *universal* social entitlements.

That at least was the theory. On the basis of his travels and observations, Tocqueville predicted that American democracy would in future have to confront a fundamental dilemma. Put at its simplest, it was this. If privileged Americans try, in the name of such and such a principle, to restrict social and political privileges to a few, then their opponents will be tempted to organise themselves, for the purpose of pointing out that such and such privileges are by no means 'natural', or God-given, and are therefore an open embarrassment to democracy. Democratic mechanisms, said Tocqueville, stimulate a passion for social and political equality that they cannot easily satisfy. The struggle for equalisation never comes to an end. 'This complete equality slips from the hands of the people at the very moment when they think they have grasped it and flies, as Pascal says, an eternal flight.'

The less powerful ranks of society, including those without the vote, are especially caught in the grip of this dynamic, Tocqueville thought. Irritated by the fact of their subordination, agitated by the possibility of overcoming their condition, they easily grow frustrated by the uncertainty of achieving equality. Their initial enthusiasm and hope give way to disappointment, but at some point the frustration they experience renews their commitment to the struggle for equality. This 'perpetual movement of society' fills the world of American democracy with the questioning of absolutes, with radical scepticism about inequality, and with an impatient love of experimentation, with new ways of doing things, for the sake of equality. America found itself caught up in a democratic maelstrom. Nothing is certain or inviolable, except the passionate, dizzying struggle for social and political equality. 'No sooner do you set foot upon American soil than you are stunned by a type of tumult', reported Tocqueville, stung by the same excitement. 'A confused clamour is heard everywhere, and a thousand voices simultaneously demand the satisfaction of their social needs. Everything is in motion around you', he continued. 'Here the people of one town district are meeting to decide upon the building of a church; there the election of a representative is taking place; a little farther on, the delegates of a district are hastening to town in order to consult about some local improvements; elsewhere, the labourers of a village quit their ploughs to deliberate upon a road or public school project.' He concluded: 'Citizens call meetings for the sole purpose of declaring their disapprobation of the conduct of government; while in other assemblies citizens salute the authorities of the day as the fathers of their country, or form societies which regard drunkenness as the principal cause of the evils of the state, and solemnly pledge themselves to the principle of temperance.'

At Sword's Point

The prose was charming, but many observers have spotted that in passages like this Tocqueville exaggerated the momentum and geographic extent of the busy levelling process that was under way in America. He had a remarkable sixth sense of probing the difference between appearances and realities, but when looking at life in the United States he seems sometimes to have swallowed whole its own best self-image. He wasn't the only nineteenth-century visitor to be seduced by the charms of the new democracy. Consider the Italian fashion of visiting the new democratic republic, to see what it was like.[25] 'Hurrah to you, oh great Country!' wrote one traveller, shortly after Tocqueville had published his great work. 'The United States is a free land, essentially because its sons drink together the milk of respect for each other's opinions ... This is what makes them beautiful, and their air more easily breathable for us who are thirsty for freedom from old Europe, where the liberties we have gained with so much blood and pain have for the most part been suffocated by our mutual intolerance.' Another Italian traveller expressed similar excitement. 'Ah, this is the democracy that I love, that I dream of and yearn for', he wrote, contrasting it with the 'presumption and snobbishness' guarded back home by the 'people of high rank'. The same visitor was struck by the way American citizens casually wore caps and hats, how they spurned moustaches, chewed tobacco and liked to chew the fat, hands in pockets. 'Simple people, simple furniture, simple greetings', he wrote, adding that Americans 'extend you their hand, ask you what you need, and quickly respond'. Still another visitor brimmed with exuberance. 'There is no lying by officials. Truth, always truth. No prejudices, no red tape. From every street corner come the cries of a people intoxicated with hope and immortal charity: "Forward! Forward!".' He added a modest prediction: 'Just as Rome impressed the seal of its laws and its cosmopolitan culture on the old world of the Mediterranean, and Romanised Christianity, so the federated democracy of the United States will prove to be the guiding model for the next political phase of humanity.'

Tocqueville was less sanguine. Many of his observations were both astute and prescient, for instance concerning the dangers of the rise, from within the heart of the new civil society, of capitalist manufacturing industry and a new social power group (an 'aristocracy', as Tocqueville called them) of industrial manufacturers whose power of control over capital threatens the freedom, pluralism and equality so essential for representative democracy. With good reason, he worried as well about the decline of public spirit within this class. He was particularly exercised by its tendency to pursue wealth for the sake of wealth and, hence, its bad habits of the heart, like cupidity and selfishness, its possessive individualism and narrow-minded cunning. The possibility that the middle classes might turn against the fledgling democratic republic was palpable, but it was distant, at least when compared to what Tocqueville understood to be by far the biggest and most immediate danger to representative democracy: the institution of slavery.

Tocqueville was the first writer to show that representative democracy could not live with slavery, as classical assembly-based democracy had managed to do, admittedly with some discomfort. He highlighted how the 'calamity' of slavery had resulted in a terrible subdivision of social and political life.[26] Black people in America were neither in nor of civil society; they were objects of gross incivility. Legal and informal penalties against racial intermarriage were severe. In those states where slavery had been abolished, black people who dared to vote, or to serve on juries, were threatened with their lives. There was segregation and deep inequality in education. 'In the theatres gold cannot procure a seat for the servile race beside their former masters; in the hospitals they lie apart; and although they are allowed to invoke the same God as the whites, it must be at a different altar and in their own churches, with their own clergy.' Prejudice even haunted the dead. 'When the Negro dies, his bones are cast aside, and the distinction of condition prevails even in the equality of death.'

Lurking within these customs was a disturbing paradox. The prejudice directed at black people, Tocqueville noted, increases in proportion to their formal emancipation. Slavery in America was in this sense much worse than in ancient Greece, where the emancipation of slaves was encouraged by the fact that their skin colour was often the same as that of their masters. Both within and outside the institutions of American slavery, by contrast, blacks were made to suffer terrible bigotry, 'the prejudice of the master, the prejudice of the race, and the prejudice of color', a prejudice that drew strength from false talk of the 'natural' superiority of whites. Such bigotry cast a long shadow over the future of American democracy, to the point where it now seemed to be faced not only with the unpalatable options of retaining slavery or organised bigotry, but also with the outbreak of 'the most horrible of civil wars'. Tocqueville's political forecast was understandably gloomy: 'Attacked by Christianity as unjust and by political economy as prejudicial, and now contrasted with democratic liberty and the intelligence of our age, slavery cannot survive. By the act of the master, or by the will of the slave, it will cease; and in either case great calamities may be expected to ensue. If liberty be refused to the Negroes of the South, they will in the end forcibly seize it for themselves; if it be given, they will long abuse it.'[27]

Tocqueville's white-skinned suspicion of black people should be noted, as should his accurate observation of the profound contradiction between slavery and representative democracy. He was right as well to be anxious about the magnitude of the problem. By 1820, at least ten million African slaves were brought to the New World. Some 400,000 came to North America, but their numbers had multiplied rapidly, to the point where all the states south of the Mason-Dixon line were slave societies, in the full sense of the term. Even in New England, where there were comparatively few slaves, the economy was rooted in the slave trade with the West Indies. Afro-Americans did the hard and dirty work of the democratic republic. They cleared forests, turned the soil, planted and tended and harvested the exportable crops that brought great prosperity to the slave-owning classes. So successful was the system of slavery that after 1819 Southern politicians and landowners and their supporters within the federal government agitated for its universal adoption. As a mode of production, and as a whole way of life, slavery went on the warpath, as Abraham Lincoln made clear in his not inaccurate claim that Slave Power was hellbent on taking over the whole country, North as well as South.

The aggressiveness of Slave Power during the 1820s and 1830s disturbed the dreams of some Americans; it forced them to conclude that the American polity required a refounding. Reasoning with their democratic hearts, they spotted that slavery was incompatible with the ideals of free and equal citizenship. These same opponents of slavery were to some degree aware of a contradiction that lurked within the contradiction. The problem, simply put, was whether or not the abolition of slavery could be done democratically, that is, by peaceful means such as petitioning and decisions by Congress, or whether military force would be needed to defeat slavery's defenders.

Slavery posed new questions that had been skilfully organised out of party politics during the gentlemanly and Jacksonian episodes of democracy in America. At the Federal Convention, for instance, Madison had spoken plainly in favour of quashing the subject. He noted that 'the real difference of interests lay, not between the large and small but between the Northern and Southern States'. Slavery formed a 'line of discrimination' that had to be erased from the debates about the shape of the new polity because it might otherwise wreck its chances of survival.[28] In the context, that proved to be a winning argument and it helps explain why the new Constitution contained a great silence about slavery – and why the decision was taken to create a Senate in which states were represented, so guaranteeing that slavery in the South would be untouchable, simply because until the middle of the nineteenth century it commanded a majority of votes in the upper chamber.

The clever resolution of the major row that erupted in Congress by the admission (in 1820) of Missouri to the Union represented a continuation of the political efforts to ensure that slavery was a non-issue. The Missouri Compromise did the trick. Since the admission of the state of Missouri to the federation threatened to upset the even division of the Senate between eleven free states and eleven slave states, a new, free state of Maine was carved from the north-eastern counties of Massachusetts. Fresh guidelines covering future admissions were accepted, on terms agreeable to the South. Questions about the future of slavery were shelved by declaring a great swathe of land in the Great Plains called the 'Unorganised Territories' as off-limits for slavery, for the time being. Constitutional engineering of this kind was clever, and it showed that the art of compromise was essential oil needed for the smooth operation of the gears of government in a republican democracy. Yet the effectiveness of the Missouri Compromise was limited, as Thomas Jefferson (himself the owner of nearly two hundred slaves and father of children with a slave) foresaw in his accurate prediction that the compromise was a bad compromise that would stir up trouble and lead, eventually, to the destruction of the federation, at sword's point. He likened the Missouri Compromise to 'a fire bell in the night' that awakened and filled him with fear. 'I considered it at once as the knell of the Union. It is hushed, indeed, for the moment. But this is a reprieve only, not a final sentence. A geographical line, coinciding with a marked principle, moral and political, once conceived and held up to the angry passions of men, will never be obliterated; and every new irritation will mark it deeper and deeper.'[29] The point for Jefferson was straightforward: it was one thing to pass government resolutions to keep the lid on slavery. It was quite another to prevent public resistance to slavery from within a vibrant civil society that contained growing numbers of citizens who found slavery sickened their stomachs, simply because in their hearts they cherished the universal values of equality and freedom.

For a time, the main political parties effectively fudged the issue. Throughout the 1830s, the Whigs (the party formed in opposition to the policies of the Democrats) certainly contributed to the camouflage. So did their opponents, led by Jackson and Van Buren, whose political campaigns consistently forced them to cultivate Southern support, so frustrating efforts to inject the issue into federal politics. Van Buren's high-wire act was typical. His resort to the argument that slavery was undesirable, but that it could not be abolished without the consent of the slave owners, worked in their favour, and his. That was why, throughout the 1830s, he denied the right of Congress to abolish slavery in the District of Columbia without the agreement of the slave states; and why he supported legislation that regulated the circulation through the post of abolitionist materials according to the different laws of the several states. It was also why he stood behind the infamous Gag Rule, adopted by the House of Representatives in 1836, which was used to put a stop to the reading and debate of anti-slavery petitions in Congress.

Those people who concluded from all this that the young republican democracy could forever dodge the question of slavery were in for a surprise. Out from underneath the fledgling system of parties and representative institutions irrupted a new and subversive force: a social movement that was dedicated to using the press and other means of civic dissent to 'democratise' the problem of slavery by showing that it was an unnecessary evil.

The anti-slavery movement was more than the Whiskey Rebellion. It was social opposition on a grand scale. It had altogether more noble aims and more mature methods that included cooperation with anti-slavery protesters across the Atlantic. Prior to the 1830s, anti-slavery opinion had been dominated by the colonisation movement, which urged the return of slaves to African colonies like Liberia. But from 1833, the year in which the Slavery Abolition Act passed through the Westminster parliament in Britain (the Danish monarchy had already set the agenda by issuing an edict in 1792), American abolitionists toughened their stance by embracing what some called 'immediatism'. In the name of representative democracy, and with a great sense of urgency, abolitionists tried to mobilise anti-slavery opinion, to pressure reluctant politicians into halting the spread of slavery to the new territories of the republic, and to set their sights on its immediate and complete abolition in the South itself. The reaction among slave owners was swift. As the leading Southern politician John C. Calhoun (1782–1850) observed, in a widely publicised speech on 'slavery as a positive good',[30] a polity where a military *coup d'état* seemed neither thinkable nor practicable left pro-slavery interests with no other option but to retaliate, by joining in the battle for public support, from both civil society and the party system.

Two Peoples

Calhoun's recommendation was arguably fatal for the pro-slavery cause, effectively because it forced its champions to concede by their actions that slavery was not 'natural', or God-given, but instead depended for its survival as an institution upon some people's control over the various resources of power, including the power of persuasion. That is not to say that the defenders of slavery simply gave up the ghost. They fought hard with guns, and with words designed to show that they, too, were democrats – of a higher, Greek kind. On the eve of a vicious civil war, a remarkable war of words spread through the American republic. There was no shortage of verbal warriors. Calhoun, nicknamed 'cast-steel man', was among those who led the charge by staunchly defending the principle of nullification, according to which states could defy majority opinions by declaring null and void any federal laws they deemed to be unconstitutional. Such attacks on the principle of majority rule were new – so new that many people feared that the enfranchised *dēmos* of the American republic, like some living cell, had begun to subdivide into two *dēmoi*. 'We are not one people, we are two peoples', declared the *New York Tribune* in an anti-slavery editorial in 1855. 'We are a people for Freedom and a people for Slavery. Between the two, conflict is inevitable.'[31]

Viperous conflict was indeed inevitable, but its contours were far more complicated than that newspaper editorial stated. On the side of the abolitionists were many Southerners – four-fifths of the members of the 130 abolition societies established before 1827 lived there – as well as many whose abolitionist views had formed in the chapels and open religious meetings of the Second Great Awakening, and who found their views mirrored in the Christian humanitarianism of Harriet Beecher Stowe's biggest-selling novel in nineteenth-century America, *Uncle Tom's Cabin* (1852). There were those who had concluded that slavery was a comparatively unprofitable mode of production; nationalists who believed that slavery was a hindrance to America's manifest destiny as a unified country; and abolitionists who favoured Northern secession as a way of saving the nation. The opponent of slavery and founder editor of *The Liberator*, William Lloyd Garrison, publicly burned a copy of the Constitution at a Fourth of July meeting of abolitionists in 1854, repeating his conviction that the Declaration of Independence, an expression of divine wisdom, had been betrayed by the pro-slavery Constitution, which amounted to a 'Covenant with Death and an Agreement with Hell'. Talk of heaven and hell was commonplace among abolitionists, the most radical of whom were religious fundamentalists. Here was a grand irony, one that had older roots and a long history yet to come: the cause of representative democracy, understood as an ideal form of society based on non-violent power-sharing among free and equal citizens, was most vigorously championed by God-fearing militants, people who condemned slavery as a sin against God and humanity because it crushed individuals' God-given ability to choose responsibly their being-in-the-world.

Anti-slavery Appeal

The call to wash away the sins of slavery inspired not only the first ever major social movement of the era of representative democracy: the syntax and organising tactics of the abolitionists were copied in other quarters, sometimes with surprisingly democratic effects.

A striking instance was the public resistance of women to slavery, including their own at the hands of men. The public claim that women were entitled to emancipation had older roots, for instance in Protestantism and the natural rights doctrines of the seventeenth and eighteenth centuries. But it was the anti-slavery issue in the United States that brought women together publicly for the first time, on an unprecedented scale, especially during the 1830s. Their gathering represented a serious challenge not just to slavery, but to a civil society built on the exclusion and silencing of women: a pseudo-civil society that allowed their names to appear in print only twice in their lives, on their wedding day and in their obituary; a society in which married women had no legal rights over their children or their inherited property or earnings; an unequal society in which women were unschooled, voiceless in Church affairs, pressured to avoid spinsterhood and generally destined for the home, where they were expected by men to play the role of hard-working mothers, and to bless life with grace, ornament and sexual bliss.

The resistance of women to duties that guaranteed their subordination was partly the work of anti-slavery preachers, who stumped from town to town to deliver the abolitionist message and to organise new local chapters, in the process calling on women to join them. Many early women activists, surviving evidence suggests, thought of themselves as good Christian or deist women whose untainted morals entitled them to raise matters that men in general, and corrupted or corruptible political parties in particular, had suppressed. These fiercely religious women entered public life in droves. For most of them, the experience was an adventure in crossing the private-public divide for the first time. They spoke in chapels and at public meetings. They helped establish abolitionist societies (whose numbers jumped to more than a thousand by 1837). Taking advantage of steam-powered printing presses and the new postal networks that now covered the republic, they drew up petitions, and had them printed and circulated in huge quantities. In the new world of American representative democracy, voting between elections, likened by John Quincy Adams to a form of 'supplication, entreaty, prayer', became customary, especially for many women, even though they were without the vote. In the years 1838–9 alone, legislatures received more than 400,000 petitions containing some two million signatures of Americans. Many signatories were women, voicing their opposition to such matters as the interstate trade in slaves, the admission to the Union of Florida and Texas as slave states, and the grip of slavery on the District of Columbia and the western territories.

During the burgeoning petition campaigns of the 1830s, resistance to abolitionism, and thus opposition to women's public involvement in public affairs, intensified. Political poison began to seep through the pores of the republic. 'A woman is a nobody', thundered *The Public Ledger* of Philadelphia in an article lampooning talk of equal rights for women. 'A wife is everything. A pretty girl is equal to 10,000 men and a mother is, next to God, all powerful.' It concluded that the 'ladies of Philadelphia' were therefore 'resolved to maintain their rights as wives, belles, virgins and mothers and not as women'.[32] Meanwhile, laws were passed by state legislatures to forbid the distribution of 'incendiary' literature. The aforementioned Gag Rule, applied by Congress with ardent support from the Jackson administration, prevented the House from discussing or even mentioning the content of anti-slavery petitions. Rewards were offered for the arrest of abolitionist leaders. Boycotts of their businesses grew common. Anti-slavery literature was either refused by postmasters or put to the torch at public demonstrations. From all over the country, reports circulated of physical and verbal abuse of women who identified with the anti-slavery cause. This mob violence and misogyny – a word from the seventeenth century that now took on a new and more pungent political meaning – had the effect of encouraging other women to join their sisters in a common cause. The struggle against the enslavement of black people widened; the word slavery applied equally to women.

The semantic change was profound. Proof of its power to subvert was the public appearance of figures like Angelina Grimké (1805–79; Figure 46). The daughter of a wealthy, slave-owning Episcopalian judge from Charleston, Ms Grimké turned her back on both the balls and dinner parties of the planter society of South Carolina, and her father's sect. She moved north, to Philadelphia, where her sister, Sarah, persuaded her to join forces with local Quakers. She soon rejected their stodgy paternalism, and said so in

FIGURE 46: Angelina Grimké, photographed around 1875 in Hyde Park, Massachusetts.

print. Uproar followed her letter on the subject of mob violence published in the most famous abolitionist newspaper, William Lloyd
Garrison's *The Liberator*.

Many thought she showed unusual literary and political talent in
her first pamphlet, *An Appeal to the Christian Women of the South*
(1836). Within its pages she denounced slavery as un-Christian.
Her reasoning was that all people were equal in God's sight. The
souls of black folks and women were as valuable as those of white
men. The enslavement of God's children by others, even if it was
sanctioned by the Constitution, was a violation of the Higher Law.
She called upon women to reject Slave Power, to act as freethinking
public agents, as citizens who had the responsibility to 'persuade
your husband, father, brothers, and sons, that slavery is a crime
against God and man'.[33]

Grimké soon pioneered the arts of public speaking before audiences of both women and men. In Charleston, she had personally
witnessed many acts of cruelty against slaves, and she was good at
conveying the horror that came over her when hearing for the first
time the screams of workhouse slaves being dragged on a tread-
mill, suspended by their arms; or the distress she felt when meeting

the young boy slave who hobbled with difficulty on legs scarred permanently by repeated whippings. Appalled by such acts of violence, and inspired by the Scriptures and abolitionist ideals, she roused and mesmerised her listeners with a potpourri of impeccably crafted rhetoric, perfumed with sentences and phrases like: 'The ground upon which you stand is holy ground, never-never surrender it . . . if you surrender it, the hope of the slave is extinguished.' She always had special words for women, too: 'I know you do not make the laws', she used to say, 'but I also know that you are the wives and mothers, the sisters and daughters of those who do.' Or departing words like: 'Sisters in Christ . . . I have appealed to your sympathies as women, to your sense of duty as Christian women . . . Slavery must be attacked with the whole power of truth and the sword of the spirit. You must take it up on Christian ground; and fight against it with Christian weapons, whilst your feet are shod with the preparation of the gospel of peace . . . Undo the heavy burdens and let the oppressed go free . . . Farewell . . .'

Such talk was a form of action. It broke decisively with the older custom of women acting through organisations like churches run by men. For all her middle-class deism, here at last was a woman in the American scene proposing something much more radical: women were entitled to act publicly, and they had the duty to express themselves as individuals, on a par with men. With that conviction, it was only fitting that Ms Grimké did several things no other woman had done before in America. Accompanied by her sister Sarah, she spoke for the first time, in the New York state town of Poughkeepsie in the spring of 1837, to a mixed-gender audience that she and others termed 'promiscuous'. A few weeks later, still on the stump, this time in Amesbury, Massachusetts, she was challenged by two young men to a public debate on the subjects of slavery and women's rights to a public voice. The first public debate between a woman and men happened, reportedly with Angelina 'calm, modest, and dignified in her manner', utterly at ease in brushing away 'the cobwebs, which her puny antagonist had thrown her way'. Then, on 21 February 1838, still in Massachusetts, she managed something just as spectacular. 'Mr. Chairman, it is my privilege to stand before you', she told the all-male members of that state's Legislative Committee, the hushed public galleries and staircases of the State House legislature on Beacon Hill heaving with well-wishers, among them ladies dressed in ruffled skirts and frothy bonnets, and with enemies, some of whom at first hissed from the crowded doorways. Invited to stand in the Speaker's place, from where she could best be seen and heard, she made it clear that the subjugation of women was an unacceptable hypocrisy. 'This domination of women must be resigned – the sooner the better.' She went on to address 'the great and solemn subject of slavery'. She spoke uninterrupted for over two hours, using the precious moment to iterate her long list of reasons why the cause of 'the negro' was just – and why all God-fearing Americans had a duty to consign to hell 'a system of complicated crimes, built up upon the broken hearts and prostrate bodies of my countrymen in chains, and cemented by the blood and sweat and tears of my sisters in bonds'.[34]

Three months later, in mid-May 1838, at a large anti-slavery women's convention in Philadelphia, Ms Grimké delivered her last public speech. During the hour-long address, a shouting and cursing crowd threw stones at the walls and windows of the building in which she was speaking. She was forced to raise her voice. 'I have seen it! I have seen it! I know it has horrors that can never be described. I was brought up under its wing', she said of the evil of slavery. The next morning, an angry crowd returned. The organisers appealed to the authorities for protection; the Mayor replied in writing that coloured people should be dissuaded from attending the convention, since it was their presence that angered the citizens of Philadelphia, and endangered the safety of all. The Mayor's letter was read out to delegates, who bravely carried on with their business. Early that evening, shortly after delegates had left the building in pairs, black women arm in arm with white women, the mob puffed up in anger. Suddenly, the public lamps in the neighbourhood were snuffed. The crowd stood silently as agitators set alight the building, ransacked its anti-slavery offices, and destroyed all the books and records and every scrap of paper they could get their hands on.

The Propagandist

The claim that slavery was devilish, that it contravened divine laws because it reduced black-skinned men and women, and white women as well, to the condition of beasts, rolled like thunder across the plains of the deeply Christian civil society. In the struggle for representative democracy, language counted. It eventually convinced governments, parties and politicians, but not before joining battle with master rhetoricians of slavery, smooth-tongues like the struggling planter from Virginia who posed as the Pericles of the South, George Fitzhugh (1806–81).

Author of two bestsellers, *Sociology for the South, or the Failure of Free Society* (1854; Figure 47) and *Cannibals All! Or Slaves Without Masters* (1857), Fitzhugh was no friend of either racist doctrine or talk of natural rights. His propaganda instead operated from the premise that it was not enough to defend slavery indirectly,

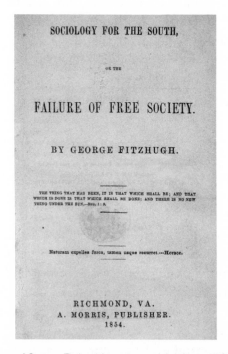

FIGURE 47: Title page of George Fitzhugh's controversial defence of Southern-style slavery, 1854.

for instance as Calhoun and others had tried to do by saying that the job of governments was to protect minorities against unbridled majorities. Fitzhugh was marginally more sympathetic to the view, later expressed by Jefferson Davis, President of the Confederate States of America, that slavery was 'established by decree of Almighty God' and 'sanctioned in the Bible, in both Testaments, from Genesis to Revelation'.[35] But Fitzhugh's preferred approach was bluntness. His starting point was that human beings were not created equal. Some were naturally endowed with superior physical, moral and intellectual qualities. Good law and government followed nature by making rulers of those who were better and slaves of those who were endowed with ordinary talents. Since 'some were born with saddles on their backs, and others booted and spurred to ride them – and the riding does them good',[36] the Southern form of government was evidently far superior to that of the so-called free states of the North. In these market-driven states, the rich and powerful had no obligations to the poor, the downtrodden and the naturally inferior. 'The men of property, those who own lands and money, are masters of the poor; masters with none of the feelings, interests or sympathies of masters; they employ [labourers] when they please, and for what they please, and may leave them to die in the highway, for it is the only home to which the poor in free countries are entitled.'

Fitzhugh admitted that there were problems in the South. State-organised industrialisation and vigorous education campaigns were urgently required to bind poor white people – 'white trash' – more tightly to the slavery system, for instance; sometimes Fitzhugh came close to saying that the best way to end wage slavery of these poor whites was to turn them into slaves as well. But the South, despite such flaws, was still a superior polity with superior potential. Resembling the prosperous and civilised slave-based systems of democracy in ancient Greece, the South made no pretence of a market in 'free' labour. 'Government is the creature of society', thundered Fitzhugh, 'and may be said to derive its powers from the consent of the governed; but society does not owe its sovereign power to the separate consent, volition or agreement of its members. Like the hive, it is as much the work of nature as the individuals who compose it.' Nature not politics was the guarantee of political community. Nature 'makes each society a band of brothers, working for the common good, instead of a bag of cats biting and worrying each other. The competitive system is a system of antagonism and war; ours of peace and fraternity. The first is the system of free society; the other that of slave society.'

The key point for Fitzhugh was that the South rejected soulless industrialism and the culture of counting-house clerks. Talk of laissez-faire and civil society based on a market in labour was sickening. Southern civility – its female grace, male chivalry and happy, dutiful blacks – made it a superior civilisation. 'There is no rivalry, no competition to get employment among slaves', Fitzhugh noted. 'Nor is there a war between master and slave. The master's interest prevents his reducing the slave's allowance or wages in infancy or sickness, for he might lose the slave by so doing. His feeling for his slave never permits him to stint him in old age. The slaves are well fed, well clad, have plenty of fuel, and are happy.' The 'beau idéal' of the Southern plantation showed that genuine democracy could work – but only if and when all citizens and subjects recognised inequality as a law of nature, so enabling the virtuous electors and lawmakers to enter into a voluntary co-partnership for the protection of the inferior, and the common good.

Tammany's Talents

The beauteous words, sown like the seeds of Cadmus in the sweet soil of the South, consolidated four years of terrible misery. An ugly struggle between two huge armies that locked horns ten thousand times, the Civil War was the first recorded war between two aspiring representative democracies, whose political elites were prone to think of themselves as defenders of two incompatible definitions of democracy. The conflict was in a way a clash between two different historical eras. The military crushing of the Southern fantasy of Greek democracy, in the name of a God-given vision of representative democracy, proved costly. Death, disability and destitution ruined hundreds of thousands of households, on both sides. There were an estimated 970,000 casualties, 3 per cent of the total population of the United States. Some 620,000 soldiers died, two-thirds from neglect and disease.

If anything good resulted from the brushfires, pillage and killings, it was that the war ruled out a return to the *status quo ante bellum*. Led by President Abraham Lincoln, the federation was restored, and the ripped lines of communication, trade and commerce were stitched together, certainly. And it is true that the blackened landscape left behind by the heat and flames of battle soon sprouted the green shoots and saplings of plants that had somehow managed to survive the war. But it is also true that the war triggered a fundamental alteration of the social landscape of the defeated South, forcing it to undergo a painful process of 'spiritual' mourning and recovery in the face of punitive Reconstruction. The Civil War also split the Democratic Party, which was symbolically a good thing because it helped smash the public identification of slavery with democracy. The victory against Slave Power sharpened democratic sentiments, destroyed old customs and institutions based on slavery; and it officially freed nearly four million slaves. Three major amendments to the Constitution also resulted: the outlawing of slavery (Article 13); the extension of federal legal protection to all citizens, regardless of their race (Article 14); and the abolition of racial discrimination in voting (Article 15).

In the slowly emerging world of representative democracy, the combined positive effect of these several changes was astonishing, and without precedent. It is true that the freed slaves soon lost their freedom, yet the Reconstruction that followed the final Yankee humiliation of pro-slavery forces, at the Virginian village of Appomattox in April 1865, pushed representative democracy in new and challenging directions. Some proved especially hazardous. During the next half-century, two intertwined forces had particularly dangerous implications for representative democracy, as it had been understood during the era of Jackson and Van Buren: big business and big government, run by parties.

It so happened that Tocqueville, when looking into the future, had worried about the same two forces. He noted that a new power group of industrial manufacturers had sprung from the heart of democratic society and now threatened its freedom and pluralism. This new 'aristocracy', as he called it, applied the division-of-labour principle to manufacturing. This greatly increased the efficiency and volume of production, but at a high social cost. The modern system of industrial manufacturing, he claimed, created a manufacturing class, comprising owners who loved money and had no taste for the virtues of citizenship, as well as a stratum of workers, who were crowded into towns and cities, where they were reduced to mind-numbing poverty.

Unlike Marx, Tocqueville predicted that each part of this new manufacturing class would press for government support of its own interests, for instance through large-scale infrastructure projects, such as the provision of roads, railways, harbours and canals, that it deemed necessary for the accumulation of wealth and the maintenance of social order. When done in the name of the sovereign people, as Tocqueville expected it would be, such government meddling in the affairs of civil society would choke the spirit of civil association and result in a new form of state despotism. Unlike past despotisms, which employed the coarse instruments of fetters and executioners, this new 'democratic' despotism would nurture administrative power that was 'absolute, differentiated, regular, provident and mild'.[37] Peacefully, bit by bit, by means of democratically formulated laws, government would morph into a new form of tutelary power dedicated to securing the welfare of its citizens – at the high price of clogging up the arteries of civil society, thus robbing citizens of their collective power to act.

Tocqueville's prediction has been much disputed, and mostly discredited. The details of the controversy do not matter here, for much more interesting is one of its deeper insights. Tocqueville worried his head that the American experiment with democracy would nurture a bad habit – the melding of money and politics in the name of 'the people' – that might well kill off democracy. It turned out that Tocqueville was right about the overall trend towards the merger of dollars and politics, but wrong about the consequences, which were wholly surprising all down the line, since they sharpened the sense of many citizens that democracy was under siege, that it was in danger of being undone, and that, at a minimum, the great deal that had been achieved now needed protection against the twin threats of private wealth and corrupt party government. The upshot during the last quarter of the nineteenth century was astonishing: the country that gave the world a compound democratic republic with elected presidents, competitive parties, civil associations and the democratic keyword OK now pushed the spirit and substance of democracy still further, into unexplored territory.

What exactly happened? Simply put, by the last decades of the nineteenth century, social life in America had been transformed by industrialisation led by big corporations. Figures like John D. Rockefeller and J. P. Morgan symbolised the new trend towards the concentration of economic power into the hands of a new class of industrialists and financiers. They were rich by world standards. The steel tycoon Andrew Carnegie reportedly earned over $20 million without paying a penny of tax; one of his steelworkers typically earned no more than $450 a year, working twelve-hour shifts a day, six days a week. The magnates lived well off their fabulous fortunes, and naturally they were interested in political power. Confident in their newly acquired financial clout, they pulled strings in the political parties, the Congress and state legislatures, and in the courts as well. Money did not merely talk. It made laws and ensured that things were done. Business meant busyness. The effect was to bankroll politics, and to encourage the political parties to join the bonanza. During this period, money touched thousands of people's lives, through jobbery so pronounced that a new name was coined to describe the new tactic of distributing money to party loyalists in the form of government jobs. Tammany Hall it was called, after the names of a legendary Native American chief and the headquarters of the Democratic Party in New York. 'How are you goin' to interest our young men in their country if you have no offices to give them when they work for their party?' George Washington Plunkitt, one of the leaders of Tammany Hall, asked in his widely read *Plunkitt of Tammany Hall* (1905). The answer at Tammany Hall was blunt: jobs were now so much the bread and butter of politics that no government could resist feeding their supporters.

Between the 1890s and the 1920s, at least a fifth of jobs in the growing government sector of that city were targeted at party faithful; if jobs handed out through contracts struck by government with private business are included, the actual figure was much higher. Tammany's talents were spread from top to bottom of the political system, including the federal tier of government. It was

FIGURE 48: *Running the 'Machine'*, an 1864 satirical cartoon, probably by John Cameron, featuring Abraham Lincoln ('All this reminds me of a most capital joke'), seated at the centre of a round-table meeting with his inner cabinet, accompanied by a 'greenback mill', operated by Treasury Secretary William Pitt Fessenden.

there, at the summits of governmental power, that the slogan 'Justice to All' – first used by president-elect Abraham Lincoln to describe his plan to allocate federal posts to supporters of his divided Republican Party – set a new trend (Figure 48). Lincoln cleaned out Washington's stables by ordering the removal of three-quarters of the 1500 or so officials whose jobs depended on previous presidential patronage. Until his assassination in 1865, he proceeded to fill the vacancies with his own favourites.

The next forty years unleashed a veritable gold rush for federal patronage. Figures are hard to come by, but in 1871 civil service employees numbered 51,000; by 1881, there were said to be 100,000 individuals listed on the federal payroll.[38] Presidents often squawked against the patronage system during this period. Former senator and twentieth president James A. Garfield (1831–81), lamenting that a third of his time had been wasted on firing and appointing officials, now felt victim of a veritable 'inundation'. 'My God!' he wailed, 'what is there in this place that a man should ever want to get into it?'[39] Chester A. Arthur (1829–86), who succeeded Garfield after his mortal wounding at the hand of an assassin, refused to meet jobseekers more than three days a week. And during his second inaugural speech, the only American president to serve two non-consecutive terms in office, Grover Cleveland (1837–1908), spoke out against 'this dreadful, damnable office seeking' and 'the demoralizing madness for spoils'; at one point, he even warned grovellers to steer clear of Washington.[40] But the brute fact was that both main parties operated a patronage system that resembled a duopoly in the business world.

Cries of opposition soon came from within the parties themselves. The most serious challenge appeared in the early 1880s from the rebel Republicans dubbed (by the *New York Sun*) the Mugwumps, a small faction of well-heeled lawyers, bankers, scholars and literary figures from a demographic group that had been pushed from public life by the spoils system. They resembled the republican gentlemen of a bygone era, proud individuals who denounced 'corruption', by which they meant government oiled by dirty money and run by uncultivated opportunists. The complaint earned them a nickname that was an old slang word for 'kingpin', from the Algonquin meaning 'great men'. The sarcasm was apt, for the bolting Mugwumps considered themselves too good for the spoils system – but also too well educated to rub elbows with the riffraff, and certainly too good to stick their hands into the political muck.

Although Mugwumps had a hand in the election of Grover Cleveland, spoils fever spread so rapidly through the youngest and most vibrant representative democracy of the nineteenth century that it is tempting to describe the whole trend as regression to the court patronage systems of eighteenth-century Europe. The key difference, of course, was that the parties were now the chief vendors of influence. At times, they resembled something like welfare states within the state. At other times, they looked more like big businesses trading in governmental power through organised cartels called 'rings' (that name was actually given to combinations of plundering politicians and party officials in cities such as Philadelphia, where the Gas Ring, centred on the municipal Gas Department, doubled as an employer of several thousand men and as a Democratic Party machine that controlled primaries and conventions, and won elections). Electoral victory for parties was synonymous with jobs and public contracts, and licences and permits for the loyal. The federal postal system, a huge employer (78,500 posts by 1896) after the demobilisation of the army, was a favourite of governing parties, especially because postmasters often doubled as agents for party newspapers, and as party organisers blessed with the power to obstruct the flow of opposition publications. Another favourite was the customs and excise service. The federal government extracted more than half its revenues from a single institution, the New York Customhouse. It employed men from all over the country and did five times more business than the largest private corporation in the country. In effect, it functioned as the New York Republicans' employment agency, a lucrative gravy train that provided jobs and income for the party faithful and backhanders into the pockets of customhouse officials.

The Customhouse symbolised the integration into the state of political parties that were designed in a previous life to be organs of civil society. The party patronage system helps to explain why, towards the end of the nineteenth century, the level of public involvement in elections reached the highest ever in American history. The point should be kept in mind when lamenting the latter-day decline of party membership and affection. In the six presidential elections between 1876 and 1896, an average 78.5 per cent of eligible voters cast ballots; nearly 63 per cent of eligible voters, meanwhile, turned out for off-year elections. Such figures were impressive, and massaged by the sense among citizens that the two-party system was evenly balanced, and that voting counted. Between 1872 and 1912, it is true that the Republicans had a monopoly grip on the presidency that was broken only twice: by Grover Cleveland's victories in 1884 and 1892. Yet the Democrats also had their fair share of office; during the same period, they won sizeable majorities in the House of Representatives in seven out of ten congressional elections. Such intense competition had the effect of arousing voter interest, and bumping up voter turnout. Election campaigns were periods of suspended animation. Everyone lived as if they were written in the subjunctive tense, not knowing the outcome of the contest, and knowing only that the way they voted might well have an effect on the outcome. The politics of surprise had democratising effects. But filthy lucre also played a big part in magnetising voters. So, too, did the emergence of party machines run by party bosses who ate, drank and slept politics.

Machine Politics

The Republicans and Democrats financed themselves through semi-compulsory taxes (called 'assessments' or 'voluntary contributions') levied on both their candidates for office and the lucky recipients of party spoils. Potential candidates paid hefty sums to secure a place on the party ticket. One contemporary account notes that candidates for judgeships were expected to pay around $10,000, senators and congressmen about $20,300 and candidates for alderman around $12,180.[41] Meanwhile, the party organisations levied 'assessments' on their beneficiaries and supporters. They were supposed to be 'voluntary', but in practice they resembled a master's instructions to his servants. This was machine politics in motion: with the help of full-time party workers, including 'henchmen' and 'heelers', party committees mailed printed assessments out to postmasters, federal judges, manual labourers working on federal or state or municipal projects, Customhouse and Internal Revenue Service employees, and others. Each handwritten letter stated the exact amount expected – usually 3 per cent of the employee's salary. If they did not cough up, follow-up letters were sent. Unsolicited visits to the tavern, home and workplace by mean-looking party workers – 'heelers' – were not unheard of.

Levies were in effect compulsory taxes that raised barrels of money to oil the party machine. Parties were large employers. In the 1880s in New York City alone, the Democrats employed over 3200 full-time field workers to run party affairs in the electoral districts. The Pennsylvania Republicans boasted that their twenty thousand regular workers made them larger than most of the private railroad companies in the state. During election periods, both parties paid daily wages as well to election inspectors and clerks, plus one-off payments to campaign supporters. In between elections, party finances were typically gathered and channelled through the state-level caucus organised by state and local bosses, county chairmen and legislators. The funds so gathered were then poured into soliciting local support by means of various forms of 'pork-barrelling' organised by the party bosses. Following a visit to the United States in 1896, the Russian political scientist and student of parties Moisei Ostrogorski (1854–1919) tried to capture the ways in which party workers resembled a cross between a feudal lord, a capitalist employer and a modern Christian missionary. Note his striking description of the figure of the ward heeler, precinct captain, county chairman, state assemblyman and Congressman, and the state boss: 'To this one he lends a dollar', noted Ostrogorski, 'for another he obtains a railroad ticket without payment; he has coal distributed in the depth of winter; he makes other gifts in kind; he sometimes sends poultry at Christmas time; he buys medicine for a sick person; he helps to bury the dead by procuring a coffin on credit or half-price. He has a kind heart in virtue of his position, and his position gives him the means of satisfying his need for kindness: the money which he distributes comes from the chest of the Machine; the latter has obtained it by the most reprehensible methods ... but no matter. With this money he can also dispense an ample hospitality in the drinking-saloons. As soon as he comes in, friends known and unknown gather round him, and he treats everybody, he orders one drink after another for the company; he is the only one who does not drink; he is on duty.'[42]

The party 'boss' – men who are rarely remembered today, figures like George Hearst in California, Tom Platt in New York, Matt Quay in Pennsylvania – was a new type of political animal. Dubbed with the Dutch word (*baas*) that was commonly used in New York as a term of respect for a master, or employer or chief, the boss was an avowed democrat, certainly. But he was also an unsleeping, devious, ruthless manipulator, a leader feared as much as respected because of his audacious strength of will, cleverness, and large purse. In an age of ever-bigger organisations, he resembled a general in charge of an army on the battlefield of elections, which were those moments when parties clashed openly using razzamatazz rather than rifles, paper stones rather than bullets. An American election campaign was a great show to behold, as the hero of Jules Verne's *Around the World in 80 Days* (1873) discovered shortly after arriving in San Francisco. Witnessing an election rally that sparked a brawl with sticks and canes flying, Phileas Fogg is informed by a hotel porter that it was just an ordinary meeting to hear from the two candidates, Mr Mandiboy and Mr Camerfield. For 'the election of a general-in-chief, no doubt?' Fogg asks the porter. 'No, sir; of a justice of the peace.'[43]

American party machines specialised in spats. They were conflict machines. Election campaigns were notorious extravaganzas and there was even a contemporary saying that 'paltics ain't bean bag'. Passions ran high; the whole democratic world seemed to burst into flames as party candidates and their machines vied for victory. The aim was to impress voters by offering them a dollar, or a few drinks, to outperform each other, for instance by mobilising clubs, staging street-corner speeches, illuminating houses, organising torch-lit parades and erecting 'liberty poles' stretching scores of feet into the air. Election tactics sometimes had a definite military ring; outsiders could have been forgiven for thinking that the party skirmishes resembled a civilised version of the Civil War, whose engagements remained strong in people's memories. Ticket splitting and floating voters were widely denounced as unpatriotic. There were bellicose campaign songs, war whoops and party rallies featuring speeches by beribboned soldiers of the Grand Army of the Republic, or by whiskery colonels 'late of the Confederate Army'.

FIGURE 49: William McKinley greeting children at the railway station in Canton, Ohio, from a stereopticon image, 1896, photographer unknown.

There were moments when party rhetoric resembled a call to worship, as in the sermons on the honest dollar and the full dinner pail delivered during the 1896 presidential election by William McKinley, standing on his front porch in Canton, Ohio, overlooking a white picket fence, to an estimated audience totalling three-quarters of a million people, ferried there by nine thousand railroad cars paid for by the Republican Party (Figure 49). Greater modesty normally prevailed. 'Tailboard campaigns' were a state-of-the-art favourite, of the kind used by the former gas meter inspector and single-tax-on-land proponent Henry George, when running (unsuccessfully) for Mayor of New York in 1886. 'The usual method', noted a contemporary, 'was to call a meeting at a street-corner, and just before the appointed hour to draw up a truck, from the "tail" of which one speaker after another addressed the crowd that came.'[44] Other favourites included filling streets with marching bands and campaign processions. Travelling glee clubs were also popular; hailing originally from eighteenth-century Britain, these Americanised versions of choir societies that sang part songs proved effective in drawing and entertaining large crowds. During the 1896 presidential campaign, in Indiana's Sullivan County, the Republican Glee Club, pulled by six horses, moved about on a giant wagon fitted out with a roof, curtains, a small organ mounted behind the driver, flags, benches and chairs for forty singers and – to hammer home McKinley's campaign slogan – a long string of pails chocked with food.[45]

Party Allergies

The antics of the parties understandably aroused the ire and sarcasm of those – especially women – still excluded from the whole process, partly on the grounds that they were not reliably 'rational'. 'No hysteria about it – just patriotic loyalty, splendid manly devotion to principle', chuckled the greatest orator of the suffrage movement, Anna Howard Shaw (1847–1919), after witnessing men cheering, screaming, singing 'the "Hown Dawg" song' and throwing and kicking their hats into the air until five o'clock in the morning at a Democratic National Convention, held in Baltimore.[46]

The attack on the all-male party boss system might have been expected from the woman who had made history in the United States, by becoming the first female Methodist minister, but she had a point. Masculine hypocrisy shielded by parties indeed served as a political brake on women. So, too, did another blockage within the arteries of the American experiment with political parties: the elementary lack of public accountability of these party machines and the bosses who ran them.

Here was the problem. The rocky American road to government by party competition was a bold first in the history of representative democracy. It potentially ensured that elections would not degenerate into acts of conquest, that winners would be inclined to exercise self-restraint by appealing for support among losers. During the nineteenth century, American democrats of various persuasions came to agree on one thing: a party-less democracy was a contradiction in terms, and that is why they scoffed at George Washington's view that party government was 'alternative despotism of one faction over another'.[47]

Representative democracy was indeed unthinkable without parties. But now imagine something new in the history of democracy: the profound disappointment with political parties felt by growing numbers of nineteenth-century Americans. By the 1880s, many citizens began to see something new, a 'softer' despotism run by unelected party bosses lording, in the name of 'the people', over parties skilled at dispensing sinecures and extracting money and bullying support from candidates and supporters alike. With hindsight, it is clear that this soft party despotism was a threat to democracy – and that it was a close cousin of the hard party despotism that sprang up in the twentieth century, using not just money, patronage and cunning, but fists, terror and totalitarian propaganda, to rule whole countries otherwise as different as Russia, Italy and Germany. The late nineteenth-century American version of party rule was admittedly more impressionable; its face was prettier and it was subject ultimately to voter rejection. Yet the boss system still produced dangerously anti-democratic toxins, which is why, by the early years of the twentieth century, millions of Americans had already decided to act, to spare the health of the republic.

The urgent need to drain off the poison in the pork barrels was confirmed by the dramatic assassination, in July 1881, at the Washington railway station, of President James A. Garfield by a crazed government clerk who had recently been sacked. There were loud calls to do something, initially by putting an end to the corrupt sinecure system. Civil service reform – introducing rigorous professional standards to slash the grip of party machines on government – was one kind of practical response.

The Pendleton Act (1883) established an independent Civil Service Commission charged with classifying federal jobs and administering examinations. The clean-up was reinforced two years later by the election of reform-minded Grover Cleveland to the presidency (1885–9). Known as the Veto Mayor of Buffalo, New York, where earlier in his career he ended the practice of closing government offices early (at 4 p.m.) and rid the city of corrupt sewerage and street-cleaning contracts, Cleveland cussed 'this dreadful, damnable office seeking'. He doubled the number of jobs covered by the civil service reform, all the while admitting that the whole boss system was 'a disagreeable necessity, I assure you'.[48] The remark underscored the contradictory long-term effects of the Pendleton Act and Cleveland's reforms based on the principle of 'the application of business principles to public affairs'. While by 1900 there were 100,000 positions subject to more rigorously professional standards, the decline in the numbers of government office holders who could be dunned for party contributions forced the parties to scratch around for funds elsewhere – to cuddle up to the Rockefellers and Jay Goulds, the Levi Mortons, Henry B. Paynes and other big men of big business.

The contradiction was palpable, and quite a few observers noted during this period that the deadly mix of democracy and dollars, big parties and big business, was having undemocratic effects upon the whole governmental system. James Bryce, the historian of democracy and British minister in Washington, who also happened to witness the 1884 presidential contest between Cleveland (Democrat) and James G. Blaine (Republican), was shocked to discover their convergence. 'Neither party has any principles, any distinctive tenets. Both have traditions. Both claim to have tendencies . . . All has been lost, except office or the hope of it.' For some decades it had been said by many citizens that Republicans expected all government to be active and generous, while Democrats hoped to keep it grudging and stingy ('that though the people support the Government, the Government should not support the people', as Grover Cleveland famously put it at the time). But Bryce the outsider saw things clearly. Party power, gathered in the hands of cigar-smoking men who sported campaign buttons and rolled logs, collected dollar votes and handed out gifts from bottomless pork barrels, fed more than mouths. Party power strengthened the impression that politics was a corrupt business in which the quickest route to success was upstairs, into the backroom party headquarters marked by a sign over the door that read 'Never Closed'. 'Yes, many of our men have grown rich in politics', confided George Washington Plunkitt. 'I have myself. I've made a big fortune out of the game, and I'm gettin' richer every day.' Things looked different down below, as the newly founded Farmers' Alliance and Industrial Union in Oregon made clear in one of its first statements. 'The power of trusts and corporations has become an intolerable tyranny', said its members, quickly adding that big business had 'almost exhausted the public domain; and the corruption of the ballot has rendered our elections little less than a disgraceful farce.'[49]

The image of the go-getting candidate and professional party boss as wealthy salesman trading on behalf of big business bothered not just farmers and labour activists in Oregon; it upset millions of other Americans as well. Something had to give in the young democracy – as it soon did, as an abreaction that was later repeated in many different countries, with many different effects. America was the first young representative democracy to experience backlashes against the whole system of representation, in the name of 'the people'.

Various stirrings outside the parties, among the marginal groups of civil society, provided a first taste of things to come. Farmers squeezed by rapid industrialisation and a downward spiral of prices and credit yelped. Small-town America grew fretful about the decline of Christian society. Industrial workers found themselves struggling for the right to organise to protect their jobs and wages, and to cut the length of their working day. There was widespread unease about the restriction of the franchise, especially among women, blacks and poor people in general. So, during the 1880s, the first calls for a 'new politics' became audible. The mottled voices included supporters of Henry George's single tax, readers of Edward Bellamy's best-selling socialist utopia *Looking Backwards* (1888) and proselytes of Christian cooperation, through what was called the Social Gospel. While divided by deep disagreements about matters of tactics and vision, all of them fretted about the fate of little people in a big polity that gave free rein to monopolies based on urban capital and party-dominated government.

From out of the cauldron of resentment bubbled Populism. By 1890, its non-partisan campaigns had begun to shake the whole system. The Populists' candidate in the 1892 presidential elections was an ex-Civil War general from a humble farming and abolitionist background, James Weaver (1833–1912). Calling for a graduated income tax, the eight-hour working day and a citizens' alliance with black people of the South, Weaver urged the steadfast to vote as they prayed, and was rewarded with more than a million votes. A dozen Populist Congressmen went to Washington. Three states (Colorado, Kansas and North Dakota) returned Populist governors.

Support for the Populists was cross-class and socially mixed. Populism was big-tent politics backed by dirt-poor farmers, black and white; hard-pressed local merchants; small-town editors and miners; cowpunchers and cattlemen with whiskered chins and broad-brim hats and a strong dislike of immigrants. Women were highly visible and were powerfully present on Populist rostrums. They included speakers against Money Power and Monopolies; die-hard prohibitionists determined to rid the West of moonshine and Wall Street; and writers like Sarah Emery, whose influential *Seven Financial Conspiracies* linked the decline of America with the disappearance of citizen participation. The Populists saw themselves as reversing evil trends. In undertones of Christian redemption, they called for a stop to the humiliation of the little person; their aim was to bring hope to millions of Americans through a pentecost of politics inspired by sources as diverse as Jefferson, Bellamy and the New Testament. The style was raw, but effective. Its talk of power most definitely worried the powerful, even if the Populist sense of history was a bit thin. 'We seek to restore the government of the Republic to the hands of the plain people with whose class it originated', declared the Populist convention in Omaha in 1892. The delegates railed against Money Power and 'governmental injustice'; they warned (as if they had been reading Marx) that the country was splitting up into two great classes, 'tramps and millionaires'. Political innocence was now a virtue. Seizing power – becoming 'as we are in name, one united brotherhood of freemen' – was now a necessity.

Progressivism

Like a blast of shotgun pellets at first light, the Populists set the big political animals scattering in all directions. Populism quickly won electoral support during the first half of the 1890s, but as a third party it lacked funds, candidates and organisational savvy. It was eventually to split and fizzle out, especially after the majority of delegates to the Populist convention in St Louis in 1896 voted to support the 'Demopop' ticket headed by William Jennings Bryan. Yet though barnstorming Bryan went on as Democratic candidate to lose the election, the spirit of Populism penetrated the whole political system. Its resistance to Big Money and Big Parties was to morph into a more long-lasting challenge to the old politics, with the consequence that from around 1900 the American democracy was remoulded by a highly contradictory but remarkable phenomenon called Progressivism.

The resistance to Big Money and Big Parties produced an unstable mix of trends. Contemporaries sympathetic to Progressivism liked to describe it as a concoction of overlapping reforms, including opposition to political corruption, greater public accountability of government and its efficient expansion to relieve social and economic distress. Progressives disliked wastefulness, disorder and incompetence. They railed against monopoly franchises, kickbacks and bribery. They were nauseated by the stinking contrast between dilapidated tenements crowded on rubbish-strewn streets and million-dollar mansions set amidst fine boulevards and pleasant parks. Progressives wanted governments – city, state and federal – to put an end to the prostitution and alcoholism bred by poverty. They favoured planned government intervention in defence of the public interest – to bring down high streetcar fares, to improve sanitary conditions and safety at dangerous railway crossings. Few of them spotted the deep tension between two quite different trends that they helped to unleash: the attempts to reinvigorate citizenship through the efforts of the sovereign people, and the struggle to press home the antithetical principle of efficient, top-down government by experts and specialists. Progressivism proved to be an incoherent affair. It was as if Americans tried to govern themselves by simultaneously heeding the conflicting advice of Demonax and Plato – or Tom Paine and Alexander Hamilton. The consequence was that American democracy was to beat yet another path into unknown territory, this time by wrestling with the same grave tension between planners and citizens that continues to rack and test existing democracies today.

What did Progressivism look like in practice? It had several faces. One of them was revealed during the years from roughly 1900 to the mid-1920s, which witnessed remarkable efforts to address the problems of injustice within civil society as a prelude to boosting popular participation in government. Many people who thought of themselves as progressive were sure that the best remedy for boss rule and corruption lay in building citizens' coalitions. That conviction produced a wide variety of civic efforts to stretch the boundaries of civil society to include groups, especially women, blacks and the urban poor, whose everyday lives currently shamed American democracy. W. E. B. Du Bois's *The Souls of Black Folk* (1903) criticised governments' call for patience and their preoccupation with piecemeal improvement of the manual skills of black workers. Du Bois proposed more radical measures, such as equal educational opportunities and efforts to rid daily life of white bigotry. In 1909, he and other Progressives, black and white, launched the National Association for the Advancement of Colored People (NAACP), which began a long (and still unfinished) campaign to abolish segregation, to end the disfranchisement of black people and to promote their civil and political freedoms.

Progressive reformers, or at least some of them, dug in their heels for the empowerment of women. The backbone of the women's movement during this period was most definitely white and middle-class, whose ranks were swelled by a jump in the numbers of women in certain professions, such as teaching, and in voluntary clubs and organisations, as well as in higher education. By 1910, when around 5 per cent of college-age Americans attended tertiary institutions, some 40 per cent were women. The activists among them joined organisations like the General Federation of Women's Clubs, a volunteer service network run by and for women; there was as well the National Consumers' League, founded in 1899, and the body that spearheaded efforts to organise women into trade unions and to reduce women's working hours, the Women's Trade Union League, established in 1903. Many Progressive women read Henry George's *Progress and Poverty* (1879), which quickly sold over three million copies, and *Women and Economics* (1898), written by the feminist Charlotte Perkins Gilman. Reformers clustered around Florence Kelley (1859–1932), the founder of the National Consumers' League and first factory inspector appointed by the state of Illinois, who agitated for labour laws that protected children against exploitation by employers. Other women put their efforts into the politics of birth control, support for which was voiced by a wide spectrum of sisters, from the Lithuanian-born anarchist Emma Goldman (1869–1940) to figures like Margaret Sanger (1879–1966) and the lawyer and feminist socialist Crystal Eastman (1881–1928), all of whom were united in their outright opposition to the established obscenity laws that prevented the dissemination of contraceptive information and devices.

The new feminism was symbolised as well by the heavy involvement of young and single middle-class women with a religious bent in the so-called Settlement House Movement. Taking its cue from London's famed Toynbee Hall, the movement aimed at the self-empowerment of the urban poor, as pioneering figures like the Nobel Peace Prize winner Jane Addams (1860–1935) demonstrated at Hull House, a battered mansion in the heart of a large Chicago slum. By 1895, there were more than fifty such settlements, each in their own way considered as social laboratories, as templates of a new social order that stood in stark contrast to the rotten reality of an America corrupted by inequality.

The settlement supporters gathered statistics and used first-hand observations to publicise their cause, helped by a new species of journalists dubbed 'muckrakers'. Writers like Lincoln Steffens, Ida Tarbell and Jacob Riis saw themselves as public journalists writing for a public hungry for the facts of life in contemporary America. True to their name, they saw nothing sacrosanct about privacy. Publicity must be given to the private wherever and whenever 'the public interest' was at stake, they thought. To this end, they used new investigative techniques, such as the interview; under hails of protest (they were often condemned as busybodies and meddlers) they took advantage of the widening circulation of newspapers, magazines and books made possible by advertising, and by cheaper, mass methods of production and distribution, to write long and detailed articles, even entire books, to provide often sensational exposés of grimy governmental corruption and waste, business fraud and social deprivation. The Pennsylvania-born journalist Nelly Bly (1864–1922) did something daring but dangerous: for Joseph Pulitzer's newspaper the *New York World* she faked insanity to publish an undercover exposé of a women's lunatic asylum. The muckrakers openly challenged political bosses and corporate fat cats. They questioned industrial progress at any price. They took on profiteering, deception, low standards of public health and safety. The muckrakers complained about child labour, prostitution and alcohol. They called for the renewal of urban life – for an end to slums in cities. By around 1905, the muckrakers were a force to be reckoned with, as William Randolph Hearst demonstrated with his acquisition of *Cosmopolitan* magazine; its veteran reporter, David Graham Phillips, quickly launched a much-publicised series, called 'The Treason of the Senate', which poured scorn on senators, portraying them as pawns of industrialists and financiers, as corruptors of the principle that representatives should serve all of their constituents.

Many Progressives grew adamant that efforts to expand civil society and protect its members from humiliation required more popular participation in government. There was a decided break here with Populism, which as a semi-organised party had raised hopes and expectations of empowerment of 'the people', paradoxically by channelling the participation of the disaffected into the hands of a political party. The patchwork of people, ideas and policies that came to be called Progressivism was different. It experimented with new methods of open government. 'The people are finding a way', proclaimed the Progressive publicist William Allen White, who noted with excitement the rapid spread of schemes of 'fundamental democracy'.[50] It was not quite clear what 'fundamental democracy' meant to him, although the evidence shows that he was not the only one to spot that the list of American innovations grew excitingly long during this period.

It was as if American democrats had suddenly grasped that their cherished system of representative government offered unlimited scope for the art of innovation – that democracy could be democratised, using democratic means. In each case, the stated aim of the inventions was to help citizens control their representatives. Progressives tried, for instance, to tie the hands of party bosses by working for the introduction of the secret ballot, which was usually called (for reasons that we shall see) the Australian ballot, from where it was imported (from Tasmania) and first adopted in the state of Massachusetts. The new voting method was designed to rid elections of the corrupting effects of oral balloting and voter intimidation and bribery, and to do so by printing at public expense official ballots containing the names of all candidates, distributing these ballots at polling places run by election officials, and asking voters to mark their ballots in secret, then to place them in a sealed box that was later opened and the ballots counted by politically neutral officials.

Progressives also championed the direct election (rather than the appointment by states) of senators, the campaign for which first succeeded in the states of Oregon and Nebraska, and eventually made its mark at the federal level (in 1913) with the ratification of the 17th Amendment to the Constitution. It was trumpeted as a great victory for 'the people', their deserved triumph over the ailing system of state-appointed senators that had been adopted at the 1787 Constitutional Convention, partly on the grounds that republican gentlemen senators elected for longer periods by state legislatures would be better representatives by virtue of their insulation from the self-interested people of their own states.

The proposal for direct primary elections within parties was among the pet proposals of Progressives. Several different varieties were eventually adopted, depending on whether the initial voting for a preferred candidate was closed to registered members of the party; or whether it was instead more or less open to registered voters of any party, or non-party affiliation. The experiment sometimes resulted in mixed systems, as in West Virginia, where primaries for the Democratic Party became closed affairs and Republican primaries were opened to independent voters. In each case, however, the declared aim of the reformers was to break the grip of party bosses and big money by ensuring that the nomination of potential candidates for office was subject to formal rules that guaranteed greater internal openness and accountability, either to the party membership or to the electorate as a whole.

An intriguing invention from this period, one designed to keep party-disciplined representatives on their toes by pressuring them from the outside, was the recall mechanism. The principle was simple. If duly elected representatives, from the point of view of citizens, behaved irresponsibly or foolishly in between elections, then they ought to be recalled before their terms expired. The recall mechanism was a dismissal procedure, a way of giving the boot to representatives who turned out to be duds. It was strongly championed by groups like the Direct Legislation League of Los Angeles, led by a medical doctor-turned-property developer, Dr John Randolph Haynes. In speech after speech, he deplored 'inefficiency, extravagance and corruption' and saw himself as a defender of 'the mass of citizens' rendered 'helpless between elections'. It was he and his supporters who managed to win approval for the inclusion of a recall clause in the Los Angeles city charter of 1903. At the state level, Oregon was the first (in 1908) to adopt the same measure. Seventeen more states were to follow suit. In each case, the recall rule took aim at bad behaviour variously described as 'violation of oath of office', 'malfeasance or misconduct while in office', or simply 'lack of fitness' or 'incompetence'. The recall mechanism allowed the use of a petition drive to collect a statutory number (usually between 10 and 40 per cent) of signatures from registered voters; if the minimum level of support was achieved, the matter then had to be placed on a ballot. An election was held and (depending upon the election result) the controversial official was either removed from office, or allowed to complete the originally designated term, as if on a suspended prison sentence.

Meanwhile, a modern American version of the ancient Greek rule that citizens can initiate laws or amendments by referendum was approved in 1898, in the state of South Dakota, where it had strong support within the trade unions as a valued weapon in the arsenal of what was called 'a people's legislation'. Unknown to South Dakotans, the initiative principle, as it came to be called, had home-grown roots in the 1777 Georgia state constitution, which provided for the adoption of amendments with voters' consent. Progressives never managed to codify the initiative in federal legislation, but it did come to be adopted widely at the state, county and local levels, throughout the country; and during the twentieth century it was to be used by a remarkably wide spectrum of interests. The initiative came in two forms. The 'indirect initiative' specified that voters were mandated to submit petitions to the legislature for action. The more common 'direct initiative' specified that any matter could be drafted by any voter, but required the initial signature of usually between 5 and 15 per cent of the registered voters before it could be put on the ballot, either at the next scheduled election, or at an election called especially to consider the proposition.

A Toolmaker for Democracy

There were places where Progressive recall and initiative measures had powerful effects. Oregon quickly won the record for the most state-wide initiatives (there were 318 between 1904 and 2000), the highest average initiative use (6.6 per general election), and the most state-wide initiatives on the ballot in a single year – 27 in 1912.

The driving force behind its reputation as a laboratory of democracy was a frail, pale, softly spoken man named William Simon U'Ren (Figure 50). Known affectionately as 'Referendum

FIGURE 50: William Simon U'Ren.

U'Ren' for his single-minded devotion to the cause, he was born in 1859 in Lancaster, Wisconsin, the son of a blacksmith who, with his wife, had emigrated from Cornwall, in England. Young U'Ren accompanied his family westward to Nebraska, then to Colorado, learning the blacksmith's trade from his father. By his mid-twenties he had earned a law degree in Denver, and then moved to Iowa, Hawaii and California, before settling in Milwaukee, Oregon, in 1889, by which time he had been a blacksmith and miner, a newspaper editor, a quiet champion of vegetarianism and a Republican Party worker, in addition to practising law.

In 1892 a severe asthma attack forced him to abandon his law practice. Having no family in the area, he was nursed back to health by the Lewellings, a local family of cherry farmers. His hosts were reformers, 'good government being to us what religion is to most people', wrote the lady of the house. Another family member showed U'Ren a copy of James W. Sullivan's recently published book, *Direct Legislation by the Citizenship Through the Initiative and Referendum*; U'Ren, now thirty-three, found his life's calling. As he later told an interviewer: 'Blacksmithing was my trade and it has always given color to my view of things. I wanted to fix the evils in the conditions of life. I couldn't. There were no tools. We had tools to do almost anything with in the blacksmith shop;

wonderful tools.' He added: 'In government, the common trade of all men and the basis of social life, men worked still with old tools, with old laws, with institutions and charters which hindered progress more than they helped it. Men suffered from this. There were enough lawyers: many of our ablest men were lawyers. Why didn't some of them invent legislative implements to help people govern themselves: Why had we no tool makers for democracy?'[51]

With financial help from the Lewellings, U'Ren set to work on forging the required tools. He brought together representatives of the state Farmers' Alliance and labour unions to form the Oregon Direct Legislation League, which elected him as secretary. In 1894, U'Ren was also elected chairman of the state's Populist Party convention, and won approval for his initiative and recall platform. That same year, the League published a pamphlet explaining initiative and recall and distributed 50,000 copies in English and 18,000 in German. In 1896, U'Ren won a seat for the Populists in the state's lower house and in the following year worked the legislature – without success – to gain approval for initiative and recall. Warned by his enemies that he might well end up in purgatory for his wheeling and dealing, U'Ren famously replied, in his quiet and croaky voice: 'I'd go to hell for the people of Oregon!'

U'Ren went on to outflank the legislature by reorganising the League, broadening its support base. In addition to farmers and trade unionists, the new seventeen-member executive committee included bankers, the Portland *Oregonian* newspaper editor, Harvey W. Scott, and the president of the state bar association (that was unusual, for attorneys' associations were notorious during the Progressive era for opposing initiative and recall). U'Ren lost his bid for the state senate in 1898, but the following year his initiative and recall amendment was finally accepted. Under Oregon's constitution, amendments had to be approved by two successive sessions of the legislature. U'Ren had to wait until 1901 for his moment of triumph, when the initiative and recall proposal finally passed through the Oregon legislature with just a single dissenting vote. A year later, voters ratified it by an eleven to one landslide margin.

U'Ren was sure that initiative and recall would open the door to other Progressive reforms. Until his death in 1949, aged ninety, in the city of Portland, he joined forces with sponsors of scores of initiatives. In 1906, U'Ren supported an initiative to ban free railroad passes, which the railroads routinely handed out as gifts to politicians, and which, he publicly confessed, he himself had once received. In 1908, he proposed initiatives to make Oregon the first state with popular election of US senators, and to reform election laws. Both passed by overwhelming margins. Other early initiatives that bore his hand were a 1906 constitutional amendment extending initiative and recall powers to local jurisdictions, which was approved by three to one; and a 1908 amendment that gave voters power to recall elected government officials. His hand was present in the victory of labour unions in a 1912 initiative that established an eight-hour day for workers on public works projects, and two other measures prohibiting private employers from hiring cheap convict labour from state or local jails.

In 1910, with strong public backing from U'Ren, Oregonians passed an initiative to establish the first presidential primary election system in the nation. The margin was small (43,353 to 41,624), but two dozen other states copied it within six years. The closeness of the 1910 vote showed that voters were not always quite as ready for reform as U'Ren. His 1912 initiative, proposing a unicameral legislature, was defeated by a greater than two to one margin. A 1914 full-employment initiative, sponsored by the Socialist Party and backed by U'Ren, also failed. The proposal was advanced for its time, for it would have set up a job-creation fund derived from an inheritance tax on estates worth more than $50,000 (a huge fortune in those days). The state labour commissioner would have had the power and duty to employ any citizen demanding work in a 'Department of Industry and Public Works'. The measure failed, at 57,859 to 126,201. There were still other initiatives, like the proposed enfranchisement of women, which had to be bitterly defended. Oregon was one of two states (the other was Arizona) where women gained the right to vote by an initiative. It lost on the first try in 1906, and lost again, by an even bigger margin, in 1908. In 1910 suffragists tried a different approach: an initiative giving only female taxpayers the right to vote, a compromise that was rejected by about the same margin as the 1908 suffrage amendment. Finally, in 1912, Oregon suffragists led by U'Ren's acquaintance, Abigail Scott Duniway, tasted sweet victory after a long and difficult struggle. Their measure passed by a slim margin. Leading the fight against women's suffrage were the liquor and saloon interests, which (rightly, in this instance) feared women would vote for Prohibition. In 1914, the first year Oregon women voted, a Prohibition initiative passed by a wide margin. After an initial setback, women also provided the slim 157-vote victory margin (out of over 200,000 votes cast) for a 1914 initiative that abolished the death penalty in the state of Oregon.

Governmentality

Since legislatures would not always adequately represent them, recall and initiative supposed that people must be able to push through laws they desire, and to get rid of laws they oppose. 'What is this magical transformation', a prominent Oregon champion of initiative later asked, 'that makes voters too stupid to make decisions for ourselves, but suddenly capable of making wise decisions when it comes to electing politicians to govern us?'[52] Whatever is thought of the question, or the bubbling energy that question gave to early uses of recall and initiative, there is no doubting their originality and the radical, often contradictory effects they triggered, as subsequent events in Oregon proved.* Progressives like U'Ren clearly saw themselves as the best friends of civil society, as firmly on the side of fluid majorities and minorities of people battling

---

* Examples of successful Oregon initiatives have included a procedure to set up independent, locally owned 'People's Utility Districts' to market water and power (1930); approval (in 1937/8) of an order to clean up the Willamette River, which was heavily polluted by pulp and paper mills and sewage; and of the 'Townsend Plan' old-age-pension initiative that proposed making monthly payments to senior citizens if they promised to spend their entire allotment each month, so helping to stimulate the economy. Then there was the approval, by a margin of nearly two to one in 1952, of the principle (championed by a student at the University of Oregon at Eugene, Clay Myers, a leader of the campus Young Republicans) of periodic reapportionment of the state's legislative and congressional districts, whose boundaries had not been redrawn for over fifty years; and (with strong support from senior citizens) a 'denturism' initiative (1978) that broke dentists' monopoly by allowing denture technicians to sell and fit dentures at a lower cost. The 1990s saw the rise of an initiative proponent called Bill Sizemore. Soon nicknamed Mr Initiative, he provoked the ire of Progressives (liberals) because of his support for literally dozens of initiatives aimed at them, including tax cuts, labour reform and term limits. His opponents, primarily labour unions,

against government. By contrast, there were many early twentieth-century supporters of the Progressive cause who hedged or fudged their bets. It was not always clear what or whom exactly they had in mind when they spoke of 'the people'? Did they mean majorities? Did they mean everybody? Or did they in fact mean *themselves*?

The truth is that many Progressives treated the people mostly as a convenient phantom. They paid much lip service to 'ordinary Americans': to blacks, poor white farmers in the boondocks, railway and lumber workers dying for the whistle to blow, the new poor huddled in the cities. But when they spoke of 'the American people' they typically meant people like themselves: upright, talented, sanctimonious teachers, editors, professionals, business leaders, native-born middle-class citizens with sensible views, sober habits and strong convictions about what had to be done to protect or nurture American values and the American way of life. Progressivism spoke of the people, certainly. But it most definitely spoke with a middle-class accent schooled in the original Federalist vision, championed by Alexander Hamilton and others, of a prosperous continental republic managed by men of talent and good breeding. Progressivism, one could say, was a species of republican elitism, which helps to explain why, during the period leading up to World War One, the 'populism' of the Progressives struck alliances and did deals with government, often to the point of questioning 'the people' and representative democracy itself.

did battle by sponsoring initiatives designed to curtail the resort to initiatives, including (in 2002) the proposed banning of payment for signature gatherers. Voters adopted the proposal, but a court challenge ensued. The dispute illustrated the growing entanglement of ballot initiatives and the Oregon Supreme Court, over a third of whose cases in the year 2000 involved challenges to ballot titles. The irony, unanticipated by U'Ren, that the 'Oregon system' of initiatives would hasten the reliance on the judicial branch of government, was compounded by widespread complaints about their reductive and polarising effects, with complicated issues boiled down to black or white propositions and campaign slogans like 'better government', with voters encouraged to vote selfishly, with their pockets, rather than using their heads. And speaking of pockets: average costs of campaigning for an initiative rose from around $860,000 in the 1970s to around twice that amount, $1,700,000, in the 1990s. When combined with the practice of paying signature gatherers (dubbed 'mercenaries') around $2–3 per signature – a practice sanctioned by the 1988 US Supreme Court ruling that banning payment was contrary to the First Amendment – the effect has been to press the initiative process firmly into the arms of big money.

The 'governmentality' of many Progressives was evident in their strong attachment to the belief that the ills of the American democracy could be cured by the elevation of competent officials (they had in mind men and occasionally women) to positions of power. Progressives favoured tax reforms, better utility services and effective health regulations; they stood for city governments liberated from greedy special interests, corrupt businessmen and party bosses. The rule of competent specialists and experts would bring 'good government' based on what President Theodore Roosevelt (1901–9) called the 'gospel of efficiency'. Progressives thought government could be used as a tool of popular empowerment. Good government meant frugal and expert-driven government *for the people*, not bossing by wasteful, vested private interests. Some Progressives were adamant that talk of government *by the people* was now obsolete. They believed that citizens were often muddleheaded creatures, simpletons confused by old-fashioned popular suspicions of executive power that were traceable to the bygone era of 1776. 'The true remedy for American misgovernment', said Henry L. Stimson (soon to be Secretary of War under President William Taft), was 'exactly the opposite direction from that indicated by the advocates of direct democracy. The elected officials must have more power, not less.'[53]

Not everybody accepted what in effect was an epochal effort to redefine democracy – by stretching it to mean government by representatives who were substitutes for citizens incapable of governing themselves. Resistance to rule by educated elites was understandably strong among the surviving adherents of Populism, who considered that all matters of government involved moral issues, that 'the people' were well qualified to speak and decide all matters for themselves, and that, especially if government were made less complicated, there would be no need for the rule of the competent, simply because all citizens could become experts in public affairs.

Seductive was the faith in simplicity, but Progressives with an elitist bent were mainly to have their way in policy matters. The trend towards democratic elitism was set in dashing style by the rise to prominence of the Wisconsin Idea, championed by 'Battling Bob' La Follette (Figure 51). Bolting against a Republican Party

FIGURE 51: The Wisconsin Idea of good government: a *Chicago Daily Tribune* cartoon (29 December 1911) featuring 'Battling Bob' La Follette, by John T. McCutcheon.

effectively corrupted by its close ties to the lumber and railroad companies, La Follette enjoyed three consecutive terms of office (1900–1906) as state governor. Tapping expert advice from economists, educators and political scientists, he rammed through a set of much-talked-about reforms. They included a state railroad regulation commission to set fair freight rates; an improved civil service; and a pure-food law. The reforms included a graduated state income tax that assessed the rich at a higher rate; conservation measures; state banking controls; a water franchise act; and labour protection laws. The Wisconsin Idea spread through other states; when Woodrow Wilson became governor of New Jersey, he implemented many of La Follette's reforms, as did Hiram Johnson in California. With the presidency of Theodore Roosevelt (who was ricocheted into office by the bullets that struck down President William McKinley, in September 1901), Progressivism became a synonym for vigorous federal government interventions in the affairs of business and other institutions of civil society.

No stone of private vice – big parties and big business – was to be left unturned by the public virtues. Progressivism was against profiteering, dishonesty, bosses and 'robber barons'. It was generally against 'interests', a keyword that stood not only for octopoid companies like the Southern Pacific Railroad and the venality of 'trusts' like Standard Oil but, more deeply, for the pernicious values of free-market economics, possessive individualism and growing social inequality. Progressivism stood firmly for 'disinterestedness', for a society based on hope, hard work, conscientious administration, professional expertise, social altruism, the common weal, good government in pursuit of the public good. Convinced of the need to turn the wheels of progress, Progressivism stood for building codes, fair taxation regulations, the reduction of working time, workers' safety and compensation laws; and it stood as well for accident insurance, aid for farmers, scientific management of government departments, new health care arrangements, mandatory school attendance, government meat inspection, improved roads and transportation safety schemes. There was even talk of 'gas and water socialism', and action to see it into practice.

Phantom Democracy

By the 1920s, the Progressives had achieved much. They had strengthened the appeal of modern democratic institutions – open party competition, periodic elections, limited terms of office, civil liberties such as freedom of assembly and the press – to a society wounded by civil war less than a generation before. Progressives had questioned the power of corrupt bosses within party politics, publicised the damaging effects of big business and laid the foundations for the later recasting of government into the New Deal version of a welfare state. Progressives rightly claimed responsibility for important taxation and social reforms. And despite the fact that the Progressive Party, founded in 1912, imploded just five years later, Progressives stood squarely behind four vital constitutional amendments: the empowerment of Congress to lay and collect income tax (Article 16; 1913); the direct election of senators (Article 17; 1913); controls on the production and transportation of alcohol (Article 18; 1919); and women's suffrage (Article 19;

1920). Progressivism also launched an uphill battle to expose the deeply corrupting effects of money on party politics – a battle that has still not been won today. Its firm support for the Tillman Act (1907) soon led to the introduction of prohibitions on corporate donations to political parties, campaign spending limits in congressional elections, and the compulsory filing by national party committees of their contributions and expenditures.

The new public disclosure rules were among the first of the era of representative democracy, but they were born toothless. No independent enforcement agency was set up; citizens had no access to filed reports; penalties for non-compliance were left undefined; and no one was ever prosecuted for their failure to comply with the law. For all its successes, Progressivism had another downside: it took the sting out of popular politics, especially by expanding the publicly visible role of specialists, professionals and experts in matters of government. Gone were the days marked by the sumptuous display of pep rallies, bonfires and parades. The direct election of senators and the use of the recall and initiative had certainly kept the pulse of representative democracy beating, but by the early 1920s astute observers began to note a profound change in the political spirit of the republic. Popular involvement in parties and government seemed to have declined. Public spectacles had gradually given way to 'advertised' forms of administration and the concentration on 'policy'. Some spoke favourably about the permanent decline of the illusory ideal of democracy; many others sighed a deep, melancholy sigh at the changed political climate.

No one better exemplified the trend towards administered democracy than America's most distinguished syndicated columnist and political commentator, Walter Lippmann (1889–1974). A founding editor of *The New Republic* and youthful adviser to President Woodrow Wilson during World War One, Lippmann spoke for many men of middle-class comfort during these years by bidding a gloomy farewell to the ideal of an informed public of citizens capable of reasoning for themselves about matters of public concern. His best-selling *The Phantom Public* (1925) caused a sensation. It fiercely questioned populists' and Progressives' belief in representative democracy and what he dubbed its myth of 'the sovereign and omnicompetent citizen'. The American reality was otherwise, insisted Lippmann, who talked and wrote as Plato might have done, had he been a journalist working in the early decades of the twentieth century.

Most citizens give little time to public affairs, Lippmann said. They have but 'a casual interest in facts' and 'a poor appetite for theory'. They act upon the simplified pictures in their heads; their signposts are 'stereotypes', a word borrowed from the printing industry that Lippmann invested with new meaning. Even those who try to take a keen interest in public affairs find themselves bamboozled. The eager-beaver citizen so loved by democrats and democratic theory is supposedly energetic, public spirited, intellectually curious; in fact, he or she knows little about a restless world marked by infinite complexity. And so the 'mystical fallacy of democracy' collapses. The presumption that 'the people' are a God-like, shadowy mastermind is a foolish illusion. Pulled hither and thither, amateur citizens acting in concrete situations find that they 'cannot know all about everything all the time'. Victims of stereotypy, they are forced to recognise that while they are 'watching one thing a thousand others undergo great changes'. Citizens are muddled and fuddled creatures – 'as bewildered as a puppy trying to lick three bones at once'.[54] Floundering in the 'chaos of local opinions', the average citizen resembles the theatregoer who walks into a play in the middle of the third act, then leaves before the final curtain, none the wiser.

So what was to be done? If the old vision of a political community based on government by the people, and by their expertise as equals, was now ruined, was there a positive alternative? Lippmann thought so. Given the dangers of popular ignorance in a dangerous world bristling with economic and geopolitical uncertainty, he forecast that American politics must learn to live without the fiction of an informed 'people'. Representative democracy had undermined its own founding conceit; it was an ideal ruined not by its dependence upon the bourgeoisie (that was the misgiving expressed by Marx and contemporary American socialists) but, rather, by its deluded attachment to ignorant people, whom Lippmann's contemporary, the Baltimore satirist H. L. Mencken, had waggishly dubbed the 'booboisie'.

Those who governed America had hereafter to rely on sophisticates, not sophists; they had to see that knowledgeable specialists were vital for handling the complexities of domestic and international affairs. Lippmann admitted that governing elites could never hope to become know-all Experts; the world was much too complex for that to happen, which is why public discussion, public opinion sampling and periodic, well-run elections could still sometimes provide valuable second opinions for governing elites.* Yet public debate, followed by the verdict of 'the people', could not be seen as the presumed source of sovereign authority, Lippmann concluded. Representative democracy was no longer an ennobling vision, as it had been for public figures like Andrew Jackson, Abraham Lincoln, Grover Cleveland and William U'Ren. Representation and democracy had now to go their separate ways. Government was simply a practical way of letting leaders get on with the difficult business of deciding who got what, when and how, through the crafting of 'enlightened public policy' for others.

---

* The roots of public opinion polling go back to the 1820s, for instance to the unweighted, local (usually city-wide) 'straw votes' conducted by newspapers such as the *Harrisburg Pennsylvanian*, which showed Andrew Jackson ahead of John Quincy Adams in the 1824 presidential race. Among the first country-wide American opinion polls was that conducted by the influential general-interest magazine the *Literary Digest* (the forerunner of *Time* magazine), which in 1916 used the method of mailing millions of postcards and counting the returns from readers to predict (correctly) Woodrow Wilson's election as president. The technique doubled as a circulation-raising exercise, and its accurate prediction of an election result aroused the attention of the founders of public relations, including the nephew of Sigmund Freud, Edward Louis Bernays (1891–1995). Styling himself a 'public relations counsel', Bernays spent much of his early career pushing the frontiers of sampling and public persuasion techniques beyond mere advertising methods towards what he called 'the engineering of consent'. He loved the 'ballyhoo' of public spectacles and experimented with new ways of fabricating media events, including a first ever 'pancake breakfast' with vaudeville for Calvin Coolidge in his run-up to the 1924 presidential election. Bernays was prepared to hire out his publicity guns to all who could afford him; over the years he had clients within both government and civil society, including the corporate world, but throughout he was convinced that individuals were suggestible creatures driven by dangerously libidinal energies in need of sublimation, restraint and ordering by means of intelligently crafted publicity blitzes directed by leaders. Listen to Bernays on how life is and must be in a democracy: 'The conscious and intelligent manipulation of the organized habits and opinions of the masses is an important element in democratic society. Those who manipulate this unseen mechanism of society constitute an invisible government which is the true ruling power of our country . . . We are governed, our minds are molded, our tastes formed, our ideas suggested, largely by men we have never heard of . . . It is they who pull the wires which control the public mind' (*Propaganda*, New York, 1928, pp. 9–10).

Empire of Innocence

The epitaph for democracy written by Lippmann was unmistakably sombre, a most melancholy ending to what had been a remarkable history of democratic inventions that had combined to set the United States apart from the rest of the world, by a mile.

The period after 1776 saw the creation of a new continental federation that resembled a homespun political cocoon that hatched a type of democracy entirely unknown to the ancient world of assemblies. The United States of America was easily the most promising representative democracy of the nineteenth and early twentieth centuries. The country witnessed the rise of the world's first political party system, the first peaceful handover of government from one party to another and the first grassroots political party calling itself democratic. Although it did not lead the world in extending the franchise to all men and women, as is often believed, America was the place that experienced for the first time the organised mudslinging and razzle-dazzle of election campaigning and 'the din of party strife', as President Grover Cleveland once called it. America managed to survive the shock waves produced by the assassination of two of its presidents. It weathered the storms of a brutal civil war between two hostile and opposed definitions of democracy, and effectively put to rest all fantasies about recreating the ancient world of democracy, based on slavery. In that sense, it was the first country to turn democracy into an enemy of slavery, as well as to commit itself to the long, painful and embattled process of extending rights of citizenship to people whose skin colour was darker than white. America was the first representative democracy to witness the degeneration of political parties into machines run by bosses and full-time campaigners, and financed by business fat cats. It was the first aspiring representative democracy to give free rein to experiments in civil service reform that aimed, in the name of 'the people', to inject greater 'efficiency', 'professionalism' and 'expertise' into its governing structures. America also saw the first self-conscious efforts, in the name of democracy, to cultivate civil society and civic opposition; to witness experiments with party primaries, initiative and recall and other new forms of democratic representation; and to unleash a new adversarial ('muckraking') form of journalism that threw its weight behind public efforts to expose corruption and breathe new life into the ailing system of representative government.

This was all most impressive. But there was a darker side to the rise of American democracy, specifically to do with the temptations of wielding power over other governments and peoples thought to be inferior, both at home and in the wider world. It was Edmund Burke – commenting on eighteenth-century British designs on India – who famously remarked that revolutions are the first step to the building of empires.[55] The comment pre-dated the coming of democracy to America, of course, but from the outset – as we shall now see by way of conclusion – Burke's maxim was to apply with troubling effect to the country that became the most powerful representative democracy of modern times.

Most historians of American democracy have preferred to ignore the link between empire and democracy. They take for granted that American democracy was untouched by the lure of imperial domination, until at least the end of the nineteenth century. The story runs like this: the American republic managed its affairs with no general foreign policy, save that of George Washington's strict determination to avoid entanglement in great power confrontations. The young republic was a disinterested power. It was both amateurish and *anti-imperialist*. Following the military toppling of Napoleon and the success of the American peace commissioners in rescuing America from the near-defeat of the War of 1812, the American people took advantage of their geographical isolation to fulfil their own political destiny, protected by distant British warships. Extravagant imperial fantasies certainly sometimes surfaced, like the belief (associated with the oceanographer and naval officer Matthew Fontaine Maury) that the Caribbean could become an American-owned lake; or the wacky proposal to turn the Mississippi Valley into the heart of a vast and profitable *imperium* that stretched all the way from the shores of China to those of Ireland. But such musings remained just that – or so runs the story – until America's noble innocence and splendid isolation were disturbed by the rough scramble for colonies and profits led by Britain, France, Germany, Russia and other European states.

Proclaimed innocence, described by Byron as 'heavenly ignorance / Of what is call'd the world, and the world's ways',[56] is a
curse for democracies. Like a flowering weed, it chokes off criticism
of its own illusions. It is ashamed of nothing and acts righteously,
apparently afraid of nothing, until such time as it finds itself naked,
unprotected and vulnerable to the ways of the world. Innocence
certainly flourished in the American republic throughout the nineteenth century, eventually suffering meltdown in the heat of the
catastrophic events of 1914–18. Towards the end of January 1917,
a week before German submarines were to sink four unarmed
American merchant ships and draw his country into the first ever
global war, President Woodrow Wilson declared America to be an
innocent but morally committed defender of worldwide peace.
Its 'American principles' were 'the principles of mankind', he told
the Senate. America had always opposed 'entangling alliances',
'competitions of power' and 'selfish rivalry'. It had always stood
for the principle 'that no nation should seek to extend its polity
over any other nation or people, but that every people should
be left free to determine its own polity, its own way of development, unhindered, unthreatened, unafraid, the little along with
the great and powerful'. The urgent task now, said Wilson, was
to avoid 'organized rivalries' and to promote 'organized peace'.
Balance-of-power politics had to be replaced by a community of
world opinion rooted in democratic nation-states whose governments, leaders and citizens would band together within a new
league that would promote the cause of world peace and democratic justice.[57]

It was heady stuff, but consonant with an old American tradition of claimed innocence in a tainted world. Such innocence was
written all over the words that sprang from the pages of the inaugural address (in March 1885) of President Grover Cleveland, who
told a large crowd gathered outside the East Portico of the Capitol
that the uniqueness of American democratic institutions necessitated a 'scrupulous avoidance of any departure from that foreign
policy commended by the history, the traditions, and the prosperity of our Republic'. What did the republic traditionally stand for?
'It is the policy of independence, favored by our position', he
replied. 'It is the policy of peace suitable to our interests. It is the

THE LIFE AND DEATH OF DEMOCRACY

policy of neutrality, rejecting any share in foreign broils and ambitions upon other continents and repelling their intrusion here.' Such neutrality had been championed by George Washington, Thomas Jefferson and James Monroe, and its principles were clear: 'Peace, commerce, and honest friendship with all nations; entangling alliance with none.'[58]

So deep-rooted was this old belief that the young American republic was leading the world towards peaceful democracy that Alexis de Tocqueville, with just one qualification, elevated the avoidance of 'entangling alliances' into a general principle of democratic life. 'Fortune, which has conferred so many peculiar benefits upon the inhabitants of the United States, has placed them in the midst of a wilderness, where they have', he wrote, 'no neighbours; a few thousand soldiers are sufficient for their wants.' Tocqueville warned that democracies should be permanently watchful of armies, whose officers and other ranks (unlike the armies once led by aristocrats) are gripped by material ambition, and therefore prone to disgruntlement with their lot. They come to see that war is in their self-interest, even though wars and rumours of war, like an acid, eat away the body of democracy. Fortunately, Tocqueville observed, most civilian Americans understood that war whips up animosity towards others, that it concentrates the means of administration in a few hands, as well as destroys material wealth. Privileged by geography and committed to equality, the American democracy tends to pacifism. 'The ever increasing numbers of men of property who are lovers of peace, the growth of personal wealth which war so rapidly consumes, the mildness of manners, the gentleness of heart, those tendencies to pity which are produced by the equality of conditions, all these causes concur to quench the military spirit.'[59]

The First Americans

The assessment, like the self-proclaimed innocence of a long string of American presidents, was wildly inaccurate. Leaving aside the shame of a civil war driven by two clashing definitions of democracy, the innocence that became part of the soul of nineteenth-century

American democracy turned a blind eye to its will for power over Native Americans, whose liberty – symbolised by the eagle – was virtually destroyed by the democratisation unintentionally kick-started by the revolution of 1776.

From the beginning, Congress had been irritated by the way that the Six Nations of the Iroquois Confederacy, for reasons of cultural dignity and physical survival, had long since mastered the art of balancing one group of whites against another, regardless of whether the balance was British against French, Americans against British, or French against Americans. The number of native groups who consistently supported the gentlemen revolutionaries was actually small. Lured by gifts and British promises of protection from the clutches of colonists who descended like locusts on Indian lands, the majority supported the other side, much to the annoy-ance of most prominent revolutionaries, who were quick to strike off 'savages' from their list of those eligible for universal liberty. The Declaration of Independence denounced them as 'merciless savages'. John Adams called them 'blood Hounds'. Thomas Jefferson said that white Americans were destined – had an 'expectancy' – to possess their land. George Washington likened Native Americans to wolves – 'both being beasts of prey tho' they differ in shape'.[60]

Such words implied genocide. An English traveller recently returned from America during the period dominated by republican gentlemen reported that 'white Americans have the most rancorous antipathy to the whole race of Indians'. He added: 'Nothing is more common than to hear them talk of extirpating them from the face of the earth, men, women and children.'[61] Other observers spotted the counter-trend: the resilience of Native Americans in the face of bigotry backed by muskets. These first Americans lived in material abundance – 'The life of an Indian is a continual holiday, compared with the poor of Europe', remarked Tom Paine[62] – and they liked to talk of freedom granted them by the Great Spirit. They naturally greeted mentions of kings with laughter and stub-bornly refused, in several declarations of independence, to give up their own autonomy to any earthly power.

During the next century, these qualities ensured that Native Americans did not become the passive victims of government agents after land, frontiersmen after blood, or missionaries after souls. Unlike the native peoples of Mexico and the Andes, the first Americans were not reduced to a subordinate caste. Some accepted Britain's invitation to move to Canada. Most lived skilfully on the edge of American colonial life. The so-called Proclamation Line, designed in 1763 by the British to separate Europeans from native peoples, formally defined that edge. For a time, that line, running from the border between Florida and Georgia up the eastern mountains to Chaleur Bay on the Gulf of St Lawrence, served as a safety fence, staving off white men's hunger for land. But despite valiant attempts to push encroaching European settlers back to where they were supposed to be, and though even the names of their tribes struck fear into the hearts of many white Americans, the original Americans were heavily outnumbered, outgunned and vulnerable.

From the perspective of white Americans, the westward expansion of democratic ways of life certainly bore fruit during the nineteenth century. Like the Athenian strategy of spreading citizenship entitlements by colonising the ecosystems of others, the move westwards provided land, jobs, new sources of agricultural exports and minerals, and, of course, new sources of profit. It was not 'a vast system of outdoor relief for the upper classes' (James Mill's famous definition of the British Empire[63]) but a vast field of opportunity for men and women who thought of themselves as equals in the struggle for enrichment. Conquest produced a semblance of equality. Tocqueville rightly thought that there was something very 'democratic' about it all. Colonisation westwards was done in the name of what he called the *semblable*: equality in the rush for spoils, new lives, dreams fulfilled. Never mind that the westwards push left behind trails of tears marked by trickery, extortion, intimidation, shooting, detention camps; for many settlers the point was simply that they were contributors to a grand democratic experiment. A mountain in Colorado was even named in their honour (Figure 52). In one of the newly conquered territories – the Territory of Wyoming, which later dubbed itself the Equality State – the sense that all white settlers had a common stake in land and procreation, against a common enemy within a hostile environment, even helped to empower white women. Pushed by local settler activists like Esther Hobart Morris – soon to

FIGURE 52: Rising to over 4300 metres in the Rocky Mountains of Colorado, Mount Democrat. A favourite summer climb for citizens in reasonable physical shape, it is located a few kilometres from the ghost town of Climax, once the highest human settlement in the United States.

become a justice of the peace and perhaps the first woman to hold judicial office in the era of representative democracy – soil and sex stirred up passions favouring gender equality. It is daunting to think that democracy tapped white male fears of emasculation and female threats of miscegenation, but so it was in this remote frontier of the modern world. In December 1869, shortly after the first ever Territory-wide election, land and libido joined hands to persuade the Governor of the Territory of Wyoming, John Campbell, to sign into law a bill that for the first time in America granted white women the right to vote (but not to stand for election). Three months later, bathed in public attention, some of it international, the first women jurors were called to duty in Laramie, the capital. Laws were soon passed giving married women control of their own property. In preparation for their admission into the Union in 1890, Wyoming voters approved the state constitution that re-affirmed voting rights for women (Figure 53); and, in 1924, Nellie Taylor Ross became the first woman governor in the United States.

Forged by the fears and fantasies of white settlers in a hostile territory, the changes certainly made a difference to white women. But

FIGURE 53: Women casting their votes in Cheyenne, Wyoming, in November 1888, from the front page of *Frank Leslie's Illustrated Paper* (24 November 1888).

from the perspective of Native Americans, all this energy felt like imperial conquest. White Europeans seemed much like Cervantes' Sancho Panza, whose scheme for deriving advantage from the government of an island involved selling its people into slavery and putting the profits in his pocket. Their fate was potentially worse than slavery. The ugly waves of disease and death triggered by their earliest contacts with Europeans signalled their demise; the Iroquois alone lost half of their eight to ten thousand people during the last quarter of the eighteenth century. For a period after the 1776 revolution, Native Americans, displaying extraordinary skill at playing off different groups of opponents, still believed that their own nations would earn them the respect of white American citizens. But in the end, regardless of whether they went it alone or instead chose the support of the French, the British, the Spanish, or American democrats, Native Americans were handed an unhappy fate by the fledgling democracy. In the name of that democracy, they were forced to totter on the borderline between physical extinction and cultural assimilation and promises of what Grover Cleveland famously called 'ultimate citizenship'.[64]

Purchasing Power

The young representative democracy knew another way of acquiring empire: conquest through the gentle soldier called money. Its
use, Benjamin Franklin liked to say, is the sole advantage of having
money, a principle that was first applied with real effect in the
Louisiana Purchase. In Paris on 30 April 1803, the American
envoys Robert Livingston and James Monroe signed a treaty that
gave sixty million francs to the French government and a further
twenty million francs to Americans who had outstanding claims
against the French. The sums were as vast as the land acquired,
875,000 square miles of the Louisiana Territory, which today comprises 23 per cent of the territory of the United States and includes
the wedge of thirteen states that runs north from Louisiana to
Minnesota and west to Montana (Figure 54). The formal handover
took place in New Orleans in late December 1803, when the Stars
and Stripes were raised in front of the Cabildo, to the applause of
a handful of Americans and the stony silence of French, Spanish

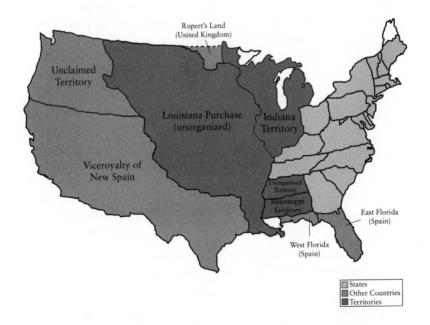

FIGURE 54: American states and territories, showing the vast Louisiana Purchase, 1803–4.

and Native American onlookers. A few months later, a white silk banner was paraded through the streets of New York City. It fired a twenty-one-word salute: 'Extension of the Empire of Freedom in the Peaceful, Honorable, and Glorious Acquisition of the Immense and Fertile Region of Louisiana'.

The banner stated what was to seem obvious to coming generations of innocent democrats: the Louisiana Purchase was an unparalleled piece of diplomacy that ranked (as the nineteenth-century American historian Henry Adams put it) 'next to the Declaration of Independence and the adoption of the Constitution'.[65] The acquisition – the word 'conquest' was never used – was seen to have rescued the republic from the bloody power confrontations of Europe, to have stabilised the foundations laid by the revolution, and thus to have defined the American destiny of making the whole world safe for freedom and equality. Thomas Jefferson, who was president at the time, had once contemplated the possibility that liberty on the continent could be secured by a family of 'sister republics', of which the United States was one, perhaps along with a creole republic of Louisiana. During the negotiations with Napoleon, who needed cash to pay for his European ventures, and who saw also that a stronger America might mean a weaker Britain, Jefferson changed his tune by threatening an Anglo-American alliance if France refused to sell. Madison warned of coming 'collisions'. Both strategies proved unnecessary. In the emerging banknote world, money proved a good man-at-arms. Without a single shot being fired, the 'empire of liberty' (Jefferson's pet oxymoron) had virtually doubled in size, at a cost in the currency of the day of less than three cents an acre.

The peoples of Louisiana never formally agreed to the tactic of dollar-bill expansion. Native Americans who lived on the land never even knew of the sale. Had they been consulted, they would no doubt have been puzzled by the very notion that their land and lives could be tied to a price tag, which raises questions about what exactly an empire of liberty meant, and how it could be reconciled with the principle of government by consent of the people.

Such questions seemed never to matter at the time, which is one reason why variants of the dollar-bill tactic were used by successive American governments during the next hundred years. In 1867, Secretary of State William H. Seward negotiated a treaty under which the United States purchased Alaska from Russia for a modest $7.2 million. Efforts during the Civil War to buy the Danish Virgin Islands were scuppered by a Senate veto; their purchase (for $25 million) had to wait until 1916. Control over territory was also acquired by the application of commercial muscle. Especially after 1875, sometimes in the name of democracy, American businessmen, bankers, industrialists and shippers openly called for easier access to global markets. Sometimes that implied direct intervention with local support, as happened in Hawaii, where the annexation of the islands (in 1898) was helped by the overthrow of the native queen Liliuokalani by American sugar planters. Control over the Panama Canal project was gained through more circuitous means. The Hay-Herran Treaty of 1903 granted the United States rights to a canal zone for the sum of $10 million plus an annual rental of $250,000; the deal was opposed by the Colombian senate, which forced the Americans to change tactics. President Roosevelt verbally attacked his Colombian opponents as 'contemptible little creatures' who opposed progress across the hemisphere. With the blessing of Washington and help from its navy, local canal promoters and *insurrectos* whipped up a local pocket revolution in favour of Panamanian independence from Colombia. Rehearsing the lines used by many later presidents, Roosevelt was unapologetic about democracy's combined use of cunning, cash and cannon. 'If I had followed traditional conservative methods', he said, 'I would have submitted a dignified state paper of probably two hundred pages to Congress and the debates on it would have been going on yet; but I took the Canal Zone and let Congress debate; and while the debate goes on the Canal does also.'[66]

The Superior Republic

Armed annexation had its full-dress rehearsal in *la intervención norteamericana*, commonly known today in the United States as the Mexican-American War (1846–8). The official reasons given for the American declaration of war on Mexico, in mid-May 1846, were at the time hotly disputed on both sides; and the territorial conflict produced widespread destruction, and the death and wounding of more than forty thousand soldiers. But for the aspiring young American democracy, the war yielded extraordinary dividends. Weakened by hip-level use of old-fashioned British muskets, the Mexican troops were outgunned and outmanoeuvred by well-equipped American and Texas Ranger troops, to the point where Mexico lost half its territory. The Americans gained undisputed control of Texas. The new border with Mexico was set at the Rio Grande River, and the United States was granted Nevada and Utah, as well as parts of Wyoming, New Mexico, Arizona and Colorado. The war whipped up dissent, certainly. Henry David Thoreau, who during this period penned his famous essay *Civil Disobedience*, was among those jailed for their refusal to pay taxes to fund a war deemed incompatible with democratic ideals; John Quincy Adams, the only son of a president also to become president (1824–8), until George W. Bush managed by a whisker to do so in the early twenty-first century, strongly criticised the war as unjust, even suffering a fatal stroke on the floor of the Congress after arguing against the award of 'swords of honor' to generals who had prosecuted the war.

There were plenty of other honest democrats with a conscience, but the victory against the Mexicans also produced from the presses of America a massive surge of proud justifications of the war. Supporters of the Democratic Party were especially vocal, and certainly the most skilled in using the press as a propaganda weapon. Nahum Capen (1804–86) was among those who came out publicly in favour of the war, with all guns blazing. The well-connected Bostonian publisher and bookseller, whose good friend, the incumbent eleventh president, James K. Polk (1795–1849), convinced him to write the first American history of democracy, heaped praise on 'the brilliant achievements' of the American army in Mexico. The victory, Capen said, was a glorious victory for 'democracy'. He likened it to the magnanimous struggle of the Athenians against the Persians, and reckoned the triumph of the United States to have similar universal significance. 'The cause of democracy is the universal cause of equal rights and freedom', he said, 'and it is placed with us, more than with any other people, to be protected, preserved, and advanced. It is not the cause of a day, but of all coming time; not of a people, but of a world.' Lest the florid language be judged a camouflage for brute power, Capen insisted that the American people and its government were lovers of peace. But he quickly added that when faced with Mexican-style governments built of 'impenetrable walls of national error, pride, and prejudice', the American democracy had no choice but to break down their defences, using power driven by force. When dealing with recalcitrant nations, democratic might was right. 'A nation cannot be sent for by the police', Capen concluded, sliding towards italics. 'It cannot be imprisoned for safety. It cannot be tried by a jury, sentenced by a court, and punished according to law. *A nation cannot be called to an account for its wickedness, or be subjected to punishment, except by war.*'[67]

The words resembled mortar in the edifice of empire. As the nineteenth century wore on, talk of democratic right, backed by the threatened or actual use of force to annex territory and people, became commonplace. It was as if innocence no longer needed the mask that once covered the face of hubris. It was Athens all over again. The aspiring American democracy quietly occupied and claimed Baker Island and Howland Island and guano-rich Jarvis Island (1857), Johnston Island and Kingman Reef (1858), Midway Island (1867), Samoa Island (1889), Guam Island and Palmyra (1898). Wake Island was seized from Spain (1899). Given this westward expansion into the Pacific, it should come as no surprise to learn that by around 1900 some serious American observers were openly describing the United States as an empire whose expansion was natural, due to its 'superior' peoples and polity.

The force used in some annexations suggested that the natural was in fact political. At first, military action seemed unspectacular, as when troops had been quietly sent to Buenos Aires in 1890 to protect American business interests (in a country that was one of the ten wealthiest in the world); and, a year later, when marines had clashed with nationalist rebels in Chile. Before long, the size and political scope of the interventions ballooned. In 1898, with strong public backing at home, American troops and gunboats, accompanied by a press corps, foreign dignitaries and well-wishers, smashed the Spanish military crackdown against popular resistance in Cuba, which despite grand promises of 'Cuba Libre' was trans-formed into an American protectorate, along with neighbouring

Puerto Rico. Then, 15,000 kilometres to the west, came the conquest of the Philippines, first by Admiral Dewey's rout of the Spanish navy, then – after four thousand American soldiers were killed in difficult battles – the military defeat of guerrillas led by Emilio Aguinaldo.

Self-styled 'anti-imperialists' at home tried publicly to warn against the fall from the grace of the early glorious republic. Their brave stance arguably smacked of the innocence of their opponents, but it fell on ears deafened by the noises of imperial ambition. 'Who will embarrass the government by sowing seeds of dissatisfaction among the brave men who stand ready to serve and die, if need be, for their country?' called President McKinley to a flag-waving crowd in Omaha during the invasion of the Philippines. His successor, Theodore Roosevelt, the first American president to ride in an aeroplane and a military submarine, the first American to win the Nobel Peace Prize and who, a year later (in 1907), despatched the new Great White Fleet navy on a world tour, to prove that America could carry a big stick, spoke the language of *realpolitik* with greater confidence. 'If we stand idly by', Roosevelt warned an invited audience in Chicago's Hamilton Club, 'if we seek merely swollen, slothful ease and ignoble peace, if we shrink from the hard contests where men must win at hazard of their lives and the risk of all they hold dear, then the bolder and stronger people will pass us by, and win for themselves the domination of the world.' Roosevelt's conclusion minced no words. 'Let us therefore boldly face the life of strife', he said, 'for it is only through strife, through hard and dangerous endeavor, that we shall ultimately win the goal of true national greatness.'[68]

With this sermon, Roosevelt announced the end of American innocence, the official entry of its democracy on to a world stage soon to be pulled apart by life-and-death struggles for power. Roosevelt was a great showman blessed with sharp political instincts that won votes; he had no fear of war and was architect of the doctrine that the United States was entitled to intervene in the affairs of other states when the corruption of their governments made that necessary. Yet unlike Professor Marvel, the clairvoyant character featured in America's most-loved film, *The Wizard of Oz* (1939), Roosevelt had no access to a crystal ball that would have let him peer deeply into the dark future. Perilously dark the near distance was: a world racked by revolutions, death camps, two global wars, economic collapse, dictatorship, totalitarian rule, bomb blasts brighter than the sun. These forces were not exactly what Roosevelt had in mind when speaking of strife, but their power to destroy power was soon to push America on to the back foot. The only remaining question was whether American boldness could protect democracy from the cold claws of destruction – whether it was strong enough to stop the strife of twentieth-century life from once again reducing the spirit and institutions of democracy to a dead word in old dictionaries.

CAUDILLO DEMOCRACY

We elect monarchs whom we call presidents.

Simón Bolívar

The business of hoisting the flag of democracy at gunpoint had its hazards, especially when tried on a world stage. The Athenians learned a thing or two about the strife of life, but this time round, under trickier modern conditions, life seemed more than willing to match Roosevelt's challenge, even to put his brand of high-minded politics severely to the test, on a world scale. Quite aside from the fact that future American invasions of different parts of the planet were to rely upon the most frightful weapons ever known to humanity – motorised tanks, jet fighters, chemical and nuclear bombs – Theodore Roosevelt's talk of tackling life's turmoil had troubling implications for the institutions and spirit of representative democracy, both at home and abroad. As twentieth-century America gradually woke from its sleep of innocence to find itself within touching distance of the centre of the world, it was forced gradually to confront the contradiction between the domineering spirit of empire and power-devolving democracy.

Imperial ventures were costly. Done in the name of democracy, they risked charges of hypocrisy and harsh snubs, blows of the kind delivered to Yankee power by a majority of Cubans during elections in mid-June 1900, shortly after American troops had occupied their island, in preparation for annexation. Imperial ventures also endangered representative democracy at home. Military intervention normally required ceding special privileges to the presidency, and to the armed forces under its control, as well as put a strain on the power-sharing arrangements of the republic, including the civil and political liberties of its citizens. 'To fight', Woodrow Wilson reportedly told Frank Cobb, the editor of the *New York World*, on the eve of America's entry into World War One, three years after he had ordered American troops to occupy Veracruz in Mexico, 'you must be ruthless, and the spirit of ruthless brutality will enter into the very fibre of our national life, infecting Congress, the courts, the policeman on the beat, the man in the street'.[1] Just hours later, Wilson bit the bullet by delivering the first ever speech by a head of state in defence of using force to protect and expand representative democracy. Standing before a special joint session of Congress, he explained that in world affairs armed neutrality was no longer a viable option for the United States. Experience showed that Germany and other states unchecked by freedom of opinion and assembly 'fill their neighbour states with spies' and 'set the course of intrigue'. Ruled by 'plottings of inner circles', they tell their people nothing, break their covenants and generally do whatever they please. Government based on 'a narrow and privileged class' is thus prone to belligerence. According to Wilson, the corollary was clear: 'A steadfast concert for peace can never be maintained except by a partnership of democratic nations.' That point led President Wilson to explain that world affairs were now at the beginning of a new age, one that would be defined either by irresponsible governments that threw aside 'all considerations of humanity and of right', or by democratic states that upheld 'the right of those who submit to authority to have a voice in their own governments'. Wilson made it clear where America would place its bets. 'The world must be made safe for democracy', he told Congress. The interests of the United States were now identical with the interests of humanity. 'We have no selfish ends to serve', he said. 'We desire no conquest, no dominion. We seek no indemnities for ourselves, no material compensation for the sacrifices we shall freely make. We are but one of the champions of the rights of mankind.'[2]

The speech is often remembered in triumphal terms, but it actually caused a great public rumpus. With the exception of an

Anglophile minority that favoured military intervention in the affairs of Europe, a big majority of Americans felt duped, if only because many of them had voted for Wilson a year before on the understanding that he would keep America out of the war. Congress itself was awash with furious rebuttals. There were moments when its chambers shook with bursts of shouting and angry applause. Several representatives condemned Wilson's decision as a victory for armed plutocracy marching to the tune of 'Onward Christian Soldiers' bearing American flags marked with dollar signs. Others said that Americans were too frightened to stand up to their president, while Robert La Follette, now battling in the Senate, delivered a four-hour speech crammed with scathing denunciations of Wilson's alleged hypocrisy, his support for Wall Street bankers and his silence about the possible starvation of many thousands of German children and elderly caused by the British blockade of its opponent.

Such was the heat of domestic opposition to a war for democracy that Wilson subsequently tried to sell his military strategy to sceptical Americans by launching a speaking tour, towards the end of which he suffered his famous cerebral thrombosis that left him mentally and physically disabled. The wider public strains produced by military forays were sometimes camouflaged in America by a type of nationalist rhetoric that indulged talk of the national interest, loyalty to country and the will to fight, all of which implied citizens' primary dependence upon the power of the American government as it elbowed and jostled its competitors in a world dominated by empires and states. At other times, there were recurrent bouts of the old feverish innocence – marked by semi-delirious talk of America's obligations towards less fortunate and suffering peoples and its God-given duties to make the whole world a better place by introducing it to 'the benefits of a Christian civilization which has reached its highest development under our republican institutions' (as President McKinley put the matter after the conquest of the Philippines). Grand ideology of this kind masked particular power interests, but it sometimes seemed to persuade voters and to win elections at home, even though its anti-democratic consequences abroad were unmistakeable. Its victims were to learn something new about modern representative democracy: that flights of political abstraction centred on the goodness of democracy could mask brute force and greed that robbed others of their own claims to self-determination. Here, in a nutshell, was an entirely new difficulty in the history of democracy as its language and institutions spread across the globe: the geopolitical problem of how to combine representative democracy at home with representative democracy abroad.

Southern Brethren

The question of how to practise democratically the principle of letting others live democratically would soon stare all representative democracies in the face. It was at first a peculiarly American problem, one that was fuelled by the vexed relations between the United States and Spanish-speaking Central and South America.

From around the time of the American invasion of Spanish-controlled Guantánamo Bay in 1898, many American politicians and diplomats, even some citizens, liked to portray the world to their south as shackled by financial corruption, untamed passions, sun-dried poverty, political disorder and intellectual muddle – all of which served as proof of the superiority of Yankee-style democracy. The cruelties of the Spanish army in Cuba, where perhaps 200,000 Cubans died in or on their way to urban camps called *reconcentrados*, seemed to confirm their point. It followed that permanent vigilance and periodic intervention would be required, if only to elevate peoples untutored in the arts of democracy. Theodore Roosevelt set the pace by complaining that recurrent troubles in the 'infernal little Cuban republic' often fuelled thoughts that the United States should 'wipe its people off the face of the earth'. But American goals were benevolent, he insisted. 'All that we wanted from them was that they would behave themselves and be prosperous and happy so that we would not have to interfere.' If Cubans continued to play the game of revolution they would 'get things into such a snarl that we have no alternative save to intervene – which will at once convince the suspicious idiots in South America that we do wish to interfere after all, and perhaps have some land hunger.'[3]

Jawboning was directed not just at Cuba. It crystallised into a Latin American policy that built on the Monroe Doctrine – the 1823 declaration that confirmed that Latin America was in the 'sphere of influence' of the United States – and came to be called the Roosevelt Corollary. In plain English, it awarded the United States the right to see itself as exclusive policeman of the region that stretched nearly nine thousand kilometres from the tropical Gulf of Mexico to the Antarctic islands of Tierra del Fuego. No European powers were welcome in the region; the American continents were closed to future European colonisation. Existing colonies or dependencies (Monroe had in mind the continuing Portuguese grip on Brazil) would remain unopposed. But any effort by Russia, France, Britain or Spain to extend their political influence into the New World would be regarded (Monroe told the American Congress on 2 December 1823) as 'the manifestation of an unfriendly disposition toward the United States' and 'as dangerous to our peace and safety'. Much was at stake, he said. The political system of the United States was 'essentially different' (Monroe meant better) from those of the Old World. It honoured the principle of non-interference with other states and its corollary, the cultivation of 'friendly relations' through the application of 'a frank, firm, and manly policy'. The United States expected all other states to behave in the same way, and it would reciprocate by refraining from interference, both in European conflicts or internal affairs and in the affairs of 'our southern brethren'.[4] The resulting stability on the American continents would bring peace and good government and benefit American corporate interests – not just in improved trade, but also in key fields such as the extraction of primary resources, banking and industrial investment.

Defenders of the Corollary meant business. The earlier despatch of naval forces to Buenos Aires and Chile (during 1890–91), the full-scale Cuban intervention and the later occupation of Puerto Rico by American forces cast the die. It established the habit of intervening in the domestic affairs of its neighbours whenever the American government or its *comprador* allies decided that their investments or political hegemony needed reinforcement. In fact, the whole of Central and Latin America was to become a testing ground of the dialectics of this Yankee imperial spirit that had roots in the conquest of native peoples during the westward expansion, and in the military attack on Mexico. In the twenty-year period from 1890 to 1910, American forces invaded the region twenty times. They returned nineteen times between 1910 and 1945 and another twenty times from then until 2004.

That was a grand total of fifty-nine military interventions in just over a century. In the terms of the Monroe Doctrine and the Roosevelt Corollary, the whole of the region was regularly targeted, using a variety of methods that ranged from the deployment of troops and marines to the provision of command operations and (for the purpose of staging a *coup d'état*) intelligence services. Few countries were spared (Paraguay was among the lucky exceptions). The length of occupation varied from days to years, and the range of interests perceived by the Americans to be at stake was very broad indeed. Force was directed at a revolt led by black workers against American claims upon Haiti's Navassa Island (1891). Trade unionists were sometimes the target of occupation (Guatemala 1920; Panama 1925). Troops and ships were used several times to repel threats to American interests posed by Mexican nationalists (1914–16). In a number of countries, troops were sent to shape or reshape the outcomes or aftermaths of elections, as happened in Cuba (1906–9), several times in Panama (1908; 1912; 1918–20), and twice in Honduras (1919; 1924–5). Interventions were also commonly directed at securing investments or seizing resources, as in the Dominican Republic (1903–4), the 'Dollar Diplomacy' protectorate set up in Nicaragua (1907), in two interventions in Honduras (1911; 1912), and in the extended occupation of Cuba (1917–33).

Cádiz

In the speeches and statements of American politicians and officials, all this meddling was variously justified. Theodore Roosevelt spoke to Americans of the need for a 'reasonable and intelligent foreign policy' that would put an end to the 'crying disorders' on their doorsteps. Champions of dollar diplomacy followed the Taft administration (1908–12) in speaking frankly about the benefits of exporting capital. Still others referred to humanitarian sentiments, or even used the 'democracy' word – which in retrospect looks thoroughly cheeky, even duplicitous, considering that the tree of representative democracy actually budded throughout the region *earlier* than it did in the United States, during the 1810s, a full decade *before* Andrew Jackson's home-grown push towards democracy.

It is worth pausing for a moment to see why Spanish America blazed a trail in matters of democracy. The vibrant constitutional revolutions that swept through its lands during the early years of the nineteenth century proved just how marvellously tangled were the roots of representative democracy. The Spanish American revolutions showed that the basic institutions of representative government, like lemon and orange trees, could be transplanted with some success into foreign climes, despite the interesting fact that the whole transplantation exercise was utterly unplanned – so proving, once again, that in matters of representative democracy there were times when the road to heaven was paved with hellish intentions.

The revolutionary upheavals that occurred in early nineteenth-century Spanish America were not straightforward affairs, and careful attention needs to be paid to their amusing dialectics. The ruptures were inspired by the bizarre revolutionary events triggered by the 1807 advance of the troops of Napoleon Bonaparte towards mainland Spain. In the spring of 1808, in quick succession, both Charles IV and his son Ferdinand VII (who was arrested and imprisoned by Napoleon) were forced by Napoleon's forces to abdicate, thus leaving behind a kingdom that resembled a political vacuum. It was filled at first with a wild rush of local monarchist sentiment. But fashion faded fast. The granting of the Spanish throne by Napoleon to his brother, Joseph, triggered widespread feelings of insult. Rioting erupted in Madrid and a guerrilla war was sparked in various parts of unoccupied Spain. Mobs drove out, or strung up by their treacherous necks, royal officials who had dared to side with the French. Meanwhile, in an effort to take control of the situation, leading Spanish gentlemen set up scores of local juntas, self-governing bodies made up of respected clergymen, aristocrats and government officials who still proclaimed their

loyalty to young Ferdinand VII as legitimate king of Spain. The
juntas raised troops, and ran local affairs throughout the summer
of 1808, all the while searching for ways of re-establishing some
form of central government that could coordinate the opposition to
Napoleon.

A political solution came in late September 1808, at Aranjuez,
near Madrid, where an opposition government was formed to rid
the country of its French occupiers. The self-christened Supreme
Central Junta for the Government of the Kingdom declared
Ferdinand VII to be sovereign king of Spain. It described itself as
his guardian until such time as he returned to the throne. That was
an interesting move, since the Supreme Central Junta in effect set
itself up as the revolutionary source of authority of the absent king.
It was an upside-down version of 1776, and the move suddenly put
the Spanish American colonies on the spot. The remarkable news
that had been arriving there by wind power, several months out of
date, had at first prompted loyalist outbursts. All hands in Spanish
America seemed to be raised in favour of king, Church and tradition, in opposition to the French conquerors. But when the news
arrived that a Supreme Central Junta had been founded, it caused
great surprise, mixed with perplexity. Spanish Americans learned
that they were now to be offered a say in the future of the empire.
Battered by military defeats and wounded by unpopularity, the
rebel government based in Aranjuez had taken an unprecedented
step: in the name of 'the beloved King' Ferdinand VII, it invited its
Spanish American provinces to elect representatives and 'be part of
the Central Junta of the Kingdom's government through their representatives'.[5]

The extraordinary move, to include the peoples of the empire in
a transcontinental vote in favour of monarchy, played wicked tricks
on all parties to the deal. It was to hasten both the end of empire
and its replacement by self-governing republics. Between the spring
of 1809 and the winter of 1810, from the mountainous deserts
and wide beaches of Sonora to the rain and slush, glaciers and
permanent snow of the southern tip of Chile, the whole Spanish
American region found itself caught up in its first ever electoral
exercise. It was the biggest ever experiment in representative self-
government, and there were, naturally, hiccups galore. The election

FIGURE 55: The viceroyalties and captaincy-generals of Latin America, about 1800.

rules caused irritation among many of the public juntas that had sprung up in the provinces. The original edict of January 1809 inviting participation described the region as 'the vast and precious domains that Spain possesses'. But that contradicted the views of many Americans, who loathed all talk of 'colonies', instead insisting that there was a fundamental *equality* between what they called 'the Spains' or the 'Spain of the two hemispheres'.

Salt grit was rubbed deeper into the wounds of Spanish American patriots, who were miffed by the fact that their elite-led, insurrectionary juntas, which had been copied from the mainland model, would have to abide by the decision of the Central Junta in Madrid to restrict representation to the four viceroyalties (New Spain, New Granada, Peru and the Plate) and the five captaincy-generals (Cuba, Puerto Rico, Guatemala, Venezuela and Chile). Whole swathes of territory and people were to be left out of the vote (Figure 55). The Central Junta stacked the cards higher by allowing each of the lucky areas only one representative – in contrast to the two representatives of each of the thirteen mainland

Spanish juntas – despite the fact that the population of the Americas was much greater. Nine representatives against twenty-six: what kind of parity was that in a kingdom that spanned two hemispheres? many people in Spanish America began to ask.

It turned out that more than a hundred cities of the Spanish Americas participated in the election, proportionately many more than in mainland Spain, but the arcane and clumsy electoral methods used stirred up discontent. The vote was mainly rigged in favour of an oligarchy of wealthy notables in a minority of 'good towns'. Three potential candidates (called a *terna*) were first chosen by the aldermen of each of the municipal councils of the district in which the election was taking place. Each city's final choice was then decided by the drawing of lots. It was said that man selected and God decided (note the parallels with the ancient Greek drawing of lots, a procedure that was praised simultaneously for avoiding factionalism and enabling the intervention of providence, the ultimate guarantor of the natural order). There was then a second filtration of possible candidates. In the capital of the wider viceroyalty or captaincy-general, the Viceroy or Captain General, taking advice from the local *audiencia* of notable gentlemen, chose another *terna* from the long list of candidates selected by the cities. A final drawing of lots determined the single representative appointed by the kingdom to the Central Junta.

The elitist methods belonged to the old imperial order, and so, too, did the results. Given that representatives would be absent for a long time, the typical representative (called a *procurador*, the same word first used in the parliaments of León and Castile) was a man without family commitments, like a well-educated priest or a young civil servant with a university degree. Supported by the system of patronage operated by men of honour who controlled the municipal bodies and family cliques, these were representatives of an oligarchy who were fiercely loyal to the empire. That is why the growing perception that the Central Junta was *unrepresentative* caused trouble, and ultimately proved fatal to the Spanish empire.

The trouble stemmed partly from the fact that none of the American representatives arrived in time to take up their seats in the Central Junta, which governed for only a bit more than a year,

until January 1810. The farce was reinforced by the party infighting that racked many colonial cities and country districts. Large
families linked together by blood ties, wealth and friendship often
resembled mutual protection rackets. They were (not surprisingly)
not for giving up their power, and so they easily took a stand
against their rivals. Such divisions turned on allegations of undue
influence, but there were also disputes triggered between those
calling for more or less trust in the Central Junta, and – something
new for the colonies – quarrels over the legitimacy of a traditional
principle of representation that supposed the representative to
be bound ultimately to a tradition-based kingdom that now had
no king. Representative monarchy might for a time have seemed
plausible, but quite aside from the difficulty of reconciling representation with the (God-given) crown – the problem that originally
faced young King Alfonso IX in León – there was as well a serious
strategic problem. Simply put, the issue was whether or not monarchy could be restored using the old ways of monarchy.

The fractiousness was compounded by the contradictory signals
that arrived from mainland Spain, in slow motion, by clipper. First
came the news that the Central Junta was planning immediately to
assemble a new *cortes*. Then it was learned that the Central Junta
had appointed substitute representatives who were empowered to
deal with the affairs of Spanish America, on the grounds that war
with Napoleon and time constraints ruled out the formation of
autonomous juntas and independent elections in the provinces.
Given the strength of loyalism in Spanish America, its sidestepping
by the Central Junta, whether intended or not, in effect weakened
the case for monarchy. Then came astonishing news from the
besieged city of Cádiz. It was learned that its citizens had backed a
constitutional revolution, which had erupted in September 1810,
led by figures like the law graduate and revered poet from Madrid
Manuel José Quintana (1772–1857) (Figure 56), who declared
himself stridently in favour of independence for the provinces.
'From now on, Spanish-Americans, you are elevated to the status
of freemen', he wrote. 'You are no longer the same, you who lay
until recently under a yoke so much the heavier since you were so
far from the centre of power, looked on with indifference, wounded
by greed, destroyed by ignorance. Remember . . . that your destinies

FIGURE 56; Manuel José Quintana, later crowned national poet by Isabella II, from a contemporary sketch.

no longer depend on ministers or Viceroys or governors', he concluded, 'your destiny is in your own hands.'[6]

Fast-paced confusion spiced with peppery advice from poets had the effect of temporarily opening a chasm between mainland Spain, where the resistance to empire began, and the Spanish Americans, whose loyalty to a virtual monarchy lingered. In direct contrast to the rebellious Philadelphian gentlemen opposed to the British Empire, the Spanish Americans thought of themselves as staunch loyalists – for a time. But among the strangest dialectical turns in their twisted and tense relationship with the mainland was their zigzagging towards rebellion. Their overall position, broadly summarised, at first stuck to the letter of the old Spanish proverb, 'Ni quito Rey, ni pongo Rey' ('I do not oppose the king, nor do I establish the king'). Faced with the impracticability of that position, something had to give.

The stunning upheavals in Venezuela were a taste of things to come, in dramatic form. In April 1810, the white creole elite of Caracas voted in an open-air town meeting to oust the local governor. They declared themselves a junta that would govern in the name of the deposed Ferdinand VII. That decision caused instant strife and on 5 July 1811 a congress convened by the city council (*cabildo*) issued a declaration of independence. The language was strident, a Catholic version of the American declaration of 1776 and the secession of the United Provinces in 1581. 'In the name of God Almighty, we, the representatives of the United Provinces of Caracas, Cumaná, Barinas, Margarta, Barcelona, Mérida y Trujillo . . . believe that we cannot and should not maintain the ties that linked us to the government of Spain and that, like all the peoples of the world, we are free and authorised to depend upon no other authority than our own . . .'[7] Towards the end of 1811, just a few days before Christmas, a new constitution of the independent state of Venezuela was adopted. So began what some Venezuelan historians still call the Silly Republic: silly, because in quick time the city councils of three major cities – Coro, Maracaibo and Guayana – declared themselves in favour of continuing rule by Joseph Bonaparte. Similar loyalist outbursts erupted among commoners mistrustful of the local white republican elites. To cap things off, as if a miracle had happened, a major earthquake devastated pro-independence strongholds, while sparing virtually every locale controlled by royalist forces.

It felt to many royalists that even the forces of nature and God were conspiring against locally determined, representative government. But all hopes that monarchy, God and nature were the new Holy Trinity on Spanish American soil were scotched in late 1812 by the entry into Venezuela of the army commanded by Simón Bolívar (1783–1830). 'The Liberator', as he came to be known, was something of a George Washington figure. A wealthy cacao planter, well-travelled aristocrat and a formidable self-taught field general who understood well the historical significance of the American and French revolutions, Bolívar favoured an independent federation of Spanish Americans. He was later to liken his efforts to implement that bold vision to the ploughing of the sea. Declaring 'war to the death' against Venezuela's colonial rulers, the ploughman launched a lightning campaign through the Andes to capture Caracas, which for a time became the capital of the new Second Republic, the centre of a new federation of Venezuelan states. The victory sealed

Bolívar's reputation as the pre-eminent figure of Spanish American independence. It triggered popular outbursts of republican sentiment, so guaranteeing a frosty reaction to Ferdinand VII's return to power, in 1814. The restoration of monarchy on the Spanish peninsula was widely felt to be regressive, a turn towards absolutism. That impression was bolstered by a shared sense of physical distance from the peninsula. All of a sudden, the old tyranny of distance was replaced by a new sense that distance was the enemy of tyranny. So began a wholly paradoxical revolution in favour of representative government – a struggle against imperial monarchy that had more than a passing resemblance to the republican ideals of the American revolutionaries.

Ploughing the Sea

The half-crazed sequence of events that began with the 1807 Napoleonic invasion of peninsular Spain sparked off anti-imperial resistance not just in Venezuela, but throughout Spanish America as a whole. Broadly speaking, and with the big exception of Brazil – thanks to the astonishing vagaries of the times it remained a constitutional slave-holder monarchy closely dependent upon Portugal from 1822 to 1889, when it became a republic* – the whole of Spanish America began to plough the seas, in its own inimitable way, in search of new forms of representative self-government that later mutated into species of home-grown representative democracy.

The remarkable adventure lasted from 1810 until around 1830, and it turned Spanish America into the freest place on earth, on paper at least. The constitutional revolutions were indigenous

---

* When French troops entered Portuguese territory, its royal family had already set sail from Lisbon for Rio de Janeiro, from where they ruled every part of Portugal, including the colonies of Africa and Asia not under French occupation. Brazilian ports were thrown wide open to neutral and friendly (mainly British) shipping, so that without shots being fired the territory known as Brazil came to enjoy most of the trimmings of independence. Only after the monarchy returned to Europe did a serious bid for formal separation from Portugal arise. Following a brief but intense armed conflict, the older son of Portugal's King John VI, purposely left behind when his father went home, became Emperor Pedro I of an independent Brazilian slave-holding monarchy that proved for a time to be skilled at juggling conflicts and fashioning compromises among the country's power elites.

affairs, even though the United States and Europe were written all over their faces. They proved, in matters of constitutional thinking, that Spanish America was intrinsically part of the Atlantic zone of influence, even that it was positioned at its cutting edge. Although strongly influenced by the poetry of fresh beginnings sung by the French Revolution (a fabulous irony, considering that the first disturbances were triggered in solidarity with the Spanish monarchy, against French republicanism), the struggles for constitutional independence were shaped as well by the stanzas written by the American resistance to the British Empire. Praise was heard throughout the continent for the principles of independence, confederation and federation, self-government and the separation of powers. There were also expressions of deep admiration and sympathy, circulated through such newspapers as José María Blanco White's *El Español*, for the invisible constitution based on liberty of the press and independent public life in England. The revolutions were fuelled too by strong feelings for local self-government, feelings that were inherited from the old order of the Spanish kingdom and, ultimately, from the rural assemblies of shepherds and cattlemen, and from the parliaments that first sprang up in León and Castile.

The municipal reforms introduced (in 1767) by Charles III were especially important, for in the new circumstances they had unintended revolutionary effects. By approving the indirect election of magistrates and aldermen by local assemblies of deliberating citizens known as *vecinos*, the reforms in effect set the precedent for the much bolder cases of organised public action of Spanish American citizens themselves. Exactly this happened, for instance, during the years 1810–12 in various cities of Colombia, beginning with a bold declaration of independence from Spanish authority by a council of representatives in Bogotá (20 July 1810), which shortly afterwards became the capital of the newly independent state of Cundinamarca (Figure 57). Thanks to the prevailing taste for assembly government, local citizens, gentlemen who were heads of established, property-owning households, saw themselves as equally entitled to elect their own representatives, whose job it was to write down, and to defend, their new constitutions.

The combined effect of this remarkably intricate web of forces

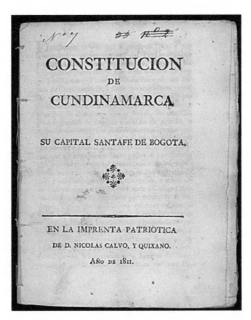

FIGURE 57: Title page of perhaps the first constitution of any Spanish American state, Cundinamarca, drawn up and agreed in the capital city of Bogotá, July 1811.

was to make the homespun revolutionaries of Spanish America unusually sensitive to the dangers of concentrated state power during revolutionary transitions, such as that of the French type, which had been marked by terror and, later, by the Napoleonic despotism that had triggered their own revolutions. The first steps towards representative democracy in Spanish America were interesting, and historically important. They proved that the region was neither 'exotic', in the sense that it was unconnected with European developments and influence, nor a poor carbon copy or copycat of earlier European history. Something new was born in Spanish America. It is an exaggeration to say that the revolutions of Spanish America were revolutions *against* the French Revolution. But the grains of truth in the exaggeration help to explain why radical constitutions were so quickly written throughout the continent (Paraguay, unusually, waited until the 1840s), always for the stated purpose of defining the new and unexpected 'liberty' and 'national independence', and to protect them against future relapses into despotism. At a time when most of the Western world, with the striking exception of the United States, endorsed monarchy, it is highly significant that not a single revolution in Spanish America explicitly embraced either monarchy, authoritarianism or some combination thereof. 'Free government' and 'national independence' were everywhere the declared aim of the revolutionaries. They wanted the creation of independent states that were structured by well-designed constitutions. These written constitutions were expected to leave no room for arbitrary government, simply because they sanctioned a strict separation of powers – that was why federalism was so often favoured – subject ultimately to popular representation and control over executive power, through periodic elections.

We have seen in the case of the United States that popular representation was a highly ambiguous notion. As a principle, it functioned in Spanish America in much the same way as it did during the gentleman-republican phase of the American Revolution. The champions of the new states of Spanish America often boasted that they had been founded on the free expression of agreement among contracting individuals who formed a 'people' or 'nation'. It was a fiction, certainly; not until much later did the peoples of the continent (there were about twenty million at the time of independence) feel themselves to be 'Colombians' or 'Costa Ricans' or 'citizens' of Mexico (whose territory stretched from Panama to Oregon). The fiction nevertheless had puissance; it made it seem as though new subjects, variously called 'the people' or 'the nation' or 'citizens' or 'freemen', were now in charge of their own earthly destiny. The constitutions written after 1810 all seemed to confirm the point that a new founding compact had fundamentally transformed the New World of Spanish America. The 1822 elections to Emperor Iturbide's Constituent Congress in Mexico, in which virtually universal male suffrage and an American-style federal system were combined with a self-appointed *generalísimo* and representation by town, estate, class and profession, were one exception that proved the rule. The other exception was the breathtaking silence of the constitution makers about women, who were regarded as an invisible and mute estate unworthy of representation. Otherwise, throughout Spanish America, all legal distinctions of class and estate among men were abolished. Slavery was outlawed. The distinction between believers in the Catholic faith and non-believers was also legally abolished; the enthusiastic profession of faith at the unveiling of the first Venezuelan constitution of 1811 was again the exception that proved that rule. Gone were the days of the Inquisition. It was farewell for ever to the world of feuding nobles, gold-hungry rulers and ruthless colonial governors. All men, sometimes even those of indigenous stock, were now declared equal before the law. They were free citizens, not subjects clinging like barnacles to the sinking ship of monarchy. They now had the vote and the right to live within 'sovereign' constitutional republics, under a brand-new form of representative government guided by periodic elections and the basic freedoms of assembly and the press.

The first constitution of Venezuela (1811) set the pace. It envisaged a federal state with a triumvirate executive branch and a bicameral legislature made up of representatives elected by 'the people'. The vote was granted to all male citizens. They were said to include 'free' creoles and 'free' coloured people aged twenty-one or above (or younger, if married), and who were blessed with small minimum amounts of cash or property (worth 600 pesos for single men, or 400 pesos for married men). 'The people shall make their constitution through their representatives', declared Article 2 of the first Chilean constitution (1812), which then added that all 'free' inhabitants of the country enjoyed equal political rights because 'only merit and virtue make individuals worthy of the honour to work for their mother country'. The first constitution of the Peruvian Republic (1823), which was conceived as a bicameral system of popular government, was framed by the same principle: 'sovereignty resides essentially in the nation and it is exercised by the officials to whom the nation has delegated its powers' (Article 3).

How exactly was the nation or the people defined? In the Peruvian case, the answer was among the most cautious of the whole region. The nation was said to include only those who were 'citizens', which meant men who were born in Peru or were naturalized, who were married or older than twenty-five, literate and who either owned some property or who engaged in a profession or a useful branch of industry. The scope of Peruvian suffrage was further restricted by a second set of stated preconditions that were designed to encourage 'industry and work, the firm foundations of real civil liberty'. Excluded from citizenship were servants, debtors, the bankrupt, criminals, the jobless, including those shut out from employment by physical and moral disabilities, gamblers, alcoholics, those men who had abandoned their wives or failed to fulfil their family obligations, or who were leading a 'scandalous life', and men who were caught trading their votes. The Indians of Peru were also excluded, in no small measure because of white fears of their potential disloyalty to the new republic, memories of the massive Indian rebellion of 1780–81 under Túpac Amaru, and their record, displayed during the struggle for independence, of fighting predominantly on the side of the king, whose loyalist forces had used their tight grip on Peru to draft Indians as soldiers. So, all things considered, the vote in Peru was to be restricted to white male citizens who either had property worth at least 300 pesos, or who enjoyed the status of 'a public professor of science' – around 5 per cent of the total population.

Elsewhere, for instance in Argentina, and especially in several of its provinces, the vision of constitutional government was far bolder than in Peru, so daring in fact that citizenship and suffrage laws were for their time more highly developed there than anywhere else in the world. 'Every free man, born in the country or a simple resident, of 20 years of age and above, or before if married, is entitled to vote', announced the *Ley de Buenos Aires* (Law of Buenos Aires) of August 1821. The electorate included not only Spanish citizens; male servants and day labourers were also deemed worthy of the vote. In several provinces, constitution makers went even further, as in Santa Fe, where in 1819 citizenship was granted (in its *Estatuto Provisorio*, under the guiding influence of public figures like Don Estanislao López) to all adult men, regardless of their class or educational backgrounds; the right to vote was explicitly denied only to public debtors and 'the enemies of the general cause of America, or the specific cause of the province'.[8] In the north of the country, Salta's electoral law of September 1823 followed suit. It granted voting rights to 'all men of the previous Spanish Americas'. And the western province of Mendoza did the same (in an electoral law of May 1827), except that its constitution writers explicitly excluded both 'notorious vagrants and bankrupts' and slaves, a reminder that when references during this period were made to all adult men, indentured labourers with black skin were judged to be minors who were not real men.

Caudillos

The Spanish American dalliance with self-government in the first quarter of the nineteenth century was astonishing, but riddled with a puzzling contradiction. The constitutional changes were impressive by world standards, yet strangely they worked against democracy and in favour of wealthy men with a hunger for power, politically ambitious men for whom government based on elected representatives was a way of ensuring *subordinación* of the represented: their quiet deference to political rulers and silent acceptance of massively uneven distributions of wealth.

How on earth could representative government in the age of 'the people' contribute to their subordination? Why in this part of the world did written constitutions and periodic elections come well before representative democracy? Was it because the hemisphere was disfigured by weak markets and widespread poverty, or because most Spanish Americans had had no prior experience with representative government, other than at the municipal level, or perhaps because they had no taste for democracy, for instance because they were Catholics unused to questioning priests and papal power (as has often been claimed)?

The seeds of democracy did in fact germinate in Spanish America, but we are about to see that it happened in puzzling and protracted ways, beginning with this striking fact: for much of the nineteenth century, the daring experiments that abolished monarchy in the name of a sovereign people handed power to home-grown elites who had mastered the art of using stripped-down forms of representative government to get their way in the world. Beginning with the path-breaking constitutions of Cundinamarca and Venezuela in 1811, these elites sided with representative government not because of some heartfelt textbook commitment to the principles and practice of power sharing, publicly accountable government and political equality. It is true that these oligarchs were hostile to the restoration of monarchy (and that where they tried to do that, as in Mexico, they failed). It is also true that these elites treated the word 'Jacobin' as a term of abuse. On paper they rejected unprincipled power grabs, which they knew could well ignite civil war fuelled by lingering rivalries between big and powerful families locked in their hereditary hatreds. These elites, it should also be noted, were afraid of concentrated power and had strong feelings for local self-government inherited from the old order of the Spanish kingdom. And although they knew and sometimes made the point that government by elected representatives was dictated by territorial size, this was not the way they usually thought about the subject either.

So why did they opt for representative government? Their principal motive for writing constitutions and embracing elections was shockingly straightforward. They had no desire for a restoration of monarchy exactly because they drew from their own experience the firm political conclusion that inequalities of social wealth and power were best sealed by government based on representation. Representative government in the name of the people, a way of governing that can be called 'caudillo democracy', was for them the best type of government because it enabled superior men to rule, their authority propped up by written constitutions and public election, backed by force of arms.

What exactly did caudillo democracy mean in this context? It was a local variant of representative democracy that was unique to Spanish America, a twisted type of republican oligarchy rooted in the people, a hybrid method of governing based on rich and powerful caudillos, strongmen who liked looking at themselves in the mirror of the people they dominated. Caudillo democracy was democratic only in appearance. It was in reality rule by those who thought of themselves as the best. Throughout the continent, everybody knew that talk of 'the best' was just a fancy way of referring to the rich and the powerful, white men of property and connections, men who had to be respected, and feared. In some parts, Chile, for instance, the best meant an oligarchy of landowning families. In other parts of the continent, in Buenos Aires, for example, it meant prominent men of the major cities and towns and their environs: rich men with interests tied up in land and/or in financial, industrial or commercial enterprises. In each case, the best were called the *parte sana* or the *personas principales*; or they were known as the 'illustrious families' headed by honourable men. They saw themselves as a cut above the rest, as the oldest and most distinguished members of their city, or their region. Landowners, merchants, clergy and military men, they were proud of their lineage. They treasured their amassed fortunes, their sons and daughters, their household manners, and their personal qualities of honour and dignity. Some of them recalled with ease and pride their grandparents' belief in what they called *pactismo*, the principle that king and kingdom were bound together by the loyal and reciprocal observance of duties and entitlements. In the new situation, they thought of themselves as guardians of a new *pactismo*, as a new aristocracy whose mission was to defend the new republics from the possible rot and decay caused by common values and interests.

Behind these old families – and often towering over them – stood the figure of the powerful leader, known as the caudillo. The word itself had its roots in the Latin *capitellum*, the diminutive of *caput*, or head. It referred to the political leaders who sprang up all over the continent, and are now familiar figures of its turbulent history: men like Antonio López de Santa Anna, famed for losing half of his left leg and half his country of Mexico to the United States during the 1840s; Juan Facundo Quiroga, whose foul temper and threats of violence ensured him permanent success at the card table; and his fellow Argentine Juan Manuel de Rosas, whose nickname 'Bloody Rosas' was not unrelated to the fact (said one obituary) that when in exile in England 'his greatest happiness seemed to be to sit on his horse and give orders'.[9] Then there were caudillos like Andrés Santa Cruz, who during the 1830s showed the creoles of his country that a *mestizo* (a person of mixed Indian and European ancestry) could govern the Confederation of Bolivia and Peru. There was William Walker, the hundred-pound pro-slavery gringo from Nashville, who in the 1850s realised his dream of compassing the weak by declaring himself President of the Republic of Nicaragua, only to be executed a few years later by the government of Honduras. And there was Francisco Solano López, who fancied himself as a new Napoleon and won an Irish lover, Eliza Lynch, who later buried him with her own hands after he lost his life during the Paraguayan War, whose terrible violence left more than half the population of his country dead.

Whatever is today thought of these figures, there is no denying their long-term impact on the political and social landscapes of the region. During the course of the nineteenth and twentieth centuries, as Spanish America groped its way towards representative democracy, caudillos exercised an extraordinarily strong political presence. Many bore sobriquets, sometimes not of their own choosing. Venezuela's Juan Vicente Gómez was called 'El Bagre', or 'The Catfish'. Perón of Argentina was dubbed 'El Conductor'. Rafael Trujillo was ambiguously known as 'El Benefactor'. Paraguay's Alfredo Stroessner was straightforwardly feared and satirised, as 'El Tiranosaurio'. The faces of these and other caudillos meanwhile became familiar to newspaper, radio and television audiences around the late twentieth-century world. Their numbers included a defiant Manuel Noriega, his fist clenched overhead, scowling at television cameras, and at the United States, just before his capture by American forces during 'Operation Just Cause', in 1989. Standing in their ranks in Havana was Fidel Castro, puffing on a cigar and stroking his grey beard while delivering a marathon address to a huge audience of *guajiros*, or country folk. And not to be overlooked was Hugo Chávez, presenting his own Sunday morning television programme from a Caracas studio, singing, reciting poetry and spouting off about the advantages of his brand of 'Bolivian socialism' and 'participatory democracy'.

It is generally agreed that these and other caudillos are unique to the constitutional experiment that took place in Spanish America. Much less agreement surrounds their origins. Sometimes caudillos are linked to their countries, as if they were products of their peculiar national character: Castro and Cuba, Díaz and Mexico, Perón and Argentina. At other times, these men of power, men whose political careers usually began locally before blossoming in national settings, are interpreted as products of Hispanic cultural values, or local temperament.

Such explanations contain some grains of truth. But taken on their own they are ultimately misleading, principally because they ignore the key fact: the first caudillos sprang up during the transition from imperial rule to popular representative government. These caudillos came in different shapes and sizes; they were known by various names (for instance, local Mexican caudillos were called *cacique*, a word taken from Arawak, meaning 'chief'); and during the course of the nineteenth century, driven by various ambitions, including the desire to swap their ranches and ponchos for government palaces and uniforms, they underwent multiple mutations. Their efforts to fill the power vacuum created by the collapse of monarchy were never guaranteed. In climbing the mountains of power they often fell short, but the ones who succeeded were always wily, resourceful and charismatic figures who were good at appealing for support from 'the people', using elections and plebiscites. Caudillos were practitioners of the arts of power based on the accumulation of followers. Nowhere else in the world did this dynamic unfold, at least not on such a scale and with such intensity – which makes the figure of the caudillo and their 'caudillo democracies' all the more interesting.

In a strange if perverted way, the caudillo was a representative of the subjects he dominated; he (they were without exception men) acted as if he had been chosen through free and fair elections. It was an utter fiction, of course, but that did not stop caudillos from imagining themselves as instruments of 'the people' they ruled: real people, the riffraff of knife-and-lasso horsemen, ranch hands and other gauchos, rough-skinned men who dressed in boots or sandals, brightly coloured, loose-fitting trousers and waistcoats, men who protected themselves against the elements by wearing woollen ponchos and hats sporting words like 'God and Country' (Figure 58). Sometimes these folk dared to display the name of their leader, which reinforced the caudillo's belief that he was not the creature of underlying social interests, or a narrow partisan of some 'political party' (those notions, in contrast to the United States, began to take root deeply in Spanish America only by the end of the nineteenth century). The caudillo rather fancied himself as a great harmoniser, as the political champion of an undivided society that now desperately needed a brand-new set of government institutions to heal the social cuts and bruises that empire and monarchy had inflicted on the body politic.

One way of seeing caudillos, roughly along these lines, was first

FIGURE 58: A gaucho supporter of the state-building faction of the Argentine Federalists, from an oil painting by the celebrated French artist resident in Buenos Aires, Raimundo Monvoisin (1845).

put forcefully by the exiled writer who later became president of Argentina, Domingo Faustino Sarmiento (1811–88). In his earlier years, Sarmiento was not much of a democrat (he said he was for 'educated government') and no fan of caudillos, but his *Civilización i barbarie* (1845), one of the greatest works in the Spanish language, proved that he was a talented writer whose glorious prose had fascinating things to say about them.[10] He pictured rough-cut caudillos as a new breed of political animal born of the power vacuum that had been opened by the struggle for independence. Black-bearded Juan Facundo Quiroga (1778–1834) epitomised the trend (Figure 59). A small, stout and bad-tempered man with broad shoulders and a short neck, a wild-looking fighter whose squinting eyes seemed to fire bullets from beneath sinister eyebrows, Quiroga was a dangerous man of 'the people' who as a boy had cut his political teeth on his father's cattle ranch in the red-soiled western province of La Rioja, in Argentina. It was there that he had learned how to rule, Sarmiento pointed out. Quiroga mastered the art of sipping maté with the lowly classes; he was a

FIGURE 59: Juan Facundo Quiroga, from a printed sketch, 1845.

man who knew how to pluck their strings, to produce the sounds he wanted to hear. He knew as well the art of scaring them witless if they dared whisper words of dissent, raised their eyebrows or showed doubt on their faces.

Like other caudillos of this period, Quiroga saw his own face in the looking-glass of these wild men of the pampas. His confidence was boosted by the fact that they depended upon him for work, and for physical protection, and that was why, at an early age, he had joined the provincial militia. Quiroga quickly rose through the ranks to become its commander; it was not long before his troops were used as a personal weapon in governing the province by crushing his opponents, particularly the 'unitarian' forces that favoured the building of a unitary Argentine state. True to his belief in 'the people', Quiroga always said he was for decentralised power: he professed support for local control, support for local industries and local ranchers, whom he backed to the hilt in a successful 1832 desert campaign to 'cleanse' their lands of Indians. Quiroga was not shy of using whichever means worked: cheating, gambling and killings were his specialities, as were attacks on women, organised rebellions and flying the flag of 'Religion or Death'. The most bizarre political move he made was to evacuate at gunpoint the city of Rioja, whose frightened residents were robbed of their homes and forced to find new lives in the countryside. Quiroga tried through such conquests to prove to his 'people' that political independence from Spain had bred crime and chaos, and that 'the rule of brute force, the supremacy of the strongest' was thus an absolute necessity. 'With him terror took the place of administrative activity, of enthusiasm, of strategy, of everything', wrote Sarmiento, before adding a chilling warning about the dangers of caudillo rule: 'Let us not deceive ourselves: terror is a means of government that produces greater results than patriotism and fervour.'

Democratic Kings

Quiroga was eventually assassinated, but according to Sarmiento that did not put an end to the problem of caudillos. He was right. Throughout the nineteenth century, in power terms, caudillos regularly acted as though they were the new kings of the republics – as if they were democratic kings who wore invisible crowns placed on their heads by popular acclaim, thanks to their political cunning, superior military skills, the spoils they handed out, and the elections they learned to contest, and to rig.

Sarmiento had a bad habit of seeing caudillos as 'pre-modern' throwbacks to the rural barbarism of uncivilised times; Spanish America was said by him to be trapped in an almighty battle between the 'small oases of civilization' represented by cities and 'the spirit of the pampa' that 'prepares the way for despotism'. The truth was that caudillo democracy – the rule of caudillos claiming support of 'the people' – was not the expression of an age-old struggle between 'civilisation' and 'barbarism'. It was a thoroughly modern child of thoroughly modern constitutional and state-building struggles, political manoeuvrings and social conflict, some of it violent, within a wide range of different settings that featured causes and causers haunted by the spirit of the 'great democratic revolution' famously analysed by Tocqueville.

To see Spanish American caudillos as political expressions of the democratic-egalitarian sentiments that flourished after the breakdown of empire is to reject more recent views of what made them tick. Caudillos were not proof of Great Man theories of history (as Thomas Carlyle and others in the nineteenth century supposed). They were certainly not throwbacks to the times of 'feudal' lords, or political madmen acting out the delirium of the masses, or (the most common academic interpretation) examples of some universal type of rule based on so-called patron–client relations. Caudillos were also not democrats, but without question they did belong to the dawning age of representative democracy. The circumstances of their rise to power were admittedly complicated, crammed with conflict and usually dirt-ridden. Holding our noses, let us therefore look briefly at just one early case, that of Venezuela.

Its short-lived Second Republic led by Bolívar was wrecked by a fellow caudillo, José Tomás Boves, who for a time successfully whipped up royalist sympathies against the white creole elite by appealing, in the name of social equality, for the support of the skilled horsemen of the plains, the cowboys (*llaneros*) who made such good soldiers that they managed to throw Bolívar and his caudillo army out of Caracas. Tail between his legs, Bolívar fled to Jamaica. From there he issued, in the form of a widely quoted letter, a bold attack on monarchy and a public appeal for finding practical ways of establishing Spanish American independence based on the principles of liberty, equality and popular sovereignty.

Such were the topsy-turvy times that every caudillo aspired to be loved and feared as a man of the people. Another rival Venezuelan caudillo of *mestizo* descent, José Antonio Páez, a functionally illiterate ranch hand in trouble with the law when the independence movement began, managed to convince the cowboys along the Río Apure that Boves (who was killed in action in late 1814) had been wrong, and that the real enemies of the people were the Spanish, not the local white elites. Páez and his loyal cavalrymen eventually linked arms with Bolívar, and together, during the years 1816–20, they pushed the royalist forces off the political map. Bolívar himself then rounded on yet another rival caudillo, Manuel Piar, who was captured, tried and executed. Camped near the mouth of the Río Orinoco, Bolívar went on to rout royalist forces in the east of the country, then mustered enough solidarity from the 1819 Congress at Angostura (present-day Ciudad Bolívar) to get himself elected as first president of the Third Republic. With Caracas still in the hands of royalist troops, he marched his armed supporters across the plains and into the Andes, to free New Granada from the clutches of colonial rule. Nearly two years later, troops commanded by Bolívar occupied Caracas after the decisive Battle of Carabobo. That allowed delegates from Venezuela and Colombia, backed by Bolívar and his troops, to meet at the border town of Cúcuta, where they signed the new constitution of the Republic of Gran Colombia, with its capital in Bogotá and Bolívar as its first president. The Bolívarian dream of integrating the continent under an American-style republican federation then marched on royalist troops in Ecuador, Bolivia and Peru. But back home in Venezuela, the illiterate caudillo General José Antonio Páez had other plans. Experimenting with the originally European politics of national sovereignty, he and his supporters appealed once again for the support of 'the people' of Venezuela. In 1829, Páez led the successful campaign to detach Venezuela from Gran Colombia. Venezuela won its freedom. Páez was twice elected president under the new 1830 constitution. But the price was exorbitant. Two decades of armed struggle against French and Spanish rule, and violence among caudillos jostling for popular support, ruined the cocoa-based export economy. It also claimed the lives of an estimated one-quarter to one-third of the Venezuelan population, which by 1830 was reduced to about 800,000 citizens.

The mind-numbing complexity of the struggles among the people-minded caudillos of Venezuela rather typified the whole continent. In the power vacuum opened up by the collapse of the Spanish empire, caudillos always encountered opposition from wealthy and influential political rivals, some of whom were in a hurry to restore peace and regular government, using whatever means could be salvaged from the dying colonial administration. In the pushing and shoving that went on, in contexts as different as Mexico, Argentina and Venezuela, aspiring caudillos recognised that the ranch or estate was their vital power base. But land was not just land. It was a source of personal wealth, a place where workers and troops could be recruited, a laboratory in which the arts of popular government could be tested, a place of retreat and a fortress in defeat. Every aspiring caudillo had to reckon on annihilation, either by competing local caudillos, or by men of wealth from the cities who favoured top-down administrative solutions. So the ambitious caudillo had to search for weapons other than land and violence. If clever and lucky, he found it in the accumulation of loyal and adoring followers.

Followers were vital assets in the battles of caudillos to widen their power base, which helps to explain why, during much of the nineteenth century in Spanish America, there was no clear-cut divide between caudillo politics and representative government. It was as if the whole region lived simultaneously in two historical periods. To the epoch that began with figures like Alfonso IX and extended through the English, Dutch and American revolutions, it owed the practice of representative self-government based on an imagined 'people'. To the era of landed wealth that stretched from post-colonial Spanish America back to old Europe, it owed the ethos of wealthy oligarchs keeping tight reins on government, with the help of a whip. Within these two-faced polities, 'democracy' found the going tough during the first half of the nineteenth century. Defined in the modern style as government by representatives elected by a people living and working as equals within a civil society, democracy was in practice very nearly strangled to death by powerful caudillos.

Appearances were admittedly deceptive. There were textbook constitutions and fine declarations in favour of liberty and equality. Voter turnout at elections hovered somewhere between 5 and 10 per cent of the adult male population, higher than in such enlightened European nations as France. Political factions and political parties hatched, bearing names like Liberals and Conservatives. There were strong reforming impulses and the first green shoots of civil societies poked through the soils of the new republics: under the English influence, for instance, Buenos Aires first outlawed bullfights as early as 1819, getting instead a cricket club whose members boasted that they were at least as good as the English. There was a sharp increase in the number of domestic and foreign merchants and manufacturers eager to take advantage of the elimination of colonial trade barriers. Efforts went into abolishing slavery, and demands for full religious toleration and questions directed against the staggering wealth and moral power of the Church grew louder. Some caudillos even learned to speak the language of democracy. That was no small achievement, considering the prevailing republican prejudices against it. 'Let history serve as our guide', said Simón Bolívar in his February 1819 report to the members of the Congress of Angostura, the town on the Orinoco that gave the world its famous bitters. 'Athens affords us the most brilliant example of an absolute democracy', he continued, 'but at the same time Athens herself is the most melancholy example of the extreme weakness of this type of government.'[11] Bolívar insisted that democracy was flawed because it could only ever deliver 'lightning flashes of liberty'. He went on to say that what the continent needed was 'republican government' based on the principles of 'sovereignty of the people, division of powers, civil liberty, proscription of slavery, and the abolition of monarchy and privileges'.

Bolívar's complaint about democracy recycled the old republican point that freedom would be crushed by mass equality, but he was mainly quibbling about words and, not surprisingly, it wasn't long before the first caudillos said so. From the decade of the 1830s, the language of democracy began to be spoken throughout the hemisphere. The word was an import via France from the United States, and when it came from the lips of leaders like Bartolomé Mitre (1821–1906), the first elected president of unified Argentina and founder of the widely respected Buenos Aires newspaper *La Nación*, it had a positive meaning. Democracy was a word used to describe not just a special type of republican government (throughout the continent, the political and constitutional language of the time remained overwhelmingly republican). The word democracy was used as well to point to a special type of *social order*, and to emphasise the advantages of the presumed egalitarian social conditions of the region when compared, say, to old Europe. That was the sense in which Mitre (with stars in his eyes) praised George Washington as 'the highest authority' of the 'extraordinary democracy' of the United States several thousand kilometres to the north. He likened the American gentleman general to Bolívar, San Martín and other southern champions of the 'democratic principles' of 'popular sovereignty, of the division of powers, of the harmonious interplay of free institutions, of the inalienable rights of the social man'. But unlike Sarmiento, Mitre also praised the creole populations of Spanish America as the vanguard of the social revolution against monarchy and empire. Gripped by a 'mission to complete the democratization of the American continent and to found a new order of things destined to live and progress', these descendants of European settlers – 'true sons of the soil' Mitre called them – proved that the southern part of the continent could cut for others a path towards a better future. 'When the revolution broke out in 1810', he wrote, 'it was said that South America would become English or French; when it triumphed, that the continent would sink back into barbarism. By the will and work of the Creole', Mitre added, 'it became American, republican and civilised.'[12]

These were puffed-up words, but especially from about the middle of the nineteenth century, in various parts of Spanish America, talk of 'democracy' appeared to be making progress. Sarmiento, following a two-month fact-finding visit in the late 1840s to the United States, became a convert of democracy, just as had happened earlier to Tocqueville. 'Someday justice, equality, and law will come to us when the South reflects the light of the North', he wrote. 'The world is changing, and so is morality. Do not be shocked! As with the application of steam to locomotion, of electricity to the transmission of the word, the United States has preceded all the world in adding a principle to human morality in relation to democracy.' Sarmiento's new conviction held for the rest of his life. 'What will Sarmiento bring us from the United States if he is elected President?' snarled a leading Buenos Aires newspaper shortly before his return from a second visit, and his inauguration as second president of a united Argentina. 'Schools! Nothing more than schools', he replied. 'We need to make all the Republic a school . . . Schools are democracy.'[13]

Elsewhere in the hemisphere, democracy had already entered the vernacular, for instance in Colombia, where at the end of the 1840s, in big towns like Bogotá, angry artisans, calling for protection of their trades through higher tariffs, ploughed their energies into networks of political clubs called Democratic Societies. Canvassing lower-class support, they shunned aristocratic terms of address such as 'Excellency' and 'Honourable' and struck up alliances with the local political faction known as the Liberals, who introduced universal male suffrage as part of a new constitution in 1853. All adult men were granted the right to vote, various government offices – including judges of the Supreme Court and provincial governors – were subject to direct popular election, while in the province of Vélez women were granted the suffrage, for the first time in the hemisphere, more than a decade before it first happened in Wyoming, five thousand kilometres to the north.

The good women of Velez were robbed of their vote before they could use it, courtesy of a bad-tempered decision of the national Supreme Court (it ruled that no province could grant more rights than were currently specified in the national constitution). The votes of newly enfranchised male voters were also discounted, but throughout Spanish America there were plenty of mid-century signs of a democratic momentum, even within the ranks of political caudillos. Still paying lip service to 'the people', they now put their weight behind the extension of the franchise and other constitutional reforms. The Argentine constitution of 1853 created a federal polity with a six-year-term presidency and vice-presidency. It established a senate, a house of representatives and a supreme court – and founded all these institutions on universal male suffrage. The Peruvian constitution of 1856 followed suit, while in Mexico the constituent Congress of 1856–7 rejected the findings of a constitutional commission, then moved to adopt suffrage rules that abolished all previous restrictions, including a ban on votes by domestic servants. The 1858 constitution of Venezuela, meanwhile, removed all literacy and tax requirements for men, and lowered the voting age to twenty. Proving that representative democratic inventions were beginning to travel the world, it specified that all future elections would be based on the 'Australian' secret ballot – three decades before it was first adopted in the United States, in Louisville, Kentucky.

Given the trends, a first-time visitor to the region might have been forgiven for thinking that it had made more progress towards representative democracy than anywhere else in the world – particularly because Spanish America did not suffer a slavery problem on the scale of the United States of America. Closer inspection reveals a different picture. It shows once again a world of power elites lording over republics marked by deep political and social inequalities.

The budding caudillo democracies were propped up in a variety of ways, not least by the skilful pursuit of pact politics. So-called *pactismo* was roughly the Spanish American equivalent of the American boss system operated by pork-barrelling parties. Governing involved deciding matters and getting things done, behind the back of the constitution, through deals that were struck by the caudillo and his supporters with the 'representatives' of prominent social power groups, and then later sometimes sanctioned through laws. Connections mattered to caudillos, and not surprisingly *pactismo* flourished during the course of the nineteenth century, simply because it was bound up with the growth of written constitutions, open societies and territorial governments that acknowledged their roots in 'the people'. Pact politics was no hangover from 'traditional' or 'pre-modern' times; it was a new way of governing in the age of representative democracy. Democratic it certainly was not. But caudillos knew that their power over others never derived simply from force, or from its threatened use. Just as important was wheeling and dealing lubricated by marriage and sperm, property and law, trust and tradition, money and gifts. Caudillo government was in this sense the art of forging deals with important persons. That was why bargains were struck with bigwigs, like the *cacique* of an Indian group, or the owner of a *hacienda*, or an alderman (*regidor*) of a town or city, or a representative of some or other association (*cofradía*). These representatives were neither publicly elected nor subject to fixed-term appointments. In the language of the time, they were 'vicars'. They were men whose power was vicarious, exactly because they claimed that they had the authority of others to speak, and to act (as the 1814 Mexican constitution put it[14]) as 'supplementary representatives' on their behalf.

Caudillo regimes rested on more than vicars; they were oiled by deep fears among caudillos that if commoners actually got their hands on the reins of government everything would be ruined. When it came to the ribble-rabble, caudillos were paranoiacs. For all their publicly stated confidence in 'the people', caudillos suffered private delusions of persecution, exaggerated self-importance and deep-seated anxieties about real people. Labelling them *canalla*, *vulgo*, *populacho* and *plebe* – all were terms of abuse – they pictured flocks of impassioned fanatics stampeding into the arms of the clergy. They spoke with disgust of ignorant peasants, especially if they were of Indian descent; and they squirmed in the presence of urban hoi polloi, and other creatures from the underworld of inferiority. They worried, correspondingly, that the world would be turned upside down by popular power. That had happened in the eighteenth-century slave uprisings in Santo Domingo and the armed Indian resistance led by Túpac Amaru in the Andes. Similar things took place (it was said) during the popular rebellion in Mexico of 1822–3 – a revolt of *la indecente plebe* and *la canalla muy abjecta* that had briefly catapulted the military commander Iturbide into power, whereupon he proclaimed himself Napoleonic emperor of Mexico. Many caudillos drew a moral from such episodes of popular rebellion: any leader who served the people would be seduced into serving something worse than nothing.

To complicate matters, many caudillos nevertheless said they could imagine the time when 'the people' might rule, as should be expected in republics founded on the liberty of its citizens under the law. Empowerment of the people was a noble goal, and that was why education, the gradual extension of civic equality and the destruction of old corporate privileges were all necessary. Yet the difficulty, caudillos reasoned, was that the 'true' people had not yet been born. That meant, in the here and now, the political problem was to steer the ship of state between the reefs of cramping domination and popular anarchy. 'We seek a strong, stable power which can protect society', said Mexico's Catholic ultra-conservative president, General Mariano Paredes Arillaga in 1846, on the eve of the American invasion of his country. 'But to protect that society we do not want either despotic dictatorship or the degrading yoke of the orator.'[15]

The problem for many caudillos was how to win over a riffraff that was basically weak-kneed ('submissive people', or *bajo pueblo*, were the words for commoners used by Mexico's leading nineteenth-century historian, Lucas Alamán[16]). Many big men of Spanish America, caudillo oligarchs like José Antonio Páez

(Venezuela), Antonio López de Santa Anna (Mexico) and Raphael Carrera (Guatemala), were sure this riffraff could be seduced into submission voluntarily; that is why they thought caudillo power could be combined with what was increasingly called democracy, which to most people on the ground meant universal male suffrage. Why were they so self-assured? The short answer is that they oozed confidence that the lower ranks would faithfully, even lovingly, defer to them, as if there was a God-given compact between rulers and ruled. This was the caudillo maxim: we rule and you keep your heads down, with your hearts open and mouths closed.

Caudillos liked to suppose that the visceral affection of the powerless for the powerful ran deep. These were the chains of bondage later imaginatively dissected in the great twentieth-century novels of Spanish American writers such as Gabriel García Márquez (*The Autumn of the Patriarch* and *No One Writes to the Colonel*) and Mario Vargas Llosa (*The Feast of the Goat*). Combining the roles of guerrilla leader, wealthy landowner, generous distributor of patronage, keeper of social order and tough man of violence, caudillos portrayed themselves as indispensable in the lives of the poor and powerless. They fancied themselves as heroes capable of taking all the difficult decisions, as dictators capable of seducing their victims. This self-assurance of the caudillos, their confidence in the erotica of unchecked power, helps explain why political caudillos (like their forefathers in the Low Countries) often thought of democracy and aristocracy as mutual prerequisites – as the leading lights in the Mexican province of San Luis Potosí had first done on 4 July 1813. 'If we find ourselves gathered in a genuine Aristocratic *Junta*', they declared, 'it is by virtue of Popular Democracy.'[17]

The erotica of unchecked power in love with its own aristocratic qualities explains why nineteenth-century Spanish American election campaigns so often resembled carnivals that were rife with declarations, formal dinners, petitions, promises and public meetings. Given the carnival atmosphere, the final act of voting often had a feeling of anti-climax about it, as if what really counted at election time was the ability of a notable candidate to dazzle and debauch his inferiors with the lavish resources he could publicly mobilise. Election days resembled hangovers and were marked by low turnout. In most cases by the middle of the nineteenth century it was below 5 per cent of the total population; very often, it dipped to below 2 per cent, while among the minority of those qualified to vote turnout seldom reached 50 per cent. Hence the odd fact that low participation rates seemed unmoved by whether or not officially there was universal male suffrage. In 1885, in Chile, where only literate men were entitled to vote, the electorate comprised about a quarter of the adult male population, with only about 5 per cent actually voting. In Argentina, where universal male suffrage had been in force since 1853, those who actually appeared to vote on polling days rarely reached 20 per cent. There were very few exceptions to this trend. One of them was the Mexican general election of 1851, where the turnout, under conditions of universal male suffrage, reached nearly 40 per cent, one-fifth of the adult population.

Wrecking Trends

For the oligarchs of nineteenth-century Spanish America, caudillo democracy was no oxymoron. That is why, shamelessly and with a minimum of fear, they could take with one hand what they gave with another, often in the name of the people. This strange trend was clear in the matter of voting rules, which remained constantly vulnerable to interference from above. Some decades in advance of the United States, Spanish American caudillos showed that there was no such thing as a Law of Evolutionary Expansion of the Franchise, as if history provided guarantees to those struggling for the right to vote. The Spanish American case showed just the opposite. It demonstrated that the fires of democratic power sharing could be extinguished by *shrinking* the franchise. Caudillo democracy began with a remarkably generous definition of who was entitled to be a citizen. As its caudillo oligarchs grew concerned about political instability and the possibility of social unrest, caudillo democracy grew mean-faced, so that in many contexts some citizens were stripped of their citizenship rights.

That representative democracy enjoyed no historical guarantees – that time could be made to stand still and historical progress brought to an end, even reversed – was made clear when universal male suffrage was gradually unpicked in the federation of Colombia, first by devolving the power to decide the content of electoral laws downwards to its member states, then (in 1886) by abolishing universal suffrage outright in the new, unitary constitution. The same wrecking trend was perhaps strongest in the Andean countries of Peru, Ecuador and Bolivia. The oligarchs there grew worried that the large Indian populations would hurl votes at their palace windows. The consequence was that universal suffrage was an epiphenomenon, as in Peru, whose 1860 constitution reverted to what was called a *sufragio capacitario*, which in plain speech meant that the right to vote was restricted to literate male taxpayers. Something similar happened in Mexico, where two-thirds of the population lived as Indian 'peons', ill paid and ill treated by a landowning oligarchy backed by the dictatorship of Porfirio Díaz, the caudillo who famously complained that his country was so far from God and so near to the United States, and who ruled (with one short interval) for thirty-five years, from 1876 to 1911. Everywhere, the consequence was that 'citizens', as they were called, were only a small, sometimes tiny proportion of the overall population.

Throughout Spanish America, many oligarchs agreed that the rule of the people was a good rule, in principle, but that in practice it should be allowed to operate momentarily and briefly, rather like the Roman custom of Saturnalia, the day when the existing oligarchy was symbolically overthrown by a rabble that was expected, for the rest of the year, to obey patrician rule. What did this mean in practice? Some of the weapons of disempowerment wielded by caudillos were sophisticated, like the reliance upon indirect suffrage, which served as a device to filter out unwanted popular potions. The tenth article of the 1821 constitution of New Granada and Venezuela was a hint of things to come. It minced no words: 'The people will not exercise [other] attributes of sovereignty by themselves other than that of participation in primary elections.'[18] Elsewhere, the control of the dangerous classes through indirect suffrage was done differently. Leading families arranged that the votes of their city would rank above the rest. In the final rounds of voting, criteria such as wealth, education or literacy were applied. If any doubts about outcomes remained, the families made sure that their men supervised the elections – and counted the ballot papers.

The tactics of rigging elections were crude favourites. If one way of looking at representative democracy is to see it as a system of publicly owned and operated procedures for handling power, then the rigging of elections by nineteenth-century caudillos and their allies can be seen as an effort by them to 'privatise' the means of decision making, to place those means in the hands of the few, rather than of the many. In doing this, the fraudsters made up the rules as they went along. Voters were brought in groups to the polls from the far-distant corners of the district (thereby giving a whole new meaning to block voting). Meals, drink and gifts – and a sprinkling of silver coins – were used to buy needed ballots; many more votes were cast between sundown and sunup than between sunup and sundown. Arrangements were made for individual voters to lodge multiple votes, either at the same booth, or elsewhere. Rules were waived to allow non-registered voters, or those who were legally disqualified – minors, foreigners, soldiers, transients – to cast precious votes. Boxes were stuffed full of ballots lovingly prepared in advance. When voting was oral, *Doppelgänger* stepped forward to sound their voice. Those who had departed for other climes suddenly reappeared. And, of course, the dead were resuscitated, massaged back to life, to cast one last vote.

An odd feature of the rigged elections in Spanish America was that very often their corrupt methods were practised in full view of everybody. Just as odd was the fact, strikingly evident during the long years of rule by Porfirio Díaz in Mexico, that there was often little public protest. 'Bread, or the stick' (*pan o palo*) was the way contemporaries sometimes described his rule. That was to say that the people either accepted what was given to them by their governors, or they would face the harsh consequences of their refusal. It was as if fraud thrived on publicity. It seemed that the powerless could not live without strong leaders. Díaz himself was quite open about this. The people resembled dogs, and so long as they had a bone in their mouths they would neither bark nor bite. He often emphasised the point to others. 'I received Government from the hands of a victorious army at a time when the people were divided and unprepared for the exercise of the extreme principles of democratic government', he told the American journalist James Creelman in 1908, referring to the month of November 1876, when he appointed himself president. 'To have thrown upon the masses the whole responsibility of government at once would have produced conditions that might have discredited the cause of free government.'[19]

It followed from that caudillo way of speaking that the rougher methods had to be used to stifle popular power. Well-equipped city and rural police came to the rescue of sympathetic governors who had proved that they could deliver votes, for instance. Allegations of fraud were used against opponents. Terms of office were arbitrarily extended. Legislation to disfranchise male domestic servants and day labourers was given approval by tame, handpicked legislatures. Prospective voters were turned away from the polls, or they were detained behind bars, especially if they looked as though they were intending to vote for the wrong candidate, or the wrong party. Election results were annulled, without cause. There were pitched battles to control access to the polls, or to turn voters away. Or it happened that police disguised as rioters carried off and destroyed ballot boxes, so allowing the incumbent government to exercise its constitutional right to fill the vacant seat, with its own candidate.

The Red Despot

When all else failed, and play became rough, there were the martial arts. Caudillo democracy regularly used violence against indigenous peoples, whose refusal to be pushed aside produced great bloodshed on both sides. The grand Argentine man of twentieth-century letters, Jorge Luis Borges (1899–1986), famously remarked that while his country in the nineteenth century achieved its independence from Spain, the Spanish conquest of Argentina remained incomplete. The fancy observation cruelly applied to the whole continent. For at the time of independence, and for many decades afterwards, the caudillo oligarchs of the region fought hard to crush or eliminate their Indian opponents. The Indians themselves were haunted by terrible memories of how, after 1492, European colonisers had inflicted awful violence on the whole of the Americas, nine-tenths of whose people – close to one-fifth of the world's population – were killed in what amounted proportionally to the greatest death toll in human history. That was why Indians fought back, and why caudillo violence was itself bathed in fear of further reprisals. There were vivid memories as well of how colonial elites (in Venezuela, for instance) had violently resisted the imperial practice of *gracias al sacar*, which permitted non-white men to buy corporate privileges – and the status of being white – from the Crown. Haunted by such ghosts, caudillos dug in their heels. They were usually opposed to talk of enfranchisement of native Indians, or of legal recognition of their claims to property and liberty. Caudillos seemed always prepared as well to drop the talk – to leave the original occupants of the land for dead.

Caudillo democracy harboured violence in another way. As a mutant form of representative democracy, caudillo government had many peculiar qualities, but none so queer as this: it proved that rulers could win the friendship of the people by implicating them in the violence used to rule over them. That at least was the novelty of the world's first ever durable caudillo democracy, the political dictatorship in Argentina cleverly crafted by Juan Manuel de Rosas (1793–1877).

The despotism that he and his supporters put in place between 1829 and 1852 did not spring from some grand political philosophy. Rosas was not a timeless political genius. He was very much a man of his times, a figure who resembled an explorer pragmatically cutting a new path towards the future, using the maps and compasses of the new age of democratic representation. Rosas proved that 'democratic caesarism' was possible.* He showed that the tools of periodic elections and voting could be combined with republican talk of 'the people' to recruit them into an army of supporters of a

---

* The phrase 'democratic caesarism' was the title of a most interesting, still untranslated work by the Barcelona-born Venezuelan diplomat, former customs officer, scholar, journalist, publisher and director of the national archives Laureano Vallenilla Lanz, *Cesarismo democrático. Estudios sobre las bases sociológicas de la constitución efectiva de Venezuela* (Caracas, 1919 [1991]). Writing during the caudillo dictatorship of Juan Vicente Gómez, with whom he was closely associated, Vallenilla Lanz abhorred the tendency of the human condition towards 'spontaneous anarchy'. He argued that the figure of the strong caudillo leader – the 'necessary gendarme' – was needed when building a political order committed to effective government and stable social relations. The experience of turbulent disorder in post-colonial Venezuela had taught that 'the caudillo has constituted the only force of social order'. The lesson had far-reaching implications for the future, Vallenilla Lanz supposed. With the advance of republican

strong caudillo, who then rode over them on horseback, armed with muskets, cannon and swords, all the while continuously appealing to them for their votes.

How did he manage it? To begin with, Rosas was a textbook caudillo. He came from an old established family of elite creole landowners and office holders, and he had married well, into the Buenos Aires upper class. He was at a young age taught the arts of managing his father's ranch and soon left to forge his own career, at first in the meat-salting industry. He later became a big property owner and leading expert in the buying and selling of land, investment opportunities and estate management. Like other caudillos, Rosas complained bitterly about cattle rustlers and the mobs of idlers and vagabonds that hampered business exploitation of the land. So he came to see his own ranch, which produced hides for export and salted meat, as a state in miniature, as a combined business and political laboratory that could fashion an orderly society from the rabble that roamed the vast pampas. Rosas liked to insist that dealing with uncouth gauchos and peons, vagrant *montoneros* and savage Indians, required force mixed with persuasion. Hence his favourite reminiscence, the story about the day on his ranch when he spotted a swirl of dust on the horizon. Figuring instantly that it was a rustler making off with his cattle, he jumped on his horse, took off in pursuit, captured the rustler, then brought him back at gunpoint to be given a hundred lashes. With the punishment administered, Rosas invited the man to join him at table for lunch, during which he offered him a job, as ranch foreman. The astonished gaucho readily accepted and, naturally, became a devoted lifelong Rosas follower.

Like so much in his career, the story spun by Rosas was probably half-history, half-fiction, but certain was it that the political business

---

democracy, the 'ignorance and fanaticism of the popular masses' could be contained and refined only by means of strong-armed leadership that motivated people to shift for themselves, to pull themselves up into the dignity that comes with the enjoyment of equality with others. Vallenilla Lanz urged and predicted that the 'democratic Caesar' was vital for empowering the masses. Acting as 'the representative and the regulator of popular sovereignty', the great leader would be a genuine expression rather than a denial of truly representative democracy. Borrowing from the principles of Hobbes and Popular Sovereignty, democratic caesarism would in practice combine into a new and higher harmony various opposites that were once thought to be irreconcilable antagonisms: democracy and autocracy; leadership and equality; individual greatness and collective self-discipline; the power of the people and rule by a single representative (ibid., pp. 96, 94, 79, 145).

experiment he conducted put him in a strong position within the battlefield of unresolved political struggles between the so-called 'Unitarios', who favoured an integrated Argentina, and others, the so-called 'Federalists', who worked to maintain some kind of decentralised vision of the country. As a provincial caudillo hell-bent on defending his own interests in Buenos Aires, the most powerful province of the country that would soon become Argentina, Rosas initially sided with the Federalist Party, which he promptly absorbed and destroyed, with the help of a network of powerful friends, relatives, business clients and military contacts. The election of the Federalist Manuel Dorrego (in August 1827) as governor of Buenos Aires suited Rosas, who was offered the post of Commandant General of the Rural Militias in the province. Following the overthrow and execution of Dorrego by a Unitarian military coup, Rosas slid into his saddle. He became unrivalled political leader and chief military strategist of the Federalist forces, which in 1829 routed their Unitarian opponents.

The victory allowed the thirty-five-year-old Rosas to enter Buenos Aires on horseback, surrounded by his own militia, to assume control of the province. Dressed like a rooster puffed up with proud machismo, he was cheered by a wide spectrum of interests – from city labourers to British merchants and local warehouse owners. It came as no great surprise to many that a few weeks later, on 6 December 1829, he was elected governor and granted emergency powers, with the support of a virtually unanimous vote of the House of Representatives.

The die of democratic caesarism was cast. During the next two decades, Rosas set about building a politically unified Argentina that combined representative government with the rough-hand ways of the ranch. He later reminisced that he had been saddled with the task of bringing order to 'a hell in miniature', an Argentina whose face was pocked by political anarchy, financial instability and disintegrating morale. He fancied himself as a great exterminator of unwanted vermin. 'For me the ideal of good government would be paternal autocracy, intelligent, disinterested and indefatigable', said the man who liked to dress in hat and poncho, enormous silver spurs on his heels, whip in hand, ready to mount his horse at any moment. On one occasion, in Palermo, near

Buenos Aires, one balmy autumn evening under a clump of ombu trees, famous for their wide, creeping roots and hollow trunks, he delivered a passionate speech to his supporters in proto-democratic language. He said what he always said: that his ideal was a government led by 'autocratic dictators who have been the first servants of the people'.[20]

This was about as sophisticated as his political thinking became, for what really interested Rosas was winning and maintaining power. This he managed to do – and with great success – by combining popular support with the arts of total government. The result was a taste of things to come, in Europe, Asia and elsewhere. With the legislature wrapped around his fat little finger, Rosas moved to ban alternative parties. Rival loyalties in both government and society were snuffed out. The property of his opponents was confiscated. The University of Buenos Aires was virtually shut down. The administration, the police and the army were purged of hostile elements. At every opportunity, Rosas practised pact politics by offering special perks and privileges to little *rosistas*: local justices of the peace, military officers, administrators, ranch owners, big merchants and anybody else who seemed loyal to their leader. New infantry and artillery units were built up. Nearly half of the annual government budget was eventually devoted to the military, while for reasons of paranoia his personal militia of gauchos and *montoneros* was broken up, absorbed into the new army, or stood down and sent back to their ranches.

Rosas sometimes feared his enemies, but he was also highly skilled at wielding fear as a weapon of government, especially by exploiting popular horrors of chaos. Backed by a militant political club called the Sociedad Popular Restaurador, Rosas cracked down on his opponents. Among them was the young Argentine poet and prose writer Esteban Echeverría (1805–51). He was hounded into exile in Montevideo for writing *El matadero*, a political allegory that was promptly banned but in time became famous for its portrayal of the Argentine people as trapped like animals in the pens of Rosas' slaughterhouse. Echeverría was lucky to survive, for Rosas and his supporters had already teamed up with the police and local cut-throats to form a new private police force called the *mazorca*. It was in effect a death squad: its job was to carry out selective assassinations (an estimated 2000 people lost their lives in this way) and to sniff out and hunt down 'group enemies', like the Jesuits, who were then terrorised into leaving the country.

A new army was mobilised. At the end of the 1830s, prompted by a rebellion in the south of the province sparked by a slump in rural exports, Rosas used his red-capped troops to crush his opponents outright. Dissenters were treated harshly, through a revamped legal system, to the point where Rosas became chief justice of the regime. Seated alone at his desk, often late into the night, he sifted silently through the evidence, read police reports, then handed down a verdict by writing on the files such phrases as 'fine him', 'imprison him', 'to the army', or 'shoot him'. 'Cut his throat' was his favourite: it revealed his rancher's conviction that people should be put to death just like cattle, by the knife.

The press and the pulpit, meanwhile, were encouraged to cultivate the public image of Rosas as a strong and brave leader, as a one-man government, as a saviour of the people, as a lovable demagogue who should be feared. He was referred to as the Restorer of Laws and praised for his many achievements. The list of alleged successes was long. It included the policy of increasing the lands available for settlement, promoting the export of salted beef and hides, and stopping the cycle of civil wars among the provinces. The list extended to forging a loosely defined confederation of Argentina dominated by Buenos Aires, reducing foreign debts, launching war and (from 1843) a nine-year blockade on neighbouring Uruguay, as well as protecting the country against foreign enemies, like the French navy, which imposed its own blockade on Buenos Aires in 1840.

Through all of the dramas, Rosas acted the part of the stern demagogue, and he often did so to perfection. Working seven days a week, backed by a personal staff of three hundred at his principal residence in Palermo, surrounded constantly by scribes, he had an astute sense of the importance of *mise-en-scène* when exercising power – so astute that it prompted the British minister Henry Southern to report that Rosas himself was aware that he wielded power more absolutely than any monarch sitting on a throne.[21] Rosas excelled at encouraging public demonstrations of solidarity by people who mattered, rigged popularity contests of the kind that took place in July 1835, when the best-known and most powerful ranchers, accompanied by their farm workers, travelled from all four corners of the province to Buenos Aires, to stand guard outside the governor's mansion, to show their 'deference' and 'respect'.[22] In the same month, at a *fiesta* held in Tapalqué in honour of Rosas, an Indian leader waxed eloquent in his favour. 'If it weren't for Juan Manuel', said the chief, as if he were speaking about his brother, 'we would not live as we do, in fraternity with the Christians. As long as Juan Manuel lives, we will all be happy and live a quiet life alongside our spouses and children. The words of Juan are at one with the words of God: all who are assembled here can testify that everything that Juan has told and advised us has proven to be true.'[23]

Praise the Lord. It was high recommendation of the lowest order, but wherever possible the demonstrations and *fiestas* were turned into media events – thanks to the personal control that Rosas exercised over newspapers like the *Gaceta Mercantil*, which was widely read, often aloud to others, throughout the province.[24] Rosas also knew (as his Indian admirer knew) that it was important to have God on his side, to make the people think that to resist him was a sin. 'When I decided to make the terrible sacrifice of climbing onto the seat of government', he reminisced, with no trace of modesty, in his second presidential acceptance speech in April 1835, 'I accepted the investiture of A POWER WITHOUT LIMITS, which despite ITS ODIOUSNESS, I considered ABSOLUTELY NECESSARY for such a large undertaking. Do not think that I have overlooked my limited capacities, my weaknesses, or the *extended power that the law, based on your vote, almost unanimous in the city and the countryside, has given me* – No: my hopes have been based on special protection from heaven, and on your virtues and patriotism.'[25] The man of God and the people naturally snuggled up to the clergy. Many responded by wearing red ribbons and preaching in his favour, as well as by organising processions through the streets, with portraits of Rosas held aloft, later to be displayed at the rosemary-scented altars of the local church.[26]

This was not just organised religion, but a new style of politics that belonged to the dawning age of representative democracy. For

FIGURE 60: Poster from the 1830s featuring the Argentine caudillo Juan Manuel de Rosas as the 'Exterminator of Anarchy'.

all his utter contempt for his subjects, Rosas was a man of the people. Official posters of him were in great demand. Among the most prized, titled *The Exterminator of Anarchy*, is one showing Rosas, the red despot, in full military dress, preparing to kill a seven-headed serpent, which represented the chaos allegedly caused by the Unitarios during the 1820s (Figure 60). His followers were naturally instructed to dress in *rosista* uniform, always sporting the colour red – the colour of the Federalist forces. Women were urged to dress in red, to carry red flowers (preferably red roses) and to wear red ribbons in their hair. The style for men was openly macho. All the rage were fierce faces, hirsute chests, red caps, red bandannas and red silk badges bearing murderous slogans such as 'Long Live the Federation! Long Live the Federalists! Death to the Unitarians!'.

Among the most cunning features of the regime run by Rosas was its clever use of the 'soft' weapons of representative government: elections, plebiscites and petitions. Rosas was fond of comparing himself to the captain of a ship drifting in troubled waters. He said repeatedly that he needed emergency powers, and that he could only sail the ship of state well if he had the direct backing of its crew, 'the people'. So he did all that he could, not only to simulate a permanent state of emergency, but also to portray himself as the saviour of the state and its people. Hence the priority he gave to outflanking parliament by conducting a permanent 'dialogue' with 'his people'.

Elections were put to good use. The aim was to get a near-unanimous result, which is why the Great Exterminator personally vetted and approved candidates, appointed soft-touch electoral officers and justices of the peace to run polling booths. Fanfare surrounded the campaigns. Single-page poems praising Rosas variously as the Caesar of Argentina, as the country's Achilles, as a modern Cincinnatus, simply worded and printed in great quantities, were planted in the hands of street crowds. Rallies organised by *rosistas* resembled festivals, often with displays of fireworks. Voters could have been forgiven for thinking them to be plebiscites. The voting spree held during the autumn month of March 1835 was typical. The parliament had just granted Rosas unlimited executive powers, so he chose to confirm the decision by asking registered voters to express their opinion – *sí* or *no*. To give them a good chance of casting their votes, the poll was stretched over a three-day period (26–28 March). Voting was confined to Buenos Aires. The *Gaceta Mercantil* reported that 'the opinion of the inhabitants of the countryside was not consulted because apart from the delay that this would have caused, time and again unmistakable evidence has demonstrated that the sentiments that motivated all the inhabitants of Buenos Aires are universal'. The report went on to note that in a district of Buenos Aires a huge crowd had gathered on the last day. Standing before a church, where final votes were to be cast, 'both sexes and all classes' milled and mingled, carrying olive branches, willows and red flags. A giant portrait of the Great Citizen (*Gran Ciudadano*) had been placed on the gates at the entrance of the polling booth. Loud music was played, and individual voters, all men, standing before the crowd, swore their oaths of allegiance to Rosas. After votes had been cast in this way, an electoral officer, clutching a list of votes cast, led a procession of the people through the streets, accompanied by a band and the giant poster of the Great Citizen, who was later declared the official winner of the election, with 9316 votes in his favour and just 4 votes against.[27]

There was obviously a danger that the wee word fraud would be hurled like a stone at such plebiscites, which is why Rosas relied upon his favourite simulated act of direct democracy, the petition. Rosas told those close to him that he believed that the natural order of things tended to unanimity: in other words, that harmony of opinions was normal in a good political system.[28] It followed that 'the free expression of public opinion' (as he put it in a wonderful leap of imagination) would always work in his favour. The only remaining political problem was then to find the proper means of divining public opinion. Rosas sanctioned 'spontaneous' pleas and petitions by people, among them mothers and widows, who queued for hours and sometimes days in the courtyard of his *quinta* in Palermo. Petitions organised from above were also commonplace, as in 1840, when a campaign was mounted in the face of yet another – cunning and successful – effort by Rosas to renew his absolute power by threatening to resign if he failed to win solid public support. Local authorities throughout the province rallied behind the Great Citizen. They urged notables to draft and sign petitions that backed the return of Rosas with unlimited executive powers. So in the city of Concepción petitioners included justices of the peace, policemen, a lieutenant colonel, priests and members of a self-styled Rosas 'Restoration Society'. The resulting petition involved a remarkable twist in the meaning of representation. It produced 1163 petitioners in favour of Rosas, of whom only 318 had signed in person.

War and Dictatorship

Luckily for the Argentine people, Rosas was defeated militarily by an alliance between his domestic opponents and Brazilian troops; in February 1852, he departed on a British ship, to spend the rest of his years among his former European adversaries, to be buried on the southern coast of England, in Southampton. Other peoples of Spanish America were less lucky, if only because caudillo republics were prone to degenerate into violent despotisms that menaced more than just their subjects at home. Especially after the failure of early efforts, like those of Bolívar, to build a post-imperial federation of free republics, something like a United States of Spanish America, caudillo governments and their subjects found themselves in the devil's company of geopolitics. The question confronting these republics was whether an elected government that paid lip service to 'the people' could be combined with a system of armed territorial states that acted as if they were 'sovereign' powers.

The big military men who ran the caudillo dictatorships of Spanish America easily answered the question. They were sure that, just as nature abhors a vacuum, so state politics moves to fill gaps and to take advantage of opportunities. These caudillos knew instinctively that the mechanisms of representative government had both 'inside' and 'outside' dimensions, that political manipulation at home could be enhanced by dalliances and skulduggery abroad. The populist dictatorships for which Spanish America later developed a global reputation had deep roots in the nineteenth-century world of interstate wars and political intrigues. These dictatorships were not just home-grown, based on the domestic armed power of the caudillos over 'the people' whom they flattered and feared; they were also creatures of war, and of rumours of war. Dictatorships were products of a caudillo politics that kept nodding in the direction of 'the people' and the 'sovereignty of the people' – but a politics that tried constantly to shore up the popularity of regimes at home by taking advantage of the military mistakes and weaknesses of their neighbours. That is why strong-minded dictators, who often privately cursed and despised the *canalla* and the *vulgo*, did all they could in their public appearances to flatter and stroke their plumes – by appealing for their support in coping with 'emergencies', exploiting international tensions and combating foreign enemies.

A simple reading of the constitutions of Spanish American republics of this period reinforces the impression that they were peace-loving polities, islands of subtropical calm in a vast ocean of isolation. The brute reality was that caudillo republics found themselves nagged constantly by their neighbours, and by the irresistible temptation to snatch military gains from weaker states

FIGURE 61: State boundaries (approximate and disputed) in Latin America, c. 1850.

(Figure 61). Border disputes were chronic. Threatened invasions were frequent, and actual military engagement was common. So too were *coups d'état* and emergency edicts (called *pronunciamentos*), which grew to be routine features of life in the Spanish republics. Matters were not helped by the constant military interferences of the United States in the region. The overall militarisation of political life that resulted was not a matter of foreordained necessity, a genetic defect of representative democracy or democratisation *per se*. The reasons were peculiar to the Spanish American context. Since the civil societies of these polities were often weak, its caudillo governments rarely managed to extrude organised violence from civilian life, or to subject armies and police forces to constitutional control and public monitoring. The nineteenth-century Spanish republics failed to *democratise* their means of violence on any scale.[29] And so caudillos, backed by armies recruited from the regions in which great families enjoyed influence, jostled for dominance, unhindered by the niceties of the rule of law. Caudillos were good at spotting power vacuums and political opportunities. They filled them creatively, using force, especially when the constitutional order seemed shaky, and when social pacts were crumbling.

The violent turbulence that cut like a sword into the tissues of the early Mexican republic was an early exemplar of the wider trend. Between 1824, the year of a new republican and federalist constitution, and 1857, which saw the introduction of another new constitution that abolished slavery, introduced a bill of rights and restricted clerical and military privileges and property rights, only one president, Guadalupe Victoria, completed his term of office and handed over executive power to an elected successor. The period was punctuated by the suspension of the constitution (in 1833) by the conservative caudillo president, Antonio López de Santa Anna Pérez de Lebrón. He was the man made famous by his ruthless cruelty, the burial of his amputated leg at great public expense, and the imposition of a new charter, the so-called Seven Laws, that raised the property qualifications for voting, strengthened the powers of the presidency, and militarised the federal government.

Similar trends were evident throughout Spanish America. Domestic politics in Peru and Bolivia was thrown into turmoil by the War of the Pacific with Chile (1879–83). The very existence of the fledgling Uruguayan republic was repeatedly thrown into question by the ongoing rivalries between Argentina and Brazil. Local federalist forces in collusion with Argentina besieged Montevideo from 1838 to 1851; that conflict in turn produced deep tensions between two warring political factions, the Blancos and the Colorados, whose struggles plunged the country into political intrigue, civil war and dictatorship. In quick succession, Uruguayans suffered three military invasions at the hands of Brazil: in 1851, against Manuel Oribe, ostensibly to ward off Argentine influence in the country; again in 1855, at the request of the Uruguayan government and Venancio Flores, leader of the Colorados, who had traditionally been supported by the Brazilian empire; and once again in 1864, against the government of Atanasio Aguirre. In Argentina, geopolitical rivalries with neighbouring Brazil and Uruguay fuelled violent clashes between the provinces and the supporters of federalism and centralisers based in the commercial centre of Buenos Aires. The violence persisted into the 1890s, and it had disfiguring effects on the face of government by consent.

As happened elsewhere, war tempted Argentine leaders to invoke the use of the constitutional procedure known as intervention. This meant, simply, that in cases of political emergency, when government was brought to the brink of collapse, parliaments were suspended, or they were stacked with trusties, sometimes at the point of a gun, so that the president could then ensure a majority for his own party in the legislature. Such manipulation was not an Argentine speciality. In many parts of the continent the growth of presidential power backed by (threats of) violence was encouraged by inter-state rivalries. War was bad for representative democracy – just as it had been bad for assembly democracy. Constitutional amendments that granted substantial powers to the executive, at the expense of assemblies and citizens, were commonplace. Harbouring deep fears of what caudillos liked to call 'popular licence', these amendments actually gave licence to the bad practice of entrusting considerable powers to the executive, in order better to define and discipline 'the people', if need be through the barrel of a gun.

The degeneracy of the 'liberal' free trade and strong state regime led by the coffee caudillo Justino Rufino Barrios (1835–85) in Guatemala showed what could happen. With the backing of big planters and middlemen, his regime disbanded Church properties and promoted market freedoms. Vast tracts of land stolen from the Q'eqchi' people were granted to German and other immigrants. Coffee exports soon tripled in these years, thanks in no small measure to an anti-vagrancy law of 1878 that forced indigenous peoples to work on local coffee plantations at harvest times. Many subjects began to feel the pinch as Barrios prepared for war, equipping his armies with state-of-the-art American weapons, in quest of his dream of recreating a Central American Confederation. The war cost his subjects dearly. On paper, it seemed to favour representative government; in practice it nurtured a government of fear and obsequiousness, symbolised by its reputation for ferrying its detainees around in cages, so that all 'the people' could see with their own eyes, and feel within their own guts, that they were the prey of a regime acting in their own name.

The scale and intensity of the geo-military violence was some-times shocking, as in the long war against Uruguay, Argentina and Brazil led by the Paraguayan caudillo Francisco Solano López (1826–70), who ruled his country with whips and branding irons, as if it were a large estate in the business of death. The six-year conflict known as the War of the Triple Alliance was in its own way as physically and emotionally devastating as the civil war that erupted around the same time in the United States. But this conflict was driven by no noble purposes, like the abolition of slavery. It was a bleak rehearsal of the horrors of World War One.

The long war between Paraguay and its neighbours had numer-ous causes, all of them traceable to the jostling for territory, resources and power among the four states, with the British stand-ing in the background, hungry to pick up the spoils, especially minerals. The catalyst was the entry of Brazilian troops on to Uruguayan soil in October 1864, to oust the government of Atanasio Aguirre. A few months later, the government of Paraguay, backed by the largest standing army in Spanish America, declared war on both Brazil and Argentina. The puppet government of Uruguay sided with Brazil and Argentina, to form the Treaty of the Triple Alliance. So began their protracted military struggle against tiny Paraguay. The war that followed was strange, and devastating. Frontal assaults against fixed battlefield positions were combined with ironclad warships firing on wooden paddle steamers. Lances, spears and hand-to-hand fighting were supplemented by the use of high explosives, breech-loading rifles and observation balloons. At one point, the Paraguayan army even experimented for the first time in the world with a bizarre weapon that resembled a tank: an armoured locomotive that attacked Brazilian forces positioned out-side Asunción. The conflict turned out to be the bloodiest in Latin American history; it quickly came to resemble the proverbial battle between the pair of cats in Kilkenny, Ireland, which fought till only their tails were left. Around 50,000 of the 123,000 Brazilian troops who fought in the war lost their lives. Argentina lost more than half of its 30,000 combatants. The Uruguayan army of 5600 men (some of whom were mercenaries) was reduced to less than half its size.

In an effort to save his state, Francisco Solano López conducted

FIGURE 62: Scene from the Battle of Tuyuti, 24 May 1866, during the War of the Triple Alliance, from a painting by Cándido López.

a people's war (Figure 62). He conscripted every able-bodied man, including children as young as ten, and forced women to perform all non-military labour. His opponents followed suit (Figure 63). By 1867, Paraguay had lost 60,000 men to battle, disease or capture. Another 60,000 soldiers were called to duty. Slaves were conscripted. Infantry units composed entirely of children went into battle, sometimes wearing false beards and armed with sticks.

FIGURE 63: A boy soldier of the army of Argentina, during the War of the Triple Alliance, photographer unknown.

Women were forced to work behind the front lines. Shortages of equipment and supplies grew so pressing that Paraguayan troops went barefoot and half naked into battle. The slide into unreality was compounded by Solano López's deluded conviction that he was victim of a vast conspiracy. He retaliated by ordering the execution of thousands of his remaining troops, hundreds of foreigners and scores of top government officials. He even signed death warrants for his mother and sisters. He eventually retreated to the northern jungles of his country, where he hid for fourteen months, there to witness the painful cession of large patches of territory to Brazil and Argentina. His country virtually died destitute around him. The numbers of casualties remain hotly contested, but it is today estimated that some 300,000 Paraguayans, mostly civilians, perished. Up to 90 per cent of the male population may have died. Of the estimated pre-war population of 525,000 people, only 221,000 Paraguayans survived, of whom only some 28,000 were men. In early March 1870, Solano López was himself fatally wounded by a Brazilian trooper's spear as he tried to escape, by swimming down a jungle stream. His last reported words were: 'I die with my country' (*Muero con mi patria*). The caudillo should have added a few honest words: 'at the expense of the people, who have been robbed of their rights to good government, their villages, their industrial wealth, their loved ones, along with their lives'.

This Country . . . Has Never Voted

The abyss that stood between republican democratic constitutions and the cruel reality of caudillo power prompted harsh conclusions from some contemporary observers of the scene. Among them were British writers who took an interest in the history of democracy. In his widely read *Popular Government*, first published in 1885, the comparative jurist and historian Sir Henry James Sumner Maine (1822–88) used the Latin American experiment with republican power-sharing to draw the conclusion that representative democracy was in practice an unworkable ideal – that efforts to overthrow monarchy were bound to produce misery, at the hands of the mob.

The Belfast-born politician and historian James Bryce (1838–1922), a close confidant of American President Theodore Roosevelt, was somewhat more charitable, but not generously so. His overall tone was somewhere between sceptical and dismissive. The reasons given by Bryce are interesting for what they reveal (in 1921) about his views on the meaning of representative democracy and its preconditions. His main emphasis was on the instability of the Spanish-speaking republics, which 'have crowded a series of vicissitudes and experiences which, for their number and the light they throw upon certain phases of human nature in politics, find a parallel only in the republics of ancient Greece and in those of mediaeval Italy'. The big majority of Spanish American republics he considered to be 'forms of Tyranny, *i.e.* illegal despotisms resting on military force'. Various reasons were given for the failures of representative democracy. He included the apathy and 'unlettered ignorance' of the aboriginal Indians and a large part of the *mestizos*. He mentioned the corresponding monopoly on politics of 'knots of intriguers and adventurers', above all men inclined 'to rule by the sword'; and he had things to say about the 'long welter of revolutions and dictatorships' that had been stirred up by ignorance, lawlessness and military habits nurtured by international strife. Bryce pointed to a few promising cases – Chile, Uruguay and Argentina – which in his view implied (note the Eurocentrism) the possibility of disseminating 'the ideas and mental habits of Europe and the United States into the Spanish American population'. In these three exceptional countries, there was plenty of 'pure European blood' to feed the springs of 'men who lead in public affairs . . . persons of standing and reputation . . . as well as of statesmanlike capacity'. There was also the growth of prosperity and stable government fostered by the growth of an industrial bourgeoisie aided by European capital. Of significance as well was 'the protecting and steadying influence of the United States'. According to Bryce, the whole of Spanish America suffered a weakness or outright absence of one or more of these three preconditions. Hence the unavoidable conclusion: free, self-governing institutions can never work on a people unfit to comprehend or use them. With a few possible exceptions, the ideal of representative democracy was wasted on Spanish

America. 'The people did not rule in these republics because they could not rule.' So Bryce drew 'the moral of the whole story' of the quest for democracy in the southern half of the western hemisphere: 'Do not give to a people institutions for which it is unripe in the simple faith that the tool will give skill to the workman's hand. Respect Facts. Man is in each country not what we may wish him to be, but what Nature and History have made him.'[30]

The lines oozed condescension, but it turns out that Bryce was wrong about the past, the present and the future. Rather a victim of his own European bigotry, which in retrospect looks quaint and utterly misguided, he failed to say anything about the history-making constitutions that were crafted during the early years of the nineteenth century, and that were the most advanced documents of their time. Lacking a good grasp of the phenomenon of caudillos and the circumstances of their birth, Bryce also could not understand how the mechanisms and spirit of representative government served as a glove for the fist of caudillo power exercised in the name of 'the people'. Put simply, Bryce made the double mistake of supposing that the institutions and spirit of representative democracy were thoroughly benign, and that they had been deformed by the historical backwardness and vulgarity of Spanish America. The truth was otherwise. Representative government conducted in the name of the people was no utopia. The moon of representative democracy had a dark side, one that revealed its vulnerability to self-corruption at the rough hands of power-hungry caudillos like General Rosas.

Bryce's European prejudices also prevented him from spotting that the self-corruption of representative democracy could be reversed, that caudillo government could be broken up, and democratised. It is of more than passing interest that the very period in which Bryce was writing witnessed important new efforts to push the political systems of the region towards more effective and egalitarian forms of representative democracy. In Chile, for instance, parliamentary government had taken root following a nasty armed conflict (in 1891) triggered by disputes about the dictatorial powers of President José Manuel Balmaceda, whose defeat and subsequent suicide enabled forces such as the Democratic Party to mobilise wide sectors of the population, in support of genuine universal suffrage.

In Mexico, during the same period, the whip-hand campaign by the Liberal Union to restrict effective suffrage had failed; following major disturbances sparked by a fraudulent election in 1910, the thirty-five-year dictatorship of Porfirio Díaz promptly collapsed. A widely influential document published in San Luis Potosí had denounced violations of the constitution as a species of tyranny. 'The legislative and judicial powers are completely subordinated to the executive', it had complained. It added that 'the division of powers, the sovereignty of the states, the liberty of the common councils, and the rights of the citizens exist only in writing in our great charter'. It went on to remind Mexicans that in their 'democratic Republic, the public power can have no other origin nor any other basis than that of the will of the people, and the latter cannot be subordinated to formulas executed in a fraudulent manner'. There were huge gains for campaigns to build more effective political representation, especially by encouraging the founding of free trade unions, freedom of association of other groups, and the inclusion of a whole array of previously excluded social groups in government policy making.

Behind the push to reshape caudillo democracy stood the inspired figure of a Mexican democrat with a difference: opposition leader (and later president) Francisco Madero (1873–1913). Frail in body and delicate in health, here was a man who understood that representative democracy stood no chance of survival unless the sickness induced by caudillos wielding absolute power was cured, using political remedies never before tried. Madero (Figure 64) was convinced that representative democracy could not be imported into Mexico as if it were a commodity; it was not a plot that could be hatched in secret, or a weapon that could be packed in soldiers' rucksacks and discharged through the barrel of a gun. Democracy was a state of mind, a feeling, a disposition. It had to come from within citizens themselves. That is why he devoted a considerable part of his energies to changing perceptions of power, for instance by building a network of 'anti-re-election' clubs that campaigned for free and fair elections, and for the immediate political retirement of the Mexican dictator, Porfirio

FIGURE 64: Francisco Madero (centre) and his wife, Sara Pérez, 1911.

Díaz; and why much of his short life was an experiment with spir-
itualism. Democracy was for him the opposite of cunning,
lawlessness and apathy, and that was why it demanded a radical
change of mind and heart, Madero told others. He came to feel
that he had a special vocation as a 'writing medium', a man whom
the spirits had taken by the hand, in order to communicate with
humanity. The apostle of democracy stopped smoking, destroyed
his private wine cellar, abandoned siestas and gave up eating meat;
at one point, partly to escape the swelling crowds that greeted him
with *vivas* wherever he went, Madero spent forty days and forty
nights in the desert, under the Milky Way, near a ranch he called
'Australia'. He signed his articles using various names, including
Arjuna, the prevaricating prince who was tutored in the arts of
action by the god Krishna, in the Hindu classic the *Bhagavad Gita*.
For Madero, the personal was political. That conviction blessed
him (as it would later bless Mahatma Gandhi) with a profoundly
felt faith in the power of magnanimous leadership. 'I have been
chosen by Providence', he wrote. 'Neither poverty, nor prison, nor
death frighten me.'[31] The words gave him great inner strength,

which was lucky because Madero's success in humbling the Mexican dictatorship in 1911 was rewarded with election to the presidency, and with a bullet through the neck in the middle of the night – courtesy of a plot co-organised by the American ambassador, Henry Lane Wilson.

Meanwhile, in Argentina, where such organised violence began to pass out of fashion, voting for men was made compulsory in 1912. That was the year in which one of its influential senators remarked, famously, that his country, 'according to my convictions, formed after a detailed study of our history, has never voted.'[32] Local suffragettes and men without the vote took heart from the appeal by Julio González for more and better representative democracy. On the eve of World War One, the old system of rigged government by elites known as 'The Agreement' was finally abolished. Faced with a rising tide of non-violent resistance that included the strategy of boycotting polls known as 'revolutionary abstention', President Roque Sáenz Peña agreed to allow the passage of legislation that established secret, compulsory and universal (for men) suffrage. That was a big blow against caudillo politics. Great attention was hereafter paid to improving the methods of the two-chamber assembly that comprised a Chamber of Deputies plus a Senate chosen by the provincial legislatures. There was rising interest in the role of the presidency, and there was widespread agreement that its powers needed to be defined carefully, and radically trimmed. Chosen by an electoral college modelled on that of the United States, the president was able to hold office for a six-year, non-renewable term, during which time, it was agreed, the incumbent could exercise various powers, including the appointment of ministers who were still answerable to the legislature.

After 1916, under the presidency of the leader of the Radical Civic Union, the school teacher-turned politician Hipólito Yrigoyen (1852–1933), Argentina moved rapidly from theory to practice, towards a power-sharing, full-motion representative democracy (Figure 65). Compulsory voting was practically introduced; we know that the custom was traceable to the roundups with red paint-soaked rope in advance of sessions of the Athenian *ekklesia*, but in Argentina it had a new shape, and a powerful sting. The issuing of an enrolment card (a so-called *libreta de enrolamiento*)

FIGURE 65: Scene from an election rally of well-dressed supporters of the Radical Civic Union (Unión Cívica Radical), Buenos Aires, 1922.

drawn from the pre-existing military conscription list was an administrative convenience, of course; but when supplied to voters it had higher purposes. It was designed to put a stop to the caudillo racket of shamelessly bribing and intimidating powerless voters. Obligatory voting was also defended in terms of correcting low voter turnout (which had usually hovered between 20 and 30 per cent of eligible voters) and preventing governments from being run, as in the United States, by party 'machines'. There were strong words as well from politicians and government officials about the importance of moulding the adult male population – nearly a third of them had not been born in Argentina – into a much more tightly integrated nation of citizens.

Universal male suffrage was reintroduced; women had to wait for their votes until 1947 (when the government of Juan Perón finally enacted a national suffrage law). Meanwhile, electoral rights and other citizenship entitlements were extended to recently naturalised European immigrants, many of them part of a rapidly expanding urban working class in an economy soon to become the fourth-largest in the world. Voting was by the Australian secret ballot and, perhaps for the first time anywhere in the world, fingerprinting of voters was used to put a stop to the old caudillo trick of voters turning themselves into impostors by turning up to vote for a second time, or several more times, under an assumed name.*

The simple method of fingerprinting was an invention of the Croatian-born Argentine citizen Juan Vucetich (Figure 66). Its adoption reportedly injected into elections a strong sense of fairness among voters. Adding one more luscious irony to the history of democracy, it proved that state-sponsored techniques for prosecuting crimes against the social order committed by trade unionists, immigrants and so-called anarchists could cut both ways, that a surveillance technique could be redefined for different purposes, in support of representative democracy. The use of fingerprinting had a wider significance. Contrary to Bryce and other sceptics, it showed that the advance of representative democracy

---

* The fingerprinting of voters, a technique used today to counter corruption and register people's identity, is an invention traceable to Juan Vucetich (1858–1925). Born Ivan Vučetić on the Dalmatian island of Hvar, in what was then the Habsburg Empire and is today the Republic of Croatia, Vucetich emigrated to Argentina in 1882. Drawing on the early work on fingerprinting by the British polymath Francis Galton, Vucetich pioneered the methods of what he initially called *icnofalangométrica* (derived from the Greek term for 'finger track measurement'). He later renamed the method using the more accessible term 'dactyloscopy' (*dactiloscopía*, from the Latin for 'finger description'), by which he meant the technique of comparing and classifying the pattern of dermal ridges or papillar lines on the pad of a human finger. Vucetich believed that no two fingers have exactly the same dermal ridge, and that the pattern of dermal ridges of each individual is unique. On this basis, he won international fame for his efforts to solve one of the most infamous murder cases in late nineteenth-century Argentina. Two small children had been stabbed to death in their beds in the village of Necochea, in Buenos Aires province. The case proved vexing to the authorities. No person had witnessed the crime, and interrogations had yielded contradictory evidence. With the assistance of Vucetich, the prosecution demonstrated a perfect match between a bloody fingerprint left on a door jamb and the children's mother, Francesca Rojas, who promptly confessed to her crime. Vucetich was soon hailed locally and internationally for his pioneering contribution, which predated by a full decade the use of such evidence in criminal trials in London and Paris. He was appointed head of the new La Plata Office of Identification in 1890, and he later published *Dactiloscopía comparada: El Nuevo sistema argentino* (Comparative Dactyloscopy) (La Plata, 1904). Vucetich was convinced that the ability to develop reliable and easy-to-manage bureaucratic archives of fingerprints had many potential applications beyond crime solving, including civil uses such as immigrant-tracking systems, the registration of prostitutes and the elimination of corruption from election procedures. In support of his research and path-breaking methods, he travelled widely, including to North America, Europe and China, where the Peking (Beijing) City Police formally adopted the Vucetich system.

FIGURE 66: Photograph, signature and thumbprint of Juan Vucetich, from *Homenaje a Juan Vucetich* (Buenos Aires, 1938).

was not just a centre-to-periphery affair, a gift of Europe to the world. The Vucetich invention proved that Europe and the United States had no monopoly on innovation, and that vital democratic inventions could happen just as easily elsewhere in the world, off the beaten track.

The Laboratory

Easily the most impressive democratic power-sharing experiment happened in the tiny neighbouring state of Uruguay wedged between Argentina and Brazil on the Plate estuary. At the time of its independence in 1830, Uruguay had a population of only 75,000 people, spread thinly across a graceful landscape made up of lush, gently undulating grasslands, many *arroyos*, or small streams, gently rounded hills oddly called *cuchillas* (knives), and a coastline dotted with wild palms, lagoons and white sandy beaches.

Born of the anti-imperial resistance kick-started by the sequence of events that began with the 1807 Napoleonic invasion of peninsular Spain, the territory called Uruguay was among the modern world's first and most successful representative democracies. The Uruguayan experiment proved that caudillos were not all cut from the same cloth, and that there were some grains of truth in the well-known distinction between 'barbarous caudillos' and 'cultured caudillos' drawn by the Bolivian writer Alcides Argüedas

(1878–1946).[33] The Uruguayan experiment also defied the Marxist thesis that a vigorous and independent class of market-driven town dwellers is vital for the growth of parliamentary democracy. The formula 'No bourgeois, no democracy'[34] simply did not apply to this frontier territory that had long been coveted and disputed by the Spanish and Portuguese empires; within the region, the February 1811 rebellion against colonial rule was in fact led by creole landowners who had been born locally of Spanish descent. They stood against the fortified port city, Montevideo, many of whose merchants, military officers and town dwellers wanted to retain at least a nominal allegiance to the Spanish king, Ferdinand VII. It was countryside against city, caudillos and gaucho cowboys against bourgeois families and urban folk (called *ausentistas*) whose interests were bound up with the countryside.

The flames of conflict were fuelled by a cocktail of ideas drawn from Spanish translations of Thomas Paine and various American constitutional documents, all articulated by their most eloquent and prominent defender: a soft-spoken caudillo named José Gervasio Artigas (1764–1850). A former general in the local Spanish army who threw away his epaulettes, adopted civilian dress and trained his followers' guns on the Spanish and the Portuguese, then on the Argentines and Brazilians, Artigas criticised concentrated power and championed federalist forms of government based on elected representation. Through his secretary and ghostwriter, a cousin and priest named Miguel Barreiro, Artigas issued eloquently written calls for the public recognition of the 'rights of man and citizen'. He championed the right to bear arms and to resist despotism, to enjoy religious freedom and the right to own and use land, and he wanted that right extended to Indians and *mestizos*. Later Artigas issued a set of directives known as the 'Instructions of the Year Thirteen', which included a declaration of independence from mainland Spain, proposals for elected assemblies, written constitutions and an American-style confederation of all the provinces making up the former viceroyalty of the Río de la Plata (the Plate), plus a demand for the political and economic autonomy of the Banda Oriental region, including its freedom from the clutches of Buenos Aires.[35] Artigas and his troops fought tooth and nail for these republican principles, but, despite winning important strategic battles, he eventually (in 1820) suffered defeat at the hands of Portuguese troops, who went on to capture Montevideo and annex the Banda Oriental as a Brazilian province. Artigas immediately fled into exile, into neighbouring Paraguay, where he lived comfortably, a guest of the local dictatorship, until his death in 1850.

For many of his later admirers, Artigas was something of an enigma, a pliable symbol of many different values and moods. Although he refused an invitation by his followers to return to Uruguay, whose independence as a sovereign state he never favoured, Artigas earned a lasting reputation among many Uruguayans as the great Protector of Free Peoples (the sacred words chiselled into a stone panel inside his mausoleum in central Montevideo). He was one of those courageous losers who became a national hero, in spite of everything. The ideas he vented were not altogether original; they resembled a rocket in the big explosion of statements and declarations of independence and constitution making throughout the Spanish Americas of this period. But the way Artigas articulated these ideas undoubtedly kept alive, and positively shaped, the difficult struggle for Uruguayan independence, which was achieved finally in 1828, aided by Britain, which favoured a buffer state between Argentina and Brazil to protect its commercial interests.

The written constitution of the new state was approved officially on 18 July 1830, after having been ratified by Argentina and Brazil, whose collaboration formed a very early example in the era of representative democracy of supra-national constitution making. The new constitution established a representative form of republic. It was called the Oriental Republic of Uruguay, so named after the original designation of the territory as the Banda Oriental, the eastern province of the former Viceroyalty of the Río de la Plata, which was dissolved in 1810 when independence was declared. The constitution announced (in Article 4) that 'sovereignty in all its plenitude resides fundamentally in the Nation' and it extended the right to vote to all resident tax-paying literate men who had reached the age of twenty, without being seduced by the wicked charms of alcohol. The constitution made Roman Catholicism the official religion, but provided guarantees of freedom of worship for the Swiss German Evangelicals, Waldensians and Anglican minorities. It divided

the territory into nine administrative jurisdictions, known as departments, each headed by a governor appointed by the president and
each having an advisory body called a Citizens' Council (*Consejo
de Vecinos*). The constitution divided the government into the
executive, legislative and judicial powers. It established a bicameral
General Assembly that was charged with the appointment of a
Supreme Court of Justice and the election of a president, who was
to be in charge of the executive branch of government for a non-
renewable four-year term. The president (the first was General
Fructuoso Rivera) was granted considerable powers that were tamed
somewhat by an 1834 amendment that provided for impeachment
(*juicio político*) of ministers appointed by the president for 'unacceptable conduct'. The General Assembly comprised a popularly
elected body called the Chamber of Representatives, whose members
served a three-year term of office. There was also an indirectly elected
body called the Chamber of Senators consisting of nine members,
each one selected for a six-year term by an electoral college in each
of the departments. For a time, these senators assembled (sometimes in joint sessions with the Chamber of Representatives) in
an elegant House of Commons-style debating chamber located in a

FIGURE 67: The author in the opposition benches, in the House of Commons-style
General Assembly, from whose balcony (to the left of the picture) newly elected presidents
of the republic customarily greeted crowds gathered in Montevideo's Constitution Square
(November 2005).

wood-panelled, white-painted room on the first floor of the old town hall of Montevideo (Figure 67).

There were understandably more than a few contemporaries who concluded that the 1830 constitution had been crafted by the hand of technical perfection. Some observers were convinced that it was a world-class constitution, even (some thought) touched by the hand of God. The bitter truth was that hard times soon came. Fighting hands had their way with its constitutional niceties, and for the rest of the nineteenth century, as elsewhere in Spanish America, political efforts to run government by constitutional standards were periodically wrecked by armed struggle among various local and regional caudillos. The continuing tensions between the commercial interests in the port town of Montevideo and the rest of the country, where caudillos and their armed bands still held sway, eventually gave birth to one of the oldest two-party systems in the world of representative democracy. So named because of the coloured badges worn by their adherents, the Blancos (the Whites), later officially known as the National Party, were formed out of groups of landowning caudillos. The Colorados (the Reds) were backed mainly by groups of urban and commercial bigwigs. Despite efforts on both sides to bring about pacts between the warring groups through power-sharing arrangements (called *coparticipación*), the tensions between these proto-parties were to bring the country to the brink of civil war several times during the nineteenth century, and again during nine months of fierce fighting in 1904. The failure of either side to get the upper hand, combined with a decisive show of army force in 1904 by Colorado Party President José Batlle y Ordóñez (Figure 68) against his National Party opponents, put a stop to the violence and enabled a new 'fuzzy' compromise based nominally on a two-party system. With that came the consolidation of effective governmental power, with long-lasting democratic effects that were to be felt throughout the whole social order.

The reforms championed by José Batlle y Ordóñez (1856–1929) were at the cutting edge of politics in the region. They demonstrated for the first time anywhere in Spanish America that it was possible to use the institutions of representative government to create a more egalitarian society – in effect, to produce a form of representative

FIGURE 68: José Batlle y Ordóñez, savouring morning newspapers during his European sabbatical from politics, Paris, 1910.

democracy that rested on more democratic social foundations. Batlle's vision of a welfare state democracy had deep roots. Born of good political blood – he was the son of General Lorenzo Batlle, former president of the republic (1868–72) and prominent figure in the Colorado Party – Batlle was deeply influenced through his education by European (especially French) radical ideas. In his early years, he was critical of militarism and participated in the 1886 Quebracho revolt against the caudillo government of General Máximo Santos. A champion of a free press, Batlle founded (in 1886) an opposition newspaper, *El Día*, which continued to publish until 1993. He often referred to himself as a believer in the innate dignity of humankind. In pursuit of humanist ideals, and helped by a most unlikely adviser (an immigrant anarchist from Calabria named Domingo Arena), Batlle worked hard to strengthen, reform and personally control the Colorado Party. During his two terms as president (1903–7 and 1911–15) he also used state institutions to break the political grip of the rural caudillos – a vital step, he thought, towards the democratisation of Uruguay.

Consistent with his humanist pragmatism, Batlle backed far-reaching reforms that made Uruguay the first welfare state in Latin America. With popular support, in the name of democracy, he championed new forms of state regulation of social life. Rather like 'Battling Bob' La Follette and other Progressives in the United States, he thought the job of government was to produce a more equal society, in this case by modernising and sharing the fruits of agriculture, as well as by responding to social demands, using the means of representative democracy. Batlle was convinced that greater social justice could be extracted from a booming market economy that was based on wool and refrigerated meat exported through the newly refurbished, world-class port of Montevideo. The Batlle policies were the political expression of a profound transformation of social life in the country. They spelled death to the old elitist, segmented social order dominated by bitter conflicts between urban oligarchs and rural caudillos. They signalled the birth of a much less rigid and more diversified civil society enlivened by the dramatic growth of new social groups like merchants, teachers, office workers and manual labourers, as well as by foreign immigration so massive that, between the 1870s and 1910, Uruguay's population doubled to just over one million inhabitants, nearly a third of whom lived in Montevideo.

The social changes were dramatic, and even though they later happened, if unevenly, throughout the whole continent, Uruguay quickly developed a reputation as a political laboratory. Thanks to Batlle's far-sighted energies, whole legislative programmes were committed to greater social equality. Batlle personally defended women's legal rights in a series of articles that appeared under the pen name 'Laura'. Divorce laws were passed in 1907 and 1910 (divorce with cause and by mutual consent), while in 1912 women won the right to file for divorce without specific cause. It was a victory for the burgeoning local women's movement.

Divorce law reform was a slap in the face to the Church, which was forced to concede quite a few other powers during this period. The move to separate God and government was not intended to get rid of God from human affairs; it was instead a vote of no confidence in the ability of men of God to govern. In 1909, religious education within public schools was abolished, despite the vigorous opposition of a newly formed Catholic-oriented party, the Civic Union of Uruguay (Unión Cívica del Uruguay – UCU). In the name of democracy, the governments headed by Batlle defended more than the separation of Church and state; they also abolished capital punishment and worked towards curbing the undue political influence of the military in social affairs. The whole point, thought Batlle and his supporters, was to create a more civilised society, which meant as well taming the power of both greedy employers and extremist trade unions, especially by introducing labour market reforms. Batlle fought tooth and nail for the eight-hour working day (finally enacted by his successor in 1915), unemployment compensation (1914), night work restrictions (1918), retirement pensions (1919) and enforceable occupational safety standards (1920). Efforts to apply the principles of the American economist Henry George in the field of agriculture were scuppered by the organised resistance of a new pressure group called the Rural Federation (Federación Rural), a front for large landowners. Batlle had tried to curb their power by introducing progressive taxes on land use, plus a surcharge on inheritance taxes. Instead, he had to make do with modest government interventions, for instance by establishing a series of institutes dedicated to research and development in such fields as dairying, livestock, horticulture and forestry.

Quite a few of Batlle's reforms had the intended effect of *reducing* the scope of market mechanisms in the name of democratic equality. Representative democracy, he reasoned, demanded that key services be in the hands of elected government. Government was better placed than business to promote greater social equality, to stimulate domestic capital accumulation, and to combat foreign remittances that served only to weaken the country's balance of payments. Under Batlle's direction, government became heavily involved in the field of education. He said repeatedly that the poorest deserve the best, that education was the right of 'all, without distinction of social class'; at one point, he shocked some citizens by suggesting that the talented poor should be given the opportunity to become scholars, while the untalented rich should plant potatoes.[36] This was the spirit in which high schools were created throughout the country (in 1912), free high school education was soon approved (in 1916), and strong government backing was given for the policy of universal access of all women to the University of the Republic. New state enterprises flourished. A private savings and loan company (BROU) that printed money was nationalised in 1911. The following year, the government took control of the generation and distribution of electricity, in the form of the State Electric Power Company. The Mortgage Bank of Uruguay was nationalised, while in 1914 a large private railway company was purchased, thus laying the tracks for the future State Railways Administration.

Double Simultaneous Voting

Most interesting is that Batlle saw Uruguay as a democratic laboratory, a place in which the creation of a welfare state required the invention of new institutions of representative democracy. He had a fine grasp of the dialectics of representative government. Batlle knew that caudillos like Bolívar and Artigas had been its decisive champions during the struggle for independence from the Spanish monarchy. But he recognised that most caudillos had quickly abused the mechanisms of representative government, using them as a convenient ladder for climbing above 'the people', then treating them as a hindrance, as shit, to be kicked away at the moment that victory over other opponents had been secured. Encouraged by reading the works of authors such as Sarmiento, Batlle was sure that the old caudillo way of doing politics had to get off its high horse. He found unacceptable that during the first seventy-five years of Uruguayan history, four elected presidents had declared martial law. But this did not lead him to draw revolutionist conclusions. He instead saw that the mechanisms of representative democracy needed strengthening, so that they could be used to rid democracy of what he spittingly called *caudillismo*.

Such were the times, and his powerful sense of historical mission, that at the end of his first four-year term of office in 1907, Batlle took a sabbatical from politics. Like Tocqueville, but instead sailing from the New World back to Old Europe, he spent four years travelling in England and on the Continent, and through Palestine, Syria and Egypt. Dressed in crumpled suits and badly knotted ties, the huge man with a gruff voice met statesmen (initially he headed up the Uruguayan delegation at the Second Hague Peace Conference of 1907) as well as journalists, businessmen, professionals and citizens; he read widely, scribbled constantly and studied different systems of government and law. The insights gleaned during his European sojourn were put to good use. Following his re-election as president to a second term of office (1911–15), Batlle worked hard to change the rules of the political game. He started by hosting a constitutional convention.

Inspired by what he had found in Europe, Batlle pushed for the replacement of the presidency with a nine-member collegial executive called a *colegiado*. Figures like Rosas he found so repulsive that he was sure that what was badly needed in Uruguay was a cabinet-style mechanism of making executive decisions, a new means of give-and-take bargaining at the top that involved healthy compromises and the open expression of differences of opinion. 'There is no doubt that the most advanced peoples in every age recognised at some time the inconvenience of domination by a single man and attempted executive government by various men', he said. That was because concentrated executive power always meant 'force, action, speed in attacks', 'warlike power'.[37] Batlle's reforms understandably aroused opposition. Although the principle of collegial leadership was eventually to win acceptance, in the short term his vision of more humble government caused a deep split in the ranks of his own Colorado Party; that allowed the opposition National Party, led by Luis Alberto de Herrera, to torpedo it in the water, shortly after its launch.

Batlle meanwhile put his energies into supporting an early version of a Uruguayan speciality: a new method of voting called the 'double simultaneous vote' (*doble voto simultáneo*). The nifty method was in effect an application of the principles of proportional representation to political parties themselves. Aiming to show that representative democracy was a method of publicly managing disagreements, it allowed citizens when casting their votes to express their support simultaneously for both a party and their favourite faction within it. Thought up by a French professor, Joseph Borély, in the years just before 1870, details of the scheme quickly travelled across the Atlantic, towards Uruguay, where just several years later the first pilot schemes were tested, and its principles taught in the law faculty of Montevideo's University of the Republic.[38]

Here is how it worked: during any election campaign, whether in small-scale municipal elections or elections for the presidency, each party (known in Uruguay as a *lema*) was entitled to field several candidates, each representing a particular faction (*sublema*) of the same party. The actual composition of the *sublemas* could vary, depending on the context in which each was used. For instance, it might be a pair of candidates bent on winning as a team the post of mayor and deputy mayor of a city; or an ordered list of candidates from different factions of the same party, each seeking a seat in a legislature; or a full-blooded campaign by two or more party candidates for the highest office of state. On polling day, with each voter entitled to vote for one candidate, the winning party was to be the one that attracted the most votes (calculated by adding up the votes for its various *sublemas*). Yet within the winning party, it was the *sublema* with the most votes that would win. In other words, candidates from the same party would have a common interest in maximising its total number of votes, even though the aim of each candidate was to outdo their rivals by winning the maximum number of votes for themselves.

The beauty of the double simultaneous vote was that it meant several things to more than a few people. That was a reason why in Uruguay it proved popular with Batlle and his supporters, and why it was first included in an electoral law of 1910. The double simultaneous vote system was designed to block the rise of third parties and to consolidate the two-party system in Uruguay, mainly by preventing ticket splitting and rolling together general elections and the American system of primaries. Batlle and others thought that allowing factions within the same party to run rival lists of candidates, and to accumulate enough votes to take office, would not degenerate into American-style razzamatazz. Openly competitive party lists would, instead, offer an important incentive to minorities, the emerging trade union movement and rural poor, for instance, to vote for one of the two main political parties. By using this system, the most socially disadvantaged voters were less likely to waste their votes and more likely to have a collective say in making and unmaking governments. Put differently, the double simultaneous vote was a way of calming social tensions and postponing the dangers of civil war; voters who favoured a particular party would not be forced to shut their mouths and pinch their noses when voting for candidates unrepresentative of their views. Batlle personally expected another advantage to flow from the adoption of the double simultaneous vote: by legitimating internal party differences, it would publicly expose cloak-and-dagger backroom dealing, so proving that there was no such thing as an Iron Law of Oligarchy at work within parties. This was the point: Uruguay would proudly set the pace of political reform for other countries, and it would do so by encouraging multiple candidates to run within the same party, and to leave the final decision not to party bosses, but to citizens themselves.

Batlle's efforts to extend the use of the double simultaneous vote, to disarm aspiring caudillos by making the presidency dependent upon the majority faction of the governing party, was defeated in 1916, in Uruguay's first ever open election based on the secret ballot and universal male suffrage.[39] The prior reforms that he had successfully backed nevertheless made their mark on the new constitution of 1917, which was approved by plebiscite. It formally separated Church and state, adopted proportional representation and the secret ballot, as well as abolished the death penalty. It recognised a two-chamber legislature called the General Assembly, which comprised a Chamber of Representatives based on constituencies determined by the numbers of adult males resident in the country's nineteen departments; and a Senate, whose members were elected at large from a countrywide vote. The constitution also granted a revised version of Batlle's wish for a collegial executive. A new body called the National Council of Administration was set up. It consisted of nine representatives (six from the majority party and three from the minority party) elected for six years by direct popular vote, one-third retiring every two years. It was empowered to supervise the new welfare state by appointing ministers and exercising all powers not expressly granted to the president. The new constitution also adopted the principle of universal male suffrage, which had first been used in a general election the year before, in 1916 – a full two years before it was practised in the United Kingdom, the supposed home of parliamentary democracy.

One other trend-setting invention in the Uruguay laboratory is worth mentioning. From 1925 onwards, elections were placed under the non-party jurisdiction of a newly created Electoral Court. The body was born with teeth. It bore a paradox, in that the independent judicial body was an example of an unelected institution so vital for enforcing the rules of the game of representative democracy. Batlle himself must have smiled at the belated success of a political vision that he had long been championing. The founding of the Electoral Court was not just an important breakthrough in the consolidation of representative democracy in Uruguay. It produced the amazing spectacle of venal and openly corrupted politicians willingly agreeing the need for a 'clean' organisation that would clamp down on their wheeling and dealing.

Political cynics said the new Court confirmed the old adage that even thieves need periodically to sit down together, to agree to the common rules of their thievery. But the innovation worked. The Electoral Court enforced the method of decentralised vote counting at thousands of vote-counting tables. Aside from supervising the entire registration and voting process, and registering parties and candidates, it also had the final say in all election disputes; in the event of gross irregularities, it had the power to annul an election result. It supervised the various departmental electoral boards and the National Electoral Office in Montevideo, which had the responsibility for organising and maintaining the Civil Register of all eligible voters in the country. Before an election, through a grant of money decided by the General Assembly, the Electoral Court allocated campaign costs among the political parties, in direct proportion to the number of votes they had received in the previous election.

The principles of rotation of office-holding and democratic compromise were reinforced by experiments with various power-sharing procedures. Save for voting, judicial magistrates and members of the police and armed forces were banned from party-political life. The president of the republic and members of the Electoral Court were not permitted to serve as political party officials, or to engage in political election propaganda. All electoral boards at the departmental level were publicly elected. A two-thirds vote of the full membership of each chamber of the parliament was needed to repeal or to adopt any new election law. To reduce manipulation by incumbent governments, and to stabilise the electoral cycle, measures were also adopted to hold all national and local elections on the last Sunday in November, every five years. The Court supervised efforts to redistribute electoral spoils from winners to losers, most notably through co-participation rules that guaranteed the minority party representation within all areas of government, including appointments within state ministries and to the boards of directors of public enterprise. The new Electoral Court targeted electoral fraud by issuing eligible male voters with a registration card bearing their photograph and fingerprint. The innovation was courtesy of Vucetich, and it had been tested on prostitutes, who were in fact the first group in Uruguayan society to be compulsorily issued with an identity card, so prompting the local joke that women actually got the vote before the men of the country.[40]

The Return of Caudillos

The reforms associated with Batlle were impressive by world standards. Political and social developments in several other Spanish American countries were equally inspiring, and they appeared to be the climax of a most interesting century of experiments with representative government. The wholly unexpected break with imperial monarchy had triggered a long political journey, commencing with the careful crafting of republican constitutions that overlapped with the growth of power-hungry caudillos, territorial rivalries and war, a terrorist dictatorship that operated in the name of its people, the rise of party competition, lots of electoral tomfoolery and fraud and, finally, serious efforts to put an end to the violence and bossing of *caudillismo* by pushing reality in the direction of the textbook principles of representative democracy.

It is no accident that the push towards power-sharing institutions in Uruguay, and throughout Spanish America more generally, happened from the end of the nineteenth century until around

1930. This was after all a period which saw a great growth spurt of globalising pressures, especially in terms of flows of capital and trade and people, as well as the more general nurturing of civil society institutions, like trade unions, business associations, political parties and religious bodies. It was above all a period in which the practical ideal of universal suffrage came of age. Governments and dominant social classes everywhere found it hard to resist popular pressure. 'The people' were now a force to be reckoned with, and so political reforms gathered pace, leading some observers to conclude, in contradiction of James Bryce and other masters of condescension, that a new age of representative democracy was now dawning in Spanish America.

Then came a triple hammer blow. The combined forces of a global war, the implosion of markets and political infighting crippled the young representative democracies of Spanish America. There was something utterly modern about this de-democratisation process. Certainly it was not understandable through the rather simple-minded explanations offered by the first Greek writers and speechmakers who ruminated on why democracies collapse. They supposed the chief culprit was *hybris*: the insatiable appetite for power that invariably brings misfortune, to gluttonous rulers and ruled alike. Pericles, Plato, Thucydides and others reasoned that power greed was an ailment of the human condition; and so they concluded that democracy would inevitably succumb to gluttony. But the explanation was excessively general, and prejudiced by its dislike of democracy. In Spanish America, during the first decades of the twentieth century, different, more detailed forces were at work. Beginning with the outbreak of World War One, the collapse of the core institutions that had for some decades underpinned globalisation had especially devastating effects upon the democracies and would-be democracies of the region. It was as if a spiteful Europe had decided to take its revenge on Spanish America for its earlier disloyalty – a revenge that took the form of trade restrictions, disinvestment of capital, the disruption of communication links, the severance of social ties and, worst of all, the outbreak of the world's first ever military conflict that prepared the way for an even more devastating bout of global violence during the years 1939–45.

The destructiveness of World War One and the extended depression produced by the Wall Street Crash of 1929 sabotaged the young democracies of Spanish America – and that of Brazil as well. It was as if some strange, new anti-democratic weapon had exploded, producing poisonous fallout on a world scale. Its toxins had strong effects throughout the hemisphere. Young representative democracies went into terminal decline. The mockery of democracy became a sport. The mechanisms of elections, party competition and power sharing suddenly seemed unfair, ineffective and unresponsive to many people, not only to the swelling ranks of new voters, but especially to landed property owners and their military allies. These conservatives had wanted democracy to behave itself, to uphold the rules of the game. When they found it was unsuited to that purpose, they dug in their heels and insisted that government should reflect the prevailing socio-economic order, rather than serve (as Batlle had thought) as some kind of counterweight to it.

The consequence was that representative democracies fell like tender buds in a snap frost. In Chile, the wealth-promoting autocratic government of Carlos Ibáñez fell apart. So dependent was the country on its primary commodity exports, copper and nitrates, and on foreign loans and investments used to fund public works, that ruin followed the virtual collapse of export markets and capital imports. Investment and debt repayments ground to a halt, and by 1930 the country was gripped by worsening unemployment, the collapse of public works and deep cuts in wages and salaries. Strikes and street demonstrations against the government's handling of the crisis swelled. Ibáñez replied with press censorship and force; but when, in July 1931, a young Santiago medical student, Jaime Pinto Riesco, was shot in cold blood by a policeman who had tried to snatch the newspaper he was reading with his friends, public opinion boiled. Ibáñez, trying to save his skin, resigned. Wild scenes of public jubilation followed. 'What overthrew the dictatorship was not a revolution', a leading Santiago newspaper commented, 'but quite the opposite. It was the irresistible force of public opinion which sought to put an end to a revolutionary situation and restore constitutional and legal normality.'[41] The times were unfortunately dead against such happy outcomes. Eighteen months after the fall of Ibáñez, with markets in a state of near-collapse, Chile had witnessed two general strikes, several *coups d'état*, one mutiny of the navy and nine different governments.

Similarly ominous forces gripped Argentina. In late December 1929, President Hipólito Yrigoyen miraculously survived an assassination attempt. A few months later, ill and confined to bed, he was deposed by a well-prepared military coup led by José Félix Uriburu, who had the backing of the landowning class, army fascists and conservatives, and by parts of the population suffering unemployment and runaway inflation in the wheat and beef export economy, one of the world's biggest. News of the coup prompted wild celebrations in downtown Buenos Aires. In neighbouring Uruguay, crippled by adverse trade balances, spiralling debt service payments and the depreciation of the peso, Dr Gabriel Terra, its president, abolished the collegiate executive power, dissolved Congress, won a rigged election and then (since it was 1933) dressed himself up in the clothes of a dictator. The destabilising events of the late 1920s and early 1930s impacted as well on Brazil, where a strongman of wealth in the caudillo tradition, Getúlio Vargas, was installed by the military as 'provisional president'. He stayed fifteen years, to forge a populist dictatorship supported by the army, millions of rural poor, urban workers and the middle classes.

These and other cases of dictatorship proved that in Spanish America representative democracy, originally a European invention, was deeply dependent upon another European invention: a market economy whose greedy recklessness could make redundant both capital and labour, with devastating social consequences. The plague of dictatorships proved as well that modern democracy was governed by another thoroughly European rule: representative democracy in any one country could never survive by 'going it alone', but only when democratic politicians and citizens joined hands as equals, stood firm and stuck together in solidarity, within a wider political community of like-minded governments that were prepared, in times of adversity, to come to each other's rescue.

Unfortunately for democrats, that never happened in Spanish America (as it later did in Europe, in the shape of the European Union). With the death by strangling of the hopes and dreams and schemes of democrats like Madero, Yrigoyen and Batlle, caudillo dictators of various shapes and sizes picked up their pistols and slipped back into their political saddles, to rule much of the region for the next fifty years.

THE EUROPEAN GRAVEYARD

It was the best of times, it was the worst of times, it was the age of
wisdom, it was the age of foolishness, it was the epoch of belief, it was the
epoch of incredulity, it was the season of Light, it was the season of
Darkness, it was the spring of hope, it was the winter of despair, we had
everything before us, we had nothing before us, we were all going direct
to Heaven, we were all going direct the other Way . . .

Charles Dickens, *A Tale of Two Cities* (1859)

It is time to return to Europe, to face some bittersweet truths about
parliaments, peoples and big powers.

From the last quarter of the eighteenth century until roughly
1930, the tiny peninsula at the western end of the Asian landmass
made a mark on the world out of all proportion to its physical
size. Europe became synonymous with dynamic thinking, practical
innovation, the long-distance conquest of peoples and territories.
In the shape of steam engines, threshing machines, locomotives,
automobiles and military tanks, Europe shook the world with
its own inventions. It unleashed the might of industrial capitalism,
mobilised mass armies and triggered a wave of movements – against
Slavery, for the Nation, Socialism and Peace – that radically transformed the way many people thought about life. During the same
period, loud calls for democracy filled Europe's fields, streets and
buildings; there were new words like 'democrat' and 'democratism'
and the period even gave birth to a subversive verb for describing
the movement of whole societies towards political and social equality: *democratise* (it came from the French *démocratiser*, perhaps

courtesy of the Dutch). Gripped by the feeling that 'the people' had finally mounted the stage of history, large numbers of Europeans grew convinced, or began to hope, that just as their region was the birthplace of representative democracy, so Europe was now destined to become its heartland, perhaps even a place from where brand-new forms of democracy could bring light to the rest of the world. Hear the hope in the words scribbled in London in 1846 by the great champion of Italian statehood, Giuseppe Mazzini. 'The democratic tendency of our times, the upward movement of the popular classes', he wrote, hiding away from the continental authorities who wanted his arrest, 'is henceforth no Utopian dream, no doubtful anticipation. It is a fact; a great European fact, which occupies every mind, influences the proceedings of government, defies all opposition.'[1]

The dreams of democrats like Mazzini were to be crushed by the juggernaut of events that ended in the disastrous global war of 1939–45. It was not simply that market slumps and big power rivalries in Europe helped kill off representative democracy elsewhere, for instance in Spanish America and Brazil. Of greater consequence, when measured in terms of global impact, was that Europe suffered dystrophy, becoming a hellish place where almost every nineteenth- and early twentieth-century experiment with representative democracy *failed*. If Alexis de Tocqueville had been American, and if he had decided during the 1930s to travel eastwards by steamship across the Atlantic, to observe the mechanics of democracy in Europe, there is no doubt that he would have been tempted to compare its bizarre misfortunes to the miserable fate of a character in a short story by the young German writer who specialised in depicting the dark side of Europe, Heinrich von Kleist. His *Michael Kohlhaas* (1810) captured the anti-democratic spirit of Europe more than a century before its menacing triumph: hounded and hunted, hemmed in on all sides by powerful authorities that despised its ideals, representative democracy in Europe was a loud cry for freedom and justice against tyranny, a call for equality that was met with arrest, then rewarded with execution on the scaffold of power politics. The consequence was frightful: the European peninsula descended into darkness, dragging the whole world into a rats' alley, a hell of social strife and political despotism that very nearly reduced representative democracy to the bones of an extinct political species.

A Herd Confus'd

To understand why Europe came close to being the graveyard of representative democracy, we need to get to grips with the large-scale sequences of events through which its spirit and institutions were first nurtured, then failed to mature, with consequences that cast a long shadow over the earth and its peoples.

We have seen already how Europe was the place where representative assemblies took root, in many different forms. These parliaments established the practice of government through consultation, and this custom – in some contexts – was linked to the reliance upon written constitutions and, beneath them, the principle that government is only ever legitimate when it rests upon the active consent of its citizens. Among the principal champions of this principle of government by the consent of the governed were republicans. Inspired by Greek and Roman ideas, they first rose to power in the early Italian citizen-states. Republicans liked to speak of 'the people'. But who exactly 'the people' were remained moot. It turned out that republicanism was a subtle ideology of inequality. 'And what the people', asked John Milton, 'but a herd confus'd, a miscellaneous rabble, who extol Things vulgar?'[2] There were some rare exceptions to this republican prejudice against commoners; the tiny Swiss mountain canton of Graubünden, where pride in self-government ran high, was one of them.[3] But it wasn't typical. In the name of 'the people', republicans typically thought in terms of the rule of brute beasts by the best, of the government of commoners docile to the yoke by citizens refined by reading and learning, secure in their ownership of property, proprieties and printing presses.

Enter the rabble of beasts, the flesh-and-blood commoners, the rough-talking women and men dressed in tattered clothes, surviving on simple food earned each day through hard labours that stretched from dawn until dusk. It is tempting to despise or romanticise these people, but one thing is clear: if democracy minimally involves efforts by ordinary folk to establish their equality with others richer and more powerful, then there is no way of excluding rough-hewn commoners from the story of the disparate beginnings of representative democracy in Europe.

The vital contributions of the downtrodden to the widespread disturbances and semi-organised revolts that dotted early modern maps of Europe are proof of this point. Here is just one randomly chosen example: from Córdoba in Spain, in the spring of 1652, came news that typified times in which the bulk of the population was acted upon by the powerful, except for those moments when, like a snake, it suddenly hissed and struck back at those who had disturbed its peace and quiet. 'Mourning inconsolably, a poor Gallegan woman crossed the *barrio* of San Lorenzo, displaying the corpse of her son, who had just perished of hunger, and called out for justice with wild cries', ran the story, retold by a twentieth-century historian. 'A powerful revolt suddenly erupted. Indignant local women wildly scorned their men's cowardice; they called on them to act against injustice and evil. The men gathered knives, pikes, halberds and axes, then marched as a body towards the house of the Corregidor (who upon hearing of the uprising had already fled to Trinity Convent). The men broke down its doors, ransacked the house, and destroyed everything inside. The swelling crowd, urged on by the women within its ranks, surged through the streets shouting insults and complaints against nobles, placemen, benefice holders, even against bishop Don Pedro de Tapia. They attacked houses and granaries, helped themselves to wheat stored in the church of San Lorenzo and also from the houses they assailed.'4

How are we to make sense of such crowd actions? The revolt of the good women of Córdoba was revealing of the styles of action preferred by the powerless before the age of representative democracy in Europe. The evidence – scanty fragments of eyewitness accounts that survive from an age without historians, journalists and newspapers – shows that these were not mindless outbursts. The mobs were not fickle morons or victims of frenzy. Their actions were not gusts of passion but part of the 'moral economy' (as the great English social historian E. P. Thompson once put it) of people who had had enough, who had decided that they had to teach the powerful a lesson or two for the injustices they guarded. Throughout Europe, the powerless commoners kicked their fat bottoms with big boots. They challenged the powerful with rough-and-tumble actions, with deeds that were typically small-scale, confined to local areas, targeted at local authorities, and that lasted normally only for brief periods. Until the end of the eighteenth century, the commoners knew nothing of the language of democracy. But they did know about bargaining by collective riot: satire and mockery, violence directed against people and calculated damage to things.

Surviving reports, such as they are, suggest that those who went on the rampage (many were women) did so always with a sense of purpose – and sometimes with a brawling sense of carnival humour. Rowdy meetings, marches, petitions, lootings, burnings, moral harangues, often laced with religious themes: all of this was understood as an arrow over the heads of the powerful, a warning that they should not go too far, that the status quo should be preserved, or that there needed to be a return to times past. To get their point across to the local authorities, temporal and spiritual, the commoner rebels often parodied the political symbols of their opponents. Actions were seldom spontaneous or unpremeditated reactions to felt injustices; the resistance of commoners was often fuelled by thoughtful exasperation, the culmination of negotiations with authorities with closed minds and cloth ears. The rebels sometimes appealed to an imagined 'good king'; often thought of themselves as spiritual equals of their opponents; and they usually tapped into support from the local communities in which they lived, which is why the rebels liked to time their protests to coincide with holidays or officially authorised gatherings.

It is wrong to think of the commoners as powerless people. While they had no civil liberties or rights to cast votes, the weak had powerful weapons. Their resistance normally began as unsolicited grumbling in places like bakeries, alehouses and markets. Bellyaching at the authorities easily turned into cursing, the brandishing of harsh words that drew power from the widespread belief that they had the backing of God. From cursing it was only a few heartbeats to talk of 'necessity hath no law' and more desperate tactics: launching appeals to named individuals for help; making representations or circulating petitions; or publicly 'shaming' the local authorities for their misdeeds, such as a new tax on beer or altered grazing and firewood arrangements. If everything else failed, scores were then settled by direct action: forcible seizures of marketed food or assaults on its sellers; burning effigies of figures judged to have outraged public morality; or marking out sites of injustice, usually through physical attacks on the dwellings of the alleged perpetrators, or the place where an alleged offence took place.

Mortal Gods

The defensiveness and geographic dispersal of these early rebellions of vengeance stood in marked contrast to the revolutionary clamours to come. The many-headed monsters and brute beasts were about to organise themselves in different ways, and with different goals. There was, however, no sudden moment of change, and, indeed, the old rambunctious protests survived for a long time, even into our own day. But by the middle of the eighteenth century, throughout the European peninsula and its adjoining islands, the struggles of commoners to stand up and be counted changed form and direction. The old politics of clinging to the past through grumbling, shaming, vengeance and intimidation fell into decline. A new, forward-looking politics of combination with others sprang up. Local protests were linked to other local protests. With the help of improved roads and the printing press, protest came to be organised and coordinated across great distances. The protesters, sometimes backed by burgher militias, began to speak in the name of a newly imagined subject: 'the people'. There was also a new target: *governments*. Political authorities were seen increasingly as culpable – as sackable, even electable – by a people that was not simply a rhetorical invention of self-serving constitution writers or pamphleteers, but an organised, armed reality, an articulate force that was willing to press home its claims upon power. The change was momentous, so profound in fact that it can safely be said that the invention and spread of territorial states were to change everything in the history of representative democracy.

It is well known that the territorial state was an invention of early modern Europe. Its first appearance, in such Renaissance city republics as Venice and Florence, and its subsequent spread throughout the European region, then to the whole world, led to the concentration of government resources in a few hands. The architecture of politics changed. Territorially defined governments, fed by their control of taxes, legal expertise, administration and the means of violence, began to wield enormous power over their subjects. They were usually called states. Scholars disagreed about whether they were 'the actuality of the ethical idea' (Hegel) or 'the admission that this society has become entangled in an insoluble contradiction with itself' (Engels) or, more accurately, a set of powerful institutions that 'monopolises legitimate violence over a given territory' (Weber). There was more agreement that states were a new kind of association among persons, a new form of power not based on blind obedience but, rather, exercised partly through law, and hence limited in certain cases by a constitution. It was agreed as well that states were rooted in a particular territory, which defined their jurisdiction, and that in their capacity to act they enjoyed as well a definite measure of personality. States were juristic persons in international law. In popular thinking, they came as well to be regarded as a quasi-person, as a body of rules, offices and powers with an identity distinctly separated from, and standing watch over, the identity of those whom they ruled.

The hard-nosed political thinker of the English Revolution Thomas Hobbes (1588–1679) famously described states as Mortall Gods. That nicely captured their tremendous power to shape and reshape the lives of their subjects. States turned people into taxpayers; into objects of law and civil administration; and into policemen and soldiers and victims of war among states. It has been customary in European political thinking (as the work of scholars such as Max Weber shows) to emphasise these and other *duties* of subjects to these newfangled states. But that is to tell only half the story, for the remarkable thing about the whole centralising and dominating thrust of European state building is the way that it both prompted resistance to its claims and helped concentrate, centralise and redefine those claims as potentially *democratic* demands, for instance in the shape of voting in periodic elections.

In Europe, representative democracy resembled a plant that grew in the hothouse of the territorial state. It was fed by many nutrients, including the renaissance of interest in Roman politics that took place during the fifteenth century. That republicanism emphasised that states could not be considered legitimate unless they cultivated *citizens* who considered themselves as the source of sovereign power. So-called republicanism championed the principle of 'popular sovereignty', but during the course of the seventeenth and eighteenth centuries its strongly elitist understanding of 'the people' was decisively corrected by the entry of commoners into state-organised politics. Their uphill battles for recognition were hard-fought. The great transformation of rebellions by commoners into sophisticated demands for political representation, in the name of 'the people', took time. It was no overnight affair, and it suffered constant setbacks. There were no guarantees that it would succeed. That it managed to do so was a tribute to the staying power of common people. They chipped away at local rocks of power with the stubborn desperation of miners trapped underground, with nowhere to go but up.

Three Europes

The great excavation undoubtedly involved a change of heart, in favour of the belief that political equality was possible, that feisty commoners – craft workers, farmers, labourers, fishermen – were capable of governing themselves, if need be by joining forces with aristocratically minded burghers, or even by shoving them out of the way, in the process forming brand-new ways of handling power, such as the right to form trade unions, by pushing towards a universal male franchise, and by government legislation designed to protect the downtrodden from exploitation by the powerful.

The extent to which commoners managed to become self-governing citizens very much depended on whether or not they lived under a state. To be stateless was to be treated like dirt at the mercy of the plough. Citizenship was equally conditional upon the type of state that existed, in particular whether and to what extent it was open to influence from pressures from below. Absolutist states, those in which the means of governing were concentrated into the hands of just a few, with a king or queen at the top, everywhere proved menacing for the principles and practice of representative democracy. In a way, the fate of commoners was determined by where they were born, and where they subsequently lived. Territory pre-decided their chances of becoming citizens.

Consider for a moment the striking differences between the western, east-central and eastern parts of Europe.[5] In the long and bitterly contested transition from medieval to modern times, each of these regions tasted life under an absolutist state that tried in different ways to preserve certain elements of the feudal heritage, support the growth of market production and exchange, and build up its own governing institutions. But here the similarities ended, for the methods, goals and degree of coherence of absolutist states, as well as the level of resistance of commoners to their power, varied greatly from region to region. Much depended on the dynamism of their respective economies, geopolitical situations and the strength of the inherited medieval infrastructures of power and representation.

In the western region of Europe, for example, the mechanisms of representation born of the medieval way of life only abandoned their resistance to state builders gradually and grumpily. There were frequent rebellions by the nobility, the urban bourgeoisie, the peasantry and other commoners, so that absolute states only appeared in this part of Europe by the seventeenth century. Whereas all European absolutist states were hellbent on subordinating and 'policing' their subjects through the deployment of various techniques of control from above, in practice various local autonomies, representative mechanisms and civil freedoms were nowhere eliminated. The dogged independence of a prickly civil society was displayed time and again. In the field of commerce and exchange, for instance, the typical form of western mercantilism was the independent capitalist company organised under state protection. Striking as well was the resilience of parliamentary institutions, the survival of various local mechanisms of representation, and the bureaucratisation of the nobility by means of the sale of offices (which had the effect of opening the way for the infiltration of the state apparatus by bourgeois and professional groups). Not surprisingly, the lifespan of absolutist states was relatively short in western Europe. Sometimes, with the help of commoners, they were overthrown relatively early, as happened (we have seen) in the Netherlands and England. They only survived the eighteenth century in 'semi-peripheral' territories, like Spain, Portugal and southern Italy, kingdoms that were disadvantaged by the relocation of the centre of the world political economy to the Atlantic region.

Things were very different in the eastern region of Europe. There absolutism developed earlier, lasted much longer and served as the great demiurge of politics and social life. The rise of an absolutist state in Russia between the reigns of Ivan III and Ivan IV (1462–1584) had serious consequences for the whole population, including its commoners. The Russian state eliminated virtually every independent 'freedom' and local autonomy. Whereas western absolutism subordinated society to the state, eastern absolutism nationalised it. Russian absolutism developed through such organisations as the *oprichnina* championed by Ivan the Terrible. It was a terrorist state within the state that monitored all potential opposition, exterminated the boyars and confiscated their lands, and prevented the formation of any independent bourgeois stratum. The process of state building went unhindered by the weak and short-lived Estates Assembly (*zemskiy sobor*), which was not properly speaking a parliament, since it was created from above by a decree of Ivan IV. The state also created a unified 'service nobility' (called the *pomeshchiki*), and it did so by politically incorporating it into the bureaucracy or army, and subjecting it to the ultimate power of the Csar. The state prolonged peasant serfdom and it was dominant in all key industries (especially iron, steel and shipbuilding) and exercised a near-monopoly on foreign trade. It was also the decisive factor in the Russian conquest of vast swathes of territory stretching to the Pacific, a colonisation that resulted in an empire comparable to the empires built by the western European powers during the sixteenth and seventeenth centuries. While the *conquistadores* were expanding the Western world economy all the way to the Indies, the Cossacks, after their first expeditions to Siberia (during the years 1581–4), advanced as far as Kamchatka, thus outlining the possibilities of an alternative world economy. Meanwhile, the Church in the Russian lands was subordinated from the outset to the state, according to a harsher version of the pattern laid down by the Byzantine Empire. For all these reasons, representative democracy never happened in these lands. Russian absolutism successfully eliminated or prevented the growth of social power groups and representative mechanisms independent of the state. Aside from a single major shock to its foundations, the so-called 'Time of Troubles' that erupted between 1605 and 1613, and apart from the periodic uprisings by peasants who could stand things no more, Russian absolutism proved remarkably stable for a period lasting four centuries.

The absolutist states of middle Europe were built under the impact of waves of historical events that pounded the region from Asia Minor, as well as from the two expansionary regions of western and eastern Europe. Squeezed between these two zones, and forced to defend themselves for several hundred years against repeated Ottoman invasions from south-eastern Europe, the states of east-central Europe – the Polish-Lithuanian Kingdom, Brandenburg-Prussia, and the Habsburg dynasty – displayed a peculiar and unevenly distributed mixture of both western and eastern characteristics. Whether or not representative and democratic institutions took root in this region, thereby clearing spaces for the involvement of commoners as citizens, very much depended on whether these east-central European states were more 'eastern' or 'western'.

There were plenty of signs of institutions of the west European type, even if their roots were shallower and damaged to some degree. Towns developed, although they were fewer in number and less autonomous than their western counterparts. The nobility was a force to be reckoned with, and sometimes its powers were overgrown. Parliaments were active, but they were typically much less representative than those in the west, and certainly much more resistant to the pressures exerted by commoners. State builders in this middle region of Europe accordingly had to reckon with pre-existing networks of social power, even if they were less dynamic and energetic than those of western European societies.

The various state-building strategies used to handle these peculiarities resulted in hybrid state structures of three varieties. As we have seen already, the Polish-Lithuanian Kingdom, the one most highly charged with western characteristics, was the dominant political force in this region of middle Europe until the last decades of the seventeenth century. It assumed the unusual form of a self-governing republic run by the nobility. The hands of its elected rulers were continually tied by the parliament, the *Sejm*, which consistently manoeuvred to exclude from its ranks both the commoners and the interests and representatives of the Polish towns. It was a painful irony that the power of the parliamentary nobility, its 'aristocratic democracy', served as well to block the revolution in military weaponry and strategy that took place under absolutist states elsewhere. The price of noble power was high: Poland suffered military defeat and disappeared from the maps of eighteenth-century Europe.

The Brandenburg-Prussian state was something of an opposite model of government. Its military and bureaucratic structures closely approximated eastern absolutism. Mechanisms of representation were comparatively undeveloped, and the state systematically swallowed up the nobility (making the Junkers an exemplary western variant of the eastern 'service nobility'). It also pursued mercantilist policies, and greatly expanded its military capacities. It proved to be a highly flexible absolutist state; under pressure from Napoleon's troops in 1806, its rulers managed to put the ideas of 'revolution from above' into practice.

The Habsburg state occupied an intermediate, 'semi-western' position between its Polish and Prussian neighbours. For nearly four centuries, the Habsburg dynasty managed to squeeze the whole southern part of east-central Europe into a Russian-style imperial conglomerate. During the eighteenth century, it developed an eastern-style programme of 'enlightened' reform from above. Yet the Habsburg state was never fully centralised along eastern lines. There were considerable (if unevenly distributed) freedoms for the nobility, town burghers and even the peasantry. And while western-type resistance to the strengthening absolutist state was dealt with in Bohemia (1620) with a truly 'eastern' brutality – virtually the whole of the Czech nobility was murdered – subsequent social resistance, for instance in Hungary in 1670, resulted in something of an uneasy compromise between state and society, a compromise that proved impossible in the region of eastern Europe.

Patriots

Given this uneven distribution of states with more or less absolutist qualities, it should come as no surprise that positive talk of democracy and the growth of representative forms of government that were open to popular pressures from below first happened in western Europe, in the Low Countries. Following the 1648 treaties of Westphalia, which formally confirmed the important Dutch declaration of independence against Philip II of Spain in 1581, the Low Countries became divided into the autonomous United Provinces in the north, a Habsburg-controlled Spanish Netherlands in the south, as well as a semi-autonomous Luxembourg and several other city-states. The region came to resemble an international system of mini-states. The pattern was consolidated in 1650 by the failure of Stadtholder William II to take over the entire north; and by the close alliance of the Dutch republic with England, its old enemy across the North Sea, following the crowning of William III of Orange. The system of states served as the framework within which a flourishing economy – Europe's most vibrant – brought unprecedented prosperity to parts of the population, especially to the urban merchant oligarchies, whose wealth stemmed from their trade connections with Scandinavia, the British Isles, north Germany and remote parts of the earth.

The Dutch states system also bred popular resistance to unaccountable power. Brave new talk of *het Volk* flourished; and for the first time in modern Europe, the word democracy began to vibrate in the heads and hearts of philosophers and publicists. Baruch de Spinoza (1632–77), born in Amsterdam, a humble lens grinder and Dutch philosopher whose parents were exiled Portuguese Jews, was among the first European thinkers to speak positively of 'democracy'. 'We can conceive of various kinds of democracy', he commented, 'but my intention is not to treat of every kind, but of that only, "wherein all, without exception, who owe allegiance to the laws of the country only, and are further independent and of respectable life, have the right of voting in the supreme council and of filling the offices of the dominion".'[6] Spinoza's spirited defence of 'democracy' against 'oligarchy' admittedly had no room for women, children, dissolutes and those 'slaves who are under the authority of men and masters'. But still its verbal praise for democracy was significant, a measure of how, in fits and starts, during the course of more than a century after 1650, 'the people' – not only middling burghers with aristocratic pretensions, but also growing numbers of artisans (like Spinoza) and commoner upstarts – began to clamber on to the political stage.

The Dutch alliance between burghers who liked reading newspapers while puffing on pipes stuffed full of tobacco and plainer people subsisting on bread and potatoes, gin and stuff they called coffee and tea, was something new. The coalition that crystallised during the eighteenth century probably never formed an outright majority of the adult male population; while it drew together Protestants and Catholics, tenant farmers, bakers, innkeepers, haberdashers, gin sellers, ironmongers, cooks, grocers and the occasional tax collector, the alliance failed to make serious inroads into the ranks of hard-core Orange loyalists among the more numerous poor, including people like the shipwrights, dockers and sailors of Rotterdam and Amsterdam.

In the context, that failure did not much matter, for the remarkable influence of the Dutch democrats was out of all proportion to their numbers. Proof of their tactical prowess came during the early 1780s, when those who called themselves 'Patriots' in the American style recognised the United States of America and came within a whisker of establishing their own self-governing, federated republic. Straddling local towns and rural communities, spurred on by pulpit and press, they took up arms, convened public meetings and circulated petitions that called on their fellow (male) citizens to stop paying their taxes and to withdraw their consent to the Prince of Orange and his hangers-on, including Britain, whose declaration of war on the country (in 1780) fanned the coals of local resentment against 'aristocracy', which by now was a term of abuse.

In mid-1785, the Patriots did something remarkable: forming themselves into an elected rival government called the 'Constituted', they backed a bold new written constitution for the United Netherlands. Known locally as the Leiden Draft, it was principally the work of the publicists Pieter Vreede and Wybo Fijnje, whose stirring opening paragraph called for a people's government by representation. 'Liberty is an inalienable right, adhering to all burghers of the Netherlands commonwealth', they wrote. 'No power on earth, much less any power derived truly from the people . . . can challenge or obstruct the enjoyment of this liberty when it is so desired.' The proposed constitution railed against unproductive rentiers, crippling taxes and incompetent military men. It called on the men of the Netherlands to recognise the primacy of self-evident natural rights over all inherited historical powers and offices; and the proposed constitution affirmed the principles of popular sovereignty ('the Sovereign is no other than the vote of the People'), the responsibility of elected officials to their electors, religious toleration and guarantees of freedom of speech (described as the 'foundation of a free constitution'). Patriots were enraptured. Determined to demonstrate that they meant business, they called on all citizens to join an armed non-denominational Free Corps led by elected officers, who were bound always to act in the name of the Dutch people, whom they addressed as people for the first time. 'O fellow countrymen! Arm yourselves, assemble together and take charge of the affairs of the land for these must be your affairs' was the way things were put by one of the most respected Patriot leaders, a frustrated aristocrat with American sympathies named J. D. van der Capellen. 'This land belongs to you – the entire Netherlands people, and not solely to the Prince and his grandees, but to you the descendants of the free Batavians.'[7]

This was a tipping point in the history of representative democracy. For Patriot revolutionaries like van der Capellen rejected the view that government was naturally the domain of uniformed nobles, or the private property of wealthy burghers. They thought of themselves as guided by Christian principles, and were especially attracted to the doctrine of Christian brotherhood, which implied that everyone had a stake in government. Legitimate government for them required equality of representation. Exactly that thought inspired the remarkably bloodless revolutionary takeover of many towns of the United Provinces in the mid-1780s by single-minded democrats clutching muskets and white lilies, and sporting black cockades and ribbons tied in a 'V' (for *Vrijheid*, or 'Freedom'). By the autumn of 1786, the city of Utrecht was governed by an elected Patriot council and protected by several thousand Free Corps troops, themselves governed by an elected commission of tribunes. These new governing bodies constituted an attempt to build a representative democracy within a state run by the Orange monarchy; given what was at stake, the Patriots wasted no time linking arms with their counterparts in neighbouring towns, to form a regional assembly that claimed the authority of the States of Utrecht.

Excitement mounted when the Patriots bloodlessly took over Amsterdam, the largest and wealthiest city in the country. The newly formed Amsterdam Council ordered the city's bridges burned, to prevent intervention by the forces of the House of Orange, all public expressions of sympathy for which were banned. The use of the colour orange was forbidden; a decree was issued to prevent the display of carrots in markets unless their grassy green tops were visible; and a thoughtless chef who went heavy on the saffron in his cakes was arrested and charged with sedition. Fighting between Patriots and Orangists meanwhile erupted in various parts of the country, but the whole experiment in moving towards a popularly based representative democracy – the very first such experiment in Europe – failed. It ended in blood mixed with tears and broken hearts.

The Patriots were hampered by their military inexperience. The tiny state of less than two million people had been accustomed to having others do the fighting on its own land, and this weakness was compounded by their own (understandable) unwillingness to coordinate their resistance on a countrywide basis, for fear of upsetting particular villages, towns and regions jealous of their traditions and newly acquired local freedoms. The Patriots also mishandled their geopolitical destiny. Proud of the successful overthrow of monarchy in the early 1580s, convinced that, come what may, God would help them hold fast yet again to their precious democratic liberties, the Patriots underestimated their role as a second-order power sitting in the cockpit of a big-power Europe.

The Patriots annoyed their Prussian neighbours by quietly accepting money, artillery and vague diplomatic support from France (vague, because a French minister was on record as saying 'it is impossible to undertake anything or concert anything with democrats'). But their greatest bungle came when they arrested Princess Wilhelmina, herself very much a Hohenzollern, as she tried to enter and retake The Hague. The King of Prussia flew into a rage, before ordering a sizeable Prussian military invasion in October 1787. The old rhyming German adage rang true: 'Gegen Demokraten hilfen nur Soldaten [Soldiers are the only remedy for democrats]'.

Like a newborn calf trapped between the legs of fighting bulls, the young Dutch experiment with representative democracy was very nearly kicked to death. Its suffering was a taste of things to come, in the whole of Europe; the unhappy outcome proved that democracy could only survive when freed from the monkey business bound up with border confrontations among quarrelsome states. Following the Prussian invasion, Dutch Patriots were arrested, their properties burned, looted and confiscated; more than 40,000 fearful refugees were hounded into exile. Eight years later, the country was invaded once again, this time by French forces bent on establishing a Batavian Republic. The republic was to give way to a French satellite Kingdom of Holland (1806), only then to be gobbled up for a time by France (1810–13) before finally being split into a bifurcated kingdom that nominally included both the south and the north of the previously divided states. The Dutch republic was no more.

Jacobins

The forcible rout of Dutch democrats was a serious setback for the cause of representative democracy. Yet defeat harboured a victory by unleashing a powerful trend that seemed for a time to be unstoppable, a new habit of the heart that proved mightier than the force of mustered armies: the powerful conviction that 'the people', down to its lowest ranks, were entitled to govern themselves.

The change of heart was evident in the remarkable spread of the noun 'democrat' throughout Europe. It was a Dutch coinage of the 1780s, which was not surprising when it is considered that the first recorded positive usage of the word 'democracy' first happened in the Dutch revolt two centuries before. Then, as we have seen, it was a spouse of aristocracy. In the brand-new context of the bashed-up Dutch Revolution of 1784–7, the marriage fell apart. The new word 'democrat' was suddenly counterposed to another new word: 'aristocrat'. 'Two great parties are forming in all nations', observed a well-travelled young patrician from Rotterdam, G. K. van Hogendorp (1762–1834), himself no friend of democracy or democrats. 'For one, there is a right of government, to be exercised by one or several persons over the mass of the people, of divine origin and supported by the church, which is protected by it. These principles are expressed in the formula, State and Church.' Van Hogendorp continued: 'To this is opposed the new system, which admits no right of government except that arising from the free consent of those who submit to it, and which maintains that all persons who take part in government are accountable for their actions. These principles go under the formula, Sovereignty of the People, or Democracy.'[8]

Van Hogendorp, who was later to help draft the 1814 Dutch Kingdom's first constitution that restored the House of Orange as a national monarchy, feared that the formula was revolutionary. He was right. It certainly had incendiary effects in disturbances not only in the Low Countries, but also in other hot spots of Europe, for instance in Switzerland and Ireland. But the formula undoubtedly had its greatest early triumph in the French Revolution. An earthquake that sent shock waves from Paris to the shores of Portugal, the Russian steppes, the towns and villages of Scandinavia and all the way into the heartlands of the Ottoman Empire, the spectacular events of 1789 introduced millions of Europeans to the idea that government could be 'for the people'. Contemporary politicians, poets, philosophers, journalists and other witnesses were dumbfounded. All agreed that strong new words of description were needed. A jumble of natural metaphors resulted. 'Bliss was it in that dawn to be alive, / But to be young was very heaven' was William Wordsworth's version in *The Prelude* (1805). His German counterpart Friedrich Klopstock wrote that the face of France had broken into a smile of 'blue serenity in a vast stretch of sky'. Others, like the English poet Coleridge, spoke of 'France in a rage raising her gigantic limbs'. Edmund Burke was most struck by the theatricality of the events. His earliest known thoughts about the upheaval are contained in a letter to his Irish friend Lord Charlemont, dated 9 August 1789: 'What Spectators and what actors!' he wrote. 'England gazing with astonishment at a French struggle for Liberty and not knowing whether to blame or to applaud!'

Burke's metaphor was apt, for the Revolution indeed proved to be a spectacular stage performance clotted with countless actors of many different shapes and sizes, moving in all directions, united by the sense that nothing would ever again be the same. Four years into the Revolution, with the Terror in full sway and his own death just a few months away, Maximilien Robespierre's fiery speech on democracy, virtue and terror to the Convention on 5 February 1794 registered the pulse of events. Climbing down to the podium from his favourite place amidst the high tier of seats people called the Mountain, the firebrand leader took just five minutes to deliver to the delegates his report on the meaning and progress of the Revolution. 'When, by prodigious effects of courage and of reason', he thundered, 'a whole people break asunder the fetters of despotism to make of the fragments trophies to liberty; when, by their innate vigour, they rise in a manner from the arms of death, to resume all the strength of youth . . . they can neither be checked by impregnable ramparts, nor by innumerable armies of tyrants leagued against them.' It followed that if a people 'do not reach the heights of their destiny it can only be the fault of those who govern'. The people (Robespierre meant himself) could do no wrong: 'to love justice and equality the people need no great effort of virtue; it is sufficient that they love themselves'. So everything depended upon how they were governed. Robespierre spat out his contempt for 'all the vices and absurdities of Monarchy', and went on to say that in a country the size of France the prime virtue of equality could flourish only under a form of 'democratic or republican' government by representatives. The ancient Greek model of democracy was obsolete. 'Democracy is not a state in which people, continually meeting, regulate for themselves all public affairs', he told the delegates. It was more accurate to say that the democracy enacted by the Revolution was of an entirely new type, proudly made in France. 'Democracy', he growled, 'is a state in which the sovereign people, guided by laws which are of their own making, do for themselves all that they can do well, and by their delegates do all that they cannot do for themselves . . . Democracy is the only form of state which all the individuals composing it can truly call their country.'

The performance was unquestionably a *tour de force*. Radical delegates were reportedly reassured by its forthright severity, especially because it was no secret that four years of living through what Robespierre called 'the tempest of revolution' had left its leader physically exhausted and mentally depressed. There were, of course, those who hung like puppets on his every word, who worshipped every inch of the ground he walked on. But most delegates knew that the rhetoric streaming from the lips of the man who symbolised the Revolution was tricky. The force of the speech sprang from his titanic attempt to pin together the subjects of representative democracy, terror and republican revolution. These words in effect became synonyms in the violent struggle against the old order. Hence Robespierre's warning about the dangers of political regression. 'A nation is truly corrupt', he said, 'when . . . it slides from democracy into aristocracy or monarchy; this is the death of the political body by decrepitude.' And hence Robespierre's prediction, one that proved to be as inaccurate as it was bombastic: 'The French are the first people in the world to establish a true democracy, by calling all men to enjoy equality and the fullness of civil rights; and that, in my opinion is the real reason why all the tyrants allied against the Republic will be defeated.'[9]

Robespierre's boast played to the high drama of the moment. While discredited in some circles by its association with the practice of terror (Figure 69), the French Revolution nevertheless put 'Democracy' at the centre of an appealing, if eclectic, vision of a good society that contained many voices from the European past: the assembly *dēmokratia* of the Greek city-states; the struggle for representative councils and parliaments; the ideals of the Levellers; an American declaration of independence from colonial domination; commoners' protests against the powerful; revolutionary talk

FIGURE 69: George Moutard Woodward's engraving, *A Democrat* (1791), featuring a bug-eyed, cockaded Jacobin, standing aside a gibbet, a copy of Tom Paine's *Rights of Man* stuffed into his coat pocket.

of 'democrats' in the Low Countries. The Revolution combined these voices into a new anthem sung by a chorus of angry voices denouncing 'aristocrats', 'monarchy' and unelected privilege. It was not (as posterity often claimed) the first ever moment in modern European history to talk positively about democracy, or to transform the word from a literary device into a political weapon; the burghers of the Low Countries had already done that more than a century before. The French events after 1789 instead injected astonishing energy into the language of democracy by altering its meaning, from a type of self-government based on equal representation, to a type of social order in which hereditary power over others is abolished and egalitarian virtues flourish. The French Revolution was supposed to be total. Robespierre was emphatic: the people of the French nation were to break *all* their chains.

The champions of the Revolution rejected sterile bookish views (expressed, for instance, by the Chevalier de Jaucourt in the *Encyclopédie*) that democracy was 'one of the basic forms of government, in which the people as a body enjoys sovereignty', a form of government that flourished in the tiny city-states of an ancient

world that had forever been destroyed by a combination of decadent forces.[10] Sprinting in the footsteps of their American
counterparts, whose gentlemanly republicanism they otherwise
detested, the French revolutionaries set out to prove that democracy could work in France, a state defined by a vast territory, large
numbers of citizens and highly complex social relations. The revolutionaries, as if acting in defiance of gravity and suspended in the
air by upward pressure from the streets, moved through the forum
known as the Convention to abolish monarchy, before a breathless
public, using the new invention called the guillotine, to slice off the
head of Louis Capet. But that wasn't enough. Convinced that
although the king was now dead the spirit of royalty and 'aristocracy' lived on in the institutions, hearts and minds of the country,
the revolutionaries pushed to quicken the pace of events, fighting at
every turn against those they labelled Girondins, speculators,
bureaucrats, hoarders and monopolists. 'Those who make revolutions by halves', declared Robespierre's close political friend
Saint-Just, 'dig their own grave.' The Revolution demanded swift
action to impress doubters and crush enemies. The regeneration of
humanity through republican democracy justified sacrifice. Force,
the midwife of victory, was indispensable to the enforcement of

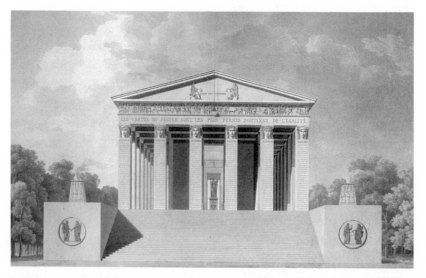

FIGURE 70: Project for a Temple to Equality by the architects Jean-Nicolas-Louis Durand
and Jean-Thomas Thibault, 1794.

FIGURE 71: *Le Peuple mangeur de Rois*, statue of the French people, 'Devourer of Kings', proposed by the newspaper *Révolution de Paris*, 1793.

justice with liberty for all. Redemption required fearless repression. The new democratic man – women were quickly pushed out of the revolutionary nest – demanded audacity, even in fields like architecture and sculpture (Figures 70 and 71). The people had to be made, turned into what they should be.

The revolutionaries were from the beginning split over the issue of whether or not the whole people could participate directly in matters of government, and what that would mean. A full generation before the American Civil War, a struggle between two imagined goals – assembly democracy and representative democracy – erupted. The majority of deputies to the Constituent Assembly that met between 1789 and 1791 favoured the security of persons and property and accepted representative government because for them liberty meant the autonomy of individuals from government, rather than direct participation in some hypothetical 'government by the people'. In a speech of 7 September 1789, Emmanuel-Joseph Sieyès, the famous author of the pamphlet *What is the Third Estate?*, put it like this: monarchy and landed property are exhausted forms of representation. Populous modern civil societies, with their division of labour and commerce and exchange, require a different system of representation, a truer form of representative government that changes the meaning of democracy. 'The people can speak, can act only through its representatives.'[11] The famous Declaration of the Rights of Man and of the Citizen captured the spirit of this new, modern compromise between democracy and representation, the principle of representative democracy first outlined several decades earlier by the Marquis d'Argenson. 'The law is the expression of the general will', said the Declaration. 'All citizens have the right to participate personally, or through their representatives, in its formation.'

The bitter dispute within the Convention between those standing behind the principles of representative government (the Girondins) and those who instead said they favoured a new type of society based on the direct voice of 'the sovereign people' (Robespierre and other Montagnards, the radical republicans who seized control during the great Terror that gripped the country) was never resolved. The proposal by Saint-Just that the will of the people should be concentrated in the central government at the expense of the primary assemblies, and that all deputies had to be elected by all the people, was rejected only for technical reasons, to do with the difficulty of organising elections on a vast territorial basis. So both sides drew the conclusion that the survival of democracy in France required the regeneration of 'the people'. Enter Robespierre: a new type of political leader brought to power by the anti-parliamentary riots of 31 May–2 June 1793.

Robespierre was a curious political animal, a proud little man filled with murderous instincts, something of an eighteenth-century Masaniello. Born in Arras in 1758, the green-eyed son of a brewer's daughter was a poor man's lawyer with a sharp mind, a clever man who consistently put principles before profit, and both before friendship and human affection, a ruthless political creature with the life and death of democracy very much on his brain. With one leg in the Convention and the other planted squarely in the revolutionary clubs and cells of Paris, Robespierre clawed his way to the summit of power by presenting himself as the great reconciler of direct and representative democracy. He was 'the people'. A half-generation before General Rosas in Argentina, Robespierre won first prize in the race to become the first democratic dictator of the era of representative democracy. Partly through luck, but partly through tactical prowess, he positioned himself to play the role of guide within a political void, the great champion of democratic progress against aristocratic decadence. Robespierre welded an alliance between the popular *sans-culotte* movement and militant segments of the middle class, then moved fast to root out all dissent. Obsessed with unanimity, which he considered a prime revolutionary virtue, he thought and acted like a fanatic, an obsessive who believed that the leading role of 'the people' and the 'general will' necessitated not only the provision of radically new policies like public education, poor relief and the universal suffrage, but something more: the root-and-branch elimination of vices such as 'faction' and 'particular interest', through force of arms, whenever necessary. Robespierre was adamant that the Revolution had to treat virtue, terror and democracy as triplets. 'If virtue be the spring of a popular government in times of peace', he snarled, 'the spring of that government during a revolution is virtue combined with terror: virtue, without which terror is destructive; terror, without which virtue is impotent. Terror is only justice prompt, severe and inflexible; it is then an emanation of virtue; it is less a distinct principle than a natural consequence of the general principle of democracy, applied to the most pressing wants of the country.'

The Revolution and Europe

The profound excitement aroused by the Revolution in favour of democracy rapidly spilled over into various parts of Europe, like molten lava and steaming ash after a great volcanic eruption. The extent to which the fallout sparked fires of support on foreign soils has often been exaggerated; great care needs to be taken when trying to assess the impact of democratic ideals and institutions spawned by the French events. Contemporaries who expressed sympathy for the Revolution, especially intellectuals, typically thought of it as an epochal moment, as a clean break with the corrupted past, as a giant leap upwards, into the air, on to a higher historical plane. That reaction was especially strong within the German lands, where philosophers like Immanuel Kant thought of the Revolution, in cosmopolitan but ethereal terms, as something like a metaphysical fact of relevance for the whole world. The revolutionaries' own denunciations of despotism added liquor to the cups of the tipsy. 'The National Convention', read the decree issued by La Révellière-Lépeaux on 19 November 1792, 'declares in the name of the French nation that it will grant fraternity and aid to any people that may wish to recover its liberty.' People living under oppressive regimes, anywhere in Europe or in the rest of the world, were in effect invited to take matters into their own hands. Kings and clerics and landowners were warned. Insurrection for the sake of democratic liberty was no longer a crime: the right of all peoples to remake themselves into democrats was now universal.

In retrospect, it is unclear exactly who were supposed to be, or were in fact, the beneficiaries of this right. There were plenty of outspoken voices favouring this right in cities like Milan, Warsaw, Brussels and Utrecht. But in 1789, illiterate peasants and other commoners still comprised the big majority of Europe's population. In the central-eastern half of the continent there were few cities, limited trade and commerce and only a small middle class that read newspapers. More serious was the fact that those who ruled Europe's populations through absolutist states and empires, including so-called 'enlightened despots' like King Frederick the Great, had little interest in allowing the spirit of democratic liberty to flourish, as it had done in France and Britain and the Low Countries through the subterranean development of printing presses, reading circles, clubs and *salles de lecture*. The rulers of Russia, Prussia, Saxony, Sweden and Spain had all favoured active military intervention to crush the Revolution alive. When their moment of opportunity came, there were crackdowns aplenty, as in Russia, where Catherine the Great (1729–96), who had warned that 'the affairs of France were the concern of all crowned heads', revealed her true reactionary instincts by spying on, arresting and imprisoning her democratic opponents. The principle for handling democrats was outlined by Joseph II, the Holy Roman Emperor and ruler of the Habsburg lands from 1780 to 1790: 'Everything for the people, nothing by the people.'

The backlash tempted the French revolutionaries into resorting to military force, which they did in April 1792 by declaring a war for democracy on Prussia and Austria. So history repeated itself – Athens versus Melos – this time on a continental scale. Spread from the streets of Paris, democracy was not negotiable; not surprisingly, the spirit of militarism and talk of *pays ennemis* and *pays conquis* flourished. Dressed in bright uniforms topped with red, white and blue cockades, democracy went on the march. Its rumblings could be heard all across Europe. Just as democratic Athens radically altered the way that wars were fought, so revolutionary France completely changed the face of militarism. Gone were the niceties of limited warfare in the aristocratic style, quaintly symbolised by the estimated 145 tons of luggage that used to accompany the Duke of Cumberland into battle. Warfare became total. Mass conscript armies backed by a war economy and the priceless frenzy of citizens in arms tried to deliver results on a scale never before imagined. The fighting produced the largest empire since the Middle Ages, and the greatest conqueror since Charlemagne (Figure 72), but it quickly became trapped in the practical exigencies of conquest and occupation. At home, the Revolution provoked a savage attack on all manifestations of 'aristocracy' and 'counter-revolution', culminating in the killing fields of the Vendée, where at least 250,000 men, women and children were slaughtered in 1793–4. Abroad, annexation in the name of democracy was either carried out through the signing of a treaty (as happened in the Rhineland)

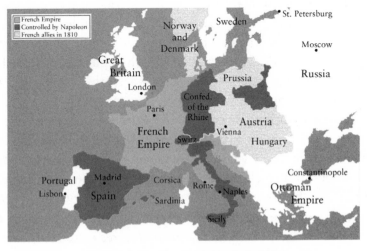

FIGURE 72: The Napoleonic Empire in 1812.

or territory was simply grabbed and broken up into arbitrarily defined, French-style departments, without consultation, as the people of Belgium (in 1795) and Piedmont (in 1802) discovered.

It is true that there were places, like the Batavian Republic and the Helvetic Republic, where the Napoleonic armies claimed that the birth of a sister republic was the work of its most 'advanced' patriots; and there was Poland, where French forces, led by the flamboyant Murat, received a tumultuous welcome (to this day Napoleon has a line in Poland's national anthem). But the bigger truth was that French control over territory, resources and people was always the primary imperative. Territorial self-determination by citizens was arranged on French terms. Republican constitutions designed to bring order and guarantee certain basic freedoms – subject to strong executive authority and a limited property franchise, *à la française* – were imposed. Administrative systems based on departments and districts, cantons and communes were put in place, along with a local press, sympathetic to French orthodoxy, of course. Property held in the seigneurial system of vesting power in landed lords, who extracted contributions from peasants under their jurisdiction, was broken up. Every effort was made to dissolve the power of the Catholic faith; and there was much talk of men being born and remaining free and equal in their rights.

Whatever locals thought of these French innovations counted for little, for the fundamental point was that the reforms were imposed by conquest, not accepted through publicly negotiated consent. Democracy played no role in the export of democracy. Especially after 1793, when the French republic expanded its military campaign and found itself at war with most monarchies of Europe, the logic of brute conquest prevailed. In practice, the revolutionary slogan 'Guerre aux châteaux, paix aux chaumières' ('War on castles, peace to cottages') meant what the Committee of Public Safety meant when (on 18 September 1793) it instructed the commanders of French armies to live off the land and its people, to 'procure, as far as possible from enemy territory, the supplies necessary to provision the army, as well as arms, clothing, equipment, and transport'. *Commissaires militaires* were charged with extracting taxes and supplies on the spot. Huge sums were expected.

In 1798, in the Helvetic Republic, the cantons of Fribourg, Soleure, Zurich and Berne were collectively assessed and ordered to pay sixteen million livres, one fifth of which had to be handed over within five days, under threat of punishments that included the taking of hostages and the compulsory billeting of soldiers. The first annexations by the French army, in Avignon and the Comtat, were timid, halting adventures. It was not long before the search for military resources became the prime purpose of occupation, as when the revolutionaries marched into northern Italy for the purpose of providing a new granary for the French armies and new funding to pay off the costs of war. Civilians were seen as fair game and officers, knowing the unreliability of food convoys, turned a blind eye to the bad behaviour of their troops, despite the grave risks of military indiscipline. The people's army bit into the flesh of the peoples they occupied. In the name of ballots, they billeted themselves using bullets. Horses and cattle were rounded up. Fields were stripped to feed starving battalions. Troops smashed their way into homes, where they helped themselves to money, bedding, clothing, wine, food and kitchen utensils. There was drunken abuse, wanton vandalism and beating and rape of anybody who stood in their way.

Few troops were ever brought to justice and little gratitude ever flowed from the conquered. Countless Italians, Belgians, Spanish and Rhinelanders understandably saw the conquest with the eyes of conquered people. They saw equality bathed in misery, fear mixed with poverty, but no liberty or fraternity; there was real force in the stone later hurled by Lord Byron, who complained that democracy was 'an Aristocracy of Blackguards'.[12] The sheer size of the French armies, plus their youth, hunger and military inexperience, spread fear and stirred up national resentments among the local communities through which they passed. The French effort to sow the seeds of democratic revolution by military force had the unintended effect, as we have seen, of triggering the collapse of an imperial monarchy in Spanish America. In Europe, it failed to do that. It certainly altered boundaries, triggered reforms and altered institutions, but it did not manage to win minds, let alone hearts. It bred resentment and resistance and the consequence, not surprisingly, was that the whole trend towards representative democracy stalled. It was as if History had taken a strong dislike to its principles. War in the name of democracy promoted petty tyranny or authoritarianism, as well as clampdowns on press freedom, public assembly and other civil freedoms. At the end of the Revolutionary and Napoleonic Wars in 1815, not one government in the whole of Europe could be described as a representative democracy – if by that we mean, as was meant at the time, a civilian government subject to openly contested elections and voting by adult males.

Brother Gregory

Europe's biggest ever democratic revolution manifestly failed to achieve its stated goals, at least not within its own time framework. It nevertheless harboured some grand surprises. As usual, war took the world by the scruff of the neck and dragged it in unexpected directions.

The cocktail of military conquest and democratic ideals produced a marked tipsiness within various bodies politic of Europe, sometimes with comic effect. In the northern regions of Italy, for instance, the French attack on monarchy in the name of the people pricked popular confidence in existing authority. Old loyalties weakened. Existing laws seemed arbitrary. Respect for superiors felt like humiliation. And the little word 'democracy' suddenly became respectable, even on the lips of earnest men of God. A figure named Luigi Barnaba Chiaramonti (1740–1823), two years before his elevation to the papacy as Pius VII, was among its prominent champions. Born in Cesena, he studied at a college for nobles at Ravenna and at sixteen entered a Benedictine monastery near his hometown. After ordination, Brother Gregory, as he was now called, taught at Parma and then Rome, where he was appointed abbot of San Callisto monastery by Pope Pius VI, a friend of the family. Chiaramonti was elected pope in the magnificent Venetian church of San Giorgio on 13 March 1800 – just in time to deal with Napoleon, the military autocrat who was at that moment hellbent on transforming the Roman Church into a vassal of the revolutionary empire.

Pius VII did everything he could to resist. He refused

Napoleon's demands that he expel all subjects of nations at war with France and participate in the continental blockade against Britain. The greatest moment of triumph of Brother Gregory came in the year 1804. At the coronation of Napoleon in Notre-Dame, he tasted the ultimate pleasure of spiritual victory, by forcing the French dictator to place the emperor's crown on his own head.

In poor health and forced to spend five years under French arrest, Pius VII eventually caved in to the emperor's designs, though he did so only after numerous dogfights, including the refusal of all negotiations with Napoleon. Pius VII was a pontiff with a difference. He could indeed fairly be described as the first prominent Christian democrat, a staunch Catholic believer in representative government and civil and political rights, including the universal male franchise. His affection for representative democracy stretched back to the years 1785 to 1800, when he had been Bishop of Imola, a town near Bologna in the northern part of the Papal States. On Christmas Eve 1797, inspired by the revolutionary disturbances that had erupted when Napoleon's troops had stormed through Lombardy the year before, the good Monsignor preached to his diocese. 'Most beloved brethren,' he began, 'the form of democratic government adopted among us is not inconsistent with the Gospel.' Sprinkling his words with quotations from St Augustine, Jesus and St Paul, he told his flock that 'civil equality' would encourage each person to cooperate with their fellows, and that this would bring harmony to the political community. His conclusion aroused the anti-clericalist suspicions of the French authorities: 'Be good Christians and you will be excellent democrats.'[13]

After the service, that same evening, Christmas had a special meaning for many citizens of Imola. Convinced that their good bishop was right, that representative democracy could clasp hands with the constitution and the Catholic Church, some citizens denounced 'traitors' and unbelievers. Someone gave a speech in the main street of Imola, saying that festivals, like Christmas or the public celebration of the arrival of spring, were important for fostering the idea of a good Creator, whose only aim was the happiness of the people. Others replied that the gospels demanded that priests be democratic, and that priests could play a vital role in creating 'a democratic base' that would 'democratise the People'. There was much talk of education for democracy, even strong comparisons of the education of children by parents with the political education of citizens, their conversion into dedicated democrats. For many that night in Imola, the word democracy seemed to have magical properties; it meant liberty, equality, respect for the law, happiness, universal consensus, the love of one's homeland, rather than masters and tyrants. Some spoke excitedly of a recently published dictionary of democratic terms; it had caused a minor sensation by warning its readers to be on the lookout for 'masked democrats', like ambitious and hypocritical rich men who called themselves friends of the people the better to deceive them.

One citizen of Imola, inspired by the bishop's sermon, reportedly predicted that Tuscany and Naples would go 'democratic'. A printed proclamation nailed to a wooden door declared that any republic in Italy should aim to be 'a democracy, one and indivisible'. Hand-distributed leaflets announced forthcoming town events, including a theatrical production called *The Democratisation of Heaven*. There was to be a grand ball in honour of the Napoleonic armies: no 'ladies' or '*seigneurs romains*' were welcome, read one leaflet, since 'the party is to be democratic'. Later that evening, in a town procession, a smiling couple, recently engaged and shortly to be married, held up a sign daubed with the words Democratic Fecundity. That moment was probably a first in the history of democracy. And at a nearby coffee house someone called on servants to risk everything by addressing their masters and mistresses as 'citizen'. One member of the local popular club shouted: 'Facciamo uno governo democratico!' Those present spontaneously chanted in reply: 'La democrazia o la morte!' Democracy or death: the old words had fresh energy, a brand-new sound. Democracy was no longer just a word to describe long-forgotten small cities of the ancient world, or a dead definition in the works of philosophers like Montesquieu, who wrote with his quill: 'one of the basic forms of government, in which the people as a body enjoys sovereignty'. In the streets and cafés of Imola, democracy had become a vital principle: a new type of political regime that ideally combined political representation and the universal suffrage of men with a way of life in which the values of equality flourished, freed from hereditary guff and aristocratic perks.

Social Democracy

So the French push for representative government had definite, if unintended, successes. The French events sparked excited talk of 'democracy' – and even the first practical steps towards parliamentary government based on more open elections. In the German states, beginning with Prussia in 1808, elections to assemblies began to be based on some version of male, property-restricted suffrage. The experiments culminated, in early 1848, in the so-called March Demands (*Märzforderungen*) for freedom of the press, trial by jury, a national German parliament and – the demand most dangerous to princes and emperors – arming 'the people' under elected officers. During the temporary unification of that same year, the German Union Bundestag sanctioned elections based on independent adult male suffrage, although the individual German states retained the power to define what 'independent' and 'adult' meant. After unification in 1871, despite Bismarck's efforts to grind democracy into the ground, Germany experienced unbroken parliamentary government for half a generation.

That wasn't all. For it was within the German states that the spirit of the French events triggered something remarkable: the language and politics of democracy were projected into the heart of social life. The child of *social* democracy was born of hard times. During the 1840s, sometimes called the 'Hungry Forties', many regions of Europe were hit hard by crop failures and famine combined with inflation and unemployment. Suffering was worst in Ireland, but hunger stalked many German regions, reinforced by a crisis of the traditional crafts caused by sudden industrialisation and the rapid spread of market economics into the heartlands of country and city life. Trapped in the jaws of destitution, commoners in the German lands cried out. In the spring of 1848, whole villages marched on the castles of princes; a string of strikes in factories and on railway construction sites caused a public sensation. Workers' societies (*Arbeitervereine*) sprang into action, organising

FIGURE 73: Shot-maker at work behind a barricade in Berlin, from a drawing by Robert Kretschmer, April 1848.

rallies peppered with placards, leaflets, caricatures, petitions; and in towns and cities, journeymen, labourers, apprentices and tradesmen took to the streets, sometimes to build barricades, in the name of brotherhood (Figure 73).

The commoners had come of age, helped along by the tireless courage of humble characters like Stephan Born (1824–98). The fourth son of struggling Jewish parents from Lissa (today's Poznan), Born moved to Berlin when he was a young teenager, in search of a life (Figure 74). Granted naturalisation as an assimilated Jew, he confronted local prejudice by changing his name from Simon Buttermilch and started an apprenticeship, as a typesetter, an occupation he thought would earn him a living and quench his thirst for reading. In December 1846, after involvement in a Berlin craftsmen's literary association that organised lectures for workers and offered them training in the art of public speaking, Born celebrated the end of his apprenticeship by setting off on his own worker's version of a grand European tour. He wandered from Leipzig, Magdeburg and Hamburg all the way to Paris and Brussels, where he met Karl Marx and Frederick Engels, whose communism he came to accept, for a time, until the sudden disturbances in Germany in the spring of 1848 changed his mind.

Hurrying back to Berlin, Born wasted no time in founding the

FIGURE 74: Stephan Born, typesetter, working-class journalist and early proponent of 'social democracy'.

first workers' association in the city. Designed to raise workers' awareness and to give them an independent public voice, the Central Committee for Workers spearheaded efforts to form an extra-parliamentary regional network of workers' and artisans' clubs, the Workers' Fraternity, whose founding congress (some called it 'the workers' parliament') of August 1848 elected him vice-president. Born wanted to put his typesetting skills to good use, which he did by publishing two newspapers: the thrice-weekly *Das Volk* (The People), the first ever publication for workers in Berlin, and the Leipzig-based monthly *Die Verbrüderung* (The Fraternity). Both publications contained cutting-edge ideas and proposals, and Born's own contributions, some of them published anonymously, caused quite a stir, for a good reason. He made plain his attachment to what he called 'political democracy', by which he meant demands for a written constitution drafted by elected representatives of the people, religious freedom, universal education, and equal votes for all adult men who had reached the age of twenty-four. Unusual was the way Born saw these political demands as a stepping stone to what he called 'social democracy' (*soziale Demokratie*). Born was no philosopher, and he made it clear that he had no time for -isms; he said that 'dreamers who foam with rage' and visionary utopias like 'tear-dampened and love-sick

Socialism' were not his thing, simply because most workers (Born included women) favoured immediate action that would protect their rights as workers against present-day miseries, and against future slavery at the hands of unelected, self-appointed representatives of workers.

Marx and Engels were among those who heaped abuse on him as a petit-bourgeois class opportunist, but Born saw things differently, arguably with clearer vision into the future world of trade union ideals, trade union-backed parties and the era of 'functional representation', of joint economic boards, tribunals and representative councils, that flourished briefly after World War One in Germany, Czechoslovakia and other central European countries. His fundamental point was that class inequality was incompatible with self-government. Representative democracy could not function properly unless the social conditions of voters were roughly equal; it certainly could not be combined with unregulated markets, simply because the raw and unequal power division between capitalists and workers always worked to the disadvantage of the commoners. The problem with market competition is that some people always lose. That is why, Born concluded, workers needed to organise themselves, to combine for the purpose of pressuring governments into restricting and regulating markets, for the sake of social justice.

A plan for taming the force of markets was first outlined in several midsummer editions of *Das Volk*. The proposals, in effect a defence of representative democracy through what Born later called 'practical social policy', were far-reaching, even by today's standards. Born called on governments of all German states to set up workers' ministries, departments run by representatives elected by workers themselves. Funded by direct taxes on the propertied classes, these ministries would regulate working hours, enforce a minimum wage and provide for injured and unemployed workers and other people in need. For the sake of social democracy, Born concluded, governments must do all they could to protect the powerless, to encourage them to shift for themselves, as equals. Free education for all was desirable. So, too, was support for workers' self-help associations, workers' freedom of travel and residence, and the establishment of networks of public libraries.[14] For good measure, Born called upon governments to provide free legal support for workers, a resource he certainly could have used a few months later, when the German authorities hounded him into exile in Switzerland, where he remained for the rest of his days.

Csarism

Picked at random from the several dozen states that dotted the nineteenth-century maps of Europe, the cases of Italy and Germany illustrate some of the long-term regional trends that were kick-started during that century by the French Revolution, and the 1848 revolutions that followed. Monarchs, landowners, generals and churchmen were for a time thrown on to the back foot; their nervousness was expressed in the popular anecdote featuring Austrian Emperor Ferdinand I, whose court physician, following a routine check-up, remarked that his majesty had an excellent constitution (despite suffering up to twenty seizures a day, which made ruling difficult). 'Why do you talk about constitution?' snapped the Emperor. 'Say nature, if you please!'

Such were the times that wherever and by whatever means the grip of absolutist states was loosened, some or other type of government based on parliamentary representation appeared, though usually with a heavily restricted franchise; as in Spanish America, elections continued to be rigged using various forms of electoral geometry.* It is true that elections enabled workers and social democratic demands to gain a toehold, usually through the formation of associations and movements (such as Chartism in Britain),

---

*The best-known Sicilian novel, Giuseppe Tomasi di Lampedusa's *The Leopard* (1958), wonderfully recaptures the mid-nineteenth-century trend. Faced with a forthcoming plebiscite on Italian unification, Prince Don Fabrizio, convinced that the times are against him, privately urges his otherwise hostile local subjects to vote 'yes'. The pilgrims who visit his study for advice on which way to vote are confused. Some think the prince is being ironic, that it is impossible for him to be in favour of what they call the Revolution. Other supplicants, having listened to his earnest advice, conclude that he is a turncoat, or perhaps a half-wit ignorant of the age-old proverb about preferring a known evil to an untried good. The day of the plebiscite comes, the votes are counted and by that evening a large crowd has gathered at the town hall, to hear in silence the result read out from the balcony by the prince's trusty aide: Voters, 515; Voting, 512; Yes, 512; No, zero.

Suffrage by Decade

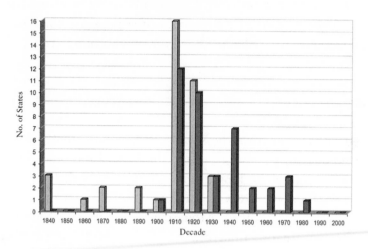

FIGURE 75: Full franchise victories for men (light shading) and women (dark shading) by decade in Europe, 1840–2000.

trade unions and labour parties. Yet nowhere in nineteenth-century Europe did women win the right to vote at the state level (though there were breakthroughs in more local settings, as on the suitably named Isle of Man, where unmarried women and widows who owned property were first granted the vote in 1881). The enfranchisement of women began only during the early years of the twentieth century, first in Finland (in 1906) and then in Norway, Denmark, Iceland, Austria, Germany, Luxembourg and Great Britain, usually with property, marital, age or education restriction. Throughout Europe, manhood suffrage (as specified in laws and constitutions) typically came much earlier than that for women (Figure 75), though normally well after the initial adoption of parliamentary government. There was generally an inverse relationship between the advent of parliamentary government and the coming of effective male suffrage: the longer it took to establish parliamentary government, the shorter was the time of arrival of full male suffrage.

The rule reflected the long-term pressures for inclusion of 'the people' – and the slow softening-up of older forms of authority, especially landed monarchy, empire and military rule. Nevertheless, the struggles for representative democracy were often uphill battles, as in Greece, where revolutionaries singing the praises of popular independence formally wrested autonomy from the Ottoman Empire in 1832. Contrary to expectations, the movement for independence was carried out in the name of an imaginary Greek 'nation', not democracy. 'I detest democracy,' said Adamantios Koraes, the most prominent champion of the Greeks' cause, 'as Plato, Aristotle and all the ancient philosophers did. The more prudent Americans detest it too.' He went on to say (in 1825) that oligarchy may have been the 'regime of the wicked', but democracy was most definitely the 'regime of fools'.[15] Those words set the tone of ambivalence about representative democracy among wealthy and powerful Greeks. By European standards, manhood suffrage triumphed early in their country, in 1843. But it came in restricted form, tempered by an intermediate body of elite voters, while for the rest of the century efforts to secure parliamentary democracy were upset by coups and uprisings, fuelled by intense struggles between the champions of authoritarianism and the supporters of parliamentary government. It was not until 1923, following the Greek defeat in the vicious Greek–Turkish War of 1919–22, that the military removal of King George II and a subsequent plebiscite to abolish the Greek monarchy finally prepared the way for parliamentary government based on popular election.

The rough Greek road to representative democracy showed that the European trend in favour of people's right to vote was only one of several competing trends, that the push towards representative democracy was fraught and fragile. Just as in Spanish America and the United States, the shaky appearance of representative democracy in Europe confirmed that there were no 'iron laws' governing its growth. Yet nineteenth-century Europe revealed to the world something altogether more terrible. It proved not only that representative democracy had no historical safety guarantees of success, or trans-historical saviours. The disturbing truth was that in several parts of Europe there were rich and powerful people who were so frightened of democracy that they did all they could to strangle its spirits and institutions to death.

Take the case of Russia. There, the word democracy had a pejorative sense throughout the nineteenth century (and was only later valued through its misuse, to legitimise the 'democratic centralism' and 'socialist democracy' of communist politics in the first decade of the next century). This was not, to deal with some oft-repeated clichés, primarily because of the geographical setting of Russia at the margins of Europe and Asia, or Russia's missing bourgeoisie, or the endemic mysticism of Russian intellectuals, or because the conscious universe of the peasant majority of the population was somehow limited by its deep love affair with the dark richness of Russia's fertile soil.

Whatever truth lies buried in these clichés is minor compared with the cleverly repressive role played by Russia's despotic form of government. The fate of Aleksandr Radishchev (1749–1802), the first modern Russian democrat and famous author of the ode 'Liberty' and *A Journey from St Petersburg to Moscow* (published in the early summer of 1790[16]), served as a lesson to all would-be democrats in the Russian lands. Born into a moderately wealthy noble family with landholdings in Saratov province, and later educated in law and philosophy at the University of Leipzig, Radishchev joined the civil service and rose to become head of the St Petersburg Customs House. He soon grew hostile to absolutist government, and saw himself by contrast as a member of the minority of enlightened aristocrats who loved liberty and therefore took the side of the peasant majority against their political oppressors. Initiator of the Russian tradition of intellectual martyrdom that includes figures as varied as Herzen, Bakunin, Piotr Struve and Solzhenitsyn, Radishchev was condemned to personal hardship and suffering for his rapturous glorification of liberty, in the name of the people. Alarmed by the radicalism of the French Revolution, Catherine the Great saw in Radishchev's public denunciation of serfdom a threat to the state. She pronounced him 'a rebel worse than Pugachev' (the soldier who had proclaimed himself Peter III, led a Cossack and peasant rebellion against Catherine, then suffered arrest and transportation in an iron cage to Moscow, where he was executed). Radishchev was promptly arrested, tried and condemned to death. Catherine later commuted the sentence to ten years' exile in Siberia. Under the reign of Paul I, Radishchev was released and his privileges as a nobleman were restored in 1801. The following year he committed suicide.

The csarist drive to push people like Radishchev over the edge ultimately had its roots in the unique process of state building in early modern Russia. As we have seen, the development there of bureaucracy, a standing army, economic protectionism and the centralisation of taxation and legal powers paralleled the growth of territorial states elsewhere in Europe. In matters of territorial state building, there was nothing exceptional about Russia. What was different, when compared with the Low Countries, France and Britain, was the type of state that resulted. In the Russian lands, those who wielded power through the state structures did so without major competitors. Among the first acts of Russian absolutism, during the reign of Ivan III, was the consolidation of territory and resources, for instance through the occupation of the independent and self-governing city of Novgorod (1478). Its leading strata, the merchants and the boyars, were deported, their property confiscated, and the local boyar self-government (*guba*) was replaced by direct csarist rule.

The reorganisation of Novgorod was directly modelled on Moscow, where all sub-centres of power – the boyars, civil servants, merchants, soldiers, artisans and peasants – were subordinated to the central units of administrative and military power. The old nobility blessed with free estates (called *votchina*) lost their autonomy and were transformed into a 'service nobility' that was utterly dependent on the whims and mercies of the Csar. Even the richest merchants were in effect his agents. In the centuries to come, the Novgorod takeover was often repeated. From Tsaritsyn to Arkhangelsk, and from there to Ufa and further to the east, all towns and social strata in the newly colonised Russian territories were incorporated into the power structures of the centralising state; there were no towns or cities that resembled Amsterdam, Barcelona or London. Noblemen became civil servants or military officers; social rank and bureaucratic hierarchy were melded. Under Peter the Great and his offspring, the state exercised dominance in the field of foreign trade and in all key industries, especially those (shipbuilding, iron mining and steel production) linked to war. Economic growth fed state power, and not vice versa, as for instance happened in western Europe.

The same pattern of dominating centre crystallised in the field of Church–state relations. Around 1480, monks began pawing through manuscripts, on behalf of Ivan III, in search of a new governing formula. A Byzantine state, centred on the principle of Moscow as the 'Third Rome' and bathed in the mysticism of the autocrat, was born. The fate of the Russian people was hereafter supposed to be tied to God's vicar on earth, the 'Csar of all Russians', the bearer of 'true' power to the 'true' unity of the people. There was said to be an indissoluble pact: the Csar was duty-bound to uphold and support the Orthodox Church, whose chief duty, conversely, was to worship the state and lead the Russian people towards a holy life based on correct, orthodox beliefs. In practice, this pact was completed (in 1721) by Peter the Great (1672–1725) with the creation of the Holy Synod. It confiscated much of the Church's wealth and consolidated the permanent integration of religious orthodoxy and political power guided by the personal power of the Csar.

It was on this autocratic basis that modern Russian history dispensed with power-sharing, representative assemblies. The weak, short-lived Estates Assembly (*zemskiy sobor*) was created by Ivan IV for tactical reasons, to win over the nobility of the territories under Polish and Lithuanian influence. That explains why, after the assembly (in 1649) had legally sanctioned the binding of serfs to the soil for ever, it withered away. One consequence of the absence of parliamentary power sharing was that Peter the Great (and later Catherine the Great, Paul I and Alexander I) had free hands to embark on top-down reforms designed to meet the political and economic challenges coming from the western parts of Europe, especially the military pressures for French-style 'democracy'. The Russian monarchs performed various tricks. Paul I (who reigned from 1796 to 1801) reintroduced corporal punishment for disloyal civil servants and nobles, and generally cracked down on all dissent, until drunken officers murdered him. His son Alexander I tried softer authoritarian methods. His government survived the occupation of Moscow by Napoleon's troops – Moscow was burned to the ground, which forced the starving French troops to retreat – and set free landless serfs in the Baltic provinces; he also founded a state school system and set up an advisory body called the Council of State. The species of despotism that resulted was most definitely not some extra-European phenomenon (as the prominent twentieth-century Czech writer Milan Kundera famously claimed), as if the invention of civil societies, parliaments and representative government was quintessentially 'European'. By the time of the French events, and for a century afterwards, the Russian political system used thoroughly European methods to dispense with the paraphernalia of representation. It demonstrated that an Eastern European path to the modern world – without representative democracy – was possible. By the end of the nineteenth century, csarist Russia had in fact outpaced France to become the world's fourth-largest steel producer and fifth in overall industrial output – without any help or interference from democrats and democratic ideals. But that lack had its price: snared in the pincers of despotism, Russia was shaken periodically by revolts of the peasantry, as well as an intelligentsia determined to win over 'the people' to its cause.

For all these reasons, nineteenth-century Russia witnessed the birth of a distinctively local version of the ideology of populism. Known as *narodnichestvo*, it was the Russian substitute for parliamentary representative democracy, a bastardised version of democracy whose fetish of 'the people' bore more than a passing resemblance to the caudillo democracy that sprang up in nineteenth-century Spanish America. Russian populism, defended by an intelligentsia that considered themselves the only free beings in a political order of slaves, called for Russian unity and government through the Russian people, in opposition to the combined power and authority of the Csar, the Church and the landed nobility. Populism was born not simply of a bad reaction to the French revolutionary ideals of 'democracy'. Populism registered and absorbed those ideals by acknowledging that the commoners were no longer to be treated like scum. It praised them and spoke constantly of the 'people's will'.

Yet buried in the politics of Russian populism was a metaphysical, almost apocalyptic presumption: that a clean revolutionary break with the past was both necessary and possible, and that the consequent upheaval would result in revelation, a stripping away of twisted and dehumanising power structures, followed by a clarification of the true nature of things and, finally, human emancipation. Populists emphasised the people's tellurian qualities. They generally disliked industrialisation. They were not friends of technical progress, and rejected as false the whole modern idea of the liberation of humanity through the domination of nature driven by markets and science. The populists saw no need for representative mechanisms, for they thought of themselves as bearers of the unchanging essence of the Russian people. That is why state-organised capitalism guided by parliamentary democracy was for them a miserable chimera, an unworkable vision that was bound in practice to produce delusion and unhappiness, founded on slavery.

What, then, was the alternative? The populists were often at their own throats; no generally agreed vision surfaced. Although they dominated the opposition to csarism during the second half of the nineteenth century, especially from the 1870s, the populists never formed an organised political party and refused a coherent doctrine. It was a movement comprising various organisations and factions, including the anarchists, the Nihilists and the Social Revolutionaries. Their ranks contained regicides, anti-capitalists, and eccentric figures like Petr Tkachev (1844–86), who reportedly urged the rebirth of Russia by eliminating every person over the age of twenty-five. The populists suffered frequent setbacks, as in the summer of 1874 when peasants failed to embrace their ascribed role as 'the people' by handing student populist agitators clad in peasant clothes over to the Csar's police. The harsh realities of csarism nevertheless kept them going, at times united, above all in their emphatic rejection of representative democracy.

Populists typically described themselves as 'apolitical', meaning that they had no truck with 'plutocracy' or 'petit bourgeois' or 'bourgeois' electoral politics and its corresponding fantasy of taking up seats in a parliament. Populists put their faith in a new revolutionary subject – the peasants and small producers – and they were convinced that Russia could leapfrog the age of industrial capitalism and representative government. The typical populist was a Janus, Lenin wrote, 'looking with one face to the past and the other to the future'.[17] Most embraced a version of Aleksandr Herzen's alternative – originally medieval – vision of the natural harmony of the *mir*, the free association of peasants, empowered periodically to redistribute arable land and through its decisions granting each and every peasant an equal say in determining how to live their lives as equals. Populism stood for the protection of the people in the *mir* by the *mir*. It imagined the new Russia as a decentralised confederation of self-governing units, as a new type of post-democracy freed from the evils of serfdom, industrialism, capitalism and the violence of the territorial state.

The point was to change the world by upending old Russia. Tens of thousands of young populists heeded the call (first spelled out in 1868, in a famous article by Bakunin in the émigré journal *People's Cause*) to 'go to the people'. Others known as 'Jacobins' drew the conclusion that 'the people' were incapable of liberating themselves, and that, since their role could only ever be that of a negative, destructive force, they needed, as a lion needs a tamer, strong leadership provided by a tightly organised vanguard that would help fashion revolution out of the chaos sparked by popular uprisings. Then there were populists who were so convinced that the Russian state (as Petr Tkachev explained) was 'suspended in thin air' and 'absolutely absurd and absurdly absolute' that its rulers deserved assassination.[18] Their first two attempts to kill the Csar and the csarist system with one violent blow – a plot to blow up the emperor's train, and an explosion in the Winter Palace prepared by Stepan Khalturin – failed. It was third strike lucky. On 1 March 1881, a bomb thrown by the Russified Pole Ignacy Hryniewiecki, a member of the underground party called 'The People's Will', struck down and killed Alexander II. Many populists were overjoyed; but their spirits soon slumped. The regime of Alexander III arrested and executed five accomplices (Hryniewiecki was killed by his own bomb), flatly rejected calls for a freely elected National Assembly, then tightened the screws of repression. Violence fed despotism. Russians were forced to wait in the queue for parliamentary democracy – for half a generation.

The Westminster Model

Among the grand paradoxes of the French Revolution is that peoples spared French military assault or occupation tended to be most receptive to its best and boldest democratic claims. It was not that ignorance bred sympathy. The dynamics are better described as a learning process, for what took place in lands not directly touched or conquered outright by the French armies – the otherwise quite different cases of Spanish America and Russia under Alexander I show – was the recognition that the tide was turning in favour of full political equality and, simultaneously, turning against the Jacobin way of doing politics. In the age of poor communications, geographic distance from the Napoleonic armies certainly helped governments to survive, sometimes through reform. So, too, did the sea, which served as a rampart against land-based armies. In nineteenth-century Europe, as in ancient Greece, the Arcadian Law applied: the possibility of democracy in any territory was inversely proportional to the military pressure on its borders. That was a key reason why Britain – fresh from a victory off Cape Trafalgar (21 October 1805) that protected it from French military invasion and ensured that it became the world's dominant naval power – proved to be the most successful parliamentary democracy, the most consequential example of what George Orwell called a 'maritime democracy'.

The French events shook the local political system to its foundations, but with surprising effects. Given that Britain and France were at war from 1793, it was difficult for English, Scottish and Irish radicals to declare their open support for the French precedent, at least not without risking the charge of sedition. The support was to come all the same. In England, admiration for the French experiment extended to political leaders like Charles James Fox, influential scientists such as Joseph Priestley, and writers like Tom Paine, whose trumpet blast in defence of the Revolution, *Rights of Man* (1791–2), outsold any book ever published, including the Bible, and earned him honorary French citizenship and a seat in the National Assembly. William Wordsworth was not alone in his conviction that to experience the new dawn at close range was bliss and heaven. In the soil of cities and the countryside of Britain, radicals planted the tree of democratic liberty, sometimes with astonishing success: in 1797, at Spithead, near the Isle of Wight, even the sailors of the Royal Navy mutinied in solidarity with the new French aims by ordering their officers ashore, running their ships by committee, and demanding (successfully) better wages and working conditions.

For the first time since the civil war of the 1640s, but now on a much larger scale, radical reformers and campaign groups like the Sheffield Corresponding Society (founded in December 1791) and the London Corresponding Society (founded in January 1791) backed universal manhood suffrage. The next year, a circle of Whigs, led by Charles Grey and James Maitland and supported by twenty-eight Members of Parliament, formed a reform group called the Society of the Friends of the People. Most astonishing of all was the summoning of a British Convention, which met in Edinburgh in November 1793, in open defiance of Pitt's government. Through the use of spies and the agency of Lord Braxfield and the Scottish courts, draconian sentences were imposed on the radicals' leaders. Groups like the London Corresponding Society were gagged, its network of links with Midland and northern cities weakened. In matters of style and substance, the government of Pitt emerged the winner – for a limited time.

Despite various local republican outbursts, Britain retained its monarchy, but at the price of monarchy. Its system of government was never again the same, simply because the style and substance of the radical democrats were to have powerful subterranean effects on both daily life and the governing institutions. Among the most obvious were the civil initiatives against the slave trade, mounting pressures for the inclusion of the urban middle class of property owners and professionals in the political system through the extension of the franchise, and the birth of the cooperative and self-help movement among artisans and workers and their families. Just as in Germany, so in Britain there was talk of social democracy.

The sublimated radicalism of the French events also produced a noticeable upturn in the quantity of public irreverence towards politicians and parliament. The country had for a long time been famous throughout Europe for its political wit, most memorably in the sharp-tongued humour of politicians like John Wilkes (1725–97), the man well remembered for first publishing verbatim accounts of parliamentary debates, and for running for parliament in defence of the principle that voters, rather than the House of Commons, had the right to determine their representatives. When during a public speech a constituent had called out that he would

FIGURE 76: Preparing to hang and burn a prime minister in effigy in the streets of Westminster, London, 1756.

rather vote for the devil, Wilkes had famously replied: 'Naturally.' He then added: 'And if your friend decides against standing, can I count on your vote?' Combative wit of that kind was deeply democratic. It was almost a sport, a conspiracy between the combatants, born of mutual antagonism but mitigated by snappy humour, and by a gamble that well-timed wit would prevail. In the aftermath of the French events, the public art of embarrassing politicians by giving them verbal hell spread into the ranks of commoners. The sport was sometimes mastered by whole communities, including the radical flax workers of Dundee, who gave it a brand-new name: heckling (the word came from their day-time jobs of 'heckling', or splitting and straightening flax or hemp fibres, in preparation for their spinning). Other commoners repeated the old custom of burning effigies of prime ministers (Figure 76), or they carried placards daubed with words like 'Equal Representation or Death', as happened in Manchester in the summer of 1819, when sabre-wielding troops injured hundreds of demonstrators and trampled or skewered to death more than a dozen people, following an order to disband a crowd of several tens of thousands. The same radical spirit chopped down at the Peterloo

FIGURE 77: An anonymous etching, *Dreadful Scene at Manchester Meeting of Reformers, August 16, 1819* – the Peterloo massacre.

massacre (Figure 77) resurfaced in the Chartist struggles to win political acknowledgement of the claims of male workers. And of epochal importance was the growing public involvement of women, not only in the anti-slavery movement but also in social campaigns against alcoholism and prostitution that prepared the ground for their – eventually successful – demand for full political inclusion as citizens.

The passing of the controversial Reform Act in 1832 by the government of Lord Grey was a signal of vital things to come in British politics, certainly a watershed, a moment when it became obvious to many that the dreaded French disease had begun to eat deeply into the old body politic of the British Isles. The Reform Act 1832 put an end to the old oligarchic order. On the eve of the French Revolution, the size of the electorate in England and Wales had been around 214,000 people – less than 3 per cent of the total population of some eight million. According to the 1831 census, the situation was no better, while in Scotland, according to the same census, only about 4500 men were registered as voters, out of a total population of some 2.6 million. Thriving industrial cities like Manchester, Birmingham and Leeds did not have a single

Member of Parliament, whereas in parliamentary terms most boroughs and counties were massively over-represented. There were some cracking examples, like the Wiltshire borough of Old Sarum, whose electorate in 1800 comprised eleven voters, all of whom were landowners who lived elsewhere. The right to vote was everywhere restricted to men above the age of twenty-one, provided they met property qualifications. Those who owned property in several constituencies were rewarded with multiple votes. Indirect election to parliament by town corporations was sometimes practised. Landed property owners were especially skilled at getting their political way, above all by wielding their power and influence in constituencies known as nomination or pocket boroughs, so called because they were in the deep pockets of their wealthy patrons. There were even recorded cases, for instance in New Shoreham during the 1770s, where local patrons formed themselves into an organisation, the 'Christian Club', that regularly auctioned off the job of representing the borough to the highest bidder.

The old parliamentary system sometimes paid well, and it made no pretence to be democratic, which was the starting point of the Reform Act 1832. Amidst talk and fears of a revolutionary upheaval, and despite massive opposition from Tories, especially in the House of Lords, the Act forced the aristocracy to share power with the new middle classes. It took away seats in the House of Commons from towns that had suffered decline and depopulation during recent centuries (the so-called 'rotten boroughs'). It granted them instead to the large industrial cities. The vote was granted to all men who either owned or leased property, or who were tenants-at-will paying an annual rent of £50. The number of voters was more than doubled. A system of voter registration, administered by overseers of the poor in every township or parish, was introduced. Special courts were established to resolve disputes concerning voter qualifications. Multiple polling places within the same constituency were given the go-ahead. The old custom of dragging out elections over five or six weeks was abolished, in favour of polls lasting a maximum of two days. The Act overall bade farewell for ever to a parliamentary racket that ensured, at one point, according to a contemporary observer, that out of the 514 parliamentary gentlemen who represented England

and Wales, about 370 were hand-selected by just 180 rich property-owning patrons.[19]

Colonies

According to its preamble, the Reform Act 1832 was designed to 'take effectual Measures for correcting diverse Abuses that have long prevailed in the Choice of Members to serve in the Commons House of Parliament'. Despite its impressive achievements, the machinery built from the legislation quickly showed up its grave defects, which in the eyes of many could only be remedied by drawing up a new political agenda for dealing with the unfinished business. The Act preserved an old prejudice by explicitly disenfranchising women (Figure 78). The vast majority of people were still unable to vote. Polling places remained in short supply, bribery of voters remained rampant, and elections continued to be prolonged and corrupted affairs.

Faced by defects, setbacks and disappointments, some part of

Figure 78: *The Rights of Women*, a satirical attack by the English caricaturist George Cruikshank, 1853.

the British spirit of democratic radicalism went into exile. To understand how this emigration happened, it is vital to see that the history of representative democracy was sometimes shaped by a queer rule, according to which radical innovations took place not at the powerful centres of social and political life, but rather at their weak margins. That 'law of innovation at the margins' certainly applied in the British Empire, in whose colonies, against titanic odds, there developed a powerful momentum for progressive forms of 'responsible' and 'representative' government.

The thought that an empire could resemble a political laboratory in which elements could be mixed together to form new democratic compounds seems utterly implausible. We have already encountered the problems posed by empire to the Athenian democracy. Ponder now the tensions between the meanings of the two little words 'empire' and 'democracy'. They are not exactly happy family members, or even friendly neighbours. They seem to have a deep mutual aversion, as if – to our minds – they were ends of magnets in a state of strong repulsion. Think of representative democracy: a form of polity, a whole way of life in which power relations are seen widely as contingent and transformable and therefore permanently in need of public checking and humbling through such mechanisms as periodic elections, liberty of the press and parliamentary government. Now think of empire: a form of geographically extended polity whose diverse lands and peoples are held together, and ultimately controlled, by a centrally positioned ruler, an emperor (from the Latin: *imperator*) or imperial group. Those who rule empires claim to be representative of some or other universal jurisdiction. They cling to their privileges by projecting on to their subjects ideological claims to superiority based on religion, or law or race, or history, or refined manners. They back up these claims, ultimately, by their monopoly over the means of violence. In other words, empires are dominant powers whose rulers are prone to measure their strength against all their rivals combined. Pericles put it very well: the strength of democratic Athens at the beginning of the Peloponnesian War, he said, lay in her possession of naval forces more numerous and efficient than those of the rest of Hellas.[20]

Exactly that superiority complex helps to account for why

empires have developed a bad name, especially in modern democratic circles, where the word itself is saddled with connotations of
monarchy, conquest through violence, and subordination of different peoples through monopolistic power that acknowledges no
limits and actively disregards the sovereignty or independence of its
weaker constituent units. Empires have normally had such qualities, and so their poor reputation as anti-democratic is justified.
And yet – and the qualification is vital – empires are not all cut
from the same cloth. From the standpoint of representative democracy, three different types of empires should be distinguished. Like
the twentieth-century Soviet empire, some set out explicitly to
crush all opposition by exercising centralised control over their
subjects; parties, elections and parliaments were rigged in favour of
the ruling imperial power. There were, by contrast, empires such as
that run by the Ottomans, which combined a measure of centralised control with substantive power-sharing with its subjects,
for instance through the convening of representative assemblies
known as *meshwerets*. The Portuguese empire similarly operated in
Goa through a system of locally controlled village councils (*com-
munidades*). A strong measure of devolution of power, with
elections and parliamentary institutions, was an important feature,
within Europe itself, of the multinational Austro-Hungarian
Empire. Then there have been empires that have had the wholly
ironic effect – despite their violence of conquest, their centralised
administration, their greed and vanity – of functioning as midwives
of new democratic institutions.

For a time, the British Empire most definitely belonged in this
latter category. To see why requires an understanding of the two
cycles through which Britain rose to imperial dominance. The first
stretched from the defeat of Louis XIV to the American
Revolution. During this period, British power reached its zenith in
the Seven Years War (1756–63), when Canada and India were both
conquered. But her naval and commercial supremacy bred foreign
enmity as well as colonial rebellion; and in the War of American
Independence (1775–83) she had to fight against a formidable
coalition of powers that included the United States, France,
Holland and Spain, with a coalition of powers like Sweden, Russia,
Prussia, Denmark and Austria grouped together under the banner

of armed neutrality. Britain grew to be isolated and her first empire was shattered. It was to be rebuilt – this was phase two – through superior tactics and naval power and heaps of imperial confidence in the struggle against Napoleon's 'democratic' armies. 'However great France may be', crowed Pitt in 1802, Britain 'had a revenue equal to all Europe . . . a navy superior to all Europe, and a commerce as great as that of all Europe . . . and', he added laughingly, 'to make us *quite gentlemen*, a *debt* as large as that of all Europe.'[21] To some English eyes, the war effort against Napoleon was a life-or-death struggle to free the whole of Europe from the tyranny of democracy. The conflict was in fact a titanic struggle to form the first ever world empire. 'Two nations of overgrown power', wrote Thomas Jefferson in 1807, 'are endeavouring to establish, the one an universal dominion by sea, the other by land.'[22] He was right to anticipate that the victory of the British against French democrats would have consequences for the whole world. The nineteenth century indeed proved to be the golden age of British naval and economic supremacy. British manufactures and capital, and the cultural and political example of British institutions, spread all over the globe, and the British navy maintained a rudimentary world order almost everywhere outside the European continent.

Like all previous European empires, *Pax Britannica* went for straightforward aggrandisement dressed up in lavish appeals to world unity based on its own superiority; great empires and little minds always went ill together, and this one was no exception. Henry V (1081–1125) dreamed of a Christendom united in its crusade against the Turks. The principles of international Catholicism were fiercely championed by a confederation of states (Austria, Spain, the Netherlands, Naples, Milan, Bohemia, Portugal, Hungary) clumped under the House of Habsburg. Gustavus Adolphus (1611–32) fought battles and defended territories in the name of Protestantism. Catapulted into Europe and beyond by the events of the French Revolution, Napoleon breathed new life into the old language of democracy promotion both, in the process crowning himself with the ancient title of Emperor of the French.

Compared with all these narrations of dominant power, the British Empire sailed the globe and planted its feet under fluttering flags marked with seemingly grander, more arrogant ideals. There were eighteenth-century mercantilist noises about the links between population and wealth, and the need to stave off Britain's feared population decline. There was as well political economists' talk of the worldly benefits of market commerce and the progress of knowledge; references to the Christian qualities of British rule; the advantages of 'secularity' over superstition; and theories of the biological disadvantages of the 'lower races' under its tutelage.

Such presumptions were not just self-contradictory. They stood at right angles to the principles of parliamentary government – as influential public figures in Britain and throughout the empire spotted. Edmund Burke's famous parliamentary speeches on the dangers of what he called 'geographical morality' – the practice of governing according to double standards that wrongly suppose that a 'free country can keep another country in slavery'[23] – set the tone for those who not only wished to see greater equality of power-sharing at home, but who had concluded as well that the nurturing of representative democracy abroad could help the cause of representative democracy at home. It was as if they preached a new rule, that as the reach of government lengthened, the functions and forms of government had everywhere to become less concentrated, so that the subjects of power gained a measure of control over their own destinies. Some figures like Jeremy Bentham (1748–1832) openly criticised the behaviour of colonisers who were busily building up despotic institutions in parts of the empire. Others tried to sting the body of empire with the charge that it was a class-ridden polity, 'a vast system of outdoor relief for the upper classes', as James Mill famously put it. Still others took the side of the aboriginal peoples of the empire.[24] Then there were those who acted on these ideas, doing so by injecting, wherever possible, the vaccine of representative government into the body politic of the empire.

During the course of the nineteenth century, British government officials began to distinguish between three types of sub-government within the empire. 'Colonial possessions' were seen to include 'crown colonies', in which the Crown had command over legislation, with day-to-day administration carried out by public officers controlled by Westminster. There were colonies that possessed representative institutions, but did not enjoy 'responsible government' because, although the Crown had no more than a veto on legislation, Westminster retained control of public affairs in the colony. Finally, there were colonies blessed both with representative institutions and responsible government, subject only to the Crown's veto on legislation and Westminster's control over the colonial governor.

British North America

It was within this last group of colonies that impressive – by the standards of the day – innovations took place in matters of representative democracy. For reasons of politics and money, or accident or whim, things were done abroad that could not be done at home. The rule that the government of colonies at a distance required, if only for the sake of effective administration, granting them some measure of self-government played a forceful role.

Consider developments in the British North American colonies that later formed themselves into Canada. Following the British military defeat of France, a Royal Proclamation of 1763, issued by George III, defined the Province of Quebec and appointed its first governor with orders to convene a legislative assembly, when conditions allowed. That was the catch, because it so happened that the big majority of subjects (some 95 per cent) were either so-called 'Indians' or French-speaking Canadians, whose legal status quickly caused a local ruckus. Colonial authorities sought the opinion of London, who ruled in favour of the French-speakers, noting that the conquered were not subject to the 'Incapacities, Disabilities and Penalties' imposed upon Catholics at home.

Following the Quebec Act of 1774, the French-speaking Canadians were allowed to live under the civil code known as the *Coutume de Paris*, which replaced English common law, reinstated the seigneurial system of land tenure, and generally reinforced the Canadians' strong affection for the old French colonial principle of 'chacun parle en son nom et personne au nom de tous' ('each one speaks on his own behalf and no one on behalf of everyone'). The originality of these colonial arrangements – the sanctioning of a bilingual, Catholic-dominated polity with its own legal traditions – was nothing short of remarkable.

The changes pointed towards a 'multicultural' democracy (a later Canadian speciality) and they were consolidated by the Constitutional Act of 1791, which renamed Quebec as Lower Canada, acknowledged its differences, while at the same time (because of pressure from the English-speaking settlers) introduced both a parallel land tenure system along English lines and – to the great surprise of many observers – a local house of assembly. That in turn enabled (in 1792) free elections to be held, subject to a property-based franchise that enabled anyone who had reached the age of twenty-one – male or female, French- or English-speaking – to vote, so long as they owned a minimum of property or paid annual rents and had not been convicted of treason, or a serious criminal offence. The upshot was that propertyless tenants paying a minimum annual rent of £10 – a modest sum for the times – were eligible to vote, as were women who met the same tenancy or property requirements. In a settler society where property ownership or tenancy was common, and English common law did not apply, large numbers of women evidently voted, for the first time anywhere in the British Empire. In the town of Trois-Rivières, where, during the election of 1820, a local judge noted that 'here women vote just as men do, without discrimination', one man entered the polling place only to be told that he could not vote because he had placed his property in his spouse's name. Red-faced, he was ordered to bring his wife to the polls, since she was the qualified voter in their family.[25]

Elsewhere in the region, with the backing of imperial power, cutting-edge experiments took place in abundance during the course of the nineteenth century. Geopolitical and geo-commercial concerns led to the establishment of the smallest legislative assembly in British North America, in the colony of Vancouver Island. A fur-trading post inhabited by employees of the Hudson's Bay Company, its forty-odd electors, male freeholders owning at least twenty acres of land, voted in seven members in the first elections of August 1856. On the other side of the continent, meanwhile, the franchise had already been stripped of its property bias. Two years earlier, Nova Scotia became the first colony in British North America to adopt near-universal male suffrage – without so much as a whisper

FIGURE 79: New citizens: merchants of Yarmouth, Nova Scotia, 1855, a year after winning the right to vote.

or whimper of revolution (Figure 79). The local assembly adopted a law entitling all British subjects aged twenty-one or older to vote, so long as they had lived in the colony at least five years. A peculiarity of the law is that it incorporated an older law that granted the vote as well to freeholders who owned property that annually generated revenue of at least forty shillings. This had the effect of guaranteeing that recent immigrants of British stock could exercise political power – if they owned property. On the margins of empire, numbers were important, so long as they were of the right stock. (It is worth remembering that exactly a century before, with Britain and France at war, the anxious authorities in the colony of Nova Scotia solved the problem of loyalty to empire by burning down the homes and confiscating the land of 10,000 French-speaking Acadians, who were herded on to ships and scattered like bad seeds among the Thirteen Colonies of New England and the West Indies.) The government of the tiny maritime colony of Nova Scotia drew back from a truly universal male franchise. 'Indians' and all people in receipt of financial aid from the government were forbidden the vote.

By contemporary world standards, such restrictions were minor, especially when placed in the context of another, first-time political achievement in British North America. This took the form of a new confederation negotiated by the colonists themselves, without the use of revolutionary violence. The political motives that drove the union of colonies were mixed. They ranged from improved military defence and local (and Westminster) beliefs in self-government to the development of a more cost-efficient, coast-to-coast railway system. Important as well was Lord Durham's conviction that a union of the different parts of Canada would both dilute its French qualities and prove, within the bounds of the British Empire, that Canada was different from the United States. The combined effect of these different and conflicting motives was to spark intense political bluff and bluster. It lasted nine years, until 1873, when voters in Prince Edward Island finally agreed to join the Confederation. The key agreement, the British North America Act, was admittedly a child of closed government. Bringing together Nova Scotia, New Brunswick and the Province of Canada, it was defined in secret and negotiated in camera. Mainly the work of colonial politicians and businessmen, supported by prominent London financiers and officials, it was given Royal Assent on 31 March 1867. It confirmed the Tory wager of John A. Macdonald and other so-called fathers of confederation that a new constitution was possible through their own efforts, not Westminster's, and that this could happen without consulting the subjects of the empire.

The fathers were right on the first point, but wrong on the second. The times they were a'changing, and the negotiators were quickly forced to get in step. Although the 1867 constitution was adopted on the nod, the process of confederation had definite democratising effects. It certainly contradicted the oft-repeated claim that no democracy was ever built democratically. There was serious trouble in New Brunswick (where two elections were fought over the issue) and in Nova Scotia, which agreed to join the confederation only after London offered favourable policies in matters of trade, taxation and fishing. Voters were consulted in the straggler provinces of Newfoundland (where an overwhelming majority voted against joining the Confederation), British Columbia and Prince Edward Island, whose citizens were the last to sanction the new union, which was the first ever act of confederation within the British Empire.

The Bunyip Aristocracy

Elsewhere in the empire, equally astonishing things happened. The land called Australia hardly seemed the place that would be remembered for its gifts to representative democracy. Not only was it established as a dictatorship under British military rule over white people who themselves violently ruined the lives of the indigenous peoples, but here was as well a strange and topsy-turvy biosphere, definitely a weird place, as Charles Darwin put it when visiting, a continent where 'an unbeliever in everything beyond his own reason might exclaim, "surely two distinct Creators must have been at work"'.[26] Aside from amazement at marsupials, black swans and eucalypts that retained their leaves and shed their bark seasonally there were also, from the time of the first colonisation, a few fantasies about the regenerative powers of the country. 'I beheld a second Rome, rising from a coalition of banditti', recorded Lieutenant James Tuckey during the long journey of another shipload of convicts to Port Phillip Bay and Hobart Town in 1803–4. 'I beheld it giving laws to the world, and superlative in arms and in arts, looking down with proud superiority upon the barbarous nations of the northern hemisphere.'[27]

Such views of the young military dictatorship were initially rare, and often considered extreme, although as the century unfolded the reality of difference and a tough-minded sense of democratic freedom began to take root. *Marching Song of Democracy* (1901), an experimental composition by the Australian-born Percy Aldridge Grainger (1882–1961), captured this robust hopefulness: written originally to be performed by a chorus of men, women and children singing and whistling to the rhythmic accompaniment of their tramping feet, as they marched in the open air, it expressed the radical conviction that the sunburned continent called *terra australis* could make important contributions to the world. That it subsequently did so had much to do with a contrary trend that dominated the first colonies, in New South Wales and Van Diemen's Land, especially before 1850: the emergence of a landowning gentry with aristocratic prejudices, a class that treated the French Revolution with disdain, and so made

FIGURE 80: Son of Irish convicts and champion of male suffrage, Daniel Henry Deniehy.

a determined effort to recreate the imagined manners and powers of the British aristocracy.

Families with precious surnames like MacArthur and Wentworth, Franklin and Macquarie, acted the part of a squirearchy. They passed and then guarded laws as magistrates. They founded exclusive private schools and endowed churches; and they acted as patrons and governors of local communities. They made friends with Tory governors of the colonies, and they loved to dine with like-minded gentlemen at clubs, such as the Union in Hobart and the Australian in Sydney. This bunyip aristocracy, a sarcastic term invented by a Sydney-born journalist and politician, Daniel Henry Deniehy (1828–65),* was in fact a class of impostors. They thought

---

*Daniel Henry Deniehy (see Figure 80) deserves to stand among the unsung, forgotten heroes of the era of representative democracy, if only for his inventive talk of 'bunyip aristocracy'. Of tiny physique and chronically in poor health for most of his life, Deniehy was the son of former Irish convicts who prospered after their term of confinement had expired. His parents arranged for him to complete his secondary education in Europe, where he met leaders of the Young Ireland Party and found himself attracted to Chartist principles. Returning to his hometown Sydney in 1844, he studied law and quickly made a name for himself as a gifted orator, a competent barrister, and outspoken critic of the 1853 New South Wales Constitution Bill, whose aim was to create a powerful unelected upper house and a

of themselves as almost too good for the God-forsaken southern colonies. They fantasised that people of fine British breeding were entitled to rule as they ruled elsewhere, in Ireland, the Caribbean and India. The bunyip aristocracy detested bad blood. It despised aboriginals, black-sheep parolees and rough-bred swagmen as much as it hated convicts. It harboured doubts about many immigrants who had arrived on its shores – rotting apples like Chartist sympathisers, religious dissenters, Irish patriots, and all those whose liberalism had been burned into them by bad memories of class rule and intolerable wrongs in the old country. The bunyip aristocracy was predictably suspicious of the camps of bickering gold miners that produced not just uncouth rich upstarts, but also political rebels, which is why, supported by pastoral allies and some merchants, lawyers and doctors, this would-be aristocracy, during the 1850s, set about sealing its powers against the riffraff by drafting new property-based constitutions – only to fail, by a whisker. The consequence was that Australia, in contrast to settler societies like Argentina and Uruguay, never developed a down-under version of caudillo democracy.

substantial property-based franchise for the lower chamber. Active in the ranks of the New South Wales Electoral Reform League, he championed adult male suffrage and fiercely opposed the extension of rich families' control of the vast grazing lands of inland New South Wales. He accused this squatter class of 'Botany Bay magnificos' of maltreating Chinese immigrants, of behaving like 'political oligarchs' who 'treated the people at large as if they were cattle to be bought and sold in the market'. In a public speech in Sydney's Victoria Theatre on 15 August 1853, he made reference for the first time to the bunyip, the howling, human-flesh-eating beast of aboriginal legend that supposedly dwelled in creeks, swamps and billabongs. For many white people, the bunyip symbolised a fear-ridden figure of imagination, which is exactly what Deniehy meant by the phrase 'bunyip aristocracy': the landed oligarchs of New South Wales were make-believe monsters whose non-existence could be demonstrated simply by disbelieving stories of their existence. The exquisite ridicule turned heads and helped to ditch the proposal. It also resulted, in 1857, in his election to the New South Wales Legislative Assembly. The following year, adult male suffrage was adopted, and with that victory Deniehy turned to journalism and literature, and to drink. In 1859, he founded and edited a radical newspaper, *Southern Cross*, then edited the Melbourne-based *The Victorian*. For a time, he lectured on modern literature at the University of Sydney, Australia's first university, and regularly contributed to the Irish-Australian *The Freeman's Journal*. In October 1865, in the country town of Bathurst where he was practising law, he died of complications caused by alcoholism, aged thirty-seven.

Arithmetic and Democracy

It turned out that there were several ways of trapping the bunyip. In the colony of South Australia, first settled in 1836 and later called by many the Paradise of Dissent, the spirit of aristocracy was extinguished by settlers who thought of themselves as fair-minded, God-respecting men and women of the improving classes. Coming from the other side of the world, these invaders of a vast desert landscape with a coastline fringe blessed with Mediterranean seasons thought of themselves as more English than the English, as people whose disappointment with their mother country and old Europe could be harnessed to build a new society and government, an improving order that would bring Englishness closer to the blue heaven of perfection. Of middling-class stock, they believed the past to be corrupted, and looked with passion towards the future. They were enthusiasts of civil liberties, social opportunity and equality among all Christian sects, including German-speaking Lutherans, whom they offered assisted passages across the ocean. These English middling classes believed they were free within the laws they applied to themselves, that they were protected by habeas corpus, that they had a right to an elected parliament, trial by jury and a press that guaranteed the free circulation of public opinions. Many of them consequently felt ashamed of their robbery and ruination of the aboriginal peoples they conquered.

These English men and women – merchants, bankers, small industrialists, mine owners, doctors, farmers and freeholders, shopkeepers, salaried clerks, independent skilled craftsmen and tradesmen – disliked talk of good blood because they believed in self-improvement through hard work, self-discipline and attainment by merit. They were fascinated by the discoveries of natural history, the successes of machinery, and by the new techniques of crop rotation, medicine and steam power. These middling classes shrewdly pursued wealth, some with deplorable arrogance masked as self-assurance, but many of them were born philanthropists who detested social conditions that produced prostitution and drunkenness, paupers and vagrants. These English citizens loathed the old convict system, which was deliberately never used in South

Australia. They disliked the violence-ridden interstate rivalries of old Europe, and thought of their geographic isolation, their protection from the rest of the world by a great Southern Ocean and a vast inland desert, as a political blessing. They did not necessarily believe in the priority of rights of property over the rights of persons; and they objected strongly to talk of upper-class families and their 'natural' ability to judge best the interests of the whole society. Many of them were passionate egalitarians, and they knew by heart either the words or the intended meaning of the famous remarks of Lord Henry Brougham (1778–1868), after whom one of the prominent streets of the colony's capital city, Adelaide, was subsequently named. Said the outspoken Lord who scorned the ruling classes, counted among his good friends such leading Radicals as William Hazlitt and Lord Byron, and who as Lord Chancellor was instrumental in helping pass the Reform Act of 1832 and the Anti-Slavery Act in the following year: 'If all the castles, manors . . . and broad acres were brought to the hammer and sold at fifty years' purchase, the price would fly up and kick the beam [hit the ceiling] when counterpoised by the vast and solid riches of those middle classes, who are also the genuine depositaries of sober, rational, intelligent and honest English feeling.'[28]

Locution of that kind convinced the settlers of South Australia that they could change the world in their favour by experimenting with new methods of government. Their early search for greater proportionality – for a closer mathematical relationship between votes cast and elected representatives – was their first of several gifts to the world of representative democracy.

Shortly after the founding of the new colony, there were robust debates among the settlers about the subject of arithmetic and democracy, or how best to represent individuals and groups in parliamentary assemblies. The debates targeted a core principle of representative democracy, one person, one vote, and the upshot was that many colonists grew convinced that the principle suffered a malady. To see why, let us pause and draw back for just a moment from South Australia, to consider the old complaint, first heard in nineteenth-century Europe, that we human beings have transformed ourselves through the ages into creatures of calculation, virtually to the point where we can think and act in no other way than that of a machine. 'Perhaps all the morality of mankind has its origin in the tremendous inner excitement which seized on primeval men when they discovered measure and measuring, scales and weighing', wrote the German anti-philosopher Friedrich Nietzsche (1844–1900), in the same generation that the South Australian colonists were pondering the subject of electoral representation. Similar concerns about the bad effects of humans' embrace of calculation surfaced in the writings and teachings of the most controversial philosopher of the twentieth century, Martin Heidegger (1889–1976). No friend of representative democracy, he pointed out that there were ancient Greeks who thought that the capacity to speak with others was a basic feature of the human condition, that this capacity for speech enabled human beings to become creatures of calculation, *arithmein*, animals with the ability to reckon, to design and to redesign things, people and situations. For Heidegger, there was something inherently wrong with the human will to reduce complex phenomena to questions of number. He liked to cite a line from the Romantic poetry of Friedrich Hölderlin: 'Is there a measure on the earth? There is none.' Those who think otherwise, said Heidegger, fall foul of the truth that the world and all that is within it defies the will to measure it. They wrongly suppose that individuals, groups, organisations, whole societies are the same, or can be made to be so. The quest for standardisation (so Heidegger concluded) is defined by a hidden political agenda: by defining people and things that are not the same as equivalent, as sufficiently similar that they can be summed, compared and evaluated, the will to standardisation reduces life to calculation, to control, to the forcible elimination of differences.

Heidegger was no angel. His rejection of standardisation fell into the arms of apolitical disillusionment – and, for a time, support for the Nazis, whom he (foolishly) expected to break the mould of standardisation. Yet even today there are some who continue to be troubled by democracy's love affair with arithmetic. Don't they have a point? Doesn't democracy blindly worship numbers? Remember the old Greek adage that geometry should be taught in oligarchies because it demonstrates the proportions within inequality, whereas in democracies instruction in arithmetic should be promoted because it teaches relations of equality. And ponder for a few seconds the working principle so dear to the era of representative democracy: one man, one vote. Surely only measuring men could reason like that? Doesn't that hallowed principle display a fetish of quantity: reckoning, computation, enumeration, accounting, the belief (mobilised in opinion polls and election predictions) that doubt and uncertainty can be banished from the world? Surely by embracing this metaphysical spirit of calculation, democracy was infected with the very will to equivalence, mastery and control which democrats otherwise found abhorrent?

The middle-class settlers of South Australia rejected such conclusions. In 1840, in the capital city of Adelaide, they introduced, for the first time anywhere in the world, a new voting system based on the principle that representative democracy could harness man the measurer for purposes other than the steamrolling of some by others. The Adelaide experiment recognised that the principle of majority rule had created a Frankenstein, the real possibility of domineering government caused by 'enthroning the majority as sovereign, by means of universal suffrage without King or Lords', the words used by a shareholder in the South Australian experiment, John Stuart Mill.[29] The new voting system in Adelaide was designed to stop Frankenstein's monster in its tracks, to give freer voice to the views and interests of minorities; it chimed with the colonists' love of arithmetical precision – and their strong affection for democratic fairness.

It was no coincidence that among the chief backers of their scheme was Rowland Hill, who later became famous as the inventor of a new postal system that treated all letters as equal, so long as they were franked with the one penny postage stamp. The system of one letter, one stamp overlapped with the conception of a political system based on the idea of one man, one vote and its corollary, the right of each person to be different. Hill was at the time Secretary of the Colonization Commission of South Australia, and quite familiar with the principle that representation should be proportionate to the opinions of different members of a body, which had been applied, as early as 1821, to the Birmingham-based Society for Literary and Scientific Improvement, in which both he and his father, Thomas Wright Hill, had been prominent members.[30]

With his backing, the 2000 or so adult residents of Adelaide, women among them, had successfully petitioned (in the name of their 'rights and privileges') the colonial authorities for their own government. The first local government in Australia was formed on 31 October 1840, with the election of the first ever mayor, James Hurtle Fisher, three aldermen and fifteen councillors to the new Adelaide Corporation. The election of a local government by ratepayers, using a simplified form of proportional representation, was not only a first for Australia, but also a first for the world. The experiment openly contradicted the widespread belief in parts of old Europe that representative democracy could be a celebration of popular unity, or that it would degenerate into the unthinking custom of voters behaving like lost sheep vulnerable to political wolves, like priests and demagogues.* The South Australian experiment was driven by the desire to release different opinions and ways of life from captivity within blandly calculated visions of representative democracy based on some presumed undifferentiated unity of 'the people'. Adelaide voters (whether they included women is unknown) were invited to form themselves into as many 'electoral sections' or 'quorums' as there were seats to be filled. Two such 'quorums' stepped forward. One group of ratepayers declared themselves for Mr William Senden. A group of workers,

---

*In a remarkable passage in his posthumously published memoirs, Alexis de Tocqueville tellingly described the sheepish behaviour of newly enfranchised voters in his home district, during the first election based on universal male suffrage in France, in April 1848: 'We had to go in a body to vote at the town of Saint-Pierre, a league away from our village. On the morning of election day all the electors, that is to say the whole male population over twenty years old, assembled in front of the church. They formed themselves into a double column in alphabetical order; I preferred to take the place my name warranted, for I knew that in democratic times and countries one must allow oneself to be put at the head of the people, but must not put oneself there. The crippled and sick who wished to follow us came on pack horses or in carts at the end of the long procession. Only the women and children were left behind. We were in all a hundred and seventy persons. When we got to the top of the hill overlooking [the chateau of] Tocqueville, there was a momentary halt; I realised that I was required to speak. I climbed to the other side of a ditch. A circle formed around me, and I said a few words appropriate to the occasion. I reminded these good people of the seriousness and importance of the act they were going to perform; I advised them not to let themselves be accosted or diverted by people who might, when we arrived at the town, seek to deceive them, but rather to march as a united body with each man in his place and to stay until they had voted. "Let no one," I said, "go into a house to take food or to dry himself (it was raining that day), before he has performed his duty." They shouted that they would do this, and so they did. All the votes were given at the same time, and I have reason to think that almost all were for the same candidate' (*Recollections* (New York, 1971 [1896]), pp. 119–20).

meanwhile, unanimously elected their foreman as a councillor. Both were declared duly elected. The remaining seats were filled by the traditional block-vote method. Each voter who had not already helped elect a member by way of the 'quorum' was invited to cast votes for whichever candidates they preferred. Multiple votes were allowed and the candidates with the most votes were then declared winners.

Under the Southern Cross

The South Australian colonists, having managed to do without aristocracy, later gave other gifts to the new world of representative democracy, including a constitution that was ratified by a general election using a path-breaking version of the secret ballot; the full enfranchisement of women; support for aboriginal voting; and the active endorsement of a new federation based on the universal franchise that resulted (in 1904) in the election of the first national labour government in the world, led by Chilean-born John Christian Watson.

Elsewhere in the Australian colonies, bunyip aristocrats had their snobbery dynamited towards the heavens by popular protests. One flashpoint was the Victorian gold-mining settlement of Ballarat, where by the early 1850s hard-living miners with shaggy hair and rough hands had grown fed up with the high cost of the obligatory miner's licence (which had to be paid whether or not gold was found). Like earlier rebels in the Low Countries and the American colonies, the miners detested their lack of political representation and it felt to some (as the fiery Scotsman Tom Kennedy put it) that they were dealing with the 'very rags and tatters of a British Government' clinging to power through thuggish methods, like the 'bloody licence tax' and the local police custom of chaining unlicensed diggers to eucalyptus trees.[31]

In November 1854, at a site named Bakery Hill, a rowdy public meeting of 10,000 miners voted unanimously to form the Ballarat Reform League. Its charter called for 'honest Government' and 'wholesome laws'. The League's demands echoed those of the working-class Chartists back in Britain, which was not surprising considering that its secretary, John B. Humffray, had been a

Chartist before his emigration from Wales. The miners' charter went on to say that 'the people are the only legitimate source of all political power'. It added that 'taxation without representation is tyranny' because 'it is the inalienable right of every citizen to have a voice in making the laws he is called on to obey'. The charter demanded five political reforms: manhood suffrage; the abolition of property qualifications for members of the colonial legislature; the payment of members of parliament; short-duration parliaments; and 'full and fair representation'.

The miners quickly moved to a collision course with the colonial authorities; they in turn prepared to go fox hunting, in the style of English gentlemen. Blood was about to soak the local summer soil. The authorities secretly decided upon government by artillery; on 30 November 1854, sensing that they were about to be slaughtered, the miners replied by building a stockade of wooden slabs, on the slopes of Bakery Hill, at a goldfield site known as Eureka (Figure 81). The next day, towards dusk, under their own newly made flag that featured the Southern Cross represented by a near-white rectangular cross studded with five near-white stars, on a dark blue background, the miners knelt to chant an oath, as if they

FIGURE 81: Miners swearing allegiance to the republican Southern Cross flag, Eureka, Victoria, December 1854, from a watercolour by Charles Doudiet.

were monks with the weight of the world on their shoulders: 'We swear by the Southern Cross to stand truly by each other, and fight to defend our rights and liberties.' The government's troops, nearly three hundred cavalry and infantry dressed in scarlet shirts and white caps, showed no mercy. Next morning, just before daybreak, they spent ten minutes storming through the stockade. The Southern Cross was torn down and burned. Five soldiers died. Twenty-four digger democrats were killed; perhaps twenty were injured, with many more broken hearts arrested.

The scale of the violence was piffling by European standards, and Lieutenant-Governor Sir Charles Hotham did his very best to dump the matter into forgotten files by thanking Her Majesty's troops for putting an end to mob rule spread by 'strangers in their midst'. With warrants hanging over their heads for 'treasonable and seditious language', and acting to 'incite Men to take up Arms, with a view to make war against Our Sovereign Lady the Queen', the digger democrats and their supporters seemed to have emptied their barrel of hopes. What nobody anticipated was that the Eureka stockade so profoundly frightened the colonial authorities in London and Melbourne that they were forced to make concessions, with many positive and long-lasting effects.

Within a year of the uprising, juries in Melbourne acquitted all thirteen diggers tried for treason. A royal commission recommended dropping the hated licence system, while the adoption of a new 'miner's right' costing only a pound a year (the old licence cost a pound a month) effectively enfranchised all adult men in the colony. The district of Ballarat won the right to elect two representatives to the colony's Legislative Council. And just to beggar belief, two rebel diggers – Peter Lalor and John B. Humffray – were elected unopposed.

The Australian Ballot

The unexpected radical effects didn't end there. Arguably the most important consequence of the blood spilled under the Southern Cross was the boost it gave to the adoption of a small but globally important invention that soon won the blessing of the Colonial Office in London: a new type of secret ballot that came to be

FIGURE 82: An early nineteenth-century ballot box used for the election of the Board of Guardians of a privately run workhouse in the Welsh parish of Forden, Montgomeryshire.

called, in the United States and elsewhere around the world, 'the Victoria ballot', or 'the Australian ballot'.[32]

This is roughly how the change from bullets to ballots happened: in early 1856, just before a new constitution enabling self-government was handed down from London, the Victorian Legislative Council agreed a new method of voting, probably reinforced by similar moves in neighbouring Tasmania and South Australia. The measure was a brand-new version of the secret ballot, adapted to the conditions of representative democracy down under. Back home, in Britain, as elsewhere, the principle of the secret ballot had been practised in gentlemen's clubs, learned societies and other voluntary organisations, including workhouses (see Figure 82). It was on the list of key Chartist demands, and George Grote, the great champion of Athenian democracy, had spoken in its defence in the House of Commons. Versions of the secret ballot – the practice of voters carrying into the polling station their own bit of paper containing their voting intention, usually handed to them by one of the candidates, sometimes folded in an envelope – already existed (for instance) in the Canadian colony of New Brunswick and in the American states of New York and Massachusetts.[33] There is no doubt as well that the

FIGURE 83: A voting scene, as depicted on a coin issued by Licinius Nerva, around the time that he became a Roman praetor in 114 BCE. One voter, standing to the left of a *pons* (or voting bridge, designed to make the act of voting a public act while ensuring the secrecy of an individual citizen's choice), is being handed a ballot by a bare-chested attendant below. On the right, another voter puts his ballot in a *cista*, or voting urn.

art of casting a vote without others knowing one's intentions had much older roots, traceable to the earlier age of assembly democracy, for instance in the Greek custom of concealing with the grip of a hand a copper or clay ballot, and in the series of ballot laws, passed in the second half of the second century CE, that made voting secret in all the assemblies of the late Roman republic (see Figure 83).

The type of secret ballot that took root in southern Australia was different, and it was backed by an odd assortment of friends, ranging from rough-tongued workers threatening revolution to smooth-talking liberal intellectuals and radical lawyers, including Henry Samuel Chapman (1803–81), who had spent time as Colonial Secretary in Tasmania before moving to Melbourne, where as a barrister he had defended the Eureka rebels, pleaded successfully for their amnesty, and in early 1856 drafted the legislation that introduced the secret ballot to Victoria. The newly enfranchised diggers were fully behind Chapman's proposals, as were workers and journeymen afraid of being bribed or bullied into voting a certain way by their employers. So, too, curiously, were parts of the bunyip aristocracy and middle class, who were in their own way afraid that the advent of adult male suffrage would lead to bullying from below, by 'the people' prying into their

FIGURE 84: *The Poll*, an etching by Thomas Rowlandson, 1780.

private lives, by demanding to know how they voted. Support was strong as well among people, teetotalling Christians for instance, who were not just sick to the back teeth with rigged and riotous election contests that used the system of so-called 'open voting', but who thought the act of voting should more closely resemble an act of prayer, standing alone with one's conscience, before God.

The teetotallers had a point. Until the advent of the Australian ballot, electoral contests everywhere in the world of emergent representative democracy were feverish struggles for power, conducted in broad daylight, among intimates who were often inebriated. That was the point of the satirical etchings and engravings of 'election entertainments' by eighteenth-century British artists like William Hogarth and Thomas Rowlandson (Figure 84). Since the business was carried out in public by means of threats, nods and winks and Chinese whispers, candidates had a fair idea of the voting trends during the day; in Spanish America, as we have seen, the result was usually known days or weeks in advance. If contests proved to be cliffhangers, a candidate and his supporters would simply go fishing or hunting for voters. Candidates laid on cabs and buggies to fetch their own voters. Plying them with grog and grub was also a favourite device. 'The old custom of a personal house-to-house canvass has, in our cities, degenerated into a visiting of liquor saloons and "corner groceries"', reported Henry George (1839–97), the American political economist who married an Australian and was best known for his best-selling *Progress and Poverty* (1879). 'The candidate is expected to visit each groggery in his district, to present his card, and leave on the bar a ten or twenty-dollar bill, for which no change is given, while all the loungers about the place are called on to take a drink. In some places the custom is for him to pay for a keg of beer.'[34] Customary, too, was the tactic of supplying them with voting papers – any old scrap of paper would do – and filling out their choices for them, especially if they were illiterate or too careless or drunk to sign their name next to that of their preferred candidate. The practice of delivering the voter, ballot in hand,

FIGURE 85: Poster issued by the Society for Promoting the Adoption of the Vote by Ballot, Manchester, 1866.

to the Returning Officer, himself not beyond a pint's bribe, was also rampant. The voter was less a rational animal than a prized victim.

The Australian ballot put a stop to most of this tomfoolery, as contemporary reports and a pictorial broadside (proudly inverting the image of the Australian colonies as an uncivil wasteland) made clear (Figure 85).[35] The methods were simple in both design and purpose – and easily transferable to other parts of the world, where they are today familiar to several billion people. With the announcement of an election, the government and its officials were responsible for printing and promptly delivering, on foot or by donkey, camel or horse and carriage, official ballot slips and ballot boxes. For the double purpose of providing voters with greater ease of access, and to make life harder for organised bribery, a network of polling stations was established within each constituency. The exact number of stations was proportionate to its size, and in South Australia, beginning in 1856, stations were by law located at a minimum distance from public houses (presumably to dissuade the bribed and boozed from staggering into the arms of the political devil). The date and opening and closing hours of the polling day were strictly set in advance, usually from 8 a.m. until 6 p.m. (a Saturday was eventually chosen as polling day in South Australia, for the maximum convenience of voters who worked full time). On the day of election, location signs were plastered throughout the neighbourhood, to guide citizens to their destination. On the prearranged hour, a local constable opened the doors of the polling booth, while one or two others sauntered about in the background, billy clubs and handcuffs at the ready. As voters arrived, they were ushered, one at a time, towards a table where their names were marked off on the electoral roll that had been put together by election officials, aided by postmen, foot constables and mounted police, who had sometimes ridden hundreds of miles across a vast outback landscape. The compilation of reliable electoral rolls through house-to-house canvasses of a highly mobile population was obviously a vital condition of success of the new Australian ballot. The principal experiments in this field were conducted not in Victoria, but in neighbouring South Australia, which had the world's first salaried electoral officials (from 1858), introduced a system of continuous enrolment of voters (rather than once a year, or on the eve of elections), and appointed, in all but name, the first ever

Chief Electoral Officer in the dawning age of representative democracy, William Robinson Boothby.*

*Like the Argentine-Croatian inventor of fingerprinting, Juan Vucetich, William Robinson Boothby may look to us a dour and dull character, yet the success of representative democracy depended on the creative efforts of men like them. Born in England in 1829, Boothby emigrated with his family to Adelaide, South Australia, in 1853, shortly after graduating from the University of London. A year after arriving in the colony he entered the civil service and was quickly promoted to sheriff, a post he held until 1903. He became the most distinguished civil servant of his generation in the colony – and the figure who was responsible for implanting the most advanced species of the Australian ballot into Australian soil. Boothby played a central role in implementing the Electoral Act of 1856, which included provisions for the new ballot (Tasmania passed a version of the legislation on 4 February 1856; Victoria followed suit six weeks later, on 19 March; South Australia followed a month later, on 18 April), as well as the more innovative Electoral Act of 1858. It provided for each voter to place an X alongside the name of his preferred candidate, rather than crossing out unwanted names. The 1858 Act also guaranteed a genuinely secret ballot by specifying that the ballot paper should show 'no other matter or thing', aside from the listed names of the candidates and the Returning Officer's initials on the back; and it prompted new legislation (in 1859) that included measures for transferring voters' names from one constituency to another when they changed their place of residence, as well as the requirement that local registrars should inform the electoral office of deaths. Both innovations were designed to ensure that the rolls could be kept as comprehensive and accurate as possible. It is worth noting that these procedural innovations implied – as a necessary condition of the smooth and efficient conduct of elections – compulsory enrolment (that was introduced at the federal level in Australia in 1911) and the compulsory voting by citizens (a measure first introduced in 1915 in Queensland, and at the federal level in 1924, although aboriginal people were required to register and to vote only in 1984). From 1856 to 1903, Boothby supervised every parliamentary election in South Australia, including the 1896 election, when adult women (including some aboriginal women) voted for the first time. He provided expert advice to every relevant public inquiry about the conduct of elections, and supported the introduction (in 1890) of postal voting that enfranchised seamen, the sick and the infirm, and later worked to the benefit of women voters, who disproportionately used the provision. Boothby's quiet passion for improving the mechanics of the Australian ballot system seemed to stem less from his principled commitment to representative democracy and much more from his attachment to a mid-nineteenth-century version of the English Utilitarian doctrine of crafting social cohesion and happiness through governmental regulation. Boothby disliked the rumpus – the brass bands, abuse and pelting of candidates with rocks, rotten eggs and dead animals – caused by the emergence of party politics, and followed with great interest the abolition of public nominations (1856) and the introduction (in the same year) of a 'gagging clause' that was designed to prevent South Australian politicians from opening their mouths publicly during election campaigns. Boothby was a firm believer in the top-down responsibility of government for the everyday wellbeing of its citizens – for their 'policing', as Adam Smith and other eighteenth-century figures liked to say, using a term that has since faded into obsolescence. Boothby, a man of patience who played cricket for South Australia, clearly liked regulated order based on statistics (in this he was supported by one of his younger brothers, Josiah Boothby, who was a South Australian government statistician and superintendent of the census). His commitment to 'good government' through more effective policing of the population was evident in other fields, for instance in his role, from 1869 onwards, as comptroller of the Adelaide Labor Prison. Boothby's reforms were thoroughly Benthamite. In the name of abolishing physical cruelty against prisoners and improving their 'welfare', he abolished the barracks system, improved prison accommodation, used prisoners on public works and drafted a new Prisons Act in 1869–70. Following an inspection tour of European prisons in the years 1876–7, he also arranged for the planting of olive groves in prisons, for

FIGURE 86: Sketch of orderly polling arrangements under the Australian ballot system, Victoria, 1889.

The Australian ballot had other important features. Each voter (it was always to be a man, for nearly four more decades) was asked to state his name in full and then carefully handed a printed ballot paper. On one side it contained the names of all the candidates, hierarchically arranged and alphabetically listed; whatever extra space existed was not for writing messages or obscenities on the paper, for in that case the vote was deemed spoiled. In Victoria, the ballot paper contained the voter's number in the electoral roll, on which were registered the names of all qualified voters, arranged in alphabetical order. (In Tasmania and South Australia, the practice of numbering was deemed a violation of the secrecy principle, and was understandably scrapped.) Near the entrance to the polling station, individual compartments or booths, sometimes equipped with curtains that could be drawn, created a private space for carrying out the most public of acts: standing alone, marking a ballot paper, using a pencil (see Figure 86). For those unable to write, but who could read, the ballot paper was foolproof; and those voters who were illiterate or otherwise visually impaired could ask for help from one of the polling station officials. In the case of Victoria, voters were asked to draw a line

the purpose of rehabilitating prisoners through their production of olive oil. He published *The Olive: Its Culture and Products in the South of France and Italy* (Adelaide, 1878). Boothby died at his home in North Adelaide on 12 July 1903. A federal electorate was named after him.

FIGURE 87: Casting a vote in a referendum on Australian federation, using the Australian ballot method, 1898.

through the names of all those candidates they did not intend to vote for; that request was quickly found to be potentially confusing to voters, so that in South Australia, in 1858, for the first time in the world, voters were asked simply to place a mark in the square alongside the candidate(s) they supported – to punch out a chad, as Americans would later say.

Then came the moment of reckoning, the ultimate act, the instant when voters dropped their marked and folded ballot paper into a large, oblong, padlocked box, under the watchful eye of the Returning Officer, his deputy, perhaps a Poll Clerk and several scrutineers nominated by the competing candidates (see Figure 87). The Australian ballot was designed to ensure one man, one vote, and no more. But given that those who count the votes ultimately determine who wins elections, the new system put in place quite strict arrangements. With the voting over, and the doors of his own and all other polling stations in the constituency closed, the Returning Officer unlocked the ballot boxes (including those delivered from other stations) and set to work counting the votes, helped by his deputy, in the presence of the scrutineers. The candidate with the greatest number of aggregate votes, at all booths in the district, was declared the successful candidate. As soon as the poll was officially declared, the Returning Officer sealed up all the ballot papers and posted them to a central point, usually the Clerk of the Legislature, who, after keeping them for the time prescribed for disputing the election results, disposed of them, usually by burning.

This was not yet the age of time- and space-busting communications technologies and delays and mishaps continued to plague the whole system, which was by no means perfect. The Australian ballot discriminated against illiterate and sightless voters.[36] The public monitoring of the count by Returning Officers and their assistants supposed, on occasion naively, that election officers were incorruptible, that for instance they would never use false-bottomed ballot boxes. And fraud among voters certainly persisted, some of it to be admired for its ingenuity. Among the cleverest was the so-called 'Tasmania dodge', which involved bribing individual voters to bring out their unmarked ballots after they had placed a blank sheet of paper in the ballot box. The vote buyer then filled out the ballot paper, passed it to another artfully bribed dodger, who cast the marked ballot after receiving a fresh ballot paper, which was then brought outside for another round of bribery.

Despite such hiccups, the Australian ballot that was pioneered in Tasmania and Victoria helped put an end to many dirty tricks. Locals were justifiably proud of their invention. Welcomed by many as a 'brilliant success', as a means of increasing the power of voters and thus a remedy for 'caste, fashion, and fear of offending those above us in the social scale',[37] it boosted the growth of organised, machine-like parties dedicated to getting out the vote. It added to the gathering pressures to enfranchise women, to encourage them to indulge without fear an orderly indoor ritual now that drunken and violent contests in the open air were a thing of the past.[38] Not surprisingly, the new ballot system was soon adopted in other Australian colonies, beginning with South Australia, the only colony where an election was held to decide its own constitution. The Australian ballot was copied by Venezuela (1858), New Zealand (1870) and Britain (1872), from where it spread across the Atlantic to American cities and states, beginning with Louisville, Kentucky, and Massachusetts in 1888.

A Polynesian Republic

Let us pause to take stock of what so far had been achieved on the tiny European peninsula and its adjoining islands. By the middle of the nineteenth century there were signs everywhere in Europe that the ideals and institutions of representative democracy had an assured future. Much had happened that was of local and world significance, beginning with the invention and popularisation of dangerous catchwords like democrat and democratisation, and their contrast with aristocrat and aristocracy, which in some circles were now foul-smelling euphemisms. Thanks to the pioneering work of Spinoza and others, the language of democracy sounded much more positive, especially when fused with talk of representation, representative government and the distinctively European neologism, representative democracy. Halfway through the nineteenth century, representative democracy had become encased within territorial states and markets, both of them gifts of Europe to the world. Like a drum beating the tune of the future, revolutionary events in the Netherlands and France had sounded the entry of 'the people' on to the public stage; attempts were under way by workers to 'socialise' democracy by calling into question the fetish of money, private property and markets; even a Catholic pope had spoken in favour of representative democracy, whose most durable version, the Westminster model of government, had spawned remarkable inventions within its far-flung empire. It promoted the toleration of different languages, faiths and legal codes within virtually self-governing dependencies (as in Canada); the vigorous extension of the male franchise, and the application of a new system of secret voting called the Australian ballot. In New Zealand, despite strongly felt prejudices among Europeans that indigenous peoples were untrustworthy, ignorant and, like a flock of sheep, easily led astray by rogue politicians, adult Maori men, backed by London, secured universal suffrage in 1867 – a full dozen years before their white Pakeha colonisers.

It was the margins of the British Empire that produced arguably the most fundamental reform to come, a change that would affect a majority of the world's population: the extension of voting rights to all women living within a geographic territory defined by a government with laws.

The first breakthrough in women's suffrage happened as if by a miracle, in the oddest of places, in the southern Pacific Ocean, on a remote volcanic island positioned halfway between Chile and New Zealand. Named after the young midshipman who was the first European to spot its towering cliffs (in July 1767) aboard His Britannic Majesty's *Swallow*, captained by Philip Carteret, Pitcairn's (later Pitcairn Island) was separated from the human world by a string of archipelagos to the tropical north and the vast southern waters stretching to the ice floes of Antarctica. Carteret had been prevented from landing on the island by treacherous surf. His report reached Captain James Cook, the Englishman at the centre of the scramble by Europeans to make their mark on this part of the world. Cook searched for the little ocean jewel, but in vain.

The honour of European 'discovery' of the island was left to a dedicated band of mutineers. It is recorded that a French-style revolution against tyranny broke out in the mid-Pacific on board the armed English ship HMS *Bounty* during the night of 28 April 1789. Accused of 'tyrannical conduct, harsh and opprobrious language, ungovernable passion, and a worrying and harassing temper',[39] Lieutenant William Bligh and those loyal to him were thrown off the ship. The revolutionaries headed for Tahiti. There they fetched supporters and supplies, then sailed a circuitous route through the warm waters of the mid-Pacific, in search of a new home, at a safe distance from the clutches of the British navy.

Lieutenant Fletcher Christian, his eight mutineers and seven Tahitian men and twelve Tahitian women broke through the rough surf of subtropical Pitcairn on 23 January 1790. Amidst the abandoned ruins of a Polynesian settlement – they found stone adzes and gouges, cliff drawings depicting animals and humans, and roughly hewn stone gods guarding sacred sites and burial grounds – the rebels carved out a new life. The experiment had all the elements of the kind of utopia that exercised the imagination and energy of many people during the century to come. Countless Victorian sermons were to praise its virtues as well. Guided by the energies of Christian – the son of the coroner of Cumberland and a well-educated man of Isle of Man descent who had been to school with

William Wordsworth – the Pitcairners built an English-style village of wooden houses circled around the Edge, a small grassy platform that overlooked the bay where the *Bounty*, stripped of its contents, had been burned and sunk, to erase all traces of their ancestry. The settlers lived well, and were fruitful. Coconut, banana palms, mulberry and breadfruit trees were plentiful on the island of red soil. The community had brought with them chickens, pigs, sweet potatoes and yams, enough to support themselves and their offspring. Many children were born, and the population doubled in half a generation.

For the European men, it was a pleasurable experiment in the polygamous mixing of races, seemingly on their terms. There were reports of attempts by some Tahitian women to flee the island, even 'a conspiracy of the women to kill all the white men when asleep in their beds'[40] – and of revenge murders by both sexes. Thanks to the self-taught schoolmaster and pastor, a cockney orphan named 'Father' John Adams, Christian morals later prevailed, or so said many parsimonious Victorian parsons, whose sermons praised the use of the single Bible and Book of Common Prayer rescued from HMS *Bounty*. Perhaps, indeed, the Pitcairners were a Christian community. That would help to explain why, like their counterparts back home in Europe, they attended church on Sundays and said grace before each meal, but also bickered, persecuted each other and picked up guns. A criminal justice system administered by a bench of three elders was introduced (in 1829), but two years later things had so degenerated that the whole community, worried about dwindling resources and expanding numbers and split by conflicts fuelled by alcohol distilled from the native *ti* plant, opted for relocation back to Tahiti. But their roots were found to be rotten. Five months later, unimpressed by unChristian Tahiti, the nomads of the mid-Pacific returned to Pitcairn, tails tucked between their legs.

Contagious diseases and a strange 'inflammatory fever' contracted in Tahiti took their toll. Then came the biggest trauma: the experience of tyranny. In October 1832, a ship arrived carrying a megalomaniac named Joshua Hill, who claimed he had been sent by the new British government. London was at least twenty weeks away by clipper, and the islanders were tempted into respecting his wishes. Hill promptly appointed himself all-powerful Governor of the Commonwealth of Pitcairn. The consumption and distillation of liquor were banned;

'lousy foreigners' were expelled from the island. Labelled a *naysey* (the local *patois* for a bad-tempered person), and warned that he should stop putting on airs (*donner-wah-wh-har*), Hill retaliated by turning against everybody. Pie-eyed by his own powers, he forbade any contact between the islanders and visiting ships. Hill preached on Sundays with a loaded musket at the pulpit. He built a prison, introduced a treason law, conducted trials without witnesses and meted out floggings and arbitrary imprisonment for all misdeeds ... until the islanders, who discovered from a chance visitor that they had been duped, banished the tyrant from their midst, at the point of a musket.

The political woes of the Pitcairners were eased by the unexpected arrival, on 29 November 1838, of the sloop HMS *Fly* captained by Russell Elliott. Not much is known about Elliott and his political tastes, except that he proved to be a nineteenth-century Demonax, with a genuine appetite for representative democracy. A delegation drawn from the ninety-nine islanders explained to him their fierce desire to preserve their territorial independence against the growing numbers of vessels – sealers, whalers, East India Company merchant vessels, as well as armed ships of the Royal Navy – that now trawled the mid-Pacific seas. The delegates described the islanders' permanent fear of invasion. 'There having been cases of recent occurrence', reported Elliott, 'where half the ruffian crew of a whale ship were on shore for a fortnight, during which time, they offered every insult to the inhabitants, and threatened to violate any woman whose protectors they could overcome by force, occasioning the necessary concentration of the men's strength for the personal protection of the females, and thereby great damage to their crops, which demanded their constant attention; taunting them that they had no laws, no country, no authority that *they* were to respect.'[41] The delegation conveyed as well the painful business of past island rivalries, the rapes and murders, and their recent experience of tyranny.

The picture presented to Elliott resembled the state of nature famously sketched in Thomas Hobbes's *Leviathan* (1651). It was indeed an island riddled with deathly power struggles, but Elliott's recommendation stood at right angles to Hobbes's talk of the need for an all-powerful, sovereign Leviathan. It is known that Elliott held strong anti-slavery views. He had spent some years chasing ships carrying slaves on the high seas, and it is probable as well that he was in deep sympathy with the 1832 legislation extending the vote to middle-class men. Whether or not he had Chartist sympathies is unknown. Why exactly he recommended a fully democratic constitution remains unclear, but that is what he did.

On board the *Fly* he drafted and then witnessed the signing into law of what would later be impressively titled the *Codex Pitcairnensis*. Dated 30 November 1838, it was an odd document, in more ways than one. Constitutionally speaking, it was an acknowledgement by the islanders of their status as a British possession in which they were subjects of the Crown – and citizens of a fully self-governing republic! Acting without the authority of London, Elliott sanctioned their use of the Union Jack, to be flown as an ensign of British protection. Pitcairn Island thereby became a British colony, 'answerable . . . to Her Majesty's Government'.

At the same time, Elliott granted the islanders' wish for a written constitution. The new document – in contrast with its unwritten counterpart in the motherland – specified the fundamental rules of self-government. Free and fair elections for the post of Magistrate, in effect the president of the republic of the Pitcairn Islands, were to be held on 1 January of each year. The Magistrate, who had to be native-born and who was required to swear an oath before the assembly of citizens, was to govern through a council consisting of two represen-

FIGURE 88: The schoolhouse and parliament building, Pitcairn Island, 1850.

tatives, one appointed by the head of state and the other to be elected by a simple majority of the island's voters, who would assemble for the New Year's Day elections in the island's schoolhouse, which would double as their parliamentary assembly (Figure 88). Administering justice with the help of written-down laws, churchwardens appointed on a monthly basis, and juries of seven citizens, the Magistrate (according to section 1 of the constitution) was 'not to assume any power or authority on his [sic] own responsibility, or without the consent of the majority of the people'. Who then was entitled to vote? Perhaps reflecting their own vulnerability to fatal diseases transmitted by outsiders, or their ebullient sense of confidence in their offspring, who were compulsorily schooled from the age of six, *Codex Pitcairnensis* specified that the age of political maturity began either at fifteen (for those who were married by law) or eighteen (for those still single). Denizens who had resided on the island for five years would be granted the right of citizenship automatically. These criteria were rather unusual for the times, but the genuine originality of the constitution sprang from the third line of the preamble. It specified, in matter-of-fact prose, that elections for government office would be 'by the free votes of every native born on the island, male or female . . .'.

The enfranchised women of Pitcairn quickly fixed the gaze of outsiders (Figure 89). 'The female descendants of the Otaheite women

FIGURE 89: Pitcairn citizens, 1871.

are almost as muscular as the males, and taller than the generality of the sex', ran one contemporary report. It added that the new citizens were 'well-looking', that they wore flowers in their ears, and were literate.[42] Feeding upon the fascination and fantasies of others, the citizens of Pitcairn understood how special they were. They proudly explained their novel system of government to the outside world. At home, they invented rituals to celebrate their achievements. 'At twelve o'clock (noon) a number of musketeers assembled under the flagstaff, and fired a volley in honour of the day', reported a visitor to the island exactly sixty years to the day after the arrival of the first European settlers. 'After dinner males and females assembled in front of the church (where the British flag was flying), and gave three cheers for Queen Victoria, three for the Government at home, three for the Magistrate here, three for absent friends, three for the ladies, and three for the community in general, amid the firing of muskets and ringing of the bell. At sunset the gun of the *Bounty* was again fired, and the day closed in harmony and peace both towards God and man. It is voted that an annual celebration be observed.'[43]

Celebrations aside, the breakthrough on Pitcairn had limitations. No woman candidate for Magistrate stepped forward and the constitutional innovation produced no ripple effects elsewhere. In any event, the experiment in self-rule (or 'petticoat government', as detractors like Sir William Denison, Governor General of New South Wales, called it) ended unhappily. In 1896, evidently because a lenient sentence was given to a Pitcairn citizen after she threw her illegitimate baby into a well, the British authorities, at the behest of the Governor of New South Wales, ordered direct rule. The first experiment in enfranchising women was ruined.

Shrieks in Paradise

It is worth asking an obvious question: why did women win the vote so much earlier in places remote from the heartlands of modern European wealth and power? Was it because they somehow managed to convince men that they could bring a much-needed feminine touch to otherwise uncivil, rough-and-tumble frontier zones, where women's suffrage could cancel out the votes of working-class or non-white men? Was it because women were in short supply, and could therefore command their price with men who needed them to pitch in to work outside the household, for instance in agricultural labour? Or was the plain truth that men depended sexually upon women to bear children within sparsely populated frontier zones, territories in which the colonisers themselves were often outnumbered by aboriginal peoples?

Each of these factors undoubtedly played a role; the extent to which they did so very much depended on the context, and especially on the refusal of local women to bow down to men armed with misogynist prejudices. Common to each of the earliest electoral breakthroughs – Pitcairn Island (1838), Vélez (1853), Wyoming (1869), Utah (1870), the Pacific municipality of Franceville in the New Hebrides (1889), New Zealand and Rarotonga (1893) – was an unusually strong sense of mutual interdependence among men and women who thought of themselves as living on the edge of the world, within settler societies that were proud of their achievements but worried by their geographic isolation and capacity to survive the challenges of a testing environment. Solidarity fused with pride and anxiety, laced with a few strokes of luck, certainly played a vital role in the dissenting paradise of South Australia, whose white women fought successfully at the end of the nineteenth century to become the first in the world to win both the right to vote and to stand for election – with voting for aboriginal women and a generous postal-ballot package favourable to all women thrown in for good measure.

Their victory was nourished by a local spirit of Englishness that was especially strong among freethinking, God-fearing middle-class women, dubbed 'shrieks' by their opponents. The suffragists sprang from civil society. There were local intellectuals like Catherine Helen Spence, poet, novelist, penfriend and acquaintance of John Stuart Mill, a battler whose writings and public speeches spoke of free women devoted to democratic fairness, and who provoked a hostile local press by likening the Mediterranean climate of her home city on the coast of South Australia to ancient Athens. The suffragists had the backing as well of groups like the Women's Christian Temperance Union, formed in 1886, dedicated to fighting drunkenness. Like its predecessor, the Total Abstinence Society, it was staffed with energetic women who quickly built up a loose network of supporters grouped in local 'unions' and Methodist and other non-Conformist chapels. Through trial and error, these women learned to lobby clergy, politicians and prominent local figures, to convince them that family disruption and poverty were caused by insobriety – and that women, the bearers of good morals, needed the vote in order to sober up society.

Standing by their side was the Social Purity Society. Established in March 1883 and enrolling members of both sexes, it campaigned (as its constitution stated) 'with the object of shielding the purity of both sexes, raising the standard of morals, and abating the moral and physical evils resulting from various practices'.[44] Mincing no words, its members spoke of 'evil influences' and the need to combat them through 'the formation of sound public opinion' for the purpose of 'the restoration of the fallen'. From there it was only a short step to pledging itself to the cause of women's suffrage, which it did in June 1888, backed by activists of the fledgling United Labor Party, which specialised in highlighting the conditions of working women. 'Women of South Australia! Sisters! Wives! Mothers!' read one of its one-page campaign sheets. 'The extension of the suffrage to women has always been one of the principal planks of the Labor Platform, and in the teeth of bitter opposition . . . the Party and its adherents have secured the recognition of EQUALITY OF THE SEXES.'[45]

The only remaining little matter to be settled was whether the local parliament of men would be willing to share power by granting women the vote. The first sign that some of them might in fact do so came during the mid-winter session of the House of Assembly in 1885. The setting was simple but dignified: a red-brick and white-sandstone two-storey building with arched verandas, shuttered windows and a Dutch-style frontage. On the inside the Assembly had the feel of a non-Conformist chapel, with wooden-beamed high ceilings, large windows, fireplaces and gas-fired chandeliers. It was normally a place with a reputation for quiet dignity, though the afternoon session on Wednesday 22 July 1885 was an exception.

Amidst loud cheering from the floor, the honourable member for respectable North Adelaide, a consultant surgeon and university lecturer named Dr Edward Charles Stirling (1848–97), introduced a resolution. Stirling was a politician with a track record. He had been active in the successful campaign during the 1870s to admit women students to the University of Adelaide. For that he had earned the trust of many suffragists and, besides, he himself knew that it would be very short-sighted to make enemies of future constituents who showed growing determination to struggle for the vote, to the bitter end. Dressed in an elegant three-piece suit topped with a flowered lapel, Stirling stood up and faced the Speaker. His aim was to get the house to assent to the resolution, then to call upon the government of John Colton to draft, introduce and pass legislation in order to implement its bold terms. 'That in the opinion of this House', read Dr Stirling to a hushed floor, 'women, except while under couverture, who fulfil the conditions and possess the qualifications on which the parliamentary franchise for the Legislative Council is granted to men, shall, like them, be admitted to the franchise for both Houses of Parliament.'

With those words, there were more loud cheers from the floor; a faint buzz even descended from the crowded Strangers' Gallery crammed with shrieks warned by the serjeant-at-arms to bite their tongues. That was the beginning. The end was a long time coming. For want of the necessary support, lack of will and poor whipping of members – one of them was even in the bad habit of retiring to bed early, and so often missed crucial divisions on the floor – six legislative initiatives in the House of Assembly proved fruitless. Two similar efforts in the Legislative Council also came to naught. Nine years passed, during which time a new House of Assembly was built and opened for business, in June 1889.

The gathering social movement in support of women's suffrage stood united in its impatience. Petitions continued to pour in from throughout the colony: from far-flung towns with aboriginal names like Onkaparinga, Wallaroo, Gumeracha and Wooroora. At a public meeting held in Adelaide's Albert Hall, Catherine Spence put and defended a motion before supporters of the Women's Suffrage League, Women's Christian Temperance Union and the Women's Trades Union. 'That as no country can be called free where one half its people are disfranchised', read Spence, 'in the opinion of this meeting the time has arrived when the suffrage should be granted to the women of South Australia.'[46] The motion was carried unanimously. Elsewhere in the British colony, women speaking at public meetings reiterated the fundaments of the struggle. This was a battle about both means and ends. Women were pushing for votes for the sake of their dignity as women. This was a struggle against outmoded views of women's proper place in the fields of society and government. It was a fight for the education and improvement of women. Women were not just sexed animals. They were *gendered* beings. Women were neither 'naturally' nor 'conveniently' fitted for the privacy of the home. A woman's place was in the home *and* in society and politics. She was entitled to an equal share of the public realm, because only in that way could she ensure that her different concerns, about the birth and nurturing of children, or the rights and wrongs of prostitution, for instance, were impressed upon men. That implied that men, the wielders of dominance in matters 'public', would hereafter be encouraged to take an interest in matters 'private'. So votes for women were not simply a means of the empowerment of women. Votes for women implied a different – more civil and democratic – kind of society.

There were weaknesses in the suffragists' tactics and vision. How exactly women were to wrest social and economic power – especially jobs, income, wealth – from men remained less than clear, although champions of women's trade unions at least envisaged a pathway towards a world – they called it 'socialism' – where women were not just more equal with men, but all men and women were more equal. There was also the problem that the suffragists did not speak with one voice. Yet despite such weaknesses, there was still enough confident unity within the ranks of the suffragists to frighten many politicians. The wreckers in parliament dug in their heels, especially when confronted with the sixth and final version of the Adult Suffrage Bill 1893, which was introduced into the lower house during the first week of July. It provided for full adult suffrage, but tagged on a referendum clause designed to stop full suffrage dead in its tracks. Two questions were to be put to the adult male and female voters of the colony: 'Do you wish the franchise for the Legislative Council to be extended to women?' and 'Do you wish the franchise for the House of Assembly to be extended to women?' In order to succeed, the bill demanded that an absolute majority of *both* men and women would need to be secured.

The parliamentary politicking that transpired proved the truth of Virginia Woolf's well-known remark that the history of men's opposition to women's emancipation is more interesting than the story of that emancipation itself. The bill sparked bitter rows outside the parliament. *The Country* newspaper likened the shrieks to aboriginals and 'negroes': 'THE SUGGESTION THAT WOMEN ARE EQUAL TO MEN IS ABSURD', it ranted, in the next breath acknowledging one exception: 'Early ripening is a faculty they have in common with negroes. Up to twelve a nigger boy is probably ahead of a white boy; from twelve to fifteen, possibly equal; at fifteen he stops. But nobody would say that because a negro boy was ahead of a white boy at twelve that therefore he was equal, for after fifteen he is hopelessly behind.'[47] Tension continued to mount within the House, where skirmishes went on for three months. The bill went through a third reading, only to be killed by the final vote – Ayes 24, Noes 23 – that failed to produce an absolute majority. For the suffragists it was back to square one.

Then, on 4 July 1894 – the symbolism of the date was not lost on the politicians – the Attorney General, John Hannah Gordon, described as 'a consistent Liberal, with a tendency . . . towards the left',[48] introduced a new version of the Adult Suffrage Bill 1894 in the upper house. It had only two clauses. Women were to be granted the right to vote on equal terms with men for both houses, but (as in Wyoming) they were forbidden to sit in either house. Gordon was known for his superb oratory, and supporters of the bill thought its chances of passing were improved by that moderate second clause, which is why, in a wholly surprising move, a gentleman representative named Ebenezer Ward successfully moved an amendment. The clause that forbade women to stand for parliament was struck out. South Australia was to go beyond Wyoming and New Zealand, where the previous year women had been granted the right to vote, but not the right to stand for election.

It was a cunning move by Ward. The son of a Baptist minister, Ward had a reputation for political skill, but also bankruptcy, indolence and showmanship. He was certainly no friend of women. Many remembered how his former wife Matilda had bravely sued him in a nasty four-year divorce, charging cruelty and adultery; and more than a few of his colleagues spotted that the tactic he was using was wholly duplicitous. His aim was to scare the wavering men in his ranks, to frighten them off the petticoat trail. The whole point was to bury, once and for all, in a deep hole, efforts to legalise women's votes.

We have seen many times, in matters of democracy, that the power of unintended consequences is greater than the power of will and design. Through a comical sequence of events, Ebenezer Ward soon discovered the force of that rule, both inside and outside parliament. Outside, within the restless civil society, all sorts of militant but remarkably peaceful actions took place. On the day, 23 August 1894, that the Legislative Council read the Adult Suffrage Bill 1894 for the third time, then gave it final approval and passed it on for consideration by the lower house, a sense that an era was ending began to grip the politicians. Business was leavened by the arrival, on the steps of parliament, of a monster petition wrapped in a golden bow – the colour of the local suffragists. Comprising grey paper sheets neatly stuck together with adhesive to form a roll that was 400 feet long, it contained the names of 11,600 prominent individuals (and some organisations) who supported the Women's Suffrage League campaign for the right of women to vote and to stand for office, on equal terms with men (Figure 90).

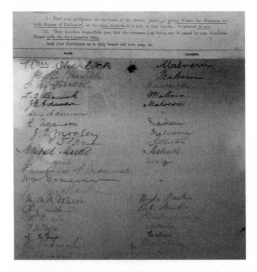

FIGURE 90: A page from the 400-feet-long petition for the full enfranchisement of women, South Australia, 1894. The first two signatories are the author's great-grandfather and great-grandmother, who is pictured opposite (Figure 91) with the author's grandfather, in the year she voted for the first time.

FIGURE 91: A shriek in paradise: Matilda Hooper Charlick (1853–1929).

The giant petition was later that day passed to the House of Assembly.[49] For sixteen weeks the chamber debated the bill's clauses with great intensity. Punctuated by the arrival of no fewer than eight other public petitions against women's suffrage, all the arguments pro and con were rehearsed. The men who thought everything was on the line tried every trick in the book. The general rule was that those who had least to say took the longest time to say it. Fatigue fluttered over the members. At one point, a wavering Honourable James Howe tried to slip off to bed. He was tracked down and brought back into the chamber, whose division bells were rung, doors locked and a vote on the second reading then held – and quite narrowly won. By Monday 17 December 1894, the day earmarked for the bill's final reading, the suffragists scented victory. Ladies poured into the Strangers' Gallery. But towards midnight, a bitter battle broke out over a proposed amendment to give to women the entitlement to a postal ballot. Like exhausted wrestlers, the politicians grew delirious. Well after midnight, debate was adjourned.

The Speaker (Sir Jenkin Coles) took the chair at 10.30 next morning. Wrangling resumed instantly. At least one honourable member, contemptuous of the bill, was accused of being a good reason for why women's suffrage was necessary. Another was charged with stonewalling business in order to let supporters of the bill straggle into the house. The principal objections and counter-objections to the bill were once again raised – for the last time, it turned out. If women could vote, said one gentleman, then there would be no end to domestic quarrels, even the destruction of the sanctity of the home, courtesy of easy divorce and free love. The household of Queen Victoria, who wielded the vote over an empire, had proved otherwise, came the reply. The great body of women are politically ignorant, are they not? asked another. The answer: thanks to the spread of education, women are realising that men are not their superiors, and that their exercise of political rights would awaken a strong sense of political duties. The suffragists – the 'trousers-wearing section' – at least one honourable member dared say on behalf of others, are mainly 'disappointed, childless creatures who have missed their maternal vocation; ill-favored ones, who will never get an opportunity of exercising it . . . the bitter-hearted . . . the cranks and fadmongers; the followers of the teetotal parsons . . .'. They were presumptuous do-gooders 'who fish for the souls of the soiled in the back alleys of the slums'. Came the reply: this is upside-down nonsense, if only because for thousands of years women have been treated like serfs, which is why today it is still supposed that they are fit mainly for cooking their husband's food, bearing his children, washing his clothes, mending his socks. Then came disconnected bits of rough rhetoric, hurled around in the chamber like knives in a kitchen. What kind of world is it where a son has more rights than his mother, from whom perchance he has inherited his best qualities? someone asked. Others chipped in. What good would come from the cry of 'no taxation without representation!'? Should we really contemplate the consignment of marriage and the family to a mere memory from the Palaeozoic era? (This question bred cries of 'Hear, hear'.) Shouldn't women be granted their full political rights so as to protect us from war and its effects? Another asked: why should the cause of 'democratic innovation' be stifled, especially at the hands of men who were cast-iron reactionaries, pampered and stroked by 'their feminine clients'? Then there was the cocktail of envy and xenophobia that whetted the lips of a member who asked: are 'our women more incapable of exercising the franchise' than 'the negrowomen of Wyoming'?

Over an hour later, a division was called. The ladies in the gallery hushed as the results were read out. Ayes, 31 . . . Noes, 14. It was a decisive statutory majority of 17 for the Ayes.[50] In London, six weeks later, Queen Victoria gave Royal Assent to the bill. A registration drive began and on Saturday, 25 April 1896 women voted for the first time in the general elections for the House of Assembly. 'That the children of franchise were out on the warpath on Saturday was plain enough', reported a male writer for Adelaide's *Observer*. 'Carriages, cabs, carts, trolleys, lorries, and drays were rushing in all directions as fast as the devoted horses, wondering what it was all about – as it was not a race day – could put their legs to the ground, carrying voters male and female to the polling places . . . Women were everywhere, and their presence in the streets, and leavening the lumps of humanity in the crowded polling places, no doubt had a refining influence . . .'

The *Observer* noted the 'level-headedness and self-possession' of South Australia's new voters, as well as the 'intense excitement' and fun of it all. At the Adelaide Town Hall, makeshift voting booths were made from wooden doors set in a three-sided fashion, with a calico curtain in front. The structure caused some confusion to the newcomers. 'One woman remained there so long recording her vote that the Deputy Returning Officer had to go and ask what was the matter. She turned round and said indignantly, "I have been knocking at the door here ever so long and can't make any one answer."' The new citizen thought the door at the back would be opened, and that someone would fetch her voting paper. Some of the good ladies persisted in going into the same box in pairs, and were surprised on being told that in the age of the Australian ballot it was not the correct thing. 'One old lady who was purblind came with a companion to coach her. Another was heard to say, "Me husband told me to plump for Paddy Glynn. Which is his box?" evidently thinking that each candidate had a voting crib for his [sic] own use. A very candid elector with a sense of humour said he [sic] had "two butchers [beers]" at one candidate's expense and voted for the other. One lady said she liked a certain candidate, his manly speech, his sensible sentiments, but she could not vote for a man who parted his hair in the middle.'[51] After all the poppycock she and other women had been put through, she had a point.

Back at Westminster . . .

The British experiments in responsible government and democratic innovation highlighted the strange point that empires were sometimes capable of planting the seeds of representative democracy. Equally strange was the fact that the seedlings were sometimes brought back by clipper and transplanted to the soil of Britain, occasionally with breathtaking effect.

The life of the South Australian suffragist Muriel Matters (1877–1969) symbolised this boomerang effect. She is one of those unsung heroines whose modest works later helped make possible in Britain what taunting crowds and sneering police and politicians had once dismissed as utterly utopian: women's right to choose, and to reprimand, those who govern them. Muriel Matters (Figure 92)

FIGURE 92: Muriel Matters in prison dress, Holloway women's gaol, London, 1908, photographer unknown.

was born and raised in Adelaide, where she studied music at university and became an actress and elocutionist. She later noted that her interest in women's suffrage had been stimulated, at the age of fourteen, by reading Ibsen's play *A Doll's House* (1879), which was soon staged in Melbourne, at the same time as in London (where it was initially banned) and five years before its premiere in Paris. But Matters always said that her views had been shaped as well by the path-breaking legislation that had granted all women – including aboriginal women – in South Australia the vote and the right to stand in 1894. So it is not surprising that when she set off for England, sometime during the southern autumn of 1905, intent on furthering her musical career, things turned out quite differently.

Settling in London, she became acquainted with its leading social reformers, including the infamous anarchist Prince Kropotkin. Matters soon afterwards joined the Women's Freedom League, for whom her earliest and most daring act was to padlock herself to a metal grille in the Public Gallery of the House of Commons, hiding the key well inside her knickers. She then began to interrupt proceedings by delivering a speech, the first in that parliament by a woman. Female courage finally prevailed, helped by male double standards. Too embarrassed to snatch back the key, officers were forced to remove the metal grille. Matters was dragged away, in triumph, the 'vile grille' trailing behind her, attached to her body by a 'burglar proof chain', which later had to be filed off by a blacksmith. She was then ejected from the building – her arrest inside would have required her trial at the Bar of the House – and promptly charged with disorderly conduct, and later imprisoned.

Upon release, the wild colonial girl spent several years travelling throughout England, living in a caravan, delivering speeches and campaigning for such reforms as free kindergartens, children's courts, equal pay for equal work, and for women's right to vote. 'We did what we did', she reminisced, 'because we had to attract attention some way.'[52] So in mid-February 1909, on the opening day of parliament, she proved that flying machines could be more than weapons of war, that they could join the fight for representative democracy. Aiming to lift campaign morale, Matters hired a piloted Zeppelin airship daubed with the words 'Votes for Women'

FIGURE 93: Muriel Matters' Zeppelin, from the *Daily Mirror* (London), 17 February 1909.

(Figure 93). As she ditched pounds and pounds of suffragist leaflets on to the residents of Westminster, Women's Freedom League activists on the ground below were arrested, but not before attempting to interview ministers in Downing Street, and at the House of Commons.

These were daring acts, and, although women had still to wait two decades for their political rights, they helped consolidate the appeal of the system of government that came to be called the Westminster model. It was indeed parliamentary government with a difference. Under popular pressure from below, the system that crystallised during the nineteenth century – some named it the Mother of Parliaments – was not only exported to many different countries and settings, both inside and outside the Commonwealth. It also enjoyed a high reputation within Europe itself. In the Westminster system, parliament was composed of three different units: the Crown, the House of Lords and the House of Commons (also known as the Lower House). There was a dual executive. There was the ceremonial executive, the Crown, which possessed some constitutional 'reserved' powers as well as performed symbolic functions;

and a political executive, a head of government called the Prime Minister, who performed the basic governing functions, helped by members of a cabinet of ministers drawn from parliament.

The Westminster model was based on several other important principles: those of shared power, responsible government, representation and parliamentary sovereignty. *Shared power* meant that the elected legislative assembly was not the only parliamentary actor. The Crown and the House of Lords were also part of parliament and the approval of all three actors was deemed necessary for the final approval of legislation. That was the meaning of the phrase *responsible government*, which referred throughout the nineteenth century to a system in which there was a fusion of political power rather than the separation of powers that accompanied presidential systems of the Spanish American or United States types. Responsible government signified the presence of the executive within an elected legislative assembly and the power of that assembly to remove, or to confirm, the political executive (but not the monarch) in their position. A formal legislative vote that expressed a lack of confidence in the political executive was supposed to remove them from their position, or trigger a new election. That followed from the point that the executive was collectively responsible for the activities of government.

Under the Westminster model, the authority to remove a government from office or call a new election rested with the Crown, which reserved for itself a limited number of 'prerogative' powers. In practice, the Crown acted more and more on the basis of what transpired in the House of Commons. That was in accordance with the other key Westminster principles: representative government and parliamentary sovereignty. *Representative government* in nineteenth-century Britain was based on the notion that those who served in government held office as a result of elections. Voters organised through political parties chose people to represent them in the parliament. Throughout the century, controversy simmered over what representation meant. Most accepted that the word 'represent' meant to make present something that, in fact, was not present. Representatives enabled an indirect voter presence in the legislative process, in three ways: as a delegate, in which representatives voted for the views of (a majority of) their constituents, regardless of their personal views; as a trustee who took the position that he (it was always men until 1928) had been elected to exercise his best judgement, based on his perceptions of what was most appropriate; or as a party representative, who voted as a loyal member of a particular party.

In practice, a hotchpotch of all three understandings of representative government fed both the Westminster model and the doctrine of *parliamentary sovereignty* on which it ultimately rested. According to this unwritten but widely repeated doctrine, the powers of parliament within a unitary state were unlimited. Walter Bagehot, author of what came to be a classic nineteenth-century study of the unwritten British constitution, expressed the theory succinctly. Since the constitution is unwritten and the state is unitary, parliament is the sovereign body, he noted. It could make and unmake laws, change the form of government; if it so chose, it could interfere with the course of justice, even snuff out the most sacred rights of citizens. If it chose (say) to withdraw the right to vote from all men with red hair then in principle it would be quite within its rights; no separate 'constitutional court' could stop it in its tracks. Bagehot went on to indicate that in practice parliamentary sovereignty had become concentrated in the Commons. Democracy had begun to make its mark. 'The ultimate authority', he observed, 'is a newly-elected House of Commons. No matter whether the question upon which it decides be administrative or legislative; no matter whether it concerns high matters of the essential constitution or small matters of daily detail; no matter whether it be a question of making a war or continuing a war; no matter whether it be the imposing a tax or the issuing a paper currency; no matter whether it be a question relating to India, or Ireland, or London . . . a new House of Commons can despotically and finally resolve.'[53]

The Century of Reforms

The House of Commons was to spearhead important reforms throughout the nineteenth century. It was as if the Westminster model vaccinated itself against the French disease, to stop its spread through the British Isles, by administering a dose of its poison to its own body politic. The slow but steady democratisation of power, in the spheres of both government and civil society, has sometimes been described in terms of the cumulative growth of citizenship entitlements, beginning with *civil* rights, like habeas corpus, the private ownership of property, and liberty of the press, then extending to *political* rights, particularly the entitlement to vote and to serve on juries, through to *social* rights, guaranteed by such social policies as unemployment insurance, compulsory education and child endowment.[54] The description is a bit too simple, if only because it understates the bitter conflicts, setbacks and repressive policies – like the treatment of the poor as criminals destined to become inmates of the dreaded 'Poor Law Bastilles' – that were part of the gains for citizenship. It nevertheless captures the long sequence of path-breaking reforms and legislative initiatives that was to mark off Britain in the nineteenth century as *the* model parliamentary proto-democracy in Europe.

The century was to see reforms that had the effect of dramatically widening the opportunities to elect political representatives. The repeal of the Test and Corporation Acts (1828) removed the political disabilities imposed on non-Anglican Protestants in the seventeenth century, so that Dissenters could hereafter sit in parliament and participate in local government. Despite huge opposition, new parliamentary legislation entitled Catholics to sit as Members of Parliament (1829). The Reform Act (1832), which brought Britain to the verge of revolution and took two years to reach the statute books, extended the franchise to those who did not own landed property. Municipal governments were made more answerable to electors (1835); slavery was finally abolished and slaves and apprentices set free throughout the British colonies (1839); and (a demand of the Chartists) the property qualification for MPs was abolished (1858).

The long struggle by Jews to take their seats in parliament, triggered in 1847 by London MP Lionel Nathan de Rothschild, who refused to take the oath which included the phrase 'on the true faith of a Christian', was finally won after eleven attempts in the House of Lords to have the oath changed. Examinations (instead of connections with the 'right' people) for entrance into the civil service (except the Foreign Office) were introduced (1871). Despite strong opposition from landlords and employers, the 'Australian', or secret, ballot was introduced at all elections (1872). The vote was extended to urban working men (1867) and then to most adult males (1884). All boroughs with fewer than 15,000 inhabitants lost their MP; those with fewer than 50,000 inhabitants lost one MP; constituencies were reorganised so that (out of a total of 670) there were 647 single-member constituencies (1885). Local government was reorganised: the old local government boards (around 27,000 of them) were replaced by elected County Councils equipped with extensive powers that covered such matters as policing, bridge-building and road maintenance. When it was found that many of these new bodies were too cumbersome to cope with the rising demands on their services, they were replaced by smaller, elected District and Parish Councils, for which unmarried women were entitled to vote (1888), then to stand as candidates and to become elected councillors themselves (1894).

Various reforms, meanwhile, were introduced to widen partici-pation within the actually existing civil society, and to reduce or eliminate at least some of its many incivilities. Social democratic pressures – what Tocqueville had called a 'great democratic revo-lution' – began to pinch their way into the once-hallowed privacy of the market. The Hobhouse Factory Act (1831) prohibited night work for workers under the age of twenty-one; and it became ille-gal to employ boys and girls under the age of ten in mines (1842). The 1842 Railway Act, the first piece of railway legislation, was designed to improve safety for passengers and employees; follow-up legislation (1844) required railway companies to provide a minimum service of one train each way per day, stopping at every station, charging no more than a penny a mile for third-class passengers and travelling at the breakneck speed of not less than 12 miles per hour. To prevent what the law described as 'reckless speculation', companies were compulsorily registered and required to issue prospectuses and publish their accounts regularly (1844). The Church of England lost its monopoly over marriage services and non-Anglicans won the civil right to marry either in their own church or in registry offices (1836).

Following the Public Health Act of 1848, Boards of Health were set up – compulsorily in towns where either more than 10 per cent of the population petitioned for one, or where the death rate exceeded 23 per 1000 population. Local authorities were later made responsible for the prevention of 'overcrowding' and the provision of sewers, street cleaning and water (1866). Stamp duties on newspapers were reduced, and then abolished (in 1855), along with excise duties on paper (1861), thus ending the 'war of the unstamped' against government efforts to remove unstamped newspapers off the streets. Divorce courts were established (1857), and although women were granted limited access to divorce they were able to repossess their property (if they had any) after a legal separation, or upon the granting of a protection order following the husband's desertion. They were later (1882) deemed separate owners and administrators of their property after marriage. Trade unions were recognised as legal bodies endowed with rights to own property and monetary funds (1871), and to engage in peaceful picketing without being charged with conspiracy (1875). In cases of breach of contract, workers, who were subject previously to criminal law, together with their employers, were placed on an equal legal footing, as subject to civil offence proceedings (1875). All workshops and factories employing more than fifty workers were subject to regular visits by government inspectors (1878). And in the so-called 'dangerous trades', employers were obliged by law (1897) to compensate workers who were injured, or the dependants of workmen who were killed at work.

Nations and Nationalism

The combined effect of these many changes was to enhance the reputation of the Westminster model of parliamentary government for its openness, flexibility, fair-mindedness and respect for the laws. Those who swore by this reputation were exaggerating, of course. Westminster was not the 'Mother of Parliaments' (that honour belongs to the *cortes* of León); other countries (such as Finland, 1907, Norway, 1913, and the United States, 1920) arrived earlier at full parliamentary democracy; and despite the kick up the backside they received in the American colonies, British champions of the Westminster model had a bad habit of ruling as if the so-called white man's burden justified pomp, cruelty, murder and discrimination against peoples in crown colonies otherwise as different as India, Rhodesia and Nigeria.[55] But still it is true that by the end of the nineteenth century, depending on how and with whom it was compared, Britain was for many other Europeans a shining model of how representative government founded on a civil society was to be nurtured. The trouble was that sinister European forces – easily the most dangerous was nationalism – were about to block the way. Europe was about to be turned into the graveyard of representative democracy.

The beginning of wisdom about the failures of representative democracy is to see that Europe was the place where a clutch of questions unknown to assembly democrats was first asked. What is a nation? Do nations have a right to self-determination? If so, is the national identity of citizens best guaranteed by a system of representative democracy, in which power is subject to open disputation and to the consent of the governed living within a carefully defined territory? And what of nationalism? Does it differ from national identity? Is it compatible with democracy?

Such questions, and the answers they prompted, were first detectable during the ninth century CE, with the end of the Carolingian Empire that covered half of Europe. Following the death of Emperor Charles III the Fat in 888 CE, a new sense of collective identity, national awareness, began slowly to emerge as a powerful force throughout the European region. It was first championed by sections of the nobility and the clergy, who used derivatives of the old Latin term *natio* – one that had formerly been used to describe people who travelled beyond their homelands, to reside and study – to highlight their sharing of a common language and common historical experiences. The 'nation' did not refer to the whole population of a region, but only to those classes that had developed a sense of identity based upon language and history, and had begun to act upon it. Nations in this sense were seen as distinctive products of their own peculiar histories.

From the fifteenth century onwards, the term 'nation' was employed increasingly for political purposes. According to the classic definition of the eighteenth-century French writer Denis Diderot, a nation is 'a great number of people who dwell within a certain territory which is confined by borders, and who obey the same government'.[56] Here 'nation' described a people who shared certain common laws and political institutions of a given territory; a nation was a people who had a state in their hands. This political conception of 'the nation', understood to include citizens who were entitled to participate in politics, and to share in the exercise of sovereignty, had fundamental implications for the process of building states. As struggles to control state power began to take the form of organised confrontations, often in parliaments, between monarchs and the privileged classes, some of these classes began to describe themselves as advocates of 'the nation', in the political sense of the term. They insisted, in opposition to their monarch, that they were the representatives and defenders of 'national liberties' and 'national rights'. If the sovereign monarch came from a different nation – as in the Low Countries during the war against Habsburg Spain – then such claims were sharpened by another factor: the struggle for liberties was transformed into a movement for national emancipation from what was called foreign tyranny.

During the eighteenth century something even more dramatic happened to talk of 'the nation'. It underwent a democratisation. The struggle for national identity was broadened and deepened to include the less privileged and commoners. Self-educated middle classes, artisans, rural and urban labourers, and other social groups began to demand inclusion in 'the nation', and this necessarily had anti-aristocratic and anti-monarchic implications. From now on, in principle, the nation included everybody, not just the privileged classes; 'the people' and 'the nation' were supposed to be identical. The rumpus sparked by Tom Paine's *Rights of Man*, the most influential European attempt to 'democratise' the language of national identity during this period, well illustrated this trend. *Rights of Man* sparked bitter public rows about the merits of monarchies and republics. Its insistence that each nation was entitled to its own system of representative government drew attention to the explosive links between national identity and representative democracy. 'What is government more than the management of the affairs of a nation?', he asked. 'It is not', answered Paine. 'Sovereignty as a matter of right, appertains to the nation only, and not to any individual; and a nation has at all times an inherent indefeasible right to abolish any form of government it finds inconvenient, and establish such as accords with its interest, disposition, and happiness.'[57]

That kind of insistence that people had a basic right of national self-determination subsequently enjoyed a long life. Nineteenth-century Europe saw the emergence of two great powers (Germany and Italy) based on the principle of national self-determination, and the effective partition of a third (Austria-Hungary after the Compromise of 1867) on identical grounds. The same principle was at work in the two revolts of the Poles in support of their reconstitution as a nation-state, and in the formal recognition of a chain of lesser independent states claiming to represent their sovereign nations, from Luxembourg and Belgium in the west to the Ottoman successor states in south-eastern Europe (Bulgaria, Serbia, Greece, Romania). During the twentieth century, especially after World War One, the principle of national self-determination enjoyed great popularity among international lawyers, political philosophers, governments and their opponents, all of whom supposed that if the individual members of a nation so willed it, they were entitled to freedom from domination by other nations, and could therefore legitimately establish a sovereign state covering the territory in which they lived, and where they constituted a majority of the population. From this angle, the democratic principle that citizens should govern themselves was identified with the principle that nations should determine their own destiny. This in turn produced within more than a few European languages a convergence of meaning of the terms 'state' and 'nation'. The terms came to be used interchangeably, as in such official expressions as the 'law of nations' or 'nation-state', and in the commonplace usage of the term 'national' to designate anything run or regulated by the state, such as national service, national health insurance or national debt.

It followed from this way of thinking that a shared sense of national identity, in Hungary and Russia no less than in Germany or Ireland or Spain, was a basic precondition of cultivating representative democracy. But what did national identity mean? some asked. The usual answer was that it was a particular form of collective identity in which, despite their routine lack of physical contact, people felt themselves bound together because they spoke the same language or a dialect of a common language; inhabited or were closely familiar with a defined territory, so that they experienced its flora and fauna, its mountains and plains with affection; and because they shared a variety of customs, including memories of the historical past, which was consequently experienced in the present tense as pride in the nation's achievements, or a sense of shame about the nation's past and present failings.

National identity so defined was a specifically modern European invention. It proved to be a powerful force. It was able to infuse citizens with a sense of purpose, with a measure of confidence and dignity, with a feeling of being 'at home'. By giving them the ability to make sense of everyday life, to share with others a common-sense understanding of everything ranging from food and songs and jokes to the looks on others' faces, national identity equipped members of a nation with a sense of belonging, a sense of security in themselves, and in each other, as equals. National identity had a definite democratic feel about it. To be a member of a nation was to be entitled to self-government. It also enabled people to say 'we' and 'you' without feeling that their 'I', their sense of self, was slipping through their fingers.

So how well did Europeans handle this new talk of nations and national self-determination? When the winds of national feeling blew, did the people, like a beautiful bird, grow wings and fly their way to the land of representative democracy, blessed by territorial independence? Unfortunately, they did not. Here much can be learned from the French Revolution, which was a fundamental tipping point because it revealed the potentially murderous implications of the democratic-sounding doctrine of national self-determination. The Revolution destroyed faith in the divine and unchallengeable right of monarchs to govern. It sparked a struggle against the privileged classes in the name of a sovereign and 'democratic' nation of free and equal citizens. The trouble was that those who acted in the name of the sovereign nation grew tempted to emphasise the importance of citizens' faithfulness to *la patrie*, to their state, itself the guarantor of the nation, itself said to be 'one and indivisible'. At the beginning of the Revolution, the motto of the crumbling *ancien régime*, 'Un roi, une foi, une loi' ('One king, one faith, one law') was replaced by 'La Nation, la loi, le roi' ('The Nation, the law, the king'). The Nation was supposed to make the laws that the king was responsible for implementing. But when the monarchy was abolished in August 1792, the Nation – also known as 'the people' – suddenly became the titular source of sovereignty. 'Vive la Nation!' cried French soldiers one month later at Valmy, as they flung themselves into battle against the Prussian army. Everything that had once been royalist had suddenly become national. The Nation even had its own emblem, the tricoloured national flag, which replaced the white flag of the House of Bourbon. The new spirit of nationalism had surfaced. The struggle for national identity had turned fundamentalist, bringing with it a lust for the power and glory of the nation-state. The first nationalist dictatorship of the era of representative democracy was born.

The formation of rough-handed states oiled by nationalist appeals to the nation was Europe's Greek gift to itself, and to the rest of the world. So, too, was the experience, especially common among the peoples of central-eastern Europe, of the misery that came from statelessness and bossing and bullying at the hands of more powerful nationalists. Nationalism and statelessness proved that the doctrine of national self-determination was a cuckoo in the nest of representative democracy. They flung that doctrine into a smouldering crisis, for they revealed that single-minded believers in a nation are always at risk of being seduced by the language and power fantasies of nationalism. Nationalism was a hungry scavenger. It fed upon the pre-existing sense of nationhood within a given territory, transforming that shared national identity into a bizarre parody of its former self. Nationalism was a monomaniacal, pathological form of national identity. Impatient with peoples' different and often conflicting sense of their own national identity, nationalism squeezed nations into Nations. That was why, as Albert Camus remarked, some Europeans decided that they loved their nations too much to be nationalists.

The history of Europe during the nineteenth and twentieth centuries shows that nationalism had a fanatical core. In contrast to national identity, whose boundaries were never fixed and whose tolerance of difference and openness to other forms of life was therefore qualitatively greater, nationalism required its adherents to believe in themselves, and to believe in the belief itself, to believe that they were not alone, that they were members of a community of believers known as the Nation, through which they could achieve great things. Nationalism required both its believers and their leader-representatives (as the French scholar Ernest Renan put it in a lecture at the Sorbonne in 1882 called *Qu'est-ce qu'une nation?*) to participate in a continuous referendum, 'un plebiscite de tous les jours'. The level of ideological commitment required by nationalism helps explain why it was driven by a bovine will to simplify things, by the kind of instruction issued by Bismarck: 'Germans! Think with your blood!'

Things could be put this way: if representative democracy was ideally a continuous struggle against compulsory simplification of the world, then nationalism was a continuous struggle to undo complexity, the desire not to know certain matters; it was a chosen ignorance, not the ignorance of innocence. It always had a tendency to crash into the world, crushing or throttling everything that crossed its path, to defend or to claim territory, to think of land as power and its rightful inhabitants as a single fist prepared to defend themselves against 'foreigners' and 'enemies'. Nationalism had nothing of the humility of national identity. It felt no shame about the past or the present, for it supposed that guilt only belonged to foreigners and 'enemies of the nation'. Nationalism revelled in macho glory, and it therefore tried to fill the heads of young and old alike with stories of noble ancestors, heroism and bravery in defeat. It felt itself invincible, waved the flag and, if necessary, eagerly bloodied its hands on its opponents.

At the heart of nationalism – this was among the most peculiar and deeply anti-democratic features of its 'grammar' – was its simultaneous treatment of others as the Other who is everything and nothing at the same time. Nationalism was tossed constantly between the horns of fear and arrogance. Whether in the Balkans or in Scandinavia, in Russia or in Britain, nationalists warned constantly of the menace posed by aliens to their own precious way of life. The Other was the knife in the throat of the Nation, a permanent danger to its society, or its state and constitution. Always panicky, permanently driven by friend–foe calculations, nationalists suffered the haunting conviction that all nations were caught up in an animal struggle for survival, in which only the fittest animals survive. Yet nationalism had another face. It was not merely fearful of the Other, but strangely arrogant, portraying people treated as the Other as inferior rubbish, as a worthless zero. The Other was disliked and despised, seen as unworthy of respect or recognition because of its smelly breath, strange food, unhygienic habits, weird religion, or its babbling and incomprehensible language. People who were Other proved by their habits that they did not belong. It followed that they had few if any entitlements, not even when they formed a majority of the population resident in any given territory. From the point of view of nationalists, wherever a member of their Nation was, there was the Nation. Hence the temptation to taunt and spit at the Other, to label them as shit, to discriminate against them, to prohibit the public use of their minority languages, or even, in the extreme case, to press for their expulsion, so that a more homogeneous Nation could get on with the job of governing itself.

It was true, as Vladimir Ilyich Lenin (1870–1924) liked to say, that in the European region the nationalism of a conquering nation was not the same as the nationalism of those whom they conquered, and that conquering nationalism always seemed uglier, hence more culpable. It was true as well that nationalism could be more or less militant in its desire for self-determination and territory, and that there were many bees in its bonnet, ranging from attachment to a language or a religion to the active commitment to building states and altering territorial boundaries, through acts of war. But when all was said and done, nationalism, with its single-minded arrogance, was a permanent threat to representative democracy – as was spotted by the famous Irish historian William Lecky (1838–1903). A few years before the end of the nineteenth century, he noted with alarm how the spirit of nationalism was fuelling a 'great growth of militarism'. The democratic struggles for the universal franchise and national self-protection had begun to link arms with universal military service. 'Universal service tends strongly to weld nations together, to strengthen the patriotic feeling, to form a high standard of civic duty and of self-sacrificing courage, to inspire the masses of the population with the kind and the intensity of enthusiasm that is most conducive to the greatness of nations.' But welding nations together meant strengthening the power of states and armies, which clashed head-on with the principles and practice of representative democracy. The latter supposed that 'all ideas of authority and subordination are discarded'. It was a system 'in which the skilful talker or demagogue naturally rules, in which every question is decided by the votes of a majority'. By contrast, universal military service required 'the strictest despotism and subordination ... passive obedience without discussion or remonstrance'.[58]

Something had to give, and proof that it did came during and after World War One, with the brazen herding and murdering of peoples – all in the name of the pseudo-democratic doctrine of self-determination. In 1915, on the southern fringes of Europe, huge numbers of Armenians were hunted from Turkey; and after the crushing defeat of the Greek army by the Turks, in Anatolia in 1922, Greece expelled some 400,000 Turks, just as the Turks were expelling perhaps 1.5 million destitute and panic-stricken Greeks from the lands of Asia Minor, where they had lived with others since the time of Homer. Though few people at the time realised that all this was the beginning of a new and more dangerous herding and murdering of peoples, something was now finally clear: nationalism was the language of uncompromising struggle, the obsession with the purity of Nations, murderous, the muscled hand willing to grab territory and build or keep or 'cleanse' states, if need be through organised murder and war.

Total War

On the rocky road that wound towards World War One, the Westminster model of parliamentary government managed, by using hook and crook, to shield itself against much of the nasty business of nationalist bickering and imperial power rivalry that racked continental Europe from the time of the French Revolution. The British state was itself formed of a compromise among nations, and by dint of running an empire that straddled the globe it could afford, especially after its military defeat of Napoleonic France in 1815, to stay away from major involvements in violent European struggles for territorial expansion and national self-determination. That did not, of course, make Westminster-style parliamentary government immune from other dangers, including a new kind of violence and frightful destruction that dropped from the air – as the residents of Folkestone, a small coastal town in southern England, were among the first to find out.

A warm, sunny Friday afternoon, 25 May 1917, was the day when the Westminster way of life was to taste a new threat to parliamentary democracy, one that was unknown to the nineteenth-century imagination. Without warning, throngs of Folkestone shoppers readying for the Whitsun weekend were startled by the crack and thunder of explosions. According to on-the-spot reports, children were the first to scream. Fires exploded from shattered buildings. Streets instantly iced with finely shattered glass. Horses dropped dead between their carriage shafts. A queue crumpled before a greengrocer's shop. A wine merchant returned to his shop to find a decapitated customer. 'Zepps! Zepps!' a lone pedestrian had shouted, mistakenly supposing that Zeppelins had just dropped yet more high-explosive bombs on innocent English civilians. Two minutes later, their work completed, a dozen silver Gotha biplanes pulled away, glinting in the vast blue sky, heading home from southern England to Germany. Ninety-five people were left dead, 195 injured. And so the citizens of Folkestone had their first taste of strategic civilian bombardment – victims of one of the first Guernicas of the twentieth century.

The mechanised power relationship between the bomber and the bombed – masked raiders, like Jove, hurling thunderbolts from the sky at their hapless victims below – symbolised the new challenge of war to democracy in much of Europe during the following two decades. Nineteen days after the Folkestone assault, a squadron of Gothas dropped almost 10,000 pounds of bombs on London. This time, 432 people were injured and 162 killed, including sixteen children whose bodies were torn apart as they huddled in the basement of their nursery school. Londoners found themselves virtually defenceless, but military commanders and politicians, blind to the historical significance of the new weapons of war, saw no great need for alarm. The Earl of Derby, the War Minister, told the House of Lords that since not a single soldier had been killed, the bombing was without military significance.

The new killing machines of the Great War, strategic bombers, machine guns, big guns, tanks, mortars that fired deadly gas, some of it smelling like fresh-mown hay, were to prove the minister mistaken. 'The War had become undisguisedly mechanical and inhuman', noted a fictional infantry officer in a story by Siegfried Sassoon.[59] That was more accurate, for the Great War resembled a state-owned factory where corpses were manufactured on a European scale. It was extraordinary technical ingenuity, matched by terrible effects upon conscripts and civilians alike. The technical prowess of European states and their armies in matters of killing was to define the twentieth century as the most murderous in recorded human history. The pattern was set by the Great War, which claimed twenty-nine million battle casualties. By the end of the century, wars of various kinds had claimed an estimated 187 million people – the equivalent of one-tenth of the world's population in 1913. The Great War set another trend, in which the burdens of war weighed ever more heavily on civilians. Not only was it the most 'democratic' of wars – sixty-five million people were mobilised for battle – but civilians, like defenceless pawns on a chessboard of cruelty, became the favourite targets of military calculations that dissolved the old distinction between 'front' and 'home'. During the 1914–18 war, civilians comprised a staggering one-twentieth of the victims. During the 1939–45 war, the proportion rose to two-thirds; by the end of the century, perhaps nine-tenths of the victims of war were civilians.

The Disintegration of Democracy

The long grave dug by the Great War contained more than enough room for the bones of parliamentary democracy. The violent suffering and devastation had various political effects, among which were powerfully organised efforts to rid the world of representative democracy. They very nearly succeeded.

Things initially looked different. Contemporary observers could have been forgiven for thinking that the end of the Great War was a glorious dawn for representative democracy; war, often the midwife of democracy, seemed to be firmly on its side. Politicians dressed in top hats and frock coats suddenly looked like creatures from the past. Dukes, emperors, sultans, pashas ran for cover as the once-powerful autocratic empires of Russia, Ottoman Turkey, Austria-Hungary and Hohenzollern Germany crashed to earth. In December 1918, with revolution in the air, the National Congress of Soldiers' and Workers' Councils in Germany voted decisively in favour of parliamentary institutions as the foundation of a new constitution. Backed by the United States, the Paris peace agreement of the following year seemed to herald a new age of parliamentary democracy; ten new republics were born virtually overnight, each of them brandishing new democratic constitutions. The charters of states like Finland, Greece, Poland, Lithuania and the Irish Free State declared, in muscular language, that sovereignty resided in the 'nation'; others spoke of 'the people' as the source of all authority, but the meaning was identical. 'Austria is a democratic republic. Sovereignty is vested in the people' read the first article of its new constitution. The constitution of the neighbouring Weimar Republic affirmed its commitment to representative democracy by repeating the point that sovereign authority belonged to 'the national self-consciousness of a self-organising people'.

Within less than a decade, events proved that such sentiments were quixotic, words with no grip on the unstable realities of the region. Most parliamentary democracies in Europe began to look like democracies without democrats. Why? Certainly not because Europe suffered outbursts of collective insanity triggered by psychopath dictators, as many contemporaries liked to believe. The reasons lay elsewhere. Constitutional delirium – the naive belief of politicians, lawyers, diplomats and government officials that good constitutions could overcome bad political and social conditions – was among the many causes of the death of representative democracy. So, too, was the presumption that well-designed parliaments could provide leadership strong enough to make lions lie down with lambs. Corporate disinvestment, economic collapse and mass unemployment played a paralysing role, as happened in Spanish America and Brazil, more or less at the same time. Unregulated markets were bad for representative democracy: their collapse sent shock waves through the region's civil societies. Heaving with rising expectations and dashed post-war hopes, seething with nationalism, party political squabbles, anti-Semitism and the spread of paramilitary violence, societies turned into uncivil societies. Social implosion handed opportunities to those who spotted a basic weakness in the theory and practice of representative democracy, a malady that had earlier been exploited by the French Jacobins, General Rosas in Argentina and the Russian populists: the vulnerability of representative democracy to subversion at the hands of demagogues appealing to 'the people'. A sign of sinister things to come was Hitler's reminder to Chancellor Brüning after leading his NSDAP (the National Socialist German Workers' Party) to a near-victory in general elections: 'it is the fundamental thesis of democracy', said Hitler, 'that "all power derives from the People"'. He then acted on that principle, to destroy representative democracy, helped by an acquiescent majority of the German population and fellow travellers and appeasers throughout Europe.

Geopolitical pressures added to the misery of democrats. Easily the deadliest forces were nationalism, its friend–foe dogmas, and their lubrication of life-and-death struggles among states locked in bids for imperial splendour. The period 1918 to 1939 was arguably the only one in European history when something approaching a 'pure' form of territorial nation-state sovereignty prevailed. With the collapse of empires on European soil and pitifully weak fledgling international regulatory bodies like the League of Nations, it turned out that the Woodrow Wilson government's remedy for the European sickness – its insistence that each nation was entitled to govern itself, and that peace would come when Europe was governed by sovereign states that doubled as representative democracies – played into the hands of pettifogging, power-hungry nationalists. Tensions within and among states reached breaking point when Western intervention failed to crush the Bolsheviks in the Russian civil war. The wave of strikes, mutinies and insurrections that swept through Europe during 1918–19 triggered not only civil war in Finland and street fighting in Germany; it spawned widespread fears of Bolshevism within governing circles that promptly did deals with the devil. Events in Hungary showed the face of the future: in early 1919, the parliamentary republic headed by Count Mihály Károlyi was ousted by a government sympathetic to the Bolsheviks, led by Béla Kun. It lasted just months; watched by Britain, the United States and other Entente powers, the Romanian army invaded Hungary, forcing the communists to flee. The invasion brought to power the regime of Admiral Horthy: supported by the landed gentry, authoritarian but fiercely anti-communist, it ruled by means of terror, with full diplomatic recognition from the Allies. Representative democracy had found a new friend: hypocrisy.

Then there were the causers of the democratic sickness. Intellectuals were among its gravediggers; they helped swing the prevailing mood in Europe towards fatalism, the belief that all signs pointed towards the replacement of parliamentary democracy by a yet-to-be-defined alternative. Especially from the mid-1920s, many writers, thinkers, journalists indulged talk of 'the crisis of democracy', and weird things were said.[60] The Austrian modernist Robert Musil, author of the unfinished masterpiece *The Man Without Qualities* (1930–32), was convinced that the star of representative democracy had fizzled. 'I do not fight against fascism,' he said, 'but in democracy for her future, thus also against democracy.' The writing machine H. G. Wells told Oxford summer-school students that the coming age of collectivism demanded 'enlightened Nazis' willing to match the spirited courage of continental fascists. The young Romanian intellectual Emil Cioran similarly praised the visionary energy of the totalitarian attack on 'democratic rationalism'. Journalists at *The Times* of London added their shilling's worth. 'Recent Spanish Governments have tried to conform to the parliamentary type of republican democracy, but with scant success', they commented, as if to say that British policy of non-intervention in Spain was justified by the clear superiority of Westminster institutions. 'It may be', they added, 'that the system of parliamentary Government which suits Great Britain suits few other countries besides.'[61]

It was as if the old European tradition of bellyaching against representative democracy had finally come of age. Many intellectual critics aimed below the belt, insisting (with the German historian Heinrich von Treitschke) that it was axiomatic that nature had made all organisms unequal, and that there was something thoroughly 'unnatural' about democracy. Some preferred to quote Edmund Burke's old remark that democracy was a recipe for degenerate government by the stupid, that 'democratists' (a strange word that was roughly his equivalent of the French word *démocrates*) were shameless creatures of ambition, and that 'in a democracy, the majority of the citizens is capable of exercising the most cruel oppressions upon the minority, whenever strong divisions prevail in that kind of polity, as they often must'. Liberals claimed that the essence of democracy is the unity of private and public interests, the triumph of the state over the freedoms of civil society (that was originally Hegel's complaint, repeated by Tocqueville); favouring liberty over equality and fearing the mob, liberals were convinced that talk of liberal democracy was oxymoronic (in contrast to our times, when the phrase 'liberal democracy' rolls off the tongues of politicians, journalists and scholars as if it has always been accepted currency). Still other intellectuals echoed the objection that democracy tends to lawlessness, that it is 'unconstitutional' (Fichte) because its belief in a sovereign people violates the separation of legislative, executive and judicial powers. It was also said that the whole democratic thing had been contaminated by its association with representation, that representative democracy was a fraud because it sold short 'the people', the true source of authority; or (the opposite complaint) that because democracy could not admit of representation, it was in practice dysfunctional, and certainly could never work in large states. Some socialists and most communists, meanwhile, accused it of being a bourgeois affair, a mask for class exploitation; anarchists (like Georges Sorel) said that democracy was an illusion fed by servility, while Prince Kropotkin warned that representative democracy was a recipe for a new type of despotism run by political parties, elected politicians and governments. The German scholar Max Weber (1864–1920) crafted the cleverest attack, in the form of a powerful interpretation of Europe as the birthplace of a universal trend towards bureaucracy. The trend was irreversible, Weber explained, because complex problems are best defined, handled and resolved by technically sophisticated experts and officials in large-scale organisations. For reasons of technical efficiency and effectiveness, the grip of large bureaucratic corporations managed by industrial entrepreneurs had become just as much an 'iron necessity' as bureaucratic command in the field of electoral politics, government administration and fighting wars. Given this irreversible concentration of the means of power in the hands of a few people, Weber insisted, the government of European states now demanded skilled, devoted, cool-headed political leadership. Elections, political parties and parliaments could help in this respect, by serving as training grounds for new leaders. But according to Weber the whole eighteenth-century vision of building states guided by the principles of representative democracy was now utterly exhausted. 'Such concepts as "the will of the people", "the *true* will of the people", have long since ceased to exist for me', he said to a former pupil. 'They are *fictions*. All ideas aiming at abolishing the dominance of humans by others are "utopian".'[62]

In the life-and-death power struggles of the period 1918–39, the language games of intellectuals hostile or unsympathetic to democracy suddenly sprouted devils' horns. Among the chief foes of democracy during this period were the champions of *purple tyranny*: strong states ruled by monarchs bent on turning back the tide of universal suffrage and parliamentary democracy. The Great War did not sweep away monarchies, as many predicted, or hoped; whereas at the outbreak of the conflict there were 19 continental monarchies and 3 republics, at its end, with newly independent states on the scene, there were 16 republics and still 14 monarchies. In 1923, the trend continued, for instance in the newly independent state of Albania, where Bishop Fan Noli's democratically elected government was overthrown by Ahmed Zogu, who subsequently proclaimed himself king (under the name Zog) to govern without an elected parliament. In Yugoslavia, the constitution of the country was rewritten after the 1929 royal coup staged by King Alexander (who had earlier acceded to the throne because his elder brother was deemed unfit after kicking his servant to death, in a fit of rage). The new constitution transferred executive power to the king, who hereafter appointed half the upper house of parliament directly and guaranteed that legislation became law with the approval of one of the houses alone, so long as it had the king's approval. The new electoral system introduced by Alexander effectively reduced the number of voters, restored open balloting in rural constituencies and bullied public employees into voting for the governing party.

Few genuine monarchies in fact survived the shocks produced by the devastation of the Great War and the intense egalitarian pressures generated by struggles for representative democracy. That was why a second type of anti-democratic trend proved much more worrying for the friends of representative democracy: *armed dictatorship* operating in the name of 'the people'. 'Until the post-War era', the English scholar J. A. Hobson observed in 1934, 'democracy, in the sense of popular self-government, was making such advances in most countries of the world as to be considered the natural goal of political evolution. Even those who distrusted it believed it to be inevitable.' Hobson contrasted the past with the present. 'Now democracy is in several countries displaced by dictatorship, and everywhere it is discredited.' He then posed a disturbing question. 'Is this a merely temporary set-back, due to emergencies carried from war into an unsettled peace, and calling for unusual exercise of arbitrary power by rulers, to be laid down when normal conditions are resumed?'[63]

Many political figures and observers in the European region saw nothing temporary in the turn towards military dictatorship. 'I am convinced', said the Portuguese dictator António Salazar in 1934, 'that within twenty years, if there is not some retrograde movement in political evolution, there will be no legislative assemblies left in Europe.'[64] He meant it, and he was not the only one for whom the big boss power of the state seemed to be Europe's fate (Figure 94), despite all the earlier contrary signs. Following the Great War, mainly because of pressure applied by the victorious Allies, it was true that parliamentary democracy appeared to come of age in many parts of Europe. Between 1919 and 1921, most restrictions on voting were lifted and – with the extension of the vote to women in most countries – suffrage became nearly universal, for the first time. But as pressure for the inclusion of the previously dominated lower classes grew, the inherited bureaucratic structures of government began to be pulled and stretched by multi-party systems that sometimes produced wild swings from one political grouping to another. Hanging on a hair, governments came and went, at an alarming

FIGURE 94: *Power*, by the Bohemian-born illustrator, writer and Expressionist painter Alfred Kubin (1903).

rate; after 1918, there were hardly any European countries blessed with governments that lasted longer than twelve months. Some parliaments suffered a nervous breakdown; made fractious by the multiplication of angry parties and the constant collapse of executive authority, it was not uncommon to witness chambers ruined by representatives spitting insults, or throwing chairs, as if they were attending a carnival of asses. With civil societies weak and split down the middle by ethnic and national divisions, the resulting social tensions and political conflicts soon took their toll. Parliamentary democracy imploded, prompting calls for strong leadership. Emergency decrees flourished. The hour of martial law had arrived.

Consider for a moment Poland, where free elections not only failed to create a stable government, but, whipped by hyperinflation, they actively bred disorder. In the 1922 legislative elections, 29 per cent voted for right-wing parties, 30 per cent for the centre, 22 per cent for the left and the rest for national minority representatives. Soon afterwards, the President of the Republic, Gabriel Narutowicz, was assassinated. Talk of the need to 'sanitise' (*sanacja*) the country flourished. Polish patriot Marshal Józef Piłsudski, former democrat and commander-in-chief of the army, stepped into the political vacuum. Staging a *coup d'état* in 1926, he moved immediately to change the electoral laws, to use the army and state administration to rig the outcome of elections (gaining 46.8 per cent of votes in the 1930 elections). It was Poland for the Polish people – minus the main opposition leaders, communists and fascists alike, who were arrested and put on trial – and in 1935 a new constitution that legalised dictatorial practices was adopted.

Similar things happened elsewhere. In Romania, where party conflict gradually intensified during eighteen years of universal suffrage using the secret ballot, parliamentary government was abolished by a *coup d'état* in 1938. The survival of parliamentary democracy in the region was further jeopardised by economic backwardness, which tempted certain 'reformers' or 'national radicals' of the political establishment to experiment with state planning and investment in the economy. Well-placed political figures like the Bulgarian colonel Damian Velchev, the Hungarian Gyula Gömbös and the Polish colonel Adam Koc all imagined their states as 'modern' political regimes freed from the curse of democratic elections. Distancing themselves from the propertied classes, they manoeuvred to strike alliances with the lower and lower-middle classes, so as to work towards a new form of well-armed, one-party government that would intervene in the economy and develop income redistribution policies by taking wealth from Jewish entrepreneurs and aristocratic landowners. Internally divided and facing stiff competition from more radical right-wing parties – like the Hungarian Arrow Cross and the Romanian Iron Guard – these reformers never managed fully to get their way. But their influence was strong enough to ensure that, by the outbreak of World War Two, the candle of parliamentary democracy had been all but extinguished.

The notable exception in the region – Czechoslovakia, then seventh-largest economy in the world and a thriving and stable parliamentary democracy – was destroyed from the outside by a third form of anti-democratic politics never before experienced in the history of democracy: *totalitarianism*. It first appeared in Russia and Italy and soon spread to Weimar Germany, whose permanent crisis paved the way for the rise of Hitler. The mould was cast by

Russian events and Bolshevik tactics. 'We'll tell the people that its interests are higher than the interests of democratic institutions', said Lenin in December 1917. He quickly delivered on his promise. The Constituent Assembly was dissolved and press freedom was abolished; a new constitution bid *dasvidania* to 'dead bourgeois parliamentarism' and the Cheka secret police set to work, amidst much huffing and puffing about crushing the bourgeoisie and granting workers control of industry, through newly formed soviets. Confronted with objections that the Bolsheviks were violating their own constitution, Lenin simply replied (in 1920) that the crushing of 'bourgeois democracy' required 'democratic dictatorship', 'nothing more or less than unlimited power resting directly on force, not limited by anything, not restrained by any laws or any absolute rules'.[65]

What was so new – so menacing – about totalitarianism, whether in its Soviet or Nazi form? Put most simply, totalitarianism was a simulation of representative democracy. Whether as a movement or as a regime, its institutions, methods and ethos paid homage to the great popular upsurge that dated from the French Revolution. The Bolshevik Declaration of the Rights of the Toiling and Exploited People (1918) and the Nazi big talk of a *Volksgemeinschaft* embodied the totalitarian sentiment that 'the people' could and should no longer be ignored, and that, on the contrary, their needs and desires needed to be acknowledged, shaped and reshaped into a force that would have world-historical effects. This was achievable through the iron fist of self-discipline, organisation and uncompromising political rule. Totalitarianism was rule of the masses, for the masses, by the leaders of the masses.

As a way of ruling others, totalitarianism cultivated belief in an all-encompassing ideology, a grand *bricolage* of ideas and symbols and stories that functioned as a shield against the push-and-pull pressures of the world around it. Delivered as political theatre (Figure 95), totalitarian ideology seemed to have a life of its own. It provided answers to every question. It served as the grid that defined up and down, back and front, the directions left and right and straight ahead. Belief in the ideology was compulsory, even when its content was changed, often randomly and at the whim of those in charge. Some themes remained relatively constant in the totalitarian worldview, including the repeated emphasis on

FIGURE 95: *Dem Deutschen Volke:* Adolf Hitler practising for his public speeches by striking poses in front of his personal photographer, Heinrich Hoffmann.

the unstoppable rise of the masses on to the stage of history, and the apparently contrary idea: that the Party was their life and soul, the guarantor of their safety, their prosperity, their future.

Totalitarian regimes were more than one-party, dictatorial regimes of the Polish or Portuguese type. The Party deemed itself right, always, even when its Leaders changed directions and reversed last night's decision next morning. Absolute loyalty to the Party required constant vigilance – and a well-developed knack of second-guessing things. The leading role of the Party meant that any dissent had to be tracked down by the secret police, punished and eliminated. 'Discipline must be accepted', said Mussolini, referring proudly to the *fasces*, the Roman axe-head symbol of penal power. 'When it is not accepted, it must be imposed.'[66] Totalitarianism was paranoid, and for that reason well armed and well guarded. Its secret police, typically operating in the shadows of the state, were empowered to do anything to secure Party discipline and loyalty. Arrests in the night, blackmailing, disappearances, murder: all of this was normal. But so, too, was the creation of an unending supply of enemies by the Party and its police. Among the paradoxes of twentieth-century totalitarianism was the way in which it grew more frenzied *after* its domestic enemies had been defeated. This followed from the fact that the Party had its 'objective' enemies: flesh-and-blood individuals and groups whose subjective identity was secondary to their objective position in the order of things. The regime had opponents, even if and when they protested their innocence. The categories of objective enemies were multiple and flexible and changed through time – they included police informers, imperialist spies, Trotskyite traitors, Jews, homosexuals, Titoists, gypsies, agents of bourgeois nationalism – but their enforced definition and elimination meant that totalitarian regimes were necessarily hunting their subjects constantly. Lawlessness prevailed. All loyalties and group organisation had to be pulverised, sifted continuously in the winds of surveillance and elimination.

Totalitarianism was terrorist, no more so than in the institutions that served as its own laboratories of power: the concentration camps. It was there that the true character of the regime was displayed. The camps were not houses of correction or labour camps. They operated as places in which totalitarian power conducted crazed experiments with the bodies and souls of their victims, who forfeited their rights to have rights of any kind, not even the simple right to escape through suicide. On the side of the regime, nothing was prohibited. Everything was permitted. Bizarre inversions resulted. The unimaginable became real; reality became unimaginable. The aim, if aim it can be called, was always the same: the reduction of the inmates to nothingness, their transformation into inert molecules of matter so as to prove, to friends and enemies alike, the invincibility of the regime.

Why Democracy?

It was this mentality that made totalitarianism, whether black or brown or red, so dangerous to the idea and substance of power-sharing representative democracy in Europe. In the name of lifting the common man and woman on to the stage of history, with promises that they would be propelled forwards, towards an earthly utopia of freedom and solidarity, totalitarian movements and regimes quickly wrecked the structures and foundations of representative democracy. Totalitarian power stood for the destruction of civil society. It tolerated no differences, worshipped violence, encouraged cynicism and practised lawlessness. It rejected as illogical market production and exchange, and it did so by claiming that the Party State was everything, individuals and groups nothing. Freedoms like those of habeas corpus and public assembly, free speech and casting votes in secret ballots, all of this and more it regarded as so much 'bourgeois' rubbish, as discredited monuments of a bygone era, as worthless fuel to be thrown on the fires of invincible power. Totalitarianism was aggressive, a type of reckless government in love with its propensity to strike fear into the hearts of its opponents, at home and abroad. That meant war and – for its opponents – making a last stand, if necessary 'on the beaches . . . on the landing grounds . . . in the fields and in the streets . . . and the hills', as the Prime Minister of Britain, Winston Churchill, was famously to say (on 4 June 1940) in a desperate speech in the House of Commons, which was soon to be destroyed by Nazi bombs.

The experience of total war, and the real threats posed by purple tyranny, armed dictatorship and especially totalitarianism, soon prompted Churchill to reflect on the value of parliamentary democracy. The prime minister was no natural-born democrat. He was in fact a political man saddled early with a reputation for haughty remarks against 'uncivilised tribes', a politician who had reacted badly to the looming universal franchise, who liked to say that when eagles are silent parrots jabber, and who later allegedly quipped that the best argument against democracy is a five-minute talk with the average voter. His views were changed by his direct confrontation with Hitler; on the floor of the House of Commons, Churchill vowed that he would side with the devil if his opponent chose to invade hell. 'I say that in the long years to come', he told VE Day crowds in London on 8 May 1945, 'not only will the people of this island but of the world, wherever the bird of freedom chirps in human hearts, look back to what we've done and they will say "do not despair, do not yield to violence and tyranny, march straight forward and die if need be – unconquered.'''

Much the same spirit fuelled Churchill's much quoted, poorly contextualised statements about democracy in a House of Commons debate over the future powers of the House of Lords. Now Leader of His Majesty's Official Opposition, Churchill had been ill and absent from debate on the Attlee government's new legislation to curb the powers of the upper chamber. Taking advantage of his absence, the Leader of the House and Lord President of the Council, Herbert Morrison, claimed to the Commons that 'even in his liberal days of 1910, the Right Honourable gentleman appears not to have been a very good democrat'.[67] The next afternoon, Churchill took the floor and, despite looking tired and pale, managed with his usual eloquence to lash the social democratic government with a whip of words. 'As a free-born Englishman, what I hate is the sense of being at anybody's mercy or in anybody's power, be he Hitler or Attlee', said Churchill, to heckles. 'We are approaching very near to dictatorship in this country, dictatorship, that is to say – I shall be quite candid with the House – without either its criminality or its efficiency.'

Churchill's prediction that dictatorship, unless checked, would attend the building of the welfare state attracted much uproar, and prolonged interruption. He persisted. Churchill accused the Labour government of anti-democratic behaviour. 'All this idea of a handful of men getting hold of the State machine, having the right to make the people do what suits their party and personal interests or doctrines, is completely contrary to every conception of surviving Western democracy.' Churchill sailed the waves of heckles and hearhears to explain that the government's talk of a 'popular mandate' was 'small party patter'. It supposed, wrongly, that democracy is equivalent to majority rule, 'obtaining a fixed term of office by promises, and then doing what it likes with the people'. Implicitly, the current government yearned for single-chamber government 'without regard to the wishes of the people and without giving them any chance to express their opinion'.

Churchill's argument relied on an idealised image of 'the people' as the ultimate source of political authority. He said that democracy was a system in which popular views, expressed as 'public opinion', were taken seriously by representatives working through institutions that checked governments and forced them to reconsider and abandon foolish legislation. Democracy was 'government of the people, by the people, for the people'. But it was more than that, he quickly added. It was 'a system of balanced rights and divided authority, with many other persons and organised bodies having to be considered besides the Government of the day and the officials they employ'. And so Churchill, though frail with illness, reached for his conclusion. 'Many forms of Government have been tried, and will be tried in this world of sin and woe', he croaked. 'No one pretends that democracy is perfect or all-wise.' He paused. 'Indeed, it has been said that democracy is the worst form of Government except all those other forms that have been tried from time to time; but there is the broad feeling in our country that the people should rule, continuously rule, and that public opinion, expressed by all constitutional means, should shape, guide, and control the actions of Ministers who are their servants and not their masters.'

Churchill's words would soon become world-famous – rightly so, considering that they trumpeted not just the resilient spirit of democracy trapped in a tight corner, but the rebound of its ideals and institutions, towards a new type of democracy that still today enjoys no proper name.

PART THREE

MONITORY DEMOCRACY

The Goddess of Democracy: a statue erected in Tiananmen Square, Beijing, on 30 May 1989 by students from the Central Academy of Fine Arts, who modelled it after the Statue of Liberty.

UNDER THE BANYAN TREE

Colonialism was born when modern weapons enabled small European expeditionary forces to sweep away the armies of the most populous empires in the world – and it died when these empires found their own weapons, which were not only guns.

Jawaharlal Nehru to André Malraux (1958)

On Clouds

The history of democracy is punctuated by big surprises, but none so fantastic as the escape of democratic ideals and institutions from under the rubble left by two global wars, dictatorship and totalitarianism. The breakout first happened in the Indian subcontinent, in the late 1940s. There, under toilsome conditions, millions of people used their bare hands to turn fate into destiny. Triggered by civil courage, eruptions of violence tempered by legal concessions, tenacious leadership laced with strokes of good luck, the world's biggest and most interesting, cutting-edge democracy was born. The planet had seen nothing like it before; its birth resembled a folkloric fantasy, an episode drawn from some exotic local tale. It was as if the broken-hearted spirit of democracy, banished from earth to the skies above, had suddenly summoned a cloud, thrown a saddle over its white mane, then ridden it earthwards, landing at some spot south of the snow-peaked Himalayas, where it galloped off to consummate its love for the sunlit landscape that is today called India.

The coming of democracy to the region did more than bring changes to the lives of its people. India fundamentally altered the nature of representative democracy itself. A new 'post-Westminster' type of democracy resulted, in the process slaughtering quite a few goats of prejudice. None of the standard postulates about the pre-conditions of democracy survived. They had spoken of economic development as its fundamental precondition, so that representative democracy could be practicable only when sufficient numbers of people owned or enjoyed such commodities as automobiles, refrigerators and wirelesses. Awash in poverty of heart-breaking proportions, the region managed to laugh in the face of pseudo-scientific and fatalistic propositions that had insisted that there was a causal – perhaps even mathematical – link between economic development and political democracy. Millions of poor and illiterate people rejected the view of their masters that a country must first be deemed fit for democracy. Struggling against themselves, they decided instead that they must become fit *through* democracy.

This was a change of epochal importance. In contrast to China and many other countries, not only did it show that dictatorship was unnecessary in the so-called Third World. Democrats in India demonstrated that unity within a highly diverse country could be built by respecting its differences; that, despite everything, the hand of democracy could be extended, to include potentially billions of people who were defined by a huge variety of histories and customs that had one thing in common: they were people who were not European. In this way, the region defied the common-sense rule that democracy can take root only where there is a *dēmos* bound together by a common culture. India was just the opposite. Here instead was a society brimming with different hopes and expectations about who Indians were and what their government should do for them. For this reason as well, India bearded the woolly predictions of those who said that secularism, the retreat of religious myths into the private sphere or their outright disappearance, was necessary before hard-nosed democracy could take hold of the world. Here was a region where some (repeating the teachings of the Buddha) practised the mistrust of worldly ambition and individualism, called the self unreal, spoke of the impermanence of things, and emphasised the need for individually – as opposed to collectively – organised redemption. This was a country where thirty-day, dawn-to-dusk fasts commenced after imams announced that they had just had sight of the new moon; where barefooted worshippers entered temples holding hands, listened to music clutching marigolds, later to enjoy a temple meal of daal and chapatti; a country where the Hindu majority hosted spring festivals during which people, Hindu and non-Hindu alike, wore yellow clothes, chanted mantras, threw coloured water and powder at each other, and read and performed the story of the birth of Rama.

Good Government?

These customs had convinced the British imperial masters that home rule in parliamentary democratic form was utterly impossible. In contrast, say, to the colonies of Australia or Canada, India was the white man's burden, an exotic place full of chaotic diversity and troubling manners. It was a non-country best summarised (as Kipling said in *Kim*, 1901) as 'the happy Asiatic disorder'. This muddled place was immune to purposeful change in the Western way, which meant that the British were condemned to play the role of custodians of an incorrigibly confused ancient culture in need of law and order. 'The rescue of India from ages of barbarism, tyranny, and intestine war, and its slow but ceaseless forward march to civilisation constitute . . . the finest achievement of our history', Churchill crowed. Then he grumped. 'India is an abstraction', he said, 'a geographical term. It is no more a united nation than the Equator.' This fact posed a special difficulty. 'There are scores of nations and races in India and hundreds of religions and sects. Out of the three hundred and fifty millions of Indians only a very few millions can read or write, and of these only a fraction are interested in politics and Western ideas. The rest are primitive people absorbed in the hard struggle for life.' Hence India had no democratic future. It was preposterous to suppose that 'the almost innumerable peoples of India would be likely to live in peace, happiness and decency under the same polity and the same form of Government as the British, Canadian or Australian democracies. It is preposterous', concluded Churchill, 'not because natives of India are inherently incapable of working modern democratic institutions, but because of the political, social, racial, and religious conditions of the country in which they live.'[1]

It followed that the destiny of the white sahibs of Britannia was to lord over the coloured peoples of the region. Like Mr Kurtz in Conrad's *Heart of Darkness*, they saw themselves as potentates ruling over a pagan wilderness; as with Kurtz, growing numbers of locals eventually concluded that their rulers' supreme self-confidence bordered on insanity. But for a time, local opinion did not count. The Raj was for ever. Good government meant top-down rule, guided by the Viceroy, assisted by the colonial bureaucracy and judiciary, communicating in pukka English, the only common language of the region. Good government implied a willingness of the colonial masters to take the lead, to demonstrate in practice that they were truly 'representative' of those whom they ruled. It was a strange understanding of representation that seemed drawn straight from the writings of some head-in-the-clouds professor of politics in defence of the State as the God-given bearer of all things good. The governors lived the pretence that they stood 'above politics'. They saw themselves as the true and right bearers of 'policy', and it followed from this that the involvement of locals in government, if it had to happen, was to be at most a mere advisory affair.

The Governors' Councils, set up after the thirteen-month uprising against British rule in 1857/8, served as the basic model of representation for the rest of the colonial period. The Councils were designed to enable local notables, by invitation, to proffer advice about 'native opinion' to the ruling Indian Civil Service (ICS). Much the same understanding of representation as an oligarchic affair, as unchallengeable government by like-minded chums 'in touch' with their native subjects, was evident in the British efforts to subdivide the population, for the purposes of better administration of otherwise fuzzy identities, into immutable political categories, such as 'Hindus', 'Muslims', 'Sikhs' and 'landholders'. Similar Orientalist prejudice was displayed by Lord Ripon's efforts, during the early 1880s, to introduce a measure of decentralised government. The reforms were designed to offload many petty functions of government to handpicked or locally elected 'native boards' that would administer – and be asked to pay for – such matters as sanitation, roads and schools.

This was not only administration on the cheap with the help of a select group of unpaid notables drawn from a tiny minority of house proprietors, mainly traders and professionals whom Lord Ripon had described as 'public spirited men whom it is not only bad policy, but sheer waste of power to fail to utilize'.[2] It was also a strategy of divide and rule, a method of keeping Indians in their stables, blinkered and distant from the centres of governmental power. The top-down model of representation was above all meant to guarantee that the rulers ruled, and ruled well, according to their own rules, with minimum interference by the divided and confused objects of 'policy'. The prejudice was displayed openly in the 1919 Government of India Act. For the first time, with local resistance rising, the principle of direct elections was accepted as desirable at all levels of administration; and, at the provincial level, Indian ministers, chosen from among the legislators, were allowed to take charge of certain 'transferred' policies.

Yet devils lurked deep in the details. In provincial affairs, only one in ten Indian men and one in two hundred Indian women over the age of twenty-one – less than 3 per cent of the entire population – were entitled to vote in elections. Their lucky representatives were virtually powerless. The so-called 'transferred' policies for which they were responsible were strictly limited to 'nation-building' activities, such as education, industry and agriculture, and local self-government. Coercive and extractive powers – control over the police, the courts, prisons and land revenues – were kept on the desks of the unelected provincial governor and his appointed executive councillors. Meanwhile, at the central level, the government of India remained irresponsible. The Viceroy was in effect a local untouchable, certainly not a figure controllable by the Council of State, the electorate for which (in 1930) was in any case just 40,515 eligible voters, out of a British Indian population that totalled 257 million people.

A Tryst with Destiny

It seemed never to occur to the architects of these institutions that by dangling pseudo-representative institutions before the noses of the natives they would incite tremendous resistance among Indians, who would sooner or later use these same institutions to dig the graves of empire and claim their own dignity. Lord Morley's famous remark, before the House of Lords in London, that he would resolutely block the creation of any colonial institutions that might lead 'to the establishment of a parliamentary system in India',[3] rather typified the arrogance of a whole generation of colonial governors convinced that they were in India to stay.

So self-assured were they that the decision was taken, during the early 1920s, to construct a new Parliament House in the capital, New Delhi (Figure 96). Cast in huge red- and cream-coloured sandstone blocks cut from the hills of neighbouring Rajasthan, the new structure was deemed an architectural gem that time would never tarnish. Designed by two prominent imperial architects, Sir Edwin Lutyens and Sir Herbert Baker, who were responsible for the overall planning and construction of New Delhi, the foundation stone of Parliament House was laid on 12 February 1921 by Queen Victoria's son, His Royal Highness the Duke of Connaught. Fresh from a polo competition final in his honour and a grandiloquent State Ball the previous evening, the duke was not exactly in a modest mood. 'All great rulers, every great people, every great civilisation have left their own record in stone and bronze and marble, as well as in the pages of history', he said to his lucky audience. He urged them to recall such precedents as the Acropolis in Athens and the city of Rome – he naturally refrained from mentioning lokshahi, the new political word for democracy that had Indo-Persian roots, and that had recently come into local circulation – then went on to predict that the 'new representative institution' would 'mark a vast stride forward in the political development of India and of the British Empire', and that it would stand as a powerful symbol of 'India's re-birth to yet higher destinies'.[4]

With these superfine words, Indian labourers were drafted in from all over the country, to get on with the job, under the Union Jack. Construction took six years. No expense was spared; the costs mounted to over 8.3 million rupees, but cost inflation seemed unimportant, for the architects, knowing that architecture and power are twins, placed the building somewhere on a time scale that stretched from Athens to imperial India via the Houses of Parliament in London. Sir Herbert Baker, who had already built the parliament for the Union of South Africa, commented that his aim was 'to build according to the great elemental qualities and traditions, which have become classical, of the architecture of Greece and Rome and to graft thereon structural features of the architecture of India as well as expressing the myths, symbols, and history of its people'.[5] A message from His Majesty the King-Emperor read out at the formal opening of the building expressed the parallel hope that the new building 'would inspire the Princes and people of India with the ideals of brotherhood and service by which alone the peace and prosperity of my subjects may be secured'.[6]

The massive circular edifice was subsequently much criticised locally. Delhi's subjects joked that it looked like a bullring, or a gasometer, but the architects were confident that anything in the rectangular style might encourage two-party government, and foster divisions along strictly religious lines. With a circumference of one-third of a mile and covering an area of nearly six acres, the building was set amidst rolling lawns dotted with palms and rose gardens enclosed by an ornamental red sandstone wall. The giant edifice housed two chambers: the horseshoe-shaped, grey marble-pillared Central Legislative Assembly, and the upper Council of

FIGURE 96: The colonnade veranda on the first floor of Parliament House, New Delhi.

States. Each chamber was laid out in the English style, with a Speaker's chair, an arc of comfortable seats for the representatives, a table for officers of the chamber, and boxes and galleries for distinguished visitors, government officials and approved members of the public. Bordering the Assembly and the Council was a third space, the Princes' Chamber, where the rulers of the various states of undivided India could chat, relax, doze. The three rooms were fastened together by the Central Hall, a green-carpeted, magnificently domed conference hall where mingling princes and members of the two houses of parliament could sip tea and converse, before and after business. The whole interior featured three open-air courtyards, fountains filled with coloured fish, ornamental *jali* carved from white marble, and panelled walls and furniture chiselled from teak cut in Burma. Modelled on Westminster, the Central Legislative Assembly was decorated (like the House of Commons) in green leather and green carpet; the upper chamber, the Council of States, mimicking the House of Lords, was resplendent in red leather and red carpets. Electric brass fans were installed to cool tempers, local symbols (*chhajjas*) were carved and fitted to shade the walls and windows, while various inscriptions in several languages seemed designed to summon the humility and respect for the laws made in this house of power. In the magnificent Princes' Chamber, a dome was inscribed with two gold-coloured lines in Persian. 'This lofty emerald-like building bears the inscription in gold', ran the translation. 'Nothing shall last except the good deeds of the bountiful.'

The words contained a deep ambiguity – that bad deeds would not survive the cruel judgements of time – but few in the ranks of the occupying power seemed to notice, or to care. At the opening ceremony, on 18 January 1927, His Excellency the Viceroy, Lord Irwin – the man with a withered left arm who later became a principal architect of appeasement of Hitler – waxed eloquent about the durable beauty and everlasting political significance of the imposing structure. He could not have known that twenty years later, in a much more impressive ceremony, held just before sunset on 14 August 1947, the Indian tricolour would be raised over the Parliament, to flutter in the late monsoon sky blessed by a rainbow; and that later that evening, just before midnight, Jawaharlal

Nehru, boyishly slim, dressed in a white achkan with a red rose in his lapel, would rise before excited members of the Constituent Assembly to declare that the struggle for full independence from British pomp and cruelty was over.

The four-and-a-half-minute speech delivered by Nehru became the most famous ever made by any Indian. Those who heard it live, or on radio, recalled its dream-like quality. Its words combined humility and ambition and the yearning, expressed in crisp English spoken with an upper-class accent, to start something new in a world broken and battered by war, cruelty and subjugation. 'It is fitting', he said softly into the All India Radio microphone, 'that at this solemn moment we take the pledge of dedication to the service of India and her people and to the still larger cause of humanity.' The world had become One World, noted Nehru. Not only were peace and freedom now indivisible; events had proven that disasters now had universal effects. So the pledge made by Nehru was an historic contract to wipe away the tears of all human beings, to bring democracy to the world, to exercise power and freedom responsibly, beginning with India herself. 'Long years ago,' he said, 'we made a tryst with destiny, and now the time comes when we shall redeem our pledge, not wholly or in full measure, but very substantially. At the stroke of the midnight hour, when the world sleeps, India will awake to life and freedom.' He added: 'This is no time for ill-will or blaming others. We have to build the noble mansion of free India where all her children may dwell.'

For the next fifteen years, Nehru and the Congress Party worked hard (as he told the French author and statesman André Malraux) to meet the challenge of creating a just state by just means. What exactly did this mean? Nehru envisaged an Asian democracy that would not be just a replica of the West. It would be a new type of self-governing republic that would kill three birds with one stone. It would snap the chains imposed by its colonial masters; resist the temptation to create new colonies abroad; and it would set about unpicking the threads of 'internal colonialism' at home by creating a new nation of equal citizens. Indian democracy was to be a first ever experiment in creating national unity, economic growth, religious toleration and social equality out of a vast and complex social reality, a reality whose inherited power relations based on caste status, language, hierarchy and accumulated wealth were to be subjected to the power of public debate, party competition and periodic elections.

The Great Soul

The practical odds were stacked against the Congress vision. True, the tough nut of relations with Britain was cracked in favour of the new republic of India staying within the British Commonwealth. Yet the newly independent country was hardly a country. Although the British had laid the foundations of a continental political order, its 'stateness' (said by many scholars to be an essential condition of representative democracy) was up for grabs. Portugal and France still maintained territories on Indian soil. The maharajahs and nawabs of the princely states proved tetchy and difficult to integrate

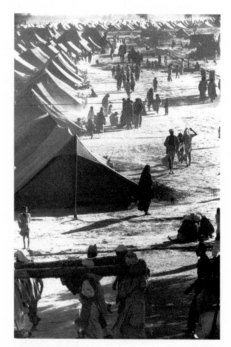

FIGURE 97: A refugee camp of 300,000 people, at Kurukshetra, the Punjab, photograph by Henri Cartier-Bresson, 1947. The site appears in the great Hindu epic – the *Mahabharata*, where it is related that many thousands of years ago a great battle took place between good and evil.

into the new Indian Union. The country had been ravaged by several years of organised killing that resulted in the so-called Partition of 1947 (Figure 97). Its causes remain disputed, but the effects of the largest single migration in history were ugly. Women and children were raped and kidnapped. Hapless refugees were machine-gunned. Trains arrived at their destination in silence, brimming with corpses. Well over ten million, and perhaps as many as fifteen million people crossed borders, and a million or more became the victims of murderous assaults. The carnage forced tense negotiations with Pakistan on such vexed issues as the subdivision of territory, the armed forces and finances. In the disputed territory of Kashmir, war soon broke out with Pakistan. The Indian army brutally put down rebellions by the Muslim rulers of the Hindu-majority principalities of Hyderabad and Junagadh. Then came the moment when the old waves of free-spirited resistance to unjust power seemed finally to crash with fury on the rocks of an ugly reality. On 30 January 1948, Mahatma Gandhi was assassinated.

Gunned down at a prayer meeting by a Hindu extremist named Nathuram Godse, who had been angered by his victim's sympathy

FIGURE 98: Nehru announcing Gandhi's assassination to a weeping crowd, Birla House, Delhi, 1948, photograph by Henri Cartier-Bresson.

for Muslims, Gandhi's death appeared to spell doom for the would-be democracy (Figure 98). Was India's destiny not freedom with equality, but revenge, hatred, murder? At the time of his death, Mohandas Karamchand Gandhi (1869–1948) was, and is still today, revered as one of the greatest twentieth-century champions of democracy. He was very much a rebel product of the British Empire. From a modest caste of traders and money-lenders, Gandhi travelled to England to study law. After briefly practising in India (1893), he emigrated to Natal, South Africa, where the mistreatment of Indian immigrants by white colonials prompted him to found the Indian National Congress, to retreat to a communal farm outside Durban, where he read Thoreau and corresponded with figures like Tolstoy and Ruskin. It was there, in South Africa, that he put theory into practice by experimenting with *satyagraha* ('firmness in truth') campaigns of non-violent non-cooperation with the imperial government.

The thin, bespectacled lawyer soon returned (in 1915) to the political turmoil of India, where he initiated and signed, with Nehru and others, a pledge not to obey the Anarchical and Revolutionary Crimes Act (the 'Rowlatt Act' of March 1919). The pledge was backed by a committee dedicated to practising *satyagraha* as widely as possible. Following the cold-blooded massacre of nearly four hundred *satyagrahis* in the town of Amritsar on 13 April 1919 – an event that can be seen in retrospect to have sealed the fate of the British Raj in India – Gandhi assumed moral leadership of a movement united by its conviction that political independence was desirable, and necessary. Gandhi went further, by humbling himself before the voteless peoples of the subcontinent. Convinced that self-government could never be won by the efforts of unelected, self-regarding, English-speaking elites that believed that the British had ears for moral appeals at dinner-party conversations, or through delegations or petitions, Gandhi worked instead for the self-empowerment of the powerless millions who inhabited India's towns, villages and countryside.

Unlike Mao Tse-tung, who in neighbouring China had become convinced that the struggle against imperial domination required fixing the sights of a gun on the highest offices of state, Gandhi was a man of civil society. He was persuaded that violent means easily turned into soul-destroying ends, that they were therefore dangerous to the cause of freedom. So he shunned the methods of 'princes and potentates' (his phrase) in favour of the emphasis on non-violent, 'bottom up' active resistance nurtured by old traditions, such as Muslim–Hindu unity and *swadeshi* (self-reliance on indigenously produced goods and services). For his efforts and great personal suffering, he was dished up much abuse. Colonial administrators frequently regarded him as a trouble-making Gujarati vegetarian spendthrift bent on keeping India backward. His narrow-minded foes publicly nicknamed him 'Mohammed Gandhi'. In the end, their views did not count because Gandhi's indefatigable courage earned him the sobriquet of Mahatma ('Great Soul'). It was under that saintly title that he campaigned, through spells of imprisonment, fasting and sickness, for an India that was rid of the social evils of indentured labour, child marriage, untouchability, religious arrogance and poor sanitation.

Gandhi's egalitarian instincts evidently had both 'Western' and 'Eastern' sources – he often described himself as a *vishvamānav*, a man who belonged to the universe – but that did not guarantee their self-consistency. Saintly Gandhi was, but contradiction-free he was not. In matters of non-violence, he recognised that there were times – for instance, when women were threatened with rape – when those who turn the other cheek need physically to defend themselves if they are not to end up on the cross of sacrifice. Gandhi's views on democratic self-government were similarly equivocal. His commitment to such democratic virtues as truthfulness, participation, social equality and the toleration of differences – the values of a democratic civil society – was bold and unswerving. His vision of the political institutions needed by a self-governing India was much less clear. Nehru was just one fellow Congressman who openly expressed his disapprobation of Gandhi's frequent references to the return of the golden age of Ram Raj in post-independence India. Strange as it may sound, Gandhi's political thinking retained a strongly anti-political quality. Convinced that the defenders of independence should heed the call to 'Go to the villages!', that India needed above all to build an interconnected system of small, autonomous, self-governing 'village republics', each guided by an annually elected *panchayat* that combined legislative, executive and judicial powers, Gandhi either neglected or rejected outright talk of the need for a written constitution, or for parliaments, political parties, courts of law, periodic elections. It was as if he belonged to the age of assembly democracy. In his first and only book, *Hind Swaraj* (1908), Gandhi had even declared himself in favour of the rule of 'a few good men'. During the two decades (from 1920 until the early 1940s) when his spirit was dominant within Congress, he practised this rule by using questionable techniques of seduction and coercion – long silences, dramatic fasts and penances – to get his way with the party's Working Committee, also known as the High Command. And at the time of independence, with the same elitist stricture in mind, he urged the dissolution of the Congress Party. Good men were to guide India to self-rule, or so Gandhi thought.

The tensions between this anti-political vision of a post-colonial state broken down into self-governing village republics and Nehru's model of an independent constitutional state based on parliamentary self-government were obvious to contemporaries. Although Gandhi's vision of India had nothing like majority support among the population, he remained until his death a force to be reckoned with. So, tragically, but ironically, Gandhi's assassination spared India the personal row that would inevitably have erupted between the two most prominent and respected leaders of the Congress-led movement for emancipation. His death also spared the new government a major power struggle in the drafting and adoption (on 26 November 1949) of the new constitution, whose principal hand was an old political foe of Gandhi's, the political leader of the 'untouchable' caste and law minister, Bhimrao Ambedkar.

'We, The People of India' began a document subsequently renowned for its length and sweeping breadth. When judged by the inherited standards of representative democracy, it was a remarkably forward-looking document that pointed well beyond the Westminster model. Its soberly written preamble described India as a 'sovereign democratic republic'. It stood for social, economic and political justice for all its citizens; liberty of thought, expression, belief, faith and worship; equality of status and of opportunity; and fraternity that would assure the dignity of 'the individual and the unity and integrity of the Nation'. A whole section of the new constitution contained what were called 'directive principles of state policy'. These obliged governments to set goals for enhancing the welfare of citizens, such as a minimum wage (Article 43), reserved jobs for those from the disadvantaged Scheduled Castes and Scheduled Tribes (Article 46), and free and compulsory education for children (Article 45). The new constitution prohibited arbitrary arrest and detention without trial (Article 22). It abolished 'untouchability' (Article 17) and 'discrimination on grounds of religion, race, caste, sex or place of birth' (Article 15). It declared Hindi in the Devanagari script to be the official language, but sanctioned the continuing use of English and other minority languages (Articles 343, 350). The document guaranteed freedom of citizens to 'practise any profession, or to carry on any occupation, trade or business' (Article 19) and drew a bold line through the employment of children under the age of fourteen (Article 24). The constitution guaranteed freedom of religion and reserved the right of the state to intervene in otherwise self-organising religious institutions, for instance to promote the equality of access and social welfare of their believers (Article 25). Provision was made for the appointment by the President of a Supreme Court with sharp teeth (Article 124); the establishment of a two-chamber parliament, known respectively as the Council of States (whose seats were to be filled by representatives nominated by the states) and the directly elected House of the People (Articles 79–81). The constitution provided for the setting up of an independent Election Commission to supervise, direct and control elections (Article 324). And it specified (Articles 83, 326) that full adult suffrage would be the basis of biennial elections for the Legislative Assembly of each state and five-yearly terms for the House of the People.

We Want No Caesars

Preparations for the first free parliamentary general elections began. Sukumar Sen, a mathematician-turned-civil-servant, was appointed as the first Chief Election Commissioner.* All adult women and men were simultaneously entitled to cast votes for the first time. There was tremendous popular excitement – and huge uncertainty about the future, for that is one of the distinctive experiences of moving towards democracy. No matter whether they succeed or fail, transitions to democracy are moments of hyper-uncertainty. Social groups previously unaware of their strength and excluded from politics suddenly get a whiff of political power. They sense that they can change things. The powerless prepare to swap places with the powerful. All that was once solid and taken for granted begins to melt into thin air. Rumour mills work overtime. Everybody speculates in this or that way about what will or will not happen. Nobody actually knows what the future will bring, which is why all eyes are often on leaders, or potential leaders, who sense within them enough power to feel their way towards the new.

---

*Following in the footsteps of William Boothby, Juan Vucetich and other unsung electoral experts, Sukumar Sen was nominated by Jawaharlal Nehru as India's Chief Election Commissioner in March 1950. Born in 1899, the son of a district magistrate, Sen was educated at the prestigious inter-faith Presidency College in Calcutta and at the University of London, where he was awarded a gold medal in mathematics. He joined the Indian Civil Service in 1921 and served in various districts as a judge before being appointed Chief Secretary of West Bengal, in 1947. Details of Sen's life remain obscure – he left behind neither papers nor memoirs – but his enduring love of mathematics and problem solving made him the ideal expert to oversee India's first general elections in 1951–52. The geometric scale of the exercise was colossal. The aim: to create a new electoral system that extended a fair vote for 4000 seats to 176 million Indians aged twenty-one or over, of whom about 85 per cent could not read or write. The methods: in quick time, 224,000 polling booths were built; two million steel ballot boxes were, meanwhile, manufactured and delivered to site; 16,500 clerks were hired on six-month contracts to type and collate the electoral rolls, on a constituency basis; 56,000 presiding officers and 280,000 support staff were appointed to supervise the voting; and 224,000 police officers were placed on duty outside polling stations. Sen had to solve other simultaneous equations, using new methods. Multiple ballot boxes installed at each polling station were designed to help voters who were predominantly illiterate. Each party was allocated its own box marked by a pictorial symbol: an elephant for one party, an earthen lamp for another, a pair of bullocks for the Congress Party. Helped by Indian scientists, Sukumar Sen also coordinated a scheme for preventing impersonation by fingerprinting each voter; the indelible ink, of which nearly 400,000 phials were used, lasted at least a week. In the interests of a fair and equal franchise, Sen also confronted patriarchal barriers to women's participation in the election. The diffidence of many women to allow their names to be entered on the electoral register – preferring instead to be X's wife or Y's mother – was criticised by him as a 'curious senseless relic of the past'. He instructed his officials to record the actual name of such women voters, but they sometimes refused. About 2.8 million women voters were consequently turned away. The public uproar that followed was judged by Sen to be a 'good thing' because he predicted – correctly – that it would help to corrode male prejudice against women.

Nehru's leadership skills are important for understanding how democracy came to India, despite everything. Such skills today remain a neglected topic among democrats, especially those who think leadership is equivalent to demagogy, hence incompatible with 'the rule of the people'. Nehru confounded the association of leadership with bosses and bellwethers. His considerable skills certainly played a key role in the country's first general elections, which began in October 1951 and – such was the scale of things in the world's largest democracy – took six months to conduct. Convinced that great causes and weak leaders go ill together, Nehru flung himself into the great 'choosing day' (the words of Walt Whitman) with energy to match. He travelled night and day some 25,000 miles, mostly by DC3 aeroplane, to urge India's voters, 85 per cent of whom were illiterate, to cast a vote for their own future (Figure 99). Both Madison and Hamilton, champions of republican government on a continental scale, would have been astonished to witness an election in which 75 political parties wooed the votes of 176 million adult women and men (for the first time in the history of the subcontinent the franchise was universal). There were 489 seats in the federal parliament and 3375 seats in the various state assemblies to be filled. For the first time, the public legitimacy of the Congress Party was put mathematically to

FIGURE 99: *Hasten Slowly*, an election cartoon by Shankar, with Congress President Purushottam Dan Tandon driving bullocks, a symbol of the Congress Party, and Nehru piloting a plane, 15 July 1951.

the test. The examination produced good results. On a voter turnout of 60 per cent, Nehru's party claimed victory in 18 of the 25 states and won an outright majority of seats (364 of the 489) in the lower house of the Lok Sabha (House of the People). On the strength of the Westminster-style first-past-the-post system, the overall vote for Congress amounted to only 45 per cent, yet the calculations were such that the government of India could plausibly claim that it had been democratically elected. The socialists were routed. The communists claimed second place – not such a bad result for a fledgling democracy, which had more hard-core Stalinists than the Soviet Union, and probably more fellow-travelling reds than fellow-travelling democrats. Nehru himself, facing a Hindu *sadhu* who tried to throw turmeric in the face of Nehru's alleged 'appeasement' of Muslims, meanwhile romped home in his own Uttar Pradesh constituency of Phulpur, by a thumping margin of 233,571 votes to 56,718.

From the moment of electoral triumph, leadership counted hugely in the Indian experiment with democracy. His own power-sharing predilections proved decisive, even infectious. His power of inspiring others around him to become little Nehrus was impressive. Reflecting splits within the Congress Party, the new prime minister deliberately appointed a cabinet that included many shades of Indian opinion. Nehru personally saw himself as playing the role of bridge between the socialist left wing and Hindu right-wingers who talked of dismissing Muslim officials, banning trade unions and generally promoting the interests of the Hindu majority. This was not simply a self-interested balancing act, or an exercise in retaining his leadership of the big-tent politics within a Congress Party that was to retain control of central government for nearly three decades. More was involved than that. As his best critic and India's most celebrated cartoonist K. Shankar Pillai pointed out, Nehru saw himself at the crease, facing some tricky bowling and determined fielding (Figure 100). Nehru wanted to observe the rules of the political game. The cultivation of political openness was an important goal to him. So, too, was the nurturing of secularism – not the secularism of the French or American constitutions, but something far more innovative, in effect a principled even-handedness that guaranteed the equality of all religions,

FIGURE 100: *Gallant Stand*, a cartoon by Shankar, featuring Nehru and Patel at the crease, with Jaya Prakash Narayan bowling and democracy as the umpire, 26 January 1950.

which implied the need for government policies to correct the imbalances of power among them.

Nehru's views on religion were paradoxical, yet they proved decisive in shaping the Indian transition towards a new form of post-Westminster democracy. There were times, mainly before becoming prime minister, when Nehru spoke like an atheist rationalist. 'Senseless and criminal bigotry struts about in the name of religion and instils hatred and violence into the people', he wrote for a speech someone else delivered on his behalf when he was ill in October 1923. Three years later, he told a Muslim friend that India could not 'breathe freely or do anything useful' until it rid itself of the 'terrible burden' of religion; and that that would require 'a course of study of Bertrand Russell's books'.[7] There was, however, another Nehru, the leader who grasped that cultures of the sacred would not wither away, and that therefore the problem was how to strike a new – democratic – compromise among India's multitude of faiths. Nehru thought of India as a secular democracy that resembled a once ancient, now modern palimpsest bearing traces of many faiths and ways of life. India should be a large canvas of many different colours – not a grey melting-pot country, and certainly not (to use an opposite image) a patchwork quilt of loosely connected or cantankerous faiths kept from each other's throats ultimately by the gun barrels of the state. Nehru was firmly opposed to any form of religious or ethnic fundamentalism. He favoured an Asian democracy crowded with cultural and religious distinctions that were horizontally interconnected. The canker of communalism turned his stomach. Partitioning was not his thing. That is why he vigorously resisted proposals, put forward by representatives from several religious minorities, including Muslims and Sikhs, for India to embrace a Swiss-style system of proportional representation and a ministry comprised of representatives from each and every party in the legislature. It was also why he had no truck with prejudice against Islam. A two-nations policy – one for Muslims and one for Hindus – stuck in his throat. It offended his very idea of India, and of democracy as a way of promoting respect among people of different religious suasion. So long as he was prime minister, he told an approving, large crowd in Old Delhi in 1952, he would do everything to prevent the spread of communalism. 'If any person raises his hand to strike down another on the ground of religion, I shall fight him till the last breath of my life, both at the head of the government and from outside.' Nehru meant it.

Backed by a big majority of the Congress Party, Nehru also meant business in matters of open and representative government. How to explain Nehru's democratic instincts? His choice to craft legitimate governing institutions through ballots and not bullets or bullying was the product of a long-running preoccupation with the subject. In his early years, he had quickly grasped the irony of British rule over the Indian subcontinent. The irony was this: although democracy was not their departing gift, they had broken the back of the pre-modern local order, with its limited kingship, its Brahmin social customs, its archipelago of villages gripped by a strong sense of social hierarchy. The British had begun the work of cutting into the social flesh of India – for instance, by outlawing the old patriarchal custom of *sati*, the cruel Hindu ritual of widows immolating themselves on the funeral pyre of their husbands. The British masters had as well cemented the foundations of a large-scale state defined by a limited, bowdlerised version of representative government. The British thereby confronted all

Indians with the fundamental question: shall the future form of government be more or less despotic or democratic?

Nehru was sure of his answer to that question. There was more than a grain of truth in his critics' description of him as the last liberal Englishman in India. It is commonly pointed out that he had a passion for chocolate cake, pies and ice-cream sundaes; that he preferred the company of Lord and Lady Mountbatten and other English friends (Gandhi once jokingly said that Nehru spoke English when he talked in his sleep); and that he had been educated into the manners of Harrow and Cambridge. It was for such reasons (as he wrote about himself) that Nehru was a political leader whose instincts were too aristocratic to favour either the crudity of political autocracy or the vulgarity of fascism. He might indeed be described (in European terms) as a conservative liberal democratic guild socialist, as exemplified by his remarks (in an unfinished review of Bertrand Russell's *Roads to Freedom*, 1918) that 'present-day democracy, manipulated by the unholy alliance of capital, property, militarism and an overgrown bureaucracy, and assisted by a capitalist press, has proved a delusion and a snare', whereas 'Orthodox Socialism does not give us much hope' because 'an all-powerful state is no lover of individual liberty ... Life under Socialism would be a joyless and soulless thing, regulated to the minutest detail by rules and orders.'[8]

Nehru was an Eastern democrat with Western qualities. He believed in fair play (the Indian capitalist and admirer G. D. Birla famously observed that Nehru was 'like a typical English democrat who takes defeat in a sporting spirit'). He was equipped with a sharp analytic mind (his Communist Party opponents nicknamed him 'the Professor') that had easily spotted the hypocrisy in the British Government of India Act of 1935. It had granted the vote to only 36 million out of India's 300 million people. Driven by the spirit of divide and rule, not pluralism, it had allocated seats in the national parliament disproportionately to religious and linguistic minorities; and it had denied the vote altogether to the poor majority. Nehru and the Congress Party were determined to reject such arrangements as hypocritical half-measures. Unlike the enemies of democracy who came before and after him, they had long ago drawn the implication that the universal franchise now had to be won. They cherished the widening struggle for parliamentary rule and the universal franchise in both Britain and the Indian colonies. They took heart from a major slip of the tongue in a report by the local Constituent Assembly, which admitted that in India although the voter's 'judgement may be faulty, his reasoning inaccurate, and his support of a candidate not infrequently determined by considerations removed from a high sense of democracy, he is yet no better or worse than the average voter in many parts of Europe where adult franchise has been in force for some time'.[9] Nehru couldn't contain his sarcasm towards such talk. 'Democracy for an Eastern country seems to mean only one thing', he wrote from prison sometime between June 1934 and February 1935: 'to carry out the behests of the imperialist ruling power and not to touch any of its interests. Subject to that proviso, democratic freedom can flourish unchecked.'[10]

The last phase of British rule, when, for instance, the military dictatorship arrogantly presided over the Great Bengal Famine of 1943 by diverting food (on Churchill's personal orders) from tens of thousands of starving civilians to lucky Tommies, proved to Nehru just how degenerate unchecked power could become. He knew personally about loss of freedom – he had suffered a grand total of 3262 nights in eight different prisons – which is why, having been trained as a lawyer, he called lawlessness by no other name. He strongly disliked bossing and violence, and had rock-ribbed feelings for civil liberties, consolidated by his first ever public speech, in mid-June 1916, in defence of the publisher and leader of the Home Rule League, Annie Besant, who openly defied the censorious Press Act.

Despite political disagreements, Nehru stood alongside Gandhi's insistence that independence was conditional upon the activation of India's millions of poor. Through his three terms as prime minister, Nehru continued to describe his policies as 'socialist'. By that he meant a commitment to state planning of industry and import substitution, tempered by his democratic liberal conservatism and good measures of local insights and habits. While he had a tendency to romanticise the undernourished, struggling wretched of the Indian earth, his commitment to their empowerment was passionate and unflagging. He had been impressed (during a visit to Ireland) by the Sinn Féin tactic of boycotting British goods and had absorbed something of Gandhi's faith in the self-reliance of the village, symbolised by the spinning wheel, homespun clothes and salt. Nehru had within his guts a dislike of colonialism – a dislike so visceral because it offended his democratic sensibilities. He knew that the equalisation of social power would not happen naturally, for instance through 'market forces'. Breaking even was not the same as giving everyone an even break. That is why Nehru was suspicious of 'free trade' and international capitalism. It was why he regarded state enterprises and projects like dams and factories as the 'new temples' of modern India. It was also why he was an unswerving champion of what came to be called the reservation system, the new set of rules designed to guarantee job and opportunity quotas for the downtrodden 'Scheduled Castes' and 'Scheduled Tribes', whether in schools and colleges, or in the public sector industries, the civil service, and in parliament itself.

What is especially interesting about Nehru is that, unlike almost all other post-colonial leaders of the twentieth century, he understood that the struggle for democracy could be damaged by tutelary figures acting as if they were dispensing *prasad* to adoring crowds. He was no Indian caudillo or bunyip aristocrat or European dictator. He worried about the dangers of power-drunken Caesarism, and on one remarkable occasion, when it looked as though he would probably succeed Gandhi as head of the Congress Party, he even penned a pseudonymous attack upon himself. Calling himself 'Chanakya' – Chanakya (c. 350–275 BCE) was a local political writer famous for saying that reckless kings will always fall prey to their foes – Jawaharlal Nehru said that Jawaharlal Nehru had 'all the makings of a dictator in him – vast popularity, a strong will directed to a well-defined purpose, energy, pride, organizational capacity, ability, hardness, and, with all his love of the crowd, an intolerance of others and a certain contempt of the weak and the inefficient . . .'. Nehru asked Nehru whether it was 'his will to power that is driving him from crowd to crowd'. His conclusions about himself – that he was capable of sweeping aside 'the paraphernalia of a slow-moving democracy' – were harsh. 'From the far north to Cape Comorin', he wrote, 'he has gone like some triumphant Caesar, leaving a trail of glory and legend behind him . . . His conceit is already formidable. It must be checked. We want no Caesars.'[11]

A great test of this principle was the second general election, in 1957. It produced even better results than the first. The Congress Party enjoyed a landslide victory. It won 65 per cent of seats in the state legislatures and 75 per cent of seats in the Assembly. In spite of sweet success, Nehru showed few signs of being tempted to turn himself into a 'dictator of the battlefield of elections' (as Max Weber and others had predicted would be the fate of all parliamentary democracies of the twentieth century).[12] Nehru certainly had plenty of alibis within reach. Here was a polylingual democracy that resembled Babel, a polity riddled with religious and communal violence, illiteracy, widespread poverty and mal-nourishment, a subcontinental republic – it seemed – tottering on the edge of the abyss. The Indian polity contained every conceivable racial type; thirty-five languages spoken by more than a million people; and it was home to every faith known to human-kind. Faced with such complications, Nehru demonstrated a remarkable resistance to the siren call of big boss man politics. At election rallies, when his supporters enthusiastically shouted 'Pandit Nehru Zindabad' (Long Live Pandit Nehru), he urged them instead to chant different words: 'Jai Hind' (Victory to India) or 'Naya Hindustan Zindabad' (Long Live the new India). He was equally opposed to playing the Hindu-leader nationalism game. A telling moment – the dramatic and widely publicised fast-unto-death of a southern Telugu-speaking Gandhian, Potti Sriramulu – was his strong public support for the creation of a Telugu-speaking Andhra Pradesh, and for a new body called the States' Reorganization Commission, which had recommended in 1955 the redrawing of India's internal boundaries, mainly along linguistic lines.

Nehru the democrat had no interest in becoming the sullen or moody Political Leader who had contempt for the masses and their own moods. He seemed to enjoy the rough 'n' tumble that was to become a hallmark of Indian elections, with their drummers and street dancers, firecrackers, processions, and winners carried aloft. 'Why don't you go and live in the country whose flag you are carrying?' he called out at a crowd sporting hammer-and-sickle

young Asian democracy could or should behave in a unipolar world dominated by the United States, and bristling with arms. Should India try to stick to its founding Five Principles? Was it better to behave in 'realist' ways, picking and choosing pragmatically from a variety of conflicting and ever-changing priorities? Did its democracy instead have a responsibility to intervene militarily in situations where innocent people were suffering rape, homelessness and murder? Should India strive to be a new superpower?

The answers to such questions were to remain controversial. Nehru's staunch but contradictory anti-imperialism suffered other weaknesses, including a taste for fantasies about the state as the great protector and ultimate liberator of the Indian people. The preoccupation of Nehru and the Congress Party with bureaucratic state planning of investment fed this trend. He had a native mistrust of foreign capital – it was as if every foreign company resembled the East India Company, which traded in order to rule – and he regarded local Indian capital as excessively concentrated, for which the remedy in both cases was state planning. Guided by the new constitution, which spoke of the 'directive principles' of state policy, a permanent Planning Commission was created, with Nehru as its first chairman. So began a series of Five-Year Plans that aimed to use state power to grant permits, issue licences, specify quotas and build steel mills, dams and institutes of technology, all in the name of shutting out foreign capital and fostering growth in the towns and the countryside. The successes were mediocre. Critics like Rajaji (who turned his back on Nehru to set up the pro-free enterprise Swatantra Party in 1959) slammed 'the Hindu rate of growth' (around 3 per cent, several times lower than many other Asian countries during this period). Expansion of output was certainly not enough to rescue the majority of Indians from pauperisation. In the agriculture sector during the 1950s, production actually fell to the point where India resorted to grain imports, a striking measure in a country where four-fifths of the population tried to grub and gouge a living from the land.

These failures of overstaffed, under-reactive 'socialist' state planning would later pressure Indian governments into adopting policies of deregulation, cutbacks of bloated state budgets, foreign investment and export-led growth. The dirigisme that came to dog

Indian democracy was compounded by corruption, at both the top and bottom of the system. At the bottom, corruption grew like a fungus in the crevices of everyday life. Bribery and democracy acted as if they were twins. Citizens found themselves dodging fines and legal action by 'giving tea' to police officers. 'Making the file heavy' – adding some rupee notes to speed up an application for some or other service from government – became routine practice. Special favours, for instance persuading officials to waive excess baggage charges at an airport, for a price, were equally common. Then there were the organised money-making rackets, within areas 'protected', at the point of a gun, by local criminal gangs, backed by the police or courts; or the political rackets, some of them directly related to electoral politics, beginning with unscrupulous 'vote banking' by crafty politicians and party officials. A favourite trick was to convince desperately poor people to move from the countryside into the city, where as homeless people they were housed in multi-storey slums, issued with electoral cards, instructed to vote the right way, in return for which the same voters might receive, say, free electricity or running water as a reward.

Towards the top of the system, 'civilised' corruption assumed such forms as the payment for posts like that of local police commissioner, or civil servant in some or other ministry. In the Church of England, stipends and pensions supplied to ensure a service were christened prebends. Within the Indian democracy, bribes and kickbacks were labelled with sugary names like 'trust' and 'working together' and 'providing services'. At the highest levels of government, some corruption undoubtedly stemmed from the choices Nehru made in pursuit of a 'just state using just means'. Given the immediate problem of crafting state institutions under pressure from potentially implosive or damaging domestic and international forces, Nehru and the Congress government understandably chose to rely upon the bulk of civil servants and armed services personnel who had served the British Raj. They put their faith in them, and this trust, in a state that issued regulations, quotas and licences for all sorts of business deals, handed civil 'servants' all sorts of opportunities to get rich quick, on a plate, or under the table. By the end of the first decade of constitutional government, Indian democracy, not surprisingly, was rocked by its first bribery and corruption scandals. Jayanti Dharma Teja, who had established a large shipping business with Nehru's help, defaulted on loan repayments and fled the country, to the safety of another democracy, Costa Rica. Shady dealings in the field of life insurance forced the resignation of Nehru's Finance Minister, T. T. Krishnamachari. Popularly known as TTK, he had consistently defended himself in parliament as a 'pillar of democracy', especially against his fiercest parliamentary critic, Feroze Gandhi, whom he had called 'a barking dog'. When Krishnamachari was finally trapped, his nemesis seized the moment. 'Mr Minister', he said, in the style of a true Indian democrat, 'you called me a dog, and termed yourself the pillar of democracy. Now I'll do to you what a dog does to a pillar!' Meanwhile, Nehru's old friend and long-standing private secretary M. O. Mathai was forced out after becoming entangled in the worst kind of allegations – spying for the CIA and piling up a private fortune.

Emergency

Amidst the mess, Nehru kept his hands clean, even though tongues wagged about his judgement of political character. He sometimes referred to his civil servants as the 'steel frame' of an independent India, but the industrial simile concealed the tough truth that the new state's structures were not embodiments of the public service ethic, let alone a Westminster notion of government ministers held responsible for supervising a non-partisan, expert civil service. The state structures instead had a large appetite for centralisation, bribery and arrogance. It came as no surprise that these qualities of government continued to flourish well after Nehru had departed the scene. During the 1970s, the booming oil industry sector was lubricated by tight money links that fastened government officials, the oil agency ONGC, foreign suppliers and their fixers. Much the same happened in the arms industry. Rumours circulated that the Defence Minister Shri Jagjivan Ram was in the habit of accepting 'stones' (diamonds) supplied by arms suppliers, who legitimised purchase entries in their account books by listing them as 'diamonds for tool cutting'. In 1971, one lucky ex-army captain, R. S.

Nagarwala, surely hit the boardgame jackpot by cleverly imitating the telephone voice of the new prime minister, Indira Gandhi, proceeding past go to collect six million rupees in cash from Mr V. P. Malhotra, the unsuspecting chief cashier of the State Bank.

Bizarre these incidents certainly were, but they were revealing of the authoritarian qualities of the Indian state that were cleverly exploited by Nehru's daughter. There had never been a plan to create a 'democratic dynasty', as it later came to be called, but it was the unexpected death of Nehru's successor, Lal Bahadur Shastri, a mere two years into his term of office, that signalled the start of something new in Indian politics – a second phase of parliamentary democracy in which many worried that democracy itself would be gobbled up by dictatorship.

After being chosen leader of Congress, with the backing of the powerful provincial party men known as the Syndicate, Mrs Gandhi turned on them. She was only the second woman to lead a representative democracy – Sirimavo Bandaranaike of Ceylon was the first – and wasted no time proving that she was capable of more than fly catching or twiddling thumbs (*makhi marna*, as the Indians say). With exquisite precision and impressive determination, she set about transforming the governing party, especially after its lacklustre performance in the 1967 elections, which it won with a reduced majority and the loss of control over eight state legislatures. Her project involved walking a tightrope across a political abyss, towards the land called the Indian People. It was a ploy new to the Indian electorate, but an old trick that belonged to the era of representative democracy, as we have seen in the different cases of Jacobinism in France, General Rosas in Argentina and the American critics of Tammany Hall. The chosen strategy of Mrs Gandhi was straightforward, if risky. It involved appealing over the heads of the Congress apparatus, directly to the society, and especially to its millions of poor. The aim was to win power for herself and for a new-style Congress government by disrupting the so-called 'vote banks' system, through which local party barons organised whole groups of voters, in return for which they received this or that preferential treatment by the central leadership of Congress.

The trouble was that Mrs Gandhi began to act as if she wore the

Koh-i-noor (the diamond that was once believed to grant its owner the right to rule the world). She demonstrated her resolve to shake up the whole political system by hurling the rhetoric of the left at her opponents. She seemed determined to replace the charisma of her father with some kind of Caesarist rule. Through posters, loud-hailers, and television and radio sets, the slogan 'Abolish Poverty' ('Garibi Hatao') was plastered everywhere. Compulsory vasectomy schemes were started. Constitutional protection for the privileges of the regional princes was abolished; the banks were nationalised; and she surprised millions by calling a general election one year early, thus breaking the traditional synchronisation of regional and central elections.

The effect for a time was to fix all eyes on her government – in essence to 'nationalise' Indian politics by distracting attention from regional and local concerns. For this display of populism Mrs Gandhi was rewarded with a handsome landslide victory, one that was bigger than any before, or since. Then came military conflict with Pakistan. Mrs Gandhi's swift, iron-fisted approach in the events that resulted in both victory and the secession of Bangladesh was again rewarded with rich electoral successes, this time in the 1972 regional elections. The way was now open to shrink democracy into elections and Congress itself into an election-winning machine that resembled a large, lumbering elephant with Mrs Gandhi in the saddle, garlanded with flowers, under a parasol, looking down imperially on the intrigued and admiring crowds.

But were Indian voters so intrigued, so admiring? Did they buy the view that India was Indira, and that Indira was India? Some bystanders began to ask what any of these reforms had to do with democracy. Others joined in. The first signs appeared that power-sharing democracy had taken root in Indian soil – that a lively, loquacious civil society using democratic freedoms to act at arm's length from both Congress and the state had been born. The cocoon of party politics in which the Asian democracy had been wrapped soon burst. Dissent ruptured the belief, inherited from the British Raj, that the head and hoof, haunch and hump of Law is obedience. Older beliefs in karma – in their crudest form, the stip-ulation that individuals wishing to improve their prospects in the next life must properly fulfil the caste roles assigned to them in this life – were shoved aside. To the surprise of many observers, there was a flourishing of a democratic ethic, of the belief that patterns of life on earth are shot through with time, that their power relations are utterly contingent, and that they can and sometimes must be transformed. Those who liked to say with a sigh that no man or woman could escape their fate (*kismet*) held their tongues. Street protests erupted. Angry faces filled television screens. Political thinkers like Rajni Kothari – the earliest and most insightful home-grown Tocqueville of the Indian scene – pondered the nature of democracy for the first time since independence.[14]

Local communities mobilised. A 'People's March on Parliament' and other massive demonstrations ensued. Millions began to feel that parliamentary democracy was becoming an empty shell – and that they could free themselves from the Great Wheel of Things by cutting the cords of despotism. Mrs Gandhi's personalisation of Indian politics backfired. In the name of democracy, she and her cronies were blamed personally for all that was perceived to be wrong with India.

Her response was dictatorial. Summoning up powers that the Constitution (Articles 352–360) had cleverly borrowed from the British Empire, Mrs Gandhi manoeuvred the president into declaring a state of Emergency, on 26 June 1975. That morning, as the government cut off electricity in Delhi to halt the production of newspapers, the Bombay edition of the *Times of India* published an obituary of 'D'Ocracy – D. E. M., beloved husband of T. Ruth, loving father of L. I. Bertie, brother of Faith, Hope, Justice, expired on 26th June'. Many readers found the news frightening; and they no doubt concluded that the death of democracy was less a sudden seizure and more the culmination of a process of manipulative politics set in motion some years earlier by supposedly democratic men. The Emergency was not exactly martial law, but the army certainly puffed its uniformed chest and strutted through streets, weapons cocked. Judicial procedures and democratic rights were suspended. Public gatherings of more than five citizens were banned. Some members of parliament found themselves behind bars. The communist government headed by E. M. S. Namboodripad in the southern state of Kerala – among the first ever freely elected such governments in the world – was sacked. There was spreading talk of the constitution as a millstone around the necks of those who wanted to improve the lot of India. President's Rule, an Emergency power enabling direct rule from the centre of a province, was used with painful frequency; during the first two decades of independence, such rule had been used twenty times, whereas during the next two decades, from 1967, President's Rule was invoked seventy times, a trend for which Mrs Gandhi was heavily responsible. Federal initiatives burgeoned. Parliament and cabinet were consistently bypassed. Sidestepped as well were the old structures and party faithful of Congress. Mrs Gandhi cultivated a brand-new power base: the so-called Youth Congress run by her trusted younger son, Sanjay, himself surrounded by young men of dubious backgrounds, dressed in smart suits and wide ties, the midnight's children of Nehru's India, all keen to hallucinate on whiffs of political power. Governmental power, meanwhile, moved rapidly towards the centre of the centre – to the Prime Minister's Office in Delhi, a city that in turn Mrs Gandhi decided to adorn. Like the British before her, she moved to make her own physical mark on the capital by commissioning Jagmohan, the Lieutenant Governor of Delhi, to 'Make Delhi Beautiful'. Her picture was posted everywhere. Slums were bulldozed. Trees were planted. The Emergency was to endure – and to be remembered.

Remembered it was, but not in the way that the Leader's advisers and flatterers had expected. Such was their confidence that they managed to convince Mrs Gandhi to go to the polls in 1977. The Leader was misled. Dressed in fine hubris, she came to the election table, only to be forced to eat humble pie. The election aroused tremendous passions and gave a voice to groups – farmers, the poorer castes, untouchables – whose voices previously had not counted for much. They rounded especially on the new authoritarianism and its policies, symbolised by the abusive vasectomy programmes championed by her son, Sanjay. Votes piled up against her to the point, for the first time in the history of Indian democracy, where Congress lost control of the central government. The Janata Party, a motley alliance of various forces, swept the polls, winning a majority of parliamentary seats. Morarji Desai became the first non-Congress prime minister of India, and many Congress Party loyalists – backed by a spirited poster campaign that featured

FIGURE 101: Election poster featuring the heroic Congress Party rescuing the distressed damsel of Democracy, 1980.

democracy as a damsel in distress – deserted Indira Gandhi, who herself lost her own parliamentary seat (Figure 101).

The new non-Congress government quickly descended into serious bickering; it fell apart after two years. New elections were called, and in the summer of 1980 a humbled and visibly more nervous Mrs Gandhi crawled back into office. In quick succession, the two souls of democracy – the yearning for civil and political freedom and the felt need for predictable order – had made their mark on the Indian polity. Indian citizens had set an example that others elsewhere in the world would soon follow. They had demonstrated that the arrogant could be humbled, taught (as Spinoza once put it) that they could not make a table eat grass, and that dictatorship could be defeated using democratic means.

Civil Society

The rejection of dictatorship by the voting poor and their supporters resonated with a country whose favourite sport is cricket, that levelling game of games marked by patience, wrist-work and cunning, and by outcomes that sometimes change with startling speed, surprises that prove that calculated certainty is unreliable, that the underdog can come out on top, that the principle of the survival of the strongest and fittest is by no means absolute. But in the overthrow of the Emergency more was at stake than doosras, leg byes or a catch in the slips. It triggered a new dynamic, in which the levelling ethos of democracy began visibly to make its mark on old attitudes towards social inferiority. The poor demonstrated that the act of voting can sometimes have instant empowering effects, that election days can be their days, when they get shot of the rich and powerful who tower over them.

But what happens the morning after? That was the key question that worried Dr Ambedkar (Figure 102) on the day (25 November 1949) that the Indian Constitution was adopted. 'In politics we will be recognizing the principle of one man one vote and one vote one value', noted Ambedkar, who was born into a poor untouchable community. 'In our social and economic life, we shall, by reason of our social and economic structure, continue to deny the principle of one man one value.' Something would have to give, he predicted. 'How shall we continue to deny equality in our social and economic life? If we continue to deny it for long, we will do so only by putting our political democracy in peril.'[15]

FIGURE 102: Necklaces with lockets bearing the portrait of the chief architect of the Indian Constitution, Bhimrao Ambedkar (1891–1956), at a stall near his memorial in Mumbai, 2007, photograph by Gautam Singh.

Both question and prediction had roots in the fields of nineteenth-century social democracy, for instance in the thinking of rebels like Stephan Born, but in the Indian context they resembled a razor wielded with dramatic effect by the caste-ridden poor – the majority – against the pseudo-inevitability of their life's lot. Dr Ambedkar spoke against what he called *bhakti*, the bad habit of degrading oneself by following the path of devotion and hero worship. In effect, he begged the poor to cast their votes against caste. He urged them to rise up through democracy, to use the suffrage to shake off their suffering, to bid farewell to the age of helplessness, to see that only they themselves could win the struggle to live in dignity and self-respect. Proof that it was possible in practice to mobilise this spirit of democracy came with several new developments. They were to demonstrate that the new Asian democracy was not just the world's largest democracy – a tiresome cliché – but also its most dynamic and potentially most innovative form.

The defeat of martial law first of all demonstrated that popular mobilisation 'from below' might well be able to change things, or at least prevent bad things from happening. It was no coincidence that from the time of Mrs Gandhi's dictatorship India witnessed the birth of a civil society energised by a kaleidoscope of social groups and networked 'grass roots' movements, all of whom felt the need to make their mark on government policy by breaking up the patronage-ridden Congress system. Especially from the early 1980s, some of these civil initiatives focused on ethnic questions, as in the Punjab and Assam; or dealt with matters of tribal identity, as in the Jharkhand and Chhatisgarh movements; or came as struggles for public recognition by the so-called backward classes in Gujarat, Uttar Pradesh, Bihar and elsewhere. Other initiatives took the form of rice-and-chapatti actions, as in the upsurge of peasants and agricultural labourers in the Telengana and Naxalbari movements, and in the formation of the Bharatiya Kisan Union by middle-caste farmers in north India.

Civic initiatives began to spread rapidly, in the process spawning new public institutions. An example is the way sexual violence, unfair practices like *triple talaq* (divorce decided by a husband uttering the word *talaq* three times, spaced over his wife's three consecutive menstrual cycles) and other family justice matters began to be raised and dealt with, especially by Muslim women, through a variety of newly formed personal law boards and courts known as *lok adalats*. The first of these local people's courts was established in Chennai in 1986. Operating parallel to the established judiciary, they were an important political innovation, and proved to be popular with citizens. Inspired by Article 39-A of the Constitution, which specified that the legal system should promote justice, on the basis of equal opportunity, and in particular provide free legal aid, by suitable legislation or schemes that ensured that citizens were not disadvantaged by economic or other disabilities, the *lok adalats* were a new extra-parliamentary means of deciding who got what, when and how. Designed to settle disputes quickly, free of charge and through compromise, so that enmity, time and unnecessary expenditure were kept to a minimum, the decisions of these parallel courts were final. Not surprisingly, with the passage of time their scope gradually widened, from matrimonial affairs to matters such as traffic offences, employment grievances, bank loans and compoundable criminal cases.

The political geography of Indian democracy was further altered by new initiatives aimed at defending the environment, or reshaping the course of economic development. Groups organised at the local and regional levels began to demand a say in decisions that previously, under the Nehru model of growth, were monopolised by planners, economists and scientists, behind firmly closed doors. Unchecked industrialisation and economic growth suddenly became controversial; civil society groups took up matters ranging from the unregulated growth of shrimp farms dotting the Indian coastline to choking traffic in Delhi and the tarnishing of the Taj Mahal by pollution from a nearby oil refinery. The new pace was set by the large and vigorous movement in the Narmada Valley against the construction of the Sardar Sarovar dam, plans for which had fascinated Nehru. The protesters used mainly Gandhian methods of non-violent resistance, including declarations of their willingness to drown in the face of submergence. Their courage and discipline were greeted with repression and violence by the Gujarat authorities. Some small local initiatives became nationally famous, like the mobilisation of the Maharashtra village community of Ralegaon Shindi by Annasaheb Hazare and her supporters; once barely able to produce less than a third of its own food, the village set about building embankments and storage ponds that so recharged the local water-table level that crop productivity rose dramatically. Less well-publicised initiatives – the 2005 Rajasthan water consultation on ground water management, for example – promised not only more sustainable and more equitable patterns of growth. Such water consultation initiatives qualified as a new organ of political representation for civil society, a mechanism that in effect moved beyond the parliament-centred, Nehru-led Congress model of democracy.

The shift coincided with a dramatic increase in the numbers of non-governmental organisations. By the year 2000 there were an estimated two million Indian NGOs, so many of them staffed or led by women that (according to some wags) the parents of a young man looking for a good bride no longer found themselves offering her a plot of land, an air conditioner or a car, but sums of money to start her own NGO. The growing public visibility of women was not just a middle-class affair. Their heavy involvement in group actions among the historically disadvantaged lower castes, especially the *dalits* (untouchables) and the castes officially named the Other Backward Classes (OBCs), symbolised the growth of a great democratic upsurge within the lower ranks of Indian society. Unlike any other democracy on the face of the earth, the Indian poor – despite the absence of compulsory voting arrangements – began to turn out at election time in proportionately greater numbers than the affluent middle and upper castes. In the first two general elections, overall voter turnout was under 50 per cent. Beginning with the 1977 elections, the first held after the Emergency, the figure reached around 60 per cent, where it consistently remained, the increase due largely to the growing political involvement of the poor. In states like Uttar Pradesh, *dalits* and other members of the lower castes were much more likely to vote than the affluent, where voter apathy proportionately rose. Such figures suggested something remarkable about the country: that support for democracy grew stronger in the bottom half of the socio-economic scale, that the humblest of India's most humble became disproportionately convinced that the ballot box was a means of redemption.[16]

Quotas

The introduction of quota arrangements and an upsurge of regional parties helped to consolidate the trend towards a post-Westminster democracy. The principle of quotas had roots in the era of representative democracy, for instance in the form of minimum representation for (say) islands and densely or sparsely populated regions. There had been experiments (from 1867 New Zealand was the prototype) with special or reserved parliamentary seats for indigenous peoples; and rules had been applied for the purpose of providing special representation for minorities defined by their ethnic, religious, regional or linguistic identities. But it was in India, following the defeat of the Emergency, that quotas came to play a special role, one more vigorous, powerful and far-reaching than anything experienced in the age of representative democracy. With the 1980 Mandal Commission Report, whose recommendations began to be implemented a decade later by the V. P. Singh government, all state institutions were required to set aside places and jobs for groups whom the Constitution had originally called the Scheduled Castes and Scheduled Tribes. Government also had to make room for the so-called 'backward classes' (the mainly Shudra castes, estimated by the Commission at 52 per cent of the population).

Designed to bring greater equality and openness to Indian society, the reforms had the unintended effect of stimulating caste consciousness. The winds of change whipped up fires of protest, particularly in northern parts of the country among lower-middle-class, upper-caste youth, many of whom had seen their future in a government job. Their reaction against what they dubbed 'Mandalism' symbolised the beginning of a new kind of democratic caste struggle that had the effect of turning the categories inherited from the colonial period on their heads. The disadvantaged castes and tribes were now to be represented in public institutions in proportion to their actual numbers in society. Since government was the employer of the big majority of waged and salaried workers in India, the new reservation system also had the effect of snapping the patron–client chains once forged by Congress. For the sake of

FIGURE 103: Mayawati garlanded by supporters of her Bahujan Samaj Party in Lucknow, June 2005, photograph by A. K. Singh.

democracy, many concluded, limits had to be enforced on the power of certain citizens for the sake of empowering others.

The legal requirement to reserve spaces in the parliament and the state legislatures, and in public sector employment, including education, had a felt and visible impact on all of these institutions. The caste-consciousness effect was consolidated by the vote hunger of regional caste-based political parties headed by iridescent figures who brought a certain abracadabra quality to Indian democracy. One of them was Mayawati (Figure 103), the first woman to become chief minister of the large state of Uttar Pradesh; she was a leader who loved sometimes to wear a golden crown and, verbal sword in hand, to deliver thumping speeches about the importance of creating an 'egalitarian society', without discrimination based on caste or creed. Another iridescent leader was the political boss of Bihar, Laloo Prasad Yadav, famous for spicing his speeches with songs from Bollywood films after alighting from his helicopter, pet parrot on his shoulder. Calling for more than jobs, and bearing names like the RJD (Rashtriya Janata Dal), the SP (Samajwadi Party) and the largest *dalit*-based party, the BSP (Bahujan Samaj Party), these parties stirred up controversies in civil society and intensified political competition, both in the states and at the centre of Indian politics. A record thirty-one different parties, most of them elected from the regions, filled the national parliament following the

1996 general elections. Playing the role of spoilers and bargainers, many of these parties had in effect a one-point programme – to get hold of government by elbowing others out of the way. Their single-mindedness soon proved effective. Despite undergoing splits and 'unity efforts' and splits again, these splinter parties pushed the young Asian democracy to the point where, from the mid-1990s, no government in Delhi was formed without their help. Poverty implied political power. It meant holding on to reservations; resistance to atrocities; and winning and holding office, against better organised opponents.

Panchayats

The kaleidoscopic effects of extra-parliamentary politics and the empowerment of the poor were compounded by another striking development: the 1993 agreement by the Indian parliament to extend democracy 'downwards' and 'sideways', by introducing local self-government to India's 600,000 villages and towns.

The so-called *panchayat* reforms were publicly justified in democratic terms. Their architects argued that participation in local government could empower the less powerful members of Indian society. It was said as well that diverse local problems could be better handled by more accountable and socially sustainable 'decentralised planning' anchored at the local level, rather than in the remote regions of central government. These sentiments were fed by a strong sense within government circles that the old Congress model of poverty alleviation and bureaucratically organised 'trickle-down' economics had failed, and that a new departure required breaking the grip of rural elites on the use and distribution of resources, especially water and common pastures.

Despite the obvious irony that the reforms were introduced from above without much clamour, on behalf of the excluded, in their defence the scale of the changes was impressive, and not just on paper. In the countryside, the drive to create a new three-tier structure of local government resulted in the formation of some 227,000 'village councils' at the base; 5900 higher-level or 'block councils' comprising representatives drawn from the village councils; and standing above these over 470 'district councils'. Similar structures (municipal corporations and councils) were erected in the cities, so that the ranks of the country's elected representatives – some 500 MPs and 5000 state representatives – were swelled by another three million newly elected men and women representatives. The effect was to create a huge number of new spaces in which the downtrodden, especially women, *dalits* and tribal people known as *adivasis* (literally, 'original inhabitants') could contribute actively to decisions about who got what, when and how. All *panchayat* posts were subject to the deliberations and watchdog powers of village assemblies and to the constraint of free and fair election on a universal basis, normally on a five-year cycle. One third of the seats were set aside for women. *Dalits* and *adivasis* were also guaranteed seats in proportion to their actual numbers in the local region. Sometimes they found themselves in a clear majority.

Voter turnout in these *panchayat* spaces was generally higher than for state and national elections, despite flaws in the design and implementation of the new structures – the failure of fiscal decentralisation to keep pace with political decentralisation, for instance. The inability of local governments to legislate or to take either the states or the central government to court over jurisdictional disputes – in other words, the absence of the powerful body of local government case law that there is in the United States federal system – proved to be a hindrance to local empowerment. Meanwhile, every trick in the book was flung at the weak by the strong. Village assemblies were often not convened; when held they were often improperly conducted, or inquorate, or their records were falsified, so enabling village oligarchs to get away with blue murder. Women candidates and voters were frequently harassed, especially in areas where purdah was observed. Elected women representatives were disproportionately under-represented, thanks to the tactic of replacing them with proxies, usually their husbands. Elected local government leaders (called *sarpanches*) from the reserved castes were physically prevented from taking up office ('sitting on the Sarpanch Chair'), or forced to defer to the upper-caste deputy chair. Leaders were denied access to telephones and offices. They were called insulting (lower-caste) names; barred from entering upper-caste homes; and excommunicated from village ceremonies, such as the award of prizes, the hoisting of the national flag, and delivering welcome speeches to visiting music and theatre troupes. Tougher tactics were common. The favourite was playing the foul game of pinning the tail of incompetence on the quota-system donkey by obstructing local development projects, or by embroiling lower-caste or women *sarpanches* in real or imagined funding scandals. And, when all else failed, the dominant castes threatened – and often used – violence. Citizens were kidnapped, lives were taken, homesteads burned, women raped, usually with impunity, sometimes with the help of local police and shadow-world gangsters.

Banyan Democracy

Despite such goings-on, the *panchayat* reforms survived; in many areas they thrived, thanks principally to the powerful cycle of changes that had pushed Nehru's India towards a new kind of democracy under the subcontinental sun.

Indian democracy was no tropical version of the Westminster model of government. It had supposed that citizens' needs could be championed primarily through elected parliamentary representatives organised by political parties and civil servants, without a written constitution. By contrast, the break with empire pushed the young Asian democracy into uncharted waters. It sailed towards a compound form of representative government, one defined by many new qualities. India proved that one of the lessons the history of democracy teaches us is that history sometimes teaches us the wrong lessons. India showed not only that democracy could surmount violence and carnage; it proved that democracy could thrive within a society that lacked a homogenous *dēmos*, a civil society shackled by poverty and illiteracy and crowded with all sorts of cultural, religious and historical distinctions.

India demonstrated as well that a democracy could experiment with new mechanisms designed to introduce greater public accountability in the making of decisions by government, at all levels, in all fields. In virtually every case, the new accountability mechanisms were purveyors of the principle that periodic elections were not enough, that citizens' interests must be represented not just through general elections and debates and decisions in the central parliament, but as well through a wide variety of post-Westminster processes. On the long and interesting list of innovations were a robust written constitution, the creation of a three-tier system of government driven by stronger local self-government and the more explicit division of powers between states and central government. Of equal importance were the introduction of compulsory quotas for representing groups previously excluded from politics; a stronger role for judicial review through the courts; the constitutional exemption of parts of the country from laws made in federal or state parliaments (as in the so-called Fifth Schedule amendment that protects the rights of indigenous peoples to the land they live on); and experiments with *satyagraha* campaigns of non-violent resistance. And of vital importance was the application of new power-checking mechanisms, including *lok adalats* and water consultation schemes, but also extra-parliamentary inventions like participatory budgeting; 'yellow card' reports on government services issued by citizens' groups; the handling of public disputes through railway courts; fiercely fought student election campaigns; and the invention of public-interest litigation, a new method of defining the public interest by enabling individuals and groups – women who were being abused by their husbands, or prisoners suffering mental illness, for instance – to have their grievances presented on their behalf to the courts by public-spirited individuals, or by the courts themselves.

How significant were these various innovations dating from the time of the Emergency? It is hard to visualise their compound effects, to find a language in which to speak about them. Perhaps banyan democracy is a good term, if only because the much more complex patterns of representation of citizens' interests began to resemble, in form at least, the multi-trunk tree with aerial roots that grows throughout the subcontinent, a giant tree known in English as the banyan tree, whose interlinked roots and branches and massive canopy are often used as a symbol of the unity that came from diversity (Figure 104). Among the largest trees on earth – they can reach more than 30 metres in height and 200 metres in diameter, to cover an area of several hectares – the

FIGURE 104: A banyan tree, from a watercolour by an unknown artist (c. 1825).

banyan is sacred, especially to Hindus and Buddhists. Enshrined in ancient Hindu myth as the 'wish-fulfilling tree', it is described in Sanskrit as 'many-footed', or as 'one with many feet', a reference to its aerial roots and aura of immortality that stems from its extraordinary capacity for growth, expansion and regeneration. The tree is mentioned as well in the Buddhist Jataka tales, for instance in the story of Savitri, who courageously entered into a debate with Yama, the God of Death, and won his life back. Minor deities are still believed by some Indians to dwell in the branches of the banyan, whose defacement or destruction is considered a sin. It is also a useful tree. The English name for the banyan tree comes from 'banyans' or 'banians', the Hindu traders who were often seen resting or carrying out their business in the shade provided by the massive tree canopy. In contemporary India, many communities have a banyan tree that provides fruit for humans in times of food shortage, shelter from the elements, a place to sleep and relax and chat, as well as a space where the community can meet to discuss and decide important matters. So, to speak of the banyan tree when trying to understand the local democracy is not only to underline the path-breaking historical importance of the Indian experiment with democracy; it is also to underscore the much greater 'depth' and 'span' of this form of democracy, certainly when compared to the Nehru model of self-government. The point is that following the defeat of the Emergency, democratic ideals and power-sharing mechanisms began to extend sideways and downwards, into the nooks and crannies of Indian government and society. Households and villages, states and whole central government departments began to be touched by their presence. So did corporations, castes and the rest of civil society. Banyan democracy had deep roots, many trunks and tall branches that stretched not only upwards, but outwards as well. The sacred banyan tree symbolised the coming of democracy to India: not only did India now feel more democratic, but democracy itself came to feel more Indian.

Stars

Among the most important implications of the banyan model of democracy was that parties and politicians could not be relied upon fully to address citizens' needs – and that other public channels were vital for representing their concerns, and dealing with their grievances.

The collective sense that elections, parties and parliaments were not everything, and that democratic politics mattered to everyone, including the poorest of the poor, was undoubtedly animated by the astonishingly high degree of media saturation of Indian life. Less than a generation after gaining independence, the country that began with high levels of illiteracy was heavily hooked on books, magazines and the biggest and liveliest newspaper industry in the world. Audiences for radio, television and theatre became huge; the media landscape even made room for star musicians. There was the world-renowned sitar player Ravi Shankar; the folk singer Gaddar, famous for an early hit song about the rickshaw pullers of Hyderabad, a *dalit* musician revered by peasants in Andhra Pradesh and other states for living a life on the run, in and out of jail, questioning police brutality, celebrating the efforts of the poor to resist the rich; and there was the remarkable female singer M. S. Subbulakshmi, known as MS, loved publicly for her many classical and folk compositions, and for memorable charity concerts given in support of women's groups, hospitals, sanatoria and public sector employees.

Of monumental significance in understanding how India managed to push itself towards a banyan democracy was its thriving film industry. The subject of movies and democracy is often neglected, but the entertaining fact is that the two came to have a special affinity after Indians won independence from the British Empire. The scale, dynamism and genuine popular appeal of the industry were breathtaking. Movies were first produced locally during the 1920s, but markets were small. By the time of independence, 250 films were being produced annually; by 1990, when India had long overtaken the United States as the world's leading producer of films, more than 900 new films were screened each year in more than 9000 theatres.

The growth spurt of cinema brought out the priggish in force. Indian film was derided as a mere pleasant distraction from unpleasant realities, as ocular opium for the toiling masses. Many prominent early Congress movement figures certainly thought that films corrupted Indians with sex and violence and a sense of unreality. That is why they supported the establishment of a Censor Board. Nehru evidently did not frequent the cinemas; and Gandhi, who was said to have only ever half-watched one film in his life, stubbornly declined invitations to view a 1930s classic, *Achut Kanya*, a love tale featuring a Brahmin man and a *dalit* woman.

Democracy is admittedly no fairy-tale world, but the backlash was hardly fair, indeed uncomprehending of the forces unleashed by the pageantry of popular cinema. For a start, Indian democracy produced one of the great masters of an elliptical form of twentieth-century neo-realism, Satyajit Ray, news of whose death (in 1992) brought his Bengali birthplace of Calcutta virtually to a standstill, with several hundred thousand mourners gathered outside his home. Showered by scores of awards, including an Oscar for 'lifetime achievement', Ray directed more than thirty major films. Many feature strong, intelligent, independent women, whose lives are interwoven with a society crammed with poverty and wealth, misery and hope, envy and generosity, conflict and accommodation. Ray made detective films, historical dramas and outstanding children's films (based on stories written by his grandfather); and sometimes his work touched directly on matters of basic importance to the survival of democracy itself. Inspired by the Norwegian playwright Henrik Ibsen, Ray's award-winning *Ganashatru* (Enemy of the People, 1989) was an exemplary tale of how disasters can be averted through citizens' stubborn use of their practical intelligence, even in the face of humbuggery. A small town in Bengal stands on the cusp of an outbreak of a life-threatening mystery illness. A wise doctor employed at the town hospital grows convinced that the source of contamination is a local temple, whose 'holy water' is being served to unsuspecting pilgrims. The good doctor goes public, but when he proposes that the temple be closed down temporarily, so that the source of contamination can be repaired, the sky crashes on his head. His brother, who leads the town's municipal government, reacts badly. So, too, does the builder of the temple, an industrialist who spearheads a campaign of whispers and threats designed to convince the local community that the doctor is an enemy of the people.

The work of Satyajit Ray was often described as 'art cinema', to distinguish it from the rough-and-tumble feature films that came to be the great popular passion of Indian citizens. The grip of these films on Indians' imaginations undoubtedly helped banyan democracy take root. With their love stories, unrestrained fights, chases and tears, their blazing colours and song-and-dance routines, these films cut through the divides of caste, gender, religion, class and language. While the biggest box office hits were in Hindi, a language understood throughout much of the country, nearly as many were produced in Tamil, and still more in the languages of Marathi, Bengali, Telugu, Malayalam and Kannada. Film helped citizens to feel publicly represented, in the language, religion or region of their choice.

Cinema undoubtedly served as a means of advancement for talented Muslims, who wielded great influence as the scriptwriters and master creators of the fusion music and richly poetic lyrics that made Indian films both original and special. Of importance as well was the way that popular cinema served as a platform for 'stars' to function as potential rivals of elected politicians, keeping them on their toes. It was not just that stars inspired tens of thousands of fan clubs, many of them better organised (and certainly much more fun) than political parties. The stars themselves went into politics. An example was M. G. Ramachandran (1917–87), who became chief minister of Tamil Nadu on the basis of his prior fame as 'MGR', the megastar who played characters skilled at rescuing the poor and championing their self-respect. MGR's much talked-about policies, for instance the provision of midday meals for pupils in all government-run and -aided schools, proved so popular that his death prompted extreme reactions. In his home state of Tamil Nadu, there were dozens of suicides and a month's rioting and looting; a million mourners attended his funeral and several hundred thousand people had their heads tonsured, as a mark of respect and devotion.

There were times when the public adventures of stars left elected politicians looking grubby and greedy, or simply unrepresentative of citizens' hopes and fears. The prototype of the new development, the growth of unelected representatives revered by Indian society, was the son of a famous Hindi poet of Allahabad, Amitabh Bachchan. It was no accident that his rise to fame during the 1970s coincided with rising mistrust of politicians and parliaments. Baritone-voiced Bachchan specialised in playing the disgruntled hero battling (and winning) against a system of power; he was the honest police officer encircled by corrupt superiors, or the underworld gangster with a heart of gold. Bachchan featured as well in hit films like Manmohan Desai's *Amar Akbar Anthony* (1977), a comic story of three brothers separated in childhood and brought up as Hindu, Muslim and Christian respectively (the brothers are reunited in the end, naturally). Following an accident while filming a fight scene, millions of Indian citizens prayed in temples for his recovery. Their prayers were answered. Bachchan went on to become a Congress MP – his parliamentary victory margin (68.2 per cent) was the highest ever in Indian history – but with scandal hovering around his ears he quit politics early, to return to the screen. Following some box office flops and fraught business deals, he managed to relaunch himself, as the massively popular presenter of *Kaun Banega Croropati?*, India's rendition of the British television game show *Who Wants to Be a Millionaire?*.

Shining India?

The growth of a star-studded society wrapped in a colourful mix-ture of media tales imparted a definite resilience to the banyan democracy. It reinforced the common sense that there was no alter-native to the democratic coexistence of castes, creeds, cultures, colours, cuisines, customs and costumes. Within a parliamentary system in which political corruption flourished – several studies showed that by the early years of the new millennium around a quarter of all 543 Indian members of parliament were facing crim-inal charges, half of them elected from the four northern states of Jharkhand, Bihar, Madhya Pradesh and Uttar Pradesh – a resilient political culture of stardom put India's politicians on their toes by offering alternative role models. By multiplying the public channels of extra-parliamentary representation of people's private concerns, it also undoubtedly helped Indian democracy survive its second big test: a challenge from a government of demagogues bent on using questionable tactics to put an end to the principles and practices of democratic coexistence. The full force of the assault was felt in the spring months of 2004, during the most bitterly fought general election in Indian history. The battle consolidated the trend away from the Congress-dominated party system inherited from the Nehru period. But more was at stake than the question of whether a two- or multi-party system was good for democracy, or whether Congress could recover from defeat. For the election struggle frightened many observers into thinking that democracy itself might suffer an untimely death.

The fear had deep taproots. By the end of the 1940s, Congress had successfully transformed itself from the umbrella organisation of the resistance movement into a governing party at the centre of Indian political life. Under the tutelage of Nehru, it had functioned as a 'big tent' party. Its aim had been to agglomerate as many parts of the Indian electorate as possible, to form a hegemonic bloc that no competitor could unseat. Although it never managed to win an absolute majority of votes in any general election, challengers, like the free-market Swatantra Party, which lasted from 1959 until 1974, found the going tough. Yet the first electoral victories against

Congress, for instance in West Bengal and Tamil Nadu during the 1960s, were portentous. A dense forest of regionally based parties slowly sprang up, organised by politicians hungry for office and eager to take advantage of voters – religious believers, speakers of minority languages, ethnic groups – who felt muzzled or squeezed out by the 'catch-all' strategy of Congress. So instead of (say) a three-party system defined by a right wing, a middle-of-the-road social democracy and a left wing dominated by communists, the Indian party system began to be defined by Congress versus the rest – with the latter splintered into scores of razor-edged shards defined by their visceral opposition to others because of their caste, spoken language, or religious faith. In the Indian jargon, a myriad parties went hunting for 'vote banks'.

They did so not out of any inclusive political principles, as Nehru had done when appealing for support for Congress, but rather by targeting particular self-centred loyalties. This politics of exclusion dug much dirt. The struggle for votes sometimes went hand in hand with unseemly parliamentary conduct and behind-the-scenes backstabbing, even (as in Chandigarh in early 2005) the use of *lathi* and water cannon by police against dissident parliamentarians wearing black arm bands and protesting against 'the murder of democracy'; and in some states, Bihar for instance, pockets of lawlessness spread as parties fought like gangs, replete with 'self-defence committees' run by fearless dons (called *dabang*) prepared to kidnap and murder in support of their aims.[17]

Such incidents were most definitely not understandable as the return of primitivism, as outsiders (repeating colonial prejudices) sometimes claimed. This was a thoroughly modern, cutting-edge phenomenon, an unsavoury form of exclusivist politics that not only had its roots in the efforts of the British, during the colonial era, to categorise people for the sake of better administrative control. The politics of exclusion was also the poisonous fruit of a democracy that had been dominated by one party – a toxin that not only triggered the delirious pushing and elbowing of a myriad splinter parties against Congress. It induced a much more dangerous reaction: the formation of a new, potentially dominant party, a middle-class party impatient with democracy, a power-hungry group both anxious about its possible fall from power and, gushing with nationalist enthusiasm, a party that favoured a more confident and streamlined, happier, even 'shining' India, defined as 'essentially' a Hindu nation.

The rise during the 1990s of a viable coalition of more than a score of parties led by the nationalist Bharatiya Janata Party (BJP) sent shivers down the spines of many Indian citizens and politicians, with good reason. Virulently anti-intellectual, the party with fiercely Hindu roots called into question more than the old one-party system and the gaggle of regionally based parties it spawned. To begin with, the BJP quest for dominance dragged Indian politics into the world of communicative abundance by embracing the slickest, most intensive media operation in the history of democratic India. With Congress still convinced of its own political superiority, but now lacking grass-roots organs and actually stuck in the era of the public rally and radio and newspaper coverage, the BJP began mobilising its cadre organisations. These included the Vishwa Hindu Parishad (World Council of Hindu Churches) and the much-feared Rashtriya Swayamsevak Sangh (Organisation of National Volunteers), a shadowy network of more than two million Hindu activists, whose military salutes and daily parades in khaki uniforms were modelled on the 1920s military drills of the Italian fascist movement.

Tapping into these parent bodies, the BJP pointed the gun of media politics at their opponents. It harnessed big campaign financing, secret backroom planning, slick press statements and photo opportunities. It went celebrity hunting and experimented with disinformation and negative imaging, trial balloon policy announcements, and saturation campaign advertising that a leading BJP politician (L. K. Advani) likened to the 'carpet bombing' of India's 675 million voters, almost half of whom were between the ages of eighteen and thirty-five – and one hundred million of whom were first-time voters. 'This is Atal Behari Vajpayee, prime minister of India, and I am calling to tell you . . .' were the opening words of the pre-recorded message heard by most of India's thirty million mobile phone subscribers during the general election campaign that unfolded during the first months of 2004. Countless e-mail addresses received similar messages. Walls and billboards were plastered with BJP imagery. BJP government successes were trumpeted by slick television ads crafted by the suitably named global media company Grey Worldwide. Millions of printed messages in scores of languages fluttered through a galaxy of letter boxes. Satellite communication links targeted the pockets of the Indian diaspora. GIS mapping was used for the first time, to quantify the political colour of constituencies: the area size and population of villages, the numbers of male and female voters, and how they had voted in the past. In states like Bihar and Uttar Pradesh, mapping and measuring were given a thuggish boost outside polling stations by the appearance of hundreds of vigilante squads armed with video cameras.

'Brand management' and 'spin' and 'click of the mouse' tactics trumpeted various messages. It was said that Vajpayee and the BJP had made India's economy shine and capable of competing with neighbouring China; that Indians should feel proud of their country after decades of second-rate leadership; and that, following the first nuclear tests in 1998, India was now heading towards superpower and 'world guru' status in the arts, sciences and the economy. Parts of the BJP began to suggest that all this required changes in the rules of the political game. Many took it for granted that the personalisation of government and politics, above all in the figure of A. B. Vajpayee (Figure 105), was a good thing; whether performed in traditional *dhoti* or colourful T-shirts, his centre-stage role spawned BJP calls for the creation of a presidential system of rule. Other rule changes, including proposals to strengthen the

FIGURE 105: Prime Minister A. B. Vajpayee, addressing a meeting organised by Sikh citizens to honour him for making India a nuclear power, Delhi, May 1998.

'winner takes all' first-past-the-post system and to tighten the laws
governing parliamentarians' defection from their party's ranks –
the practice of 'party hopping' – were floated. The BJP leadership,
using the old political tactic of studied ambivalence, began to speak
of the 'ills of the present system of parliamentary democracy . . .
fashioned after the British model nearly five decades ago'. There
was talk of how the same system 'has failed to deliver the goods'
and of how 'the time has come to introduce deep-going changes in
our structure of governance'. Vajpayee in particular rounded on
parliament for its muddled incompetence in handling serious policy
business. He even accused 'the present system of parliamentary
democracy, which we borrowed blindly from the British' as being
the chief cause of India's poor economic performance.[18]

The BJP dream of ridding politics of politics, of cutting the
cackle of public debate, was backed by the lack of intra-party
democracy, and by cunning top-down attempts to convince the
heartlands of BJP support – the well-educated, professional, urban
middle classes – that India was indeed suffering 'too much democracy'. The tactic was daring. It flatly contradicted the belief of
many Western analysts that middle classes have a natural liking for
democracy. The BJP tried to prove just the opposite: it set out to
demonstrate that in the case of 'shining India' the class drawn from
the middle world of small industry, provincial professions and
country trading and banking could actively turn its back on democracy. The party strategists had plenty of evidence on their side. It
was not only that the Indian middle class had doubled in size from
less than 10 per cent of the population in 1984 to around 20 per
cent in 2004. Of potentially greater significance was the fact that
public opinion polls reported that a majority of this class was
prepared on their doorsteps to indulge nostalgia by claiming that
the Emergency had been good for India, exactly because state
officials worked without asking for *baksheesh*, streets were cleared
of demonstrators, and because hoarders, black-market dealers and
misfit politicians were put behind bars. Of greatest significance was
that a sizeable chunk of this middle class (according to an early
1990s survey conducted in Madras, Mumbai, Delhi, Calcutta and
Bangalore) was willing to draw the conclusion that democracy was
merely a state of mind, and that with an eye on the future minds

could be changed. When asked whether they accepted that 'progress' in India now required 'a dictator', a clear majority of middle-class citizens said they agreed.[19]

Democracy is indeed a state of mind, a case of wishful thinking, a little dream, but how could millions of comparatively wealthy, perfectly civilised men and women with a good education think in this way? Indians of all castes and backgrounds would wrestle with this question for years to come, but by the early years of the twenty-first century the BJP tacticians knew they were on to something. For the plain truth was that among the ambiguous legacies of Nehru's India was that it spawned a sizeable middle class whose idea of progress was an unexciting version of narrow-minded materialism. This was the same class that Tocqueville had worried about when predicting the future of democracy in the United States. For their Indian counterparts, living well meant making heaps of money and piling up assets, including the peace of mind that comes from knowing that one's children will marry up the social scale. Progress implied abandoning the word altruism to the dictionary, giving the cold shoulder to the poor, embracing the conviction that India was an incorrigibly unequal society. Being middle-class – according to some members of this class – meant throwing off the yoke of the Nehru period, when government, in the name of democracy, did everything it could to crush the rise of an independent, money-hungry bourgeoisie.

Hence the indifference towards democracy within parts of this upper-caste middle class, which developed a definite fascination for strong, personalised power, combined with a taste for rule by experts and administrators. Its admiration for personal gain through hard work and no-nonsense efficiency was underpinned by the sentiment that most members of parliament were either untrustworthy or unrepresentative, and that the political system as a whole was the breeder of corruption, hence in need of 'purification'. Getting richer quicker required a freer market. A freer market implied a stronger Indian state. A stronger state required strong leadership, less compromise, less dissent and more direction, if need be from a strong and steady hand.

Talk of an excess of democracy and calls for its 'purification' meant various things to various people, but in some middle-class quarters it implied a decisive rejection of the 'kedjeree' qualities of Indian life. Calls for loosening the grip of banyan democracy on Indian life implied not just disregard for the poor. It required strong disapproval of the principle of affirmative action, of reservation system rules designed to extend a helping hand to women and men of the lower castes. The 'purification' of India demanded an end to the official pandering to minorities (the 1986 Shah Bano fiasco was a favourite target of BJP derision*). It required, above all, a stemming of the rising tide of new groups, like the *dalits* and tribal peoples, the Other Backward Classes (OBCs) and Muslim Indians, by reminding everybody that India was in essence a Hindu country. Hindu nationalism – for that is where this middle-class coolness towards democracy led – thus set itself the goal of confronting Indian secularism head-on. The basic point was to transform India into something like a turmeric polity, pushing it towards a stable, well-ordered, better managed political community infused with the properties of *haldi*, a symbol of 'Hinduness' and, conveniently, India's best-known aromatic spice used in curries: a bitter, peppery, deep-yellow ingredient supposed to cure anaemia, counter ageing of the body and keep away harmful bacteria.

What was the recipe for turmeric nationalism? At a minimum, it demanded hostility towards people who only knew how to use forks to scratch their backs. That meant turning a blind eye to the evident under-representation of certain groups, for instance Indian Muslims, who counted for some 12 per cent of the total population, and yet whose numbers in the Lok Sabha during the period 1952 to 1998 averaged only 6 per cent, a figure that consistently declined after 1980. Hindu nationalism also jettisoned the belief that Indian democracy was special because it rested upon either the principled or pragmatic acceptance of diversity. It was to be each for themselves, of course with the help of others who returned the favours, even if they were crooks.[20] Rallying around the family of

---

*In 1986, the Supreme Court of India ruled in favour of a Muslim woman's claim for alimony, in defiance of customary Muslim personal law. Conservative Muslim voices howled and the electorally sensitive government of Prime Minister Rajiv Gandhi (Nehru's grandson) moved to quash the decision. There were two casualties of the overturned ruling: the cause of equality for India's Muslim women and the strength of Nehruvian secularism, with its emphasis on the state's active commitment to the dignity of, and equal respect for, all faiths.

organisations collectively known as the 'Sangh Parivar', and politically led by the BJP, the new middle-class zealots of 'Hinduness'
called on those dissatisfied with the riffraff of Indian society to
band together, to show that strength lay in unity, especially in the
face of a rising tide of filth. The strategy was designed to produce
not just electoral results, as it did, especially by divining support
from among entrepreneurs, the urban middle classes, upper-caste
graduates and voters within the Hindu belt and the western state
of Gujarat. In the extreme, Hindu nationalism also promised or
threatened organised bigotry and pogroms against minorities.
Worst of all, it colluded in unleashing the spectre of state-sponsored
violence, as in fact happened (during 2002) in Gujarat.

A Life of Contradictions?

Some spoke of the violence in Gujarat as Indian democracy's
torched Reichstag. That language proved to be much too strong,
but there could be no doubting that the banyan democracy had
unleashed forces that confounded the belief of some scholars that
democracy had irreversibly entered the Indian political imagination. Triggered by the (possibly accidental) burning of Hindu
activists in a railway coach near Godhra station in late February
2002, the savagery claimed well over a thousand (mainly Indian
Muslim) lives. The cruelty coincided with hostile talk of 'backward', 'illiterate', 'obscurantist', 'pre-modern', 'fanatical' and
'terrorist' Muslims; and there were loud calls to send them 'back to
Pakistan'. The Gujarat violence certainly prompted memories of
the Partition pogroms, but in fact the planning and execution of the
murders were very much an early twenty-first-century affair.

The violence that gushed from the founts of Hindu nationalism
represented a full-blown rejection of the secular policies of accommodation that dated from the Nehru period. Secularism had never
meant erecting walls between government and civil society, so that
the faithful might enjoy their religious freedom untouched by
others. The whole point of secularism was to use a panoply of government devices to bestow public dignity upon believers, to protect,
nurture and to *equalise* their religious freedoms. Sometimes this

policy of equalisation implied refraining from intervention, in order to leave such matters as worship, inheritance, marriage and divorce to religious leaders themselves. At other times, the policy implied direct intervention, as happened through the Hindu Code Bill, which radically altered personal laws associated with Hindu beliefs. Financial disbursements, meanwhile, flowed from government to Muslim clergy and to mosques, and considerable sums were spent on enabling believers to make the annual Haj pilgrimage to Mecca. The cultural and educational institutions of other faiths received heavy subsidies, sometimes to the point where they came close to resembling apparatuses of government.

Hindu nationalism rejected all talk of the equality of faiths. Emboldened by media propaganda and support groups like the RSS, BJP nationalists favoured the use of state structures to champion just one faith, itself defined in bowdlerised ways. By their words and deeds, they reconfirmed the point that if democracy can be thought of as a continuous struggle against simplified perceptions of the world, then nationalism is the attempt to undo complexity; it is the will not to know certain things, a chosen ignorance, not the ignorance of innocence. Luckily for India, the wilful ignorance of Hindu nationalism displayed no unity on the question of democracy and its future. Aside from those who favoured some form of dictatorship, there were nationalists who saw that democracy understood as 'one person, one vote' could mathematically suit the Hinduist cause; strongly critical of what the BJP President L. K. Advani first called 'minorityism', they calculated that if Hindus could be convinced to vote en bloc then majority-rule democracy could be twisted like a knife into the body politic, to extract gains for sectional interests.

For these nationalists, banyan democracy could be used to fashion a democracy with turmeric qualities. But there were turmeric nationalists who disagreed with this strategy, and who instead found themselves attracted to early twentieth-century Hindu thinkers who dreamed of replacing the infantile version of representative government introduced by the British with local forms of assembly democracy. Some BJP nationalists liked to quote Hindu revivalists (like Sri Aurobindo and Radha Kumud Mookerji) who claimed that democracy had been invented in India, for instance in the religious assemblies of the age of Asoka (the third Emperor of the Maurya dynasty who lived and ruled until 232 BCE).[21] Others drew from this claim political implications that were either evolutionary or revolutionary. Evolutionists saw democracy as having made a long journey westwards from its birthplace in India through Greece to the British Isles, before returning home again to India, where its defenders were now using democracy to shake off all vestiges of the Raj. Hindu revolutionaries talked in more apocalyptic terms. Getting rid of the 1950 constitution was a pet theme. 'The Constitution is not the product of our soil; a minimum addition is required to make it more responsive', said the BJP's K. N. Govindacharya. 'Consensus, instead of majority-minority concept, suits the country better.'[22]

It was not altogether clear what that meant beyond a vague call for the construction of some form of corporatist state based on religious imaginings that would weaken or kill off vote banks, interparty bickering, 'minorityism', corrupt deputies and sterile and time-wasting parliamentary debates. It was as if turmeric nationalists, chanting a hymn drawn from the Hindu founding text, the Rig Veda, yearned to sacrifice the thousand-eyed, thousand-headed primeval monster of India's banyan democracy, in order to recreate a new and better world where the People are ruled by Brahmins.[23] The rejection of banyan democracy was accompanied by a profound suspicion of India as a country with a plural civil society protected by a polity based not on inherited status, but on the numerical preponderance of votes and multiple channels of representation. The celebrated Trinidad-born Indian novelist Sir V. S. Naipaul pointed to one possible future when commenting on the 1992 anti-Muslim pogroms sparked by the destruction of the Babri Masjid, Babur's Mosque, in Ayodhya, Uttar Pradesh. 'Ayodhya is a sort of passion', he said. 'Any passion is to be encouraged. Passion leads to creativity.'[24]

Whether the efforts of armed BJP thugs to burn Muslims alive in their homes, to knife them in the streets and to scald them with acid bombs all counted as an example of creative passions is most debatable. For what was at work here, and later took over in more organised form in Gujarat, was manifest hatred for others perceived as different, inferior, disposable, hatred backed up by the guile of mainstream party politics. Disturbing was the way turmeric nationalism made a bid for respectability using clever campaign tactics. The deliberate cultivation of contradictory messages to different audiences was a favourite. So, too, were BJP efforts to soften and publicly conceal the contradictoriness, either by doing nothing (following the Gujarat killings) or by delayed action. There was also the cunning tactic of launching policies through contrived ambiguity, as when (in 1998) Vajpayee and other BJP top dogs called for a national debate about the merits of Christian conversions after Hindu thugs had razed churches and attacked Christian communities in tribal regions of India. This was dog-whistle politics for dogs and dog lovers alike, and its undoubted champion whistler was Prime Minister Vajpayee himself. 'I believe in an India that is plural, liberal and secular', said the master of studied ambivalence, several months before the 2004 election, to a stadium full of Indian Muslims in Delhi. Three years earlier, in New York, the respectable and civilised face of Hindu nationalism told an adoring audience of expatriate fellow RSS members the exact opposite. 'My soul is *swayamsevak* [literally: 'volunteer', but also the name given to all RSS activists]. Only second to that am I the Prime Minister of India.'[25]

There were many Indian citizens from all walks of life who found themselves disturbed by such rhetoric. Some were disgusted by the substance and symbolism of an incident in mid-April 2004: a sari stampede in A. B. Vajpayee's constituency of Lucknow, where Lalji Tandon, Vajpayee's election manager, cunningly decided to celebrate his birthday on the eve of the election by giving away free saris to 20,000 poor women. The incident perverted the meaning of election promises: twenty-one poor women were killed and many others injured in the crush triggered by their badly supervised rush for personal dignity and public respect. The astonishing – wholly unanticipated – thing about the slickest and grimiest electoral campaign in India's history was the way it triggered strong anxieties, feelings among many Indians that a brave new dawn of organised deception had arrived, that banyan democracy was in a tight corner, even that Indian citizens might somehow be destined to suffer the fearful indignity of being crushed into rubble by the steel hand of a state ruled by a single party, with a leader backed by informants, media strategists, police and soldiers. Most remarkable was the way that opponents of the BJP campaign tactics rallied to bell the cat, as Indians say. The great poke in the eye given to the BJP government led by A. B. Vajpayee in the 2004 general election was a stunning result. Compared with the previous election, the BJP lost forty-four seats; its popular vote dropped to little more than 22 per cent. The overall vote tossed out the first non-Congress government in the Indian republic's history to have completed a full term. The election saw a huge turnout of India's poor. Their many millions of votes not only guaranteed the formation of the country's first ever coalition government made up of a number of small regional parties, in alliance with the Congress Party. Something more important was achieved through the ballot box. For the second time in the history of Indian democracy – the Emergency was the first – the poor and their supporters demonstrated that India could live what Bhimrao Ambedkar had called 'a life of contradictions', that the power of citizens to give a democratic kiss of life to a dying democracy was no philosopher's fantasy.

SEA CHANGES

The perils of uncontrolled power are perennial reminders of the virtues of a democratic society. But modern democracy requires a more realistic philosophical and religious basis, not only in order to anticipate and understand the perils to which it is exposed, but also to give it a more persuasive justification.

Reinhold Niebuhr (1945)

The history that is closest to us is always the hardest to summarise. Hence these awkward questions: when future historians look back on the victory of democracy in India, how will it be remembered? What will they say more generally about the worldwide rebirth of democratic ideals and institutions during the decades after 1945? Will they conclude that it was representative democracy as usual, or might they instead propose something startling: that India and its banyan democracy were no Asian anomaly, but a worldly experiment that pointed the way towards a global transformation of democracy? And concerning the democracies that resulted, how well did they measure up to the standards of our historians? When all was said and done, what were their strengths and weaknesses, and how well overall did they fare? Did they manage to survive?

Miracles

One point is striking when trying to guess answers to such questions: there was a global dimension to the breathtaking escape of democratic ideals and institutions from the clutches of cruelty and

FIGURE 106: Researchers cast their ballot at the most remote of Australia's polling stations, in the Australian Antarctic Territory.

dictatorship, totalitarianism and total war. For the first time in its history, the lived language of democracy became familiar to most people; that meant, for the first time ever in human history, democracy went on trial in all four corners of Planet Earth. There were precedents for the spread of democratic ideals and institutions into new settings, certainly; and after 1945 there were various setbacks for democracy, at various times in several regions, principally in the oil-rich states of the Middle East and in sub-Saharan Africa. Yet the impressive fact was that for half a century after 1945, democratic miracles happened on every continent.

Democracy came for the first time to frozen Antarctica (Figure 106). It took root in the warmer soils of the Indian subcontinent, while further east in Asia, as if through alchemical reaction, the military occupation of Japan triggered an astonishing top-down democratic revolution (Figure 107). It succeeded in no small measure because millions of ruined, malnourished people grew contemptuous of their defeated imperial masters, tired of war and more than willing as citizens to bite the American hand that for a time fed and harshly ruled them. Protected by a new constitution that renounced belligerency as a sovereign right of the state, Japanese people, for the first time on any scale, began to speak the language of *min-shushugi*. Elsewhere in east Asia, a proud and lively democracy sprang up in Taiwan. Driven by dogged resistance to brutal dictatorship, it disproved the European prejudice that 'Asians' were by nature deferential, or that they equated the whole

天 降 る 贈 物

FIGURE 107: A gift from heaven – democracy by parachute – by the Japanese cartoonist
Kato Etsuro, 1946.

idea of 'democracy' (*min zhu*) with gambling, prostitution, family
breakdown and other forms of Western decadence. Taiwan instead
showed that democracy with 'Asian' characteristics was possible,
even that millions of people could quickly embrace their right to
cast a free and fair vote – to throw a ticket (*to pian*) as the
Taiwanese like to say – as sacrosanct. The Taiwanese experiment
arguably had a larger significance: with the Chinese dragon breathing fire down its neck, Taiwan, lacking diplomatic recognition by
most of the world's states, defied the modern textbook rule that
democracy could survive only in a 'country' defined by 'sovereign'
territorial borders.

At the other end of the Asian landmass, in equally hostile sur-
roundings, the new settler state of Israel, founded in 1948 as a
rescue operation from European genocide, was no less remarkable.
It was a parliamentary democracy with a difference. Infused with
the spirit of Judaism, it included a sizeable minority of Arab Israeli
people. It also featured elections based on proportional representation, a directly elected prime minister, a strong independent
judiciary, a free press and a robust civil society. Like Taiwan, it was
hardly a textbook democratic state: if anything, powerful bodies

such as the Jewish Agency, which handled Jewish immigration, and the Jewish National Fund, which owned substantial amounts of land in the name of the Jewish people, functioned almost as states-within-a-state.

No less remarkable was the way democracy landed on the southern tip of Africa, freed finally of white racist presumption. In mid-February 1990, millions of people around the world, glued to their television sets, watched Nelson Mandela walk from prison to freedom, after twenty-seven years, one hour late. Dressed in a light brown suit and tie, Mandela punched the air in a victory salute and waved to well-wishers before slipping into a silver BMW sedan, which whisked him to Cape Town, forty miles away. There he was greeted under a boiling sun by an estimated crowd of 250,000 citizens, some of them dangling desperately from tree limbs, to catch a glimpse of their leader for the first time in their lives. As the cavalcade nudged towards the Grand Parade, in the heart of the city, citizens erupted in song, clenched fists, danced, waved green, black and gold flags; at one point, with megaphone calls to move back inaudible, scores of people took turns to stand or sit on the boot of Mandela's car. So great was the crush that marshals took more than two hours to deliver him to the podium, where for several minutes he stood calmly, nodded slightly to the assembly, before raising his hands for quiet. Punctuated by roars from the huge crowd, his twenty-minute speech repeated solemn words that he had used nearly three decades before: 'I have fought against white domination and I have fought against black domination', he said in a strong, clear voice. 'I have cherished the ideal of a democratic and free society in which all persons live together in harmony and with equal opportunities. It is an ideal that I hope to live for and to achieve. But if needs be, it is an ideal for which I am prepared to die.'[1]

What brought on all these changes? As at every moment in its history, the diffusion of democracy had multiple causers and causes. In the half-century after World War Two, the hand of electoral democracy touched virtually every part of the earth, often in random and unpredictable ways. There seemed to be no normal pathway – just as there was no clear pattern of causation. The dialectics of democracy defied all scientific laws, for instance those that supposed there to be a causal link between democracy and a strong middle class ('no bourgeois, no democracy', in the pithy phrase of Barrington Moore[2]); or a close affinity between Protestantism and democracy; or its dependence upon lofty levels of literacy and formal education. The rule was that there was no rule; whenever and wherever democratisation happened, it happened in thoroughly contingent ways. Stochastic modelling and computer simulation could not predict exactly when and where democracy had succeeded, or where next it might triumph. And no single factor could explain any case. Explanation – the attempt of the mind to satisfy its mastery of worldly things and events – seemed rather suspect. True to her old self, the figure of democracy remained an enigma. Guarding her secrets carefully, she appeared in different ways at different times, always accompanied by groups of different friends.

It was exactly this elusive, random quality of democracy that heightened the sense after 1945 that democratic ideals and institutions had become a global phenomenon, driven by all sorts of forces. Among the most powerful was undoubtedly what came to be called 'people power': the resolve of citizens to put an end to bossy government that had exceeded its limits, abused its authority and failed to deliver on its promises. Threatened by public disillusionment with violent state power, dictators everywhere began to feel the pinch. More than a few renamed themselves democrats, as happened in Indonesia, where during the 1950s the authorities began to speak of 'guided democracy'. Many dictators were forced into retreat or on to the back foot, sometimes in situations of high drama that doubled as media events. There was Nehru's 'Tryst with Destiny' speech – one of the first great rhetorical performances in this new phase of the history of democracy. Its rhetorical power was matched by the stirring 'Ich bin ein Berliner' speech of John F. Kennedy, broadcast on radio to millions of people around the world, during the last week of June 1963. Forgiven by locals for likening himself in bad German to a jam doughnut, the American president forcefully emphasised the indivisibility of freedom and the eligibility of the world's democrats for Berlin citizenship. 'Freedom has many difficulties and democracy is not perfect, but we have never had to put a wall up to keep our people in, to prevent them from leaving us', he said, to wild applause.[3] Much the same conviction, that democracy was a powerful weapon against the violence of governments shored up by walls, prisons and armies, later turned millions of heads in the direction of a prominent Czech playwright, whose brave defiance of the state authorities had led to his arrest; flung into prison, where he fell seriously ill, Václav Havel found himself at the centre of an international campaign for his release. The world's media, meanwhile, directed their microphones and cameras to less well-known figures; several quickly became global celebrities. One young man, carrying just a shopping bag, single-handedly fought a column of Chinese army tanks, one day after a massacre in Tiananmen Square. One woman, Aung San Suu Kyi – her name in Burmese means 'a bright collection of strange victories' – stood down a firing squad after troops, who had been ordered to cut short her life, suddenly lost their will to pull the trigger (Figure 108). She walked through their ranks, gracefully alone and unafraid; she was later placed under house arrest, where she remained for a long time, unforgotten by millions around the world.

The decades after 1945 witnessed plenty of setbacks, to be sure. According to one observer, a third of the world's thirty-two functioning democracies in the year 1958 (there were only twelve in 1945) had lapsed by the mid-1970s into some form of authoritarianism; another

FIGURE 108: Aung San Suu Kyi, at a rally in the Burmese state of Arakan, 2002.

noted that in 1962, the year Bob Dylan recorded 'See That My Grave Is Kept Clean', thirteen of the world's governments were products of a *coup d'état*; by the mid-1970s, with the appearance of Dylan's 'Shelter From The Storm', the number of military dictatorships had nearly trebled, to thirty-eight countries.[4] The trend was marked by unpleasant moments, and things sometimes turned nasty. In Athens, in mid-November 1973, several hundred students from the Athens Polytechnic tried to breathe spirit back into the old body of *dēmokratia*. Barricading themselves within their campus, the student leaders used their pirate radio station to protest against the military government of Colonel Papadopoulos. 'This is the Polytechnic!' ran their continuous message. 'People of Greece, the Polytechnic stands at the forefront of our struggle and your struggle, our common struggle against dictatorship and for democracy!' In the early hours of Saturday, 17 November, the dictators replied. A French-made AMX 30 military tank smashed through the campus gates; several dozen students and their supporters were shot, some by military snipers atop buildings (Figure 109). But the violence, not for the first time in the history of democracy, spawned a stunning surprise: victory for the students, who suffered the painful pleasure of witnessing a palace coup by military hardliners under Brigadier Dimitrios Ioannidis, who provoked a foolish military confrontation with Turkey in Cyprus that quickly led to the collapse of the Greek military junta.

FIGURE 109: Greek army tank about to crush the gates of the Athens Polytechnic in the early hours of 17 November 1973.

The Greek surprise confirmed that the anti-democratic trend was unsustainable, that authoritarian governments everywhere seemed destined to suffer setbacks, or outright defeat. Military power suddenly seemed puny, partly because the men who ruled through armies bent on trampling citizens under foot began them-selves to draw back from the brink; it was as if senior officers had decided that they wanted to be professionals, mere members of armed forces uninvolved in the dirty business of government. That sentiment was boosted by the resolutely peaceful intentions of their opponents. Given the terrible violence of the twentieth century, most democrats now seemed to want a world without barbed wire and cattle prods, tanks and tear gas, to live lives untroubled by the fearful sounds of big boots crashing and crunching the streets. 'As a rule,' said the incorruptible Polish democrat Adam Michnik, 'dic-tatorships guarantee safe streets and the terror of the doorbell. In democracy the streets may be unsafe after dark, but the most likely visitor in the early hours will be the milkman.'5

The remark figuratively rang true for millions of people in many different global settings, including Portugal, where, shortly after midnight on 25 April 1974, young officers in charge of the Movimento das Fôrças Armadas (MFA) pulled off a perfectly planned move against their leaders. Military units took possession of key ministry buildings. The post, telephone offices and broad-casting stations were occupied, along with the country's airports. By late morning, with the dictatorship of Marcello Caetano well and truly cut off from the outside world, huge crowds gathered in the streets of Lisbon to cheer the soldiers on duty. As if to celebrate the new spirit of democracy, fresh red carnations were slipped into the well-oiled barrels of their former opponents' rifles. Caetano surrendered that afternoon. A transition to democracy had begun. Much the same fate awaited neighbouring Spain, whose military government fell apart following the death (in November 1975) of the dictator General Franco, whose rise to power was linked to the civil war that led to a 'white terror' of harsh reprisals against his opponents, including widespread executions and disappearances, consignment to concentration camps, enforced exile and on-the-spot execution of many tens of thousands of citizens. Public disgust for this kind of military violence surfaced a decade later in the

Philippines, where in the middle of the night a change of regime was triggered not by military officers, but by civilian electoral officers, who refused to carry on counting ballot papers after many grew convinced that the results were about to be rigged, in favour of the military government led by General Marcos. Similar sentiments enthused half a million demonstrators who marched (in September 1988) through the streets of Rangoon, the capital of the Burmese dictatorship; some carried the American Stars and Stripes and one group of citizens even gathered at the front entrance of the American embassy, where they recited Abraham Lincoln's Gettysburg address word for word, in haltingly clear English.[6]

Latin America

The gut sense of citizens that authoritarian government had overstepped the mark was notably strong in Latin America, the birthplace of caudillo democracy, where military dictatorships collapsed like buildings on fire. Uruguay blazed the trail by returning to constitutional democracy during the darkest moment of World War Two, thereby consolidating its reputation as the principal democratic laboratory of Latin America. Brazil soon shuffled towards electoral democracy, as did Costa Rica, the small Central American republic with a population of mostly Catalan, Basque and Galician descent. Following a civil war fought in the years 1948–9, the new government of José Figueres Ferrer did something that had probably never before been attempted in the history of democracy: to prevent any future possibility of a military *coup d'état*, it abolished its own army and created instead a Public Security Force, a police force commanded by elected officials. The country went on to become the most successful electoral democracy in the region.

During 1945 and 1946, elections ushered in popularly elected governments in Argentina, Peru, Colombia and Venezuela. There followed a temporary shift towards what came to be called 'bureaucratic authoritarianism'; the anti-democratic die was cast in the early 1960s in Peru, where the armed forces barged their way into an election and rigged the result. At the beginning of the

FIGURE 110: 'Democracy yes, hunger no!': a public rally in Bolivia during the late 1970s.

1970s, eight out of ten countries in the region were governed without recourse to free and fair elections. But then the democratic pendulum again swung forcefully forwards, such that by the end of the following decade nine out of ten governments were popularly elected.

The process of democratic renewal was kick-started in Ecuador, whose military junta made the stunning announcement that it would seek to withdraw from politics; a new constitution was quickly drafted and elections in 1979 produced a civilian government. Similar things happened in Bolivia (Figure 110), where after a rocky start a civilian president was finally elected in 1982; and in Peru, whose citizens voted in a new Constituent Assembly, a new constitution and a new civilian president during a two-year period. Thereafter, in the early 1980s, the pace of democratisation quickened throughout the hemisphere. A civilian president took office in Honduras in January 1982; Guatemalans elected a Constituent Assembly in 1984 and a new president the following year; and in El Salvador a bitterly fought election in 1984 catapulted José Napoleon Duarte into the office of president. Meanwhile, the political party (PRI) that had ruled Mexico for more than half a century survived a presidential election by the skin of its teeth; in the following year (1989), it lost control of a state governorship, for the first time.

During the same period, Brazil began to shake off the most violent and criminal dictatorship in its history. In August 1974, before a gathering of loyal supporters, General Geisel spoke of the need for 'slow, gradual, and secure decompression'. The *abertura*, or political opening, was at first confined to elite groups – there were no guarantees of the right to strike, but freedom of the press was re-established, along with habeas corpus, amnesty for political prisoners, the freedom to form political parties and direct elections for state governors. There was talk in military circles of 'relative democracy' and of the possibility that one day there would be the 'full re-establishment' of democracy. The old popular wisdoms at the centre of Brazilian political language – proverbs like 'Voting doesn't fill your stomach' and 'In politics it's not the facts but the versions that count' and 'Those who feel persecuted should complain to the bishop' – began to give way to serious public discussion about the merits of democracy. 'We have hot soup on the table', Air Force Minister Délio Jardim reportedly said, 'and what is interesting is that no one wants to upset the table.'[7] The changes finally resulted (in early 1985) in the appointment of Brazil's first civilian president since the beginning of dictatorship two decades earlier.

Velvet Smiles

The whole of Latin America watched in the meantime with amazement the bloody spectacle of Mrs Thatcher's questionable British war on the Malvinas islands turn into an unquestionable rout of the brutal Argentine military government, followed by the subsequent election (in 1983) of a new civilian government and president. While the restoration of electoral democracy proved painful for many citizens, simply because it confronted them for the first time with grisly details of the 'dirty war' they had suffered at the hands of the dictatorship, there was great public jubilation. In a widely reported speech, newly elected President Raúl Ricardo

Alfonsín summed up the mood with a grandiloquent claim: 'With democracy', he said, 'people are fed, educated and healthier.'

The end of military dictatorship everywhere left behind blood mixed with bitter tears, but during this period the rejuvenation of democracy came as a grand surprise to almost everyone. Sometimes the rebirth came swaddled in public joy, as happened in neighbouring Uruguay, where in November 1980, in a remarkable demonstration of 'people power', a decisive majority of brave adults (57 per cent) stood against their own military government in a plebiscite to decide on a new constitution biased towards executive power. At the end of a long day, when voting had been supervised by mostly fair-minded government officials, tempers flared as thousands of voters poured into polling stations at closing time, demanding that ballot boxes not be destroyed by the reigning military government. After two tense hours, their democratic wish was granted. It was obvious to everybody that the military – many of whose senior officers were secretly committed to a return of democracy – had blundered badly.

The military government tried in the weeks before to bury its subjects in an avalanche of propaganda. Television, radio and newspapers had been crammed with sinister warnings. A vote against the proposed constitution was a vote against the Fatherland, it was said. In a dour televised speech, the fat-faced president had asked: what kind of government do you want? His answer to his own question, that nobody in their right mind could possibly favour 'irresponsible parliamentary government' because what was needed was 'executive power that can pass laws necessary for Uruguay', smacked of dictatorship. So, too, did the warnings of his supporters that without a new constitution the Fatherland would go down the road of 'subversion' and 'communism' and 'permanent strikes' and 'terror in the streets'. Government propaganda even warbled a love song for the American President, Ronald Reagan, who was said to be very much in favour of the status quo, and against constitutional change. The whole display of organised deception misfired. In a very large turnout (85 per cent) by world standards, Uruguayan voters resoundingly said 'No!' But since there was still martial law, citizens could not take to the streets. So they dressed up in yellow, the colour of the democratic opposition, and heeded the advice of a well-known Montevideo private radio station owner, Germán Araújo, to use their own mouths to spread what they called a 'smile revolution': simple curls of the lips to demonstrate their magnificent triumph to friends, colleagues and strangers in the streets.[8]

The Uruguayan victory proved that when large numbers of people individually feel the need to change their lives spectacular things can happen, especially when they band together, fearless and determined to make the world a better place. And so we come to what was arguably the biggest victory for the ideals, 'spirit' and institutions of democracy: the extraordinary 'velvet revolutions' that erupted in central and east Europe during the summer and autumn of 1989.

There was little agreement about the factors reckoned to be responsible for jump-starting the changes. Some said the tipping point was the decision of the authorities to allow East German summertime tourists to pass into Austria, and hence into the West. Others said the critical moment was in fact the decision of the East German authorities not to use violence against demonstrators, thereby avoiding a Tiananmen solution to opposition to the communist regime. Still others emphasised background developments, like President Reagan's military confrontation with the Soviet Union and the rise to power (in March 1985) of Mikhail Gorbachev.

All revolutions inspire attempts to pinpoint their magical beginnings, but the clear fact was that the astonishing changes that happened in central-eastern Europe from the summer of 1989 were by any standards breathtaking in scope, and quick. The outbreak of the Velvet Revolution in Czechoslovakia in mid-November 1989 proved exemplary. Its name was poached from the 1960s New York experimental rock band, the Velvet Underground, which was ironic considering that the first day of the revolution was littered with terrible violence. A crowd of 15,000 students had gathered peacefully outside the Pathology Institute in Prague to commemorate the death of a student victim of the Nazi occupation fifty years earlier. The commemoration had the Communist Party's blessing, and the list of speakers, both official and unofficial, had been organised by the university council of the Communist Youth

Union. The students were to march to the Slavin cemetery in the Prague district of Vyšehrad, where they would gather at the graveside of the nineteenth-century poet K. H. Mácha. And it was agreed with the authorities that the customary candles would be lit, wreaths and flowers laid, the national anthem sung, after which the procession would disperse quietly.

The final clause in the contract proved to be the sticking point. Instead of melting into the autumn darkness, thousands of students, feeling their spines straightening, spontaneously marched towards Wenceslas Square. Tension rose suddenly when the police temporarily halted their ranks at the Botanical Gardens. In the distance, police orders were barked. The demonstrators began to sing the national anthem. A flying wedge of grim-faced police wielding truncheons cut into the ranks of the best brains in the country. Scuffles broke out. Shouting and chanting erupted. The sound of clumping boots was temporarily drowned by cries of 'We are unarmed!' and 'No violence!' The demonstrators somehow managed to shake off their opponents, and to march on defiantly, towards Wenceslas Square. Scores of curious bystanders, like monks coming to prayer, silently joined in. So did actors and theatre staff. Friday night café patrons downed their drinks and joined the throng. That gave courage to the young demonstrators. They repeatedly chanted in defiant tones: 'Join us! Join us! The nation's helping itself!'

As the protest snaked its way through central Prague, state television and radio stations issued a communiqué that complained that the day of remembrance had been 'hijacked by anti-social elements, well known to the police'. It denounced those chanting slogans hostile to the socialist state, and described them as uninterested in 'dialogue, reform, or democratisation'. It concluded that 'the forces of order were obliged to take necessary measures to restore peace and order'.[9]

The arrests continued. But as the student demonstration reached the National Theatre, its numbers suddenly mushroomed to more than 50,000 people; after all the years of isolation it was as if people could not get enough of each other's company. The protest had sprouted wings, which is why, at around eight o'clock, as it entered the street named Národni Třída, it was greeted front and back by walls of white-helmeted riot police determined to stop the marchers from reaching Wenceslas Square.

The crowd suddenly realised that it had lost its escape route – and that it was at the mercy of the riot police. It braced itself, waiting for hell to break loose. Many trapped and panicky demonstrators began once again to chant, 'No violence! No violence!'; others taunted their captors with 'Freedom! Freedom!'. Once again came the bullhorn order to disperse. The crowd now knew that this was a sick joke, since there was nowhere to go. Many trembled, sat down, to sing the national anthem, followed by 'We shall overcome'. Keys were jangled. A handful of young women gave flowers to the unsmiling police. Hundreds of candles were lit. 'No violence! No violence!', 'Freedom! Freedom!' the believers in candle power chanted, yellow light flickering on their faces.

'Noise Is Fashionable'

Thus began the Velvet Revolution and the sequence of landmark events that combined to produce a great political upheaval: public talk of the need to stand up to the communists, even to defeat them, for instance through strike action and public hearings about police brutality; the defacement of statues and tearing down of communist red stars; the crowds that attended day-and-night vigils, to light votive candles at bloodstained sites before standing back in silence, as if in prayer; the formation of a new citizens' umbrella group called Civic Forum; its press conferences, held in the smoky caverns of the Magic Lantern Theatre, where its elected representatives demanded that pluralist democracy replace the power-mongering, lies and corruption of the old order; the first trolley car creaking through Prague's narrow streets, daubed with the words 'Havel to the Castle'; the Civic Forum appeals to Presidents Bush and Gorbachev; the countrywide string of giant demonstrations designed to force the government to its knees; the sudden resignation of President Jakeš; and the moment of greatest public joy: the weekend of massive peaceful demonstrations on Letná Plain, high above the Old Town Square, when a million people were thrilled to hear the master dramaturg Václav Havel announce the end of communism. Dressed in black, wearing reading glasses, rocking nervously to and fro on his left leg, the wispy-haired man of the people delivered the greatest performance of his life. 'The Civic Forum wants to be a bridge between totalitarianism and a real, pluralistic democracy, which will then be sanctioned by a free election', he shouted into the microphone, engulfed by a vast tidal sea of expectant faces. He added: 'We want truth, humanity, freedom as well.'

'Our jaws cannot drop any lower', exclaimed Radio Free Europe.[10] Communism's time was up. The timescale of events that had been boastfully predicted in the Prague scene had come to pass. The political job of getting rid of communism and beginning a transition to democracy had taken ten hard years in Poland. In Hungary it had taken ten months. In neighbouring East Germany the revolution had taken ten weeks. In Czechoslovakia it had taken just ten days. So forceful and widespread were the changes that for a time they seemed unstoppable, like a boulder tumbling ever faster down a slope of unlimited possibilities. Their rumblings continued for many years, with strong aftershocks being felt well beyond the original avalanche.

During the early months of 1997, the first green shoots of a new October Revolution could be detected in the Serbian capital Belgrade. President Milošević subsequently indicted for war crimes, fell silent. He and his Lady Macbeth kept out of sight as many huge demonstrations erupted in Republic Square, accompanied by flowers, whistles, placards, flags, gleeful children, musicians, actors, dancing, the singing of patriotic hymns. For many consecutive evenings, during the state-controlled television news programme, thousands of citizens joined in with 'noise is fashionable' actions. They flung open kitchen windows and clanged pots and pans, or honked their car horns in unison, or assembled peacefully in the streets, blowing whistles or playing trumpets and clarinets. When the programme ended, the racket stopped at once. Weather permitting, the noisemakers then walked in small groups through the frozen streets of Belgrade. The promenade was important to them, and not just because it was a cherished Balkans custom. Walking symbolised the reclamation of public space, new civil freedoms, a yearning for a civil society protected by law. Routes and assembly points were usually decided and coordinated by mobile phone. Favourite pathways included a circuit of the university courtyard, on to the education ministry, past the editorial offices of *Politika*, then over to the egg-splattered premises of Serbian Television. Sometimes the marchers walked in circles, acting like prisoners in a jail courtyard. Sympathisers supplied food, tea and coffee; everybody was urged to avoid alcohol. Police cordons failed to stop the actions. Not only did the promenaders manage to build what they called 'cordons against cordons', but their numbers swelled with each passing evening.

The strategy of organising peaceful grass-roots resistance in support of the principles of free elections and open constitutional government – democratic 'refolutions' they were sometimes called – usually enjoyed outside funding and support, especially from civil society organisations and European- and American-funded bodies and foundations. The tactic often worked, especially when pushed along by radically uncompromising 'conscience groups' (*Otpor* ('Resistance') in Serbia and *Kmara* ('Enough!') in Georgia were examples). Coordination by an obvious leader or a single candidate blessed with a sixth sense of knowing how and when to get people to cooperate with each other publicly also helped. The refolution tactic spread. In November 2003, parliamentary elections held in Georgia were denounced as grossly rigged by many local and international observers. Anti-government protests swelled. Speaker after speaker called for an end to kleptocratic government. On the opening day of the new parliamentary session, opposition demonstrators led by Mikheil Saakashvili occupied the parliament building, fragrant roses in their hands. President Eduard Shevardnadze, whose speech was interrupted, fled the building, surrounded by bodyguards. He then declared a state of emergency, but his crack military units refused to support the government. Shevardnadze resigned; the streets of Tbilisi gushed with euphoria. The Rose Revolution in favour of democracy and the existing constitution – some Russian and pro-Russian politicians called it a 'made-in-America coup' – had begun.

A few months later, in the neighbouring region of Ajaria, a second Rose Revolution erupted. Towards the end of 2004, in frostbitten conditions, public demonstrations in Independence Square in the Ukraine capital Kiev attracted up to a million citizens wearing orange clothing and orange ribbons and waving orange flags, the chosen colour of the campaign run by the opposition candidate, Viktor Yushchenko. After losing a run-off election, whose result was hotly disputed, his supporters set up a giant twenty-four-hour tent city, engaged in sit-ins, sing-ins and dance-ins and other forms of non-violent protest – to be rewarded a few weeks later by a decision in their favour by Ukraine's Supreme Court. In a free and fair second run-off election, Yushchenko won a decisive victory and was 'publicly inaugurated' in front of hundreds of thousands of his supporters, courtesy of the Orange Revolution.

The bold style of democratic refolutions soon began to travel well beyond the borders of Europe. For the first time, loud calls for democracy and 'people power' were heard in the Central Asian republic of Kyrgyzstan. The springtime of 2005 coincided with the outbreak of a Tulip Revolution, a term that ousted President Askar Akayev himself used in a speech, in which he warned that force would be used to prevent any outbreak of a 'colour revolution' in his country. It still happened. Following the irruption of violence and the occupation by demonstrators of government buildings in the southern city of Jalal-Abad, things happened fast. Braving police attacks, public protests against corrupt, authoritarian government spread throughout the country. An opposition congress called a *kurultai* voted in the city of Osh to set up a parallel parliament, or 'people's council'. There were reports that policemen, including high-ranking officers, had exchanged their uniforms for civilian clothing, and had joined the opposition. Then came the dramatic news that President Akayev had escaped from the country by the seat of his pants, with his family, by helicopter. He eventually tendered his resignation; he and his family members were stripped of many privileges. New presidential elections were held in July 2005 – by which time, a Cedar Revolution had broken out in Lebanon.

By the standards of the times it was certainly among the most dramatic pushes towards democracy. It was also the most fraught, mainly because of outside military interference by Israel and Syria, Iran and the United States. As in ancient Athens, democratisation was triggered by an assassination. Former Prime Minister Rafik Hariri was murdered in a grisly car-bomb attack in mid-February 2005. His death instantly triggered huge public protests peppered with demands for the withdrawal of the Syrian military and political presence in Lebanon. Millions of fingers of blame for the murder were wagged at the Syrian dictatorship and the pro-Syrian president, Émile Lahoud. The Lebanese government, fearing the worst and knowing that it was linked by media to protests in cities as far apart as Sydney, Montreal, San Francisco, Düsseldorf, Paris and London, held back from using force against the anti-Syrian demonstrators on the streets. Decked out in red and white scarves and hats and pro-Hariri blue ribbons, the opposition was encouraged, and drew closer together. It repeated calls for free and fair parliamentary elections. That meant the removal of the Syrians from Lebanon, and in Beirut it prompted a very large counter-demonstration, in support of Syria, by predominantly Shi'ite supporters of Hizbollah. But exactly a month after the assassination of Hariri, at the site of his grave in Martyrs' Square, in the heart of the city he had helped to rebuild, the largest demonstration ever seen in Lebanon was held.

Everybody who witnessed that determined spectacle of a million people standing shoulder to shoulder had no doubt that democracy was not just a European thing. On that Monday, 14 March 2005, it was as if the ancient Syrian-Mesopotamian spirit of assembly had suddenly revived. So many citizens jammed the city centre that tens of thousands were turned away. Veiled women linked arms with women dressed in tight jeans and with pierced navels, under fluttering Lebanese flags. Many demonstrators, young and old, painted their faces with crescents or crosses, some with one on each cheek. Druze, Shi'ites, Christians, secularists, Sunni Muslims and lots of people who simply empathised with their fellow Lebanese citizens stood there defiantly, bathing in the winter sunshine, filled with high expectations. 'Democracy is spreading in the region not because of George Bush, but despite him', wrote the well-known newspaper columnist Samir Kassir, who was shortly to be murdered by pro-Syrian thugs. The jubilant crowd did not know that it, too, would soon be punished. 'Freedom, Sovereignty, Independence', they chanted. 'Truth, Democracy, National Unity.'

They would very soon be rewarded with the departure of the Syrians, fresh elections, and a new government – but at the price of a devastating military invasion by democratic Israel in July 2006.

The End of History?

Just how things had changed on a world scale can be measured by rereading the classic American novel *Democracy*, written in the late nineteenth century by Henry Adams. Its heroine, Madeleine Lee, found herself fed up with the corrupting effects of power struggles, intrigues and general wheeling and dealing in Washington, DC. 'Democracy has shaken my nerves to pieces', she said, resigned, with a deep sigh. 'I want to go to Egypt.'[11] Under pressure from the great post-'45 democratic transformation, not even dictatorships like Egypt's proved to be safe havens for those afraid or sick of democracy. There was talk of democracy in Jordan, Tunisia and Senegal; while in Algeria, in 1989, the Islamic opposition party FIS won a majority of seats in a free and fair election (the results of which were quickly annulled by military intervention, which plunged the country into a murderous uncivil war, from which its people tried to recover, facing great difficulties). So momentous were the (apparent) changes that questions inevitably came to many people's lips: what exactly did these grandiloquent changes mean? Did they signal the beginning of something new on the face of the earth, perhaps even a global victory for representative democracy?

Answers came fast, sometimes with great public effect. There were observers, most famously the American pundit Francis Fukuyama (b. 1952), who announced that something fundamental was indeed happening in world history (Figure 111). In the summer of 1989, he published an essay that exuded confidence that ideas count in politics – by proposing the bold conjecture that all major opposition to 'liberal democracy' had crumbled.[12]

Climbing like a giddy Sherpa Tenzing to the 'standpoint of world history', Fukuyama maintained that the 'triumph of the West, of the Western *idea*', was anticipated long ago in the collapse of empires and the crushing military defeats of fascism. The successful

FIGURE 111: Francis Fukuyama at the Centre for the Study of Democracy, London, 1999.

Westernisation of Japan and South Korea, and the re-Westernisation of Germany and Italy, proved that there was nothing at all inevitable about totalitarian states attempting to forge a new 'people' on the anvil of national superiority. The end of fascism confirmed the importance of a type of government that is 'liberal insofar as it recognizes and protects through a system of law man's universal right of freedom, and democratic insofar as it exists only with the consent of the governed'. According to Fukuyama, the trend towards liberal democracy was confirmed by the collapse of military dictatorships, as well as by the political experiment called European integration, which showed just how dangerously unrealistic was the so-called 'realism' of nineteenth- and early twentieth-century conceptions of sovereign states struggling for survival and superiority in a world system of states.

Then (said Fukuyama) came the crisis of communism. The last decades of the twentieth century proved that 'the class issue has actually been successfully resolved in the West'. Market-driven consumerism had triumphed, as evidenced by 'the peasants' markets and color television sets now omnipresent throughout China, the cooperative restaurants and clothing stores opened in the past year in Moscow, the Beethoven piped into Japanese department stores, and the rock music enjoyed alike in Prague, Rangoon, and

Tehran'. Just as significant was the fact that Marxist-Leninist ideology proved to be clueless when confronted by the power of Western science and technology and the rise of 'bourgeois consumerism' linked to free markets protected by liberal democracy. Fukuyama cited the example of China, where the de-collectivisation of agriculture and increased production of consumer goods began with the 1978 reforms championed by Deng Xiaoping and sanctioned by the historic third plenum of the Tenth Central Committee of the Chinese Communist Party. In the Soviet Union, Gorbachev's *perestroika*, although initially carried out in the name of improving 'socialism', similarly hammered the last few nails into the coffin of Marxism-Leninism.

Fukuyama worried that things could turn sour in Russia, especially if it became snagged in the Slavophile nets of 'great Russian chauvinism'. He fretted, too, about rising levels of ethnic and nationalist violence and the shyness of Islam towards market exchange and liberal democracy. He pondered as well the strange possibility that the stupendous victory of Western liberal democracies might well produce a self-satisfied restlessness among their citizens, a smug boredom with the way things had turned out. But these misgivings merely demonstrated to Fukuyama that 'it is not necessary that all societies become successful liberal societies, merely that they end their ideological pretensions of representing different and higher forms of human society'. So ended his grand summary of the times, using grandiloquent language. All big ideologies of the past had now crumbled, like so many moth-eaten mantles from times bygone. Imperialism, nationalism, communism, fascism, realism, military dictatorship had been pushed to the wayside; under pressure from the forces of scientific and technical progress and market production, liberal democracy had triumphed, this time on a global scale. Something like the 'end of history' was unfolding before the eyes of the world. Clocks would not stand still; and people would not stop growing to maturity, falling in love, having children, growing old and dying. But the combined effect of these trends implied, at least in the world of ideas, that representative democracy in liberal form was no longer faced with serious political competition. The liberal democratic principles that governments should share power with their citizens, respect their civil rights and guarantee private ownership of property and free markets, had triumphed. This was no ordinary and uninteresting historical moment, no flash-in-the-pan development. Liberal democracy was here to stay. Perhaps – Fukuyama's concluding thought was avowedly speculative – we were standing at 'the end point of mankind's ideological evolution' and the corresponding 'universalization of Western liberal democracy as the final form of human government'.

A Third Wave?

Few people actually read Fukuyama's essay, but striking was how well he managed to turn heads, from all directions. He himself belonged to the advisory board of a well-known American think-tank called Freedom House, whose documents in effect summarised the mood of the times by repeating the end-of-history thesis. One of its best-known surveys spoke of the twentieth century as the Democratic Century. It purported to show that in 1900, when monarchies and empires still predominated, there were no states that could be judged as electoral democracies by the standard of universal suffrage for competitive multi-party elections (Figure 112). There were merely a few 'restricted democracies' – 25 of

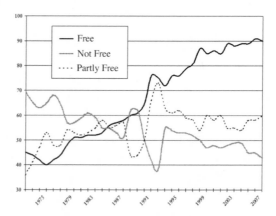

FIGURE 112: The rise of democracy: US-based Freedom House graph showing the number of 'free' democratic states and significant disputed territories around the world. The three categories ('free', 'partly free', 'not free') indicate the levels of political rights and civil liberties, 1973–2007.

them, accounting for just 12.4 per cent of the world's population. By 1950, with the beginnings of decolonisation and the post-war reconstruction of Japan and Europe, there were 22 democracies accounting for 31 per cent of the world's population; a further 21 states were 'restricted democracies' and they accounted for 11.9 per cent of the world's population. By the end of the century, the report observed, the spirit and institutions of democracy had arrived on the shores of Latin America, post-communist Europe and parts of Africa and Asia. At least on paper, out of 192 countries 119 could be described as 'electoral democracies' – 58.2 per cent of the globe's population. Eighty-five of these countries – 38 per cent of the world's inhabitants – enjoyed forms of democracy 'respectful of basic human rights and the rule of law'. So the report found that the ideal of democracy was now within practical reach of the whole world. 'In a very real sense', ran the conclusion, 'the twentieth century has become the "Democratic Century" ... A growing global human rights and democratic consciousness is reflected in the expansion of democratic practices and in the extension of the democratic franchise to all parts of the world and to all major civilizations and religions.'[13]

Words of this kind found confirmation in perhaps the most original attempt during this period to make sense of the progress of representative democracy: the detailed account provided in *The Third Wave* (1991) by scholar and policy adviser Samuel P. Huntington (1927–2008).[14] Using maritime metaphors, Huntington said that 'modern democracy', born of two earlier 'waves', was now experiencing an unusually strong 'third wave' of development. This point about wave development was very interesting, even if the simile was not quite right, for he wanted to say that experiments with democracy rarely happen on a one-off basis. Huntington stressed that democratisation typically happens in clusters, bunched like grapes on the stalks of simultaneity. He pointed out as well that democracy has no historical guarantees. Time has no single track; history is not unidirectional, so that waves of democratisation typically remain vulnerable to tidal reversals, with democracies sliding towards some or other form of non-democratic rule.

As might have been expected of someone of conservative

persuasion, Huntington defined representative democracy in a rather minimalist manner, and in a way that supposed that political elites play *the* central role in establishing and maintaining democracy. For him, its essence was the popular election of the top government decision makers within a state that has obviously demarcated borders. Its modern form clearly differed from 'democracy of the village, the tribe, or the city-state'. Democracy came to mean a type of government defined by the rotation of leadership through periodic elections. Huntington's definition followed that famously sketched in 1942 by Joseph Schumpeter (1883–1950). The 'democratic method', said the Moravian-born economist, 'is that institutional arrangement for arriving at political decisions in which individuals acquire the power to decide by means of a competitive struggle for the people's vote'.[15] The modern birth and maturation of democracy in this sense was at first slow, according to Huntington. 'In 1750 no democratic institutions at the national level existed in the Western world.' But soon afterwards democracy came to be 'associated with the development of the nation-state'.

The 'first wave' of democratisation had its roots in the American and French Revolutions, he said, and it ended shortly after World War One. It registered the emergence, for the first time, of about thirty countries with 'at least minimal' democratic governing procedures. The beginning of the end of this first long wave of democratisation was Mussolini's easy disposal of Italy's fledgling and rather corrupted democracy in the early 1920s. It was the prelude to a shift away from democracy and either the return to more traditional forms of authoritarian rule, or the introduction of mass-based totalitarianism. The rebirth of democracy in the period after 1945 came in two stages, or so Huntington claimed. The 'second wave' of democracy proved to be quite short. It had petered out by the early 1960s but – to everybody's surprise – the setbacks were themselves set back in an extraordinary renaissance of democracy that looked like persisting well into the twenty-first century. The new democratic tide was first felt in southern Europe. 'In the fifteen years following the end of the Portuguese dictatorship in 1974', commented Huntington, 'democratic regimes replaced authoritarian ones in approximately thirty countries in

Europe, Asia, and Latin America . . . Although obviously there were resistance and setbacks, as in China in 1989, the movement toward democracy seemed to take on the character of an almost irresistible global tide moving on from one triumph to the next.'

Sensing the fickleness of democracy, Huntington, unlike Fukuyama, desisted from making firm predictions about how things would turn out, but he did note the two-steps-forward, one-step-backward pattern of democratisation waves. 'To date each reverse wave has eliminated some but not all of the transitions to democracy of the previous democratization wave.' The cumulative pattern, in which each wave advanced further and ebbed less than its predecessor, was interpreted by Huntington as an encouraging sign that in the years to come democracy, for a substantial number of countries, would not turn out to be merely a sometime thing. The third wave of modern democracy could keep its shape, and roll on, indefinitely. Buoyed especially by 'a rising tide of economic progress' and steered by political elites who understand (with Churchill) that democracy is 'the least worse form of government for their societies and themselves', progress towards political democracy was possible in the third millennium. That did not mean that history was automatically on the side of democracy, for history itself required divination. History 'does not move forward in a straight line, but when skilled and determined leaders push, it does move forward'.

Pigs, Mosques and Rain

Huntington's account of democratic waves bred mixed reactions. Some observers admired its panoptic sweep, its brave effort to take stock and make sense of the clutter of disparate events that combined to produce dramas of historical proportions. Many agreed with his sober reminder that democracy often enjoyed growth spurts compressed into short periods of time – and that in the past these long waves had eventually crashed against the rocks of reality, to dissipate into so much foam before resuming their place in the vast waters of time. Given these reactions, *The Third Wave* attracted a great number of reviewers, many of them praising its brilliance in bringing order to the reality of the late twentieth century, without imposing unwieldy theoretical structures and making unsupportable claims. It was seen – rightly – as a timely contribution to our understanding of the mechanics of 'democratisation', a subject that attracted systematic interest for the first time in the history of democracy.

Other observers expressed reservations, which were far from minor. Some, for instance, doubted Huntington's overall characterisation of the so-called first wave of democracy, which according to him began around 1828 (the year of the election of Andrew Jackson to the presidency of the United States) and was powered by the twin engines of Protestantism and 'economic development, industrialization, urbanization, the emergence of the bourgeoisie and of a middle class, the development of a working class and its early organization, and the gradual decrease in economic inequality'.[16] It was certainly surprising that a conservative intellectual should have come up with such a Marxist-sounding explanation of the origins of modern democracy. Money and markets were never to be underestimated in the history of democracy, certainly, but to suppose that they were the secret of modern democracy's first successes, as Huntington did, was to miss all the marvellous ironies in its genealogy. Huntington's picture of democracy as a nineteenth-century invention was plainly wrong. It ignored the long incubation that began during the medieval period – a period that lasted at least five centuries, during which *non-liberal* and *undemocratic* forces were vital in the drawn-out process of invention of what was later called representative democracy. That was not all. With good reason, some observers took issue with the questionable, rather arbitrary distinction between the second and third waves of democracy. And while Huntington was to be congratulated for showing how the language and institutions of democracy, for the first time ever, became a global force during the second half of the twentieth century, his overall account of a 'third wave' of democracy was arguably too glib, in several senses.

To begin with, Huntington's concern with aggregate trends blinded him to the fascinating mutations that took place in both the language and institutions of democracy in the decades after 1945. Mutations? What is meant in this context by the strange-sounding term drawn from genetics? Quite simply this: in the earth's biosphere, deep down in the cells of organisms, mutations are those sudden or more protracted changes in their inherited characteristics. The changes that happen in the DNA sequence of genes and chromosomes do so either spontaneously, or because they are induced by mutagens, outside factors such as x-rays and chemical agents. Many mutations prove harmless; they are simply overridden by the presence of dominant genes. Sometimes – as in the sickle-cell anaemia produced by a change in the shape of the blood cells of a person after inheriting a particular mutation that occurs in the genes of both its parents – mutations have lethal effects; compared to its delicately balanced predecessor, the mutated organism 'wobbles' and finds it hard to survive in its given environment. But mutations do not always lead to unfitness and consequent death. Mutations can be beneficial. They sometimes produce organisms much better adapted to their environment, in which case the process of competitive selection enables the altered gene to be passed on successfully to subsequent generations. These beneficial mutations turn out to be the raw material of evolution and adaptation to changing environments. Big-bottomed sheep are a much discussed example: according to evolutionary biologists, they are carriers of a rare mutated gene called 'callipyge' (meaning 'beautiful buttocks' in Greek). Inheriting the gene from their father alone, the lucky, better equipped sheep, with very little fat, has a remarkable ability to convert food into muscle 30 per cent more efficiently than normal sheep.

How exactly they manage to perform so brilliantly and why they may have dramatic implications for the human genome are matters less relevant than the riddle they pose: what exactly do the large, muscular bottoms of sheep have to do with democracy?

One answer runs like this: changes that bore a striking resemblance to mutations in the gene pool of sheep happened in the world of democracy in the aftermath of World War Two. Recall for a moment the case of India, where from the time of its first general election in 1952 the world's first ever, large-scale banyan democracy was gradually created among materially impoverished peoples of multiple faiths, many different languages and low rates of literacy; or think of the negotiated transition to parliamentary democracy in South Africa. Both were dramatic symbols and practical examples of the historic mutation of democracy. They exposed the falsity of the old European wisdom that democracy could never happen in conditions of deep poverty and chronic illiteracy; they demonstrated that democracy could flourish in the absence of consensus on social and political values and ways of life; and each symbolised the removal of racial prejudice from the very ideals of democracy, a process that had begun with the struggles against slavery in the era of representative democracy. The fact that the language, ideals and institutions of democracy, for the first time in history, became familiar to people living not only in India and South Africa, but within most regions of the earth, regardless of their wealth and income, or their skin colour, religion, nationality or civilisation, blew apart the originally white and Atlantic biases of representative democracy; it forced democrats around the world to feel embarrassment or anger whenever they heard talk of 'backward', 'uncivilised' or 'naturally inferior' peoples. But the 'indigenisation' of democracy – its embedding and mutation in contexts where formerly it was a stranger, or forbidden – did much more than this. Symbolised by pigs, mosques and rain, it unleashed experiments that changed the meaning of democracy itself.

Let us begin with pigs: the period after 1945 saw the spread of strange democratic customs into the most remote of the earth's corners, for instance to Papua New Guinea. There the spectacle of a general election held once every five years defied most European presumptions, to the point where all previous historians of democracy, had they been privileged to witness the spectacle, would have been left in a state of fascinated speechlessness.

Several weeks before an election, life ceased to be normal throughout a country made up of 1000 local groups speaking more than eight hundred languages. Hog farmers, horticulturalists and plantation labourers got on with their work, it was true. Highway bandits known as *raskols* still operated their night-time patches. Transnational companies carried on plundering the country's oil, timber and mineral (copper, gold) resources. But everyone felt a change in atmosphere at election time. There were reported sightings of a *gavman* – a government official, usually in the figure of a policeman or patrol officer, or two. Sale of alcohol was banned, though fights fuelled by local feuds and grievances still sometimes erupted. In rural areas, some families gathered to beat drums, night after night, to chase from the world the mischievous ghosts of the recently deceased. There was talk (in *Tok Pisin*, the local Melanesian pidgin and lingua franca) of the duty to respect *Mama Kwin* (Mummy Queen, Elizabeth II), a figure whom some still described as a powerful mythical creature who was 'half woman, half snake'. By this time, to ensure that nobody was left out, electoral teams had set out by road and foot and canoe and helicopter to deliver ballot boxes and electoral rolls deep into every valley, mountain range and forest.

Then came the moment of the *eleksen*, the chance given to each man and woman to 'throw a vote' before government. Excitement mounted. Every vote counted. Papuan elections sometimes hung on just a few score votes, so every effort was made by voters over eighteen (women under that age voted as well, if they were married) to get their fellow citizens out. They always appeared in huge numbers. Some dressed in cloaks of beaten bark, and many voters

FIGURE 113: Member of the parliament of Papua New Guinea Alfred Kaibe, dressed in bird of paradise feathers, a possum fur skirt and carrying a stone axe, during a debate about the problem of corruption and the importance of preserving 'traditional values', Port Moresby, July 2001.

were accompanied by a parent or friend who knew how to mark a cross underneath the photograph of their preferred candidate. Most voters normally had no knowledge of party policies, but this had nothing to do with the strictly enforced rule that prohibited campaigning and election posters and leaflets within seventy yards of the polling station. The truth was that political parties bore little resemblance to the Westminster ideals from which they had sprung. Most were small, since that made it much easier for their 'big men' leaders (Figure 113) to manoeuvre them in and out of perpetually changing governing coalitions; some parties were nothing more than printed names on paper; and still others contained 'party hopping' parliamentarians who were members of several political parties at the same time (the logic of party competition taken to extremes). The truth was that in any case few voters had access to radio or television; in some districts, only one man in ten (and two or three women) knew how to read in a country where newspapers were prized as wrapping paper, and especially by those who liked to roll long and tasty cigarettes.

Why, reliving the spirit of Juan Vucetich, were most people willing to receive a paint mark on their finger, to clutch a voting slip, enter a makeshift cardboard booth, write an 'X' underneath the picture of their candidate of choice, then to fold the slip, place it in a metal ballot box and, on their way out of the polling station, show their paint-daubed finger to the duty policeman, on guard to prevent voters from voting twice? Was it to bring to the community the long-promised airstrip, or to secure the appointment of a new local doctor, or nurse, or primary school teacher? Or perhaps to put an end to the high rates of infant mortality (in some areas of the country one in three never reached their first birthday), so that their sons and daughters could grow up and one day plant coffee, or open a shop, or do some other kind of *bisnis*? When asked why they bothered to vote, the black newcomers to the once-white world of democratic rituals used local expressions to explain something much more basic: many straightforwardly said that they wanted to keep their 'heads high' and so put behind them the colonial times, when they were 'treated like pigs'.

The mosque: in the west African country of Senegal, the transplantation of electoral democracy showed that it could meld with a predominantly agrarian Muslim society, to produce equally unusual results. Here was a country introduced to Islamic customs from across the Sahara by Berber merchants in the mid-fifteenth century; a country where electoral politics in limited form dated back to 1848, when voting rights were granted (this was rare within the French empire) by the colonial authorities to the adult men of the principal urban settlements. Under colonial conditions, voters admittedly formed a tiny minority of the population, but the culture of voting and elections gradually spread, culminating in a victory for universal (male and female) suffrage in 1956. Following independence in 1960, the government of Léopold Sédar Senghor did its best to turn the country into a one-party system. The attempt to absorb or ban opposition parties and to rig elections failed, in no small measure because of strong support for *demokaraasi* among Senegal's Wolof-speaking Muslim majority.

In a remarkable shift of cultural reference points, some party leaders and journalists and many citizens had learned to liken political parties and elections to the sacred place of worship, the mosque. On this view, parties and their leaders resemble muezzins whose job it is to stand atop the minaret to call the faithful – voters – to daily prayer. Practically anyone can become a muezzin (in Senegalese Islam, muezzins are lay characters who require only a proven ability to learn the calls), so anybody can form and lead a party. Just as happens at mosque, *demokaraasi* draws on the principle of rotation of muezzins under the supervision of the imam, the one who stands before the assembled faithful to lead them in prayer. Those who head government resemble the imam (the Arabic root of the word *imām* means 'in front of'); supported by the wider community, and supervised from a distance by the real holders of power, the religious brotherhoods, leaders are expected to guide others through life, with the help of parties, and to do so on the basis that they have been *put* in front – in a sense, chosen – by the wider community.

The supposed chain of resemblances between the mosque and democracy begged tough questions, no doubt. Muezzins never become imams; hence the analogy in many Senegalese minds harboured confusion about how imams and government leaders were chosen, and whether they should hold office for limited term.* Such difficulties aside, there was no denying that for many Senegalese people mosque democracy (let us call it the mutation) had powerful connotations. For it followed from their way of thinking about *demokaraasi* that it was more than just a mundane method of selecting a government based on the consent of the community; wrapped in sacred language, it was a whole way of life, a set of beliefs and institutions that bound people together under one God. *Demokaraasi* knew no distinction between the sacred and the profane. It resembled instead a community of believers bound together by their quest to harmonise their differences through multi-party government and good leadership, under the watchful eye of an exacting God.

And a final symbol of the mutation of democracy, rain: during the 1950s, in the east African Shambaa-speaking region of Tanganyika (later Tanzania), discussions about the relevance of *demokrasi* flourished in the countryside, initially within circles of peasant intellectuals – women and men who liked to talk politics while earning their living by farming, and who were strongly opposed to British imperial rule. What exactly was meant by *demokrasi* and what was good about it, they asked? Should each man and woman be granted a vote in elections? Or was it rule by a council of elders, or perhaps a kind of government by the best-educated? In a *demokrasi*, would old men be entitled to exercise their old freedoms, which included substantial powers over young men? Might a peasant king sit on the throne, or did *demokrasi* demand that all royalty be abolished? And what was to become of the local tradition of ruling chiefs?

---

*During the 1988 presidential elections, the Dakar periodical *Le Cafard Libéré* (13 and 20 February 1988) published a cartoon strip by Alphonse Mendy, a prominent Senegalese satirist, who dwelled on the understandable electoral confusions of an unemployed character named Goorgoorlu, or Try-to-do-Well. Battling daily to make ends meet for his family, he and his friend Tapha watch with interest four presidential candidates make their campaign promises on television. Tapha asks Goorgoorlu if he has decided which way he is going to vote. 'Of course!' replies Goorgoorlu. 'For Savané, who promises me work: for Mbaye Niang for education in the national languages for my children; for [President] Diouf, who guarantees me *demokaraasi*; and for Ablaye, who promises me rice and fish every day. I'm no longer undecided. I'll vote for all four.' Tapha points out that his friend cannot vote for all four, but Goorgoorlu keeps his cool. 'Why not? We have *demokaraasi*, no?'

The last of these questions sparked by the flint of democracy striking the iron of established power proved especially difficult to answer. Here was the tricky problem never before faced by democrats in favour of power sharing and contested elections: according to customs that stretched back into the pre-colonial Shambaa kingdom, chiefs were widely thought to possess potent medicines for making rain, so vital for plentiful crops. People believed with deep conviction that chiefs doubling as rainmakers would only use their medicines if they enjoyed the respect of their subjects. Whenever competition for power erupted (*nguvu kwa nguvu* was the way they put it) chiefs would hold back the rains and cause a ruinous drought, either to undermine their competitors' support, or to teach the local peasants a lesson for being insufficiently loyal. On this view, the chief who wields centralised power is blessed with the capacity to 'cover over the land' by healing and protecting it. The land was popularly likened to masculinity as well as to the sun, which (like men's daily fertility) shines down each and every day and has the capacity either to make crops grow, or to crack and ruin the soil. The soothing rains were likened to the moon, which waxes and wanes according to a different rhythm, just like a woman, whose fertility comes only at an appropriate time in her monthly cycle (her 'moon'). Sun and moon thus not only resembled masculinity and femininity, but also hunger and satisfaction – each with a different rhythm that could be combined into a higher, more graceful rhythm.

Seen in terms of power, the picture of the world among the Shambaa-speaking people implied something like a law of politics: when power was centralised in the hands of chiefs, who in turn obeyed the commands of a sovereign king, the sun would shine and rains would come and good harvests would be enjoyed. Sun would hold hands with rain, the masculine with the feminine and, thanks to the healing of the land and the resulting good crops, hunger would give way to satisfaction, all according to the harmonious rhythm of time. But when disputes and struggles for power erupted, for instance when subjects jostled with a chief, or against the king, the dominance of sun, masculinity and drought would ruin the land, resulting in famine and great suffering of the people. The rhythm of fertility – the fruitful union of sun and moon, land and rain, masculinity and femininity – would be interrupted. Time would lose its way. The world would find itself out of joint. The people would be abandoned, transformed from hardworking peasants with dignity into mere playthings, at the whims and mercies of unreliable rainmakers hungering after power – as, indeed, had happened during the droughts, famine, unjust settlements and open warfare sparked by German and British colonisation.

This was challenging stuff for the local friends of *demokrasi*. It reminded them that nobody in their right mind would want to punish the people with drought, followed by famine; and it forced them to think creatively about the meaning and practicability of their ideals. What they came up with was designed to break once and for all the supposed rainmaking powers of chiefs and kings, and to do so by abolishing their role – all the while acknowledging the need to respect strong local feelings about the importance of power based on unity. What was now needed, insisted the friends of *demokrasi*, was a new type of government, one that would transcend the divisiveness of Western-style representative government, with its competitive party machines permanently mobilised to enter the battlefield of elections on behalf of the rich and powerful. The solution was to be found in what was called *ujamaa*: self-governing villages that held property in common, bound together by a presidential state that kept closely in touch with its citizens thanks to newspapers – and thanks to radio, a new medium that had the added advantage of circulating weather reports from various parts of the country, at the turn of a dial revealing to everybody with ears that meteorology was not the same as mythology.

With great eloquence, a case for this more 'authentic' form of democracy was put in the speeches and writings of Julius Kambarage Nyerere (1922–99), the man appointed as First Minister by the British during the dying moments of colonial rule, and who soon became president of the new republic (Figure 114). Born into a humble Roman Catholic peasant family, Nyerere was a man of the people who had a way with words, in English but especially in his native Kiswahili (into which he translated Shakespeare's *Julius Caesar* and *The Merchant of Venice*). 'The ancient Greeks lived in small towns', he wrote in a Tanganyika African National Union (TANU) pamphlet published in 1959 and widely circulated through-

FIGURE 114: Prime Minister Julius Nyerere of Tanzania, six months after his inauguration, chats with President John F. Kennedy at the White House, 17 July 1963.

out the country. 'Each town was a complete "nation" with its own government. They did not have kings or *watemi* (chiefs). Their governmental affairs were considered and decided in a meeting of all commoners together. Authority and responsibility did not rest with a single individual or a small group of citizens, but rested with the entire citizenry together.'[17] Note Nyerere's emphasis on the solidarity of 'commoners', the importance of exercising power *together*, thus avoiding the pain and lacerations generated within the body politic when 'power' rubs up against 'power', like a rock against human skin. Democracy meant 'equality' (*usawa*). It therefore implied (note Nyerere's modern-minded rejection of the Greek model) the overthrow of all forms of slavery, including colonial regimes parasitic upon people's skin colour. Village democracy as well implied 'freedom' (*uhuru*). That key term Nyerere defined as 'the condition of living, acting and thinking without obstruction. A slave has no *uhuru*', he added. The abolition of colonial servitude demanded the development of village solidarity, equality and freedom: a kind of democracy that Nyerere and his supporters called *ujamaa* socialism.

The principles were clear enough, but that left only the political problem of how village democracy could be combined with territorial state independence. Nyerere was convinced of the impossibility of bypassing representative mechanisms in states that spanned a sizeable territory. In his inaugural speech to the first parliament of the new Republic of Tanganyika, he noted the problem: 'because we live in scattered locations, our democracy still has its flaws'. The main defect was the lingering tyranny of distance: 'it is difficult for us to meet together and to make decisions on our affairs, especially those concerning village life. Because of this, we leave matters to be decided by our chosen representatives. Often, however, because of distance we are unable to see our representatives and to ask them what matters they are discussing and deciding in our place.' So what was to be done? Nyerere replied: 'Living in villages will lead to true democracy in the matters which concern each village.'

The heartfelt answer begged a question: how would an Africanised democracy coordinate its own national affairs? Nyerere's answer: given that village-based democracy was 'as familiar to the African as the tropical sun', multi-party systems were undesirable, and unworkable. Such systems had indeed sprung up elsewhere, for instance in Europe and the United States, in the absence of equality, that is, in contexts where there were social divisions, especially between rich and poor. By contrast, TANU and other parties in Africa were formed in the struggle for independence. From the outset, 'they represented the interests and aspirations of the whole nation'. With the defeat of colonialism, the division between rulers and ruled therefore became meaningless. That left only the task of crafting a form of self-government that expressed people's desire to be treated as equals. Two-party democracy was a contradiction in terms. When countries are torn apart by the clash of interests and parties, they twist and disfigure government into a form of artificial 'football politics'. Party jostles and elbows party. For the sake of winning against their rivals, party leaders rob rank-and-file members of their freedom to speak out. Parties also deliberately stir up trouble among the public at large. Leaders bent on winning office are forced to promise things they cannot deliver. They become tricksters who care little for 'the just management of the affairs of society'. For all these reasons, party politics threatens the old African custom of 'free discussion' and concern for 'all the people' displayed in villages where 'elders sit under the big tree, and talk until they agree'. For the sake of the people, their dignity and unity, this precious custom now had to be preserved. To be better, Africa had to be different by going back to its roots: 'where there is *one* party, and that party is identified with the *nation as a whole*, the foundations of democracy are firmer than they can ever be where you have two or more parties, each representing only a section of the community'.

The whole new perspective on one-party democracy was designed to tackle difficult local problems, such as how to integrate a population that was religiously split (between followers of Islam and Christianity, for instance) and that shared no common language, except Kiswahili. The perspective supposed that fundamental differences of policy and opinion could be made to wither away, that the search for a common good could succeed, even if that required a few sharp lashes on the backs of dissenters (as happened in 1964, when, in a desperate but successful bid to save his rule, Nyerere called in the troops of his former colonial masters, the British, to crush a mutiny by his own army). Finally there was the slippery-fish question of political leadership in an *ujamaa* democracy: how important was leadership and what kind of leaders would complement self-government through a one-party system grounded in free and equal discussion?

Nyerere's thoroughly indigenous answer was revealed during his inauguration as president of the republic, on 9 December 1962.[18] It was a grand ceremony that in one way still belonged to the era of chiefs and kings, an event designed to reassure the population that power would be undivided, that an undivided democracy could 'cover the land', and that, thanks to the unifying efforts of the presidency, the separate villages of the country would be bound together into a higher unity, so bringing the rain that would fall on the land to germinate prosperity and peace.

As his entourage arrived at the National Stadium in Dar es Salaam, Nyerere was greeted by the thump, thump, thump of the drums of the royal house of Mwami Theresa Ntare. It was then the turn of Chief Petro Itosi Marealle, speaking in Kiswahili, to greet the new president and to pray that God would bless him and grant him 'might, power and wisdom and long to live'. In accordance with local custom, Chief Mazengo stepped forward to present Nyerere with a royal robe, as a sign that 'the favour of your leadership be spread all over the country in the same way as this long robe has spread all over your body'. Mounted on a dais, the president received a spear, for the protection of the people of Tanganyika, as well as a shield for their defence against enemies. After anointment by Chief Mazengo with a paste made from flour and water, President Nyerere stepped from the dais, to walk to the saluting base, accompanied by a roll on the royal drums. The new leader then took the salute before the Tanganyika Rifles and Police. The parade re-formed and gave a presidential salute. After three full-throated cheers from the troops, Nyerere climbed into his open car, then circled and departed the stadium, in a great fanfare of cheers and applause from a crowd swaying to the sonic sound of the mighty drums.

Monitory Democracy

Soon after Nyerere stepped down from the presidency (in 1985), the efforts of TANU and its supporters to govern the country through the one-party *ujamaa* democracy triggered a backlash, so that by the early 1990s constitutional amendments had given the green light to a multi-party system. Botanists and zoologists might draw the conclusion that the effort to redefine the genotype of democracy in the circumstances of Tanganyika had produced a lethal mutation – a phenotype that 'wobbled', failed to adapt properly to its new environment, and in the end proved to be incapable of effective reproduction. Even so, there was something of greater importance at work here, a bigger moral to the little stories drawn from Tanganyika, Senegal, Papua New Guinea and India: in the decades after 1945, democracy was no longer a white-skinned, middle-class Western affair, as it had been when James Bryce wrote his *Modern Democracies* (1921). Things had changed: as the world became democratic, democracy became worldly.

It is true that the many different subtypes of democracy that sprang up on every continent still belonged to the family called democracy, not only in name, but also in spirit. Political leaders and citizens who thought of themselves as democrats were still bound together by some measure of respect for non-violent, lawful government based on the consent of 'the people'; their suspicion of concentrated and unaccountable power; and their commitment to the principle that citizens are one another's equals. The mutation of democracy in environments radically different from the earlier parent democracies of Western Europe, Spanish America and the United States nevertheless had an important implication. More than at any other moment in its long and fascinating history, the meaning and practice of democracy became implicated in local everyday sentiments, languages, institutions and shifting and contested forms of power. The consequence was that single-minded, *a priori* definitions of democracy lost their meaning. It was as if democracy itself had finally begun to be democratised – to the point where anthropologists rather than political scientists were better equipped to grasp its ways. Democracy became multivalent. People began to recognise it as a way of viewing power from many different angles, a deeply contingent way of life that stood permanently on the edge of disjunction, a way of governing and behaving that had open borders, not a single condition that a people or a country had, or did not have. Hence the first conclusion in our quest to come to terms with the main trends of our times: there was something fishy about Samuel Huntington's talk of a 'third wave' of representative democracy. While it correctly put its finger on the massive rebirth of interest in democracy during the second half of the twentieth century, its use of a maritime metaphor was too limited, too bound to the surface of things, too preoccupied with waves to notice that beneath the tides and swells of the world's oceans there were (so to speak) growing numbers of different species of fish called democracy – pufferfish and predatory sharks among them.*

---

*There were so many different species, dwelling in habitats that bore little or no resemblance to the originally Atlantic model of representative democracy, that in the early years of the twenty-first century legitimate doubts were raised about the capacity of these different democracies to live peacefully together. One of the first ominous examples: in January 2006, in Palestine, the radical Muslim network called Hamas tasted victory in a closely monitored election. It was the first time in the Arab-speaking world that voters had ousted an autocratic government in a free and fair election. Born of frustration with double standards and constant victimisation of its peoples by outside forces, the new government wasted no time in committing itself to the formation of a free and independent Palestinian state. The world took note. The governments of the United States and neighbouring Israel instantly cried foul. The newly elected, Hamas-led government was denounced as 'terrorist'. Its funding was cut off and the new government generally battered from all sides, treated as an unwanted child in the world of democracy. Weapons were covertly despatched to its opponents. Several of its cabinet ministers were even arrested by the Israeli military authorities, whose political masters acted as though democracy did not much matter whenever it did not suit them. Ground back into the soils where prophets once walked, the new government of Palestine collapsed, triggering a bloody civil war, an armed Hamas takeover of the Gaza region, followed by further Israeli military invasions and fears of a wider regional war.

That was not all. Politically speaking, something much bigger was at stake. The 'third wave' metaphor failed to spot a historic sea change, an epochal transformation that began during the second half of the twentieth century, and is still taking place under our noses: the birth of a new kind of democracy, a form of 'post-representative' democracy that is distinctively different from the assembly-based and representative democracies of past times.

It is hard to find an elegant name for it, let alone to describe in a few words its workings and political implications. The strange-sounding term *monitory democracy* is the most exact for describing the big transformation that is taking hold in regions like Europe and in countries otherwise as different as the United States and India, Argentina and New Zealand. Monitory democracy is a new historical form of democracy, a variety of 'post-parliamentary' politics defined by the rapid growth of many different kinds of extra-parliamentary, power-scrutinising mechanisms.* These monitory bodies take root within the 'domestic' fields of government and civil

---

*The adjective 'monitory' derives from the medieval *monitoria* (from *monere*, to warn). It entered Middle English in the shape of *monitorie* and from there it wended its way into the modern English language in the mid-fifteenth century to refer to the process of giving or conveying a warning of an impending danger, or an admonition to someone to refrain from a specified course of action considered offensive. It was first used within the Church to refer to a letter or letters (known as 'monitories') sent by a bishop, a pope or an ecclesiastical court who acted in the capacity of a 'monitor'. The family of words 'monitor', 'monition' and 'monitory' was soon used for more secular or this-worldly purposes. The monitor was one who, or that which, admonishes others about their conduct. The word 'monitor' was also used in school settings to refer to a senior pupil expected to perform special duties, such as that of keeping order, or (if the pupil was particularly bright or gifted) acting as a teacher to a junior class. A monitor also came to mean an early-warning device; it was said as well to be a species of African and Australian and New Guinean lizard that was friendly to humans because it gave warning of the whereabouts of crocodiles. Still later, the word 'monitor' came to be associated with communication devices. It referred to a receiver, such as a speaker or a television screen, used to check the quality or content of an electronic transmission; and in the world of computing and computer science a 'monitor' either refers to a video display or to a programme that observes, or supervises or controls the activities of other programmes. In more recent years, not unconnected with the emergence of monitory democracy, 'to monitor' became a commonplace verb to describe the process of systematically checking the content or quality of something, as when a city authority monitors the local drinking water for impurities, or a group of scientific experts monitors the population of an endangered species. Such usages seem to have inspired the theory of 'monitorial democracy' developed by the American scholar Michael Schudson (interview, New York City, 4 December 2006). See his 'Changing Concepts of Democracy', *MIT Communications Forum* (8 May 1998) and the fuller version in *The Good Citizen: A History of American Public Life* (New York, 1998), to which my account of monitory democracy is indebted.

society, as well as in 'cross-border' settings once controlled by empires, states and business organisations. In consequence – India is the only case we have so far examined – the whole architecture of self-government is changing. The central grip of elections, political parties and parliaments on citizens' lives is weakening. Democracy is coming to mean more than elections, although nothing less. Within and outside states, independent monitors of power begin to have tangible effects. By putting politicians, parties and elected governments permanently on their toes, they complicate their lives, question their authority and force them to change their agendas – and sometimes smother them in disgrace.

Whether or not the trend towards this new kind of democracy is a sustainable, historically irreversible development remains to be seen; like its two historical antecedents, monitory democracy is not inevitable. It did not have to happen, but it happened; whether it will live or die must still be discussed. Certainly when judged by its institutional contours and inner dynamics, monitory democracy is the most complex form of democracy yet. Those with a taste for Latin would say that it is the *tertium quid*, the not fully formed successor of the earlier historical experiments with assembly-based and representative forms of democracy. In the name of 'people', 'the public', 'public accountability', 'the people' or 'citizens' – the terms are normally used interchangeably in the age of monitory democracy – power-scrutinising institutions spring up all over the place. Elections, political parties and legislatures neither disappear, nor necessarily decline in importance; but they most definitely lose their pivotal position in politics. Democracy is no longer simply a way of handling the power of elected governments by electoral, parliamentary and constitutional means, and no longer a matter confined to territorial states. Gone are the days when democracy could be described (and in the next breath attacked) as 'government by the unrestricted will of the majority'.[19] The bullheaded belief that democracy is nothing more than the periodic election of governments by majority rule is crumbling. Whether in the field of local, national or supranational government, or in the power-ridden world of non-governmental organisations and networks, some of them stretching down into the roots of everyday life and outwards, towards the four corners of the earth, people and organisations that exercise power are now routinely subject to public monitoring and public contestation by an assortment of extra-parliamentary bodies.

In the age of monitory democracy, the rules of representation, democratic accountability and public participation are applied to a much wider range of settings than ever before. Here is one striking clue for understanding why this is happening: the age of monitory democracy that began in 1945 has witnessed the birth of nearly one hundred new types of power-scrutinising institutions unknown to previous democrats. As we shall see, defenders of these inventions often speak of their importance in solving a basic problem facing contemporary democracies: how to promote their unfinished business of finding new ways of democratic living for little people in big and complex societies, in which substantial numbers of citizens believe that politicians are not easily trusted, and in which governments are often accused of abusing their power or being out of touch with citizens, or simply unwilling to deal with their concerns and problems. By addressing such concerns, the new power-scrutinising inventions break the grip of the majority-rule principle – the worship of numbers – associated with representative democracy. Freed as well from the measured caution and double-speak of political parties, some inventions give a voice to the strongly felt concerns of minorities that feel left out of official politics. Some monitors, activist courts, electoral commissions and consumer protection agencies, for instance, use their claimed 'neutrality' to protect the rules of the democratic game from predators and enemies. Other monitors publicise long-term issues that are neglected, or dealt with badly, by the short-term mentality encouraged by election cycles. Still other monitory groups are remarkable for their evanescence; in a fast-changing world, they come on the scene, stir the pot, then move on like nomads, or dissolve into thin air. By making room for opinions and ways of life that people feel strongly about, despite their neglect or suppression by parties, parliaments and governments, these inventions have the combined effect of raising the level and quality of public monitoring of power, often for the first time in many areas of life, including power relationships 'beneath' and 'beyond' the institutions of territorial states.

It is little wonder that the new power-monitoring inventions have changed the language of contemporary politics. They prompt much talk of 'empowerment', 'high energy democracy', 'stakeholders', 'participatory governance', 'communicative democracy' and 'deliberative democracy'; and they help spread, often for the first time, a culture of voting into many walks of life. Monitory democracy is the age of surveys, focus groups, deliberative polling, online petitions and audience and customer voting. Whether intended or not, the spreading culture of voting, backed by the new mechanisms for monitoring power, has the effect of interrupting and often silencing the soliloquies of parties, politicians and parliaments. The power-scrutinising innovations tend to enfranchise many more citizens' voices, sometimes by means of *unelected representatives* (such as human rights organisations) skilled at using what Americans sometimes call 'bully pulpits'. The number and range of monitory institutions so greatly increase that they point to a world where the old rule of 'one person, one vote, one representative' – the central demand in the struggle for representative democracy – is replaced with the new principle of monitory democracy: 'one person, many interests, many voices, multiple votes, multiple representatives'.

Caution must be exercised when trying to understand the new methods of restraining power; they are not cut from the same cloth and therefore need careful examination. The new monitory inventions are not exclusively 'American' or 'European' or 'OECD' or 'Western' products. Among their more remarkable features is the way that they have rapidly diffused around the globe, from all points on the globe. They mushroom in a wide variety of settings and there are even signs, for the first time in the history of democracy, of mounting awareness of the added value of the art of invention – as if the democratic ability to invent is itself a most valuable invention. Symptomatic of this trend is the way visionary proposals for new ways of handling and taming power have multiplied within the European region. Cases in point include the so-called Copenhagen criteria (agreed in that city at the June 1993 European Council) that oblige present and future members of the European Union to stand for stable institutions that guarantee market economies plus 'democracy, the rule of law, human rights and respect for and protection of minorities'; and the Council of Europe's 'Green Paper' list of twenty-nine suggested reforms, covering such innovations as voting rights for denizens, democracy kiosks, online deliberation schemes, 'yellow cards' for legislatures, citizenship mentors and guardians to monitor the guardians.[20]

Monitory mechanisms operate in different ways, on different fronts. Some scrutinise power primarily at the level of *citizens' inputs* to government or civil society bodies; other monitory mechanisms are preoccupied with monitoring and contesting what are called *policy throughputs*; still others concentrate on scrutinising *policy outputs* produced by governmental or non-governmental organisations. Quite a few of the inventions concentrate simultaneously upon all three dimensions. Monitory mechanisms also come in different sizes and operate on various spatial scales, ranging from 'just-round-the-corner' bodies with merely local footprints to global networks aimed at keeping tabs on those who exercise power over great distances.

Given such variations, it should not be surprising that a quick short list of the post-1945 inventions resembles – at first sight, to the untrained eye – a magpie's nest of randomly collected items. The list includes: citizen juries, bioregional assemblies, participatory budgeting, advisory boards and focus groups. There are think-tanks, consensus conferences, teach-ins, public memorials, local community consultation schemes and open houses (developed, for instance, in the field of architecture) that offer information and advisory and advocacy services, archive and research facilities and opportunities for professional networking. Citizens' assemblies, democratic audits, human rights organisations, brainstorming conferences, conflict-of-interest boards, global associations of parliamentarians against corruption, and constitutional safaris (famously used by the drafters of the new South African constitution to examine best practice elsewhere) are on the list. So, too, are the inventions of India's banyan democracy: railway courts, *lok adalats*, public-interest litigation and *satyagraha* methods of civil resistance. Included as well are activist courts, consumer testing agencies and consumer councils, online petitions and chat rooms, democracy clubs and democracy cafés, public vigils and peaceful sieges, summits and global watchdog organisations set up to bring greater public accountability to business and other civil society bodies. The list of innovations extends to deliberative polls, boards of accountancy, independent religious courts, experts councils (such as the 'Five Wise Men' of the Council of Economic Advisers in Germany), public 'scorecards' – yellow cards and white lists – public consultations, social forums, weblogs, electronic networking and civil disobedience and websites dedicated to monitoring the abuse of power (such as Bully OnLine, a UK-based initiative that aims to tackle workplace bullying and related issues). And the list of new inventions includes self-selected opinion polls ('SLOPs') and unofficial ballots (text-messaged straw polls, for instance), international treaties and criminal courts, global social forums and the tendency of increasing numbers of non-governmental organisations to adopt written constitutions, with an elected component.

Let us pause, for evidently the list of inventions is disjointed, and potentially confusing. Clear-headed thinking is needed to spot the qualities that these inventions share in common. Monitory institutions play various roles. They are committed to providing publics with extra viewpoints and better information about the operations and performance of various governmental and non-governmental bodies; because they appeal to publics, monitory institutions (to scotch a possible misunderstanding) are not to be confused with top-down surveillance mechanisms that operate in secret, for the private purposes of organisations of government or civil society. Monitory mechanisms are geared as well to the definition, scrutiny and enforcement of public standards and ethical rules for preventing corruption, or the improper behaviour of those responsible for making decisions, not only in the field of elected government, but in a wide variety of non-governmental settings. The new institutions of monitory democracy are further defined by their overall commitment to strengthening the diversity and influence of citizens' voices and choices in decisions that affect their lives – regardless of the outcome of elections.

Take just one famous example: the Truth and Reconciliation Commission (TRC) established by legislation passed by the new post-apartheid government in South Africa. Under the chairmanship of Archbishop Desmund Tutu, the TRC operated for three years (1995–8) as a power-monitoring process with a difference. It was a court-like forum for what was called 'restorative justice', for the public remembering and expression of politicians' and officials' and citizens' guilt, shame and suffering under the whip hand of murder, torture and rape. The TRC refused to let bygones be bygones, for instance by rounding up (or executing) a few political culprits and then concentrating, say, on economic reconstruction. Its starting point was that elections and elected governments alone could not handle the terrible injustices done by people to each other under apartheid. It rejected the tactic of lustration; compulsorily screening, disqualifying and purging former officials was seen (correctly) to be vulnerable to the dangers of amnesia, confabulation and political manipulation. The TRC instead took an imaginative but hard-nosed view of South African apartheid. It reckoned that nobody in the new South Africa was entitled straightforwardly to cast the first stone of accusation, that in principle there were no 'good guys' or 'bad guys', that all citizens were in one way or another deeply implicated in propping up apartheid.

The work of the TRC rested on the belief that both victims and victimisers might suffer from what analysts call 'dissociation', the painful and disabling repression of traumatic memories. That was why the TRC called on the whole of South African society, including police and army officers and members of the governing African National Congress, to own up, to bear witness to past acts of violence. The TRC recognised that the whole process of opening up and democratising memories of the past is not easy. It saw that memories are always reconstructed, and not just straightforward matters of recall, and that for that reason it is always better to prevent the denial of incriminating memories or the implantation of false memories by having an open process of publicly checking and cross-checking claims about what happened in the past. Armed with these principles, the TRC tried in practice to expose past human rights abuses and consider applications for amnesty; it also examined ways of restoring the dignity of victims and assisting the rehabilitation of the perpetrators of violence. Mistakes were made and its effectiveness was often questionable, but the TRC foresaw, correctly it turned out, that the work of publicly monitoring the evils of apartheid would help to discharge political tensions, that the balm of public 'truth-telling' would have soothing effects, like helping symbolically to heal the wounds of the victims and their loved ones. It operated on the premise that the standard machinery of representative democracy could not prevent political criminals from occupying positions of power, let alone promote a culture of respect for civil society, the rule of law and trust in government. Monitoring what had happened through public fact-finding and public shaming were seen as much more effective ways of preparing the society for a durable democracy – in effect by granting a vote to the past for the sake of the future.

Political Geography

The TRC was admittedly a particular response to the special circumstances of South Africa, but it nevertheless displayed most of the new qualities of monitory democracy in action. For what is distinctive about this new historical type of democracy is the way *all fields of social and political life* come to be scrutinised, not just by the standard machinery of representative democracy but by a whole host of *non-party, extra-parliamentary* and often *unelected bodies* operating within, underneath and beyond the boundaries of territorial states. In the era of monitory democracy, the example of the TRC suggests, it is as if the principles of representative democracy – public openness, citizens' equality, selecting representatives – are superimposed on representative democracy itself. This has many practical consequences, but one especially striking effect is to alter the patterns of interaction – the political geography – of democratic institutions.

Once upon a time, in the brief heyday of representative democracy, the thing called democracy had a rather simple political geography (Figure 115). Within the confines of any given state, democracy meant (from the point of view of citizens) following an election campaign and on the great day of reckoning turning out to vote for a party or independent candidate. He – it was almost always men – was someone local, a figure known to the community, a local shopkeeper or professional or someone in business or a trade unionist, for instance. Then came democracy's great ceremonial, the pause of deliberation, the calm of momentary reflection, the catharsis

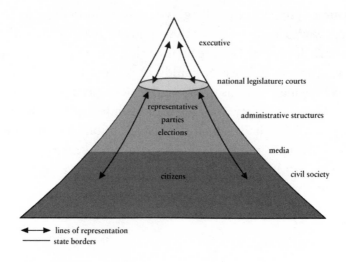

FIGURE 115: Territorially bound representative democracy.

of ticking and crossing, before the storm of result. 'Universal peace is declared' was the sarcastic way the nineteenth-century novelist George Eliot (1819–80) put it, 'and the foxes have a sincere interest in prolonging the lives of the poultry.' Her American contemporary Walt Whitman spoke more positively of the pivotal function of polling day as the great 'choosing day', the 'powerfulest scene', a 'swordless conflict' mightier than Niagara Falls or the Mississippi River or the geysers of Yosemite, a 'still small voice vibrating', a time for 'the peaceful choice of all', a passing moment of suspended animation when 'the heart pants, life glows'.[21] If blessed with enough votes, the local representative joined a privileged small circle of legislators whose job was to stay in line with party policy, to support or oppose a government that used its majority in the legislature, and to pass laws and monitor their implementation and administration, hopefully with results that pleased as many of the represented as possible. At the end of a limited stint as legislator, buck-passing stopped. Foxes and poultry fell quiet. It was again time for the swordless conflict of the great choosing day. The representative either stepped down, into retirement, or faced the music of re-election.

This is a simplified sketch of the role of elections in times past, of course; in the age of representative democracy, the lives of political parties were certainly complicated by extra-parliamentary bodies that

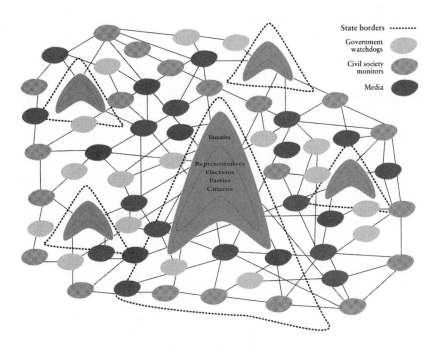

State borders ··········
Government
watchdogs
Civil society
monitors
Media

Executive

Representatives
Elections
Parties
Citizens

FIGURE 116: Monitory democracy.

included newspapers, trade unions and churches. But the sketch serves to highlight the different, much more complex political geography of monitory democracy. Just as representative democracies preserved assemblies, so monitory democracies preserve legislatures, political parties and elections, which (to the contrary) are often bitterly fought and closely contested affairs. But such is the huge growth in the number and variety of interlaced, power-monitoring mechanisms that democrats from earlier times, if catapulted into the new world of monitory democracy, would find it hard to understand what is happening.

The new democracy demands a headshift, a break with conventional thinking, an almighty wrestle with words and meanings, in order to understand its political geography. For this purpose, let us imagine for a moment, as if from an aerial satellite, the contours of the new democracy. We would spot that its power-scrutinising institutions are less centred on elections, parties and legislatures; no longer confined to the territorial state; and spatially arranged in ways much messier than textbooks on democracy typically suppose (see Figure 116). The vertical 'depth' and horizontal 'reach' of monitory institutions are striking. If the number of levels within any hierarchy of institutions is a measure of its 'depth', and if the number of units located within each of these levels is called its 'span' or 'width', then monitory democracy is the deepest and widest system of democracy ever known. The political geography of mechanisms like audit and integrity commissions, citizens' assemblies, regional parliaments, summits and global watchdog organisations defies simple-minded descriptions. So, too, does the political geography of power-disputing and power-checking bodies, such as human rights networks, trade unions and consumer councils, designed to bring greater public accountability to businesses and other civil society bodies.

Representation

Monitory democracy is no straightforward matter. Both its novelty and complexity make it vulnerable to a fistful of misconceptions, beginning with the hostile charge that monitory democracy, since it fudges the vital role of 'the people', is in fact no democracy at all.

The charge that democracy is based on the timeless principle of 'the rule of the people, by the people, for the people' is mistaken. It forgets the history of democracy; and it misses much that is interesting and novel about our times. While it is often said that the struggle to bring greater public accountability to government and non-government organisations that wield power over others is in effect a struggle for 'grass-roots democracy', 'participatory democracy' or 'popular empowerment', the terms rest on a misunderstanding of the trends.

The age of monitory democracy is not heading backwards; it is not motivated by efforts to recapture the (imagined) spirit of assembly-based democracy – 'power to the people' – as some supporters of groups like Students for a Democratic Society (SDS) liked to say during the rebellions of the 1960s. Many contemporary champions of 'deep' or 'direct' democracy still speak as if they are Greeks, as if what really counts in matters of democracy is 'the commitment and capacities of ordinary people to make sensible decisions through reasoned deliberation and empowered because they attempt to tie action to discussion'.[22] Talk of 'ordinary people' is typical of academics who usually do not know them, but the more serious point is that the reality of monitory democracy is otherwise, in that all of the new power-scrutinising experiments in the name of 'the people' or citizens' empowerment rely inevitably on *representation*. These experiments often draw their legitimacy from 'the people';* but they are not understandable as efforts to abolish the gap between representatives and the represented, as if citizens could live without others acting on their behalf, find their true selves and express themselves as equals within a unified political community no longer burdened by miscommunication, or by misgovernment.

Monitory democracy thrives on representation. Take the example of citizens' assemblies. In the early years of the twenty-first century, the most talked about case was the Citizens' Assembly on Electoral Reform in the Canadian province of British Columbia. Backed by the local legislature, the Citizens' Assembly worked for the best part of a year as an independent, non-partisan assembly of representatives charged with the task of casting a critical eye over the province's electoral system. The Assembly had 161 members; it included one woman and one man drawn randomly from each of the province's seventy-nine electoral districts, plus two aboriginal citizen representatives, as well as one representative from the province's Legislative Assembly.

---

*The point can be put like this: if the principles of representative democracy turned 'the people' of assembly democracy into a more distant judge of how well representatives performed, then monitory democracy exposes the fiction of a unified 'sovereign people'. The dynamic structures of monitory democracy daily serve as barriers against the uncontrolled worship of 'the people', or what might be dubbed demolatry. Monitory democracy demonstrates that the world is made up of many *dēmoi*, and that particular societies are made up of flesh-and-blood people who have different interests, and who therefore do not necessarily see eye to eye. It could be said that monitory democracy democratises – publicly exposes – the whole principle of 'the sovereign people' as a pompous fiction; at best, it turns it into a handy reference device that most people know to be just that: a useful political fiction. There are indeed times when the fiction of 'the people' serves as a monitoring principle, as a former Justice of the Federal Constitutional Court in Germany, Dieter Grimm (b. 1937), has explained: 'The circumstances are rare in which the fiction of "the demos" is needed as a reminder that those who make the laws are not the source of their ultimate legitimacy. Democracies need public power; but they need as well to place limits on the exercise of public power by invoking "the people" as a fictional subject to whom collectively binding powers are attributed: a "*Zurechnungssubjekt*" that is not itself capable of acting, but which serves as a democratic necessity because it makes accountability meaningful' (interview, Berlin, 23 November 2006).

The member representatives of the Citizens' Assembly were not elected, but drawn by lot. In contrast to the Greek trust in the deities as underwriters of decisions determined by lot, the Assembly members were chosen at random by a computer, from a pool that was supposed to reflect the age, gender and geographical make-up of British Columbian citizens. Granted its own budget, the Citizens' Assembly was designed to operate outside the system of political parties, and to keep its distance from the legislature, organised lobby groups and journalists. Its duty was to act as an unelected body of temporary representatives of *all* British Columbians.

The first few months' work of the Citizens' Assembly involved, with the help of various experts, a study of electoral systems in use around the world, followed by a period of consultation with civil society organisations and individual citizens. The consultations took the form of open public hearings; fifty public meetings were held and more than 1600 written submissions were received. The Citizens' Assembly then retired, in the manner of a citizens' jury, to consider its verdict. The key question was whether British Columbia should retain its existing 'first-past-the-post' method, or whether instead it should adopt a brand-new electoral system.

Members waded through the case put for preserving the status quo. There was general agreement about how the first-past-the-post voting system operated. It was an electoral system in which, to become a member of parliament, a candidate simply had to win more votes than any other rival within their constituency, and not a majority of votes cast. Some Assembly members said the system promoted strong government by ensuring that a party with a majority of seats would be able to get on with the job of governing, without having constantly to compromise with its opponents. Its critics within the Assembly saw this as its central weakness. While, in their view, the first-past-the-post system enabled voters to choose among different representatives, it also promoted the formation of governments that had a majority of seats but a minority of the popular vote (as happened in the 2004 British general election, when a New Labour government was returned to office with just 23 per cent of the popular vote, the lowest percentage for half a century, during which time every British government received less than 40 per cent of the popular vote). In such cases, said these critics, many voters were made to feel that their votes were wasted (by voting for a party that had a snowball's chance in hell of winning either a constituency or an election); and even worse was the fact, under a first-past-the-post system, that a majority of voters sometimes found themselves stuck with a government that they had never voted for in the first place.

These objections proved decisive. Following months of deliberation, the Citizens' Assembly recommended (in December 2004, in English, French, Punjabi and Chinese) that British Columbia should switch to a new electoral system called BC-STV: a form of proportional representation with transferable votes already used in countries such as Australia.[23] Copies of the recommendation were posted on a user-friendly website; hard copies were distributed to every household in the province. Amidst intense media coverage, the recommendation was put to the vote. Under the agreed terms of the original legislation setting up the Citizens' Assembly, 60 per cent of all eligible voters had to approve the proposed new system in a referendum. The set question was straightforward enough: 'Should British Columbia change to the BC-STV electoral system as recommended by the Citizens' Assembly on Electoral Reform? Yes/No'. Some voters, evidently still confused about the actual workings of the proposed BC-STV system, prevaricated. The proposal was narrowly defeated – 57.7 per cent of voters approved it – thus proving that in a monitory democracy the right to say 'no' to representatives remained an important entitlement of citizens. The government of British Columbia then announced that a follow-up referendum would be held in a few years' time, so proving that in a monitory democracy the right of representatives to reconsider and reverse decisions already taken is equally fundamental.

The Immortals

Another misconception, to do with the changing significance of elections, prevents many people from spotting the novelty of monitory democracy. It is vital to grasp that the emerging age of monitory democracy does not dispense with questions of suffrage, or voting in national or local elections. Despite the rapid growth of unelected monitory bodies and networks, it is not an era that has settled once and for all the issue of who is entitled to vote, and under which conditions (think of the emerging legal and political controversies about who owns the software of unreliable electronic voting machines[24]). In fact, some people, for instance felons, have their votes withdrawn; others, including diasporas, minority language speakers, the disabled and people with low literacy and number skills, are disadvantaged by secret ballot elections; still other constituencies, such as women, young people and the biosphere, are either poorly represented or they are not represented at all. Struggles to open up and improve the quality of electoral and legislative representation are by no means finished. And yet in the era of monitory democracy, the franchise struggles that once tugged and tore whole societies apart have lost their centrality. As the culture of voting spreads, and as unelected representatives multiply in many different contexts, a brand-new issue begins to surface. The old question that racked the age of representative democracy – *who* is entitled to vote and *when* – is compounded and complicated by questions for which there are still no easy answers: *where* are people entitled to vote, for *whom* and through which representatives?

The sea change is evident in the spread of a culture of voting into areas of life once considered 'no-go areas' for democracy. Among the striking qualities of monitory democracy is the way deliberating and voting procedures are applied to a wide range of semi-governmental and civil society institutions. Many people are already familiar with their face-to-face versions. They take for granted the election of team captains, school prefects and sororities and fraternities. The appointment, through a show of hands or a ticked ballot paper, of representatives to parents' associations, trade unions, voluntary organisations and local action committees is equally known to most people. There is rising awareness as well of the possibility and desirability of exercising rights of criticism and casting a vote in public service organisations, for instance in the areas of health and social care design and patient choice. In various parts of the world, for the first time ever, straw polls are conducted to gauge which way people would vote if they could participate in elections in the most powerful democracy, the United States. The experience of voting for representatives even extends into large-scale global organisations, such as the International Olympic Committee (IOC).

The IOC has an interesting and turbulent history. Founded in 1894 at an international athletics conference convened at the Sorbonne in Paris by the aristocrat Baron Pierre de Coubertin (1863–1937), the IOC for many decades bore a striking resemblance to an exclusive private gentlemen's club. In the era of representative democracy, it was blessed with the gentlemanly power to award the Olympics to particular cities, and thereby to shape their fates, for a time. So great was its influence that the members of the IOC were sometimes (by Greek citizens and journalists, for instance) called 'immortals'. This made sense, if only because, from its inception, the IOC had been a self-selecting body of wealthy volunteers with oodles of free time on their hands. Membership was for life. Removal from office was almost impossible; infusions of fresh blood usually came only when members joined their ancestors. Tight discipline was reinforced by the unwavering commitment to the job in hand. The IOC staged games every four years, in the spirit of amateurism, freed from the clutches of advertising and profit.

These quaint rules changed abruptly with the appointment (in 1980) of Juan Antonio Samaranch as IOC President. Olympic host cities such as Montreal had been bleeding money (it suffered a deficit of over $1 million after its staging of the 1976 Olympics), so the former Sports Minister of Spain and good friend of General Franco moved to throw overboard the IOC's long-standing – snobbishly aristocratic – opposition to commercialism. International sports federations were granted the right to determine which athletes could compete. Corporate sponsorship, endorsement deals and professional athletes suddenly came on the blocks. Cities scrambled for the big prize of hosting the Olympic Games and, with that, earning potentially massive profits from media and advertising deals, construction projects, tourism, transport and other industries.

The IOC suddenly changed flags. It went from being an exclusive not-for-profit organisation to a multi-million-dollar business that resembled the most putrid of rotten boroughs in eighteenth-century England. Its self-appointed members not only decided which cities and corporations would be rewarded with profits, but they also decided on broadcasting rights, with lucrative returns; whereas the IOC received a mere £80 for broadcasting rights in the 1956 Melbourne Olympics, it concluded a $3.5 billion deal with NBC for the same rights to all summer and winter Olympics between the years 2000 and 2008. Opportunities for bribery and corruption consequently flourished. IOC members suddenly found they had wealthy suitors, bearing lavish gifts. Under their noses they saw fine jewellery and furs, rare paintings, first-class air tickets, luxury accommodation, jobs for relatives and greenbacks in fat brown envelopes, of course.

It was all too tempting. Thanks to muckraking journalism, scandals ensued. Public outcries followed. Under pressure, against considerable odds, the IOC began to apply monitory mechanisms to its own corrupted structures. Some things didn't change. By 2002, the IOC body of 115 co-opted members included only 12 women; in that year, not one woman was among the 66 new member nominations. But some things did change. Visits by IOC members to candidate cities were banned. An IOC Ethics Commission and a World Anti-Doping Agency were formed. Reports of income and expenditure were published, for the first time. IOC meetings were thrown open to the media. A so-called Nominations Committee was set up for the purpose of more fairly deciding IOC membership, which was restricted to an eight-year term, renewable through election. Olympic athletes were granted the right to elect their own representatives directly to the IOC. The upper age limit of IOC members was reduced from eighty to seventy. And the rules of representative government were for the first time applied to its inner workings, at least on paper. The co-opted members of the IOC were required to meet in Session at least once a year. Unlike (say) the United Nations General Assembly, the Session members were expected to act as the IOC's representatives in their respective countries, not as delegates of their country within the IOC. The Session was something of a post-national assembly, a body charged with electing a President for an eight-year term, renewable once for four additional years. The Session also determined the membership of a powerful Executive Board. Elected by secret ballot, by a majority of votes cast, for terms of four years, the Executive Board functioned as the inner body ultimately responsible for managing all of the affairs of the IOC, including the recommendation of new IOC members as well as the monitoring of the codes of conduct of existing members, and of the overall performance of the IOC itself.

Founding Elections

The example of the IOC suggests that in the age of monitory democracy the spirit of elections and the custom of chastening and rotating representatives are gaining ground. It is worth repeating that this does not mean that the textbook institutions of representative democracy wither away. Since 1945 party-based democracy has in fact made a big comeback, so much so that it tricked people like Fukuyama and Huntington into thinking that nothing has changed, except for a large global leap in the number of representative democracies. They can be forgiven: following the widespread collapse and near-extinction of democracy during the first half of the twentieth century, it is indeed true that most parts of the world have since become familiar with its basic governing institutions. Conventional party-centred forms of representation do not wither away. Millions of people have grown accustomed to competition among political parties, periodic elections, the limited-term holding of political office and the right of citizens to assemble in public to make their views known to their representatives in legislatures and executives, all of this operating within the container of law-bound territorial states. In contexts as different as Sri Lanka, Nigeria, Trinidad and Tobago, Malta and Botswana, the mechanisms of electoral democracy have taken root for the first time; while in other contexts, especially those where electoral democracy is well embedded, experiments have been conducted in their refurbishment, for instance by introducing primary elections into political parties, tightening restrictions on campaign fund-raising and spending, changing the rules of the electoral game, improving voting facilities for disabled citizens and banning party hopping (a decision taken by the Brazilian Supreme Court in 2007).

For all these reasons it seemed perfectly acceptable for Huntington to speak of the spectacular rebirth of representative democracy in recent decades as a 'third wave'. Enter monitory democracy: a brand-new historical form of democracy that operates in ways greatly at variance with textbook accounts of 'representative', 'liberal' or 'parliamentary' democracy, as it is still often called. In the dawning age of monitory democracy, democracy is practised differently. Institutions like periodic elections, multi-party competition and the right of citizens to voice their public approval or disapproval of legislation remain familiar fixtures in the life of democracies. Slowly but surely, however, the whole architecture of democracy has begun fundamentally to change. So, too, has the meaning of democracy. No longer synonymous with self-government by an assembly of male citizens (as in the Greek city-states), or with party-based government guided by the will of a majority, democracy comes to mean a way of life and a mode of governing in which power is everywhere subject to checks and balances, such that nobody is entitled to rule without the consent of the governed, or their representatives.

The impact of monitory mechanisms in forcing a redefinition of democracy is evident in the advent of election monitoring. During the 1980s, for the first time in the history of democracy, founding elections in new or strife-torn polities began to be monitored systematically by outside teams of observers. The practice, admittedly, was an older invention, first used in 1857 when Prussian, French, British, Russian, Turkish and Austrian representatives jointly supervised a plebiscite in Moldavia and Wallachia; but in the new circumstances, the methods of election monitoring assumed a much more powerful and publicly visible role, on a global scale.

The effort to put into practice the principle of 'periodic and genuine elections' – as the Universal Declaration of Human Rights (Article 21.3) worded it – often proved to be a difficult business. It aimed to deter election fraud by governments, political parties, armed forces and electoral authorities, and it was led by observer teams trained or provided by intergovernmental bodies, like the United Nations, the Organisation for Security and Co-operation in Europe (OSCE) and the Commonwealth Secretariat, as well as by civil society organisations such as the International Institute for

FIGURE 117: A disabled people's voter registration meeting under a mango tree, Kologo, Ghana, photographer unknown.

Democracy and Electoral Assistance (International IDEA), the Carter Center, La Fédération Internationale des Droits de l'Homme, and the Action on Disability and Development (Figure 117). The scale of operations was at times spectacularly large, as when the UN Transitional Authority trained more than 50,000 Cambodian officials to monitor elections (in May 1993) in a country that had been wrecked by totalitarianism.

Operations sometimes had their droll moments, for instance when printed wall and tree posters announcing forthcoming elections routinely disappeared into the hands of people short of wrapping papers. There were unfunny sides to election monitoring as well. Observer bodies like the OSCE were themselves accused of corruption, of pursuing proxy government by outside forces. Monitoring was most certainly an inexact science; in the 2002 Zimbabwean presidential election, hundreds of observers openly disagreed about whether it was generally fair and free, or fiddled. Given the politically destabilising consequences of 'redoing' an election, the temptation was always strong to green-light official results. The local authorities regularly tried to massage monitors' post-election reports – or to massage the whole election process itself, as Boris Yeltsin's campaigners almost certainly did, during the 1996 Russian presidential elections, by redirecting state resources into their pockets, pressuring state television coverage of the elections and paying print journalists to come up with correct copy.

There were times when observers spoke in tongues, as in the 1996 elections in Nicaragua, which were monitored by at least eighty different foreign groups, including five separate delegations simultaneously funded by the government of the United States, which in addition despatched its own official delegation. There was plenty of incompetence and muddle, much of it caused by flying visits, excessive concentration on election day, rather than on the election process, and amateurish or ignorant monitors trying to maintain a semblance of independence in unfamiliar contexts that otherwise demanded their active cooperation with locals. Yet despite these various shortcomings, the net effect of election monitoring was to heighten globally the sense that elections mattered; that efforts should be redoubled to find and apply contextually sensitive quality standards; that election observers themselves needed watching; and that 'fair and open' methods – the elimination of violence, intimidation, ballot-rigging and other forms of political tomfoolery – were expected of all countries, including the most powerful democracy on the face of the earth, the United States, where OSCE observers played a role for the first time, in the presidential elections of November 2004.

Civil Society

Let us tiptoe quietly around the graves of Andrew Jackson and other American democrats, sidestepping what they might say, in order to deal with another misconception: the mistaken belief that monitory democracy is mainly or 'essentially' a method of taming the power of government.

Among the remarkable features of monitory democracy is the way it gradually spreads power-scrutinising mechanisms into areas of social life that were previously untouched by democratic hands. The extension of democracy downwards, into realms of power beneath and cutting across the institutions of territorial states, has the effect of arousing great interest in the eighteenth-century European term 'civil society'; for the first time in the history of democracy, the these two words are now routinely used by democrats in all four corners of the earth. The whole trend towards the 'socialisation' of democracy poses challenges, above all to uncontested rule in areas ranging from family life to employment. Such rule is checked – if and when it is checked – not just by elected governments, but also by a whole host of new monitoring institutions that have the boomerang effect of reminding millions of people of a simple democratic truth: democracy requires colossal transformations of people's characters. Their habits of heart have to change. People need to become democracies within themselves. They must recognise that there are different possible selves within themselves; they must become convinced that they can grow stronger by sorting and mustering these different selves, for self-defined ends. They must feel that they can put a stop to bossing, that they are the equals of others, that they have it within themselves to change things, or to keep things as they are. For democracy to be possible, people have to be sure that they themselves are the source of power of the institutions that govern their lives; that government and other institutions indeed rest upon the consent of the governed; and that therefore when in everyday life they withdraw their consent from these institutions, things can indeed change, sometimes in the smallest of ways, perhaps even for the better.

'Property of the People'

The intense public concern with civil society and with publicly scrutinising matters once thought to be non-political is unique to the age of monitory democracy. The age of assembly democracy saw the invention of Muslim civil societies stretched across vast geographic distances. The era of representative democracy (as Tocqueville spotted) certainly saw the rise of self-organised pressure groups and schemes for 'socialising' the power of government, for instance through workers' control of industry. Few of these schemes survived the upheavals of the first half of the twentieth century, which makes the contrast with monitory democracy all the more striking. On a scale never before seen in the history of democracy, the trend towards public scrutiny is strongly evident in all kinds of policy areas, ranging from public concern about the maltreatment and legal rights of children and bodily habits related to exercise and diet, through to the development of habitat protection plans and alternative (non-carbon and non-nuclear) sources of energy. Initiatives to guarantee that the future development of nanotechnology and genetically modified crops is governed publicly in the interests of the many, not the few – efforts to take democracy 'upstream' into the tributaries of scientific research and technical development – are further examples of the same trend. Experiments with fostering new forms of citizens' participation and elected representation have even penetrated markets, to lay hands on the sacred cow of private property.

The German system of co-determination (known as *Mitbestimmung*) is a notable example, born of desperate circumstances. With the collapse of the Nazi state, the union-free firms loyal to Hitler imploded, like a mineshaft in an earthquake. In the Ruhr, the country's coal and steel powerhouse, the defeat of Nazi rule also put an end to the brutal system of industrial relations that had produced great human suffering and loss of life among civilian foreign workers, slave labourers from the east and Russian prisoners of war. But peace brought new kinds of misery; Hitler may have been dead, but his outstretched right arm continued to ruin the lives of millions. Half the miners' homes in the region had been destroyed, or badly damaged. Many people felt physically exhausted and morally defeated. Coal production dropped to less than half the pre-war levels. During the winter of 1945–6, food shortages triggered hunger marches; and in the mines and district communes workers' committees sprang up to fill the political power vacuum caused by a society that was falling apart. The committees worked hard to rid management and local administrations of Nazi sympathisers; they tried as well to bring some semblance of order to the meagre supplies of available goods and services. Unionisation of the workforce blossomed. So did plant-level support for the reborn Communist Party (KPD); and in the first parliamentary elections in the cities of the Ruhr (in April 1947), KPD votes soared to over 20 per cent of the total.

The British occupying authorities were not pleased. They worried as much about the 'Russian danger' as about lingering Nazi influence. They reckoned that socialisation of the primary resource industries was the only progressive alternative to communism and to politically corrupted private capitalism, as the British Foreign Secretary Ernest Bevin made clear in a House of Commons speech, in October 1946. The basic resource industries, he said, needed to be 'owned and run by the German people'.[25] Sounding like Stephan Born, the words were social democratic, but what exactly they implied in practice remained unclear; in any case, various forces conspired to shape the unexpected outcome.

The outbreak of the Cold War and the decision to go ahead with the Marshall Plan (April 1948) weakened support for communism among the region's workers and put the 'democratisation' of industry on the political agenda. It was a sign of the times that the first elected state parliament of North Rhine-Westphalia introduced bold legislation to transform the mining industry into what it called a 'cooperative order'. What was envisaged? True to the newborn spirit of monitory democracy, the coal industry was to be managed democratically with the help of a 'coal council'; the mines, confiscated and held in trust, were to be transformed into 'social unions', governed by a 'shareholder assembly', comprising equal numbers of miners' and holding company representatives, and an 'executive board' with at least one 'spokesman for the miners'.[26] Following the arrest of two hundred heavy industry executives by the British authorities, the companies responded by appealing successfully to the business principle that managerial continuity was vital for running the entire industry. They proposed an alternative, watered-down plan: private companies would survive, but employee representatives would occupy half the seats of an 'advisory council' and exercise equal rights on the executive management board.

From these cluttered beginnings sprang a durable system of employee participation that was codified in three major laws in the early 1950s. Against protests by leading industrialists, the Adenauer government insisted on the right of employees to be represented, even though in practice companies retained their prerogatives over investment and capital allocation, as well as enjoyed close bilateral relations with government, to the exclusion of the unions. Two decades later, again in the face of bitter opposition from employers' associations, the co-determination procedures were strengthened. The 1976 Co-Determination Act managed to survive a subsequent challenge by the employers in the Federal Constitutional Court, which ruled in favour of a system of representation and majority rule in all German firms normally employing more than 2000 people. By law, these big firms were now required to have both lower-level works councils (dealing with such matters as health and safety, performance-related pay and redundancies) as well as supervisory boards comprising equal numbers of representatives from the side of both the company and its employees. Company representatives were to be elected either by shareholders or by company executives, at a meeting called for this purpose; employee representatives were chosen by direct election from the body of workers, or indirectly, by a secondary body of delegates elected by the workforce.

The co-determination system suffered a catch that continues to cause conflicts: according to the 1976 legislation, the powerful role of chairperson of a company's supervisory board is normally decided by a simple majority vote. In the event of a deadlock, or disagreement that forced a second ballot, the appointment of a chairperson was the sole prerogative of the company side; employees could only ever elect the vice-chairperson of the board. The rule has typically worked to the advantage of companies, for whenever boards are deadlocked the chairperson is entitled to a second vote, so ensuring that company views prevail. The system suffered other flaws, but, all things considered, co-determination demonstrates that top-down state regulation of business and markets is not the only way to deal with the irrational and power-hungry exuberance of markets – as a big majority of socialists, new liberals and other reformers supposed in the era of representative democracy.[27] In breaking with their 'governmentality', co-determination has put labour relations on an entirely new footing. It proves that democracy is not just a government affair; and it has put an end to the old *Herr im Haus* attitudes of despot industrialists who thought of themselves as industrial kings, blessed with absolute rights over their workers. The co-determination system is an important new-comer in the house of monitory democracy: an imperfect but durable form of extra-parliamentary representation, within a market economy otherwise ruled by corporate power, risk-taking, greed and the private making and taking of profits.

Watchdogs

The vital role played by civil societies in the invention of power-monitoring mechanisms seems to confirm what might be called James Madison's Law of Free Government: no government can be considered free unless it is capable of governing a society that is itself capable of controlling the government.[28] The Law has tempted some people to conclude – mistakenly – that governments are quite incapable of scrutinising their own power. The truth is otherwise. In the era of monitory democracy, experience shows that governments, unlike ducks and turkeys, sometimes vote to sacrifice themselves for the good of citizen guests at the dinner table.

Government 'watchdog' institutions are a case in point. Their stated purpose is the public scrutiny of government by semi-independent government agencies (it is worth noting that the word scrutiny originally meant 'to sort rubbish', from the Latin *scrutari*, meaning 'to search', and from *scruta*, 'rubbish'). Scrutiny mechanisms supplement the power-monitoring role of elected government representatives and judges, even though this is not always their stated aim; very often they are introduced under the general authority of elected governments, for instance through ministerial responsibility. In practice, things often turn out differently. Especially when protected by legislation, well resourced and well managed, government scrutiny bodies tend to take on a life of their own. Building on the much older precedents of royal commissions, public inquiries and independent auditors checking the financial probity of government agencies – inventions that had their roots in the age of representative democracy – the new scrutiny mechanisms add checks and balances on the possible abuse of power by elected representatives. Often they are justified in terms of improving the efficiency and effectiveness of government, for instance through 'better informed' decision making that has the added advantage of raising the level of public trust in political institutions among citizens considered as 'stakeholders'. The process contains a double paradox. Not only are government scrutiny mechanisms often established by governments who subsequently fail to control their workings, for instance in cases of corruption and the enforcement of legal standards; the new mechanisms also have democratic, power-checking effects, even though they are normally staffed by unelected officials who operate at several arms' length from the rhythm of periodic elections.

The independent 'integrity systems' that came to enjoy an important public profile in various states in Australia from the 1970s are good examples. Following repeated media exposure of fraud and corruption among politicians and police, in some cases with links to business and organised crime, monitory agencies were established to bring new eyes, ears and teeth to the public sector. The aim was to crack down on intentional wrongdoing or misconduct by elected representatives and appointed officials; fingers were pointed as well at the lax and self-serving complaints systems operated by the police, who are to democratic governments as sharp edges are to knives. Misgivings were also expressed about the reluctance of elected ministers to oversee publicly sensitive police operational matters. Two royal commissions in the state of South Australia during the 1970s led to the establishment (in 1985) of the first Police Complaints Authority. Other states followed suit, culminating in Queensland's Criminal Justice Commission (later the Crime and Misconduct Commission). Established in 1990 as a combined anti-corruption and criminal detection body, it was charged with the job of exposing corruption within the public sector, undertaking crime research, gathering evidence of organised crime, and tracking and recovering criminal proceeds.

Guide Dogs

Watchdog bodies proved popular, and sometimes effective, in a wide variety of contexts, including in India (whose Central

Vigilance Commission is mandated to propagate the principle of zero tolerance of corruption) and in Hong Kong, where in the Chinese context the Independent Commission Against Corruption (ICAC) established an important democratic precedent, evidently with a good measure of public support (according to a popular local joke, the initials ICAC stood for 'I can accept cash, but I cannot accept cheques').

Elsewhere, governments proved that they could also act as guide dogs, by fostering monitory democracy through new inventions designed to share power with civil society and its citizen representatives. The stated aim in most cases was to create new channels of representation designed to supplement the role of elections, political parties and legislatures. The guide-dog inventions were typically the result of skirmishes between civil society and government. Citizens often pressed for these monitory institutions because of unhappy experiences with governments prone to lying, trickery, bullying and violence. Governments often conceded demands for their creation for quite different motives, ranging from broadening the base of fiscal and political culpability for risky policies prone to end in a mess, through to the belief that closer public engagement makes for more 'informed' decision making and better solutions to public problems when governments act as rudders and not rowers of state institutions.

The new instrument of participatory budgeting – a Brazilian gift to the world of monitory democracy – was exemplary of 'bottom-up' schemes of representation. The first experiments took place at the end of the 1980s in the southern province of Rio Grande do Sul. Against the backdrop experience of protracted military dictatorship, a new constitution that mandated community participation in municipal government, and the renewed energy of social movements and groups within a highly urbanised civil society, city administrations in Porto Alegre and Santo André began pioneering practical experiments with the old principle of no taxation without representation.

Participatory budgeting (*orçamento participativo*, or simply OP in Portuguese) was often described by its early champions as a combination of 'direct democracy and representative democracy' (they were the words of Ubiratán de Souza, a leading supporter of the Porto Alegre scheme). It used methods of participation, election and representation that were not tied immediately to party competition and legislatures. Since OP was based on voluntary civil participation, the degree of citizen involvement in the prioritisation and co-determination of budgets obviously depended upon the turnout rate, which in turn varied according to such factors as the strength of local feeling about local matters. The voice of citizens was often muted by the power of the municipal administration to have the final say in fiscal matters. Citizen involvement was also sometimes watered down by granting explicit privileges to particular constituencies, as happened in the Young People's Participatory Budget scheme in Barra Mansa, in the state of Rio de Janeiro. The pre-selection of representatives by civil society bodies such as community associations and local parish boards had the same effect of reducing citizen involvement. Citizens' power over local budgets also varied greatly. It usually hovered somewhere between 2 and 10 per cent of the annual budget; the proportion was often a lot lower than that, though in a few Brazilian cases 100 per cent of the annual budget was actually subject to public deliberation. But even in these cases, it was the municipal government that normally determined both the size of the budget that was available for allocation, as well as approved its final details; the volume of spending was normally neither proportionate to the size of the popular vote nor determined by its deliberations. Despite all this, an interesting feature of participatory budgeting – a key point in its favour – was the clear evidence that it usually resulted in a reduced number of tax evasions and in corresponding increases in the volume of taxes collected. That kind of evidence implied that there was considerable scope for using participatory budgeting to set rates and scales of taxation, so reversing the trend towards centralised taxation that had marked the history of representative democracy in territorial state form.

'A Parley at the Summit'

In the age of monitory democracy, a great wall of prejudice surrounds the whole idea of 'cross-border' or 'international' democracy. The prejudice was built in the era of representative democracy, and almost all leading scholars of democracy today defend its supposed truth. One interesting thing about monitory democracy is that it begins to confront the wall of prejudice with a hammer. Its latticed patterns of power monitoring effectively fudge the distinction between 'domestic' and 'foreign', the 'local' and the 'global'. Like other types of institutions, including business and universities, democracy, too, is caught up in a process of 'glocalisation'. This is another way of saying that its monitory mechanisms are dynamically interrelated, to the point where each functions simultaneously as both part and whole of the overall system. In the system of monitory democracy, to put things a bit abstractly, parts and wholes in an absolute sense do not exist. Its units are better described as sub-wholes – 'holons' is the term famously coined by the Hungarian-born polymath Arthur Koestler – that function simultaneously as self-regarding and self-asserting entities that push and pull each other in a multilateral system in which all entities play a part.

The example of summits, a remarkable invention of the second half of the twentieth century, helps bring this language down to earth. A strange fact is that summits began as exercises in big power politics, as informal ad hoc meetings of heads of state or leaders of government, or foreign ministers – the kind of meetings that first took place during the fragile Soviet/American/British alliance against Hitler. Some people have said that the word 'summit' was first used to describe the so-called 'percentages agreement' at the October 1944 meeting in Moscow, when Churchill and Stalin speculated about their ratios of influence in the post-war world. The strange mathematical origin of the word (a corruption, perhaps in Stalin's virtually non-existent English, of 'sum it') was a one-off. It soon morphed into a mountaineers' term. Churchill himself long continued to advocate the tactic of high-level informal meetings in international relations. He spoke of 'summit diplomacy' and the benefits of 'a parley at the summit', which is the sense that prevailed in Geneva in 1955, when the climbing word 'summit' was used for the first time to describe a Cold War meeting of the political leaders of the United States, the Soviet Union, France and Britain.

From the end of World War Two until the time of the famous

Vienna Summit meeting between Kennedy and Khrushchev (3–5 June 1961), there were well over one hundred such summits, each using broadly similar methods. The meetings were preoccupied with the dynamics of the Cold War, and so had both a global reach and a strong bipolarity about them. Whether used as tools of amity or enmity, the early summits were also marked by a strong measure of predictability. The rule was that no statesman was willing to risk the certainty of humiliation. Hence the great attention paid to dramaturgy. 'It ended, as it began, with two firm hands firmly clasped', began the rather ritualised *Newsweek* report of the 1961 Kennedy–Khrushchev summit.[29] Such media coverage usually put ceremonial trivia on a pedestal; at one point, during the summit preparations, the question of whether Jackie Kennedy should be given a silver tea service was reportedly decided by Khrushchev with the blustering judgement that 'presents can be given even before a war'. The effect – like the old rituals of European monarchy – was to reinforce the sense among audiences that these were top-down affairs, instances of how the world was run by just a handful of men.

During the last decades of the twentieth century, the wholly surprising thing about summits was their dramatic transformation into sites where the power of representatives was publicly contested. Summits morphed into monitory mechanisms. It was a bit like what happened at the Council of Constance. Summits confirmed the rule that those who visibly exercise power over others are vulnerable to their withdrawal of consent. The change of meaning and function of summits was evident at the series of high-level meetings between Reagan and Gorbachev, including the 1986 Reykjavik gathering, where without prior consultation with NATO and other bodies the abolition of ballistic missiles and all nuclear weapons was proposed. Thereafter, summits began to be used by leaders to 'bounce' their bureaucracies into policy shifts. That had the knock-on effect of politicising government, making it clear to wider audiences, both inside and outside government, that different political options existed. That politicising effect had been forecast by the hard-nosed American statesman Henry Kissinger, who at the time of the Reykjavik meeting had warned that summits posed a great danger to conventional diplomacy because of their failure to straitjacket leaders in advance. Kissinger did not see that that advantage would be reinforced by the use of the methods of summitry to address a widening repertoire of different issues in a widening variety of geographic contexts. From the mid-1970s, for instance, leaders of the European Community began to meet twice or three times a year, an arrangement that was later formalised in the Maastricht Treaty. Other regional summits included the Summit of the Americas, convened by the Organization of American States (OAS); the African Union founded in July 2002; the biennial Commonwealth Heads of Government Meeting; and the Asian-African Summit of April 2005.

Summits were also used for the first time within specific policy sectors, sometimes giving birth to new global institutions of representation, such as the regular meetings convened by the group of states belonging to the so-called G7/G8. This body had its origins in the select 'Library Group' of finance ministers and a handful of officials and central bank governors, who first met behind the closed doors of the White House library in April 1973, without prepared papers or an agenda, to discuss the oil crisis and looming global recession. The distinctive feature of the 'Library Group' was its intention to be small, self-selecting and guided by personal contact. Only states with punch would attend. Proceedings were to be secret and no records were to be kept; the emphasis was on frank talk, unencumbered by diplomatic niceties at cocktail parties. The theory was that the weaving of person-to-person relations would lead to the unpicking of persons and problems, so making possible their resolution. The sentiments in favour of informality had been anticipated during an unplanned wartime encounter between Churchill and Roosevelt. 'The Prime Minister of the United Kingdom', said a dripping Churchill, as he hauled his chubby frame out of a bath, just as Roosevelt accidentally entered the same room, 'has nothing to hide from the President of the United States.' The same thought was expressed at the time of the Library Group meeting by a more serious Helmut Schmidt, who reportedly spoke of the need for 'a private, informal meeting of those who really matter in the world'.[30] Things were to turn out differently. The Library summit indeed gave birth to the Group of Five (which later became the G6, the G7, the G8 and the G20). But the desire of those who favoured private and informal cooperation to dispense with all rules of cooperation failed. Deliberately avoiding charters, treaties, independent secretariats and assemblies or councils with formally defined roles was one thing. Quite another was the fact that summit meetings more and more made efforts to follow the rules of annually rotating presidencies, to coordinate with other global organisations (the OECD and the IMF, for example), and to ensure smooth meetings through lengthy preparatory work, much of it handled by a new category of summit administrators dubbed 'sherpas' and 'sous-sherpas'.

The desire to avoid publicity also backfired on summits. Not only did the G7/G8 summits attract the attention of thousands of journalists eager to report stories and images of this exclusive and powerful club, but beginning with the Bonn G7 Summit in May 1985 (which attracted 30,000 demonstrators demanding greater global justice), its annual meetings provided an opportunity for civil society organisations and protesters to press their concerns related to matters as diverse as international trade and terrorism to energy development and cross-border crime – in effect, by turning rulers into culpable representatives. Attempts to transform top-down governmental summits into new channels of bottom-up representation of the interests of civil society were not confined to the G7/G8, though it was that body that attracted some of the most spectacular attention, for instance in July 2005 at the Live 8 'global awareness' concerts and field protests to encourage political leaders to 'Make Poverty History' (Figure 118).

FIGURE 118: Heads of state: demonstrators, including some wearing masks of G8 summit leaders, moving towards the perimeter security fence surrounding the Gleneagles Hotel, Scotland, 6 July 2005

Some sit-in activists banded together to form the Student Nonviolent Coordinating Committee (SNCC, pronounced 'Snick'). During 1961, it embarked upon its first campaign in support of rights for black people by launching 'freedom rides'. The tactic of empowerment was physically dangerous, but simple: activists took advantage of federal laws that guaranteed freedom of movement across state borders by travelling on buses from city to city, knowing that they were the certain targets of widespread acts of police and white mob intimidation, violence and murder. Everywhere the opponents of segregation travelled, they seemed to draw poison from a body politic infected with white racism; jeering and spitting and firebombing and direct physical attacks on protesters were typical. So great was the ruckus that there were moments when it looked as if the American democracy would suffer a major convulsion. The use of federal troops – as when President Dwight D. Eisenhower deployed the 101st Airborne Division to protect Little Rock high school students after the Arkansas school board voted in 1957 to abolish segregation – had the effect of strengthening the resolve of the movement.

Experiments with monitory tactics multiplied. Backed by local activists, individuals tried law suits against government authorities; sometimes they won important little victories that had big effects, like the white uprising of September 1962 caused by the admission to the University of Mississippi of a young black student named James Meredith, whose right to attend lectures had to be protected by regular army troops. Elsewhere, activists tired of giving in sparked off confrontations with prison authorities, publicly criticising them for the racial segregation of inmates and the iniquitous 'trusties' system, the use of lifers armed with rifles to terrorise and control other inmates, the majority of whom were normally African Americans. In Birmingham, Alabama, the Southern Christian Leadership Conference called on high school students to take part in demonstrations against the segregation of downtown businesses; a thousand responded, of whom six hundred were rewarded with imprisonment for their involvement in what would come to be called the Children's Crusade. In South Carolina's Sea Islands, the first Citizenship Schools were founded for the purpose of teaching literacy to enable black people to pass stringent voting tests that had for a long time operated to strike them off the electoral list. The pilot programmes proved highly successful. Newly formed coalitions like the Southern Christian Leadership Conference (founded in 1957) went ahead and raised funds from mainly northern sources to provide training and various forms of backing for local efforts to struggle non-violently against segregation. There were kneel-ins at local churches, boycotts of downtown businesses and marches on county buildings, 'freedom songs' and 'freedom schools' in support of the drive to register black voters. In 1963, the newly formed Council of Federated Organizations (COFO) organised mock elections, in which more than 90,000 black Mississippians voted unofficially, many of them for the unregistered 'Freedom Party'; during the course of the next year, organisers launched the Mississippi Freedom Democratic Party to challenge the whiter-than-white slate from the state's Democratic Party.

By the summer of 1963, pressures from the grass roots began to be felt publicly throughout the country, despite the reticence and resistance of parties and legislatures. After despatching troops to protect the enrolment of black students at the University of Alabama, President John F. Kennedy defended African Americans in a nationwide address broadcast on television and radio and announced that he would soon submit his Civil Rights bill to Congress. Later that summer, more than 200,000 demonstrators gathered in front of the Lincoln Memorial in Washington, DC. That was where Martin Luther King delivered his famous 'I Have A Dream' speech, and John Lewis of SNCC asked which side the federal government was on. The pace of events was quickened by the assassination of Kennedy a few months later, and by continuing nationwide media reports of white thuggery and police brutality.

Much more was to happen during the next few years: rioting in many American cities; the murder of Martin Luther King, Jr; affirmative talk of 'Afro-Americans' and 'Black Power'; the Black Panthers with their guns and 'fros and blue shirts and talk of police as 'pigs' and whites as 'honkies'; and Malcolm X, Jimi Hendrix, James Baldwin and Angela Davis. But by the summer of 1965, the opening round in the contemporary fight of black people for their rights as citizens in effect came to an end with two historic pieces

FIGURE 119: Black people registering as voters in the jailhouse of Hayneville, Alabama, 1965.

of legislation. The Civil Rights Act, signed by President Johnson on 2 July 1964, barred racial discrimination in public accommodations, education and employment. The Voting Rights Act, signed by Johnson on 6 August 1965, abolished literacy tests, poll taxes and other restrictions on voting, as well as authorised federal government intervention in states and individual voting districts that continued to use such tests to discriminate against African Americans (Figure 119).

The enactment of the double-barrelled legislation was monitory democracy in action. It proved that the powerless had power to change things, and that change had to begin in the home, the workplace and in other public fields of everyday life, before spreading across the whole of the political and social landscape of the American democracy. Shortly after signing the Voting Rights Act, President Johnson told colleagues that the legislation would lose the South for the Democratic Party for the foreseeable future. He was not entirely right. At that moment, barely one hundred African Americans held elective office in the whole of the United States. By 1989, there were 7200 office-holders, including more than 4800 in the Southern states alone. New Orleans had a black mayor, Ernest Morial, and so did the cities of Jackson, Mississippi, and Atlanta, Georgia. Southern blacks had gained top positions within city, county and state governments; and nearly every so-called Black Belt county in Alabama had an elected black sheriff. The changes had begun to be felt even at the federal level of government. Texas was represented in Congress by Barbara Jordan; the former Mayor of Atlanta, Andrew Young, was appointed by the Carter administration as Ambassador to the United Nations; while John Lewis, of SNCC fame, was elected in 1987 to represent the Fifth District of Georgia in the House of Representatives. He was to be re-elected many times, often with around 70 per cent of the votes, which was a fitting personal triumph for the son of a humble Alabaman sharecropper who had been so badly beaten on a freedom march by state troopers wielding billy clubs wrapped in barbed wire that his head wounds remained forever visible, as the scars of segregation.

Why Monitory Democracy?

Now that we have tackled some misconceptions about the contours and main dynamics of monitory democracy, let us pause finally to ask one short question: how can its unplanned birth be explained?

The motives behind the hundred or so inventions described above are complicated; as in earlier phases of the history of democracy, generalisations are as difficult as they are perilous. But one thing is certain: the new type of democracy has had both its causes and causers. Monitory democracy is not a monogenic matter, a living thing hatched from a single cell. It is instead the resultant of many forces. As in the two earlier phases of democracy, changes usually happened only when cracks developed within ruling circles, so allowing the courage of citizens and the resolve of public-spirited leaders to do the rest. Personal ambition, monkey business, power games and the quest for more effective or cheaper government – and government eager to offload blame on to others for policy disappointments and failures – have all played their part. So, too, have conservative instincts, radical demands, geopolitical considerations and market pressures. Opportunities for building 'social capital' – cultivating the connections and skills among people at local and regional levels – and the lure of winning power or revenue growth from the provision of outsourced government services have strongly motivated some organisations, especially NGOs, to push for stronger monitory institutions. Unintended consequences and plain good luck have also played their part in the early history of monitory democracy. Not unimportant either has been a factor famously outlined by Tocqueville: the contagious force of the belief among citizens and their representatives that the removal of particular grievances enables other grievances to be addressed, and resolved.

All these pressures have conspired to push actually existing democracies in the direction of monitory democracy. But one word more than any other describes the principal trigger of this new era: war. In the history of democracy, random and organised violence, war and the pity and suffering of war have often been the midwife of new democratic institutions. The same rule certainly applied to the first half of the twentieth century. Two global wars plus terrible cruelties shattered old structures of security, sparked pushes and shoves and elbowing for power, as well as unleashed angry popular energies that fed major upheavals – revolutions, usually in the name of 'the people', against representative democracy. Bolshevism and Stalinism in Russia, fascism in Italy, Nazism in Germany and military imperialism in Japan were effectively twisted and perverted mutations of democracy, understood as popular sovereignty. These were regimes whose leaders often acknowledged that 'the people' were entitled to mount the stage of history – regimes whose hirelings then set about muzzling, maiming and murdering both their opponents and their supporters. Western democracy was denounced as parliamentary dithering and muddling, as liberal perplexity, bourgeois hypocrisy and military cowardice. A third of the way into the twentieth century, democracy was on its knees. It seemed rudderless, spiritless, paralysed, doomed. By 1941, when President Roosevelt called for 'bravely shielding the great flame of democracy from the blackout of barbarism',[32] when untold numbers of villains had drawn the contrary conclusion that dictatorship and totalitarianism were the future, only eleven electoral democracies remained on the face of the earth.*

It was exactly the possibility of annihilation – the 50/50 chance that democracy would disappear along with the forests of Easter Island in the land of extinction – that galvanised minds and steeled determinations to do something, both about the awful destruction produced by war, and the dictatorships and totalitarian regimes spawned by those wars. The great cataclysms that culminated in World War Two demonstrated to many people the naivety of the old formula that people should obey their governments because their rulers protected their lives and possessions. The devastating upheavals of the period proved that this protection–obedience formula was unworkable, that in various countries long-standing pacts between rulers and ruled had been so violated that rulers could no longer be trusted to rule. The problem, in other words, was no longer the mobocracy of 'the people', as critics of democracy had insisted from the time of Plato and Thucydides until well into the nineteenth century. The most terrible events of the first half of the twentieth century proved that mobocracy had its true source in thuggish leaders skilled in the arts of manipulating 'the people'. That being so, the problem was no longer the mob, and mob rule. Ruling itself was the problem.

The problem of ruling stood at the centre of an important – unfortunately little studied – batch of political reflections on democracy in the years immediately after 1945.[33] The intellectual roots of monitory democracy are traceable to this period. They are evident in the contributions of literary, theological and intellectual figures otherwise as different as Albert Camus, Sidney Hook, Thomas Mann, Jacques Maritain and, most strikingly, in a work that soon became a classic, Reinhold Niebuhr's *The Children of Light and the Children of Darkness* (1945). Each of these authors was convinced that new times required a new understanding of democracy; each voiced fears that the narrow escape of parliamentary democracy

---

*The surviving parliamentary democracies included Australia, Canada, Chile, Costa Rica, New Zealand, Sweden, Switzerland, the United Kingdom, the United States and Uruguay. Despite its use of an electoral college to choose a president under high-security, wartime conditions, Finland might also be included.

from the clutches of war and totalitarianism might just be a temporary reprieve, even that it was 'the end of the world' (as Camus put it). They agreed that among the vital lessons provided by recent historical experience was that the mechanisms of majority-rule democracy could be utterly corrupted, to the point where they were used by the enemies of democracy, in the name of the 'sovereign people', to destroy the plural freedoms and political equality for which democracy avowedly stood. Deeply troubled, each author called for new remedies for the maladies of representative democracy, beginning with the abandonment of sentimental optimism. Opinions here divided, but all of these writers restated their support for a new form of democracy, one whose spirit and institutions were infused with a robust commitment to handling the devil of unaccountable power. The American theologian Niebuhr (1892–1971), who later won prominent admirers, including Martin Luther King, Jr, provided one of the weightiest cases for renewing and transforming democracy along these lines. 'The perils of uncontrolled power are perennial reminders of the virtues of a democratic society', he wrote. 'But modern democracy requires a more realistic philosophical and religious basis, not only in order to anticipate and understand the perils to which it is exposed, but also to give it a more persuasive justification.' He concluded with words that became famous: 'Man's capacity for justice makes democracy possible; but man's inclination to injustice makes democracy necessary.'[34]

'Equal and Inalienable Rights'

Troubled thinking about political evil undoubtedly helped inspire one of the most remarkable features of monitory democracy: the marriage of democracy and human rights, and the subsequent worldwide growth of organisations, networks and campaigns committed to the defence of human rights.

The intermarriage had roots extending back to the French Revolution, but its immediate inspiration was two major political declarations inspired by the horrors of World War Two: the United Nations Charter (1945) and the Universal Declaration of Human Rights (1948). The second was arguably the more remarkable candle in the gloom bred by the death of forty-five million people, terrible physical destruction and spiritual misery, and the mounting post-war tensions bound up with such political troubles as the bloody partition of Pakistan and India, the Berlin blockade and the unresolved future of Palestine. Drafted in 1947 and 1948, the Universal Declaration of Human Rights seemed to many at the time a mere sideshow of questionable importance. Its preamble spoke of 'the inherent dignity' and 'the equal and inalienable rights of all members of the human family'. Yet the times seemed entirely against such sentiments.

The document was born of more than one hundred meetings that stretched over eighteen months and involved difficult compromises concerning philosophical, religious, legal and political problems of great complexity. Credit for the completion and adoption of the draft belonged to the indefatigable unselfishness of a small but remarkable drafting group surrounding Eleanor Roosevelt (Figure 120). A four-hundred-page background document was prepared by a forty-year-old Canadian professor of law at McGill University, John Humphrey, a man who had been barred from military service because he had lost an arm in a childhood accident; he subsequently vowed to do all that he could to bring

FIGURE 120: Commission Chair Eleanor Roosevelt (right) engages Rapporteur Charles Malik of Lebanon (left) and Vice-Chairman René Cassin of France during a session of the Human Rights Commission, Lake Success, New York, 1947.

peace and justice into the world. The task of producing a shorter first draft was assigned to René Cassin, a disabled Jewish veteran of World War One who had responded to Charles de Gaulle's radio appeal from London by narrowly escaping from occupied France, to become de Gaulle's chief legal adviser, for which he was soon condemned to death *in absentia* by the Vichy government. Responsibility for subsequent refinements of the text passed to Peng-chun Chang, a Chinese playwright, literary critic and diplomat. He was as well a scholar of Confucianism who had earned his doctorate under John Dewey in 1921 at Columbia University, then had taken up a chair at Nankai University, from where he had fled into exile, during Japanese atrocities, by disguising himself as a woman. Peng-chun Chang was a strong, witty and resourceful character, a man who doubted that the principles of human rights could be anchored in some universal understanding of 'nature' or 'human nature'. 'Sweep the snow in front of one's door; overlook the frost on others' roof tiles', he liked to say, so expressing his conviction that the declaration of rights should embrace their different and conflicting understandings, rather than stifling them under a canopy of abstract verbal generalities.

Chang's pluralist convictions put him in some tension with the other vital core member of the drafting group: Charles Malik, a forty-year-old Lebanese man of Greek Orthodox convictions, a thinker of Thomist persuasion who quickly earned a reputation as a formidable debater and defender of the universal applicability of the principles of human rights. In August 1948, shortly before the adoption of the Universal Declaration of Human Rights by the General Assembly, the arc-nosed thinker with burning black eyes and bushy black eyebrows told American Rotarians that the declaration might turn out to be the greatest human document ever published.[35] He acknowledged its indebtedness to a long history of public declarations of support for legally enforceable rights. 'The Babylonians, nearly 4,000 years ago, had their code of Hammurabi, which established freedom within the law', he noted. 'Later the Greeks and the Romans contributed patterns for human conduct exemplified in the Justinian Code. Then after a few centuries, in AD 1215, England promulgated new liberties in the Magna Carta and toward the end of the 17th century expanded them in the Bill of Rights. France contributed the Napoleonic Code to the world and the "unalienable rights" of man, eloquently charted in the Declaration of Independence of the United States, gave new hope to people everywhere.'

Malik's potted, one-paragraph summary of the history of constitutional rights served to introduce his big point: the unprecedented cataclysms of the first half of the twentieth century had necessitated for the first time a *global* stocktaking of how to secure the rights of human beings on a *global* scale. The 1919 League of Nations Covenant (originally drafted by American President Woodrow Wilson) and the Atlantic Charter (a joint declaration in 1941 by Roosevelt and Churchill on the purposes of the war against fascism) were important beginnings, said Malik. But the new declaration of rights was the most advanced attempt yet to breathe life and meaning into the phrase 'the dignity and worth of the human person'. It was an attempt to define, protect and promote 'man's proper nature'. 'In this age of advancing governmental control, of national consciousness and sovereignty', he continued, 'it is difficult to convince man that he is not meant to be the slave of his Government.' But winning people's commitment to human rights was only half the battle. In this age of 'spreading socialism' – Malik's reference to both the Soviet Union and governments committed to state control – the art of learning to shout from the housetops that 'man cannot be absorbed by society, that he is by nature free to think, free to choose, free to rebel against his own society, or indeed against the whole world, if it is in the wrong' needed a strong helping hand. Enter the Universal Declaration of Human Rights: a new weapon to be used anywhere and everywhere against the presumption that the state had priority over the individual human being. But could this declaration of faith actually triumph over statism? Malik said he did not know. He expressed deep uncertainty about how things would turn out, but one of his recommendations proved to be inspirational for the next generation: if states reneged on their commitments to human rights, he said, human beings would have no alternative but to take things into their own hands, by nurturing and protecting human rights with the help of families, places of worship, circles of friendship and other 'intermediate institutions spanning the entire chasm between the individual and the State'.

It was in effect a call for civil societies everywhere to speak and act as if human rights mattered; its practical effect was to redefine democracy as monitory democracy. The tens of thousands of non-governmental human rights organisations that subsequently sprang up around the world deal with a wide range of rights matters, including torture, child soldiers, the abuse of women, and religious, academic and literary freedom. Their job is the advocacy of human rights through well-researched, skilfully publicised campaigns. They see themselves as goads to the conscience of governments and citizens, and they solve a basic problem that consistently dogged representative democracy: who decides who 'the people' are? Many human rights organisations and networks answer: every human being is entitled to exercise their right to have rights. In the age of monitory democracy, that conviction motivates human rights organisations to blow the whistle on rights violations. It leads them to pressure governments to do something about rights violations, not only by building up public interest in particular cases, but also by raising awareness of the vital place of human rights in the process of globalisation.

Some organisations are tiny and tied tightly to local contexts, despite their dependence upon the global language of human rights. An example is the Turkish human rights network called Mazlumder. Founded in the early 1990s by Muslim lawyers, journalists, businessmen, publishers and writers, its brief is the defence and assistance of downtrodden people – to represent those who suffer torture, discrimination and other human rights violations. Mazlumder's human rights perspective is faith-based, inspired by the precepts of personal morality, freedom, goodness, justice, right and truth that are outlined in the Qur'an. It uses ultra-modern campaigning techniques, including the printing of freedom of conscience postcards that are mailed in large numbers by supporters to government authorities, and to members of parliament. Mazlumder also uses press briefings and publishes (in Turkish) a monthly bulletin and a monthly magazine called *Universal Human Rights*; it also provides training courses; hosts press conferences that are transmitted on television, radio and the Internet; and sponsors fund-raising campaigns in support of victimised and violated people throughout Turkey and the wider region. From the time of its inception, Mazlumder specialised in high-profile 'no double standards' campaigns, including the defence of Kurdish minorities, the right of Turkish women to wear headscarves, and support for the families and relatives of the disappeared and tortured. Much of the work of Mazlumder is coordinated by lateral committees that rely heavily on the contributions of voluntary staff. It is a strictly not-for-profit network and is strongly opposed to government meddling with its work. Mazlumder officials speak with conviction about how their efforts to represent those who suffer oppression rest on the absolute primacy of human rights over government based on majority rule. 'Among the paradoxes of democracy', Mazlumder's director told the author in Istanbul, 'is that people in one country can vote in a government that then does things that destroy the rights of people of that same country, or of other countries. Free elections, multi-party systems and voting based on freedom of information are a good thing. But rights and the justice that flows from their protection are definitely prior to democracy in this sense.'[36]

Communicative Abundance

Much the same thinking pervaded most of the world's best-known human rights organisations, including Human Rights Watch, the Aga Khan Development Network and Amnesty International, a global body founded in 1961 by the lawyer Peter Benenson, initially to help 'prisoners of conscience' (Figure 121). These groups have raised new and challenging questions about the meaning and future of democracy, but let us suspend for the moment our puzzlement, to return to our starting question about the causes and causers of monitory democracy.

The fact that the intermarriage of human rights and democracy and many monitory institutions sprang to life after 1945 proved once again that war is not always (as Shelley famously said in *Queen Mab*) the statesman's game, the priest's delight, the lawyer's jest, and the hired assassin's trade, but sometimes as well an opportunity for citizens and institution builders to take things into their own hands. But if total war was the prime catalyst of the birth of

FIGURE 121: Peter Benenson, founder of Amnesty International, lighting a candle outside St Martin-in-the-Fields Church, London, in July 1981, to mark the twentieth anniversary of the founding of the organisation. The candle, wrapped in barbed wire, was designed by the British artist Diana Redhouse, and was inspired by Benenson's favourite proverb: 'Better to light a candle than curse the darkness'.

monitory democracy, then without doubt communication media are among the principal drivers of its subsequent growth.

No account of monitory democracy would be credible without taking into consideration the way that power and conflict are shaped by new media institutions. Think of it like this: assembly-based democracy belonged to an era dominated by the spoken word, backed up by laws written on papyrus and stone, and by messages despatched by foot, or by donkey and horse. Representative democracy sprang up in the era of print culture – the book, pamphlet and newspaper, and telegraphed and mailed messages – and fell into crisis during the advent of early mass communication media, especially radio and cinema and (in its infancy) television. By contrast, monitory democracy is tied closely to the growth of multi-media-saturated societies – societies whose structures of power are continuously 'bitten' by monitory institutions operating within a new galaxy of media defined by the ethos of communicative abundance.

Compared with the era of representative democracy, when print culture and limited-spectrum audiovisual media were much more closely aligned with political parties and governments, the age of monitory democracy witnesses constant public scrutiny and spats about power, to the point where it seems as if no organisation or leader within the fields of government or social life is immune from political trouble. The change has been shaped by a variety of forces, including the decline of journalism proud of its commitment to fact-based 'objectivity' (an ideal born of the age of representative democracy) and the rise of adversarial and 'gotcha' styles of commercial journalism driven by ratings, sales and hits. Technical factors, such as electronic memory, tighter channel spacing, new frequency allocation, direct satellite broadcasting, digital tuning and advanced compression techniques, have also been important. Chief among these technical factors is the advent of cable- and satellite-linked, computerised communications, which from the end of the 1960s triggered both product and process innovations in virtually every field of an increasingly commercialised media. This new galaxy of media has no historical precedent. Symbolised by one of its core components, the Internet (Figure 122), it is a new

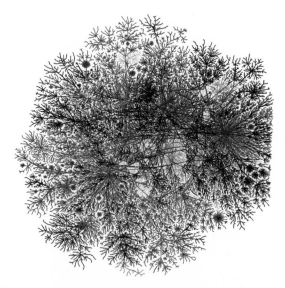

FIGURE 122: Computer graphic of global Internet traffic. Each line represents the path of sample data sent out to one of 20,000 pre-selected locations using a system called *Skitter* developed by the Cooperative Association for Internet Data Analysis, University of California.

world system of overlapping and interlinked media devices that integrate texts, sounds and images and enable communication to take place through multiple user points, in chosen time, either real or delayed, within modularised and ultimately global networks that are affordable and accessible to many hundreds of millions of people scattered across the globe.

All institutions in the business of scrutinising power rely heavily on these media innovations; if the new galaxy of communicative abundance suddenly imploded, monitory democracy would not last long. Monitory democracy and computerised media networks behave as if they are conjoined twins. To say this is not to fall into the trap of supposing that computer-linked communications networks prefigure a brand-new utopian world, a carnival of 'virtual communities' homesteading on the electronic frontier, a 'cyber revolution' that yields equal access of all citizens to all media, anywhere and at any time. Hype of this kind was strongly evident in the Declaration of the Independence of Cyberspace (1996), a document drawn up by the self-styled cyberrevolutionary John Perry Barlow, the former lyricist of the Grateful Dead and subsequent campaign manager for an infamous American vice-president, Dick Cheney. The Declaration proclaimed the end of the old world of representation within territorial states. Making hype seem profound, it claimed that computer-linked networks were 'creating a world that all may enter without privilege or prejudice accorded by race, economic power, military force, or station of birth'. Barlow said that communicative abundance heralded nothing short of 'a new social space, global and antisovereign, within which anybody, anywhere can express to the rest of humanity whatever he or she believes without fear. There is in these new media', he concluded, 'a foreshadowing of the intellectual and economic liberty that might undo all the authoritarian powers on earth.'[37]

Such utopian extravagance prompts a political health warning, not least because the new age of communicative abundance produces disappointment, instability and self-contradictions, for instance in the widening power gaps between communication-rich and -poor, who seem almost unneeded as communicators, or as consumers of media products. A majority of the world's people is too poor to make a telephone call; only a tiny minority have access to the Internet. The

divide between media-rich and media-poor citizens blights all monitory democracies; it contradicts their basic principle that all citizens
are equally entitled to communicate their opinions, and periodically
to give elected and unelected representatives a rough ride. Yet despite
such contradictions and disappointments, there are new and important things happening inside the swirling galaxy of communicative
abundance. Especially striking is the way the realms of 'private
life' and 'privacy' and wheeling and dealing of power 'in private'
have been put on the defensive. From the point of view of monitory
democracy, that is no bad thing. Every nook and cranny of power
becomes the potential target of 'publicity' and 'public exposure';
monitory democracy threatens to expose the quiet discriminations
and injustices that happen behind closed doors and in the world of
everyday life. Routine matters such as birth and death, diet and sex,
religious and ethnic customs are less and less based on unthinking
habit, on unquestioned, taken-for-granted certainties about 'normal'
ways of doing things. In the era of communicative abundance, no
hidden topic is protected unconditionally from media coverage, and
from possible politicisation; the more 'private' it is, the more 'publicity' it seems to get.

Nothing is sacrosanct – not even the efforts of those who try to
protect or rebuild what they claim to be sacrosanct. Past generations would find the whole process astonishing in its global scale
and democratic intensity. With the click of a camera, or the flick of
a switch, the world of the private can suddenly be made public.
Everything from the bedroom to the boardroom, the bureaucracy
and the battlefield, seems to be up for media grabs. Thanks to stories told by journalists, themselves unelected representatives of
publics, this is an age in which private text messages rebound publicly, to reveal the marital unfaithfulness and force the resignation
of a government minister. It is an era in which so-called reality TV
cuts from an afternoon children's programme (say) to a man on a
freeway setting his truck ablaze before turning his shotgun on the
police, and then himself, live, courtesy of a news helicopter and a
satellite uplink. These are times in which Sony hand-held cameras
are used by off-air reporters, known as 'embeds', to file ongoing
videos and blogs featuring election candidates live, unplugged and
unscripted; and this is the age in which video footage proves that

soldiers in war zones raped women, terrorised children and tortured innocent civilians. In the age of communicative abundance, the private lives of politicians, unelected representatives and celebrities, their romances, parties, health, drug habits, quarrels and divorces are the interest and fantasy objects of millions of people. And thanks to talk shows, blogs, social networking and other media acts, there is an endless procession of 'ordinary people' talking publicly about their private fears, fantasies, hopes and expectations. Some of them are sometimes lucky enough to morph into media stars, thanks to simulated elections, in which audiences granted a 'vote' by media companies are urged to lodge their preference for the star of their choice, by acclamation, cell phone or the Internet.

Helped along by red-blooded journalism that relies on styles of reporting concerned less with veracity than with 'breaking news' and blockbusting scoops, communicative abundance cuts like a knife into the power relations of government and civil society. It is easy to complain about the methods of the new journalism. It hunts in packs, its eyes on bad news, egged on by the newsroom saying that facts must never be allowed to get in the way of stories. It loves titillation, draws upon unattributed sources, fills news holes – in the era of monitory democracy news never sleeps – spins sensations, and concentrates too much on personalities, rather than time-bound contexts. The new journalism is formulaic and gets bored too quickly; it likes to bow down to corporate power and government press briefings; and there are moments when it is responsible for circulating disinformation around the globe a thousand times before accuracy is booted up. But these accusations are only half the story. For in spite of everything, red-blooded journalism helps keep alive the old utopias of shedding light on power, of 'freedom of information', 'government in the sunshine' and greater 'transparency' in the making of decisions. Given that unchecked power still weighs down hard on the heads of citizens, it is not surprising, thanks to the new journalism and the new monitory inventions, that public objections to wrongdoing and corruption are commonplace in the era of monitory democracy. There seems to be no end of scandals; and there are even times when scandals, like earthquakes, rumble beneath the feet of whole governments.

In the age of monitory democracy, some scandals become legendary, like the public uproar caused by the inadvertent discovery of evidence of secret burglaries of the Democratic Party National Committee headquarters in the Watergate Hotel in Washington, DC, and by the subsequent snowballing of events that became the Watergate Affair that resulted in threats of impeachment and the eventual resignation (in August 1974) of President Nixon in the United States. On the other side of the Atlantic, major scandals have included the rumpus in the early 1990s within Spanish politics triggered by a government auditors' report that confirmed that senior Socialist Party officials had operated front companies known as Filesa and Time Export, and that they had been paid some one billion pesetas for consultancy services that were never rendered (it was called the Filesa Affair). Then there was the nationwide investigation by Italian police and judges of the extensive system of political corruption dubbed 'bribesville' (*Tangentopoli*), the so-called *mani pulite* (Italian for 'clean hands') campaign that led to the disappearance of many political parties and the suicide of some politicians and industry leaders after their crimes were exposed. There was as well the resignation of the French foreign minister and the admission by the French president on television that agents of the French secret service (DGSE) were responsible for the murder, in July 1985, of a Greenpeace activist and the bombing of their support vessel, the *Rainbow Warrior*, a boat that had been due to lead a flotilla of yachts to protest against French nuclear testing at Mururoa Atoll in the Pacific Ocean. And not to be forgotten were the scandalous lies about the existence of 'weapons of mass destruction' spun by the defenders of the disastrous military invasion of Iraq in the early years of the twenty-first century.

Viral Politics

These and other '-gate' scandals remind us of a perennial problem facing monitory democracy: there is no shortage of organised efforts by the powerful to manipulate people beneath them; and, hence, the political dirty business of dragging power from the shadows and flinging it into the blazing halogen of publicity remains fundamentally important. Nobody should be kidded into thinking that the world of monitory democracy, with its many power-scrutinising institutions, is a level playing field, a paradise of equality of opportunity among all its citizens and their elected and unelected representatives. The combination of monitory democracy and communicative abundance nevertheless produces permanent flux, an unending restlessness driven by complex combinations of different interacting players and institutions, permanently pushing and pulling, heaving and straining, sometimes working together, at other times in opposition to one another. Elected and unelected representatives routinely strive to define and to determine who gets what, when and how; but the represented, taking advantage of various power-scrutinising devices, keep tabs on their representatives – sometimes with surprising success. The dynamics of monitory democracy are thus not describable using the simple spatial metaphors inherited from the age of representative democracy. Talk of the 'sovereignty' of parliament, or of 'local' versus 'central' government, or of tussles between 'pressure groups', political parties and governments, is just too simple. In terms of political geometry, the system of monitory democracy is something other and different: a complex web of differently sized and more or less interdependent monitory bodies that have the effect, thanks to communicative abundance, of continuously stirring up questions about who gets what, when and how, as well as holding publicly responsible those who exercise power, wherever they are situated. Monitory democracies are richly conflicted. Politics does not wither away. Everything is never straightforwardly OK.

There is something utterly novel about the whole trend. From its origins in the ancient assemblies of Syria-Mesopotamia, democracy has always cut through habit and prejudice and hierarchies of power. It has stirred up the sense that people can shape and reshape their lives as equals, and not surprisingly it has often brought commotion into the world. In the era of monitory democracy, the constant public scrutiny of power by hosts of differently sized monitory bodies with footprints large and small makes it the most energetic, most dynamic form of democracy ever. It even contains bodies (like the Democratic Audit Network and the Global Accountability Project) that specialise in providing public assessments of the quality of existing power-scrutinising mechanisms and the degree to which they fairly represent citizens' interests. Other bodies specialise in directing questions at governments on a wide range of matters, extending from their human rights records, their energy production plans to the quality of the drinking water of their cities. Private companies are grilled about their services and products, their investment plans, how they treat their employees, and the size of their impact upon the biosphere. Questions are raised about which SUVs are most likely to roll over, which companies retail the worst fast food, and which are the biggest polluters. Various watchdogs and guide dogs and barking dogs are constantly on the job, pressing for greater public accountability of those who exercise power. The powerful consequently come to feel the constant pinch of the powerless.

When they do their job well, monitory mechanisms have many positive effects, ranging from greater openness and justice within markets and blowing the whistle on foolish government decisions to the general enrichment of public deliberation and the empowerment of citizens and their chosen representatives through meaningful schemes of participation. Power-monitoring can be ineffective, or counterproductive, of course. Campaigns misfire or are poorly targeted; power wielders cleverly find loopholes and ways of rebutting or simply ignoring their opponents. And there are times when large numbers of citizens find the monitory strategies of organisations too timid, or confused, or simply irrelevant to their lives as consumers, workers, parents, community residents and young and elderly citizens.

Despite such weaknesses, the political dynamics and overall 'feel' of monitory democracies are very different from during the era of representative democracy. Politics in the age of monitory democracy has a definite 'viral' quality about it. The power controversies stirred up by monitory mechanisms follow unexpected paths and reach surprising destinations. Groups using mobile phones, bulletin boards, news groups, wikkies and blogs sometimes manage, against considerable odds, publicly to embarrass politicians, parties and parliaments, or even whole governments. Power-monitoring bodies like Human Rights Watch or Amnesty International regularly do the same, usually with help from networks of supporters. Think for a moment about any current public controversy that attracts wide-spread attention: news about its contours and commentaries and disputes about its significance are typically relayed by many power-monitoring organisations, large, medium and small. In the world of monitory democracy, that kind of latticed – viral, networked – pattern is typical, not exceptional. It has profound implications for the state-framed institutions of the old representative democracy, which find themselves more and more enmeshed in 'sticky' webs of power-scrutinising institutions that often hit their target, sometimes from long distances, often by means of boomerang effects.

In the age of monitory democracy, bossy power can no longer hide comfortably behind private masks; power relations every-where are subjected to organised efforts by some, with the help of media, to tell others – publics of various sizes – about matters that had previously been hidden away, 'in private'. This denaturing of power is usually a messy business, and it often comes wrapped in hype, certainly. But the unmasking of power resonates strongly with the power-scrutinising spirit of monitory democracy. The whole process is reinforced by the growing availability of cheap tools of communication (multi-purpose mobile phones, digital cameras, video recorders, the Internet) to individuals, groups and organisations; and communicative abundance multiplies the genres of programming, information and storytelling that are available to audiences and publics. News, chat shows, political oratory, bitter legal spats, comedy, infotainment, drama, music, advertising, blogs – all of this and much more constantly clamour and jostle for public attention.

Some people complain about effects like 'information overload', but from the point of view of monitory democracy, communicative abundance on balance has positive consequences. In spite of all its hype and spin, the new media galaxy nudges and broadens people's horizons. It tutors their sense of pluralism and prods them into taking greater responsibility for how, when and why they commu-nicate. The days (I recall) when children were compulsorily bathed and scrubbed behind the ears, sat down in their dressing gowns prior to going to bed, and required to listen to radio or television programmes with their families – these days of representative democracy and broadcasting and mass entertainment are over. So, too, are the days when millions of people, huddled together as masses in the shadows of totalitarian power, found the skilfully orchestrated radio and film performances of demagogues fascinating, and reassuring.

Message-saturated democracies, by contrast, encourage people's suspicions of unaccountable power. All the king's horses and all the king's men are unlikely to reverse the trend. Within the world of monitory democracies, people are coming to learn that they must keep an eye on power and its representatives, that they must make judgements and choose their own courses of action. Citizens are thus tempted to think for themselves; to see the same world in different ways, from different angles; and to sharpen their overall sense that prevailing power relationships are not 'natural', but contingent. Communicative abundance and monitory institutions combine to promote something of a 'Gestalt switch' in the popular perception of power. The metaphysical idea of an objective, out-there-at-a-distance 'reality' is weakened; so, too, is the presumption that stubborn 'factual truth' is superior to power. The fabled distinction between what people can see with their eyes and what they are told about the emperor's new clothes breaks down. 'Reality', including the 'reality' of the powerful, comes to be understood as always 'produced reality', a matter of interpretation – and the power to force particular interpretations of the world down others' throats.

There is admittedly nothing automatic or magical about any of this. In the era of monitory democracy, communication is constantly the subject of dissembling, negotiation, compromise and power conflicts – in a phrase, a matter of politics. Communicative abundance for that reason does not somehow automatically ensure the triumph of either the spirit or institutions of monitory democracy. Message-saturated societies can and do have effects that are harmful for democracy. In some quarters, for instance, media saturation triggers citizens' inattention to events. While they are expected as good citizens to keep their eyes on public affairs, to take an interest in the world beyond their immediate household and neighbourhood, more than a few find it ever harder to pay attention to the media's vast outpourings. Profusion breeds confusion. There are times, for instance, when voters are so pelted with a hail of election advertisements on prime-time television that they react frostily. Disaffected, they get up from their sofas, leave their living rooms, change channels, or switch to mute, concluding with a heavy sigh that the less you know the better off you are. It is only a few steps from there to something more worrying: the unwitting spread of a culture of unthinking indifference. Monitory democracy certainly feeds upon communicative abundance, but one of its more perverse effects is to encourage individuals to escape the great complexity of the world by sticking their heads, like ostriches, into the sands of wilful ignorance, or to float cynically upon the swirling tides and waves and eddies of fashion – to change their minds, to speak and act flippantly, to embrace or even celebrate opposites, to bid farewell to veracity, to slip into the arms of what some carefully call 'bullshit'.[38]

Foolish illusions, cynicism and disaffection are among the biggest temptations facing citizens and their elected and unelected representatives. Whether or not monitory democracy will survive their deadly effects is now for a brave historian of the future to tell us.

MEMORIES FROM THE FUTURE

> When I first saw pictures of the dismantling of the Berlin Wall, I had the feeling that history was running in two fundamentally different directions at once: towards democracy and towards domination mixed with blood.
>
> Yang Lian (2004)

Let us now get ready to face the future, starting with a prickly fact: during the first decade of the twenty-first century the old euphoria about democratic ideals and institutions fast began to fade. Millions of people around the world sensed trouble in the house of democracy. While most found it hard to spot exactly why this was happening, the old victory talk of democracy – of ends of history and third waves – began to feel to them like a campfire on ice. Some were caught off guard, especially given that democracy had come up trumps following its narrow escape from the cruel wars and totalitarian destruction of the twentieth century. So stunning had been its triumph that democracy seemed to have won a permanent victory over its enemies. It was said by many to be the only political game in town. That belief had served for a time to consolidate widespread commitment to democratic ideals, which around the world remained high well into the early years of the new millennium.

One report after another showed that to be true, not only for the heartlands of monitory democracy, but also for whole regions, such as southern Africa, where experiments with democratic ideals and institutions had once been given a rough ride. The Arabic-speaking world was no exception to this trend. It contained the highest density of dictatorships on the face of the earth, nearly all of them backed by carbon-hungry Western democracies. Yet while some nationalists and Islamists refused for that reason to believe in democracy and its double standards, the majority still favoured it. There was plenty of democratic spirit in the air. 'Arab Majesties, Excellencies and Highnesses, We Spit on You' read a banner held high by protesters during a demonstration in Cairo in 2006. Electoral results from the region were also impressive. In elections held during the early years of the twenty-first century, Islamists chalked up significant results in Saudi Arabia (in municipal elections), Morocco, Jordan, Algeria, Iraq, Kuwait, the West Bank and Gaza. Candidates of the outlawed Muslim Brotherhood scored remarkable victories as well in parliamentary elections held in Egypt (Figure 123). Its government played dirty, as was to be expected from a political dynasty led by President Hosni Mubarak, jokingly known to Egyptians as the last pharaoh. The arrest and assault of voters and activists before and during the elections were

FIGURE 123: In elections held in November–December 2005, Egyptian police detained hundreds of voters and restricted voting in areas contested by the Muslim Brotherhood, whose supporters (as in Bosat, north of Cairo) replied by using unorthodox methods of entering sealed polling booths to cast their votes.

widespread. The Brotherhood had responded by limiting the number of its candidates to only a third of the seats in parliament, but still they managed to win close to a quarter of all seats, a success rate that would have translated into an overall two-thirds parliamentary majority. Such predictions confirmed the elementary truth that the obstacle to democracy in the region was neither Islamists nor Islamic culture, but foreign-backed dictatorship. 'The problem', commented the exiled leader of the Tunisian An-Nahda Party, lay 'in convincing the rulers of the merits of democracy, since the shortest way to prison and the gallows in the Arab world is to win elections'.[1]

Given the massive praise for democracy, the utterly surprising thing was the strength of the counter-trend, the mounting public unease and disillusionment with democratic institutions, even a kind of melancholic depression about their future. Whatever happened to democracy? voices began to ask. Why did the global growth spurt of democratic ideals and institutions fizzle out? Was it time to think up fresh ways of breathing new life into democracy? Or was it too late for that? Was the bad moon rising over democracy a sign of rough times to come? Perhaps democracy was sliding towards another death, this time on a global scale?

Imagined History

To help digest this mouthful of questions, let us ask for help from an imaginary historian, whose job it will be, fifty years from now, to retell the story of what happened to democracy in our times. Never mind her name, or her age. Do not ask after her personal or professional details, where she lived or what she looked like. Trust only that she was sharp-minded and cool-headed, and that she was an honest soul who cared deeply about the fate of our world. Think of her as the modern-day offspring of Mnemosyne, the ancient Greek mother of all muses, as a companion from the future who inspires us to face up to our times, and to form some prudent judgements about their direction, by taking us forward in time so that we can look back on ourselves, and so imagine a range of possible answers to the questions posed.[2] Her method of encouraging us to drink from the river of memory from an imagined moment in the future – to think using the eyes she placed in the back of our heads – had the advantage of forcing us to see things that are currently less than visible, or to see familiar things with different eyes. Our muse knew that without memory all was lost. She believed firmly in the rule that misunderstanding of the present inevitably results from ignorance of the past. But she knew as well the difficulty of distancing our selves from ourselves. What was needed, said our muse, was a way of projecting ourselves into the not-so-distant future, so that we could grasp the key trends of our times by looking back at them, from a distance. That was why she practised a type of history of the present day, a kind of history that prompted thoughtfulness, a sense of wonder, even discomfort with the way things were going. She tried to prod the sacred cows of certainty, to jab and poke both common sense and nonsense, with a sharp-pointed stick of wisdom carved from the tree of historical understanding. She intended that you see her method as worthwhile. She wanted you to learn. She believed that her approach – cultivating memories from the future – could yield fascinating and relevant results.

To prove her worth, our sage put to good use her vantage point fifty years from now by seizing on the reasons why unease palpably clouded democracy's future. She was sure the democratic malaise that threatened the achievements of earlier decades had roots that ran deep and wide. It was important to look beneath appearances, she said. The malaise was confined neither to individual countries nor to particular regions. It was not traceable to ill-conceived policies, even though they often made matters worse. And the dysphoria was not simply a hangover effect of the inebriated enthusiasms that followed the collapse of communism and the string of swingeing defeats of military juntas around the world – as if the malaise was something like a return to realism after a forgivable bout of utopianism. The troubles that haunted the world's monitory democracies were not just imaginary problems 'in the head'; and they were not adequately explained by proper nouns like Thatcher, Craxi, Europe, the WTO, Silvio Berlusconi, George W. Bush, the Twin Towers, or Osama bin Laden. Contrary to a line of criticism that stretched all the way back to the Athenian democracy, the creeping pessimism about its future was certainly not part of the natural order of things, an expression of some or other 'law' of history that dictated that every generation or so democracies belly-ached about their own weaknesses. According to our guide, the causes of the stresses and strains and pinches and pains felt by all democracies lay elsewhere. They were traceable to deep-seated problems that were not easily solved by the existing system of monitory democracy. Partly they were produced by that system itself; partly they threatened it from without. But regardless of causes, these difficulties were real and formidably dangerous. She had no doubt they had life-threatening implications for the whole idea and practice of monitory democracy.

Party Government

So what were these deep-seated forces that cut like jagged knives into the body of monitory democracies everywhere? Our muse began with the most obvious: *people's deep misgivings about politicians, parties and parliaments.*

By the early years of the twenty-first century, she said, public bellyaching against politicians, parties and parliaments spread rapidly through the world of monitory democracy. It was not the first time in the history of democracy that this had happened. The greatest democracy of the nineteenth century, the United States, once experienced something apparently similar, at the end of that century, when a wide spectrum of organised resistance – from populist movements and muckraking journalism to the use of recall and referenda and the clean-up of city administrations – tried to put parties and party government on the back foot, in their proper place. Their plummeting popularity in the era of monitory democracy was driven by quite different forces: less by the feeling that parties, parliaments and politicians had become too big for their boots, and more by the sense that official 'politics' were irrelevant, or at least that they poorly represented the interests of citizens, who could in any case turn elsewhere to make their views known. Politicians, parties and parliaments began to look and feel like fossils – not quite trilobites, but certainly residues from better times.

To help us grasp what happened, our mentor reminded us that

struggles for popular self-government during the nineteenth and early twentieth centuries were mostly greeted by the rich and powerful with loathing and fear and – as in the Westminster compromise, the Crown-in-parliament system – the determination to tame or divert, or to wreck, its energies. Every trick was tried. Crude forms of manipulation multiplied. Hereditary second chambers, gerrymandering (the Austrians politely called it 'electoral geometry') and weighted votes for the propertied and educated were common. Peasants and workers were forced to mark their ballot papers under the watchful eyes of their employers' agents. Urban political machines found much-needed votes at the end of long election days – as in Turin, where (Italo Calvino recorded, through the eyes of a fictional poll watcher[3]) good nuns and priests brought the mentally ill and senile and disabled and comatose to cast votes for the Christian Democrats in national elections.

Meanwhile, our muse recalled, the constitutional powers of popularly elected assemblies were trimmed (this was the preferred strategy of Bismarck, who likened democracy to a nursery run by children). Armies were drafted in to give force to the nineteenth-century maxim that the only remedy for democracy is troops (*gegen Demokraten hilfen nur Soldaten* went the German rhyme). And instead of guns, some dissenters used sharp words, as did Thomas Carlyle (1795–1881), for whom the newfangled system of representative democracy was 'monstrous, loud, blatant, inarticulate as the voice of Chaos'; and as did Oscar Wilde (1854–1900), who used just one line to express his contempt for the tyranny of the majority: 'Democracy means simply the bludgeoning of the people by the people for the people.'[4]

In the age of monitory democracy, bellyaching against party-based democracy was expressed in quite different language, our muse explained. Almost nobody spoke against 'the people'. Growing numbers of people instead turned their backs on formal party politics, with a shrug of the shoulders, or a curse at the 'dishonesty' and 'irrelevance' of parties, politicians and parliaments. Plenty of surveys revealed the extent of the trend. Our guide admitted that figures were hard to come by in democracies such as India and South Africa, where in the year 2000 the numbers of people who said they were members of a political party was about one in ten of the voting population, far higher than for the rest of the world. More reliable evidence was provided by two surveys of changing patterns of party membership in European democracies for the period 1960–2000.[5] The data showed that during this period the ratio of political party members to the electorate as a whole shrank ever smaller. In the year 2000, it stood at less than 5 per cent, a figure considerably down on the figure of 10.5 per cent recorded among a smaller group of democracies at the end of the 1980s, with that figure in turn down by some 15 per cent from the figures gathered at the beginning of the 1960s. The trend bore only a limited relation to whether the democracy in question had been long established. By the end of the 1990s, Poland, France, the United Kingdom, Hungary and the Netherlands had the lowest ratios of all, standing at less than half the overall average, which suggested to our muse that the new so-called 'third wave' democracies, like Poland and the Czech Republic, were not temporary exceptions, but actually weathervanes that pointed to the future of all monitory democracies.

Raw numbers of party members also plummeted dramatically during this period. In the older European democracies, parties haemorrhaged members, on average by about 35 per cent during the period 1980–2000. In some countries, the scale of decline was astonishing. In France, parties lost an estimated one million members, some two-thirds of their total; while in Norway and the United Kingdom raw numbers fell by around 50 per cent of their previous total. In the early 1950s, the Labour Party had more than one million members; the Conservative Party had an astonishing 2.5 million paid-up individual members, making it one of the great political machines of Europe. During the first decade of the new millennium, Labour Party membership had plummeted to 200,000 survivors; and at little more than 300,000 supporters, Conservative Party membership was barely an eighth of its peak during the halcyon days of Winston Churchill.

Our guide moved quickly to scotch a common misunderstanding of these trends, by reminding us that there was no evidence to show that citizens were being eaten alive by the acids of selfish individualism. She noted some figures from India: when asked how strongly they trusted political parties, a clear majority said

either 'not very much' (21 per cent) or 'not at all' (24 per cent) or
that they had 'no opinion' (19 per cent). But when they were
asked whether they 'discussed politics' with their friends and colleagues 'often' or 'occasionally', a sizeable near-majority (44 per
cent) said they did, while a huge majority said that since becoming eligible to vote they turned out at 'every election' (69 per cent)
or at 'most elections' (19 per cent) or at 'some elections' (7 per
cent). Our guide also cited evidence from seven national surveys
conducted in Australia between 1984 and 1999. Asked to say
'how much interest' they 'usually' had 'in what's going on in politics', she noted that about a third (32–38 per cent) of people said
they took 'a good deal' of interest in politics. Just under half
(between 44 and 47 per cent) said they took 'some' interest, while
less than a fifth of people (15–18 per cent) said that they paid 'not
much' attention to politics. During the whole period, hardly anybody ever said they took absolutely no interest in the subject.[6]
Our muse pointed out that the Indian and Australian figures were
not exceptional. The fear that people in the age of monitory
democracy were fast losing interest in public affairs, that they
now preferred to turn their backs on others and go 'bowling
alone' (as an American scholar, Robert Putnam, had famously
claimed), was unfounded. If anything, the trend was in the opposite direction: the involvement of better-educated citizens in
various civil society organisations and their strengthened interest
in public affairs made them far more impatient with the perceived
foibles and prejudices of party politics. 'They are only out to line
their own pockets' and 'You can never trust them to do what they
say' were among the commonplace objections that slid across the
lips of many potential voters. That was why large numbers of citizens who once upon a time might have joined a party now felt
that they had lost the means of engagement with official representative politics. They simply concluded that party membership
was no longer meaningful. There was a creeping sense, in the era
of the universal franchise, that voting no longer had the significance it once had, even that not everyone's vote mattered, or that
none of it mattered.

But why did this impression gain ground? our guide asked. She
thought that some of the causes were external to parties. Easily the

most potent was the fact that in the age of monitory democracy parties, politicians and legislatures found themselves forced to compete with a multitude of power-checking, power-monitoring institutions that made the life of politicians, parties and legislatures generally far rougher than in the past. Parliaments were at a special disadvantage. They were in effect buildings without bodies; they enjoyed no collective voice, few spokespeople in defence of their public role, and were in any case often dominated by governing parties, which meant that legislatures found their reputations stained by the general dislike of politicians and parties, many of whom made matters worse by being slow to cotton on to what was happening. Most politicians and their parties had the feeling that whatever they promised or announced was rarely greeted with universal assent; on most occasions they found themselves caught in the crossfire of a host of extra-parliamentary, power-scrutinising bodies. Citizens, our muse explained, were far better equipped to grasp the uncomfortable truth: in the age of monitory democracy, the key question was no longer who voted, but where people could meaningfully vote, or find a voice through representatives with views untainted by parties and politicians. Faced with the choice (say) of supporting a human rights organisation or joining a political party, many citizens simply laughed at the latter option. They called it 'getting mixed up with the dirt of politics'.

The rough ride given to parties and politicians was made bumpier by their historic decline as employment agencies. Our guide noted that words and policy promises to voters were just not the same as offering them cash or gainful employment, as had happened in the past. The cleanup of party politics since the end of the nineteenth century had rebounded on politicians and parties: they were now the ones who looked soiled. According to our muse, their deep dependence upon external campaign funding compounded their reputation for sleaze. Many political parties lived on the verge of bankruptcy. That meant they were constantly tempted to borrow or bribe funds by illicit or outright illegal means – thus potentially embroiling themselves in well-publicised corruption scandals. Nobbling the rich, another favourite method of covering their costs and paying off their debts, normally fuelled complaints that politicians, parties and even whole governments were simply obeying the law that those who pay the piper always call the tune. Our muse noted that state funding of political parties, a common practice in some countries, harboured much the same danger; citizens reacted by seeing parties as mouthpieces of the state, rather than of 'the people'.

Our historian agreed that the public standing of parties and politicians was not helped by the Napoleonic arrogance of political figures like Margaret Thatcher, Golda Meir, Indira Gandhi, Richard Nixon, Jacques Chirac and George W. Bush, all of them leaders who seemed to believe too much in themselves, and to want too much executive power. In certain contexts, public disillusionment with party politics was fuelled by suspicions that the act of voting had been cheapened by the crafty manipulation of electoral boundaries – redistricting for partisan advantage was the polite way Americans put it – and by fears that electronic voting systems were either fiddled or flawed. But the principal cause of the unpopularity of politicians and parties, said our muse, was the stranglehold they tried to exercise over the process of representation of a growing variety of social and political interests. It was as if monitory democracy could neither live without nor live with political parties, she said. Parties indeed played a vital role in securing monitory democracy. Their job was to bring together disparate social interests, to bind together groups of voters with different opinions. But their bad habit of doing deals through behind-the-scenes lobbying, plus their predilection for occupying the 'middle of the road' by targeting voters in search of a majority, or a maximum of votes, had a high price. Evidence mounted that the middle road was seen widely as a dead end. Parties and politicians – supposedly the backbone of the system of democratic representation – seemed less and less representative of anybody, except perhaps themselves, and their buddies.

In the age of monitory democracy, our muse agreed, parties worked hard to aggregate interests. But often they did so at the price of blandly stated policies, vague visionless visions, double standards and non-commitments. Some politicians openly defended policy-free politics, saying there were important political benefits of 'flexibility' and 'keeping options open' and gradually building up an agenda, using pointillist methods borrowed from painting. In response, noted our guide, more than a few voters understandably came to be gripped by the feeling that they either did not know for whom they were voting; or that those they did vote for never delivered on their promises; or that voting once every few years seemed to bring few benefits to anybody. Our sage put it this way: many citizens accused parties of fudging the different meanings of the precious words 'yes' and 'no'. Parties, she said, quoting a favourite saying of some German citizens, were YesNo parties (*Jeinparteien*). In some contexts – countries like India and Papua New Guinea were path-breakers – politicians pushed their two-timing to the limits, by turning themselves into footloose 'party-hoppers' prepared (as happened in the Indian state of Jharkhand in 2006) to sacrifice all prior promises and principles, in order to get their hands on the levers of government power.

Our guide was sure that the compound effect of all these trends was to convince many voters that politicians were sleazy grey-haired men in suits looking after themselves (Figure 124). Survey after survey showed not only that they were disproportionately men, but that in popularity-rating exercises they usually ranked at least as low as car salesmen and real estate agents. Stories and

FIGURE 124: *Politician*, by the Lithuanian-born artist Zita Sodeika.

jokes poking fun in the face of politicians popped up in practically ever context, always with the same bite. Our muse reported a popular jibe that came from post-apartheid South Africa. A group of elderly Jewish men used to meet every Wednesday in a seaside suburb of Cape Town, for coffee and chat. They usually savoured their caffeine and sat for hours discussing politics. Their tone was usually very negative, but one day Moshe surprised his friends by announcing, in a loud and clear voice: 'You know what? I've become an optimist.' Everyone was stunned. All conversation shuddered to a halt, replaced by the rattle of cups and saucers. But then a regular named Sam noticed something wasn't quite right. He said to Moshe: 'Hold on a minute, if you're an optimist, why are you looking so worried?' Moshe said: 'Do you think it's easy being an optimist?'

Politicians were a popular butt of Australian voters. Our guide recalled that former Prime Minister Bob Hawke (who held office between 1983 and 1991) especially liked this one: on the busy Hume Highway that links Sydney and Melbourne, police discovered two dead bodies. The corpses were badly squashed, though careful examination of the evidence revealed that one was a dead possum, the other a politician. How did the forensics tell the difference? There were skid marks before the possum. Sometimes the jokes were so dark they bordered on black. From the democracy of Botswana came one about a cannibal visiting a neighbouring cannibal village, where ordinary people cost ten American dollars a head, but politicians a hundred dollars. 'How come politicians cost so much?' the visitor enquired. Replied the local chief: 'Do you know how hard it is to clean one of those?' From India came the popular joke about the citizen who spotted an epitaph in a cemetery that read: 'Here lies an honest man and politician.' 'Shame', the citizen cried, 'two people in the same grave!' And, compliments of our guide, a last one from the United States, where there was a well-known saying, popular among party candidates, that the best way to avoid suffering a loss of popularity as an elected member of Congress was not to get elected. 'I've been thinking of ways of cutting back on my work obligations; I never seem to have enough time to myself', confessed a surgeon to a colleague as they teed off for a round of golf. 'Perhaps I should specialise and only work on engineers. Their parts are numbered. Or work on aeronautical engineers. Their parts are numbered and colour-coded as well.' Trying to be helpful, his partner replied: 'I've been thinking along the same lines. But why not just operate on politicians? They have fewer operable parts, only two in fact, their mouth and their arse-hole, and they're interchangeable.'

With humour like that, it wasn't surprising that political moaning and opposition voting flourished in the early decades of the twenty-first century. Protest voting took many forms, our muse observed. Posting a blank ballot paper. Selecting the option, 'None of the Above' (electoral authorities were generally reticent about providing that choice, for fear of attracting disgruntled voters). Spoiling the ballot paper. Adding something to the ballot paper (in Sicily, said our guide, a favourite with the disaffected was to wrap a slice or two of greasy mortadella or salami within the ballot paper, then to post the 'sandwich' into the ballot box). Tearing the ballot paper to shreds, then scattering it around the polling booth. Eating the ballot paper. Mock-selling the vote, for instance by putting it up for auction, on a website. Refusing to vote altogether, especially in cases where that was treated as civil disobedience, as in Belgium, where voters who repeatedly failed to vote could be disenfranchised; or Greece, where those failing to vote faced a year's imprisonment or being stripped of public office (or, harshest of all, Bolivia, where citizens who failed to vote could lose access to their bank accounts for up to three months).

Then there was the option of voting for a minority candidate, a fringe figure who had little or no chance of election under normal circumstances. Given the low levels or dramatic decline nearly everywhere of political party membership and, especially among young people, growing disrespect for 'politicians' and official 'politics', satirical campaigns and voting against all mainstream parties and candidates flourished during the era of monitory democracy. Our sage recalled a pioneer parodist, Michel Colucci (1944–86), better known as Coluche, a famous French comedian. He attempted to run in the French presidential elections in 1981, but was forced to drop out of the race, mainly because of growing media and political pressure following polls that showed that he might command a significant share of the vote.* In Finland, a special favourite was Donald Duck, who usually did quite well in parliamentary and presidential elections, helped along by a popular magazine of that name. There were loosely networked campaigns against the ruling parties, like the Rainbow and Greens that first made their mark on Japanese local elections at the end of the twentieth century. In the Netherlands, in late 2006, a Party for the Animals (Partij voor de Dieren) understandably made history by winning two seats in the national parliament. Anti-political sentiments fuelled support for a long and lengthening list of protest figures – Screaming Lord Sutch, Ralph Nader, Pauline Hanson, Hugo Chávez, Jean-Marie Le Pen, Pim Fortuyn – all of whom, regardless of their left, centre or right policies, seemed to have had one thing in common: they claimed to champion the interests of the disaffected and unrepresented, all those who didn't identify with politicians or mainstream parties.

Phrase Struggle

Our muse wondered whether the refusal of mainstream parties and politicians was fuelled by the growth of communicative abundance. She reminded us that all monitory democracies operated within media-saturated environments. Whether they liked it or not, every twenty-first-century politician, political party, parliament and government had to factor into their calculations their opponents' use of digital media networks accessible to people through an affordable variety of media, from multiple points. Gone were the days

---

*These were among his best-known jibes: 'France has the best French politicians in the world'; 'Politicians are to politics what holes are to cheese. More cheese means more holes. But more holes means less cheese'; (concerning politicians) 'Instead of blind we say "sight-impaired", instead of deaf we say "hearing-impaired", so should fools be called "understanding-impaired"?'; 'Always remember that while the Gestapo had means to make you talk, our politicians have means to keep us quiet'; 'Besides gangster or politician, what can you do without qualifications? All that's left is to be an artist'; 'Half our politicians can't do anything; the other half would do anything'; (in a campaign speech) 'I'll quit politics when politicians quit comedy – they steal my job, so for the time being I steal theirs'; 'I'm neither for nor against politics – on the contrary!'; and 'In a dictatorship you're told: "Shut your mouth!" In a democracy it's: "Kiss my arse . . .".'

when politicians like John F. Kennedy could keep their private dalliances or pill popping quiet, or govern with the help of what they jokingly called the BOGSAT principle ('a bunch of guys sitting around a table'). In monitory democracies, the media were no longer the Fourth Estate. Politics operated entirely within media frameworks; representative government was upstaged. In the era of communicative abundance, noted our guide, an inquisitive, heavily commercial, twenty-four-seven system of *symbolic* representation sprang up. Journalists and the media portrayed themselves as 'representatives' of everything, and everybody. Politicians consequently felt the pinch of conflicting loyalties. Sometimes they gave the impression that they would rather ditch their parties and handle the media alone, surrounded by a make-up team. At other times, it was unclear whether they were representing their constituents, their party or their government, or themselves in competition not only with journalists, but with a wider media field comprising both 'ordinary people' and celebrities, some of whom turned their attention to politics. It was not surprising, said our muse, that the half-life of politicians became shorter, or that their careers very often ended in failure. Monitory democracy was an era in which politicians were easily jostled off public stages by a 'parallel government' of non-party celebrities and role models handed a microphone by communicative abundance. Marilyn Monroe, Diego Maradona, Bill Gates, Muttiah Muralitharan, Jane Fonda and Bono were on our guide's list of substitute representatives, some of them enjoying global reputations. So, too, were Kylie Minogue, John Lennon, David Beckham, Tina Turner, Michael Schumacher, George Soros, Princess Diana, Tiger Woods, Amitabh Bachchan, the cast of *Sex and the City* and Ali G.

The upstaging of political representatives by the celebrities of civil society naturally produced backlashes, our muse recorded. Some politicians complained about the 'unhealthily destructive' relationship between the media and politicians (they were the understated words of a well-known English spin doctor, Peter Mandelson). But the unsavoury truth was that politicians liked to handle the problem by copying their opponents, by morphing into media stars protected from scrutiny by minders known in Washington circles as 'flackpacks'. Our muse described the elementary rules politicians were supposed to live by: don't answer journalists' questions; see them instead as a 'cue' to say what you want. Since voters have little or no interest in details, concentrate upon the packaging. Wrap it tightly. Pay attention to dress sense. Get a loyal husband, or wife. Give the occasional speech about citizenship, or human rights abuses. Don't forget to thump the tub, to prove one's passion. Memorise by heart some policies. Be guarded, the whole time.

Some people said that the age of democratic politics and party struggle had given way to the era of 'phrase struggle' (a Mexican author, Eulalio Ferrer, had coined that lovely phrase). But according to our guide, politicians who followed the rules of phrase struggle usually looked wooden, or fake, and that made them easy targets of bad press. Websites that specialised in the tricky art of 'googling' and 'blogging' party politics, by giving legs to gossip, grass-roots comment and stories, proved especially tricky. The lives of politicians were not made easier by the use of hand-held video cameras to catch individual politicians off guard, then to upload their off-message remarks on to blogs and video sites. Then there was the constant din of Rupert Murdoch-style partisan journalism, aggressive reporting that was unaligned in fickle ways, and always prepared to ditch any particular party or political leader that did not meet its expectations, or its business interests. The media battering ensured that politicians, especially those who looked like spin statement dummies in the hands of ventriloquists, were put on their mettle, or made to look irrelevant. The impression developed that politicians and parties were out of touch, always a few steps behind public opinion, even that politicians and parties were miserably lacking in spontaneity, blandly wooden – or just self-serving dinosaurs. Hence the cutting remark of Coluche: 'I'll quit politics when politicians quit comedy – they steal my job, so for the time being I steal theirs.'

Überdemocracy

Verbal shelling on that scale sent politicians and parties running for cover; it also prompted public proposals for putting politics back into party politics. During the early years of the new millennium, our muse noted, there were loud calls for tougher public scrutiny of the fund-raising methods of parties. Some of them introduced primary elections for the first time. There were demands for extending the vote to denizens; lowering the voting age to at least sixteen (where that did not already exist); and efforts to mobilise voters and raise campaign funds by means of the Internet. Changing the electoral system and outlawing the manipulation of electoral boundaries for partisan advantage proved popular. Time and money were invested to make it easier for people to vote, for instance by providing all voters with the right of automatic, same-day voter registration. The Internet and other means of communication offered voters better information about election dates, early voting options, the location of polling places and absentee ballots (along the lines pioneered in the United States by such groups as the League of Women Voters' vote411.org). Some cities and countries saw initiatives to patch up the holes in postal ballot and electronic voting systems, for instance through legislation requiring voter verification and paper trails. Early-warning systems (called web widgets) were also built into elections for the first time; examples championed by groups like voterstory.org and videothevote.org included the electronic tracking of improprieties faced by voters and making instantly available the evidence on websites.

The stated aim of all these proposals was to give citizens a sense that they could expand their power as voters, making them feel that, although they only voted a few times in their lives, voting could be a meaningful act. The trouble – interjected our guide – was that not everybody in high places agreed that this was a desirable goal. Especially worrying, she said, was the way some politicians and parties effectively turned the tables on their critics by getting serious about top-down party politics, in effect by steering whole countries towards the twenty-first-century world that she half-jokingly called 'überdemocracy'.

She drew attention to the governing parties of Silvio Berlusconi in Italy, Thaksin Shinawatra in Thailand and John Howard in Australia, noting on the spot that these were not just local anomalies on three separate continents.* She insisted there was something of global relevance about the way these governing parties used similar techniques to win and maintain electoral support from millions of uncomplaining people. She emphasised just how few people had spotted the novelty of their governing methods. She was certain that none of these governments could be called dictatorships or totalitarian regimes in any conventional sense. In the history of democracy they were something new, she said. They were best understood as pathological reactions to monitory democracy, and that made them all the more disturbing, especially because the successes of these governments proved that monitory democracy everywhere could be transformed – remoulded by governing parties into fake forms of democracy.

The methods these governments used were straightforward enough; combined, they were lethal. Here were the how-to-do-it rules: begin by paying attention to institutions that can harm the government's electoral prospects. Snuggle up to key businesses. Bring them into the heart of government. Turn politics into

---

*Silvio Berlusconi: known globally as an unscrupulous businessman, media magnate, owner of the football club AC Milan, politician and prime minister of Italy three times (1994–5, 2001–6, and since 2008). Skilled at using government and media advertising to protect his companies and himself from prosecution – his brazen ways of running both government and his media empire prompted some Italians to speak of 'videocracy' – he quickly developed a reputation for handling truth carelessly, and for media *faux pas*, including his claims that the Italian Constitution was 'inspired by Soviets', that 'Chinese Communists used to eat children' and that right-wing female politicians were better-looking than their left-wing counterparts. Thaksin Shinawatra: one of Thailand's richest businessmen, with principal interests in media and telecommunications. In 1998, he founded the Thai Rak Thai ('Thai Love Thai') Party, which won a landslide victory in the 2001 general elections, helped by widespread vote buying and strong support from business and the rural poor. By mid-2002, Prime Minister Thaksin predicted he would remain in power for sixteen years, but in mid-September 2006, following victory in a boycotted election, and dogged by allegations of tax evasion, corruption, hostility to a free press and human rights abuses, especially of Muslim majorities living in the country's southern provinces, he was ousted by a military coup and forced into exile in England, where he bought the football club Manchester City, whose fans referred to him as 'Frank Sinatra'. John Howard: a less flamboyant figure, but never to be underestimated prime minister of Australia (1996–2007) and leader of the Liberal-National Coalition government that won successive general election victories in 1998, 2001 and 2004. In the 2007 general elections, with many voters restive about his government's pro-business bias, punitive industrial relations laws, arrogance towards indigenous people and unflinching support for the so-called 'war on terror' led by the United States (President George W. Bush once described him as 'a man of steel'), his government was ignominiously defeated, despite a booming economy; he lost his own seat, only the second Australian prime minister to do so (Stanley Bruce was the first, in 1929).

big-money politics. Say things like: 'Politics and business are inseparable, like the earth which would get too hot if it moved closer to
the sun and too cold if it moved too far away' (Thaksin). Bang on
about the importance of private initiative, cutting taxes and deregulation, the right of citizens to be themselves, to make money and
to consume freely. Round on those who are driven by the 'desire
to control everything' (Berlusconi). Hack in to trade unions and
professional associations with an independent mind. Keep an eye
on the courts; if they threaten investigations that attack the
government, accuse judges of acting dishonourably and meddling
with elected government. Insist on the principle of legal immunity
for the holders of high office. Apply pressure upon all extra-
parliamentary points of opposition. Critics of the government must
be brought to their knees, preferably in silence. Concentrate
especially upon power-monitoring bodies, like think-tanks, scientific and professional experts, human rights organisations, NGOs
and universities.

Direct threatening questions at hand-selected NGOs, especially
those giving the government a hard time. Cast doubt on their funding sources, their charitable status and their 'unrepresentative'
opinions. If that doesn't work, cut off their funds, or threaten to do
so. The point must always be to cultivate a culture of suspicion, if
culture is the right word. Punish dissent wherever it arises, particularly among scientific and policy experts who call into question
the government's integrity, or who say the evidence is against the
government. Gag them. Wheel out substitute experts, who prove
just the opposite. Always appeal for balance. Prosecute whistleblowers, or tie them up in ruinous, extended court battles.

A vital priority is executive control of political communication.
It helps to be a big player in the field of telecommunications; it is
even better to own the whole lot. When in government, build a
team of tough-minded public relations people who are good at
spinning everything. Get them to cultivate the image of the prime
minister as a dedicated, hard-working, self-made man, a leader in
whom everyone can recognise something of themselves, and what
they want to be. Grant journalists access to government plans in
return for favourable coverage. Put senior bureaucrats on notice
that they are required to report all contacts with journalists to the

prime minister's office. Stop leaks from retired or serving bureau-crats. Call it 'democratic sabotage' (Howard), and explain that leaking is bad because it wrecks the tradition of fidelity and confi-dentiality upon which the provision of frank and fearless advice by civil servants to politicians depends. If necessary, get the police to turn up on doorsteps to ask questions of suspected infidels. Pass legislation to slap bans on reporting high-priority matters, deten-tion without trial of suspects and witnesses, for instance. Pursue trouble-making journalists, especially those who refuse to divulge their sources. Have them prosecuted for libel, or contempt of court. Cultivate deaf ears to requests for disclosure of information. Ignore calls by lawyers' groups, NGOs and the press for new freedom-of-information laws, or their reform. Say often that you favour 'freedom of communication', but make it clear that there are strong grounds for withholding information, such as security, public order, fair play, the rights of business, the protection of the vulnerable, the needs of government. Starve the public of detailed stories about those who are the losers in society. Ban books. Censor the arts. Make every effort to muscle into the intellectual and artistic life of the country. Keep trusted commentators at the ready, on duty at all times.

Go on television to sign a contract with voters; say that if in the space of the next term of office the government has not properly fulfilled its promises, then it deserves not to be re-elected. Change everybody's sense of the short-term rhythm of electoral politics by planning for repeated victories. Aim to win several elections in a row, so that the rules of the political game and the whole atmos-phere of public life can be changed. Act as if the principle of checks and balances is no longer meaningful. Mobilise every (dirty) trick in the book of politics to achieve what others haven't achieved: three terms, four terms, five terms . . . six terms. If there are term limits, get them lifted. Once the trend is set, make the success story part of the appeal to go on repeating the triumphs. Satirise the dis-abilities of one's party-political opponents; be tough with those who show signs of causing trouble within the governing party. Stay calm in the face of unpromising election predictions; brush them off, as if they don't matter. Never hurry from office.

Encourage a mood swing towards petty seriousness. Cultivate a good smile, but insist that life and politics are no laughing matter; insist that government must be decisive, swift, no-nonsense business. Dissuade people from poking fun at their leaders; encourage them to get on with their daily lives. Reward 'friends', and 'friends of friends'. Turn politics into munificence. Spread the habit of political favouritism, a spoils system that hands out jobs for loyal men and women. Buy support, using contracts, jobs, returnable favours. But at the same time cultivate the sense that 'enemies' are on the loose. Draw up a list of dangerous types who don't swim in the mainstream: Islamic terrorists, communists, illegal immigrants, street criminals, pornographers, paedophiles, gays and lesbians, people who dislike business, animal rights types and other noisy minorities. Rob prisoners of their right to vote. Prove you are otherwise a good sport. Take an interest in sport. Own a team. Exploit the links between club ownership, advertising and national and global markets. Drone on about the importance of being 'practical'. Say things to cameras and microphones such as: 'The practical circumstances required us to do that.' Try an alternative: 'What we need to do is to adopt practical measures.' Or simply: 'Let's be practical.'

Encourage a collapse of faith in public protest. Show that it cannot work. Behind the scenes, get the police to threaten and intimidate would-be demonstrators; remind them that attempts to disrupt traffic, interrupt normal business and generally cause inconvenience will be dealt with harshly. Never admit that the government is wrong, even when most observers, and the government itself, know it is wrong. Never be pinned down. Use stock phrases that don't mean much, except that they serve as camouflage for political manoeuvrings. Say the right things and the wrong things, so that everyone who is listening hears what they want to hear. Analysts may call it 'dog whistling'. Some may say it is a jazzed-up version of the art of speaking out of both sides of the mouth. Ignore them; better still, question their credibility.

Find new ways of beating or sidestepping the polls. A most useful method is to moor public values in an ethereal something or other called 'the mainstream', or 'decent people', or 'working people' or 'civilised men and women' – 'the country', or 'the nation'. Speak little of democracy; make that word mean periodic elections. From time to time, dot the is and cross the ts by resorting to the language

FIGURE 125: Berlusconi: 'Everyone hates me: magistrates, journalists, pensioners, civil servants, housewives, students, professors, researchers, entrepreneurs, blue-collar workers, actors, comedians, doctors, nurses, foresters, temporary workers, intellectuals . . . but the People love me', a cartoon by Sergio Staino, *L'Unità*, 18 February 2005.

of überdemocracy: remind everybody that of course this is a country where the will of the people is respected. Be seen as a man of the people (Figure 125). Tell them repeatedly that they are in good hands, that your job is to allow them to get on with the things they really want: family, job, home, success. For those who openly disagree, who show signs of behaving like the people of old, issue warnings. If things get out of hand, call in the police; put the army on alert, but try at first to keep them out of sight. Be prepared to declare a 'national emergency', to seize control of communities, to impose a form of martial law. Emphasise to the media that the action is to be regretted. Stand firm when questioned about its necessity. Say it is dictated by common sense. Say it is what the people want.

Across Borders

The danger posed by überdemocracy was the way it behaved like a parasite, said our muse; feeding upon people's deep misgivings about politicians, parties and parliaments, it drained monitory democracy of its living substance, filling its dead shell with foreign matter. She said nothing further on the subject, instead bringing more unwelcome news, this time from a different direction. The democratic malaise, she said, was linked not only to domestic affairs. It had as well a global dimension, related to what she called *the cross-border squeeze on democratic institutions.*

She paused, before reminding us how representative democracy had been a type of self-government inscribed within a circle made up of households, local communities and national politics. She took the example of Britain. There, in the years after World War One, electorates had usually thought of themselves as living within families and local associations protected by local government and bound together by community spirit. In turn, these local dynamics were seen as linked to politics at the national level. Within this grand circle, local representatives were the cotter pin linking the family with the rest of the country. Politicians lived around the corner, knew the community and had vested interests. Usually in business, or members of a trade union, they cultivated roots, and would knock on doors and listen to the voices and concerns of local people. They also spoke in the legislature, and people listened. The buck stopped there. If they let locals down, they were given the boot.

Our muse agreed it was easy to romanticise times past, but the altered political geography of the age of monitory democracy was striking indeed. She mentioned a self-important character in Charles Dickens's *Our Mutual Friend* (1865), Mr Podsnap, who says, with complacency and self-assurance: 'Foreigners do as they do, sir, and that is the end of it.' Our guide warned latter-day Podsnaps that their times were long past. By the final decades of the twentieth century, virtually all governments, democratic or otherwise, operated within the multi-layered framework of an emerging world polity – the first ever – that unsettled democratic institutions everywhere.

Our mentor insisted that while globally interconnected governing institutions had first appeared in the age of representative democracy, they were poorly developed, usually toothless, and always at the mercy of big commerce, and big power politics. She cited the German scholar Max Weber, always an astute observer of international relations, who remarked (in 1897) that the 'trade expansion by all civilised bourgeois-controlled nations' would soon lead to a world in which 'only power, naked power' would decide each state's share in the world's resources.[7] He was not wrong. Our muse described how the period had witnessed unprecedented carve-ups of the world's land and oceans by a clutch of imperialist states: France, Italy, Germany, Portugal, Belgium, Holland, Japan, the United States and the world's most powerful political unit, Great Britain. Formal annexation had resulted. During the four decades before 1914, driven by states' search for new markets and political hegemony, a quarter of the earth's land had been formally colonised, or recolonised. The winner of the carve-up stakes was Britain, which added some 4 million square miles to its territories; France added about 3.5 million square miles, while Germany, Belgium and Italy each acquired about 1 million square miles.

The drive towards global imperialism – the word 'imperialism' itself first entered the vernacular of journalism and politics during the 1890s – was to rip representative democracy to shreds. Imperialism came wrapped in public rituals (like Britain's 'Empire Day', launched in 1902, mainly to win over captive audiences of flag-waving children), racialist language, nationalist appeals and calls for trade protection. Our muse admitted that the rivalries had triggered state-sponsored congresses and various other attempts to build new intergovernmental regulatory structures. For almost a century after the 1815 Congress of Vienna, convened for the purpose of bringing stability to a region once threatened by Napoleon's armies, the political elites of Europe had tried to keep peace and improve intergovernmental links by hosting face-to-face meetings, the forerunners of summits; between 1850 and 1913, more than one hundred such congresses were held, touching on matters ranging from submarine cables and fishing zones to the opium trade, unemployment and 'the Eastern question'. In addition to congresses, efforts were put into convening the first state-sponsored international exhibitions and fairs, like the 1851 Great Exhibition, hosted in London at the height of Britain's imperial confidence by Prince Albert. Other regulatory structures were also put in place, including the International Penitentiary Commission, the International Maritime Bureau against the Slave Trade and the Permanent Court of Arbitration.

Our guide pointed out that although such bodies were set up for the stated higher purposes of bringing legal harmony, peace and good government to the world, most of them were in fact geared to the expansion of commerce, state power and communications. Bodies like the International Central American Office, set up by Mexico and the United States for the purpose of politically integrating Nicaragua, El Salvador and Honduras, were crafted as regional bodies with strictly defined mandates. Other intergovernmental bodies had had broadly global remits, and their numbers had grown rapidly. The International Telegraph Union (ITU) and the International Commission for the Cape Spartel Light in Tangier, both established in 1865, were the pacesetters, nearly all of which, however, were not intergovernmental bodies with an independent life of their own. Member governments typically held them in tight rein, confining them to the role of forums for the exchange of information and policy coordination. It was true, said our muse, that the road to 1914 promised no shortage of proposed new global governing structures. Some successes were to follow, in the shape of intergovernmental bodies like the Allied Maritime Transport Executive (AMTE), established for the purpose of removing bottlenecks and regulating the flows of global shipping. There were even calls, in a surprising variety of contexts, for what Alfred Zimmern, founder of the School of International Studies in Geneva, had proudly called 'planetary patriotism'. But, according to our guide, the whole project of building intergovernmental structures was doomed. It failed properly to address the harsh facts of disorderly financial markets (caused by 'speculation' and what the British economist Lionel Robbins had called 'fashionable fraud'). It also failed spectacularly to deal with big-power military and diplomatic rivalries and – presaged by mass protests against immigration during the 1890s in countries like Australia and the United States – strong popular resistance to worldly values in many of the countries that had weight to throw around in the world.

National chauvinism served as an epitaph for the *belle époque* of representative democracy. By the early years of the twentieth century, the belief, spread by writers and politicians like Norman Angell (1872–1967), that the dynamic of integration was unstoppable, that it made war between highly developed industrial states effectively obsolete, fell apart. The opium dream of world peace gave way to gunboat diplomacy, then to something far grimmer: humanity's first ever global war, followed by three extraordinary decades of violence. World War One was a great setback for representative democracy. The depravity of the times was quickly plumbed by pressure groups like the British-based Union of Democratic Control – probably the world's first citizens' effort, begun in early September 1914, to subject state war-making powers to public and parliamentary scrutiny, in the name of democracy. The carnage produced by the clash of men and steel – 8 million people died and 21 million were wounded – was finally halted in 1918. Peace seemed at first to promise a new beginning. As whole empires and dozens of monarchies collapsed, the first Czechoslovak president, Thomas Masaryk, had spoken of the post-war world as a 'laboratory atop a vast graveyard'. Woodrow Wilson was in no doubt that the experiment had everything to do with making the world safe for civil liberties and political democracy. That sentiment was championed in Britain by the above-mentioned Union for Democratic Control, which by the summer of 1921 had attracted support from more than three hundred groups (mainly women's organisations, cooperatives and trade unions) with over a million affiliated members and sister organisations in several countries; in the first ever Labour government of 1924, fifteen ministers were paid-up members of the UDC. But its fortunes during this period were exceptional, for elsewhere in Europe social confusion, disappointment and political resistance to representative democracy flourished. Under pressure from nationalist demagogues, peasant radicals, unemployed workers, fascist paramilitaries, bandits and Bolsheviks, the house of representative democracy collapsed.

According to our guide, after 1945 things had initially looked bad for democracy, largely because of the onset of the Cold War; the cruel rule that democracy within states can thrive only when military pressures are lifted from their borders looked as if it would continue to have its way. But then, against stupendous odds, had come a round of intergovernmental institution building that in the history of the world had no precedent, in terms either of its scope or its depth. The new world polity that resulted was familiar to many citizens and all governments of the twenty-first century, despite the fact that its governing institutions were often ignored in textbooks, and never appeared as such on maps of the world. This world polity was an agglomeration of governing institutions caught up in worldwide webs of interdependence made possible by communications technologies that greatly reduced, sometimes nearly to zero, time and space barriers. The consequence was that governmental institutions of various shapes and sizes – local courts and governments, the parliaments of territorial states, quasi-imperial powers like China, regional bodies like the European Union, ASEAN and Mercosur, global bodies like the United Nations and the International Criminal Tribunal based in The Hague – all found themselves, despite their many differences, increasingly caught up in thickening, fast-evolving webs of links, both bilateral and multilateral.

Our muse noted some examples of the trend towards joined-up government. She mentioned local court decisions, like the order, applied (in early August 2000) by a US District Court in Manhattan, requiring an alleged war criminal and co-founder of the Serbian Democratic Party, Radovan Karadžić, to pay US $745 million to a group of twelve Bosnian women who filed a civil suit, accusing him of responsibility for killings, rapes, kidnappings, torture and other atrocities. Our guide noted as well the much-discussed impact of European integration upon the internal politics of EU member states. She pointed to the push around the world to harmonise immigration and extradition laws, environmental protection measures and the economic policies of Asian states such as China, Japan, Vietnam, Indonesia, Australia and New Zealand. And she cited a very detailed example: the 1999 OECD Convention on Combating Bribery of Foreign Public Officials in International Business Transactions, a convention that was soon ratified by nearly forty countries, including Japan, Brazil, Turkey and the world's major exporters, a convention that committed signatory countries to pass laws that criminalised the bribing of officials abroad.

Our historian was sure that the growth of joined-up government on a world scale meant in each case that those who exercised power anywhere on the face of the earth began to grow aware of the importance of feedback effects. A single event, transaction or decision somewhere within the wider system – the accession of China to the World Trade Organization and the armed attacks on Washington and New York, to take just two examples from one fateful week in September 2001 – regularly touched off a string of consequences, bounce-back and boomerang and butterfly effects, elsewhere in the world. What our guide wanted to say was that the decisions of every government, no matter how large or small, were potentially or actually *unrestricted* in scope and effect. Governments were no longer islands. What they said and did (or did not say or do) regularly impinged upon the lives of others elsewhere on the face of the earth. International relations experts called these 'spillover effects', and for a good reason. The age of homespun government and autarky was over. Despite the geographic distances and different interests that separated governments of various shapes and sizes, all of them found that they had to cope daily with the fact of their deepening interdependence.

Our muse was concerned at this point to prevent a potential misunderstanding. During the second half of the twentieth century, she said, the rapid growth of cross-border governing institutions did not point towards 'world government' in any simple sense. The pattern of joined-up government was different, and certainly more complicated.

The global polity was better described as a conglomeration of interdependent, overlapping zones of governing institutions (see Figure 126). Its inner core (A) happened to coincide with the

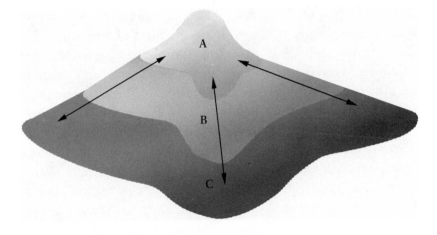

FIGURE 126: Zones of interlocking governing institutions operating at the global level.

heartlands of monitory democracy. It included the peoples of North America, Japan, South Korea, the Council of Europe countries, and Australasia, where the webs of governmental interdependence were longest and thickest, the density of efficient telecommunications heaviest, and land and sea barriers to the movement of people, goods, decisions and information consequently least meaningful. This inner core, from which thick and long webs of interdependence radiated, found itself caught up in several outer zones of political power. One of them (B) comprised the big, populous countries of India and Brazil, and quasi-imperial states like China, Indonesia and the Russian Federation. Except for Brazil and India, and possibly Indonesia, which attempted a transition to democracy in the early years of the new millennium, this zone included states that were not power-sharing democracies (our muse reminded us that China and Russia were in fact post-totalitarian regimes). Although jealous guardians of their own territorial 'sovereignty', the states within this zone were nevertheless tightly interlinked with the rest of the world, so that, for instance, India played a vital global role in the production and distribution of information technologies, while Russia, the world's second-largest arms peddler, had its most developed supplier–buyer relationships with India, China and Iran.

Then there was a third zone (C), one in which the webs of governmental interdependence were thinnest and frayed at the edges: a zone of less powerful small states, or proto-states – Nigeria, Bahrein, Bolivia, the Philippines, Thailand, among others – some of them showing signs of clustering, in the form of regional bodies like ASEAN and CARICOM (the Caribbean Community and Common Market) and through agreements like the Free Trade of the Americas. Our muse noted that a few of these governments, like Pakistan, Zimbabwe and Sudan, were failing states that tottered on the extreme outer margins of the emerging world polity, where worldwide webs of governing institutions gave way to no-go areas, in which institutions like the United Nations were unwelcome, or ineffective. These outer fringes included regimes, Burma for instance, that were hyper-jealous of their territorial integrity, and whose authorities, despite some important connections with the rest of the world, in matters of oil, drugs and guns, were openly hostile to the worldly effects of global interdependence. This outer zone, underneath and beyond the institutions of the global polity, also included the world's grim landscapes of uncivil war: a nether world of blood-soaked, land-mined, ruined and rubbled territories, like Chechnya, western and southern Sudan, and the ill-named Democratic Republic of Congo, where effective government institutions hardly existed at all.

Our muse wanted to say lots of extra things, but here she noted how the unevenly distributed global networks of government proved to be highly unstable, mainly because they were riddled with contradictions. Various fault lines regularly produced shock effects on the whole system, which is why she reported that it did not bring peace and good government to the world, let alone foster democratic institutions worldwide. She acknowledged there were times, in response to major global catastrophes, when the whole global polity became so chilled down with concern that its different components – like bundles of atoms reduced under laboratory conditions to temperatures just above absolute zero – momentarily sang together in unison. Our muse admitted as well that its multi-layered, criss-crossing institutions had certain advantages, like the give-and-take flexibility and the capacity for adaptation to changing circumstances that came with a plurality of institutions. But she remained firm, and put her point more sharply: the world polity of the early twenty-first century *destabilised* governments, monitory democracies included. Whatever advantages flowed from its clumsy, overlapping structures, this polity suffered the symptoms of what physicists called entropy, the condition of confusion, inertness and self-degradation that results from formlessness.

Our guide gave some examples. Although the world's peoples inhabited a planet shaped by over a century of global institution building – manifested in arrangements like Universal Standard Time, the International Court of Justice, and United Nations treaties, from the Declaration of Human Rights to the Law of the Sea – the lack of regional and global governing capacity remained a basic problem for monitory democracies everywhere. She went on to say that during the eighteenth and nineteenth centuries many representative democrats fought against monopolies of power, whereas monitory democrats were faced in many contexts with the exact opposite problem, the *under-concentration of power*. Monitory democracy, she said, was weakened by the lack of global driving seats and steering mechanisms, plus the ineffectiveness of many that did exist. The world polity of the early decades of the twenty-first century spawned no investment treaty and had no central bank or securities and investment commission that could have imposed restrictions on the destructive flows of hot money, risk-laundering and leveraging investments and price hikes that regularly produced market bubbles that threatened many governments, democracies included. The world polity had no properly functioning parliament through which demands from the world's population could have been peacefully channelled. There was no executive power, for instance an elected, fixed-term and impeachable president, or governing council of the world. There were no political parties that campaigned globally, on a regular basis, trying to drum up support for new policies and new institutions. There was no global criminal justice or policing system – with sharp teeth – to deal with a flourishing global (war) crime industry. And aside from the American armed forces, there was no global army or global strategy for dealing decisively with the wars and violence that regularly bedevilled the world.

There were times, recorded our muse, when funding shortages, understaffing, bureaucratic sclerosis and jurisdictional disputes at the intergovernmental level seemed to drag existing democracies into power plays that bore a striking resemblance to tragicomedy. She gave an example: the difficult business of setting up the International Criminal Tribunal for the former Yugoslavia (ICTY). The establishment of the world's first ever global war crimes tribunal (in May 1993) seemed finally to put into practice the dream of Cornelis van Vollenhoven (1874–1933), the great Dutch jurist who forcefully – but unsuccessfully – defended the need for an international criminal court during the dying days of representative democracy.[8] The birth of the ICTY nonetheless proved difficult, our muse reported. It was delayed for fifteen months because of wrangling within the United Nations Security Council; and when the Chief Prosecutor was eventually appointed, he had to pay out of his own pocket his first air fare to New York and The Hague.

He was told that there was no budget for the tribunal, and that it would have to be approved by the Advisory Committee on Administrative and Budgetary Questions (ACABQ). That body with a lovely acronym then insisted that at least one indictment would have to be issued before funding could be approved. That forced on the fledgling tribunal a safe but low-level indictment for war crimes, Dragan Nikolić. It also necessitated many irritating and time-consuming meetings about organisational – budgetary and evidential – matters with United Nations officials, and with Secretary-General Boutros-Ghali, who voiced grave doubts over the original decision of the Security Council to establish the Office of the Chief Prosecutor as an independent unit. Mechanisms were not put in place to arrest vermin like Radovan Karadžić and General Ratko Mladić. Indeed, Admiral Leighton Smith, then commander of the United Nations Implementing Force (IFOR), adamantly opposed despatching troops to catch indicted war criminals. Even in the nasty business of suspected or confirmed mass graves, noted our muse, United Nations forces refused to get involved in search or night-watch duties; at one point, the tribunal engaged the services of a willing Norwegian non-governmental organisation and their sniffer dogs to do the necessary dirty work.

The difficulty of setting up badly needed cross-border institutions was matched by their public unaccountability. According to our guide, the fledgling global polity was not quite a species of absolutism, if only because its core zone (plus countries in outer zones, like India and Brazil) harboured rich networks of monitory institutions designed to expose and oppose hubris. In the fields of cross-border politics, monitory democracy was nonetheless a rare plant. Life-and-death matters were regularly decided behind many millions of backs. Obscure, secretive structures of cross-border government and law regularly flouted the vital rules of monitory democracy: time-limited power granted on the basis of free and fair voting, the duty of power wielders to solicit different opinions and to explain and justify their actions publicly, even the obligation to resign in cases of gross mismanagement, or misconduct.

In the era of joined-up government, the powerful offered various alibis for staying quiet about their motives, and their moves. They liked to say that decisions were foisted on them by global forces (critics called this 'policy laundering'); or that the fools were those who revealed their hand to opponents and enemies (our muse called this the Rumsfeld Rule: 'In difficult situations, governments do not discuss pressing matters'[9]). Cross-border power brokers also repeated some version of Plato's rule that affairs of government were too difficult to explain to ill-informed publics. Next, our muse pointed to the alleged facts of complexity: the fragmentation of political authority, combined with a technocratic mindset among officials and a lack of public-friendly, well-trained administrative staff, ensured that many parts of the world polity were closed off from public scrutiny of any kind. Matters were worsened by references to the supposed imperatives of markets, and to what our historian called the hubris of distance: despite the noblest public-spirited motives, many leaders and managers seemed uninterested in the way decisions blocked or taken at one point on the planet regularly had long-range effects on the lives of millions of people they would never meet.

Our guide noted there were moments when all these anti-democratic alibis converged, to produce savage effects on citizens and their representatives. The in-camera tribunals set up under NAFTA (the North American Free Trade Agreement), and the 'green room' system operated by the WTO, were kangaroo courts in all but name. Deliberately avoiding public scrutiny, relying instead on techniques like distorted voting rights, money, spin, organised secrecy and legal coercion, these cross-border institutions worked in favour of the most powerful governments, the most powerful corporations, and sometimes both.* They certainly paved the

---

*The politics that took place within these arcane bodies had a distinctively eighteenth-century feel. Take the case of the tribunals set up under NAFTA: these enabled corporations to veto government restrictions upon corporate power, for instance by bringing a case before a tribunal that operated in camera. If a company considered that its commercial rights had been violated, and if the tribunal found in favour of the company and its complaint, then a government was legally obliged to make a payout to the corporation. During 2001, in a much publicised case, exactly this outcome was sought through the time-wasting suit brought by the Canadian company Methanex before a NAFTA tribunal. Methanex produced a gasoline additive (MTBE) that accidentally leached into the municipal water supply of the city of Santa Monica. Most of its wells had to be shut down. The state of California reacted by imposing a ban on the use or sale of the additive, which prompted Methanex in turn to take its case to NAFTA, claiming almost a billion dollars' compensation from the United States government. *Methanex Corp. v. United States of America* took almost four years to resolve. The 2005 Final Award fortunately dismissed all of the claims, and Methanex was ordered to pay the legal fees and arbitral expenses of the United States government.

way for decisions wholly unrepresentative of broader social interests, our muse pointed out. She said that cross-border politics looked and felt ever more like a game played among wealthy and powerful elites. Social justice was not their concern, and it was therefore not surprising, said our guide, that by the beginning of the new millennium every democratic country experienced sharp increases in their wealth gaps, to levels not seen since the late 1920s. She cited reliable evidence from the United States. By 2005, more than one-fifth of its national income (21.2 per cent) accrued to just 1 per cent of earners. America had become a country where the CEO of the giant company Wal-Mart took home, in pay and perks, nine hundred times the earnings of his average employee – a country where the estimated wealth of the Wal-Mart founders' family ($90 billion) was equivalent to the combined wealth of the bottom 40 per cent of the American population. Such trends towards social inequality gave a bad name to global governance, said our guide. They convinced growing numbers of citizens that governments at home and abroad had their own business agenda, that organisations like the IMF, the OECD and the World Bank were in the pockets of big corporations, speculators and financiers, and that hard-won citizens' rights at home were being gobbled up by unchecked worldwide 'market forces' protected by the actions and inactions of cross-border governing structures. The conclusion easily fuelled despondency, as was pointed out by the distinguished Canadian writer John Ralston Saul. Our muse recalled how he had put into words what many people sensed in their gut: governments had become so duplicitous, or so powerless, in the face of global forces that the whole world felt ever less democratic, as if it was in the grip of buccaneering forces that cared nothing for democratic checks and balances.

Nationalism

The feeling of powerlessness in the face of joined-up global government and market forces fanned the fires of old European nationalism, our navigator explained. Helped by hindsight, she spotted the way its flames licked all four corners of the earth, in countries otherwise as different as Russia, India, Venezuela, China and Iran. By the first decade of the new millennium, she said, every monitory democracy had its nationalist party, or outspoken representatives of the nationalist cause. Among the most articulate was a man whose many admirers loved to call the Father of the Serbian Nation, Dobrica Ćosić (b. 1921). Here was more than a distinguished writer, whose most famous novel, *Time of Death* (1972–5), described the fate of the Serbian people during the first year of World War One. Here was a man whose thoughts were worth remembering, said our muse, because they so fluently spoke the grammar of nationalism in all its ugly seductiveness.[10]

'It is only in great nations that the human personality, the individual can win respect', said the man of letters. 'The prior moral duty in small nations is to subordinate the individual – to the community, the people and their state. No Serb can be human unless they are a Serb, conscious of their nation.' It followed, said Ćosić, that the task of building a nation and protecting its territory by means of a state has priority over democracy. Respect for language and land, religious and patriotic customs – songs, prayers, fairy tales, the lives of saints and heroes – are far more important than voting, party competition and elections. Put differently, electoral democracy is significant for nations only insofar as it helps them decide their own destiny; it could legitimately be used (he told his close friend Slobodan Milošević) to protect a nation and build a unified state by silencing its enemies, for instance by cunningly 'rebutting their claims that we are an undemocratic country'. Otherwise, democracy is dispensable.

Ćosić was sure that this formula applied unconditionally to endangered people, like the Serbian nation. 'Can a democrat deny Serbs in Croatia and Bosnia and Herzegovina rights that are granted to Croats and Muslims?' he asked. 'Is defending the legitimate human right of Serbian people to live in their own state nationalism and "pan-Serbism"? Isn't that a fundamental democratic right?' The answer to that question was clear, insisted Ćosić. Wherever Serbs lived, there was Serbia, in need of the protection of the Serbian state. Never mind (commented our muse) that this principle falsely supposed that all Serbs were already agreed on what it meant to be a Serb; and never mind (she added) that this principle in practice involved murderous disruption of people's lives, their physical removal from land or the armed redrawing of territorial boundaries. Ćosić brushed aside such objections by saying that Serbs had long suffered bad press. 'Serbia is being slandered horribly around the world. By everyone!'

Its victimisation at the hands of hostile neighbouring nations was part of the same power game. European integration was in effect a conspiracy to undo Serbia. 'Europe is against Serbs and Serbia', he wrote. 'Europe thinks of itself as the role model of democracy. But she is also the soil that grew wars and enslavement, concentration camps, crematories and lies.' Behind Europe and its double standards stood the emergent American-led world order, a new ruling order led by people who turned 'human rights into human deceit'. Its leaders spoke of the end of history and the global triumph of democracy, but the plain truth was that this order was a 'democracy of prevaricators, thieves and perverts, villains'. The 1992 London summit on the future of Yugoslavia – said Ćosić – proved that Western democracy was but a mask for wealth, money and power. 'It was a summit of world tyrants and mediocre, mighty bureaucrats of the "new world order": totalitarian democracy and its European satellites', he snapped. 'It was a spectacle of triumphant Western pragmatism: to win victory for injustice and force at all costs. They succeeded.' Then came a parting shot. 'Communist leaders at least had rhetoric that pretended to be principled and universal', said Ćosić . 'These "democrats" speak the language of the Nazis – they lie, threaten, command, judge. The Serbian people were judged. Judged and prosecuted.'

The Hotel

Tinged with drops of self-pity and melodrama, the writer's rhetoric implied a political task: to defend the right of Serbian people to fly their flag high, to think of themselves as a single fist prepared, using guns when necessary, to defend their nation against 'foreigners' and 'enemies'. The mentality proved lethal, our muse recorded. Spurred on by a 'yoghurt revolution' led by nationalist supporters of Slobodan Milošević – the so-called revolution earned its name from the thousands of yoghurt packages thrown by an angry crowd at the parliament of Vojvodina in October 1988 – the rump state of Yugoslavia in Serbian hands propelled south-eastern Europe into a decade-long war that claimed the lives of many hundreds of thousands of people and drove several million citizens from their homes. In the age of monitory democracy, said our guide, the problem of state and para-state violence was not confined to the western Balkans. Armed states spurred on by nationalism were bad news for monitory democracy everywhere. Let loose on unarmed citizens, they inflicted great damage on individuals, groups and whole networks of monitory institutions designed to check and balance power, to put a stop to wrongdoings. In places like Burma, Zimbabwe and Chechnya, violent states and their hired hands were responsible for arresting, torturing, raping and killing journalists, human rights activists and writers. There were times, recalled our guide, when they turned against innocent civilians by using state-of-the-art methods to frighten all their subjects into submission, seemingly to prove that democracy in any form could be put to death.

Our muse offered a chilling example: the secret network of concentration camps operated by the Argentine junta during the 1970s. Its biggest camp, run by the School of Naval Mechanics, was called ESMA. Located in a chic district of Buenos Aires, within earshot of the football stadium where Argentina won the World Cup in 1978, at the very moment that its government was terrorising its own people, ESMA resembled a hotel of horrors managed by naval officers and serviced by teenage naval conscripts, and by interrogators bearing nicknames like 220, Kawasaki and Snake.

The horrors unfolded in a large, three-storey building camouflaged by well-manicured lawns and clumps of slim eucalyptus and purple-flowering jacarandas. ESMA received guests twenty-four hours a day, delivered at high speed from various parts of the city in Ford Falcons driven by naval staff in civilian clothing. Those checking in were immediately taken downstairs, to the basement, which featured a first-aid centre and a recreation room where hardworking staff spent time chatting, sipping coffee and whisky, and playing cards. After being documented, photographed and blindfolded, each guest was given orders to reassure a relative by telephone that they were in good hands. Then began their interrogation and torture – non-stop, without mercy, usually for three or four days.

There were no exceptions. Even infants and children were victims of this basement crime, which was carried out in a large room equipped with high-voltage pincers and a big tank of water in which reluctant guests, young and old, were transformed into submarines. Constant music – one song, played over and over again, all day and night, at deafening levels – helped to muffle the shouts of the torturers and the grunts and screams of the tortured. Those who survived the first round of abuse – many died during their opening interrogation – were escorted, still blindfolded, to the third floor of the hotel. There they were chained up like stray dogs, in narrow pens called 'kennels' (*cuchas*).

The third floor was a corridor leading from life to disappearance to death. It devoured nearly 5000 victims. Only 200 citizens lived to tell stories of how some of their mates were injected with sedatives on Wednesday evenings, whisked from the hotel to an air force base, loaded on to a plane, then dumped – their stomachs slit so that they would sink like stones – into the cold waters of the Atlantic. The lucky victims, those with useful skills needed to keep the establishment running, could expect to survive a little longer, on condition that they earned their keep. By night, cooped up in their kennels, shackled and hooded, writers, journalists and those with university degrees tried to sleep through loud music, kicks and punches. By day, they worked office hours in a glass-walled room called the fish tank; there, under the nose of guards who could turn nasty in the blink of an eye, they drew on the services of a librarian to write speeches, prepare press reports and even summarise books by famous authors – Sartre and Camus were fashionable at the time – for naval officers conscious of the need to do something about their ignorance. Meanwhile, plumbers, electricians and other tradesmen among the victims helped in the upkeep of the hotel. They were put to work as well outside the camp, for instance refurbishing their own confiscated properties, or others' apartments and houses, which were sold on the private market by the torturers, who doubled as a gang of money-grubbing common criminals.

The crooks naturally fancied themselves as womanisers, with

ladies dangling on their arms, even if they were injured or half dead. Civilised pretences were important, even to barbarous murderers, one of whom reportedly liked to say that he'd rather be in shit up to his elbows than shit up to his shoulders. So women prisoners were taken for the night in Ford Falcons to city bars and clubs, where they were expected to perform. Others were invited on day trips, to country resorts, where their captors offered them wine, forced them to swim and to play volleyball. Back at the hotel, the same women were treated much worse than slaves. Sometimes it happened that a woman was raped every single time she asked permission to go to the toilet. Those who suffered pregnancy were fattened up on extra rations of sandwiches and tea, moved to the labour ward on the same floor, allowed to give birth, presented with gifts, then made to bear the unbearable: the disappearance of their baby into the unknown arms of an armed forces family.

The Triangle of Violence

The odious task of recovering the bodies and missing children and testimonies of those who were disappeared for a long time dogged countries like Argentina, China, Chile and Cambodia, reported our guide. She noted that the emergence of a politics of remembering the dead was something unprecedented in the history of democracy. It belonged to the era of monitory democracy. The new politics of memory, she said, was driven by the conviction of citizens and monitory groups that armed states tend to be amnesiacs, and that therefore they could not be trusted to bring justice to the survivors and victims of their unspeakable crimes. In contrast to kangaroo courts, legal closures and imposed amnesties, this politics supposed that there was a fate worse than death – the fate of being forgotten – and that organised disappearances had set a dangerous precedent. The damage had to be undone: rats had to be flushed from their nests, and those who had been disappeared perforce deserved a permanent vote in the affairs of the living. It was necessary to see that justice was done. Public warnings against the future repetition of past crimes were also necessary. And personal responsibility for what had happened – even the responsibility of

FIGURE 127: The boarded-up, paint-splashed residence of a former Buenos Aires policeman and suspected torturer and assassin, Rodolfo González Conti, who had violated his house arrest order, September 2005.

those who kept quiet and stood by in cowed silence – needed public acknowledgement. The agony of the disappeared and their loved ones had to be remembered publicly: by silent vigils, noisy demonstrations, the building of websites and public monuments, and the setting up of memory commissions. Another common tactic was the use of graffiti, barbed wire, splashes of red paint and other daring forms of public 'outing' of suspected murderers, rapists and torturers (Figure 127); in parts of Spanish America, noted our guide, outing tactics were popularly known as *escrachar*, an old verb ('to break, to destroy') that activists invested with the brand-new meaning of 'to strike out publicly at someone's reputation for the purpose of shaming them and revealing to others the terrible things they have done in private'.

The new politics of memory proved there were positive domestic remedies for state violence but – here our muse paused, to widen her horizons and draw a contrast – twenty-first-century solutions to the problem of global violence were in short supply.

She recalled that, shortly after the atomic bombing of Hiroshima and Nagasaki, George Orwell had written: 'The great age of democracy and of national self-determination was the age of the musket and the rifle.' The present nuclear age, he continued, was of a different – more depressing – order. 'Had the atomic bomb turned out to be something as cheap and easily manufactured as a bicycle or an alarm clock', Orwell said, 'it might well have plunged us back into barbarism, but it might, on the other hand, have meant the end of national sovereignty and of the highly-centralized police state.' The mega-technology of nuclear weapons in fact had different effects. The bomb had now transformed the final Armageddon from religious prophecy into factual possibility; it had made thinkable the violent destruction of all remaining democratic states and their civilised societies. The musket and the rifle were inaccurate, yet they were controllable. But now, according to Orwell, the human species stood in danger of either destroying itself with its own grotesque weapons, or destroying democracy with a new form of servitude wrapped in a 'Cold War' peace that was not really peace at all. 'Looking at the world as a whole', he concluded, 'the drift for many decades has been not towards anarchy but towards the reimposition of slavery.'[11]

Orwell was not to know that the spirit and institutions of democracy were soon to be revived – that the new age of monitory democracy was to be born – but according to our female sage his comments on the menacing implications of the weapon that proved brighter and deadlier than a thousand suns proved to be astute. Orwell correctly put his finger on the fact that violence was perhaps the greatest threat to the spirit and institutions of democracy. Our muse reminded us that monitory democracies produced troubling amounts of violence at home – rapes, muggings, gangland crimes, bizarre Columbine High School-style murders. She recalled as well that democracies like Athens and the early United States had often been bellicose, and that the wars they waged upon other states bred hubris and disruption at home. Yet democracies also had quite a good record in not going to war against other democracies. Democracies' more recent reliance on computerised, 'risk-free' aerial bombardment – minimising the number of body bags – seemed to externalise and minimise the threat of violence. So, too, did the gathering strength of citizens' conviction that war was unworthy of heroism – that waving the flag, slipping into military uniform and going off to fight wars was the job of professionals.

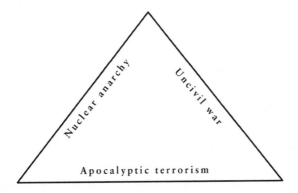

FIGURE 128: The triangle of violence.

Unfortunately, reported our muse, this did not mean that war slipped over the horizons of monitory democracies, or that it easily put an end to violence and its destructive effects. Indeed, despite the end of the Cold War, evidence mounted that in the new millennium these democracies began to fall under the shadow of what she called a new triangle of violence (Figure 128).

One side of this triangle, she explained, was the instability caused by nuclear-tipped states in the post-Cold War world polity. The United States, which could and did act as a vigilante power backed by the threat of nuclear strikes, was forced during the age of monitory democracy to co-exist with four power blocks, all of which had gone nuclear: Europe and India, China and Russia. The geometry of this arrangement clearly differed from the extended freeze imposed by the Cold War, when most parts of the world lived according to the rule that peace between the United States and the Soviet Union was impossible, but open nuclear war between them was not impossible, but unlikely.

With the collapse of bipolar confrontation at the end of the 1980s, this rule changed, said our guide. There was no evidence of the dawn of a post-nuclear age, and the freedom from the fear of nuclear accident or attack that that would have brought. Instead, said our muse, peace became possible but war much more likely, principally because a nasty form of nuclear anarchy settled on the whole world. Perhaps it was true that nuclear weapons so reduced the need for mass mobilisation of troops that they had enabled a permanent 'civilianisation' of daily life in many monitory democracies. It was also perhaps true that the probability of a nuclear apocalypse, in which the earth and its peoples were accidentally or deliberately blown sky-high, had been reduced. Perhaps. Yet our muse warned the friends of democracy that perpetual peace was nowhere on the horizon.

Why? She noted how the key nuclear powers grew preoccupied with seeing through what was called a new revolution in military affairs. This revolution was geared to electronic intelligence gathering, computerised communications networks, protective screens, and highly destructive, precision-guided or 'smart' weapons which could be used anywhere on the globe. Our guide noted that such weapons did not eliminate from battle what the early nineteenth-century military strategist Clausewitz had called 'frictions'. There were doubts too about whether the claimed level of precision of the weapons could affordably and reliably be achieved; or whether civilians uninterested in military heroism would be prepared to witness, in silent gratitude, the killing of others by remotely piloted vehicles, nano-weapons and sophisticated information systems. Major wars using these and more old-fashioned weapons remained a long-term possibility, including even the use of nuclear-tipped weapons in conflicts that originated in local upheavals and wars.

Whether nuclear conflict could be avoided was doubtful, she said. Alternative scenarios were just as likely. In the early decades of the twenty-first century, monitory democracies found themselves confronted by the real possibility that nuclear materials would be stolen or spilled, or that there would be further nuclear reactor meltdowns, or the open use of nuclear weapons. A taste of things to come, reported our guide, was governments' talk of radiological weapons and dirty bombs, the private trafficking of 'orphaned' nuclear materials and the routine dropping of depleted uranium shells on the victims of war. Meanwhile, nuclear weapons sprouted like the dragon's teeth of Cadmus. Nuclear weapons were in abundance – the arsenals of the United States and the Russian Federation alone each contained somewhere around 7000 nuclear warheads. And despite the long-standing Anti-Ballistic Missile Treaty, nuclear capacity spread, as could be seen in the entry of North Korea and Iran into the devil's nuclear lair, and in the nuclear arms races between Pakistan and India, and between Israel, Iran and the Arab states.

All this happened despite any prior agreements about the rules of nuclear confrontation and despite the fact (revealed in the National Missile Defense system planned by the American government in the early years of the new millennium) that the issue of nuclear weapons was now intimately bound up with the so-called 'modernisation' of weapons systems in general. American officials, aware that the old Cold War was over, meanwhile began to speak of a 'generic' threat, a bundle of potential dangers that might well arise at any moment, somewhere else in the world. Hence the investment, from the early 1980s, of some $60 billion in the project of developing a National Missile Defense programme designed to take aim at 'rogue' powers equipped with nuclear weapons. One trouble with this roguish project, said our guide, was that there were potentially large numbers of fellow rogues. The US State Department listed forty-four governments blessed with nuclear weapons capacity, which helped explain why the world's governing institutions were steadily plagued by newcomer nuclear governments.

The world's first nuclear confrontation unrelated to the Cold War – five tests conducted by democratic India in May 1998, followed by seven tests by Pakistan – was reinforced by a long sequence of new and equally threatening developments, noted our muse. These included North Korea's efforts to build weapons, as well as worries about the undetectable 'basement proliferation' of gas-centrifuge and laser-enrichment methods of producing nuclear weapons material. There were as well continuing doubts about Russia's ability to keep safe its nuclear weapons and materials (despite American contributions of over $2 billion per annum under the Nunn–Lugar legislation). The sinister trends included the American interest in developing 'low-yield' nuclear weapons that could be used against hardened, or deep underground targets. Things were not helped by American assurances that it would not object to China's plans to expand its nuclear arsenals, plans that in practice led to the end of the worldwide moratorium on nuclear testing, once codified in the Comprehensive Test Ban Treaty. Thanks to all these initiatives, concluded our guide, the worst fears of Orwell began to materialise during this period. There was a nuclear version of Gresham's Law: nuclear armaments bred nuclear armaments. It was true, she said, that talk of 'throw-weight gaps', 'windows of vulnerability' and 'missile gaps' no longer echoed through government corridors. Yet ominous signs were on the wall and one implication was unavoidable: all monitory democracies were endangered by a world polity that produced a rabble of self-interested nuclear powers that had no intention of getting rid of their wicked weapons.

Our guide bore more bad news. Monitory democracies, she noted, were physically threatened and morally troubled as well by the violence unleashed in uncivil wars, by armed conflicts that ripped apart political institutions, poisoned the institutions of civil society and flung their combatants into a terrible preoccupation with survival. Examples were not hard to find. They included nearly three decades of fighting in Sudan, where constant imports of arms had reached the hands of government and non-government forces, who had then conspired, in the name of acquiring land, cattle, wealth (including oil) and power, to kill at least 2.5 million people and to produce another six million refugees in their own country – internally displaced people, in the jargon of aid agencies that found themselves unable to cope with the depth and scale of the many disasters that befell the people of the region.

Uncivil wars of the Sudanese kind were marked by terrible violence and suffering. They often bordered on genocide. Those trapped in the maelstroms of violence found their existential horizons shrunk by unspeakable cruelties, said our guide. She described how armies, militias and ragtag criminal gangs raped, pillaged and murdered, to the point where sometimes all remaining pockets of civility were shredded, beyond repair. The suffering was typically fuelled by talk of 'the people' – uncivil wars often had a pseudo-democratic side to them – but above all by global flows of arms, money and gangs of men, who took advantage of the crumbling local political institutions and the jostling of competitor power groups for territory and resources. Whole populations were consequently sucked into whirlpools of cruelty. Our muse was sure that the results could hardly be thought of as 'civil war', a term that supposed that combatants engaged their opponents in a disciplined struggle for control over the key resources of territorial state power. Rwanda, Sudan, Sierra Leone, Kashmir, the Democratic Republic of Congo and many other conflicts were different. Those who fought and those who suffered made a terrible descent into hell – towards a place where violence was no longer a means to an end, but a grisly end in itself.

Uncivil wars morally troubled democrats of the twenty-first century. According to our muse they bred demands for military or 'humanitarian' intervention. Monitory democracies found themselves in a conundrum: whether or not to sail ships and fly thousands of troops to places on earth where life had become hellish. Our muse noted, with strong emphasis, just how difficult it was in the age of communicative abundance to hide from these atrocities. If democracies launched what was called 'humanitarian intervention' – as when India moved into East Pakistan – then democracies easily stood accused of meddling with the affairs of others, of behaving 'undemocratically' by inflicting violence on the lives of others. But if democracies stood by and did nothing – as every democracy did when the Indonesian military mass-murdered East Timorese citizens – then they were easily accused of double standards, and callous indifference. For an obvious reason: in uncivil war zones, people were tortured and maimed, killed and wounded, ultimately for no other reason except that they could be tortured and maimed, killed and wounded. Rivalries and jealous quarrels were projected outwards, on to others, in life-affirming acts of desperate cruelty against surrogate victims. All sober ground rules of war were consequently swept aside. The enemy was demonised as all-powerful, as a comprehensive threat, as hyper-violent. Hence, the rituals of violence against them were repeated endlessly, shamelessly. Acts of violence became gratuitous. The killers' faces looked blank. Sometimes they smiled. Their words of explanation were cynical, or took the form of clichéd accounts of their private or group fantasies.

The protagonists of uncivil war lived by elementary rules of engagement. Our guide listed them: murder and counter-murder those who were innocent. Sever the hands and genitals of the enemy. Cut out their tongues. Stuff their mouths with stones. Force the victims to swallow them. Destroy graveyards, rape women, poison or torch food, poison the land, pour into its soils the blood of the victims. Guarantee there were no innocent bystanders. Treat cruelly those who appealed for calm; punish them in the manner of the respected Hutu leader Agathe Uwilingiyimana, murdered for her moderation by fellow Hutu thugs, who left her half-naked, mutilated body on public display. Make sure that both the violated and the violent were defiled, baptised in blood, rendered accomplices of dastardly crimes. Ensure that everybody witnessed rape, torture, murder, so that they did not forget what they had seen, or what they or others had done. Trouble the democratic world with painful questions: get democrats to ask how on earth a Rwandan priest could set fire to his own church where terrified citizens had sought sanctuary? Or what class of unreason moved Bosnian Serb torturers to amuse themselves by forcing their Muslim victims to bite off the testicles of other Muslims? And, when all was said and done, drum into the heads of democrats that people who waged uncivil war were quite prepared (like Slobodan Milošević did at The Hague Tribunal, before his death from heart failure) to boast to journalists or courts of law that butchers were heroes, that victims were fictions, or that they deserved what they got – that this was no crime against humanity.

Finally – our guide apologised for the awful details – monitory democracies came face to face with a third form of violence: a new kind of apocalyptic terrorism that operated on a global scale. She recalled that the ugly phenomenon of terrorism – the word itself dated from the French Terror, the revolutionary *terrorisme* that lasted from March 1793 to July 1794 – was much older. Its 'classical' forms, she said, involved using violence to instil fear into others for the purpose of achieving defined political goals. While states (like Jacobin France and the twentieth-century juntas of Argentina and Chile) were prone to terrorism, in the sense that they used assassins and other violent undercover agents to frighten people into submission, the classical terrorist, according to our guide, was typically a non-governmental fighter who was neither a uniformed soldier nor organised in elaborate command structures. The terrorist was trained in the deadly arts of handling explosives and light weaponry, usually within urban areas. Unlike guerrillas, such as the Kenyan Mau Mau, the Algerian FLN and the Revolutionary Armed Forces of Colombia (FARC), conventional terrorists did not seek to occupy their enemy's territory, noted our muse. Like rats in a sewer, they operated in small, autonomous units, hidden away in the interstices of the local society, in order to wear down and demoralise their governmental enemy, whom they supposed, despite everything, to be capable of negotiation, concession and retreat. Propaganda of the violent deed, planting bombs in the consciousness of the people, struggling for victory by means of fear, was among their specialities.

Our guide agreed that strongly 'classical' elements of terrorism were evident in the suicide attacks on American and French military facilities in Beirut in the early 1980s, the sarin attack on the Tokyo Metro, the bombing in early 1995 of a federal government building in Oklahoma City, the simultaneous attacks on the American embassies in Dar es Salaam and Nairobi in August 1998, and the much-publicised assaults on the Pentagon and the World Trade Center in September 2001. She described how each of these planned attacks cunningly took advantage of the civil freedoms afforded by monitory democracies; each aimed at a fundamental change of the political order; and each attack unleashed violence in urban settings, without, however, attempting to occupy their territory. Yet our muse insisted that these attacks also represented a rupture with the tactics of Basque, Irish and Colombian gunmen, hijackers and bombers. The apocalyptic terrorists of the twenty-first century thought of themselves as engaged in total war against an enemy deemed unworthy of negotiation and incapable of compromise. The enemy was seen as utterly corrupted, hence deserving of annihilation through unlimited violence, bloodcurdling in its technical simplicity, witnessed by millions.

The aim, said our muse, was to choose vulnerable targets in complex systems, key symbols of American power, for instance, then to kill indiscriminately, on a massive scale. Not just embassies or airports or transport systems or crowded markets or nightclubs or hotels, but whole cities were to be paralysed, she said. The experience of Indian democracy (where in the early years of the new millennium almost as many people were killed by acts of terrorism as in Iraq) showed just how easily everyday life could be brought to a shuddering halt by the most simple weapons, such as explosives hidden in lunch boxes strapped to a bicycle. The point was neither to win over public support nor to negotiate political deals.

A deathly zero-sum game had to be played. Responsibility did not need to be claimed. Like a god, the terrorist had to be everywhere, and nowhere; it was imperative that the terror be neither graspable nor controllable. It should function as noise whizzing through the heads of its potential victims. The minds and bodies of the enemy had to be shaken to the core. It was as if – said our guide – victims and witnesses had to be buried alive, tortured in their isolation, compelled to doubt themselves into oblivion. The point was to expose the rottenness of the present-day world. No one and nothing – certainly not democratic institutions – should be spared. Nothing but catastrophe should result.

Democratic Peace?

Our historian drew back from the carnage. She predicted that when others looked back on the first several decades of the new millennium they would see in each of these depressingly violent trends the collapse of the distinction between war and peace. They would almost certainly record how the different types of violence became so tightly interlinked that people were spooked by a profoundly troubling question: were the violent upheavals of the new millennium a prelude to a global order paralysed by restless power struggles that produced universal fear, a violent order in which democracy had little or no chance of survival? Our guide did not answer the question. She simply pointed out that nobody at the time knew how to respond. Growing numbers of people understood that the urgent priority was to find fresh beginnings, to invent long-term remedies against violence, in order to prove democracy's fate had not yet been sealed – to ensure that democracy still had a future. But that was not the same as solving the problem.

As if in denial, some people, reported our sage, took comfort in the happy thought that democracies were peaceful polities, that they had an unblemished record in not waging war upon each other. Ancient Greek democrats would have found the theory astonishing. According to the splendid idea, first championed by President Roosevelt during World War One, democracies were champions of 'democratic peace'. This was the gist of their claim: within any democracy, they said, citizens enjoy good measures of freedom, including the liberty to spot dirty tricks and criticise those who govern them. When it comes to politics, citizens are unusually canny. Informed by the independent opinions of journalists, experts and civil society organisations, they spot the contradictions and doubt the alibis of warmongers; they warn their fellow citizens that war is a power game, a devil's sport that favours some, at the expense of others. Citizens are quick as well to predict the terrible effects of war. Unimpressed by talk of honour, heroism and my country right or wrong, they use their freedoms to tell others, across borders, that war is not a pretty thing, that if their democracies were to go for each other's throats then many people – and perhaps even their own democracies – would suffer bloodcurdling destruction.

That was the theory. Our guide noted how seductive talk of democratic peace managed in practice to win friends in high places. 'During the Cold War', whistled American President Bill Clinton, shortly after the collapse of the Soviet Union, 'we fought to contain a threat to the survival of free institutions.' He added: 'Now we seek to enlarge the circle of nations that live under those free institutions, for our dream is that of a day when the opinions and energies of every person in the world will be given full expression in a world of thriving democracies that cooperate with each other and live in peace.'[12]

The dream, continued our muse, was quickly turned by academics into a supposed Law of Democratic Peace. 'Democracies are peaceful and never go to war against other democracies' was the boldest version. 'Democracies almost never go to war with each other' was the more modest rendition. Both versions, said our guide, gave the impression that democracies were basically peace-loving, which was misleading, for more than a few reasons. She began with the inconvenient fact that democratic states had sometimes turned bellicose – against their democratic neighbours. The vicious attack by Israel on Lebanon in the so-called July War of 2006, she said, showed that, under circumstances of regional or global tension, democracies could grow fearful, then project their alarm on to their neighbours, by force of arms, with hugely destructive effects on citizens, physical infrastructures and the ecosystem. If serious tensions broke out between India and the United States, no love would be lost between them. Democratic states, she said, were not 'naturally' or 'essentially' peaceful; every-thing depended on whether their elected governments saw eye to eye on territory, property, money, weapons and other basic matters that had little to do directly with democracy itself.

Much depended, too, on whether citizens managed to rein in bellicose parties and leaders. When they failed – our muse here recalled a character of Herman Melville's *Moby-Dick; or, The Whale* – monitory democracy risked abuse by governments that behaved like Captain Ahab, the monomaniac who caused mayhem by hunting a feared and hated object to the last corner of the earth. The twenty-first-century record showed that democracies left more than a few victims in their wake, because sometimes they elected leaders – Ariel Sharon, George W. Bush, Tony Blair – who picked fights and started wars, often in disputed circumstances, using cooked up charges that many voters swallowed, if only for a time.

The historical record showed as well that bellicose governments could use electoral democracy to weaken democracy, for instance by invoking emergency powers and stirring up public fears well suited to dictatorship. In the new millennium, reported our muse, the drift towards garrisoned government was plainly evident during the so-called 'war on terror'. In the name of the promotion of democracy, armies were mobilised, democratic procedures manipulated and big lies told by elected leaders, in support of their decision to go to war. In the name of protecting democracy, talk of enemies and the need for 'pre-emptive action' flourished. Public demonstrations were tightly controlled, or banned. Civilians were put through dummy exercises, exposed to new systems of surveil-lance, forced to endure routine 'security' checks. 'No Joking' signs at airport checkpoints and in public buildings reminded citizens that the authorities were not joking. Police powers expanded. The dark arts of surveillance flourished. Intelligence organisations (like the US National Security Agency, so secretive that it was popularly known as the No Such Agency) assembled massive databases, in search of enemies. Magnetometers, BioWatch air sniffers, razor wire, CCTV cameras and concrete fortifications became standard features of everyday life for millions of citizens. The rules of habeas corpus were weakened; to the shame of many democrats, the old division between the torturable and non-torturable classes made a terrible comeback.

Our muse recorded that the champions of the Law of Democratic Peace found, to their embarrassment, that in such militarised circumstances their 'scientific' propositions were used against their wishes. Some American exponents of the democratic peace principle complained they had been 'Bushwhacked', which was their way of admitting that the build-up to the American invasions of Afghanistan and Iraq had proved that the principle could be used to sanction war. For if it was true that democracies loved peace, some political leaders reasoned, then that was more than enough justification for launching war on designated enemies, supposedly to transform them into democracies that would in turn shore up democratic peace with their neighbours.

The Law of Democratic Peace suddenly found itself in a topsy-turvy world where government blather about the merits of democracy, defined narrowly as electoral democracy, tarred democracy with the brush of war. Such demolatry – so our guide called it – was unwelcome news for monitory democracy. That was why some believers in the democratic peace principle tried to make amends by flipping it on its head. They claimed that 'democracies win wars', but that seemed to make matters worse, commented our muse. She quoted the two best-known champions of this view. 'Since 1815', they wrote, 'democracies have won more than three quarters of the wars in which they have participated.' They added: 'This is cause for cheer among democrats. It would appear that democratic nations not only might enjoy the good life of peace, prosperity, and freedom; they can also defend themselves against outside threats from tyrants and despots.'[13]

Even by this reckoning, commented our guide, democracies lost up to a quarter of the wars they fought. That proved cold comfort, especially in those bungled military occupations – Vietnam and Iraq were examples that she cited – where not only the global reputation of the United States, the world's leading democracy, was put on trial; democracy itself was forced to suffer a measure of disgrace. Matters of reputation were not made easier by the fact that monitory democracies, persuaded by business deals and geopolitical calculations, sometimes played noughts and crosses with despots, like Idi Amin and Saddam Hussein, Joseph Mobutu and the Shah of Iran; or by the fact that the reputation of democracies was regularly damaged by the American-led, state-of-the-art methods of fighting wars that came to be called 'asymmetric'.

Our historian spoke plainly: precision-guided bombs were usually no match for the methods practised by tightly disciplined, decentralised Hizbollah-style armies enjoying strong local support. With their high sensitivity to casualties, monitory democracies found it increasingly hard to 'win' asymmetric conflicts. True, noted our guide, there were plenty of occasions when democracies made better choices of military strategy; and it was often true that democratic soldiers fought with better-trained leadership and greater initiative. But, she said, it was equally true that democracies were under constant pressure to make wars short. Getting the messy job done in quick time seemed imperative to leaders elected for only a short time, especially when they faced re-election. Publics were understandably intolerant of casualties; monitory democracies showed signs of impatience, meting out electoral punishment to governments that became bogged down in foolish, unwinnable wars. When that happened, citizens didn't suffer fools gladly; they quickly punished their elected representatives. That is why democracies were often forced to settle for draws, or suffer humiliating losses dressed up as victories.

The Awkward Empire

The double-barrelled rule that democracies were not necessarily peaceful, and that periodically they had to learn to live with losing wars, applied strongly to the dominant democracy within the global body politic: an imperial power, the United States.

Our sage acknowledged that America was both a proud monitory democracy and an empire that differed from all previous dominant powers, in two fundamental ways. Not only was it the first such power in human history that found itself in a position, partly thanks to a measure of historical luck, to lay claim to world hegemony. It was also a dominant power guided by a revolutionary world view: a vision of democracy that had its roots in the politics unleashed by the 1776 Declaration of Independence. In these two respects, said our muse, America differed from previous modern empires, for instance the Habsburg dynasty, which was a confederation of states (stretching from Portugal and the Netherlands to Naples and Milan through to Bohemia and Hungary) that had gathered at the altar of European Catholicism. The American empire was committed to the language and institutions of democracy; and for that reason it also differed from the British Empire that peaked during the nineteenth century. British imperialists had preferred talk of Christianity and civilisation (nineteenth-century Britain was not itself a democracy, and so its leaders felt no special affinity with the term, preferring, at best, to talk of 'responsible' or 'representative' government). And even at the height of their global power, the rulers of the British Empire inclined to self-restraint. When Britain had reckoned that it could not successfully use military force, for instance in continental Europe or South America, it usually kept its finger off the trigger. Its masters sensed the folly of risking everything, including its fleet, to conquer the world.

The United States showed few signs of self-restraint. It was prone to behave arrogantly – undemocratically – despite historical evidence that all previous dominant powers produced geopolitical instability; and despite the obvious fact, said our muse, that the global polity had become far too large, and certainly too complicated, to be governed by a single power like America. Hence its actions on the global stage were often awkward. Like revolutionary France and Soviet Russia before it, America was a territorial power dedicated to transforming the whole world in its favour, even if this required using the very methods that its democratic ideology abhorred: political trickery, economic muscle, bullying and violence.

The roots of its quest for global mastery stretched back well into the nineteenth century, at least to the military invasion of Mexico during the 1840s, which was perhaps why American politicians and governments so easily felt it was their natural or God-given right to be on top of the world – to act as if the United States was the 'indispensable nation', the phrase used by a former Secretary of

State, Madeleine Albright. During the opening decades of the era of monitory democracy, said our muse, there were plenty of moments when American leaders caught a glimpse of themselves as the world's first unchallenged global imperial power. They saw things accurately, for the simple truth was that after 1989 the United States was the world's most important component – some said the hub – of the spoke-and-wheel system of global governing institutions. It was the heartland of the turbo-capitalist economy, the driving force of the global telecommunications and entertainment industries, the world champion of consumer ways of life that had gradually triumphed over the conservative asceticism of Europe.

It was also the homeland of the mightiest army the world had ever known. The Gulf War of 1991, the Bosnian pacification of 1995, the overthrow and arrest of Slobodan Milošević after the war in Kosovo: according to our guide, these and other interventions had demonstrated that decisive military action at the global level depended on the United States. So, too, for a time did the war against the government of Afghanistan, which appeared to collapse like a canvas tent under the impact of the most advanced military technology known to humanity. State-of-the art bombing; missiles fired through doorways by unmanned Predator aircraft; the interception of the enemy's telephone calls and radio transmissions; bombs that busted open the deepest bunkers: all this was technically impressive. Our muse recorded that the American war-fighting budget for 1999 was only two-thirds of what it had been in 1989, but by the early years of the new millennium the dominant power accounted for 35 per cent of the world's total military spending (Russia's share was ten times less). The United States had in the meantime consolidated its role as the biggest arms dealer, with sales in the year 2000 worth US\$ 18.6 billion, more than half the \$36.9 billion global arms trade figure. And during the Clinton presidency, the United States completed the transformation of its strategy of global containment into the capacity to fight two major regional wars (as a US Department of Defense document explained) 'nearly simultaneously'.

The dominant power had more than a million troops, men and women stationed on five continents, in more than one hundred countries. By the early years of the new millennium, reported our guide, the United States Department of Defense confirmed officially that there were some 725 military bases outside the country and 969 at home (how many secret bases there were was anybody's guess, she added). The dominant power could and did throw its weight around – in Iraq, in Serbia, in Afghanistan, in a so-called war on terror that felt to millions of people around the world more like a war *of* terror. The United States had the proven ability to act as a vigilante or rogue power. It acted tough in matters as varied as steel imports, environmental regulations, and contributions to the World Bank (our guide noted that it was the bank's largest share-holder and yet contributed only 0.1 per cent of its gross domestic product in aid, the lowest proportion among rich governments). Its leaders knew that money, information, oil, blood, steel and giga-bytes counted in world affairs. They were therefore tempted, like every previous dominant power, to act as a vigilante, to see their power as the ability, especially when push came to shove, to meas-ure their strength against all of their rivals combined. America did so partly through straightforward designs of aggrandisement and partly by appealing – here the emphasis was quite different, and contradictory – for the global observance of governing structures that promoted democratic freedom and solidarity.

By the last decade of the old millennium, said our muse, the United States, by its words and deeds, had put the ideals and insti-tutions of democracy on trial globally. She recalled the commitment of the Clinton administration to what it called 'democratic enlarge-ment'; and its willingness, as in its Kosovo intervention, to sidestep both congressional and UN Security Council authorisation of its actions. She recalled as well the behaviour of the American gov-ernment during the two-term presidency of George W. Bush, who had developed his own highly virulent version of the global impor-tance of democracy and how to achieve it, by force of arms when necessary (Figure 129). The first hints of his preoccupation were expressed, appropriately enough, in a speech delivered at the Lima Army Tank Plant, in the city of Lima, Ohio, on 24 April 2003. 'The path to freedom may not always be neat and orderly', he told his audience of workers and management, 'but it is the right of every person and every nation.' He then made a promise that prompted applause: 'Iraq must be democratic . . . One thing is certain: We

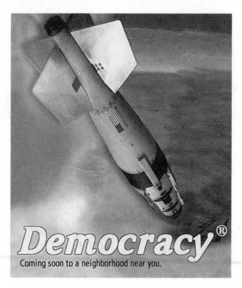

FIGURE 129: Satirical poster announcing the arrival of the American smash hit *Democracy*.

will not impose a government on Iraq. We will help that nation build a government of, by, and for the Iraqi people.' Six months later, our guide recalled, the same point was dipped in mellifluent words. In a widely quoted address to the 20th Anniversary of the National Endowment for Democracy in Washington (6 November 2003), the impromptu reasoning of President Bush had matured into something like a full-blown ideology of the transition to democracy. He said that democracy was 'both the plan of Heaven for humanity, and the best hope for progress here on Earth'. He spoke of 'the world democratic movement' and he spent some time working his way through a democracy assessment check list, awarding positive scores to Afghanistan, Saudi Arabia, Qatar and Morocco, with minus scores to China, Cuba and the Palestinians. His speech moved on to the Middle East, where 'the global wave of democracy has . . . hardly reached the Arab states'. Then came a wildly applauded promise from the lips of the President: 'The establishment of a free Iraq at the heart of the Middle East will be a watershed event in the global democratic revolution', he said. 'Iraqi democracy will succeed – and that success will send forth the news, from Damascus to Tehran – that freedom can be the future of every nation.'

Presidential speeches provided an important clue to a rhetorical turn in the Middle East policy of the United States – away from its avowed support of dictatorships in the region. The oratory revealed as well that monitory democracy now faced a misfortune: the world had fallen under the shadow of the first truly global dominant power, a power that was capable of operating in all four corners of the earth, an imperial power that prided itself on its own democracy and wielded the language of democracy to justify what it was doing in the eyes of others. Our muse agreed that America had a proven track record in the defence and creation of democratic institutions. The rescue of Europe in World War Two, and the hothousing of democracy in the Philippines, Japan and Germany were the best-known cases. So what was the problem? our guide asked. Why shouldn't the world have just made itself comfortable in the seat of presumption that American imperial power was good for democracy, its guarantor, its best hope, perhaps even its saviour?

Our muse replied: there were strong reasons for doubting the viability of America's stated global commitment to democracy. For a start, she said, the historical record showed that most militarily enforced transitions to representative democracy had failed, and that the reputation of monitory democracy was certainly not helped by wars fought in the name of promoting democracy. The point was well captured in the words of seasoned – gifted, devious – American diplomat Henry A. Kissinger: 'The choice to fight for democracy is often mistaken. Standing for democracy is inevitable.'[14] The difficulty was that most 'fight them, beat them, teach them to be less autocratic, perhaps even democratic' wars proved to be fraught, or outright failures – in about 85 per cent of cases, our muse said, citing a well-known report that had examined ninety American military interventions from 1898 to 1992. She pointed out that another report, covering more than two hundred United States military operations, including forcible interventions, peacekeeping, border control and military training, showed that democratic effects were observable in only 28 per cent of the cases.[15] The poor record of success of democracy promotion 'at the point of bayonets'[16] – she recalled the famous phrase of Warren Harding – did not at all prove that democracy was suited only to a few lucky peoples. The building of democracy no longer remained an impossibly daunting 'leap in the dark', as Lord Derby had famously claimed to Benjamin Disraeli in the 1860s. According to our historian, the record, rather, highlighted the point that successful democracy promotion was always and everywhere subject to the most stringent conditions. Self-government required the creation or preservation of a functioning government, a set of political institutions capable of making and executing policies, extracting and distributing revenue, producing public goods, and, of course, protecting its citizens by wielding an effective monopoly over the means of violence. The contradiction between the promise of self-government and the reality of forcible occupation by a power calling itself a democracy also had to be handled sensitively, for instance through a form of 'trusteeship' or 'shared sovereignty' managed by multilateral institutions that helped produce a viable, wider regional settlement. Occupation had to follow a clear timetable for withdrawal. It had to cultivate wherever possible the institutions of a civil society, including functioning markets, and – as if the list was not already long enough – the intruders had to make real efforts to cultivate local trust, not only through respect for local traditions and political aspirations, but especially by enabling the occupied population to organise and speak out against the occupiers, to subject them to the mechanisms of monitory democracy.

The American talk of a global transition to democracy was suspect in another way. It seemed to involve sleight of hand, said our muse. Ignoring the important power-monitoring innovations in the world of democracy since the end of World War Two, its official definition of democracy suffered from a shrivelled, deeply reductionist understanding of democracy, as merely a type of government based on winning a majority of seats or votes in an election. Reinforcing this reductionism was the fatuous presumption – rightly satirised by critics of 'pneumatic parliaments' (Figure 130) – that parliamentary institutions could be air-freighted into a country, erected overnight, with instant results next day. The trouble, said our muse, was that elections were held periodically in such countries as Iran, Russia and Singapore, each of which had parliaments. But, to say the least, it was rather doubtful that these polities came

FIGURE 130: Proposed exterior and interior design of a pneumatic parliament by Peter Sloterdijk and Gesa Mueller von der Hagen, designers for the firm Global Instant Objects.

anywhere near to measuring up to textbook definitions of the spirit and institutions of monitory democracy.

The chronic failure of US-backed democratic transitions, the terrible shrinkage of the norm of democracy and sheepishness about the human costs of establishing it all aroused another suspicion: that in the age of monitory democracy the political language of democracy was being used *ideologically*, misused as a great big tale of redemption or 'grand narrative' that pretended reliably to inform its believers which way was down, which way was up, and how to walk a straight line to an optimal destination. Our muse wondered how many people around the world would reject the American talk of democracy as a mask for violent power manoeuvres that had little or nothing to do with democracy, and much or everything to do with the perceived material interests of the dominant power, such as oil resources or geopolitical advantage. She pointed out that when that happened on any scale, the outright contradiction between the ideals of monitory democracy and the anti-democratic realities dragged democracy's name in the mud. She pointed out that the writing on the twenty-first-century wall came from several influential watchdog reports that documented instances of American torture, double standards and the violation of 'global values'.[17] They had warned that the whiffs of hypocrisy coming from the house of democracy might put off all prospective visitors; or worse, invite the active, radical rejection of democracy, even efforts to blow up its house wherever there were attempts to build or to preserve it. Our muse reminded us that hypocrisy had always been a sinister force in the world of democracy. It had been a recurrent feature of the history of representative democracy, especially from the last quarter of the nineteenth century. The worrying thing was that hypocrisy had begun to trouble monitory democracy – and this time on a global scale.

Her anxieties about the American empire turned the attention of our muse towards the biggest consideration of all. It was this: all past empires had tended to degenerate into hubris, so was it possible that the American empire, like the earlier Athenian and French experiments, could permanently damage, or even destroy outright, democracy at home and abroad in an orgy of hubris?

The trends made our muse nervous. There were plenty of signs that the United States was headed towards a type of government on the global stage defined by the worshipping of military prowess, in other words an empire in which armed power was reckoned the ultimate measure of greatness, while war, or preparing for war, was the exemplary common project. 'This country must go on the offence and stay on the offence', urged President George W. Bush in a press conference.[18] And so it regularly did.

Our muse gave examples. Between 1989 and 2001, the United States averaged one large-scale military invasion every eighteen months, a rate unsurpassed in its history. During the so-called war on terror, there were times when Congress fell into silent obedience, and when judges routinely adjudicated in favour of the administration's treatment of detainees, of whom there were an estimated 70,000 held outside the United States. Targeted suspects were routinely 'rendered' (kidnapped and handed over) by the American military to third-party governments for interrogation and torture, beyond the reach of American law, and the eyes and ears of the

American media. There were secret imports of qualified interrogators (in September 2002, noted our guide, a Chinese 'delegation' visited the concentration camp at Guantánamo Bay, to 'interrogate' ethnic Uighur detainees). According to our muse, the interrogation methods that became 'normal' included sleep deprivation (dubbed 'the frequent-flyer program'), simulated drowning, electric shocks to body parts, sexual taunting, and suspension from shackles. All this was done in the name of democracy! She added that some American intellectuals, like the inimitable Norman Podhoretz, were insistent that America had an international mission and must therefore never 'come home'. Policy wonks spoke of 'pre-emptive war', 'prophylactic war', 'preventive war', 'surgical war' and 'permanent war', a sure sign that the fox of war had entered the henhouse of monitory democracy.

The whole trend drew a deep sigh from our muse. She recalled some lines from Aristophanes: 'Democracy! Just where are you leading us / When people like this get appointed by the gods?' And a few lines from the cast-iron reactionary critic of the French Revolution, Joseph de Maistre: 'To hear these defenders of democracy speak, one would think that the people deliberate like a senate of sages, while in fact judicial murders, hazardous undertakings, extravagant choices, and above all foolish and disastrous wars are eminently the accompaniment of this form of government.'[19] The words belonged to two previous eras of democracy, but they echoed loudly into the twenty-first century. In the era of monitory democracy, said our guide, the United States showed that it could succumb to a narcissistic obsession with war, and with rumours of war – even that it could be the champion of war without end.

In the heartlands of the empire, as if to help things along many journalists behaved as if they were hierophants. The scope of acceptable opinion shrank. In some circles, open criticism of the 'commander in chief' amounted to lèse-majesté, as injured sovereignty, as betrayal of the nation. The military and security organisations seemed omnipresent; plenty of American civilians joined in by driving around in large, expensive vehicles that looked just like those from the First Armored Division. Among monitory democracies, noted our muse, it was only in America that soldiers and officers in uniform regularly appeared at press conferences, at political rallies, at government functions, in political photo shoots and popular movies. The militarisation of daily life, under the thumb of an imperial 'commander in chief', resembled a flourishing antibody that fed upon the cells of American democracy. Even presidential inauguration ceremonies, like the one held in January 2005, strongly resembled a military operation.

It was as if war had become America's only comparative advantage in the world. Our muse acknowledged that there were dissenters, including uncharacteristic outbursts from public figures that normally never mucked with politics. Ex-patriot Sir Michael Jagger noted, sarcastically, that America stood for liberty for all. Democracy was its style – except for people handed prison without trial. Something certain was that business boomed at Halliburton (a Texas-based oil and gas company) and he urged investors half astute to grab shares in military contractor Brown and Root.[20] Such were the times that public sarcasm splashed in the direction of the imperial presidency and the country's war efforts seemed to be absorbed easily by the sponge of official 'realism'. The unashamed voices made themselves heard: there was a realist case for America being on full alert, it was said. Maybe the country should drop the talk of promoting democracy; it was a good ideal, but certainly dispensable. The point was that American interests had to be defended. Above all, a desperate struggle to control the country's fuel supplies had to be waged. The brute reality was that, although the United States consumed 25 per cent of all the oil produced in the world every year, it had proven reserves of its own that amounted to less than 2 per cent of the global total. Hence the need for military and diplomatic supremacy in strategic, energy-rich regions, like the Middle East and Central Asia.

So our muse came to her final question: had the moment of American hubris arrived? Had its empire reached the point at which it served as a disruptive force in world affairs and openly endangered democratic institutions, including its own? That things had indeed reached this point was the conclusion drawn in the early years of the new millennium by a circle of disaffected democrats sitting in a quiet corner of a café in Damascus, talking discreetly to a journalist from the *Washington Post* about the long-term implications of the American occupation of Iraq. Our muse recorded their words for posterity.

These democrats from the birthplace of assembly democracy all agreed that American foreign policy had for the time being achieved what their President Bashar al-Assad had wanted: the silencing of public demands for democratic reforms. 'Advocates of democracy are equated now with supporters of America, even "traitors",' said Maan Abdul Salam, a thirty-six-year-old Damascus publisher and conference organiser. 'Talking about democracy and freedom has become very difficult and sensitive,' he continued. 'The people are not believing these thoughts anymore. When the U.S. came to Iraq, it came in the name of democracy and freedom. But all we see are bodies, bodies, bodies.' The point was corroborated by his friends, among them a man named Omar Amiralay, a prominent Syrian filmmaker, whose well-known documentaries were quietly critical of Assad's one-family rule. 'If democracy brings such chaos in the region, and especially the destruction of society, as it did in Iraq and in Lebanon, it's absolutely normal, and I think it's absolutely a wise position from the people to be afraid to imagine how it would be in Syria,' said Amiralay. 'I think that people at the end said, "Well, it is better to keep this government. We know them, and we don't want to go to this civil war, and to live this apocalyptic image of change, with civil war and sectarianism and blood."' For the time being, these democrats agreed, Syria's people were on their own, free to watch their government's manoeuvrings, but not to express their opinions, let alone act them out. Mohammad Yousif, a real estate salesman, predicted that many Syrians would be happy to trade American-style democracy for the smaller pleasures of life. 'We are talking and enjoying ourselves', he concluded, waving the nozzle of a traditional water pipe used to smoke flavoured tobacco. 'This is our democracy. This is our freedom.'[21]

New Enemies of Democracy

Growing unease about the world's dominant power, the democracy of the United States; sharply dipping levels of enthusiasm for fossilised parties and politicians; rising tides of protest about the anti-democratic effects of cross-border institutions and greed-ridden markets that escaped public monitoring; sullenness about the increasingly violent feel of the world; resurgent nationalism; the birth of überdemocracy; and a general confusion about what democracy was, what it might become, and what could have been done to correct the new symptoms of decadence, and so to preserve and enhance what had been achieved since the end of World War Two: our muse foresaw in the confluence of these trends the ruination of monitory democracy. She was not alone in drawing this conclusion. She noted in fact how quickly these decadent trends induced within many people a faint feeling – awareness that new enemies of democracy were on the rise, even an attitude of fatalism that democracy was definitely going to the dogs.

Was a power passing from the earth? Did monitory democracy slowly go under, drowned by forces that were partly of its making, but well beyond its reach? Our guide declined to say. She reminded us that democracy had always liked to keep a few secrets, and for that reason of respecting the wishes of her mistress our muse remained silent about the end result of the troubles of the twenty-first century. She was, however, prepared to comment on the return of an old problem with deep roots: disillusionment with the institutions and ideals of democracy.

Our guide acknowledged that the twenty-first-century coolness towards democracy was hard to measure, unevenly distributed and driven by all the forces she had so far described, including rising public disappointment with poorly performing governments, the failure to promote democracy by means of war, and the reassertion of state authority against 'terrorism', often using questionable legal and police methods. According to the new critics of democracy, whose voices could be heard in places like Caracas, Belgrade, Harare, Shanghai and Moscow, public confidence in parties, politicians, parliaments, the core institutions of electoral democracy, was waning. The critics noted the corrupting effects of organised lobbying and big-money politics; and they stressed that growing numbers of poor and immigrant people felt left out of the democratic equation. The new foes of democracy pointed to major setbacks for democrats in Russia, Kenya, Pakistan and Burma. They mocked the domineering role of the United States and sneered at the manner in which so-called democracy promotion had tangibly failed in Iraq, Afghanistan and Pakistan. The new critics also pointed out how Western monitory democracies, for the sake of expediency, regularly turned a blind eye towards unfair elections and how they had given up on democratisation, in effect making an undeclared shift in favour of authoritarian regimes that had oil and gas reserves, or served as vital allies in matters like military hardware, the drug trade or strategic proximity to China and Russia.

For the new critics of democracy, reported our guide, all these trends were proof that talk of the 'end of history' and 'third waves' of democracy was fraudulent. But there the agreement among the critics ended, she said; the new grumbling against democracy initially showed few signs of crystallising into a coherent, concerted attack on democracy, as had last happened during the 1920s. People who cursed politicians and refused them a vote, or anti-American speeches by nationalist demagogues, was one thing; taking to the streets with Kalashnikovs and killing innocents, or boarding an underground train with a rucksack packed with explosives, was quite another. In between these extremes, the grumblers came in various shapes and sizes.

There were desktop philosophers, gunmen, outspoken literary agitators and hard-line militant activists, none of them much in agreement about what needed to be done. Some critics (like the controversial French philosopher Jean-Claude Milner) accused democracy of being founded on disrespect for pluralism and, ultimately, on genocide. Others called for a return to religiosity, or to hard-nosed political 'realism', or to the writings of Karl Marx. Sometimes the critics drew the conclusion that democracy was simply a tool of American imperialism, or that it was doomed by 'shock capitalism', and by other sinister forces of globalisation. Still others dreamed of building a new post-democratic empire guided by the vision of what the Chinese government called the 'harmonious society'. Worryingly, noted our guide, most of the new foes of democracy claimed to be true friends of the people, which implied something more disturbing: if in future they managed to get their way with the world then it was absolutely certain that monitory democracy would be destroyed in the very name of democracy.

Hypocrites

The new foes of democracy were not united, but our muse warned of the need to pay attention to their claims and motives, if only because there was truth in the old adage that 'the enemy is us'. These opponents had something to say: they drew attention to troubles in the house of democracy, to the widening gap between the ideals and so-called realities of monitory democracy and, hence, to the connected problems of disappointment and hypocrisy – and their power to undo democracy, in unexpected ways.

Hypocrisy, said our guide, was the soil in which antipathy towards democracy always took root. In historical terms, democratic institutions and ways of life had been vulnerable to a wide variety of forces. Scholars since Aristotle had commonly cited factors like defeat in war, unbridgeable class antagonisms, governmental paralysis and devastating natural disasters. But these factors, whatever their explanatory power, never operated as automatic catalysts of change, she noted; these forces had no magical anti-democratic power in themselves. They undermined support for democracy only when they sapped people's confidence, or reinforced their unbelief in democratic ways of being. But for this to happen, people had to feel let down or put off by democracy; and that meant they had to have a sense in their gut that the gulf between the promises of democracy and its actual performance was so wide that democracy itself was a ruinous sham. This was another way of saying that anti-democratic sentiments always sprang up like weeds in the cracks between ideals and so-called reality, especially when democrats themselves were blind to such cracks, or tried to cover them up, for instance by telling lies, talking nonsense or using other forms of deception.

Hypocrisy was the word used by our muse to describe such cracks. What exactly did she have in mind? The word hypocrite, she explained, expressed contempt for those who failed to practise what they preached. When the word was used in the vernacular, people normally knew nothing of its origins in the world of ancient Greek drama, where the noun *hypokrisis* referred to 'feigning, dissembling', 'acting out' and 'play-acting'. It was mainly a descriptive term applied to the art of speaking in dialogue, playing a part on stage, using histrionics; in the age of assembly democracy, said our guide, the *hypokrites* was an actor, a player who legitimately dissembled on the stage, but only on the stage. That is why, during the fourth century BCE, Demosthenes had poured scorn on his bitter rival Aeschines, saying that he was a rank character, a rascal whose untrustworthiness stemmed from the fact that he had been a successful stage actor before taking up politics, and now found it impossible to restrain his skill at dissembling and impersonating others, this time in the *ekklēsia*.

Here, in the attack by Demosthenes on Aeschines, was the first hint of the powerfully negative connotations of the word hypocrisy, which in the European region, said our historian, came to bear the cross of Christianity. The Gospel according to St Matthew (23: 25) chided hypocrisy and hypocrites in ways that were utterly foreign to Greek democrats. Our muse quoted a famous passage: 'Woe unto you, scribes and Pharisees, hypocrites! For ye make clean the outside of the cup and of the platter, but within they are full of extortion and excess.' Hereafter, she continued, hypocrisy became a barbed word for judging bad people. Christian virtue and contempt for hypocrisy became conjoined twins, so unsurprisingly it was not long before the sceptics and outright opponents of Christianity laid into its own two-faced duplicities, with great effect. Our muse recalled that Cesare Ripa's remarkable book of emblems and virtues, *Iconologia* (first published in Rome in 1593), contained an example: hypocrisy was portrayed as a veiled woman, rosary beads and a mass book in hand, dressed in a cape spun from sheep's wool, but with the legs and feet of a wolf, reluctantly offering money to a beggar in the public square.

The charge of hypocrisy levelled against Christians and Christianity eventually prepared the way for the secular art of launching public attacks on double standards in public life. Christianity, our guide explained, in effect gave a gift to later forms of democracy, in the shape of lampooning, derision and biting satire aimed at knocking people in power off their perches. To accuse public figures – a party candidate or head of government, for instance – of hypocrisy was to draw attention to the way their actions violated the principles for which they avowedly stood.

'Watch their feet, not their lips' was a popular way of putting the point. Our muse reminded us that the arts of poking fun and criticism at double standards played a vital public role in healthy monitory democracies. Yet she went on to point out that the sting of hypocrisy was arguably much more painful in the body politic of monitory democracy than it ever was in the backside of Christianity. Christians who indulged in the vice of hypocrisy, after all, had a safety net: the promise of atonement for their sins, through elaborate expiation rites, such as confessing to a priest, or asking forgiveness through prayer. Things were different with monitory democracy. Except for public heckling, bad media coverage and humiliating electoral defeat, it had no equivalent expiation rite, backed by faith in a Higher Being. Monitory democracy had no merciful God, and that meant that its leaders, leading institutions and citizens were peculiarly vulnerable to the corrosive powers of hypocrisy.

Democracy, she continued, was a special political form defined by the fact that transitions to democracy always remained transitions. Democracy was never fully realised; it was always to some extent unconsolidated and defective. Democracy rested on the premise that although perfection was for the birds, steps towards self-correction, innovation and improvement were still possible. Democracy wanted to be more than it was; it was always the democracy to come, as the French philosopher Jacques Derrida liked to say. But, said our guide, it was equally true that this self-inscribed lack made democracy peculiarly vulnerable to its own failures and, thus, to the charge of hypocrisy.

Our sage cited the example of Latin America. Tapping the results of a major survey conducted in the early years of the new millennium, she reported that while just over half of the adult population (53 per cent) in Latin America thought that 'democracy was preferable to any other form of government' less than a third (29 per cent) were satisfied with how democracy currently worked in their country. Many citizens understandably blamed their fiscally weak and corrupted states for failing to promote economic development, or to deal with rising inequality, criminality, violence and drug trafficking. So that when asked who governs in their respective countries, nearly three-quarters (71 per cent) of

Latin Americans believed that they were 'governed by certain powerful interests looking after themselves'. They were right, as the figures for Mexico showed: here was a country where the richest 10 per cent of the population commanded 40 per cent of national income, with half of the population receiving just 18 per cent of the total, a country, unsurprisingly, where a huge majority of the voting population (81 per cent) did not feel represented by any political party and more than half (52 per cent) believed that citizens would govern better than politicians. According to our historian, the disturbing news from this study confirmed the point that hypocrisy was the acid of democracy: whereas just over half of Latin American citizens favoured 'democracy', a bigger proportion (55 per cent) said they would support an authoritarian government if that would 'resolve the economic problems of the country'.[22]

The Latin American ambivalence towards democracy may have been extreme, commented our guide, but it was by no means exceptional. In the era of monitory democracy, all actually existing democracies regularly produced disappointment among their citizens. She reminded us that the whole vision of publicly monitoring the exercise of power contained within it a principle of disappointment. Monitory democracy could be seen as an effective method of apportioning blame for poor political performance – a way of ensuring the rotation of leadership, guided by merit and humility. It was (ideally) a form of humble government, a way of creating space for dissenting minorities and levelling competition for power, which in turn enabled elected and unelected representatives to test their political competence and leadership skills, in the presence of others equipped with the power to trip them up and throw them out of office, if and when they failed, as often they did.

The founding principle of monitory democracy – the continuous public chastening of those who exercise power – was simple, but persuasive. Our guide took the example of periodic elections, the moment when people exercised their power to judge, sometimes harshly, the performance of their representatives. The whole point of elections was that they were a means of disciplining representatives who disappointed their electors, who were then entitled to throw harsh words and paper rocks at them. If representatives were always virtuous, impartial, competent and responsive – remarked our muse – then elections would lose their purpose.

Sleepwalkers and Fatalists

Our guide agreed that monitory democracies were blessed with different ways and means of rotating power holders and monitoring, checking and balancing power, and that when they worked well their built-in scrutiny mechanisms dealt easily with hypocrites and felt hypocrisy. Scoundrels were thrown from office, on to the streets, taunts at their back. But there were also moments when the perceived gap between promise and performance became abysmal, so intolerable to certain people that they drew the conclusion that democracy was a rotting fruit, that it was impossible to get rid of crooks and rogues, let alone to deal with the surge of global problems for which democrats and democracies had few proposed solutions, or none at all. It was at that point, as in the early years of the twenty-first century, that opponents of democracy found a voice, and began to flex their muscles.

The threats facing monitory democracy were reinforced by the strange fact that quite a few democrats never even noticed what was happening, reported our guide. Hypocrisy was a force to be reckoned with; so, too, was ignorance. During the last big organised assault on democracy, during the 1920s in Europe and elsewhere, it was the same, she said. Many people who called themselves democrats were in effect disloyal to democracy by ignoring its destruction. Time and again, they called things by the wrong name, turned blind eyes, gave excuses, stayed silent, or they simply misread the broad trends by thinking of them as unconnected exceptions. Ignorance was neither bliss nor innocence; in the circumstances, it shortened the life of democracy by encouraging a miraculous complacency that resembled sleepwalking over a cliff.

In the early decades of the new millennium, said our guide, talk of the 'end of history' and a 'third wave' of democracy had similar soporific effects. It lulled certain intellectuals, journalists, policy makers and various fat cats into the happy conclusion that the ideals and institutions of democracy had enjoyed an unprecedented growth spurt – possibly even a global victory. Scheming politicians then took care of the rest with well-spun orations that earned them a place within the archives of memorable überdemocrats. 'The Knesset's holiday is the entire country's holiday', thundered Israel's Prime Minister Ariel Sharon, during a special session (in January 2002) called to celebrate the fifty-third anniversary of the founding of the parliament. 'This is the day of Israel's victory as a fighting democracy characterized by a steadfast stand and struggle to realize the Jewish people's historic rights in its country, the fight to realize civil rights and equality of opportunity as the Middle East's only genuine democracy.' During his two tumultuous terms, President George W. Bush liked to put the same point about the triumph of democracy, but in world-historical perspective. 'As the 20th century ended', he said to generous applause, 'there were around 120 democracies in the world – and I can assure you more are on the way.' He added: 'We've witnessed, in little over a generation, the swiftest advance of freedom in the 2,500 year story of democracy. Historians in the future will offer their own explanations for why this happened. Yet we already know some of the reasons they will cite. It is no accident that the rise of so many democracies took place in a time when the world's most influential nation was itself a democracy.'[23]

It was talk of that kind that encouraged existing democracies to sleepwalk their way into deep trouble, along the way awakening enemies to the brazen hypocrisy of a new form of democracy that struggled to cope with problems for which there were no easy solutions. But, according to our guide, the new millennium brought with it more than just hypocrisy and the ignorance of sleepwalkers. It produced another reaction among citizens that was equally serpentine: it bred fatalism.

Our navigator was sure that the new millennium saw a gathering fatalism, and that it was bad for monitory democracy. The fatalist, someone who felt overwhelmed or overpowered by the world, came in two types, she said. Ignoramuses, one of the types, were straightforwardly confident, in both their ignorance and the conclusions that had to be drawn. They knew why democracy didn't stand a chance, and who ruled the world: it was the rich and powerful, or the banks or big multinational corporations, or the United States of America, for instance. And that was that. Nothing more needed to be said – and nothing more could be done, for the time being. There was another, second, species of fatalist: the more blasé type. The blasé fatalists didn't have much of a clue about whether or not democracy was a good thing, or who ran the world, and they weren't much troubled by their ignorance. They simply didn't think about such things. When asked, the blasé fatalists readily admitted their ignorance, quickly adding, with a sigh, that they didn't much care. They divined from their ignorance the conclusion that it was a waste of time worrying about who or what held the reins of power in this world. For – here the two species of fatalists joined forces – they said that there was no point in wasting words on the subject of democracy, simply because the forces that ruled the world always got their way. What is, is; what will be, will be.

Here the two types of fatalists spread their sails, to drift together on the ancient waters of Greek mythology, where fatalism appeared in the shape of old women who sat patiently spinning the threads and ropes of worldly events that were bound to happen. In the age of assembly democracy, our muse recalled, fate was represented as both external and internal to the individual. One's fate was 'spun', and so given, from the outside; but fate was at the same time intensely personal, something experienced from the inside. It left the individual no other option but to yield to what was felt outside and inside. The Romans called this inner and outer experience of necessity *fatum*. It literally meant 'a thing said', something that was reported before it actually happened. Fate was a forewarning of an event or chain of events that could not but happen. The *fatum* was irreversible. It could not be changed by a millimetre or a gramme. Fatalists were those who believed or accepted this. They embraced fate – their unfreedom – as if it were their own. Fate was *their* fate.

Our muse granted that in the early twenty-first century the gathering sense that fate had power over the lives of people was entirely understandable. A moment's reflection on the mounting threats to monitory democracy confirmed – if confirmation was needed – that human beings never fully controlled everything that happened to their lives. They regularly felt forced to go along with things, to accept what had happened behind their backs, to do things against their will. The disappointments, contradictoriness and setbacks that riddled the age of monitory democracy strongly reinforced this feeling. It was understandable that many people drew the conclusion that monitory democracy was not paradise on earth – that it promised people they would have more control over their lives, but in fact delivered much less than that. Sometimes it seemed to deliver them nothing at all. The worst thing was that from time to time it dished up terrible disappointments – the loss of their job, a beating at the hands of police, a government of fools – that produced frustrations that seemed unbearable.

So our muse was adamant: when the acceptance of fate hardened into dogma, fatalism took hold of the individual, or group, or whole societies, cruelly and without mercy. Fatalism distorted visions. It paralysed actions. Fatalism conjured necessity from contingency. It corroded the very spirit of democracy by making it seem that nothing could be done, that everything was foreordained. That was why fatalism was a principal curse of efforts to protect and nurture monitory institutions. Fatalism fed wistfulness. It seduced citizens into thoughtless indifference towards the world. It made them prey to nonsense. It tempted them into believing that they could turn their backs on politics – encouraged them to think that they could get away without access to any mechanisms for ensuring equality and freedom by monitoring and controlling power publicly.

Thinkable Solutions?

Our historian reminded us that grand-scale fatalism last flourished in the democratic world a century before, during the early decades of the twentieth century, hard on the heels of the first victories for representative democracy. By the 1930s, many young democracies, whether in Chile, Poland or Spain, found themselves overwhelmed by hypocrisy, economic crises and long-standing political resentments, including the bitter politics of war debts and reparations. Luckily, noted our muse, the essential ingredients of a 1920s-style revolt against democratic institutions and democratic values seemed to be absent in the early decades of the new millennium. There were no Soviet Unions or Third Reichs on the horizon. The thought that Russian or Serbian nationalism, or that militant support for the territorial state (*souverainisme* was the term sometimes used by French nationalists), or that Taliban militia, Burmese generals or Mugabe-style government by murder could have served as universal counter-models to democracy was laughable, she said. Fatalism, however, was no laughing matter. It was the favourite liquor of idiots. Kicking its habits was for that reason – as Charles de Gaulle reportedly commented after spotting a Free French tank daubed with the words 'Death to Idiots!' – a vast task. So what was to be done to defeat fatalism? What could have been done? Was it possible to have prevented democracy, which began as a dream and had passed through a finite life in the world several times, from once again passing back into a dream?

Our muse agreed that honest public recognition of the dysfunctions of monitory democracy was badly needed, if only to awaken sleepwalkers and wrong-foot those who poured scorn on its duplicities. Fresh eyes, more imagination and bold, practical remedies were also required. She reminded us that we were not ancient Greeks, and that nobody should therefore have expected the weaknesses of democracy to be solved by benign or angry gods. Human, all-too-human remedies – the efforts of citizens, think-tanks, universities, policy units, whistleblowers, parliaments, parties, courageous political leaders – were required. Distinctions and nuances had to be drawn, for instance between problems that were to be addressed within any given country and those that required regional or global solutions; and between solutions that had to be the work of government and those that required the initiative and dedication of people and organisations of civil society. Solutions were certainly thinkable, recalled our muse. Wherever possible, practical reforms needed to take to heart the wise maxim of one of the principal architects of European integration, Jean Monnet: half the battle in the politics of vision and improvement, he liked to say, was to find the point of leverage where bold 'small steps' (*petits pas*) produced great strides.

The principle of bold modesty recommended by Monnet, said our muse, had implications for dealing with the dry rot of representative government. There were plenty of potent remedies, principally of the kind that would have reactivated political parties at the same time as recognising their limits by cultivating many of the power-monitoring inventions that first began to appear from around 1945. Much depended upon the particular context, of course. Whether rebuilding party membership levels was a priority remained an open question, our muse thought, but she had no doubt that in general political parties had to work much harder for the support of voters. Elections could have become much fairer and more interesting and competitive, and citizens better treated, with greater respect, by parties, politicians and electoral authorities, whose job it was to reassert the principle of public ownership of elections, procedures and voting machines. Politics could have been put back into official politics, through a variety of moves, for instance by strengthening the powers of scrutiny of parliaments; tougher legislation and public control of the financing methods of parties; the compulsory staging of primary elections; the banning of party hopping; and the general strengthening of inner-party democracy. Putting into place more genuinely universal rules of political citizenship was also a vital priority. In practice, that would have meant making such moves as guaranteeing votes for felons, extending the vote to denizens, lowering the voting age and improving the basic integrity and fairness of elections and electoral systems, to ensure greater equality among votes and voters.

Everywhere and always, our sage stressed, the point should have been to reward small 'd' democrats of all parties and persuasions, and to punish those who deliberately attempted to manipulate the levers and buttons of party machines and electoral systems for personal or group advantage, by cheating and lying, pushing and elbowing their way into governmental office. The principle of rewarding and punishing certainly should have been applied as well to efforts to breathe more life and to inject purpose into the myriad non-party accountability mechanisms that became part of the landscape of monitory democracy after World War Two. In the age of monitory democracy, when the key question was not who voted but where people voted, there was a desperate need to extend voting rights and citizens' voices and rights of representation to as many different situations and institutions as possible, our guide commented. She noted that there were plenty of interesting experiments, for instance in the United States. National initiatives like the 'Red-Blue Project' tried to use the web to increase the involvement and interaction of citizens in issues that otherwise divided them. At state level, campaigns such as 'Minnesota Works Together' aimed to cultivate a shift of 'me to we' attitudes among citizens and politicians, especially by encouraging their interaction and cooperation in defining problems and finding policy solutions. In Mississippi, during the 1990s, the 'Southern Echo' campaign managed to double the number of African American elected representatives in the state legislature, at the same time as encouraging community representatives to run for seats on local schools and country boards, and as mayors, sheriffs, judges and tax assessors, all the while remaining publicly accountable to their community organisations. Similar efforts to bring greater accountability to non-party organisations and to link up and coordinate the two types of organisations flourished at city level, for instance in Los Angeles, whose SCOPE and 'Apollo Alliance' initiatives tried to foster voting among poor and marginalised communities, but also to increase their involvement in such schemes as inner-city regeneration and 'green development'.

The point of these mechanisms was to restrain and check and balance the exercise of bossy power; and, more positively, to foster social and political equality and imbue citizens with a stronger sense that their citizenship could be lived by exercising options in addition to voting a few times in their lives for candidates, or for parties or governments for which they had no special affection. The trick, said our muse, should have been to protect and to strengthen, to combine and better coordinate, the multiple mechanisms of direct and indirect involvement and scrutiny of power that had made monitory democracy so special, and so promising. These mechanisms were crucial in countering the perversions of electoral democracy, including the dangers posed by cavalier überdemocrats, and the troubles caused when cliff-hanging elections enabled the 50.01st percentile of those who voted to block or to propel major changes of policy that affected millions of people, sometimes adversely.

There was often something utterly unfair about conventional, winner-take-all party politics, our muse insisted. That was why people would have been wise to develop *other* institutions of monitory democracy – in effect, to increase the density of bodies and networks skilled at keeping power on its toes. With the help of the tools provided by communicative abundance, the aim should have been to strengthen these watchdog and guide dog institutions, at all levels within and beyond territorial states. There was no shortage of possibilities, recalled our muse. Granting power to representative bodies at the municipal, local and regional levels to issue 'yellow cards' – explicit warning notices – to one another, for the purpose of creating best practice. Financing and protecting the growth of independent, multi-voiced publics within civil society, so that the loudest or richest voices were not the only ones heard. Improved citizen representation and citizens' juries and assemblies within the operations of government, not only through court duties, but also in such fields as health, education and transportation. The rejuvenation of local government and the redesign of town halls, so that they felt and functioned much more like open public spaces. More extensive use of participatory budgeting; specialised elected councils; online deliberation systems; democracy kiosks; and technology public assessment bodies, of the kind that had sprung up in Denmark. Integrity commissions within the field of media, as well as more and better public service multi-media, including broadband Internet provision for all.

Meanwhile, the global polity needed a radical shake-up. Our guide was sure that protectionist politics would lead the world down a bleak, blind alley; given the interdependence of the world, collective action across borders was the only alternative. The principle in each and every situation, she said, should have been to apply the core principle of monitory democracy: those whose actions adversely affect others should be held publicly accountable, for the sake of everybody's well-being. She noted that it would have been possible to change the voting rules of many governing bodies, so that less powerful countries and civil society representatives had a genuine say. The creation of new monitory institutions was certainly thinkable, for instance regional parliaments (like the world's first ever example, the European Parliament), or even an elected global parliament of citizens' representatives, perhaps under the auspices of the United Nations. The list of feasible cross-border reforms included corrective taxation mechanisms, for instance covering pollution, arms sales and speculative investments that caused destabilising market bubbles. Special courts that set tough public standards for tackling criminality and environmental destruction were a possibility; so, too, was the creation of professionally staffed, full-time independent evaluation units in bodies such as the World Bank and the IMF.

New governing institutions were required to deal with the perilous triangle of violence that the world had drawn around itself – a triangle bounded by apocalyptic terrorism, uncivil war, and the worrying proliferation of new weapons systems with killing power many times greater than that of all democracies combined. Prudent government interventions in neighbouring states, designed to reduce political violence, nationalist frictions and to encourage monitory democracy, were also a valuable idea – and could have had positive practical effects, as the European Union's application of strict membership rules concerning democracy, human rights and markets, the so-called Copenhagen criteria, had shown. But our muse was certain that positive effects could also have come from citizens' campaigns against the nuclear and bio-chemical weapons industries, and against violence in general. Public vigils, noisy demonstrations, interactive websites, public monuments and memory commissions might have played a stronger role in combating violence, and outlawing torture and detention without trial. So, too, could citizens' support for organisations that campaigned against political repression, cross-border arms transfers and torture – networked organisations like Amnesty International, which at the beginning of the new millennium had more than one million members in 162 countries; and bodies like Saferworld, a London-based research and lobby group that publicised the deadly effects of global arms flows, championed community consultations and pressured bodies like the European Union into restricting arms sales to dictatorial states and armies that abused human rights.

The Return of Bipolarity

And what about America? Sending troops to its shores would have been unwise, counselled our sage. She agreed that the goal of bringing the dominant power down to earth – democratising its power – was vitally important for the future of monitory democracy. Those who attempted to do this, she said, were well advised to develop a whole host of humbling strategies, to be aware that they were facing a problem without precedent in the history of democracy, all the while keeping in mind the comparison between absolute monarchies and republics drawn by the great seventeenth-century Dutch statesman and political commentator Johan de Witt (1625–72). Our muse recalled de Witt's claim that in absolutist regimes, princes act with the bullying force of lions and the cunning of foxes, in line with the recommendations of Machiavelli. By contrast, said de Witt, those who are publicly elected to govern republics should act without hubris, like stealthy cats, which are both 'agile and prudent'. Whether the United States would prove to be the lion and fox and finally succumb, in an orgy of hubris, to the temptations of world aggrandisement, our muse did not say. But the whole matter of whether the United States could be persuaded to restrain its power in order to wield it more effectively, pressured into behaving like a cat, so that it could be a catalyst of a more dynamic, publicly accountable, egalitarian and effective set of global governing institutions, this matter was among the great, if highly dangerous, political questions of our time – or so thought our muse.

The problem of how to democratise the foreign policy of a democracy was similar to that faced by the small assembly democracies in classical Greece, except that the twenty-first-century friends of monitory democracy now had to come up with solutions on a global scale. That was a challenge, and it was by no means certain that the United States would play ball. It so happened that there was another reason for worrying about the capacity of the United States to exercise responsible leadership in the world of monitory democracy. Most observers in the early years of the twenty-first century did not spot just how short-lived was the dominance of the United States, which after just two decades of unrivalled global superiority (following the collapse of the Soviet Union at the end of the 1980s) began to feel the pinch of a major rival: China. Our guide noted that it was hard to pinpoint the moment in time when the rivalry set in. It was even harder to know how the rivalry would end, or even whether it would end in grief. But one thing was clear: a bipolar world centred on Beijing and Washington would now co-determine the fate of democracy itself.

The relationship between the two powers was at first quite unequal, noted our guide. American power was greater, but remarkable was the way that China had come far enough along the path of dominant-power status in the world polity to establish a meaningful option for the governments, businesses and citizens of the world: either the American model of power or that of the People's Republic of China. It was Athens versus Alexander the Great, this time on a world scale. One canary in the global mine-shaft, serving as a measure of tensions and rivalries between the two leading powers, was the way in which the Chinese authorities made much of the fact that so many of the world's trade and invest-ment roads had begun to lead towards their country. The great Chinese leap forward to market prosperity was lavishly celebrated. Speech after speech delivered by Chinese leaders and minor officials heaped praise on their country's economic performance. Statistics were much in vogue, and commonly used to impress, even to dazzle. China had surpassed the United States as the top destination for foreign investment, it was said. China was the number one exporter of information technology products. It was the biggest consumer of cement and steel. China was the third-largest trading power, and it had over $1 trillion of foreign reserves, the largest in the world. And so on.

Our muse had examined several well-known addresses by President Hu Jintao, a master of economic facts and figures. From 1978 to 2005, Hu liked to say, China's gross domestic product increased from US$147.3 billion to US$2.235 trillion, registering an impressive average annual growth rate of 9.6 per cent. China contributed about one-sixth of the world's economic production of goods and services, and more benefits to the world were to come. China was ready for the challenge. 'We will further deepen the reform of foreign-related economic sectors, accelerate the transformation of [our] pattern of trade growth and improve trade structure to ensure balanced growth of imports and exports', said Hu, before adding: 'We will actively introduce foreign investment, open the service sectors wider, enhance intellectual property rights protection and raise China's overall level of openness.'[24]

What kind of openness was not obvious, or so thought our muse. The devil lay in the detail. Evidently the formula involved no intended confrontation with the United States, which, after all, was by far the biggest foreign investor in Chinese markets. The United States was China's largest export market (buying around 20 per cent of its total exports) and China loaned most of the dollars it earned from trade to the American government, which used the money to cover its huge budget deficits. Caught up in the global drift towards interdependent markets and government, the property systems of the two powers were tightly interlinked. That was why no Cold War-style, empire-against-empire antagonism materialised. But here our guide noted a difference: the fact that the Chinese leadership liked to say that their commitment to open economies was 'without strings attached'. When decoded, that meant that Chinese business dropped any American-style talk of 'ethical investment', or of linking human rights and democracy to market activity in general. China was instead prepared to do business with anybody, including the ailing totalitarian regime of North Korea, the cruel military dictatorship of Burma, and the kleptocracy run by Robert Mugabe. So our muse asked: was this 'no-strings-attached' commitment to trade and investment politically naive, or was it symptomatic of something deeper, less obvious, more serious?

She was sure there was more at stake; it had to do with the Chinese resistance to the advent of monitory democracy. Our muse acknowledged that there was a long tradition in China of expressing affection for 'democracy' – *minzhu* or *min-ch'uan* – a neologism that had arrived from Europe via Japan in the late nineteenth century. Talk of democracy had thereafter featured in most considerations of the future of the 'New China'. Liang Qichao (1873–1929), the peasant boy who rose to become China's most influential turn-of-the-century scholar and journalist, had predicted that his country would nurture a flourishing parliamentary democracy. Shortly after a six-month fund-raising, fact-finding tour to Australia, he published *An Account of the Future of New China* (1902), a remarkable literary utopia that imagined, sixty years into the twentieth century, a China defined by its support for global peace, the patriotism and selflessness of its citizens, and a multiparty democracy committed to good government and respect for the constitution. Two decades later, the weekly public lectures delivered in Canton by Sun Yat-sen (1866–1925) on the arrival of democracy in China – 'the age of people's power' – had caused a sensation, partly because they pictured China as leading the world towards the climax of Four Stages of History that had begun in China, with Confucius and Mencius. Democracy had been the centrepiece of Mao Tse-tung's 1940 call to arms against Japanese occupation. 'Raise both your hands. New China is ours!' he had written, adding that the essential first task was to embrace 'democracy of the Chinese type, a new and special type, namely, New Democracy'. The age of the 'bourgeois-democratic revolution' championed by Sun Yat-sen and his band of has-been followers slavishly followed 'the old European-American form of capitalist republic under bourgeois dictatorship, which is the old democratic form and already out of date'. China would now press home 'a system of really universal and equal suffrage, irrespective of sex, creed, property or education'. He added: 'Such is the system of democratic centralism. Only a government based on democratic centralism can fully express the will of all the revolutionary people and fight the enemies of the revolution most effectively.'

In the early years of the new millennium, digging along the same vein, the leadership of the Chinese Communist Party state repeatedly paraded its democratic potentials, as it did in a rather ham-fisted but widely reported 'White Paper' on the subject.[25] Issued on the eve of a visit to China by the White House incumbent, the first ever, twelve-part White Paper was designed to take the wind out of the sails of foreign critics. According to our muse, it rather resembled a fried rice of different and conflicting principles. It presented China as a busy laboratory of 'socialist political democracy'. There was still just as much to be done as had already been achieved, claimed the document. But the experiment was working wonders. It proved that Westerners were wrong when they said that democracy could not work in a China that was too big, too poor, too complicated, its history too long, its people too afraid of violence and chaos. Democracy was 'the apt choice suited to China's conditions and meeting the requirements of social progress'. Socialist political democracy had enabled the Chinese people, proudly described by the document as one-fifth of the world's population, 'to become masters of their own country and society, and enjoy extensive democratic rights'.

Masters? Of their own country? Our muse wondered what this phrase meant. The White Paper explained that democracy in China was *socialist* because the system was wedded to the basic principle that 'the Marxist theory of democracy' had to be combined with 'the reality of China'. In the process, the document continued, China had borrowed some of the useful elements of Western democracy and combined them with China's traditional culture and civilisation. Our muse underscored the manner in which the document at times fell back on the nationalist presumption that this 5000-year-old entity called China seemed to be of one mind and spoke with one tongue in one tone. The conclusion was foregone: 'Therefore, China's socialist political democracy shows distinctive Chinese characteristics.'

Considering the criteria subsequently laid down in the document, it was a masterstroke of political illogic, or perhaps doublethink. Our muse noted how the Chinese authorities pictured China as a superior form of democracy in which 'the overwhelming majority of the people act as masters of State Affairs'. Chinese democracy was 'guaranteed by the people's democratic dictatorship'. What was that? A democracy defined by 'democratic centralism as the basic organizational principle and mode of operation'. In other words – so much for the majority as masters – Chinese democracy was 'a people's democracy under the leadership of the Communist Party of China (CPC)', a party that rose to prominence thanks to the protracted heroic struggle of the Chinese people 'in pursuing national independence, prosperity and a happy life'.

No modesty there. 'It was a choice made by history and by the people', the document concluded, but evidently the whole idea of socialist political democracy involved a type of jiggery-pokery, otherwise known as 'substitutionism'. Like the fabled bird that managed to move a mountain by resolutely carrying away stones in its beak, one at a time, the people of China, whoever they were, had taken history, whatever that was, into their own heroic hands. They had empowered their substitute, the Chinese Communist Party, to rule over them, unopposed. With one voice, the people had chosen to be forced to be free. But did the Chinese people choose death by famine, forcible displacement and the ruthless punishment of at least thirty million citizens during the Great Leap Forward? Did the people enjoy the chance, following the 1987 Thirteenth Congress of the Communist Party, to debate publicly the radical proposals for 'social democracy' (*shehui minzhu*) put by Zhao Ziyang and his supporters? Were the people in favour of the toppling of the Goddess of Democracy and the bloody crushing of an estimated four hundred Tiananmen-style protests throughout the country in the summer of 1989; and did they now vote for closure of the open architecture of multi-media communication by a censorious system of government controls that resembled a body with one head, many mouths and extremely long arms? Did the Chinese people still choose to live under a flat-footed, big-fisted one-party government that made sure that whenever there was a problem, there was a big problem? The White Paper neither posed nor answered such questions. It said only that there was a continuously improving system of 'people's congresses' and 'multi-party cooperation and political consultation', as well as 'regional autonomy for ethnic minorities'. The 'socialist market economy' was thriving. Life in China was 'not yet perfect', but it was good, and getting better. The 'democratic rights of people at the grassroots level in urban and rural areas' were expanding, as was the 'rule of law', while citizens' basic rights were 'respected and guaranteed'. There were problems, such as 'bureaucracy and corruption', but the Party leadership was aware of them, and now busily tackling them, step by step and 'in an orderly way', in accordance with 'the objective law of progress'.

Here was the recipe of Chinese success: a pinch of Marxism; a few shakes of old-fashioned, nineteenth-century European belief in evolutionary progress and science; and a generous cup of the Bolshevik principle of the vanguard party (this was what was meant by 'democratic centralism'). Stir this all together, add the milk and honey provided by the market, and finally leaven the resulting mixture with the yeast of Chinese civilisation. The result, when baked in time, was what the Chinese authorities liked to call the Harmonious Society. It was the opposite of chaos and disorder, the much-feared negatives that had often appeared in the traditional folk tales and literature of the region, and that had threatened to return during the 1989 Tiananmen events, and in the latter-day stubborn resistance and outright opposition to the Party's benign rule over the people, for the sake of the people. The Harmonious Society was the destiny of China.

Here our muse drew us back to the messy business of China's role as a dominant power. For, according to the Chinese authorities, 'the Chinese people' were doing all that they could to realise the same principle *on a global scale*. Experience had shown that it had meant only good things at home, as programme after programme of China Central Television (CCTV) proudly explained to the world. But the vision of a Harmonious Society was bound as well to bring good things to the rest of humanity: gifts like social stability, sustainable economic development, good government and continuous improvement in the level of people's mastery of their lives. China was a force for 'win-win cooperation', President Hu Jintao liked to say. The world was 'one big family' and (he told business leaders from the Asia-Pacific region) there was no alternative but to 'work together'. Harmony was 'a defining value of the Chinese civilisation', and that was why China's growing role in global affairs was wholly positive. China's widest destiny was to build 'a harmonious world of enduring peace and common prosperity'. In the Asia-Pacific and African regions, so ran the reasoning, China stood for peaceful development through its own peaceful development. According to President Hu, 'facts have proved that China's development will not stand in the way of anyone, nor will it pose any threat to anyone'.

It was all a pipedream, commented our muse, with time on her side. For the reality was that Harmony was prepared to stand against monitory democracy whenever it stood in the way of Chinese indifference towards 'good governance'. A testing ground for future explosions proved to be Africa, where China simply snubbed the efforts of leading G8 countries to tie aid and investment to 'zero tolerance for corruption' and to 'democracy'. Chinese governments proved that they were simply uninterested in such matters as human rights, the rule of law and media freedom. They insisted that growth would solve most problems, and that no single problem, whether pauperisation or poor administration, could be solved without such growth. How states governed their subjects was consequently the business of their own leaders – just as in China. The principal thing was to keep trade and investment flowing through 'a new type of strategic partnership' that fostered 'political equality and mutual trust, economic win-win cooperation and cultural exchanges' (these were words used by President Hu Jintao at the biggest ever China–Africa diplomatic event, hosted by Beijing in November 2006, reported our guide[26]). Yet what would happen if one or more partners raised objections against China's dismal political record at home? Would the Chinese authorities bite their lips, remain calm and otherwise do nothing? What exactly did the rules of Harmony and 'socialist people's democracy' counsel?

Our muse was certain that in a world marked by chronic disharmony, a passive dominant power was an oxymoron. To illustrate this conviction, she told the gripping story of China's remarkable trespassing on an important election in Zambia, a country in which China had substantial investments in the copper industry, but also in textiles, retailing and road construction. During the course of its 2006 election (Figure 131), Zambia's wildest and most entertaining

FIGURE 131: Rowing the boat: a citizen carried in a bathtub, the symbol of Michael Sata's candidacy during the Zambian general elections, Lusaka, September 2006

in memory, the main opposition candidate, Michael Sata, publicly walloped the Chinese government's maltreatment of its own workers and denounced Chinese investment in Zambia as profiteering. 'Foreign relations must benefit all concerned. It must not be one-way traffic', the chain-smoking, gravel-voiced candidate said during an interview on privately owned Radio Phoenix. 'Chinese investment has not added any value to the lives of the people of Zambia.' Sata criticised Chinese investors: 'They ill-treat our people and that is unacceptable. We are not going to condone exploitative investors. This country belongs to Zambians.'

Sata singled out the giant NFC African Mining plant, located in Chambishi in the northern part of the country, where at the beginning of each shift, spent a thousand metres under ground, poorly paid and underprotected copper miners trudged beneath a Mandarin-language big banner that read, 'Work Hard to Make the Company Prosperous'. Sata went on to hammer Chinese-run businesses. He accused them of neglecting the safety of Zambian workers. He reminded his audiences that, earlier in the year, workers had been shot at a Chinese-run mine after protesting against miserable working conditions. He threatened to run 'bogus' Chinese investors out of the country. He also dared to criticise China's so-called one-China policy and lampooned talk of 'China's peaceful reunification'. It was a policy that required direct interference with the young democracy of Taiwan, he noted.

The words of Sata had bite and considerable popular appeal, our guide reported; many pundits and several opinion polls predicted that he would be the next Zambian president. Nobody thought of him as a political angel, she noted. Nicknamed 'King Cobra' – a man judged by supporters and opponents as either ready to strike or evasive and dangerous – the charismatic Sata had risen through the ranks of Zambian politics, combining ministerial experience with a reputation for treading on toes and getting things done. Many agreed that the co-founder of the Movement for Multiparty Democracy was indeed a man of action, but some said he was a thuggish xenophobe, a politician (as one journalist put it) who was 'not good for democracy' because he could 'whip and bully a drunken and demoralised Zambia into action'. That was probably true. Yet his anti-China rhetoric seemed to strike a chord in a country where three-quarters lived in poverty (they earned less than a dollar a day) and at least half the working population was unemployed. The Federation of Free Trade Unions (FFTUZ) in Zambia announced it was throwing its weight behind Sata. Into the final days of the campaign, the topic of Chinese investment dominated newspaper headlines, radio shows and political discussions; the very mention of Sata drew loud cheers from many lower-paid Zambians, including taxi drivers, shop workers and security guards. Support for him was especially strong in the copper-mining industry, and reports of his animated 'jump on the boat' speeches sparked debate even within the ranks of his more middle-class detractors.

The rumpus grew so serious that the Chinese ambassador, His Excellency Li Baodong, felt compelled to set aside diplomatic niceties, to intervene in the debate, in effect by denouncing the candidate as a 'bad element'. Speaking a different language from that of Harmony, he said in no uncertain terms that China might have to sever diplomatic ties with Zambia if Mr Sata became president and acted on his campaign promise to recognise Taiwan. His Excellency also raised the spectre of a halt to Chinese investment in the country. And that was that. A few days later, the new bipolarity in world politics had made its mark: following a high turnout of voters, but with life in the capital city of Lusaka now halted by rioting, the Zambian Electoral Commission formally announced that Michael Sata had lost the election to the ruling incumbent, President Levy Patrick Mwanawasa, the bosom buddy of Beijing.

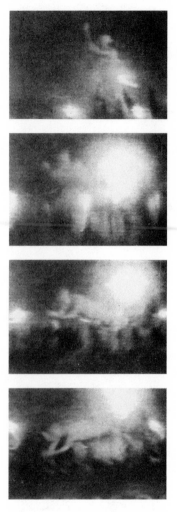

Destruction of the Goddess of Democracy: taken by an unknown citizen, rare photographs of the demolition work carried out by an army truck and tank pulling a steel cable, Tiananmen Square, Beijing, in the early hours of Sunday 4 June 1989.

WHY DEMOCRACY?

What we call the beginning is often the end
And to make an end is to make a beginning
The end is where we start from

T. S. Eliot, 'Little Gidding', Four Quartets (1942)

Imagine: democracy as we know it ruined in fits and starts by contempt for parties, politicians and parliaments, anti-American sentiments, nationalism, fake democrats, perhaps also by fear and violence, unimpeachable cross-border institutions, market failures, deepening social inequality, fatalism and disgust for the hypocrisy of whatever remained of democratic ideals and institutions. If our muse was right to foresee in these trends the sabotage of monitory democracy, what, if anything, would be lost? Who would care? Why should anybody care? In plain words: would it really matter if democracy died a fitful death?

The Democracy Thing

A curious fact is that exactly these questions were posed at a gathering of a thousand Pashtun tribal elders in the sun-scorched vineyards of Kandahar province, in southern Afghanistan, in the autumn months of 2003. The assembly, known locally as the *shura*, had been called to discuss Afghanistan's first awkward steps towards electoral democracy following the American-led invasion that overthrew the local Taliban dictatorship. The gathered representatives were reportedly served spit-roasted lamb, plus fruit and a list of instructions for dessert. Check that tents, tables, indelible ink and stationery had been delivered to polling centres, some with addresses like 'beside the Joi Nau stream' or 'near the water station pump'. Use tractors and taxis and donkeys to transport voters to those locations. Make sure that both wives and husbands could recognise the president's photograph on the ballot. 'We show them: here is the ballot, here is Karzai. Don't mark his head or put a line through his symbol – just tick the box', said Ahmed Wali Karzai, a Kandahar businessman and one of several speakers urging the assembly to cast a vote for his older brother, Hamid Karzai, the incumbent president and election front-runner. 'They don't have a clue what is going on', Ahmed Wali later commented, after the assembly had concluded its business. 'They come to us and say: "Why are we having an election? Everything is going well." Or they say: "We don't need the government. It's done nothing for us. I live in a tent. What do I care about politics?" I tell them – they often frown – it's this democracy thing.'[1]

This democracy thing: would it really matter if it withered on the world's vines during the coming years? In an age that offers plenty of other ways of handling power, ranging from secretive backroom deals to the fists and bombs of brute power, isn't monitory democracy to be seen as just one – dispensable – ideal among many others? Is it worth defending? Is it really a universal norm, as relevant and applicable to the vineyard people of Kandahar and (say) the Bekka Valley as it is to workers in Frankfurt, Tokyo and Moscow and businesspeople in Taipei and Cape Town, as well as to *dalit* women in India, or the peasant peoples of China, the Kurds of Turkey, or even to powerful bodies that operate across borders, like the WTO, the United Nations and the World Bank? Or, when all is said and done, is democracy actually just a fake universal norm – as Nietzsche thought – just one of those pompous little Western values that jostles for people's attention, dazzles them with its promises and, for a time, cons them into believing that it isn't a mask for power, a tool useful in the struggle by some for mastery over others?

Replies to these questions are essential, if only to persuade antagonists to change their minds, but efforts to do so face something very odd. It is this: more than half a century after the birth of monitory democracy, most political commentators around the world dodge questions to do with the desirability of democracy. A haughty moral silence sits on the subject at the very historical moment – paradoxically – that democracy has enjoyed a new burst of creativity. It is true that journalists, citizen activists, politicians and political thinkers commonly note that it has become, for the first time ever, a global political language. And they like to point out that its dialects are now spoken on every continent, in countries as different as India, Taiwan, Egypt, Ukraine, Argentina and Kenya. The friends of democracy take heart from think-tank reports that sing the praises of democracy using back-up evidence to prove its unstoppable advance. With a sigh of satisfaction, many people have grown convinced that it has become a global value. Although those in the know may admit that democracy is a particular ideal with particular roots somewhere in the geographic region located between ancient Syria-Mesopotamia and the early Greek citizen-states, they conclude that it has effectively triumphed over all other political values. Democracy has become its own justification. It has been embraced around the world *as if* it were a way of life that has global validity – as 'a universal value that people anywhere may have reason to see as valuable', as the Nobel Prize-winning economist Amartya Sen famously put it.[2]

The initial trouble with this view is that not everyone agrees that democracy is self-evidently valuable. Enemies of democracy are on the rise, and even pundits and panjandrums half-sympathetic to it are openly cynical about claims that it is a desirable way of life for all people on the planet. 'I know of no evidence that "democracy", or what we picture to ourselves under that word, is the natural state of most of mankind', remarked George F. Kennan (1904–2005), American diplomat, political adviser and key academic figure in the emergence of the Cold War. For him, democracy seemed 'rather to be a form of government (and a difficult one, with many drawbacks, at that) which evolved in the 18th and 19th centuries in northwestern Europe . . . and which was then carried into other parts of the world, including North America, where peoples from that northwestern European area appeared as settlers'. This way of thinking implies that democracy is a geographically specific and time-bound ideal, valued by just some people in certain times and places; not surprisingly, it rejects talk of democracy promotion and democracy as a global good, as vainglorious and undesirable. 'Misgovernment', concluded Kennan, 'the rise to power of the most determined, decisive, and often brutal natures, has been the common condition of most of mankind for centuries and millennia in the past. It is going to remain that condition for long into the future, no matter how valiantly Americans insist on tilting against the windmills.'[3]

The credo that democracy is nothing but a time-bound, geographically limited – originally Greek or Western – way of life can, of course, be put to quite a few different and conflicting uses. It can, for instance, induce the melancholy conclusion that the world is fated to be half-democratic, so that lucky people can enjoy its abundance while others less fortunate are forced to endure the misfortune of living in places where there is little, or none of it at all. Democracy is a geographic, not a global morality, and that's that. The conclusion can be a cause for celebration, of course. With more than a touch of contempt, wealthy magnificos in oil-rich consumers' paradises like Dubai and Doha commonly speak of its obsolescence. Fragrant, well-heeled, champagne-drinking members of the heavily Westernised Russian bourgeoisie are often in agreement. When asked what they think of democracy, they say something like: 'Democracy? Why democracy? Is Germany free? Or America?' If it is pointed out that at least in those countries there are free and fair elections, a vibrant civil society and a judiciary with teeth, they reply: 'We don't like that type of democracy. It would mean death for Russia. Our people don't like democracy at all.' End of story. Further questions about whether freedom is possible under a dictatorship are considered bad manners, or simply greeted with a snort and a chuckle, with mocking disapproval of the leaden curiosity of such obsolete enquiries. 'Nobody cares about anything here', they say. 'That's part of our life. We have dictatorship, and we have freedom because everyone can choose.'[4]

Things become more curious when the belief that democracy is nothing but a geographically parochial ideal fuels the inverse sentiment: that dictatorship needs to be overthrown. According to this line of analysis, if democracy is historically specific – merely one value among others – then only power stands in its pathway to unchallenged global dominance. Cunning and might could be right. Consider as an example the democracy-friendly remarks of the influential American scholar Richard Rorty (1931–2007). Like Kennan, Rorty did not mince his words. He acknowledged that modern representative democracy was a 'peculiarity' of 'North Atlantic culture'. It had no ultimate justification; philosophically speaking, it was neither True nor Right nor Universal. But when pressed to explain why he thought the 'North Atlantic' experiment with democracy was desirable, Rorty liked to reply, in one breath, that all forms of universal reasoning should be abandoned, and that democracy needed no philosophical justification at all. In ethical terms, he said, it was best if democrats travelled light. Rejecting mumbo-jumbo, they should stick to their convictions and whistle their way through the world, with an air of 'philosophical superficiality and light-mindedness'. Rorty was sure that democracy was not a substitute for theology or metaphysics. Democratic ideals should, rather, stand on their own feet. They were not desirable because they somehow corresponded or resonated with a founding 'reality' that was logically prior and given to us, an unavoidable imperative that just needed to be recognised, or obeyed, in order to take effect. According to Rorty, democracy should shun its dubious philosophical friends. It had no need of them; indifference towards old-fashioned ethics was the beginning of democratic wisdom, the trigger for realising that democracy was 'morally superior' because it was part of 'a culture of hope – hope of a better world as attainable in the here and now by social and political effort – as opposed to the cultures of resignation characteristic of the East'. So even though democracy is only one norm among others, it is self-evidently superior when put into practice. 'There is much still to be achieved', Rorty commented shortly after President George W. Bush had launched his War on Terror, 'but basically the West is on the right path. I don't believe it has much to learn from other cultures. We should aim to expand, to westernise the planet.'[5]

Westernise the planet by democratising it: in the early stages of preparing this history of democracy, during a breakfast conversation about the potentially positive effects of democracy, Rorty began by shrugging his shoulders. It was his trademark, a prelude to saying that he agreed that arguments for democracy based on its alleged beneficial consequences are notoriously unreliable. We agreed that those who favour democracy for so-called consequentialist reasons usually do so by trying to persuade others that it achieves various goals more effectively than its competitors; they say that the rightness of democracy stems from its usefulness, workability, its practicality. Some say, for instance, that democracy is a superior form of government because it maximises the opportunity of citizens to participate effectively in the making of collective decisions. Others say that democracy is good because it nurtures forms of development that are mindful of justice (that was one of the favourite arguments of the Indian scholar Rajni Kothari); or they boast that it is better than other systems at stimulating economic growth.* There are others who like to claim that democracy tames the tigers of war – that it fosters 'democratic peace' – or that it reduces so-called 'terrorist' threats to 'national security'. Still others, among them the doyen of American democratic thinkers, Robert A. Dahl, suppose that democracy fosters 'human development' more fully than any feasible alternative.

Most of these claims resemble a dog chasing its own tail, we agreed. The view, for instance, that democracy is good because it clears the way for people to participate in the making of collective decisions in effect says that democracy is good because democracy is good. Much the same can be said of the humanist view that

---

*To give a flavour of the braggadocio: a large-scale study of 224 different regimes between 1950 and 1990, 101 of them democracies, defined narrowly as regimes that hold elections in which an opposition has some chance of winning, showed that there was no such close correlation between economic growth and democracy; see Adam Przeworski et al., 'What Makes Democracies Endure?', *Journal of Democracy*, volume 7, 1 (January 1996), pp. 39–55. The study went on to draw conclusions that were quite different. 'Once a country has a democratic regime', the authors noted, 'its level of economic development has a very strong effect on the probability that democracy will survive' (pp. 40–41). They added that 'people expect democracy to reduce income inequality, and democracies are more likely to survive when they do' (p. 43). In a flight of fancy, the authors ignored non-economic causes and causers to stick out their necks to conclude: 'Above $6,000, democracies are impregnable and can be expected to live forever' (p. 41). The credibility of these time--and place-bound conclusions is shaky, to say the least. Only one thing is certain: the findings did not confirm the commonplace that democracies are friends of economic growth – even supposing that quantitative economic growth is a desirable good.

democracy fosters human development (whatever that is) more fully than any other feasible alternative. There is another problem, we agreed. When measured against practical realities, all these claims about the universality of democracy are highly doubtful. There is no evidence, for instance, that democracies consistently outperform dictatorships in achieving economic growth; and in any case too many tricky questions are left unanswered about the nature of 'human development' or the desirability of 'economic growth', or what is 'national security', for instance. So dubious are these claims, Rorty agreed, that they arguably do more harm than good for the ideal of democracy because they make it highly vulnerable to accusations of muddle and hypocrisy. The turn towards theories of 'deliberative democracy' at the end of the twentieth century provided no convincing protection against this danger, we agreed. Quite aside from problems of strategy, to do with whether and how democratic deliberation is best maximised through representative institutions, self-styled 'deliberative democrats' praise democracy as an ideal because of its requirement that when people vote they ought to do so on the basis of considered judgements of others' opinions, not by off-the-cuff or knee-jerk reactions about what is best for everybody. But exactly why citizens should act reflectively, responsively and responsibly, whether or to what extent that stipulation can come to mean the same thing, and why the principle of deliberation is to be counted as a universal norm ... all of this remains quite unclear. It is as if deliberative democracy is desirable because it maximises deliberation, which in turn has the good effect of keeping citizens busily involved in the business of deliberation.

So where did these reflections leave us? Rorty did say towards the end of our breakfast conversation that he regarded democracy as desirable – something to be valued in all four corners of a Westernised planet – because it gives hope to human beings that their lives can be freed from the curse of violence and cruelty. Persuasion rather than force, compromise and reform rather than bloody revolution, free and open encounters rather than bullying and bossing, a hopeful, experimental frame of mind: it sounded convincing, but we both knew that one trouble with his wistful meliorism is that it stood shoulder to shoulder with the contemporary 'democracy promotion' efforts of the United States and its military allies. Cosmopolitan pragmatism of Rorty's kind is not innocent; it can and does get mixed up in violent power games in devils' playgrounds, as the world discovered from daily reports of ill-fated democratisation experiments in Iraq, and in Afghanistan, where (by July 2006) new-minted members of the national parliament, most of them (like Ahmed Wali Karzai) men linked to warlords, drug dealers and human rights violators, moved around in heavy vehicles, with armed guards fore and aft, dodging daily threats and declared bounties on their bodies (US$25,000 dead; $50,000 alive).

Talk of the pragmatic superiority of democracy, when backed by military force, inevitably gives democracy a bad name. It certainly resulted, in the early years of the new millennium, in what was called 'democracy pushback', of the kind that happened in various parts of the Middle East. The harsh words against American democracy-promotion efforts spoken by Lebanese Druze leader and opposition parliamentarian Walid Jumblatt (b. 1949) may be read as the writing on the wall of democracy whenever and wherever it blindly or arrogantly supposes itself to be a universally good 'North Atlantic' value. Describing President Bush as a 'mad emperor' who thought of himself as 'God's deputy on earth', Condoleezza Rice as 'oil coloured' and Tony Blair a 'peacock with a sexual complex', Jumblatt sarcastically defined democracy as a type of imperial government in which 'their skies are American airplanes, their seas are American fleets, their bases are American bases, their regimes are U.S.-British regimes, their rivers are American boats, their mountains are American commandos, their plains are American tanks and their security is at the service of American interests'.[6]

Humility

Such rebukes are by no means innocent. They have political axes to grind, but for all their roguish self-importance they serve as a vital reminder that the age of innocent belief in democracy has come to an end. Perhaps more tellingly, such reprimands reveal a contradiction between means and ends: in effect, the belief that 'north Atlantic culture' or 'the West' (however it is defined) has a patent on the ideal of democracy, and that it is worth promoting, using military means, functions as a politically arrogant and self-contradictory dogma. Democracy becomes a life-giving medicine administered by some to others, despite the fact that they may well find it strange and distasteful, even nauseating.

Can this self-contradiction of democracy be avoided? Can democrats move to protect the ethic of democracy from its twenty-first-century opponents and doubters by coming up with a brand-new vocabulary for speaking about its global superiority? Or is democracy nothing more than a local ideal paraded hypocritically by powerful political charlatans when it suits them? We come back to our opening question: is there any way that democracy can plausibly claim to be a global ideal, applicable to all the earth's peoples, without serving as an alibi for the strong, or the pushy, against the weak? Can the ideal of democracy be democratised, brought down to earth so that it can better serve the earth and its peoples even-handedly, with less fanatical presumption, and more humility? The short answer is that it can, but what is needed is an understanding of democracy that is democratic, or at least a re-description of it that is a lot more democratic than previous old-hat understandings of democracy as a Good and Desirable Ideal.

For our forebears, the whole idea of democratising the ideal of democracy was unthinkable, let alone speakable. No democrat in their right mind would have accused the ideal of democracy of single-mindedness, of sidling up to an arrogant meta-vocabulary that had the effect of turning democracy into a Dogma by hitching its fortunes to Principles that give the impression that Democracy is an earthly Absolute, a substitute for God. It never occurred to past democrats that the haughtiness of their principles was openly at odds with an understanding of democracy that allowed for a diversity of different justifications of democracy; or that their principles were at odds with the fact that people, whether they dwell in democratic or undemocratic societies, typically live according to a plurality of conflicting and often incommensurable notions of what counts as a good life.

The proposal to democratise the ideal of democracy – to cut the swindle, to bring it up to speed with the ideals of monitory democracy – seems at first sight to make little or no sense today.

Most people simply don't get it; they find themselves bemused when the suggestion is floated that democracy needs to nurture its talents for speaking differently about itself. The chief reason for this is that in the age of monitory democracy millions of people around the world have come to believe that democracy is the continuous public chastening of power, a way of life that creates spaces for dissenting minorities and levels competition for power among citizens who are equals. It is hence hard for most people to appreciate that in times past the ideal of democracy harboured demons: grandiloquent philosophical propositions, metaphysical themes and dogmatic sentiments.

Once upon a time, until not so long ago, democracy was a dominatrix. She presented herself to the world in imperious terms, speaking in a language with strangely domineering connotations. Take the age of assembly democracy, where the word itself carried powerful suggestions of military conquest and control. Although there were no treatises by democrats in defence of the ideal of democracy, by today's standards the best-remembered Athenian speeches on the subject – the very discourses that most people, in the era of monitory democracy, still suppose to be the degree zero of thinking about democracy – sounded pompous. Not only did they picture Athenian democracy as a beautiful, harmonious whole, which it most certainly was not, but the strangest thing of all was the fact that the active friends of *dēmokratia* commonly justified democracy by linking her with empire. By the middle of the fifth century BCE power and the striving for its accumulation stood at the centre of the lives, the experiences and the expectations of the Athenians. Power politics and imperialism were seen as typically Athenian, and as typically democratic; the reputation of Athens as a busybody constantly striving to acquire more power over others became synonymous with democracy itself. Hence the well-known remarks of Pericles to mourners gathered to honour dead soldiers: 'Remember', he said, 'the reason why Athens has the greatest name in all the world is because she has never yielded to misfortunes, but has lavished more lives and labours upon warfare than any other city, thus winning the greatest power that has ever existed in history. The memory of this greatness . . . will be left to posterity forever.'[7]

Democracy as haughtiness: that way of speaking is such a nuisance in our times that there seems to be little chance that classical Greece can rescue the age of monitory democracy from its confused or sullen ignorance about why democracy is desirable. Some classicists – the shining example is Josiah Ober, the George Grote of the twenty-first century – are today investing their talents in trying to extract from the ancients a way of speaking about *dēmokratia* that resonates with our times. They say that our Greek ancestors can teach us that the great advantage of democracy lies in its capacity to solve problems by encouraging learning and innovation based on the open circulation of publicly useful knowledge.[8] Good luck to them in their efforts. Monitory democracy needs their talents, in no small measure because it will find little or no help from the age of representative democracy. Its languages of democracy were certainly plentiful; the trouble is that almost all of them contained more than a few traces of arrogance when it came to speaking about why democracy was a worthwhile ideal.

Examples of the dogmatism buried deep in the ideal of representative democracy come thick and fast. Think of an influential tract called *Government* (1820), written for an encyclopaedia by the Scottish preacher, teacher and civil servant, James Mill (1773–1836). It caused a sensation by explaining that representative democracy was the protector of private property and possessive individualism, that it conformed to the incontrovertible Utilitarian principle that 'if the end of Government be to produce the greatest happiness of the greatest number, that end cannot be attained by making the greatest number slaves'.[9] Then think of the champion of Italian unification, Giuseppe Mazzini (1805–72), for whom representative democracy was based on the Principle of Man, a foundational principle (he said) that had a 'religious' quality, in that faith in its workings was mandatory, simply because everybody and everything in the world were both its expression and potential beneficiary. Democrats were 'believers without a temple', worshippers of 'the law of continual progress' that led everywhere to the self-improvement of human beings intent on treating each other as equals.[10] And now spare a moment for Christian ways of speaking in support of democracy. Listen to just a few words from the famous speech delivered to a large anti-slavery rally in

Boston, in May 1850, by the New England preacher and campaigner Theodore Parker: 'A democracy, that is a government of all the people, by all the people, for all the people', he said, is 'of course a government after the principles of eternal justice, the unchanging laws of God'. Parker elsewhere noted that 'the democratic idea has had but a slow and gradual growth even in New England', but that it was now spreading throughout the American republic, such that 'government becomes more and more of all, by all and for all', a testimony to the fact that democracy is 'the enactment of God's justice into human laws'.[11] Finally, ponder several lines from our nineteenth-century friend Nahum Capen, the last author to attempt a full-blown history of democracy, when introducing his work: 'The History of Democracy is a history of principles, as connected with the nature of man and society. All principles centre in God', he wrote, 'the eternal source of TRUTH, WISDOM, JUSTICE AND LOVE. As the infinite attributes of Deity give existence, order and direction to the universe of being, so the faculties of man are the ordained agents of the divine will, as made known by Providence, and within the limits of humanity. In the sublime truths of Christianity', Capen concluded, 'is to be found the high standard of human conduct and endeavour.'[12]

Pity those unmoved by the Christian faith. Capen's case for why people should believe in democracy resembled the sermon of the fabled Presbyterian preacher who insisted that Jews and Muslims and those of other faiths could quit their quarrels and live together reasonably in the world if only they believed in the Lord Jesus Christ. Theodore Parker, Nahum Capen and the fabled preacher all clearly belong to a different universe from ours, as anybody but the most dogmatic Protestant Christian would today concede. Efforts to nail representative democracy to the cross of Christianity nevertheless flourished well into the twentieth century. Christian juices flowed through the speeches of many an American president, including those (most recently William J. Clinton and George W. Bush) who called upon citizens to protect and expand democracy through war.

Christian thinkers were active as well in making a case for monitory democracy. Among the first and cleverest ethical defence was one offered by the French Catholic philosopher Jacques Maritain

(1882–1973).[13] His case began with an unusual twist: 'the will of the people' is not its founding principle, he said, for recent experience had shown that the Sovereign People dogma had allowed leaders like Mussolini, Hitler and Stalin to act as if they were the sole judges of good and evil, so setting democracy on the road to totalitarian rule. Institutional limits should be placed on popular sovereignty – in favour of a 'common democratic charter' that encouraged faith in the possibility of human progress, the protection of human dignity and the conviction that human suffering and injustice could be overcome through 'political work'. Maritain called on the world to reject the dogma that the people of any single state are sovereign masters of their own sovereign house. The nurturing of 'brotherly love' across borders, extending 'civic friendship . . . to the entire human race', was now imperative, he said. But for this to happen, conventional notions of democracy had to be challenged in another way, Maritain emphasised. They indulged the mistaken belief that 'the people' could do without transcendent values, that they were soulless apes blessed by the accidents of zoological mutation and adaptation. Maritain strongly objected to the entrenched secular vocabulary of democracy. Democracy was for him the 'temporal manifestation of the inspiration of the Gospel'. On this view, democracy is rooted in God-given Being; it is the sublimate of God's creation and guidance of the earth and its peoples. 'The democratic sense or feeling', said Maritain, 'by its very nature, is an evangelical sense or feeling, its motive power is love, the essential thing in it is fraternity, it has its real sources in Gospel Inspiration.' The corollary is that democracy could not survive in purely secular form. 'The people are not God, the people do not have infallible reason and virtues without flaw.' Authority ultimately had its source in God. No person or group or people could claim the right to rule others. That is why, Maritain concluded, the voluntary re-Christianisation of the world, the 'internal awakening' of individuals who become spiritually committed to the teachings of Jesus of Nazareth, was a basic condition of reviving and quickening democracy in troubled times.

The Novelty of Democracy

The case for Christian democracy deserves respect, if only because Christians came late to democracy; the marriage of Christian ethics and the ideal of democracy was itself an important historical achievement, one that had to be built politically, the hard way, using philosophical hammers wielded by Maritain and other Christians. Their case for democracy, for all its worldly brilliance, nevertheless induces a bad feeling among Muslims, Buddhists, deists, tough-minded secularists and others. Their objection is that democracy reeks of sectarian language: it is as if Christianity has first claims on the democratic ideal. Standing behind this objection is a bigger difficulty, to do with the impossibility of straightfor-wardly combining the belief in a metaphysical First Principle (a claim that human beings are dependent upon a logically prior, inde-pendent ethical order, like a Christian God) with the most original quality of democracy as an ideal way of life. What is this novelty? Put simply, democracy as a way of life is profoundly suspicious of every type of claim to absolute power based on metaphysical First Principles and Big Talk of every description. The radical implica-tion is clear: democracy is a universal ideal because it is a basic precondition of people being able to live together on earth freed from arrogant power fed by talk inspired by principles like God, History, Truth, Man, Progress, the Party, the Market, the Leader or the Nation.

Let us pause to reconsider what we have already found in this book. The invention of the language and institutions of democ-racy in the eastern Mediterranean region well before the birth of Christ implied something revolutionary: democracy supposed that humans could decide for themselves as equals how they were to be governed. It later came naturally to many people, but the whole idea that flesh-and-blood mortals could organise themselves as equals, face to face or through their representatives, so that they could pause to decide on this or that course of action, was a sensational inven-tion. It called on people to see that life was never merely given, that all human institutions and customs are built on the shifting sands of time and place, and that if people are to avoid giving themselves over to others in the foolish belief that some are naturally superior, then they had no option but to build and to maintain flexible political institutions that ensured that questions about who is entitled to get what, when and how remained permanently open, the subject of a learning experience guided by the consent of others.

When democracy takes hold of people's lives, it gives them a glimpse of the contingency of things. They are injected with the feeling that the world can be other than it is – that situations can be countered, outcomes altered, people's lives changed through individual and collective action. The South African novelist Njabulo Ndebele (b. 1948) puts it to me like this: 'Democracy blurs the relationship between certitude and uncertainty. It gets people used to the experience of formulating a position in the morning, changing their minds by the afternoon, growing angry, sleeping it off, feeling different again about the same matter next morning. Democracy breeds possibility: people's horizons of what is thinkable and doable are stretched, and it is for that reason exciting, infuriating, punctuated by difficult, quarrelsome, ugly and beautiful moments.' I ask him what's so good about it. He replies: 'Democracy is not a good thing in itself. It is what makes good things possible.' He goes on to say that 'democracy is the closest people get to an experience of faith: the sense that against every kind of obstacle, they have to get on with things, keep searching for what in the end will work, knowing that although they don't know exactly where they are going things won't happen if their arms are folded.' Ndebele says fatalism is fatal for democracy, that people's sense of the contingency of power relations is precious, that possibility is felt most intensely when they have tasted its opposite. A character in one of his novels explains. Apartheid: 'Do you remember the experience of space, and the sense of distance and time through travel in the old days of apartheid?' She answers: 'In travelling from point A to point B, I remember not the pleasure of movement and anticipation; the pleasure of reflecting, at the end of the journey, why the journey was undertaken. What I do remember is that the intervening physical space between A and B was something to endure because of the fear of being stopped and having my existence questioned by agents of oppression.' Democracy: 'South Africa, my new home! Home, not as a building with rooms, but a country full of people, trees, mountains, rivers, houses, factories, roads, the coastline, schools and universities, military bases, museums, art galleries, theatres, research foundations, observatories, the stock exchange, the airlines . . . everything!'[14]

Ndebele was right: the thing about the ethic of democracy is that from the outset it poured cold water on karma, the belief that individuals wanting to improve their prospects in the next life must show deference to others by acting within the (caste or class) roles assigned to them in this life. Democracy as well urged people to see through talk of gods and nature and rulers claiming privileges based on some or other alleged superior quality. Democracy insisted that nobody be allowed to sit on thrones built of power backed by bogus big beliefs. It meant self-government, the lawful rule of people whose sovereign power to decide things was no longer to be given over to imaginary gods, or Tradition, or to omniscient despots, to those in the know, or simply handed over to the everyday habit of unthinking indifference, so allowing others to decide matters of importance on their behalf.

The point is worth putting a bit more abstractly: democracy is born when people are disposed to speak and act as if they are subjects of this world, in all its flesh-and-blood complexity, rather than objects dangling on some other-worldly or super-worldly dynamic. The point is sometimes stretched, to say that democracy is a thoroughly 'secular' or atheist ideal, so that democracy is only possible when people wash their hands of all traces of belief in gods, goddesses and Gods. In the history of democracy, as we have seen, fully 'secular' or non-religious governing institutions and customs are in fact a rarity. The reason is clear, but subtle. Democracy supposes the willingness of people to spot a disjunction between their transmundane and mundane worlds. It requires them to think and to act in terms of a chasm or tension that separates a higher transcendent moral or metaphysical order (whatever they think that is) and the everyday world of human beings living together within various earthly institutions. Democracy further supposes that there is no straightforward homology between these two otherwise connected worlds. It therefore implies that the mundane realities of the everyday world are 'up for grabs', that is, are capable of ordering and reordering by human beings whose eyes are fixed for at least some of the time on *this* world and not *that* world extending through, above and beyond human intervention.[15] There is an interesting flip side to the point: democracy recognises that although people are not angels or gods or goddesses, they are at least good enough to prevent some humans from thinking they *are* angels or gods or goddesses.

The Rule of Nobody

Here, then, is a new way of speaking about democracy as a global ideal, a brief answer to the big, complex and interesting question of whether or not it is a worthwhile vision: from the moment of its birth, democracy pointed the way towards a universal way of life because it took the side of people everywhere in their efforts to live as equals, to resist the arrogance of power camouflaged in grand Universal Principles and piffling prejudices.

Things could be put this way: the democratic ideal thinks in terms of government of the humble, by the humble, for the humble, everywhere, any time. Its universality, the applicability of this ideal across borders, in a wide variety of settings, whether in South Africa, China, Russia or the European Union, stems from its active commitment to what might be called 'pluriversality', the yearning of the democratic ideal to protect the weak and to empower people everywhere, so that they can get on with living their diverse lives on earth freed from the pride and prejudice of moguls and magnates, tyrants and tycoons.

Democracy thrives on humility. Never to be confused with docile meekness or submission, humility is the cardinal democratic virtue, the antidote of arrogant pride: it is the quality of being aware of one's own and others' limits.[16] People who are humble try to live without illusions. They dislike vanity and dishonesty; nonsense on stilts and lies and bullshit sitting on thrones are not their scene. Humble human beings feel themselves to be dwellers on earth (the word humility derives from *humus*). They know they do not know everything, that they are not God, or a god or goddess. Humility is the opposite of haughty hunger for power over others, which is why humility balks at humiliation. In a world of arrogance tinged with violence, humility emboldens. Unyielding, it gives individuals inner strength to act upon the world. It dislikes hubris. It anticipates a more equal and tolerant – and less violent – world.

To think of democracy as a uniquely humble and humbling ideal is to give up on the old-hat idea that democracy rests upon some or other First Principle – the Nation, History, God, Truth, Utility, the Market, the infallible Sovereign People or its Leader. To see instead that democracy is a *precondition* of the flourishing of different values and ways of life around the world is to rid democracy of its connotations of moral arrogance, sectional rule, bullying and force. To speak of democracy as a codeword for humility is to say goodbye to the worn-out nineteenth- and twentieth-century European liberal rejection of democracy as a headstrong and perilous ideal that 'by the help of a demagogue and a mystical faith in "the people" or "the masses" leads to tyranny and the rule of the sword' – a government by braying and kicking donkeys, an 'onagrocracy', as the Italian liberal Benedetto Croce (1866–1952) once put it.[17] To rid democracy of its demons, to speak of it in terms of humbling, is rather to redescribe the democratic ideal as a potentially universal check against every form of humbug and hubris, as a humble and humbling ideal that gathers strength from the vision that, although citizens and representatives require institutions to govern, *no body should rule.*

Democratic institutions – monitory democracy is so far the best-developed overall example – ideally dispense with *rule*, if by that is meant bossing others who have few or no means of redress. Under democratic conditions, nobody rules in the sense that those who govern others are subject constantly to the ideal of public chastening, tied down by a thousand Lilliputian strings of scrutiny (Figure 132). Democracy provides plenty of room for people to respect and admire authorities, and to show courtesy and respect for each other, in an astonishing variety of ways. There are democracies where men greet acquaintances with a simple gentle kiss on the cheek (Uruguay) or a firm handshake (Britain); others where they greet their fellows in the name of God (Austria and Germany) or with a high five (the United States); still others where they express their equality by bowing to each other, with a faint click of the heels (Japan). But in each case, the democrats among them are the

FIGURE 132: The chastening of power: Lemuel Gulliver, set ashore after a mutiny, regains consciousness to find himself trapped by the Lilliputians, from C. E. Brock's drawing in an 1894 edition of Jonathan Swift's *Gulliver's Travels*.

first to say that in a democracy those who exercise power should be prevented from bullying others, threatening them with violence, pushing and pulling them into different shapes, as if they are mere clay in the hands of potters, or as if (as Aristotle liked to say) they are mere pawns on a chess board.

Think of the way democracies treat their elected leaders. When they function properly, democracies can be irreverently harsh on those who make decisions on behalf of others. That leaders suffer this fate is in no small measure because democracy has the effect of breaking apart and destroying the fiction that there is, or could be, a unified body politic symbolised and held together by a Leader. Under democratic conditions, the political community is permanently subdivided. There is no 'Body Politic' and no body called 'the People' who hold it together. Whatever unity the polity enjoys is permanently questionable and constantly up for grabs, simply because the exercise of power over others is always scrutinised, contested, divided, constrained.

The contrast with anti-democratic governments, eighteenth-century European monarchies and twentieth-century totalitarian regimes is revealing. Think for a few seconds of how hard-core monarchies symbolically represented the power they wielded over their subjects. The physical body of kings like Charles I and Peter the Great was conceived in the figure of both God the Father and Christ the Son. The monarch's body was divine, and therefore immortal and unbreakable. It could not be admitted that kings died. Their bodies symbolised perfection. Like God and His Son, kings could do no wrong, which is why the violation of their bodies – through unGodly acts ranging from unsolicited touching by their subjects through to attempted regicide – was harshly punishable. The body of kings also symbolised the unbreakable quality of the 'body politic' over which they ruled. Like God, kings were omnipresent and their bodies coterminous with the polity itself. Monarchs were God-given givers of laws. But they also resembled God the Son. Sent by God to redeem humankind, kings had a 'body natural' – the sign of God in the world – as well as a body politic. Just like the persons of the Trinity, the two bodies plus the authority they radiated were one, inseparable and indivisible.

It is a strange historical fact that twentieth-century totalitarianism thrived on a version of the same fiction of a unified body politic, 'pure as a diamond', as the butchering Great Leader Pol Pot explained in a little-known 1949 pamphlet, *Monarchy or Democracy*. In the name of 'the people', but like the monarchies of old, totalitarianism put the body of the Great Leader on a grand pedestal for the grand purpose of establishing Him as the ultimate source of wisdom, strength, knowledge and power. The embalming and public display of Lenin's corpse in the Soviet Union in January 1924 was a foretaste of such practices, which reached something of a climax in the huge Memorial Hall edifice in Tiananmen Square constructed in memory of the Great Helmsman of the Chinese people, Mao Tse-tung. Those who have seen it will agree that it is no simple grave for a common corpse. It more than resembles the royal mausolea reserved for the Sons of Heaven who were at once elevated persons and divine persons, in whose bodies time figuratively stood still, for ever (Figure 133). The Tiananmen edifice preserves this custom for a revolutionary saint. It contains a marble statue and a crystal-covered sarcophagus containing Mao's embalmed remains, together with an inscription in the green marble of its southern wall: a telling phrase dedicated to the memory of 'our great leader and teacher Chairman Mao Tse-tung: forever eternal without corrupting'.

FIGURE 133: Big poster by Lü Enyi commemorating Mao's death and the completion of the Memorial Hall, Beijing, 1977.

Democrats and democracies put such embodied notions of power and leadership under a pedestal, a point well made in a subtle Chinese joke, traceable to Beijing intellectuals with democratic hearts. It tells of a bumpkin from the countryside, an old man who comes to visit his city cousin, who takes him to see Mao's tomb. 'Ai-ya', says the bumpkin. 'It's so huge! Chairman Mao of course always wanted to be just like one of us. He never wanted to distance himself from the masses. So why have they built him such a big and imposing mausoleum?' 'Oh', replies the city cousin, 'just to prove that he's really dead.'

Democracies, understood as forms of government and ways of life in which no *body* rules, dispense with the fetish of rulers. They, of course, need leaders, respect them, follow them, learn from them – but they do not worship them as Leaders blessed with metaphysical powers. Representatives are not thought to be identical with the roles they play; the bodies of leaders like George W. Bush, Ronald Reagan or Richard Nixon are not reckoned identical with the office of President of the United States. That is why, when they function properly, democracies like the United States regularly poke fun publicly at the bodies of politicians, with impunity. Halted by a traffic snarl on a freeway leading into Washington,

DC, a driver is startled by shouting. She winds down her window, to be greeted by an excited citizen carrying a jerrycan and bearing breaking news. 'The president has just been kidnapped by terrorists! They're demanding a huge ransom, otherwise they say they'll set him on fire! The government says citizens should contribute, so the situation can be resolved fast.' Replies the startled driver: 'How much on average are citizens donating?' Says the messenger: 'About a gallon apiece.'

Equality

The prickliness of democracies towards elected and unelected representatives is encouraged by the fact that democracy thrives on separations. In monitory democracies, for instance, everything seems disconnected: civil society from government, representatives from those whom they represent, executives from legislatures, majorities from minorities, civil power from military and police power, parties from voters, experts from laypeople, consumers from producers, journalists from audiences, the young from the old, workers from capitalists, lawyers from clients, doctors from patients. Both government and civil society are internally fragmented. These multiple, criss-crossing separations are necessary conditions of citizens' equal freedom from concentrations of power. Democracies try hard to take the sting out of imperiousness. They resist calls for social unity and political concord. Those who wield power are reminded constantly of their (potential) powerlessness. They are kept permanently on their toes by the push-pull dynamics set in train by differentiation.

That does not mean that democracy is defined mainly by its separation of powers, by what Montesquieu once called 'the effect of liberty'.[18] Separations were, for instance, a chronic feature of the Ottoman Empire, the European feudal order and the Qing Dynasty, all of which contained forests of concentrated power. Differentiation alone does not produce *equality*. Separations often harbour *inequalities*, and that is why democracies are different. They certainly de-centre power relations, scatter them into a complex plurality of different institutions. But when the ideal of democracy is unleashed on the world, it does something much more radical than that.

Democracy points towards the *equalisation* of power. By ruling out violent rule and by dispensing with fictions about a unified body politic, democracy strives to control winners, for instance by placing time limits on holding office, and by offering real incentives to losers. Democracies introduce a strong element of randomness in the patterns of winning and losing. They ideally require that individuals and whole groups are sometimes winners, sometimes losers. Democracies therefore thrive on the selection of those who decide matters of government and civil society through free, fair and frequent elections or other means of recall. Monitory democracies do something more: they multiply citizens' votes. They surmount the principle that dated from the age of representative democracy, the principle that said that 'each person will count for one and no person for more than one'. With its plethora of mechanisms for scrutinising and humbling power, monitory democracy instead champions a much more complex understanding of citizens and their many particular activities and interests, so that the slogan 'One person, one vote' is turned into the principle, 'One person, as many votes as interests, but only one vote in relation to each interest'.

The complex checks upon separated powers have profound implications for the way democracies think about the matter of equality. It goes without saying that the principle of the equality of people has always been fundamental to the democratic ideal. 'For by nature we all equally, both barbarians and Greeks, have an entirely similar origin . . . for we all breathe into the air with mouth and nostrils' read a fifth-century CE papyrus fragment attributed to the Athenian thinker and orator Antiphon.[19] The same sentiment in favour of equality convinced Walt Whitman that the ethos of representative democracy could not be confined to elections. 'Did you, too, O friend, suppose democracy was only for elections, for politics, and for a party name?' He replied: 'I say democracy is only of use there that it may pass on and come to its flower and fruit in manners, in the highest forms of interaction between men, and their beliefs – in religion, literature, colleges, and schools – democracy in all public and private life, and in the army and navy.'[20] The principle of equality remains vitally important in the era of monitory democracy, for instance in the equal worth of votes cast in many different settings by citizens who consider each other as equals, not only during elections, but in social life more generally. From the standpoint of the humbling ideal of democracy, a shared sense of equality among citizens needs to be visceral. One vote, one value has to be heartfelt, underpinned even by a dash of self-mockery, of the kind displayed in Nehru's attack on his own political pretensions, or in the witty reply of an elderly former Australian prime minister to a question about how he would handle his creator: 'You can be sure of one thing', he said. 'I shall treat him as an equal.'[21]

The humbling ideal of democracy implies something more than mateship. It demands that the ability of citizens equally to grasp the world around them depends crucially on their access to adequate resources. A decent education, universal access to health care and the legal protection of basic human rights are vital. It is also certain that the ideal of humble democracy demands innovative thinking and action geared to the creation of new mechanisms of universal entitlement, for instance to the empowerment of young and old people as citizens, extending rights of representation to our biosphere and the refurbishment and enhanced provision of publicly available infrastructures that are used by all people. Without equal access to 'the commons' – in matters as diverse as public transport, telecommunications and a sustainable biosphere – humble democracy in monitory form simply cannot survive, let alone thrive.

That requirement implies that democracy demands the equalisation of all its citizens' life chances. But one of the interesting effects of speaking differently – more democratically – about democracy is that simple notions of equality, understood as equal treatment and equal prospects of advancement for each individual citizen, become unworkable, even undesirable. To understand why there is this paradox – why, for the sake of equality, democracies sometimes must privilege some at the expense of others – let us imagine for a moment a totally different world: a socially undivided and homogeneous political community in which, in the name of equality, all individuals are continuously treated the same. In this paradise of pure and simple equality, resources would be divisible into equal amounts. Each citizen would benefit in exactly the same way and, since people are presumed to be so much alike in their wants and needs, no disputes would break out over the significance and effects of the equal portions given to all as equals. Differences of taste and conflicts among differing goals would be unknown. In this society of arithmetic equals, the fully centralised allocation of resources and the absence of politics would render obsolete the need for any institutions of representative government. Why would there need to be mechanisms for monitoring the exercise of power if, at the end of each day, every citizen dutifully accepted that she or he was the simple equal of each and every other citizen?

Scenarios of simple equality have often greatly bothered past analysts of democracy. 'The gradual progress of equality is something fated', wrote Tocqueville in a famous lament about the crushing consequences of the drive towards equalisation during the age of representative democracy. This 'irresistible revolution advancing century by century' in favour of simple equality, so Tocqueville thought, might well steamroll the world into a flat and simple form of equality, what he called levelling into sameness. The movement for equality would stop at nothing. It would have the unintended consequence of building a new form of state servitude brought on by the democratic quest to make and treat everybody equal. 'Does anyone imagine that democracy, which has destroyed the feudal system and vanquished kings, will fall back before the middle classes and the rich? Will it stop now, when it has grown so strong and its adversaries so weak?'[22]

Aside from his serious underestimation of the persistence of factual inequalities in nineteenth-century societies, Tocqueville's prediction failed to spot the ways in which the irremediably concrete and complex ways of democracy would remould the ideals and practices of equality into something far more complicated than anybody had envisaged in the era of representative democracy. Sameness was not to be the effect of democracy. To the contrary: in the new age of monitory democracy, awareness is growing that there are many different kinds of equalities that in turn are capable of having many different kinds of relationships with one another. The simple word equality is transformed into a much more complex grammar of equality. It becomes apparent to many people that the fractured quality of social and political life demands not only that recognition be granted to more than one practical meaning of equality. Many people realise as well that the principle of equality cannot itself serve as a basis for choosing among them. The landmark legal case of *Fullilove v. Klutznick*, 448 U.S. (1980) pointed in this direction. The case split the nine-judge United States Supreme Court into five separate opinions about whether the federal government was entitled to give preferential treatment in some part of its public works programmes to minority-owned companies. In the end, the Court held such set-aside treatment was justified, but the case highlighted a watershed clash: between equality understood in terms of equality of results or outcomes, and the quite different understanding of equality as equality of opportunity, a form of equality that typically results in unequal outcomes, in 'winners' and 'losers'.

Things become still more complicated when these different understandings of equality are applied either to individuals, or to groups, or to specific policy areas, or to large territorial areas, or to cross-border relations of power. In each case, the quest for 'equality' has different – and often unequal – effects. The scope of equality can be local or territorial or global, and these different domains often conflict with one another, so that, for instance, the act of placing singular emphasis on the equality of citizens living within a state ('all are equals in this country') easily works against citizens equipped with different needs and concerns within the same state, as well as working against citizens of other states, or those without any state at all. The implication is clear: like salt to the sea, the principle of equality lies at the heart of democracy, but it is not a straightforward Universal Principle that can be applied like a sharp saw to rough wood, or a bulldozer to uneven ground. To return to Walt Whitman's likening of democracy to fruits and flowers: the thrust of the democratic ideal, contrary to the complaints and platitudes of its opponents, is not to cut down tall poppies, to level everything to the ground. It is, rather, to ensure, through the never-ending ways and means of humbling politics, that species of poppies everywhere on the planet can flourish in fields of plants and animals otherwise at risk from harm and extinction at the hands of parasites and predators.

Hubris

It is time to say goodbye to our subject, but for a few parting words of caution about the strange elusiveness of the democratic ideal.

One of the unavoidable lessons to be learned from the history of democracy is that, when compared with the many different types of earthly regimes, democracy is utterly unique. Exactly because it means, minimally, the self-government of equals – their freedom from bossing, violence, injustice, dogmas and metaphysical claims – it demands more than humans seem willing or are often capable of giving. During the darkest moments of World War Two, the Irish man of letters C. S. Lewis (1898–1963) put his finger on the point. 'I am a democrat', he wrote, 'because I believe in the Fall of Man. I think most people are democrats for the opposite reason. A great deal of democratic enthusiasm descends from the ideas of people . . . who believed in a democracy because they thought mankind so wise and good that everyone deserved a share in the government. The danger of defending democracy on those grounds is that they're not true.' Lewis added: 'The real reason for democracy is . . . Mankind is so fallen that no man can be trusted with unchecked power over his fellows. Aristotle said that some people were only fit to be slaves. I do not oppose him. But I reject slavery because I see no men fit to be masters.'[23] The Hong Kong parliamentarian and celebrated champion of democracy Martin Lee (b. 1938) has spoken in similar terms about malefactors and fools. 'In life as in politics', he told me, 'we can never be sure that decisions taken are the right ones, which is why guarantees are needed to ensure that those who make wrong-headed decisions can be removed from office.' He added: 'Deng Xiaoping once told me: in a good political system, even men who are evil can be stopped from doing evil. In a bad system, things are worse: evil flourishes and good men are prevented from doing good, and may well be forced to do evil. I agree with that.'[24]

The democratic suspicion of unchecked power and its dangers implies something that at first sight seems shocking: democracy cannot be 'pure' or 'authentic', simply because it never manages fully to bring the tigers of power fully under control. The American satirist H. L. Mencken, known as the Sage of Baltimore, once sarcastically described democracy as government by orgasm, but that rather overstates the gratifications it brings. Democracy never breeds bliss. It is never calm, motionless, fulfilled. Democracy is not a condition achieved. It is never the same as the democracy that actually exists. The fashionable distinctions between 'consolidated' and 'transitional' and 'failed' democracies, sometimes even between 'good' and 'defective' democracies, are suspect; they should not be hardened into dogma. 'Good' democracies and 'consolidated' democracies are never blessed with divine immunity from internal corrosion and external weathering; from the viewpointpoint of those who live within these democracies, they are never good enough, never fully consolidated – never freed from the burdens of refurbishment and renewal.

The era of monitory democracy is no exception to this rule, despite its fruitful experimentation with many new methods of publicly scrutinising and controlling the exercise of power. Whether in the workplace or the fields, in the boardroom or on the battlefield, democracy continually teases people with the difference between its promises and its achievements, between its lionhearted possibilities and its sorry realities. The gap is felt especially in contexts where the word 'democracy' means things less esoteric than democratic thinkers like to suppose: places like the populous townships of South Africa and the crowded favelas of Brazil, where democracy is linked to life-and-death matters, like clean running water, honesty about HIV/Aids, gun amnesties, decent medical care, bread and a steady supply of electricity. In circumstances like this, it is hardly surprising that the majority of the world's people associate democracy with what they do not have. Citizens in India like to say that democracy is the ongoing struggle for 'BiPaSa' (*bijli*: electricity; *pani*: water; *sadak*: roads). In material terms, that expression captures correctly the esoteric point: democracies always chase democracy around corners, through halls of mirrors, across uncharted landscapes, up into blue skies. Jeremiads and failures – improvement, perfectibility – are inscribed within the very ideal of democracy. But that, believe it or not, is its great strength. Democracy is never more alive than when it senses its incompleteness. It thrives on imperfection. Those who accuse it of hypocrisy and condemn its poor performance fail to see that democracy is process. Democracy is always on the move. It is not a finished performance, only a set of actions that are always in rehearsal. It is never something that is done and dusted, never a mechanism that comes to rest, as if it has reached a steady state. Democracy must always become democracy again. It is a thing of action – not something accomplished and piled up and stored, like gold in a vault, or goods in a warehouse.

So why bother with it, given that it consistently disappoints because it demands more than humans are seemingly prepared to give? Why should people hang on to the democracy they have? Why should they strive for more democracy, given that it is never completely attainable? Today's democratic malaise feeds upon the fact that the standard answers of the past no longer work. The old presumptions that Nations are naturally democratic, or that History is on the side of democracy, or that the Christian God gave the people the power to govern themselves at the expense of others: these and other clichés are worn out. So, too, is the dogma that the Future will guarantee a higher and purer and deeper form of democracy.

When pondering the subject of democracy during the years when representative democracy was collapsing around his ears, the English novelist E. M. Forster (1879–1970) found the right track: 'So two cheers for Democracy', he had written. 'One because it admits variety and two because it permits criticism. Two cheers are quite enough: there is no occasion to give three.'[25] Let us pass over in silence Forster's faded faith in the tattered ideal of aristocracy, to note that there is in fact a third cheer for democracy, one that is becoming more pertinent with the passing of each day: the cheer that should be given for democratic power-sharing as the best human weapon that has ever been invented against the folly and hubris that always come with concentrations of unaccountable power.

The struggle against blind arrogance and stupidity caused by concentrated power is never ultimately winnable, yet it is among the struggles that human beings abandon at our own peril. Democracy is a powerful remedy for insolence. Its purpose is to stop people getting screwed. Democracy is a good weapon for publicly exposing corruption and arrogance, false beliefs and blind spots, bad decisions and hurtful acts. It helpfully injects critical thinking and matter-of-factness into the design and operation of complex organisations and networked systems; above all, it is an indispensable means of tackling problems (like climate change) for which there are currently no agreed definitions, let alone viable solutions. Democracy champions not the Rule of the People – that definition of democracy belongs in more ways than one to the Age of Monarchy and the Era of Dictatorship and Total Power – but the rule that nobody should rule. Democracy refuses to accept that those who wield power can draw their legitimacy from gods and goddesses, or tradition, or habit, or wealth, or brains, or brute power. That is why its history is partly the story of remarkable inventions designed to bring big boss men back to earth.

Hunting and gathering communities excommunicated members who aroused the wrath of the spirits by falling in love with their own arrogance. Sumerian kings sometimes had their faces slapped by priests to remind them of the importance of humility. Medieval kings in Europe were forced on occasion to swear to God that they would not abuse their power. Democrats instead preferred more down-to-earth methods, with more egalitarian effects. Greek democrats evaluated public office holders before they took up their appointments; demagogues were ostracised; complaints were brought by assemblies against officials and fellow citizens deemed guilty of misconduct; and Greek democrats popularised rules and customs like the payment of jurors, the freedom to speak frankly in public, voting machines, voting by lot, and trial before elected or selected juries.

The age of representative democracy brought new inventions. Periodic elections supervised by uncorrupted electoral commissions; requirements that politicians must resign or suffer impeachment when involved in conflicts of interest; and laws and independent media that guaranteed the right of citizens publicly to question nonsense, to speak bitterness, and to organise against their elected representatives: these tried and tested procedures were designed to keep tabs on those who stepped out of line when exercising power over others.

With the rise of monitory democracy came the conviction of millions of people that periodic elections, competitive parties and parliamentary assemblies, though an important inheritance, were simply not enough to deal with the devils of unaccountable power. So, despite all the setbacks and disappointments and unsolved problems, great attention has been paid to developing innovative methods – watchdogs and guide dogs and barking dogs – moved by the humbling spirit that enables citizens and representatives to try to keep reins on power brokers in the fields of government, civil society, and in areas in between. It remains to be seen whether these arguing and bargaining mechanisms of monitory democracy will be strong enough to prevent future rivalries, disasters and upheavals capable of tearing the world to shreds. Who today knows the formula for scrapping nuclear weapons, or putting an end to the irrational exuberance of markets, or how to move towards a more sustainable, balanced and equitable global society? As the world experiences further growth spurts in the global integration of law and government and weaponry, economic and social life, will democratic ingenuity manage to chasten cross-border power relations? Will the world witness a flourishing cross-border journalism and culture of public debate, even the expansion of a global civil society – the growth of worldwide networks of journalists, experts, elected and unelected representatives and politically unaffiliated activists skilled at articulating local injustices, taming markets, educating public opinion, mounting actions when necessary, acting in general as watchdogs of democratic life on a global scale?

We cannot yet answer these questions, but what can safely be said is that the history of democracy is not only about institutions, laws and procedures designed to chasten the exercise of power. It is replete as well with an astonishing cast of figures who helped invent the worldly ideal of democracy, personalities who saw that it had the potential to hold back the arrogant, foolish and ruthless who crave power. Many are people – the common folk of cities like Larsa, Nippur and Babylon, believers in the Qur'an who saved from extinction the spirit of assembly democracy – whose names have been rubbed out by time, and who knew next to nothing of the language of democracy. Later, there came the first recorded personalities of assembly democracy, characters like the Sophists, who hurled javelins of fun and sarcasm – and even farted in public – for the purpose of humbling arrogant authority. There was Demonax of Mantinea, the lawmaker who confirmed the right of the farmers of Cyrene to govern themselves through their own assembly; the priestesses of Athens who led prayers for the goddess Dēmokratia; the laughing democrat, Democritus, a citizen disgusted by poverty; and scholars like Abu Nasr al-Farabi, the first Muslim to speak of democracy as the Greeks had understood the word.

The history of democracy was driven as well by people who should be remembered for putting representative democracy into motion: the powdered and wigged nobleman the Marquis d'Argenson, who came close to using the phrase for the first time; Scandinavian farmers who defended their *tings*; Manegold of Lautenbach, the humble monk who thought that rebellion against tyrants was obedience to God; local Calvinists in Scotland who popularised the principle of 'covenants'; and plain-clothed commoners who applauded the public execution of Charles I. There were men of sobriety like George Grote, the hard-working banker and middle-class man of letters who published a *History of Greece* in a dozen volumes; and there were the moonshine men of Pennsylvania, who triggered the growth of Democratic-Republican societies after picking up pitchforks, tarring brushes and aiming guns at officers of their own federal government.

The age of representative democracy was driven, too, by God-fearing Christian and republican opponents of slavery, workers who refused to be wage slaves, and atheist rebels who built street barricades, raised red flags, and aimed cobblestones at glass panes, in the name of brotherhood and democratic liberty. There were the quieter types, characters who concentrated on oiling the machinery of representative democracy: William U'Ren; Juan Vucetich, William Robinson Boothby, Sukumar Sen. There were the first machine politicians of party politics, men like Andrew Jackson and Martin Van Buren; journalists like William Lloyd Garrison, the opponent of slavery who publicly burned a copy of the constitution at a Fourth of July rally, and Liang Qichao, the peasant boy who became China's most read writer. There were revered leaders like J. D. van der Capellen; Brother Gregory, elevated to the papacy as Pius VII, who forced a French dictator to crown himself; Abraham Lincoln; Father John O'Malley, the pioneering boycotter; Francisco

Madero and José Batlle y Ordóñez. There were poets, like John Milton, Manuel José Quintana and, of course, Walt Whitman, with his 'Thunder on! Stride on! Democracy. Strike with vengeful strokes.' And not to be forgotten were the brave women who broke down the doors of male prejudice: figures like Angelina Grimké, who called upon women to be citizens by rejecting Slave Power; Esther Hobart Morris, perhaps the first woman to hold judicial office in the era of representative democracy; and the fearless women who rallied in London's Trafalgar Square in defence of free speech and the vote, garbed in purple and green, spurred on by exemplars of determined courage, like the young Australian émigrée, Muriel Matters, the first woman in Britain to give a speech in the House of Commons after chaining herself to a metal grille in the women's public gallery and slipping the padlock key down her knickers.

Then there are the women and men who remain figures of our time, critics of concentrated power who breathed life into monitory democracy: Mahatma Gandhi; Peng-chun Chang, the Chinese playwright and literary critic who helped arrange the marriage of human rights and democracy; and the bearded dissidents of Moscow, Warsaw and Prague, hunched over their typewriters and huddled together on sofas in smoke-filled apartments. Not to be forgotten is Rosa Parks, the woman who grew tired of being tired; Alice Stewart (1906–2002), the fearless and much-maligned Oxford epidemiologist who first demonstrated during the 1950s that there is no such thing as a harmless dose of radiation; the young black and white American students who risked their brains under a barrage of police truncheons wrapped in barbed wire; and Buddhist monks in crimson robes, walking barefoot, keeping 'the mind mindful' as they collect rice from the faithful for the cause of survival against brutal dictatorship. There are as well the leaders: Winston Churchill, Eleanor Roosevelt, Jawaharlal Nehru, Nelson Mandela, Archbishop Desmond Tutu, Aung San Suu Kyi. And certainly not to be forgotten are the unyielding types, those who put things simply, characters like Doris Haddock (Figure 134), the office worker who, at the age of ninety, took more than a year to walk from Los Angeles to Washington, DC, a tortoise whose public speeches along the way aimed to bring into disrepute the selling of

FIGURE 134: Doris 'Granny D' Haddock (b. 1910) in front of the camper van she used during her cross-country walk in support of campaign finance reform, Dublin, New Hampshire, June 2004.

democracy to the millionaires who fund political campaigns, a little-d democrat who was fried by the sun, blown about by strong winds and skied the last hundred miles of her journey, arriving just in time to celebrate the birth of the twenty-first century by standing on the steps of Congress, before a small but enthusiastic public, to deliver a laconic address in which she pointed to the entrance of the Capitol as she issued her parting words before slipping quietly away: 'This is turning into a bawdy house.'

For all these figures, the taming of power was a way of life; it was not an inheritance to be spent, certainly not a good or service to be bought and sold in the market, for a price. These characters did not suffer fools gladly. They did not think of themselves as angels, or as deities. They refused the temptations of aggrandisement and did not much like big clichés and smelly little orthodoxies. They trusted in simple decency. They did not believe that an unequal society was inevitable. They were convinced that human beings could and should govern themselves. They detected the weaknesses of the powerful; they believed in the power of the powerless. That is why, in these testing times of monitory democracy, forgetting their democratic spirit – consigning them to the pages of the next instalment of the life and death of democracy – would be a crying shame.

NEW DEMOCRATIC RULES

The history of democracy now on your screen, or resting in your hands, took a decade to research and write. The last person to attempt a similar feat was Nahum Capen, the American historian, publisher and self-taught polymath who reportedly laboured on the subject for thirty-five years. Capen's toils were interrupted by a civil war, a bookselling and printing business (his authors included Edgar Allan Poe and Nathaniel Hawthorne), and by deep involvement in the political affairs of the Democratic Party. His plans for a three-volume history of democracy were complicated as well by a political gift from the fifteenth President of the United States, James Buchanan, Jr: his appointment (in 1857) as Postmaster at the city of Boston. Given the interruptions, it came as no surprise to one of his friends that although he was still going strong at eighty, 'thinking vigorously and writing pointedly as ever', Capen never managed to complete his manuscript. Only part of it was published, as a book of seven hundred pages, *The History of Democracy: or, Political Progress, Historically Illustrated, From the Earliest to the Latest Periods* (1874). Stuffed full of intriguing details, and especially strong on the history of political and legal ties binding the United States to its former British rulers, Capen's study of the history of democracy, perhaps the first ever published in modern times, has proved to be a hard act to follow. But I felt it necessary to try to do so, if only to correct his unashamed Anglo-American bias. Finding myself in completely different historical circumstances, under a mountain of new material of virtually unmanageable complexity, I had to move quickly to realise my goal: replacing Capen's history with an entirely fresh and certainly less partisan account of a topic that has since grown from being a transatlantic preoccupation to a subject of global importance.

Capen's history of democracy saw its subject through nineteenth-century American eyes. It was neglectful of the ancient world of assembly democracy (and openly contemptuous of the 'pride and vanity' and 'licentious habits' of Athens). It was silent about the complex origins of representative government in continental Europe, and (characteristic of its times) ignorant of important contemporary developments in the former Spanish colonies and parts of the British Empire. Written by a respected public figure who had been a willing quill of the Democratic Party since at least the time of the American military invasion of Mexico of 1846–8, *The History of Democracy* was motivated by a strong sense of the rising power of the United States, its triumph over domestic and geopolitical adversity, its breakthrough to an exciting new world of representative democracy. The book's central preoccupation was to heal the hurt caused by the horrors of the Civil War. It set out to convince its American readers that the nineteenth-century progress of democracy in the world, especially its triumph in the United States of America, was guaranteed by 'the sublime truths of Christianity'. Democracy was 'limited to no season, age, or nation'. It had an assured future, simply because it was a worldly expression of God's inscrutable design.

Capen was not alone in thinking in this way; his contemporary, the French aristocrat-turned-democrat Alexis de Tocqueville, remarked more than once that the democratic revolution of modern times, led by events in the United States, was ultimately protected by the Hand of God. Many other avowed democrats of the mid-nineteenth century agreed. This was obviously not my starting point, and in fact I quickly became convinced that my subject demanded a fundamental rethink of what would be required in trying to write a new history of democracy. Although *The Life and Death of Democracy* recognises that democracy has had much to do with people's faith in the sacred, I doubted that a faith beyond history – or the escape from time into a world of eternal essences – was the key to understanding democracy. I rejected just as firmly the opposite view, that human history is a massive jigsaw puzzle for which there are no meaningful interpretations, or that history is an unintelligible nightmare so riddled with unthinking dogma and the blind will to power that (as W. H. Auden and others have recommended) it is best left to itself. I was sure of only one thing: all the existing rules of writing about democracy and its history had to be broken. Crusty silences needed to be shattered; customary ways of thinking had to be amended, or ditched. New rules were definitely required.

Rule number one: treat the remembrance of things past as vital for democracy's present and future. Soon after beginning *The Life and Death of Democracy*, I grew convinced that the word 'history' should be posted on the mirrors or doorframes of all democrats, to serve as a daily reminder of the reasons why today and tomorrow depend upon yesterday. I began to think of my project as an exercise in extending votes to a constituency without a voice: the dead. It is in the spirit of enfranchising the past that this book makes a sustained case for bridging the gap between politics and history. With eyes on both the past and the future, it reminds its readers that things of this world never last for ever – that democracy as we know it has no built-in guarantees of survival. Less obviously, the book shows how and why democracy and history are conjoined twins. It demonstrates the vital ways in which, right from the beginning, democracy in action stirred up people's sense of the historical contingency of power relations, for instance by showing that tyrants and monarchs were not necessary in human affairs; or that prevailing opinions could legitimately be challenged and changed (through such mechanisms as constitutional conventions, judicial review and liberty of the press); or by showing that the sky would not collapse if women, slaves and the poor were treated as the political and social equals of their former masters.

The book shows that for the sake of the future much can be learned, or unlearned, from the past. Familiarity with things past can suggest what should not be done in the present, or in the future; at a minimum, it can stick a pin into the backside of those who denounce democracy as a political sickness, or who try instead to crown it with garlands of bogus praise, for example for the way it supposedly heals social tensions or generates economic growth.

The Life and Death of Democracy also aims to arouse readers' sense of marvel at the magical moments in which democracy was born, or matured, or died. It recalls forgotten characters – individuals whose words and deeds are today still capable of inspiring people in matters of democracy. The book further supposes that the act of grappling with the history of democracy makes us much more sensitive to the novelties of our times. The working formula I use is straightforward: people inevitably misunderstand the present when they live in ignorance of the past. In every line, this book tries to impress on readers that the future of democracy depends upon the past, which is always at work in the present; and it reminds them of what we would collectively lose if the world foolishly allowed democracy to slip through its hands, to wither away, or to be killed off by its rising numbers of opponents.

Rule number two: always regard the languages, characters, events, institutions and effects of democracy as thoroughly historical. Democracy is neither a naturally occurring substance nor a God-given universal. It is both a precipitate of particular times and places and a powerful contributor to people's grasp of the time-bound quality of their lives. This double-jointed quality of democracy, its dependence upon time and its role as a great driver of people's sense of their own historicity, may seem obvious after reading this book, but the astonishing fact is that most people today don't think of democracy in this way. They take democracy for granted, as if it were timeless; or (which amounts to the same thing) they treat it as if it were the foregone conclusion of prior events, as Francis Fukuyama unhelpfully did in *The End of History and the Last Man* (1992).

The presumption that democracy is a given, a part of the natural or evolutionary order of things, is commonplace in all actually existing democracies. It certainly runs deep in scholarly circles. In the course of my career, for instance, scholarly regard for democracy as an historical way of life has been the exception, not the rule. The history of democracy is treated almost as a contradiction in terms. Various factors have conspired to reinforce scholars' ignorance of democracy's past. The heavy reliance of academic researchers upon empirical methods geared to producing 'data' has produced a whole generation of amnesiacs; it is not only that the data-collection methods related to democracy are a recent invention (of the 1920s), and that they enter mainstream academic research only with such American classics as Seymour Martin Lipset's *Political Man* (1960) and *The Civic Culture* (1963), an important study by Gabriel Almond and Sidney Verba which I used to guide my very first writings on democracy. The problem with the empirical and comparative research that these books helped to inspire is that the study of democracy is confined largely to our times, and very often to a limited number of cases for which 'data' is available. The historicity of the present is thus concealed, or admitted glibly as a limitation of the data. The scholarly amnesia has been compounded by other university habits: teaching the 'classic' authors and texts of democracy without regard for their original context; fashionable academic controversies that pay little or no attention to their own time-bound character (rows over the merits of 'participatory democracy' and, more recently, 'deliberative democracy', 'agonistic democracy' and the 'quality of democracy', are cases in point). The combined effect of these different fashions and fads has been to produce something very strange: research into the way of governing and living life known as democracy suffers numbness, a loss of feeling for how democracy stimulates people's sense of the historicity of power. That numbness helps explain why no comprehensive history of the language and institutions of democracy has been attempted for a very long time – and why, in the scholarly study of democracy, there is still no work comparable to what has been produced by figures such as Adam Smith, Karl Marx, Émile Durkheim and Max Weber.

Rule number three: pay close attention to the ways in which the narration of the past by historians, leaders and others is unavoidably an historical act, which is to say that their accounts of the history of democratic institutions, ideas, characters, events and languages have an irreducibly arbitrary and time-bound, therefore contingent and tentative, quality about them. Previous histories of democracy have been intoxicated by their naive belief in timeless 'facts'. 'It is Facts that are needed: Facts, Facts, Facts', James Bryce insisted in his *Modern Democracies* (1921). Despite all that has happened in such fields as philosophy, science and linguistics since Bryce wrote these words, plenty of historians still like to suppose that they are the last historians; they think of themselves as recording angels, not as hanging judges. They imagine their impartiality stems from the fact that they deal only with facts, with what really happened, but that is a fallacy. I have elsewhere explained (in a commentary on the work of Quentin Skinner) that there is no such thing as a straightforwardly 'objective' history based on the past 'as it really was'. Those who pretend otherwise resemble tricksters bent on pulling the wool over the eyes of the living, at the expense of the dead, and the unborn.

Two of my teachers persuaded me that history is always a contrived representation, not a simple reproduction, of things past: C. B. Macpherson, who won the twin prizes of respect and fame for his theoretical efforts to guarantee a future for democracy by rescuing its past defenders from the condescension of posterity; and the great twentieth-century scholarly champion of hermeneutics, Hans-Georg Gadamer. Both teachers, who never saw eye to eye on anything but the importance of studying history, inspired me to think historically about the methods used by historians in coming to terms with the past. Throughout this book, and in previous works, I have adopted an approach that I call a 'dialogue with the dead'. Critical of all strands of political writing that rely on abstract language and formal propositions, it defends a forceful history of the present that retrieves forgotten or neglected political languages, characters, events and political institutions. The dialogue-with-the-dead approach has underpinned my earlier efforts to breathe new life into the old ideal of civil society; to show why secular forms of the originally seventeenth-century Christian principle of liberty of the press today remain alive and well; and to demonstrate the great contemporary relevance of the life and writings of the eighteenth-century political writer Tom Paine. *The Life and Death of Democracy* similarly pursues a dialogue with the dead. In supposing the importance of the past for the present and the future, it emphasises that each and every account of the past is inescapably shaped by the mental and linguistic horizons of the present day. Memories are not the gift of impartial spectators; every age and every historian look upon the past from their own different perspectives and sets of concerns. If that is so, then historians of democracy must admit the strangers of contingency and humility into their ranks. For it turns out that the simon-pure and simple facts of political history are never simple at all; and that even when apparently straightforward 'facts' – names, dates, places – win universal agreement among political historians, they are always so trivial that they cry out for interpretations of their significance. The lamp of 'Facts, Facts, Facts', contrary to Bryce, cannot guide the study of politics, political thinking and history. As in life more generally, facts invariably depend upon interpretations; interpretations depend upon narrations; narrations depend upon concepts and rules of method; and concepts and rules of method are shaped by interpretations and narrations, and by the languages, events, characters and institutions that provide the raw material ('the facts') of interpretations, narrations and ways of thinking about power and politics, understood in the broadest sense.

Rule number four: the methods that are most suited to writing about the past, present and future of democracy are those that straightforwardly draw attention to the peculiarity of their own (and others') rules of interpretation. Democracy has no need of orthodoxy or memory police. For if democracy is an unending exercise in humbling the arrogant, writing about its history should be no different. Ideally, discussions of the past, present and future of democracy must aim for openness, for example by admitting their ignorance, the deliberately conjectural qualities of their claims, and the great complexity of the causes and causers of the things they narrate.

The Life and Death of Democracy tries hard to harness such devices. For the purpose of encouraging readers to think for themselves, to make up their own minds about the subject, it switches periodically from one narrative voice to another and reverses the temporal sequence of events, so that the false sense of security provided by one-thing-followed-by-another description is broken. The book questions some standard units of historical thinking. It shows, for instance, that democracy cannot be understood through simple categories such as 'ancient', 'medieval' and 'modern'. It shows instead that democracy has different, discordant and braided tempos, and that efforts therefore must be made to track the long-term continuities, gradual changes and sudden upheavals that have defined its history. Towards the end of the story, tongue in cheek, the book even introduces a fictional narrator to remind us that imagining the future is vital for remembering what is going on in the present. Throughout, the book places great emphasis upon the messiness, the multiple causes and causers, of democracy, the secrets she keeps, her astonishing variation in time and space. The book sometimes casts doubt on its own certainties; it retells the best jokes at the expense of democracy, and gives voice to the claims of its opponents. It tries to sharpen the sense of irony of readers by paying attention to the unintended consequences that so often gave rise to democratic institutions; and it deliberately adopts the widest possible plurality of perspectives on the subject.

Stretching and sharpening the mental geography of our under-standing of democracy is one of the prime aims of *The Life and Death of Democracy*. It was spurred on by deep dissatisfaction with the parochialism of much contemporary writing about democracy. Despite many rich insights, the standard works on democracy make it seem as if its languages, institutions and ideals are still essentially phenomena of the Atlantic region. These works usually repeat the cliché that democracy originated in Athens; ignore the growing body of research on the assemblies of ancient Syria-Mesopotamia; and, as if to please the prejudices of James Bryce, Nahum Capen and Alexis de Tocqueville, remain silent about the contributions of the early Islamic world. The remarkable spread of the ideals and institutions of representative democracy in Spanish America and the British Empire is normally ignored, as is the contemporary indigenisation of democracy in places otherwise as different as India, Papua New Guinea, South Africa, Taiwan and China. In times when the world has changed democracy as much as democracy has changed the world, none of this neglect is any longer acceptable. That is why *The Life and Death of Democracy* calls for greater worldliness in the way we think about democracy. Borrowing from twentieth-century physics to depict time as a dimension of space, it makes a case for a world history of democracy, one that is no longer conceived within the confines of national and linguistic boundaries, or within originally transatlantic ways of political life and political thinking that falsely claim to be universal.

Rule number five: acknowledge that, until quite recently, most details of the history of democracy have been recorded by its critics, or by its outright opponents. Right from the beginning, cold silence and hot-blooded animosity greeted the inventors of democracy. Rather typical was the kind of abuse that lashed out from the surviving pages of its founding historian: an aristocrat named Thucydides (c. 460–400 BCE). His *History of the Peloponnesian War* emphasised again and again just how easily democracy, 'effeminate government', could be muscled aside by the immutable realities of power, politics and war. A loser who was himself exiled from Athens because the naval fleet he commanded (in 424 BCE) failed to accomplish its mission, Thucydides had a chip on his shoulder against democracy. He detested its pandering demagogues, and accused it of imprudence and political incompetence. In a world structured by cyclical time and ruled by the law that the strong always do what they can and the weak suffer what they must, democracy for him was vulnerable, irresponsible, short-sighted, selfish and fickle – negative qualities that were symbolised, in his view, by the Athenian mob that one day, under the influence of demagogues, voted to kill the entire adult male population and sell into slavery the women and children who had resisted the imperial rule of Athens, only on the next day to change its mind, thanks to the prompting of more moderate leaders.

Until well into the twentieth century, following the path first cut by Thucydides, most subsequent treatments of the life and times of democracy displayed deep ambivalence towards their subject. James Bryce's *Modern Democracies* worried that parliamentary democracies, for all their moral appeal, might well produce majorities that behaved like oligarchies, selfishly and self-destructively. A century before, François Guizot's *The History of the Origins of Representative Government in Europe* (1820–22) attacked the democratic 'principle of the sovereignty of the people' as an affront to 'the experience of the world, which has always seen the timid following the brave, the incompetent obeying the competent – in one word, those who are naturally inferior recognising and submitting themselves to their natural superiors'. That judgement resurfaced in stronger form in the classic nineteenth-century account of the rise of popular government by the English comparative jurist, Sir Henry James Sumner Maine. He concluded that if democracy had triumphed in Britain then 'there would have been no reformation of religion, no change of dynasty, no toleration of Dissent, not even an accurate Calendar'. Maine added: 'The threshing-machine, the power-loom, the spinning-jenny, and possibly the steam-engine, would have been prohibited.'

Rule number six: the negative tone of most previous histories of democracy confirms the rule that tales of its past told by historians, politicians and others often harbour the prejudices of the powerful. It sounds odd to put things this way, but one of the lessons history teaches us is that those who talk about history often teach us the wrong lessons. Given the record of deep-seated opposition to democracy among its historians, any new history of democracy worthy of the name therefore has to start again. It needs to relinquish the bad habit of thinking that the original foes of democracy were its first allies. It needs as well to bear in mind that democracy has plenty of mimickers and false or fair-weather friends; that recorded history is always a record produced by someone in some particular time and place, for some particular purpose; and that when (for instance) a president or prime minister waxes eloquent about the historic triumph of democracy, or the historic need for its promotion for the sake of peace, by force of arms, memory and power may well conspire to ruin democracy's fortunes. That is why *The Life and Death of Democracy* poses a tough question: is it possible to write about the past, present and future of democracy more democratically, using methods that include many more experiences and voices from around the world? It answers the question by issuing a warning to those who are interested in the past and present and future of democracy: history often resembles a big bag of tricks played by the living on the dead. If that is so, then those who care for democracy, and therefore have an interest in its history, must be prepared to have their prejudices challenged. They must dare to question humbug, to open themselves up to bold and unfamiliar conjectures, to recognise the need to bring democracy to the history of democracy: initially by granting a vote to events, institutions and people whose enduring contributions to democracy have been shoved aside and compulsorily forgotten, according to the rules of victors' justice, then buried by their enemies in the deep holes of the past.

A seventh and final rule: admit that the task of coming to terms with the past, present and future of democracy is by definition an unending journey, an odyssey that is permanently subject to revisions brought about by new evidence, unexpected events, different interpretations and different ways of doing history, put forward by people with fresh thoughts about democracy. During the past decade, following this rule that the quest for a 'grand theory' of democracy is both undesirable and impossible, at odds with its marvellously unfinished fluidity, my views were often altered by reading widely in several languages (for reasons of space, well over a hundred pages of endnote references were removed from the final version of the book). My views were also profoundly shaped and reshaped by contact with many hundreds of people, some of whom, for reasons of their own personal safety and the protection of their loved ones, asked to remain anonymous. Every one of them gave generously of their time in conversation; some offered documents, showed me places, sent photographs, or emailed fragments of information or opinion that they thought I might find of interest. Others read drafts of what I had written; queried my formulations; or proposed unconventional ways of interpreting the material by offering new stories, details, tips, clues. Some handed me advice so generously tough that they forced me fundamentally to rethink the direction of my whole project. I would like to thank all of them in the hope that they will see the useful marks they made on my work, and that they will forgive me for the mistakes that I have made.

Help with the overall framework of interpretation was selflessly provided by Frank Ankersmit, Wim Blockmans, Robert Dahl, Ralf Dahrendorf, Francis Fukuyama, Paul Ginsborg, John Hirst, Eric Hobsbawm, Jürgen Kocka, Thomas Koelble, Enrique Krauze, Martin C. M. Lee QC, Christine Loh, Wolfgang Merkel, Ashis Nandy, Bhikhu Parekh, Milan Podunavac, the late Richard Rorty, Pierre Rosanvallon, Hilda Sabato, Michael Schudson, Abdolkarim Soroush, the late Charles Tilly and Sheldon Wolin. For their help with materials and advice on how to think about the importance of assembly democracy in classical Athens I am most grateful to Lesley Beaumont, Rick Benitez, Alastair Blanshard, John McK. Camp, Jan Jordan, Julia Kindt, Christian Meier, Josiah Ober, Chronis Papanikolopoulos, David Pritchard, Alan Shapiro and the helpful staff of the American School of Classical Studies at Athens, the British School at Athens, and the Benaki Museum. Similar assistance with the task of making sense of ancient assemblies and other power-sharing institutions before and after Athens was freely provided by Hossein Aabedi, Abdelwahab el-Affendi, Fariba Afkari, Shmuel Eisenstadt, Sheikh Muhammad Husayn Fadlallah, Aminullah Habibi, Tom Hillard, Benjamin Isakhan, Engin Isin, Mandana Karami, Samir Khalaf, Marc Van De Mieroop, Reza Mostofi, Dariush Poor, Eric W. Robinson, Mohammad Samiei, Kenneth Sheedy and staff at the Australian Centre for Ancient Numismatic Studies at Macquarie University, the Malek Library and the National Museum of the Islamic Republic of Iran, Tehran.

My experiment with writing differently about the European origins of representative democracy was supported by Renger de Bruin, Ignacio González Casasnovas, Richard Cust, Goyita Cavero Domínguez, Burhanettin Duran, Javier Miguélez García, Dariusz Gawin, Martin van Gelderen, Jan Jerschina, Marcin Król, Ramón Máiz, Laura Miguelez, the late Jaroslav Jan Pelikan, Gerhard Ritter, Michael Saward, Orhan Silier, Quentin Skinner, Max Stackhouse, Will Storrar, Nadia Urbinati and Mark Warren. For this part of the project, I gratefully acknowledge the support given by the archivists and library staff of the Bibliothèque Royale de Belgique, Biblioteca Nacional in Madrid, Archivo Nacional de Madrid, the Hamburg Staatsarchiv, the Kunstsammlungen der Veste in Coburg, the Musée des Beaux Arts in Brussels, the Museum Boijmans Van Beuningen in Rotterdam, the National Library of the Netherlands, the Palau de la Generalitat in Valencia, and the University of Edinburgh Library. My understanding of the American experiment with representative democracy was fruitfully shaped by the advice and materials provided by Benjamin Barber, Paul Berman, Michael Edwards, Holly E. Geist, Alexander Keyssar, James Miller, Earl Taylor, Sean Wilentz and staff of the American Philosophical Society Library, the Dorchester Historical Society, the Library of Congress, the New York Public Library, the Oregon Historical Society and the Wyoming State Archives. For their support with Spanish America and Brazil, I am especially grateful to Waldo Ansaldi, Gabriela Cerruti, Inés Cuadro, Carlos Demasi, Ana Frega, Cristina Puga, Cristóbal Rovira Kaltwasser, José Nun,

Juan Rial, Ana Ribeiro, Ana Maria Rodríguez, Philippe Schmitter, Alfred Stepan, Milton Tosto and the kind assistance of the Biblioteca Nacional in Madrid and the Biblioteca Nacional de Venezuela.

Many people around the world provided expert guidance on the eighteenth- and nineteenth-century fortunes and misfortunes of representative democracy in Europe and its colonies. I am indebted to Peter Brent, David Bridges, Lea Gardam, Geoffrey Hawker, Malcom Lehman, Michael Mann, Jenni Newton-Farrelly, Mandy Paul, David Pegram, Victor Pérez-Díaz, Paul Pickering, Marian Sawer, Gerald Stourzh, Douglas Verney, Charles Vincent, Judith Vincent and Hiroshi Watanabe. Many institutions came to my rescue as well, including staff at the Australian National Library, the Bibliothèque nationale de France in Paris, the British Library, the Library and Archives of Canada, Old Parliament House in Canberra, the Parliament of South Australia, the South Australian Museum, the Staatliche Graphische Sammlung in Munich and the State Library of New South Wales. My adventures through the world of banyan democracy were assisted by Vivek K. Agnihotri, Rajeev Bhargava, Kunal Chakrabarti, Neera Chandhoke, Peter Ronald deSouza, Francine R. Frankel, Ramachandra Guha, Niraja G. Jayal, Sudipta Kaviraj, Rajni Kothari, Sateesh Kumar, T. N. Madan, Vandita Mishra, Bishnu N. Mohapatra, Ashis Nandy, Vijay Pratap, Shalini Randeria, Ash Narain Roy, Amartya Sen, Yogendra Yadav. It is a pleasure to thank as well the staff of several institutions in New Delhi, especially the Nehru Memorial Museum and Library, the Parliament Library and the Lok Sabha Secretariat.

My efforts to make sense of the history and present-day contours of monitory democracy were richly encouraged by Usep Abdulmatin, Azyumardi Azra, Patrick Burke, the late James Carey, Shin Chiba, John Clarke, Robert Cooper, Mario Di Paolantonio, Alpaslan Durmuş, Mustafa Ercan, Stephan Feuchtwang, Mark Harrison, Brian Head, H. H. Michael Hsiao, David Huang, Ronald Inglehart, Takashi Inoguchi, Clara Joewono and Elihu Katz. Generous help on the same subject was also given by Joseph Ketan, Hans-Dieter Klingemann, Lin Lihyun, Christine L. Lin, Gavin McCormack, Adam Michnik, Ferenc Miszlivetz, Godfrey Mwampembwa (Gado), Janet Newman, Kenneth Newton, Kaarle Nordenstreng, Wally Olins, Haig Patapan, Vukašin Pavlović, Ben Reilly, Roland Rich, Felix Schoeber,

Atsushi Sugita, David Steward, Lütfi Sunar, Nobuhiko Suto, Georg Thurn, Emílio Rui Vilar, Peter Wagner, Wimar Witoelar, Rwei-Ren Wu and Ryusaku Yamada. My thoughts concerning the twenty-first-century challenges to democracy were shaped by Abdou Filali-Ansouri, Samanta Casareto, Gloria Davies, Michael Davies, Tony Ehrenreich, Graeme Gill, Marlies Glasius, Paul Graham, Lucas Guagnini, Sa'eed Hajjarian, Paul 't Hart, Christopher Hobson, Shiao Jiang, Wang Juntao, John Kane, Gilles Kepel, Ben Kiernan, I-Chung Lai, Yang Lian, Claus Offe, Nnanyere Chukwu Ogo, Pablo Palomino, Sven Reichardt, Dieter Rucht, Abdulaziz Sachedina, Peter Sloterdijk, Jusuf Wanandi, Syd Wang, Luo Wen-chia and Michael Zürn. On the pressing need to rethink the advantages and disadvantages of democracy, I gratefully acknowledge the advice and warm encouragement given by Derek Butler, John Dryzek, Robert Goodin, Dieter Grimm, Nader Hashemi, Mohsen Kadivar, Patrizia Nanz, Ali Paya and Charles Taylor.

This book would not have been completed without the generous financial support provided by several organisations, including the Calouste Gulbenkian Foundation, the European Science Foundation, the Ford Foundation, the Leverhulme Trust, the University of Sydney, the University of Westminster and the Wissenschaftszentrum Berlin für Sozialforschung (WZB). Thanks are due to Heinrich Bassler and Cameron Thomson for expertly handling the research funding contracts. Maria Cifuentes de Castro, Andrew Gordon, Mike Jones and Robert Weil lived up to their reputation as world-class editors. I thank them sincerely for their patient support, their most useful comments on various drafts of the book, and their willingness to stand by me during the most challenging stages of the project. For help and advice about matters of publication I wish to thank Terence Wong-Lane, Louisa Pritchard, Rory Scarfe and Lucas Wittmann. Katherine Stanton at Simon & Schuster took charge of the design and production schedule with remarkable aplomb, thoughtfulness and professional skill. I offer a special thanks to David Daniels and Daniel Leighton, who both generously provided me with many hundreds of brilliant and wise comments on earlier drafts of the book. Nicholas Dimotakis and Giovanni Navarria offered invaluable help with the drawings and illustrations. Sue Phillpott went through the proofs with a fine toothcomb; Douglas Matthews handled the index with energy and skill. The sparkling efforts under pressure of my copy editor Richard Collins proved, in matters ranging from purple prose to historical interpretation, that he stands unrivalled, at the top of his profession. During the past decade, quite a few researchers provided me with short but vital reports on subjects I knew nothing about. I owe warm thanks to Agnes Arndt, Javier Arribas-Gómez, Baykal Binay, Ravindra Karnena, Joanna Llorente, David Mervart, Giovanni Navarria, Tina Olteanu, Brenda Suchi and Djordje Pavicević. Maria Fotou of the Centre for the Study of Democracy at the University of Westminster was more than a distinguished Research Associate: for much of the project, she tirelessly, cheerfully and with great intelligence helped me design a research strategy, provided written commentaries on dozens of disparate subjects, gathered and interpreted printed materials from various languages, hunted for illustrations and managed, with great verve, skill and diplomacy, communications with many hundreds of people located on every continent except Antarctica. I thank her warmly for correcting my excesses, lifting my spirits and teaching me to rethink my topic, again and again.

The book is dedicated to the greatest loves of my life, feisty young citizens who taught me by example much more about democracy than perhaps they realised at the time: Alice Keane and George Keane.

London and Berlin
September 2008

NOTES

BAD MOONS, LITTLE DREAMS

1 Fragmentary evidence of the wars and power struggles among the landowning aristocracy that plagued the Libyan farming city of Cyrene, plus details of the tyranny of Battus the Lame (c. 550–530 BCE) and the arrival of Demonax, the 'mediating judge' or 'arbiter' who set about empowering the poorer citizens of the city by reorganising its administrative units, is best provided in the fourth book of Herodotus, *The Histories*, translated by George Rawlinson (London, 1858): 'Hence the Cyrenians made the request and the Mantineans gave them a man named Demonax, a person of high repute among the citizens; who, on his arrival at Cyrene, having first made himself acquainted with all the circumstances, proceeded to enrol the people in three tribes. One he made to consist of the Theraeans and their vassals; another of the Peloponnesians and Cretans; and a third of the various islanders. Besides this, he deprived the king, Battus, of his former privileges, only reserving for him certain sacred lands and offices; while, with respect to the powers which had hitherto been exercised by the king, he gave them all into the hands of the people' (4.159–62).

2 Dae Hwa Chung, 'Nakchoen Nakseon Woondongeui Jeonkae Kwajeongkwa Jeongchijeok [The Process and Political Meaning of Blackballing]', in *4.13 Chongseon: Campaign Saraye Yeonkuwa Jaengjeon Bunseok* (Seoul, 2000).

3 Robert Dahl, *On Democracy* (New Haven and London, 1998), pp. 14–15. Compare the more extreme version of the same prejudice in James Bryce, *Modern Democracies* (New York, 1921), vol. 1, pp. 26–7: 'With the fall of the Roman republic the rule of the people came to an end in the ancient world. Local self-government went on for many generations in the cities, but in an oligarchic form, and it, too, ultimately died out. For nearly fifteen centuries, from the days of Augustus till the Turks captured Constantinople, there was never ... a serious attempt either to restore free government, or even to devise a regular constitutional method for choosing the autocratic head of the State.'

4 Marquis d'Argenson, *Considérations sur le gouvernement ancien et présent de la France* (Amsterdam, 1765, pp. 7–8).

5 See the Freedom House report, *Democracy's Century. A Survey of Global Political Change in the 20th Century* (New York, 1999).

6 Tyler Marshall and Norman Kempster, 'Albright Announces "Democracy Club" Plan As One of Her Final Goals', *Los Angeles Times* (18 January 1999).

7 The trend is an old one. On 30 April 1980, as the end of President Sadat's second term of office approached, the Egyptian constitution was amended, to permit the President of the Republic to be re-elected an unlimited number of times (in accordance with what might be called the principle of the immortality of dictators). The official justification of the amendment was impeccably 'democratic': 'President Sadat's term of office began before the Constitution was promulgated, and in accordance with article 190 and article 77, his term of office concludes in November 1983. This outcome, resulting from the application of this provision, is not consistent with the democratic principles which our society safeguards and seeks to further entrench . . . more importantly, this result is one which the steadfast people of Egypt reject with their hearts, minds and souls . . .' (cited in United Nations Development Programme, *The Arab Human Development Report 2004. Towards Freedom in the Arab World* (New York, 2005), p. 167). A more recent example, reported in the *Weekend Australian* (Sydney), 25–26 October 2003, pp. 10–11, was the speech to the Australian parliament, on 24 October 2003, by the Chinese President, Hu Jintao. 'Democracy is the common pursuit of mankind', said Hu Jintao, 'and all countries must earnestly protect the democratic rights of the people. In the past twenty years and more, since China embarked on the road of reform and opening up, we have moved steadfastly to promote political restructuring and vigorously build democratic politics under socialism.' And a tragic-comic example: when he met (in 2004) in his official favourite tent with Prime Minister Tony Blair, Libya's Colonel Gaddafi explained that his country, too, was a democracy. He drew an imaginary circle in the air, then said: 'This is the people and [placing an imaginary dot in the centre] here am I. I am their expression, and that is why in our democracy political parties are not required.'

ATHENS

1 In Christian Meier, *Athen: Ein Neubeginn der Weltgeschichte* (Berlin, 1993), pp. 63, 68–87.

2 Aristotle, *Politics* 1278b 9–14.

3 Throughout the period of Athenian democracy claims were made that 'moderate' Athenian democracy predated the toppling of Pisistratus, and that such democracy was traceable to a figure named Theseus. See Isocrates, *Encomium of Helen*, 32–77, and *Panathenaicus*, 126–9, which (c. 340 BCE) remarked that the democracy of Theseus had lasted no less than a thousand years before the age of Solon and the tyranny of Pisistratus.

4 Cited in Meier, *Athen: Ein Neubeginn der Weltgeschichte*, p. 217.

5 Andocides, *On the Mysteries* (Austin, 1998), 1: 96.

6 Pindar, *The Odes*, Fr. 75; compare the ode *Pythian*, VIII.95: 'Man's life is a day. What is he? / What is he not? A shadow in a dream / Is man: but when God sheds a brightness, / Shining life is on earth / And life is sweet as honey.'

7 Xenophon, *Oeconomicus*, 7.30.

8 One recorded example: in the year 333/332 BCE, the *dēmos* honoured the members of the *boule*, who in turn erected a dedicatory statue of Dēmokratia. See J. Kirchner, *Athenische Mitteilungen*, vol. 29 (1904), p. 250. The following paragraph draws from my discussion with Professor John McK. Camp, Athens, 10 February 2003.

9 *Pausanias's Description of Greece*, J. G. Frazer (ed.), vol. 1 (London, 1913), book 1, chapter 17, section 1.

10 Plato, *Republic*, 563b; Pseudo-Xenophon, *Constitution of the Athenians*, 1.10–2.

11 Lysias, *For the Invalid*, 24.20.

12 From *Rich Woman* by Eubulus, cited in *The Deipnosophists, or Banquet of the Learned of Athenaeus* (London, 1854), vol. 3, book xiv, section 46, p. 1023 (translation amended).

13 Plutarch, *Themistocles*, 4.

14 Cited in Mabel Lang, *The Athenian Citizen* (Princeton, NJ, 1987), p. 12.

15 Plato, *Republic*, 557b and 492b–c.

16 Aristophanes, *Knights*, 1063–86. Produced in 424 BCE, the scathing satire features a chorus of young aristocrats (the knights) who side with the sausage seller, Agoracritus, in his efforts to control Demos by outmanoeuvring his current overseer, a slave called the Paphlagonian. The two coarse rivals for power over Demos resort to flattery and Greek gifts: in order better to control him, they praise Demos as Tyrant and Sole Ruler of the Earth, and tempt him as well with everything from freshly trapped rabbits and cheap fish to pillows to soften the stone seats at the Pnyx. Demos appears pleased by the trickery: he is seen by Aristophanes, through most of the play, as a conceited rogue whose foolishness is compounded by his insistence that he knows precisely what is going on.

17 Jean-Jacques Rousseau, *Du contrat social ou principes du droit politique* (Paris, 1973 [1762]), book 3, chapter 15, p. 168.

18 A rereading of Lord Brougham's widely read nineteenth-century account of representation helps to clarify this surprising connection and verbal contrast between Athenian and 'modern' forms of democracy: 'the essence of representation is that the power of the people should be parted with, and given over, for a limited time, to the deputy chosen by the people, and that he [sic] should perform the part of the government which, but for the transfer, would have been performed by the people themselves' (in *Works* (Glasgow, 1860), vol. 2, pp. 35–6).

19 The Council of Five Hundred (as has been noted) dated from the time of Cleisthenes. In the era of democracy it was a body comprising citizen senators who met on the western flank of the agora in a rectangular-shaped Council House (archaeologists now call it the new *bouleuterion*) built sometime between 415 and 406 BCE, to replace the old Council House, which was then transformed into the city archives. The Council members, some five hundred of them – fifty from each of the city's ten tribes – met

each and every day of the year, except on days devoted to festivals. Their term of office was limited to one year. Surrounded by paintings and sculptures, including a carved wooden image of Demos by Lyson, the Council members perched on Council House benches arranged in a semi-circle (*Pausanias's Description of Greece*, translated by J. G. Frazer, book 1, chapter 3, section 5, at p. 5). Their job was to think up and agree legislative proposals. These citizen senators were not parliamentary representatives in the modern sense, simply because they had no power to make or to amend the laws. In matters of government, the senators, rather, resembled a steering group, or a supervisory executive. Business was a round-the-water-clock affair. The Council required some citizens, some of the time, to be full-time political animals. One of the special things about the Athenian democracy, its citizens liked to say, was that nobody privately owned its institutions. The means of government were publicly owned and administered. That principle required vigilance at all times. 'Whoever holds office in the city when the democracy has been overthrown shall be put to death with impunity' read a stone in front of the building. And so, day and night, throughout the year, matters of government were monitored by a small group of presiding senators (known as *prytaneis*) who were selected on a rotating basis from the main body of the Council. The inner circle consisted of fifty citizens, aged thirty or over, all members of the same tribe. They were paid for their services. These presiding officers were charged with supervising day-to-day administration of the government, as well as with handling any unusual incidents that took place within or outside the city. The senators were expected to serve for one-tenth of the year (one *prytany*), so that, during their duty period of thirty-five or thirty-six days, about a third of them worked overnight. While Athens slept, they kept watch.

20 Plutarch, *Solon*, 18.2.
21 Trained in music by Agathocles, Damon, son of Damonides, an Athenian of the *deme* (see note 28, p. 892) Oa, was said to have wielded considerable influence over Pericles and to have convinced him of the need to make payments to jurors out of the public treasury. Especially after 460 BCE, Damon was much in public demand. He was a well-known champion of the view that music and politics were closely related, and that music was vital for the cultivation of good citizens. He believed that the practice of music – playing the harp or singing – could allay or arouse different emotions. He believed as well that music could inculcate such vital political virtues as a sense of justice, bravery and self-restraint. Seen in this way, payment for jury service was likened by Damon to the playing of a new chord or the singing of a new note for the purpose of inducing a change of mood among citizens. His closeness to Pericles and his popularity in the assembly resulted in his ostracism around 445 BCE. Details are provided in Diels, *Die Fragmente der Vorsokratiker*, 6th edn, edited by W. Kranz (Berlin, 1951–2), 37 B4, 6, 10; and Aristotle, *The Constitution of Athens*, 27.4.
22 Aristotle, *Nichomachean Ethics*, 1130b–1132b, which contrasts this 'numerical equality' with 'proportional equality', a form of equal treatment of others who are considered as equals in some or other important respect, but not others; and Aristotle's remarks on equality, democracy

and oligarchy in *Politics* 1301a26–39: 'In the many forms of government which have sprung up there has always been an acknowledgement of justice and proportionate equality, although mankind fail in attaining them . . . Democracy, for example, arises out of the notion that those who are equal in any respect are equal in all respects; because men are equally free, they claim to be absolutely equal. Oligarchy is based on the notion that those who are unequal in one respect are in all respects unequal; being unequal, that is, in property, they suppose themselves to be unequal absolutely. The democrats think that as they are equal they ought to be equal in all things; while the oligarchs, under the idea that they are unequal, claim too much, which is one form of inequality. All these forms of government have a kind of justice, but, tried by an absolute standard, they are faulty; and, therefore, both parties, whenever their share in the government does not accord with their preconceived ideas, stir up revolution.' Against both forms of universalism, Aristotle proposed (ibid., 1302a 3–15) that the best polity is one in which a mixture of both forms of equality are cultivated. 'That a state should be ordered, simply and wholly, according to either kind of equality [numerical or proportional], is not a good thing; the proof is the fact that such forms of government never last. They are originally based on a mistake, and, as they begin badly, cannot fail to end badly. The inference is that both kinds of equality should be employed; numerical in some cases, and proportionate in others. Still democracy appears to be safer and less liable to revolution than oligarchy. For in oligarchies there is the double danger of the oligarchs falling out among themselves and also with the people; but in democracies there is only the danger of a quarrel with the oligarchs. No dissension worth mentioning arises among the people themselves. And we may further remark that a government which is composed of the middle class more nearly approximates to democracy than to oligarchy, and is the safest of the imperfect forms of government.'

23 Sophocles, *Ajax* (c. 450 BCE): 'Nothing is not to be expected. Change is the law of the world. There is always a new winner. Winter gives way to summer; night to day; storm brings peace to the moaning sea; all-powerful sleep releases what it has bound because it cannot reign indefinitely.'

24 The remark is reconstructed in Plato, *Theaetetus*, section 152a; and Sextus Empiricus, *Adversus Mathematicus*, 7.60.

25 Euripides, *Ion*, 855–7.

26 More conventional interpretations include Christian Meier, *Entstehung des Begriffs 'Demokratia'* (Frankfurt, 1970), pp. 44ff.; Jochen Bleicken, *Die athenische Demokratie* (Paderborn, 1985), p. 48; Peter J. Rhodes, *A Commentary on the Aristotelian Athenaion Politeia* (Oxford, 1981), p. 261; Richard Sealey, 'The Origins of *Demokratia*', *California Studies in Classical Antiquity* (1974), pp. 253–95; and Kurt Raaflaub, 'Zum Freiheitsbegriffe im alten Griechenland', in *Soziale Typenbegriffe im alten Griechenland* (Berlin, 1981), pp. 266–7, note 694.

27 Some details on Dēmokrates are listed in John Davies, *Athenian Propertied Families, 600–300 BC* (Oxford, 1971), pp. 359–60; and Mogens Herman Hansen, 'The origin of the term *dēmokratia*', *Liverpool Classical Monthly* (1986), pp. 35–6.

28 The system of *demes* redeveloped during the period of Athenian

democracy was complicated, and is hence difficult to summarise. When the transition to democracy first began, in the years 508/507, it is recorded that Cleisthenes had instructed that the old Ionian tribes of the region of Attica be disbanded (see Herodotus, 5.69, and Aristotle, *Constitution of Athens*, 21.2–6). Democracy required the abolition of patronage based on clans that were rooted in ancient patterns of geography, kinship and landownership, he and his supporters thought. Compulsory de-tribalisation – for instance, encouraging Athenians to use their *deme* names, so that (to take one example) an Athenian man once identified as 'Demochares, son of Demosthenes' would hereafter be identified as 'Demochares from Marathon' – was seen as a weapon useful for breaking the grip of the area's old aristocratic families, whose power had been founded upon their control of the different geographical regions of the Attica peninsula. And so the reformers announced a new configuration of identities. The peninsula of Attica, where the city of Athens and its environs stood, was subdivided into three geographical regions: the city, the coast and the inland countryside. Each region was further subdivided in new ways: into ten ridings, each broken up in turn into three *demes* (one from the city of Athens, one from the coast and one from the inland area, each group of which was called a Third (*trittyes*)). The *demes* were the smallest administrative units responsible for such matters as the supervision of communal property, the public celebration of births, marriages and deaths, the organisation of religious cults and festivals, and the keeping of registers of who was entitled to be a citizen of the assembly. Cleisthenes had in mind a pyramidal structure of governance whose foundation comprised some 139 *demes* distributed among approximately thirty ridings. In a way, the *demes* resembled contemporary American voting precincts or school districts. These constituencies were a natural geographical place: for example, a district of Athens (which was the only large city on the peninsula); a stretch of coast that included a harbour; the cultivated lands on the slopes of a mountain; or a village and its surrounding countryside. The *demes* were also political spaces. They had priests and local assemblies and a 'demarch' – a figure resembling a mayor – and their citizens were encouraged to feel that they had local identities. Cleisthenes ruled that membership of a particular *deme* was hereditary; he supposed (probably incorrectly) that future generations would forever remain in their locale. If they did not – if, for instance, they migrated from an inland village to Athens – then they would retain their *deme* affiliation, which might have had the (intended) effect of preventing regional cleavages from creeping into the polity. So despite the above-mentioned shift from 'patronymic' to 'demotic' names, the *deme* was clearly still something to do with blood: the Athenian democracy continued in its own way to pay homage to kinship. An example was the way in which the official names of citizens customarily combined references to both their kinship and their *demes*: Pericles, son of Xanthippos, of Cholargos, for instance. Cleisthenes' reforms nevertheless proved radical. They did not just aim to create small-scale political communities that would nurture citizens' powers and affections, ultimately at the most local level. In order to bind the whole body of citizens together into one polity, the new system of regions, ridings and *demes* was to be cross-cut by new 'tribal' loyalties. To complicate and fully defuse the old patterns of political loyalty, Cleisthenes – confirming the rule that most democracies are never created democratically – set about allocating the whole citizen body of Attica into larger political subgroupings. He instructed that there were to be ten new tribes (*phylai*), whose members were drawn in equal numbers from each of the three regions, their ridings and *demes*. The decision as to which ridings would be allocated to a certain tribe was (according to Aristotle's *Constitution of Athens*, 21.4) decided on a random basis, by lot. There were no opt-out arrangements: the point was to break the back of aristocratic power by creating top-level political units that each contained a cross-section of interests and were not rooted in the old systems of patronage. Membership within a tribe was compulsory and implied duties and privileges. By becoming a member of a tribe, male citizens who were eighteen years old gained certain freedoms, for instance to engage in jury service; to make their votes count in all sorts of different settings, including election to the newly created body called the Council of Five Hundred; and to use common grazing land. Tribal membership also saddled them with certain obligations, such as the duty to honour the tribe and its fictive ancestor hero in certain rituals, or to fight in the army side by side with one's tribe against the foes of Athens.

29   Leonard R. Palmer, 'The Mycenaean Palace and the *Damos*', in *Aux origines de l'Hellénisme. La Crète et la Grèce. Hommage à Henri van Effenterre présenté par le Centre G. Glotz* (Paris, 1984), pp. 151–9; and his *Mycenaeans and Minoans* (New York, 1962), pp. 97ff. Anna Ramou-Hapsiadi, Άννα Ράμου – Χαψιάδη, *Από τη φυλετική κοινωνία σιην πολιτική*, Αθήνα (*From Racial to Political Society*) (Athens, 1982) points out that the development of Mycenaean commerce and specialisation coincided with a transformation of the meaning of the word *dāmos*: whereas it once meant an area of land inhabited by people with strong family ties, it came to refer to an area inhabited by people with common interests (pp. 25–33).

30   See Michael Ventris and John Chadwick, *Documents in Mycenaean Greek*, 2nd edn (Cambridge and New York, 1973), pp. 232–5, 254–5, 264–5 and 538.

31   Details of the dispute are recorded in Palmer, 'The Mycenaean Palace and the *Damos*', p. 155, and p. 151: 'what is most striking about the Mycenaean world is the existence of a free and independent *dāmos*'.

32   *Statesman*, 291 D 1–29 A 4.

33   See Pseudo-Xenophon, *The Polity of the Athenians*, 2.19–20.

34   M. I. Finley, *Democracy Ancient and Modern* (London, 1985), p. 28.

35   Thucydides, *History of the Peloponnesian War*, 2.37–45; cf. Kurt A. Raaflaub, 'Democracy, Power, Imperialism', in J. Peter Euben et al. (eds), *Athenian Political Thought and the Reconstruction of American Democracy* (Ithaca, NY, and London, 1994), pp. 103–46.

36   Pseudo-Xenophon, *The Constitution of the Athenians*, vol. 2, 1.2. The connection between expansionist naval power and democracy puts paid to any simple 'law' that supposes a positive affinity between the sea and democracy. It is commonly observed, for instance, that whereas the Roman state, as a land-based power, later developed forms of imperial

government that matched their strong sense of territory and territorial domination, the Athenians as democrats thought primarily in terms of a wide sea that they respected because they knew they could never master it. We shall see during the course of this study of democracy that formulae of this kind – despite their revival during the past century in such works as Sir Halford J. Mackinder, *Democratic Ideals and Reality. A Study in the Politics of Reconstruction* (London, 1919) – are too simple to be believed.

37 Aristophanes, *Acharnians*, 540–54.

38 The account by Demosthenes of the assembly meeting after Philip's seizure of Elateia in 338 BCE is telling: 'Next day at dawn the Prytaneis called the Council to the Council chamber and you made your way to the Assembly, and before the Council had completed its business and drafted its proposals, the whole people was seated up on the hill. Then when the Council had arrived and the Prytaneis had announced the news they had received and brought up the messenger and he had spoken, the herald asked: "Who wishes to speak?" Nobody came forward. Though he repeated the question many times, still nobody stood up . . .' (*On the Crown*, 18.169–70)

WEST BY EAST

1 Niccolò Machiavelli, 'Of the Kinds of Republic there are, and of which was the Roman Republic', in *Discourses on the First Ten Books of Titus Livius* (1531), translated Henry Neville, book 1, chapter 2.

2 Jean Bodin, *Six Livres de la République*, translated as *The Six Bookes of a Commonwealth* (London, 1606), p. 702.

3 Consider the entry of M. le chevalier de Jaucourt on 'Démocratie' in the *Encyclopédie, ou Dictionnaire raisonné des sciences, des arts et des métiers. Tome 4ème* (Paris, 1751–65), p. 818.

4 Samuel Johnson, *A Dictionary of the English Language: in which the words are deduced from their originals, and illustrated in their different significations by examples from the best writers* (London, 1755), vol. 1; Sir Thomas Browne, *Pseudodoxia Epidemica* (London, 1646; 6th edn, 1672), book I, chapter 3, pp. 8–12.

5 Francis Fukuyama, *The End of History and the Last Man* (New York and Oxford, 1992), pp. 64, 42, and p. 134, where the 'decision to declare independence and fight Britain' of the 'American Founding Fathers' is said to have triggered the first of the 'major democratic revolutions' of modern times.

6 *Notes of Debates in the Federal Convention of 1787 Reported by James Madison* (Athens, Ohio, 1966), pp. 38–45.

7 Jean Victor Duruy, *Histoire de la Grèce ancienne*, 3 vols (Paris, 1886–91); Ernst Curtius, *Griechische Geschichte*, 3 vols (Berlin, 1857–67); translated into English as *The History of Greece*, 5 vols (London, 1868–73).

8 George Grote, *History of Greece*, 12 vols (London, 1846–56); of interest as well is Grote's review of William Mitford's *History of Greece*, in the *Westminster Review* (April 1826), and Harriet Grote, *The Personal Life of George Grote* (London, 1873).

9 Karl R. Popper, *The Open Society and Its Enemies* (London, 1952), p. 297.

10 Aristotle, *Politics*, 1304a 31–3; ibid., 1303a 22–4 and 1311a 39.

11 Isocrates, *Areopagiticus*, 7: 15–16.

12 Herodotus, *The Histories* (London and New York, 1890), Book 3, 142 (translation amended).

13 George Orwell, *The Lion and the Unicorn: Socialism and the English Genius* (London, 1941 [1981]), p. 563: 'The whole conception of the militarized continental state, with its secret police, its censored literature and its conscript labour, is utterly different from that of the loose maritime democracy, with its slums and unemployment, its strikes and party politics. It is the difference between land power and sea power, between cruelty and inefficiency, between lying and self-deception, between the S.S. man and the rent-collector.'

14 T. J. Dunbabin, *The Western Greeks. The History of Sicily and South Italy from the Foundation of the Greek Colonies to 480 B.C.* (Oxford, 1948), p. 81.

15 Aristotle, *Politics*, 1291b 20–25.

16 M. I. Finley, 'Politics', in M. I. Finley (ed.), *The Legacy of Greece: A New Appraisal* (Oxford, 1981), pp. 22–36.

17 James Bryce, *Modern Democracies* (New York, 1921), pp. 24–5.

18 The account of Wen-Amon is translated in James Henry Breasted, *Ancient Records of Egypt*, vol. iv, pp. 557ff.

19 Karl Marx, 'The British Rule in India', *New-York Daily Tribune* (25 June 1853), reprinted in Karl Marx and Frederick Engels, *Collected Works* (London and New York, 1979), vol. 12, p. 125.

20 Thorkild Jacobsen, 'Mesopotamia: The Cosmos as a State', in H. and H. A. Frankfort et al., *Before Philosophy. The Intellectual Adventure of Ancient Man* (Harmondsworth, 1949), pp. 158–9.

21 Aristotle, *Politics*, 1252b.

22 Jean-Marie Durand, 'Le *rihsum* des Hanéens', *Archives épistolaires de Mari* I/1, pp. 181–92; and Daniel E. Fleming, *Democracy's Ancient Ancestors. Mari and Early Collective Governance* (Cambridge and New York, 2004), pp. 208–10.

23 Thorkild Jacobsen, 'An Ancient Mesopotamian Trial for Homicide', *Analecta Biblica*, 12 (1959), pp. 134–6; the translation follows J. N. Postgate, *Early Mesopotamia* (London and New York, 1992), p. 278.

24 Edited and translated in Robert H. Pfeiffer, *State Letters of Assyria* (New Haven, Conn., 1935), number 62, ll.9 and 11.

25 A translation of the text appears in W. G. Lambert, *Babylonian Wisdom Literature* (Oxford, 1960), pp. 112–5.

26 Tikva Frymer-Kensky, *In the Wake of the Goddesses: Women, Culture and the Biblical Transformation of Pagan Myth* (New York, 1992), pp. 2–3.

27 Translated in Alasdair Livingstone, *Court Poetry and Literary Miscellanea* (Helsinki, 1989), pp. 30–32.

28 See Francis Joannès, 'Haradum et le pays de Suhum', *Archéologie*, 205 (1985), p. 58: 'Concerning the silver, which Habasanu during his tenure as mayor had made the town pay, the entire town assembled and spoke in these terms to Habasanu: "Of the silver which you made us pay, a

great amount has stayed in your house, as well as the sheep which we gave on top as voluntary gifts.'"

29 See the path-breaking interpretation of Marc Van De Mieroop, *The Ancient Mesopotamian City* (Oxford, 1999), especially chapter 6.

30 Mogens Trolle Larsen, *The Old Assyrian City-State* (Copenhagen, 1976), p. 163.

31 For further details of these republics (called *gana dhina*), whose assemblies appear to have been dominated by warrior aristocrats (*kshatriya*), but included as well ritual specialists (*brahmana*) and merchants (*vaisya*), but not labourers (*shudra*), see Jonathan Mark Kenoyer, 'Early City-States in South Asia. Comparing the Harappan Phase and Early Historic Period', in Deborah L. Nichols and Thomas H. Charlton (eds), *The Archaeology of City-States. Cross-Cultural Approaches* (Washington, DC, and London, 1997), pp. 51–70; Ananat S. Altekar, *State and Government in Ancient India* (Delhi, 1958); Giorgii M. Bongard-Levin, *A Complex Study of Ancient India: A Multi-Disciplinary Approach* (Delhi, 1986); Jagdish Sharma, *Republics in Ancient India: c. 1500 B.C.–500 B.C.* (Leiden, 1968); and Romila Thapar, 'States and Cities of the Indo-Gangetic Plain c. 600–300 BC', in *Early India. From the Origins to AD 1300* (Berkeley and Los Angeles, 2002), pp. 137–73.

32 The following story is told by Herodotus in *The History of Herodotus* (London and New York, 1890), books 6.43–4, and 3. 80–84. Compare the interpretations of later commentators, especially those with incurable Orientalist prejudices, like George Rawlinson, *History of Herodotus* (London, 1880), vol. 2, p. 476, note 3: 'No doubt Herodotus had Persian authority for his tale; but it is so utterly at variance with Oriental notions as to be absolutely incredible. It is not likely that even any debate took place as to who should be king. That point would be settled before the attack upon the usurper; and it is probable that Darius succeeded to the throne by right of birth.'

33 Robert Dahl, *On Democracy* (New Haven and London, 1998), p. 15.

34 Fergus Millar, *The Roman Republic and the Augustan Revolution* (Chapel Hill, NC, and London, 2002); see also Lily R. Taylor, *Roman Voting Assemblies from the Hannibalic War to the Dictatorship of Caesar* (Ann Arbor, Mich., 1966).

35 Sir Thomas Erskine May, *Democracy in Europe: A History* (London, 1877), vol. 1, pp. 27, 6. May was Chief Librarian at the House of Commons at Westminster, and later became Clerk of the House of Commons.

36 See the letter to Gobineau in Alexis de Tocqueville, *Oeuvres complètes*, edited by J. P. Mayer (Paris, 1951–), vol. 9, p. 69; and the unpublished letter to Lamoricière (5 April 1846), cited in André Jardin, *Tocqueville: A Biography* (New York, 1988), p. 318.

37 During the early stages of research for this book, in an interview conducted in Paris in May 2002, Richard Rorty urged me to adopt the interpretative rule: 'always follow the phoneme of democracy'. By this he meant to say that judgements about what to include in a narrated history of democracy should be decided by whether or not past actors or institutions distinguished themselves from others by embracing the signifier 'democracy'. In other words, his advice was: call nothing democracy

if that is not its own name. For reasons further developed in the final appendix on methods, I have not strictly followed this rule. There is a good reason for not doing so, because in matters of democracy, as with worldly matters in general (think of the way we commonly distinguish between the terms in which people describe themselves and how they are described by others), the same things often parade under different banners, often in ways not intended by their original champions. The point is summarised in the pithy remark of William Morris: '[People] fight and lose the battle, and the thing that they fought for comes about in spite of their defeat, and when it comes turns out not to be what they meant, and other [people] have to fight for what they meant under another name' (*A Dream of John Ball and a King's Lesson* (London and New York, 1896)).

38 *The Animals' Lawsuit Against Humanity* (Louisville, Ky., 2005). The fable was intended by the authors, a Sufi order named the Brethren of Purity (*Ikhwan al-Safa*), as the twenty-fifth of fifty-one 'letters' or treatises in an encyclopaedia that described the mysteries and meaning of life. In the year 1316, the text was adapted and translated into Hebrew and rendered into Latin by Rabbi Kalonymus at the request of King Charles of Anjou. The story was subsequently translated into German, Spanish and Yiddish, and remained especially popular within European Jewish communities until the early twentieth century.

39 See Abu Nasr al-Farabi, *Mabadi' ara' ahl al-madina al-fadila* (Principles of the Opinions of the Citizens of the Perfect Polity), first published around 950 CE, translated in Richard Walzer (ed.), *Al-Farabi on the Perfect State* (Oxford, 1985), section 5, chapter 15, p. 229.

40 *Kanz ul-Ummal* (Beirut, 1998), vol. 3, number 2786, p. 50.

41 An example is Bernard Lewis, 'Democracy and the Enemies of Freedom', *Wall Street Journal*, 22 December 2003, p. A14: 'The study of Islamic history and of the vast and rich Islamic political literature encourages the belief that it may well be possible to develop democratic institutions – not necessarily in our Western definition of that much misused term, but in one deriving from their own history and culture, and ensuring, in their way, limited government under law, consultation and openness, in a civilized and humane society. There is enough in the traditional culture of Islam on the one hand and the modern experience of the Muslim peoples on the other to provide the basis for an advance towards freedom in the true sense of that word.'

42 Sudayf's remark is cited in Bernard Lewis, *Islam from the Prophet Muhammad to the Capture of Constantinople* (Oxford, 1974), vol. 2, pp. 54–5.

43 See Abu Nasr al-Farabi, *Mabadi' ara' ahl al-madina al-fadila*, especially section 6, chapter 18. The following quotations are from ibid., chapter 19, p. 315; and Abu Nasr al-Farabi, *Al-Siyasa al-madaniyya al-mulaqqab bi-mabadi' al-mawjudat* (Al-Farabi's The Political Regime), edited by Fawzi Mitri Najjar (Beirut, 1964), p. 100, II, pp. 18ff.

ON REPRESENTATIVE GOVERNMENT

1 William Shakespeare, *King Lear*, Act V, Scene 3.
2 Baron de Montesquieu, *The Spirit of the Laws* (New York and London, 1949), book 2, chapter 2 ('Of the Republican Government, and the Laws in relation to Democracy'), p. 9.
3 Marquis d'Argenson, *Considérations sur le gouvernement ancien et présent de la France* (Amsterdam, 1765), pp. 7–8.
4 James Madison, 'The Utility of the Union as a Safeguard Against Domestic Faction and Insurrection (continued)', *Daily Advertiser* (Thursday, 22 November 1787): 'The two great points of difference between a democracy and a republic are: first, the delegation of the government, in the latter, to a small number of citizens elected by the rest; secondly, the greater number of citizens, and greater sphere of country, over which the latter may be extended.'
5 Cited in Pierre Rosanvallon, 'The History of the Word "Democracy" in France', *Journal of Democracy*, 6, 4 (1995), p. 143.
6 From a speech by James Wilson to the Federal Convention (6 June 1787), in Max Farrand (ed.), *The Records of the Federal Convention of 1787*, 4 vols (New Haven, Conn., and London, 1937), vol. 1, chapter 13, document 18, pp. 132–3.
7 The following quotations are from Thomas Paine, *Rights of Man*, part 1 (London, 1791 [1925]), pp. 272–4.
8 François Guizot, *Histoire des origines du gouvernement représentatif, 1821–1822*, 2 vols (Paris, 1821–2), translated as *The History of the Origins of Representative Government in Europe* (London, 1861), part 1, lecture 1, p. 12.
9 A. F. Pollard, *The Evolution of Parliament* (London, 1920), p. 3; an identical claim is made by Alan F. Hattersley, *A Short History of Democracy* (Cambridge, 1930), pp. 78–9.
10 From the account provided by the English chronicler William of Malmesbury, in *Rolls Series* ii, pp. 394–5, and p. 398: 'Rid the sanctuary of God of the unbelievers', Urban II reportedly said, 'expel the thieves and lead back the faithful. Let no loyalty to kinsfolk hold you back; man's loyalty lies in the first place to God.' See also Dana C. Munro, 'The Speech of Pope Urban II at Clermont, 1095', *American Historical Review*, xi (1906), pp. 231–42.
11 According to the Real Academia Española's eighteenth-century *Diccionario de Autoridades* (Madrid, 1737), vol. 1, pp. 627–8, the old word *cortes* has three richly overlapping root meanings: *corte* refers to the city or town where a monarch resides and holds his or her councils (*consejos*) and tribunals (*tribunales*), a usage that has its origin in the Latin *cohors* (referring to a yard, or enclosure, or troops of one-tenth of a legion); *corte* also refers to the whole body of councils, tribunals, ministers and officials whose job it is to advise and to serve the monarch; and *cortes*, which refers to the city council whose representatives are empowered to make proposals and demands, and to grant services to a monarch. The new meaning of *cortes* that crystallised around the initiative of Alfonso IX was effectively a distilled synthesis of all three of these meanings.

12 Real Academia Española, *Diccionario de Autoridades*, vol. 5, p. 392.

13 The Icelandic assembly of Thingvellir, dating from around 930 CE, has often been celebrated as the most ancient legislative assembly of the European region. The view is mistaken. Its members indeed assembled on an open plain, listened to the proposals of the wise man Ulfljøt but – the surviving evidence suggests – they normally accepted those proposals through acclamation, with no debate or controversy. Such rule by acclamation was thoroughly in accordance with the rules of feudal assemblies, as has been pointed out by Antonio Marongiu, *Medieval Parliaments. A Comparative Study* (London, 1968), part 1; and Walter Ullmann, *Principles of Government and Politics in the Middle Ages* (Harmondsworth, 1961).

14 Marichalar and Manrique, *Historia de la Legislación y Recitaciones del Derecho Civil de España* (Madrid, 1861–76), vol. VII, pp. 455–6.

15 Cited in Roger Bigelow Merriman, 'The Cortes of the Spanish Kingdoms in the Later Middle Ages', *American Historical Review*, vol. 16, 3 (1911), p. 482, note 29.

16 Johann Friedrich Böhmer, *Acta imperii selecta* (Innsbruck, 1870), p. 130.

17 Niccolò Machiavelli, *The Prince* (published originally as *De Principatibus* [Florence, 1532] (Cambridge and New York, 1990), chapters ix and xix; and the nuanced commentary by Quentin Skinner, *The Foundations of Modern Political Thought*, vol. 2: *The Age of the Reformation* (Cambridge and London, 1978), pp. 353–4.

18 Charles F. Adams (ed.), *The Works of John Adams*, 10 vols (Boston, 1850–56), vol. 6, p. 469.

19 Henri Pirenne, *Belgian Democracy: Its Early History* (Manchester, 1915), pp. 134–47.

20 The song by Bob Dylan is 'It's Alright, Ma (I'm Only Bleeding)' (1965).

21 From one of the earliest guides to the religious life, written around 400 CE, *The Rule of St Augustine* (New York, 1976), chapter 7, section 3.

22 Manegold of Lautenbach, *Liber ad Gebehardum* (Hannover, 1891), pp. 308–410; see also his *Liber contra Wolfelum*, edited by Robert Ziomkowski Leuven (Paris and Dudley, Mass., 2002).

23 Günter Stemberger, 'Stammt das synodale Element der Kirche aus der Synagoge?', *Annuarium Historiae Conciliorum*, 8 (1976), pp. 1–14.

24 J. H. Robinson (ed.), *Translations and Reprints from the Original Sources of European History* (Philadelphia, 1912), series I, vol. III, 6, pp. 31–2.

25 From the sermon in support of the National Covenant by John Hamilton, in *Diary of Archibald Johnston of Wariston, 1632–1639* (Edinburgh, 1911), vol. I, p. 326.

26 *The Confession of Faith of the Kirk of Scotland: or THE NATIONAL COVENANT, with a designation of such Acts of Parliament as are expedient for justifying the union after mentioned* (Assembly at Edinburgh, 30 August 1639, Session 23).

27 Alexander Henderson, *The Bishops Doom. A Sermon Preached before the General Assembly which sat at Glasgow anno. 1638. On occasion of pronouncing the sentence of the greater excommunication against eight of the bishops, and deposing or suspending the other six. By Alexander Hamilton, moderator of that and several subsequent assemblies. With a*

Postscript on the present decay of church discipline (Edinburgh, 1792), pp. 17–18.

28 See the biographies written by Luther's friend Philip Melanchthon (in 1548) and Luther's enemy Johannes Cochlaeus (in 1549), translated and reprinted in Elizabeth Vandiver et al. (eds), *Luther's Lives. Two Contemporary Accounts of Martin Luther* (Manchester, 2002); details of Calvin's treatment at the hands of Jerome Bolsec are found in Bernard Cottret, *Calvin. A Biography* (London, 2002).

29 All citations are drawn from *Areopagitica. A Speech for the Liberty of Unlicenc'd Printing*, in E. H. Visiak (ed.), *Milton. Complete Poetry and Selected Prose* (Glasgow, 1925).

30 Act of Abjuration, in E. H. Kossmann and A. F. Mellink (eds), *Texts Concerning the Revolt of the Netherlands* (Cambridge, 1974), p. 225.

31 Sophocles, *Antigone*, 1. 296.

32 Plutarch, *Lives: Cleomenes*, chapter 27, section 1.

33 Diogenes Laertius, *Diogenes*, Book 6, section 50.

34 The following quotations are from Jean-Jacques Rousseau, *Considérations sur le gouvernement de Pologne* (completed in 1772 but unpublished (Indianapolis and New York, 1972)), pp. 27, 42, 2.

35 *The Kings Cabinet Opened: or, Certain packets of secret letters & papers, written with the Kings own hand, and taken in his cabinet at Nasby-Field, June 14. 1645. By victorious Sr Thomas Fairfax* (London, 1645).

36 See the anonymous pamphlet *A Key to the Kings Cabinet; or Animadversions upon the three Printed Speeches, of Mr Lisle, Mr Tate, and Mr Browne, spoken at a Common-Hall in London, 3. July 1645. Detecting the Malice and Falshood of their Blasphemous Observations made upon the King and Queenes Letters* (Oxford, 1645), pp. 2ff (italics in original).

37 This and the following quotations are drawn from William Cobbett, *Complete Collection of State Trials*, vol. 4 (London, 1809), pp. 995, 1074.

38 The quotations and details are drawn from the official account, *King Charls. His Speech Made Upon the Scaffold At Whitehall-Gate, Immediately before his Execution, On Tuesday the 30 of Jan. 1648* [sic] *With a Relation of the maner of his going to Execution. Published by Special Authority* (London, 1649).

39 *Vant Swingelsche Calff, etc.* (Paris, 1580): 'These uneducated weavers and furriers have learned from their preachers how to debate, and they take particular pleasure, though without reason and understanding, as it would take too long to explain, in comparing Democracy with Oligarchy, Polyarchy, Aristocracy, and, best of all, Monarchy . . . The Ghenters say openly that they do not want to see any more four-cornered caps, long robes, and velvet capes: that is, clerics, learned doctors, and nobles.' Rounding on the stupidity of the 'common people' (*ghemeyn puepel*), the mean-spirited Catholic author drew a sour conclusion that touches on an opening theme of this book: 'Without clerics and learned doctors we shall soon have a more dangerous and horrible confusion than ever there was in Babylon.'

40 Sir John Oglander, cited in Christopher Hill, *The English Revolution 1640* (London, 1940), part 4.

THE AMERICAN CENTURY

1 See the anonymous entries 'Democracy' and 'Democratic Party' in *The Encyclopaedia Britannica*, 11th edn (Cambridge, 1910), vol. viii, pp. 1–3.

2 Thomas Jefferson, 'First Inaugural Address', 4 March 1801, reprinted in Saul K. Padover (ed.), *The Complete Jefferson* (Freeport, NY, 1969), pp. 385–6.

3 George Cabot to Timothy Pickering, 14 February 1804, in Henry Adams (ed.), *Documents Relating to New England Federalism, 1800–1815* (Boston, 1877), p. 346.

4 Thomas Paine, *Common Sense* (Philadelphia, 1776 [1925]), p. 148. Paine had probably read, or heard about, the early eighteenth-century historical novel, attributed to Francis Midon, *Memoirs of a Most Remarkable Revolution in Naples, or, The History of Massaniello* (London, 1729).

5 James Madison ('Publius'), 'The Utility of the Union as a Safeguard Against Domestic Faction and Insurrection (continued)', *Daily Advertiser* (Thursday, 22 November 1787). Madison's usage of the word democracy was wholly conventional, as can be seen by comparing the brief entry on 'Democracy' in the Scottish-produced *Encyclopaedia Britannica; or a Dictionary of Arts and Sciences* (Edinburgh, 1771), vol. 2, p. 415: 'DEMOCRACY, the same with a popular government, wherein the supreme power is lodged in the hands of the people: such were Rome and Athens of old; but as to our modern republics, Basil [Basel] only excepted, their government comes nearer to aristocracy than democracy.'

6 James Madison, *Notes of Debates in the Federal Convention of 1787* (New York, 1987), pp. 322–3, 369 and 64; the quotations that follow are from ibid., pp. 106, 483, 322–3, 308, 39, 306, 107, and 235.

7 Alexander Hamilton and James Madison ('Publius'), 'Method of Guarding Against the Encroachments of Any One Department of Government by Appealing to the People Through a Convention', *New York Packet* (5 February 1788).

8 *Records of the Federal Convention of 1787*, edited by Max Farrand (New Haven, Conn., 1911–37), vol. 3, pp. 86, 28, 73, 368; vol. 2, p. 333n.

9 The words are taken from Washington's farewell address (17 September 1796), reprinted in John Rhodehamel (ed.), *George Washington: Writings* (New York, 1997), p. 969.

10 *Marbury v. Madison*, 5 US (1 Cranch) 137 (1803).

11 Merrill D. Peterson, *The Jefferson Image in the American Mind* (New York, 1960), p. 699.

12 German Republican Society, 'To Friends and Fellow Citizens, April 11, 1793', in Philip S. Foner (ed.), *The Democratic-Republican Societies, 1790–1800: A Documentary Sourcebook of Constitutions, Declarations, Addresses, Resolutions, and Toasts* (Westport, Conn., 1976), pp. 53–4.

13 Cited in Sean Wilentz, *The Rise of American Democracy* (New York and London, 2005), p. 54; see also his *Chants Democratic: New York City & the Rise of the American Working Class* (New York, 1984), pp. 38–9.

14 See the accounts of this critical period in Philip S. Foner (ed.), *The Democratic-Republican Societies, 1790–1800: A Documentary Sourcebook of Constitutions, Declarations, Addresses, Resolutions, and*

Toasts (Westport, Conn., 1976), pp. 6–7; the *American Daily Advertiser* (Philadelphia), 20 May and 21 December 1793; the *New-York Journal*, 18 January 1794; and *Principles, Articles and Regulations Agreed upon by the Members of the Democratic Society in Philadelphia, May 30th, 1793* (Philadelphia, 1793).

15 George Washington's letters to Burges Ball (25 September 1794) and to Edmund Randolph (16 October 1794), in Rhodehamel (ed.), *George Washington: Writings*, pp. 885 and 887.

16 Further details of the young republic's biggest corruption scandal are discussed in John Keane, *Tom Paine: A Political Life* (London and New York, 1995), pp. 170ff.

17 From the Minutes of the Democratic Society of Pennsylvania, 9 October 1794, in Foner (ed.), *The Democratic-Republican Societies, 1790–1800: A Documentary Sourcebook of Constitutions, Declarations, Addresses, Resolutions, and Toasts*, p. 96. Compare Thomas Jefferson's expressed sympathy for resistance of 'the democratic societies' to 'the fraction of the monocrats' led by George Washington, in a letter to James Madison, 28 December 1794, in Robert A. Rutland (ed.), *The Papers of James Madison*, vol. 15 (Charlottesville, Va., 1985), pp. 426–9.

18 Thomas Jefferson to John Taylor, 4 June 1798, in Julian P. Boyd (ed.), *The Papers of Thomas Jefferson* (Princeton, NJ, 1950–), vol. 30, pp. 300, 389.

19 During the eighteenth century, the old word 'blackamoor' ('black Moor') was doubly derogative. It referred to slaves with very dark skin who were thought to resemble the dark-skinned Muslims of North Africa. In the context of a slave-holding society like the United States, to be a Muslim and a Negro was to be in a most unfortunate condition.

20 Thomas Jefferson, 'First Inaugural Address', 4 March 1801, reprinted in Padover (ed.), *The Complete Jefferson*, p. 385.

21 Walt Whitman, *Thou Mother With Thy Equal Brood* (1872), section 4, in *Walt Whitman. Complete Poetry & Selected Prose and Letters* (London, 1938), p. 412.

22 Gouverneur Morris to R. R. Livingston (1805), in David Hackett Fischer, *The Revolution of American Conservatism* (New York, 1965), p. 96.

23 James Sterling Young, *The Washington Community, 1800–1828* (New York, 1966), pp. 51–7.

24 The following quotations are from Alexis de Tocqueville, *Democracy in America*, edited by Phillips Bradley (New York, 1945), vol. 1, pp. 57, 69, 261, 285, and vol. 2, p. 263.

25 The quotations are drawn from Dr Torrielli, *Italian Opinion on America as Revealed by Italian Travellers, 1850–1900* (Cambridge, Mass., 1941), pp. 22, 100–101, 78–9.

26 This section draws upon Tocqueville, *Democracy in America*, vol. 1, pp. 370–97.

27 Tocqueville, *Democracy in America*, vol. 1, p. 397 (translation amended).

28 James Madison, *Notes of Debates in the Federal Convention of 1787*, edited by Adrienne Koch (New York, 1966), p. 295.

29 Thomas Jefferson to John Holmes, 22 April 1820, in *The Works of Thomas Jefferson* (New York and London, 1904–5), volume 12, pp. 158–160.

30 John C. Calhoun, '"Remarks on Receiving Abolition Petitions" in the U.S. Senate, February 6, 1837', in *The Papers of John C. Calhoun*, edited by Clyde N. Wilson, vol. 13 (Columbia, SC, 1980), p. 394: 'those who imagine that the spirit [of abolitionism] now abroad in the North, will die away of itself, without shout or convulsion, have formed a very inadequate conception of its real character; it will continue to rise and spread, unless prompt and efficient measures to stay its progress be adopted'.

31 *New York Tribune* (1855), cited in Eric Foner, *Politics and Ideology in the Age of the Civil War* (New York, 1980), p. 53.

32 Quoted in Arthur Calhoun, *A Social History of the American Family*, 3 vols (New York, 1945), vol. 2, p. 84.

33 Angelina Grimké, *An Appeal to the Christian Women of the South* (New York, 1836).

34 Angelina Grimké, 'Speech Before the Legislative Committee of the Massachusetts Legislature, February 21, 1838', reprinted in *The Liberator* (Boston, 2 March 1838).

35 Cited in Dunbar Rowland, *Jefferson Davis. His Letters, Papers and Speeches* (Jackson, Miss., 1923), vol. 1, pp. 286 and 316–17.

36 George Fitzhugh, *Sociology for the South, or the Failure of Free Society* (New York, 1854), pp. 179, 223, 26–7, 246.

37 Tocqueville, *Democracy in America*, vol. 2, p. 385

38 Morton Keller, *Affairs of State: Public Life in Late Nineteenth Century America* (Cambridge, Mass., 1977), p. 245.

39 H. Wayne Morgan, *From Hayes to McKinley* (Syracuse, NY, 1969), p. 128.

40 Thomas Reeves, *Gentleman Boss: The Life of Chester Alan Arthur* (New York, 1975), p. 293; Morgan, *From Hayes to McKinley*, p. 446.

41 William M. Ivins, *Machine Politics and Money in Elections in New York City* (New York, 1887), p. 57.

42 Moisei Ostrogorski, *Democracy and the Organization of Political Parties* (New York, 1902), vol. 2, pp. 379–80.

43 Jules Verne, *Le tour du monde en 80 jours* (Around the World in 80 Days) (New York, 1962), p. 180.

44 Louis F. Post and Fred C. Leubuscher, *Henry George's 1886 Campaign* (Westport, Conn., 1976), p. 105.

45 Michael Schudson, *The Good Citizen. A History of American Civil Life* (New York and London, 1998), pp. 155–6.

46 Cited in Aileen S. Kraditor, *The Ideas of the Woman Suffrage Movement, 1890–1920* (New York, 1981), p. 109.

47 Quoted in Harold J. Laski, *Parliamentary Government in England* (London, 1938), p. 100.

48 This and the following quotations are from John L. Thomas, 'Nationalizing the Republic, 1877–1920', in Bernard Bailyn et al., *The Great Republic. A History of the American People*, 3rd edn (Lexington, Mass., 1985), pp. 580, 579, 575.

49 Cited in Murray C. Morgan, 'The Tools of Democracy and the Woolly Rhinoceros Eaters', *Puget Soundings* (March 1972), pp. 14–15.

50 Quoted in Thomas, 'Nationalizing the Republic, 1877–1920', in Bailyn et al., *The Great Republic. A History of the American People*, p. 605.

51 Quoted in Morgan, 'The Tools of Democracy and the Woolly Rhinoceros Eaters', *Puget Soundings* (March 1972), pp. 14–15.

52 Bill Sizemore, quoted in David Santen, 'Ballot Ballet', *Metroscape* (July 2002), pp. 5–12.

53 Henry L. Stimson and McGeorge Bundy, *On Active Service in Peace and War* (New York, 1948), p. 58.

54 Walter Lippmann, *The Phantom Public* (New Brunswick, NJ, and London, 1993 [1925]), pp. 15–28.

55 Edmund Burke, 'Speech in Opening the Impeachment (16 February 1788)', *The Works of the Right Honourable Edmund Burke* (London, 1899), p. 402.

56 George Gordon, Lord Byron, *Don Juan*, canto xvi, stanza 108.

57 Woodrow Wilson, Address to the Senate of the United States: 'A World League for Peace' (22 January 1917).

58 President Grover Cleveland, 'First Inaugural Address', 4 March 1885.

59 Tocqueville, *Democracy in America*, vol. 2, chapter 22, p. 279.

60 Quoted in Richard Drinnon, *Facing West: The Metaphysics of Indian-Hating and Empire-Building* (New York, 1980), pp. 70, 97–9, 102–3.

61 Quoted in Alden T. Vaughan, 'From White Man to Redskin: Changing Anglo-American Perceptions of the American Indian', *American Historical Review*, 87 (1982), p. 942.

62 Thomas Paine, *Agrarian Justice Opposed to Agrarian Law, and to Agrarian Monopoly* (London, 1819 [1795/6]), p. 5.

63 James Mill, 'Article Colony', *Supplement to the Encyclopaedia Britannica* (Edinburgh, 1824).

64 President Grover Cleveland, 'First Inaugural Address', 4 March 1885: 'The conscience of the people demands that the Indians within our boundaries shall be fairly and honestly treated as wards of the Government and their education and civilization promoted with a view to their ultimate citizenship, and that polygamy in the Territories, destructive of the family relation and offensive to the moral sense of the civilized world, shall be repressed.'

65 Henry Adams, *History of the United States of America during the Administrations of Jefferson and Madison* (New York, 1889–91), vol. II, pp. 48–9.

66 Cited in Bailyn et al., *The Great Republic. A History of the American People*, p. 660.

67 Nahum Capen, *The Republic of the United States of America: Its Duties to Itself, and its Responsible Relations to Other Countries* (New York and Philadelphia, 1848), pp. 27, 144, 154 (italics original).

68 Theodore Roosevelt, 'The Strenuous Life', a speech delivered at the Hamilton Club, Chicago, 10 April 1899.

CAUDILLO DEMOCRACY

1 Cited in Bernard Bailyn et al., *The Great Republic. A History of the American People*, 3rd edn (Lexington, Mass., 1985), p. 667.

2 Woodrow Wilson, 'War Message' (2 April 1917), in *War Messages*, 65th Congress, 1st Session, Senate Document Number 5, Serial Number 7264 (Washington, DC, 1917), pp. 3–8.

3 Cited in Bailyn et al., *The Great Republic. A History of the American People*, p. 659.

4 All quotations are from James Monroe's message to Congress (2 December 1823), reprinted in J. D. Richardson (ed.), *Compilation of Messages and Papers of the Presidents, 1789–1897* (Washington, DC, 1907), vol. 2, p. 287.

5 *Real Orden* (Sevilla, 22 January 1809), Archivo Histórico Nacional, Madrid, *Estado* D71.

6 From the 'Manifesto of the Regency Council' (14 February 1810) composed by Manuel José Quintana, in Fernández Martín, *Derecho parlamentario español. Colección de Constituciones, disposiciones de carácter constitucional, leyes y decretos electorales para diputados y senadores, y reglamentos de las Cortes que han regido en España en el presente siglo* (Madrid, 1885), t. II, pp. 594ff.

7 *Acta de Independencia* (Caracas, Venezuela), 5 July 1811.

8 David Bushnell, 'El Sufragio en la Argentina y en Colombia hasta 1853', *Revista del instituto de Historia del Derecho*, 19, 11–29 (1968), p. 22.

9 Obituary of Juan Manuel de Rosas, *The Times* (London), 15 March 1877, p. 5.

10 Domingo Faustino Sarmiento, *Civilización i barbarie. Vida de Juan Facundo Quiroga* (La Plata, 1938 [Santiago, 1845]), pp. 179 and 35.

11 Simón Bolívar, 'Report to the Congress of Angostura [February 1819]', in David Bushnell (ed.), *El Libertador: Writings of Simón Bolívar* (Oxford, 2003), p. 27.

12 The following paragraph draws upon my interview with Hilda Sabato, Buenos Aires, 17 November 2005. The quotations are from Bartolomé Mitre's *Historia de San Martín y de la emancipación sudamericana* (Buenos Aires, 1877–88), p. 1; Bartolomé Mitre, *Historia de Belgrano* (Buenos Aires, 1859), vol. 1, pp. 404–5, 4th edn, 1887); and Bartolomé Mitre, *The Emancipation of South America* (London, 1893), pp. 19–21.

13 Domingo Faustino Sarmiento, *Sarmiento's Travels in the United States in 1847* (Princeton, NJ, 1970), p. 116, and 'Discurso a los maestros', in *Obras completas* (Santiago and Buenos Aires, 1885–1903), vol. 21, pp. 244, 247–8.

14 Drawn up at Apatzingán, Morelos, by delegates including Andrés Quintana Roo and Carlos Bustamante, the *independentista* Mexican constitution of 1814 called for popular sovereignty, republican government, abolition of slavery, equality before the law, representative government and the withdrawal of state support for the Roman Catholic Church, which was, however, to remain the state religion. The document spoke of the importance of special forms of representation: 'When the circumstances of an oppressed people make it impossible to elect deputies according to the constitution, supplementary representation [*representación supletoria*] established with the tacit will [*tácita voluntad*] of its citizens is legitimate' (Constitution of Apatzingán, 22 October 1814, article 8, reprinted in Ernesto de la Torre Villar, *La Constitución de Apatzingán y los creadores del Estado mexicano* (Mexico City, 1964), p. 381).

15 Cited in the *Guadalajara Reporter*, 18–24 October 1997.

16 Lucas Alamán, *Historia de México (1849–52)*, 6th edn (Mexico City, 1972), vol. 5, p. 463.

17 From the collection of historical documents in the Archivo General de la

Nación (Mexico City), vol. 445, document XIV, f. 1.

18 Article 10, Constitution of New Granada and Venezuela (Cucuta, 1821), in Luis Mariñas Otero, *Las Constituciones de Venezuela* (Madrid, 1965), p. 199.

19 James Creelman, 'President Díaz: Hero of the Americas', in Lewis Hanke (ed.), *History of Latin American Civilization*, vol. 2 (Boston, 1967), p. 259.

20 From the interview with Rosas by Vicente G. and Ernesto Quesada (Southampton, 1873), in Arturo Enrique Sampay, *Las ideas políticas de Juan Manuel de Rosas*, pp. 215, 218–19. The Palermo speech is described in the correspondence of Enrique Lafuente to Félix Frías (18 April 1839), in Gregorio F. Rodríguez (ed.), *Contribución histórica y documental* (Buenos Aires, 1921–2), vol. 2, pp. 468–9.

21 The first-hand account of Rosas's appears in the letter from Henry Southern to Lord Palmerston (27 January 1850), in the Palmerston Papers, GC/SO/251, Historical Manuscripts Commission (London).

22 From the report in *La Gaceta Mercantil* (Buenos Aires), 19 July 1835.

23 The speech is transcribed in Antonio Zinny, *La Gaceta Mercantil de Buenos Aires, 1823–1852, resumen de su contenido con relación a la parte Americana y con especialidad a la Historia de la República Argentina* (Buenos Aires, 1912), vol. 2, pp. 243–4.

24 See the letter from Henry Southern to Lord Palmerston (16 July 1849), in the Public Record Office (London) collection, Foreign Office, General Correspondence, FO 6 (1823–52), 144: 'The "Gazeta Mercantil" which is immediately under his care . . . is read every day in every corner of the country by the district authorities; the judge of peace reads it to the civilians, and the military commandant to the persons connected with the Army. The Gazette is in fact part of the *simulacrum* of government, which is kept up with a perfection of which only a man of the force of character, and of the inflexible and untiring nature of General Rosas is capable.'

25 Antonio Zinny, *La Gaceta Mercantil de Buenos Aires, 1823–1852, resumen de su contenido con relación a la parte Americana y con especialidad a la Historia de la República Argentina* (Buenos Aires, 1912), vol. 2, p. 236. The capitals and italics are found in the original text.

26 See John Anthony King, *Twenty-Four Years in the Argentine Republic* (London, 1846), pp. 259–60: 'For a more effectual establishment of his authority, and as a further means of intimidation to the weak, Rosas, in the year 1839, caused a portrait of himself to be mounted in gorgeous trappings, upon a triumphal car, and thus drawn through the streets of the city. This instrument of tyranny was sometimes drawn by the wives and daughters of the men of the *Massorca*, and at other times it was drawn by a procession of noisy wretches, who rent the air with the accustomed shout, "Viva la Federación, mueran los salvajes Unitarians". But this was not all . . . The picture was conveyed from church to church, at each of which it was received by the priests with a show of even devotional respect. It was conveyed through the sacred aisles amid the sounds of the organ, the anthem, and of prayer. It has been consecrated with incense, decorated for the celebration of high mass, and placed upon the altar by the side of the crucified Saviour; and thus with sacrilegious rites,

and disgusting hypocrisy, worshipped, through fear, almost as a deity.' See also Andrés Lamas, *Escritos políticos y literarios durante la guerra contra la Tiranía de D. Juan Manuel de Rosas* (Buenos Aires, 1877), p. 266, where it is recorded that in 1839 Fray Juan González told his flock: 'If it is right to love God Our Lord, so it is right to love, obey, and respect our Governor and Restorer of the Laws, D. Juan Manuel de Rosas'.

27 *La Gaceta Mercantil* (Buenos Aires), 1 April 1835.

28 Marcela Ternavasio, *La revolución del voto. Política y Elecciones en Buenos Aires, 1810–1852* (Buenos Aires, 2002), pp. 202, 206, 232–3.

29 The process of democratising violence is discussed in John Keane, *Violence and Democracy* (Cambridge and New York, 2004).

30 James Bryce, *Modern Democracies* (New York, 1921), vol. 1, pp. 187–206.

31 Francisco I. Madero, *La sucesión presidencial en 1910: El Partido Nacional Democrático* (Mexico City, 1908), pp. 179–85, 230–41.

32 From the speech by Julio V. González, to the Chamber of Senators (1 February 1912), quoted in Natalio Botana, *El orden conservador: La política argentina entre 1880 y 1915* (Buenos Aires, 1985), p. 174.

33 Alcides Argüedas, *Los caudillos bárbaros* (Barcelona, 1929) and *Los caudillos letrados* (Barcelona, 1923).

34 Barrington Moore, Jr, *Social Origins of Dictatorship and Democracy. Lord and Peasant in the Making of the Modern World* (Boston, 1967), p. 418.

35 Comisión Nacional de Homenaje a Artigas, *El Congreso de Abril de 1813, a través de los documentos* (Montevideo, 1951).

36 [Batlle], 'Instrucción Para Todos', *El Día* (4 December 1914).

37 [Batlle], 'El P. E. Colegiado', *El Día* (18 December 1911).

38 The key work is Joseph Borély, *Nouveau Système Électoral. Représentation proportionnelle de la majorité et des minorités* (Paris, 1870).

39 The blow against the double simultaneous vote was not fatal; it had strong roots and considerable reach. The method was later copied in some provinces of Argentina and in presidential elections in Honduras, and progressively incorporated into Uruguayan law in 1934, 1935 and 1939; and despite its reform in the 1982 Political Parties Law (which allowed each party to present three tickets, or single candidates, each representing a different *sublema*, for executive and legislative posts), and its restriction in the constitutional reforms of 1996, the double simultaneous vote is still used today. But its twentieth-century use showed that it had certain practical drawbacks. It supposed that citizens voted primarily for parties, and it banned ticket splitting; voters were effectively forced to choose their preferred candidate by voting only for candidates from the same party. Its other much debated disadvantages are said to include: a tendency to promote bad-tempered party divisions; to discourage intra-party and public debate when choosing presidential candidates; and to allow politicians who receive only a minority of the overall vote to rise to the highest office of state. Exactly that happened when the double simultaneous vote was adopted (in 1991) in the province of Santa Fe, in Argentina. In gubernatorial elections held in 2003, the former mayor of Rosario and socialist candidate, Hermes Binner, won 556,603 votes while his main opponent,

the Peronist candidate Jorge Obeid, former governor and Mayor of Santa Fe City, received 319,887 votes. Obeid was, however, declared the winner, thanks to the cumulative votes of the other Peronist *sublemas*. The tactic – mostly opportunistic – of multiplying *sublemas* in order to gather votes meant that nearly one in fifty voters was a candidate for election. At the end of November 2004, faced with anomalies of this kind, the double simultaneous vote law was abandoned in Santa Fe, in favour of a voting system based on compulsory primary elections followed by a closed-list main election, using the method of first past the post for executive posts, and a form of proportional representation for legislative elections.

40 Interview with Ana Maria Rodríguez, Ana Frega, Inés Cuadro and Carlos Demasi, Montevideo, 15 November 2005.

41 *El Diario Ilustrado* (Santiago), 24 August 1931.

THE EUROPEAN GRAVEYARD

1 Giuseppe Mazzini, 'The democratic tendency of our times', *People's Journal* (29 August 1846), p. 1.

2 John Milton, *Paradise Regain'd*, in E. H. Visiak (ed.), *Milton. Complete Poetry & Selected Prose* (Glasgow, 1938), Book 3, pp. 375–6.

3 For a century after 1520, the tiny alpine republic known locally as the Freestate of the Three Leagues – and today in its three native languages as Graubünden, Grigioni, Grischun – managed to preserve a form of self-government based on a confederation of multi-religious communes, a republic whose God-fearing citizens decided matters of common concern through public assemblies. It has often been said that Freestate citizens were the first modern Europeans to live in a democracy, but that is misleading. It is true that there were some Freestate citizens who thought of themselves as living in a democracy, a word that they used in positive terms for the first time anywhere in Europe. But quite aside from evidence that they did not mean to include servants and poorer and unfree peasants, and that they strictly excluded women as non-citizens, on the republican ground that they did not and could not bear arms, it is clear that the small handful of Freestate citizens who put quill to paper used the word democracy in its classical, assembly-based sense. Unlike peoples of the Low Countries, the Freestate citizens had no notion of democracy as *representative* democracy. This is evident in the Latin tract in support of forced conversion to Protestantism, written in 1577 by the Protestant minister and historian Ulrich Campell (1509/1510–82), who described the Freestate as a place 'where a democratic magistrate flourishes, that is, the part of the population with the larger number of votes is recognised as the supreme magistrate, and rules' ('De officio', Staatsarchiv Graubünden, B721, 27–8). The same Greek bias is evident in a German-language tract, written in 1618, *Grawpündtnerische Handlungen dess M.DC.XVIII jahrs* (1618). It praises the Freestate confederation for granting its common citizens the power 'according to his majorities, to create laws and to abrogate them, to form alliances with foreign princes and estates, to regulate peace and war, and to deliberate concerning all other matters pertaining to higher and lesser authority'. It added: 'The form of our government is democratic [*Democratisch*]; and the election

and removal of all kinds of magistrates, judges and officers, both here in our free and ruling lands and in those lands subject to us, lies with our common man.' Between 1620 and 1639, talk of democracy died away. The Freestate lost its autonomy, drowned under the rising tides of European power politics and confessionalism of the Thirty Years War.

4 Juan Díaz del Moral, *Historia de las agitaciones campesinas andaluzas – Córdoba* (Madrid, 1984), pp. 68–9.

5 See the masterful essay by Jenö Szücs, 'Three Historical Regions of Europe. An Outline', in John Keane (ed.), *Civil Society and the State. New European Perspectives* (London and New York, 1988), pp. 291–332. The essay originally appeared in Hungarian as 'Vázlat Európa három régiójáról', *Történelmi Szemle*, 24 (1981), pp. 313–69.

6 Benedict [Baruch] de Spinoza, 'Of Democracy', in *The Chief Works of Benedict de Spinoza (Tractatus Theologico-Politicus, Tractatus Politicus)* [1670] (London, 1891), vol. 1, chapter xi.

7 Quoted in Simon Schama, *Patriots and Liberators: Revolution in the Netherlands 1780–1813* (New York, 1977), p. 67.

8 G. K. van Hogendorp, *Brieven en Gedenkschriften* (The Hague, 1876), vol. 3, pp. 60–61.

9 Maximilien Robespierre, *Discours et rapports à la Convention* (Paris, 1965), pp. 213ff.

10 Chevalier de Jaucourt, *Encyclopédie ou Dictionnaire Raisonné des Sciences, des Arts et des Métiers* (Paris, 1754), p. 816; cf. the famous remark made by Jean-Jacques Rousseau that the growth of large-scale modern states and empires, mounting inequality and the corrupting effects of luxury and market specialisation all heralded the obsolescence of democracy: 'Were there a people of gods, their government would be democratic. So perfect a government is not for men' ('The Social Contract or Principles of Political Right', Book 3, Chapter 4, in G. D. H. Cole, *Rousseau. The Social Contract and Discourses* (London and New York, 1913), p. 56). For good measure, he added: 'If we take the term in the strict sense, there never has been a real democracy, and there never will be. It is against the natural order for the many to govern and the few to be governed. It is unimaginable that the people should remain continually assembled to devote their time to public affairs, and it is clear that they cannot set up commissions for that purpose without the form of administration being changed.'

11 Emmanuel-Joseph Sieyès, *Écrits politiques* (Paris, 1985), p. 47.

12 George Gordon, Lord Byron, 'My Dictionary', in *Letters and Diaries 1798 to 1824*, edited by Peter Quennell (London, 1950), vol. 2, p. 605: 'It is . . . difficult to say which form of Government is the *worst* – all are bad. As for democracy, it is the worst of the whole; for what is (*in fact*) democracy? an Aristocracy of Blackguards.'

13 Quoted in J. Leflon, *Pie VII: des abbayes bénédictines à la papauté* (Paris, 1958), p. 434; the points that follow are drawn from a remarkable clutch of Jacobin newspaper articles, pamphlets and books that appeared in the late 1790s, including two works by Giuseppe Compagnoni, 'Il Vocabolario Democratico', *Monitore Cisalpino* (18 May–22 August 1798), and *Elementi di diritto costituzionale democratico, ossia principi di giuspubblico universale* (1797).

14 *Das Volk* (Berlin), number 5, 10 June 1848, pp. 18–19; and number 11 (which outlines a 'People's Social Charter'), 27 June 1848, pp. 41ff.

15 Adamantios Koraes, *Ephemeris ton Athenon* (Athens, 3 August 1825)

16 A. N. Radishchev, *Puteshestvie iz Peterburga v Moskvu, Volnost* (St Petersburg, 1790), translated as Aleksandr Nikolaevich Radishchev, *A Journey from St. Petersburg to Moscow* (Cambridge, Mass., 1958). A flavour of Radishchev's themes is provided by a dream, in which the author sees himself as the Csar, to whom Truth has appeared in the guise of a pilgrim, saying: 'Know that you have it in your power to be the greatest murderer in the commonweal, the greatest robber, the greatest traitor, the greatest violator of the public tranquillity, the most savage of enemies in directing your ferocity against the lives of the weak. You will be to blame if a mother weeps over her son, or a wife over her husband, slain on the field of battle . . . You will be to blame if the fields lie fallow, if the plowman's fledglings starve at their mother's breast, withered from lack of healthy food.'

17 V. I. Lenin, *Collected Works* (Moscow, 1960–66), vol. 2, p. 507.

18 From P. N. Tkachev's 'Open Letter to Engels', in *Izbrannye sochineniia na sotsialno-politicheskie temy,* edited by B. P. Kozmin (Moscow, 1932), vol. 3, pp. 88–98.

19 Dr T. H. B. Oldfield, *Representative History of Great Britain and Ireland*, cited in Sir Thomas Erskine May, *The Constitutional History of England Since the Accession of George the Third: 1760–1860* (London, 1896), vol. 1, pp. 361–2.

20 Thucydides, *History of the Peloponnesian War*, Book I, 143, I.

21 *Diaries and Correspondence of the Earl of Malmesbury* (London, 1844), vol. 4, p. 147.

22 Letter to James Maury, 21 November 1807, in E. A. Bergh (ed.), *The Writings of Thomas Jefferson* (Washington, DC, 1907), vol. xi, p. 397.

23 Edmund Burke, *Debates on the Passage of the Quebec Act* (House of Commons, London, 31 May 1774), and *Speeches in the Impeachment of Warren Hastings* (House of Commons, London, 16 February 1788): 'these gentlemen have formed a plan of *geographic morality*, by which the duties of men, in publick and in private situations, are not to be governed by their relation to the great Governour of the Universe, or by their relation to mankind, but by climates, degrees of longitude, parallels not of life but of latitudes; as if, when you have crossed the equinoctial, all the virtues die, as they say some insects die when they cross the line; as if there were a kind of baptism, like that practised by seamen, by which they unbaptize themselves of all that they learned in Europe, and after which a new order and system of things commenced.'

24 Jeremy Bentham, *Letter to Lord Pelham, Giving a Comparative View of the System of Penal Colonization in New South Wales, and the Home Penitentiary System, Prescribed by Two Acts of Parliament of the Years 1794 & 1799* (London, 1802). The same point was made by Cornewall Lewis, *An Essay on the Government of Dependencies* (London, 1841), ed. Lucas 1891, p. 289: 'A self-governing dependency (supposing the dependency not to be virtually independent) is a contradiction in terms.' See also James Mill, 'Colony', in *Essays* (London, 1828); and, in relation to India, see the declaration of the Parliamentary Committee of 1833: 'It

is recognised as an indisputable principle, that the interests of the Native Subjects are to be consulted in preference to those of Europeans, whenever the two come in competition' (R. Muir, *The Making of British India, 1756–1858*, p. 305). Under Buxton's chairmanship, the same sentiments surfaced in the House of Commons Select Committee on Aborigines in 1837 and, in the same year, the powerful Aborigines Protection Society was formed.

25 Catherine Cleverdon, *The Woman Suffrage Movement in Canada* (Toronto, 1950), p. 215. Despite concerns about the impact of election rowdiness and violence upon 'the weaker sex' – during a by-election held in Montreal between 25 April and 22 May 1832 three Canadians were shot dead on one day by British troops – the enfranchisement of women who were propertied or tenants survived for many decades, until the union of Lower and Upper Canada into the Province of Canada, which disenfranchised women in 1849. Section 41 of the British North America Act (1867) entrenched women's exclusion from the vote, so triggering struggles across the new confederation to undo the injustice, led by suffragettes and their supporters, who organised themselves into bodies like the Women's Enfranchisement Association of New Brunswick, the Manitoba Equal Suffrage Club and the Women's Christian Temperance Union. It was not until 1900 that most women property owners could exercise their votes in municipal elections. Women in Manitoba were the first to win the right to vote in a provincial election (in January 1916). Total war – always the fickle catalyst of democratic politics – subsequently changed many men's minds: following the Military Voters Act (1917), the first women to vote in national elections were servicewomen known as the Bluebirds.

26 Quoted in A. J. Marshall, *Darwin and Huxley in Australia* (Sydney, 1970), p. 44.

27 James Tuckey, *Account of a Voyage to Establish a Colony at Port Phillip in Bass's Strait* (London, 1805), p. 190.

28 *Speeches of Henry Lord Brougham, upon questions relating to public rights, duties and interests: with historical introductions* (London, 1838), vol. 2, p. 600.

29 John Stuart Mill, *Dissertations and Discussions* (London, 1921 [1838]), p. 311; compare his *Autobiography* (London, 1961 [1873]), p. 220: 'Minorities, so long as they remain minorities, are, and ought to be, outvoted; but under arrangements which enable any assemblage of voters, amounting to a certain number, to place in the legislature a representative of its own choice, minorities cannot be suppressed.' The stem cells of the principle of protecting minorities against majorities can be found in the parliamentary debates on the first Reform Bill (see Praed's motion in *Hansard* (London, 1831), vol. 188, p. 1075). It is possible that the South Australian colonists were aware of the work in Geneva of Victor Considérant, the prominent Fourierist, who in the years after 1834 publicly campaigned for a similar method of election that enabled the expression of what he called 'constituencies of opinion'. His plan was submitted to the Grand Council of Geneva in 1846, and reprinted as *De la sincérité du gouvernement représentatif ou exposition de l'élection véridique* (Zurich, 1892). Among the very first statements of the principle

of representation of minorities was a parliamentary speech delivered by Mirabeau on 30 January 1789. 'A representative body', he said, 'is to the nation what a chart is for the physical configuration of its soil: in all its parts, and as a whole, the representative body should at all times present a reduced picture of the people – their opinions, aspirations, and wishes, and that presentation should bear the relative proportion to the original precisely as a map brings before us mountains and dales, rivers and lakes, forests and plains, cities and towns. The finer should not be crushed out by the more massive substance, and the latter not be excluded; the value of each element is dependent upon its importance to the whole and for the whole' (cited in Simon Sterne, *On Representative Government and Personal Representation* (Philadelphia, 1871), pp. 50–51; see also *Oeuvres de Mirabeau* (Paris, 1834), p. 7.

30 Rowland Hill's support for the introduction of proportional representation is recorded in George Birkbeck Hill, *Life of Sir Rowland Hill* (London, 1880), vol. 1, p. 223, and in Catherine Helen Spence, *Autobiography* (Adelaide, 1910), p. 17. See also the *Preface to the Laws of the Society for Literary and Scientific Improvement*, reprinted as Appendix B in the first volume of George Birkbeck Hill, *Life of Sir Rowland Hill*, p. 69.

31 Cited in Manning Clark, *A History of Australia* (London and Sydney, 1995), p. 257.

32 The probability that the Victorian initiative was influenced by the same initiative in the colony of Tasmania is explored in Terry Newman, 'Tasmania and the Secret Ballot', *Australian Journal of Politics and History*, vol. 49, 1 (2003), pp. 93–101. See also John Hirst, *Australia's Democracy. A Short History* (Crow's Nest, 2002); the informative website organised by Peter Brent, http://www.enrollingthepeople.com; and Edward Wakefield, 'The Australasian Ballot', *The Forum*, vol. 8 (1889), pp. 148–58. The Melbourne lawyer Henry Samuel Chapman (1803–81) had a strong hand in the process of drafting both the Tasmanian and Victorian legislation that introduced the new secret ballot system. Chapman was something of a well-travelled philosophical radical who had run a radical newspaper in Canada, had lived in New Zealand and Tasmania and was elected to the Legislative Council of Victoria in 1855. See R. S. Neale, 'H. S. Chapman and the "Victorian Ballot"', *Historical Studies*, 12 (1967), pp. 506–21.

33 See the report on the Massachusetts legislature in the *New York Times*, 17 January 1853, p. 1: 'Orders were to-day [Saturday 15 January 1853] introduced in the Legislature of Massachusetts, to consider the expediency of repealing so much of the Secret Ballot Law as makes it obligatory upon voters to deposit their ballots.'

34 Henry George, 'Money in Elections', *North American Review*, 136 (1883), p. 210.

35 Many observers have subsequently exaggerated the spring-cleaning effects of the Australian ballot. Yet bribery undoubtedly continued, and may even have increased, which is one reason why *The Times* of London denounced the ballot immediately after its introduction as a 'dead failure' and a 'vile system' ('The Ballot in Australia' [13 January 1857]). The ballot nevertheless put voters in a much stronger bargaining position,

both to command their own price and to take bribes from whomever they wished, at least until the advent of legally monitored party politics, which replaced buying votes with promises and programmes. The evidence from Britain is summarised in C. O'Leary, *The Elimination of Corrupt Practices in British Elections* (Oxford, 1962), pp. 155ff. A similar trend in India was noted during the 1970s by A. H. Somjee, *The Democratic Process in a Developing Society* (New York, 1979), p. 118: 'Tempted by the cash offered by both sides . . . the voter often decided to accept money from whoever was willing to offer it. The acceptance of cash from both sides liberated the voter, as it were, from the obligation to vote for one or the other side because of money. The electorate had certainly come of age in the art of using the secret vote.'

36 Alexander Keyssar, *The Right to Vote. The Contested History of Democracy in the United States* (New York, 2000), pp. 142–3, reports that the early use of the Australian ballot in the United States was 'an obstacle to participation by many illiterate foreign-born voters in the North, as well as uneducated black voters in the South'.

37 *Melbourne Argus* (27 September 1856).

38 The link between the Australian ballot and the enfranchisement of women was noted by the British Prime Minister William Gladstone: 'It was one thing to ask that women should have imposed on them the duty of going up to the open poll and recording their votes in public, and quite another to ask that they should be allowed to enter a quiet compartment of the polling-place and record an independent vote under the saving shelter of the ballot' (cited in Justin McCarthy, *A History of Our Own Times* (Leipzig, 1880), vol. 4, p. 317.

39 Sir John Barrow, *A Description of Pitcairn's Island and its Inhabitants* (New York, 1854), p. 295.

40 Walter Brodie, *Pitcairn's Island, and The Islanders, in 1850*, 2nd edn (London, 1851), p. 108; see also the note containing details of at least a dozen murders, 'Meeting of the Bounty and Story of Pitcairn Island 1790–1894', *John Angus Nimmo Papers (1939–1990)*, NLA MS 9488, folio 1 (Australian National Library, Canberra).

41 The following account draws upon the letter by Russell Elliott, dated 25 January 1839 (Callao), reprinted in Brodie, *Pitcairn's Island, and The Islanders, in 1850*, pp. 82–3; the report of the signing of the constitution by Elliott, 30 November 1838, reprinted in ibid., pp. 84–5; and Thomas Boyles Murray, *Pitcairn: The Island, the People, and the Pastor* (London, 1857), pp. 144–5.

42 Barrow, *A Description of Pitcairn's Island and its Inhabitants*, p. 282; see also the letter written by Arthur Quintal, Jr, to the Reverend S. C. Damon, seamen's chaplain at the Sandwich Islands (11 January 1844), reproduced in Nathan Welby Fiske, *Aleck; the Last of the Mutineers; or the History of Pitcairn's Island*, 2nd edn (Amherst, 1845), p. 159.

43 Brodie, *Pitcairn's Island, and The Islanders, in 1850*, p. 153.

44 From the 1889 *Report of the Social Purity Society* (Adelaide, 1890), p. 1.

45 *Women of South Australia!* (Trades Hall, Adelaide, 1894).

46 *Register* (Adelaide), 15 March 1893.

47 *The Country* (Adelaide), 28 July 1894.

48 See Graham Loughlin, 'Gordon, Sir John Hannah (1850–1923)',

Australian Dictionary of Biography, vol. 9: *1891–1939* (Melbourne, 1983), pp. 53–4.

49 South Australian *Parliamentary Debates* (House of Assembly), 23 August 1894, p. 1086. It is worth noting the contemporary estimate that the Women's Christian Temperance Union was responsible for collecting more than two-thirds of the signatures.

50 South Australian *Parliamentary Debates* (House of Assembly), 18 December 1894, p. 2951.

51 *Observer* (Adelaide), 2 May 1896, p. 41.

52 From the interview with Muriel Matters, 'A Woman Who Dared', *Southern Sphere* (1 July 1910), p. 12.

53 Walter Bagehot, *The English Constitution* (London, 1867), p. 270.

54 The classic (if controversial) account of the historical growth of citizenship rights in Britain is T. H. Marshall, *Citizenship and Social Class* (Cambridge, 1950).

55 People who today suppose that the experiments that British governments allowed to happen in places like Canada, Australia and New Zealand were typical, that the Empire run by Westminster was on balance a training ground in the arts of Westminster-style government, should ponder the words of the enlightened, practical imperialist, the self-declared 'British race patriot' Lord Alfred Milner (1854–1925), whose last great act of public service was to head a mission to Egypt, where serious rioting prompted the British to search for a way of reconciling the British protectorate established in 1915 and local demands for self-government. 'I attach much more importance, in the immediate future of Egypt', concluded Lord Milner, 'to the improvement of the character and intelligence of the official class than I do to the development of the representative institutions with which we endowed the country in 1883. As a true born Briton, I, of course take off my hat to everything that calls itself Franchise, Parliament, Representation of the People, the Voice of the Majority, and all the rest of it. But, as an observer of the actual condition of Egyptian society, I cannot shut my eyes to the fact that popular government, as we understand it, is for a longer time than any one can foresee at present out of the question. The people neither comprehend it nor desire it. They would come to singular grief if they had it. And nobody, except a few silly theorists, thinks of giving it to them' (*England in Egypt* (London, 1920), pp. 378–9).

56 *Encyclopédie* (17 vols, Paris, 1751–65), vol. 11, p. 36.

57 *Rights of Man. Part First*, in Philip S. Foner (ed.), *The Complete Writings of Thomas Paine* (New York, 1945), p. 341.

58 William Edward Hartpole Lecky, *Democracy and Liberty* (London, New York and Bombay, 1896), p. 261.

59 Siegfried Sassoon, *The Complete Memoirs of George Sherston* (New York, 1937), vol. 2, p. 143.

60 The following references are from Robert Musil, cited in D. Luft, *Robert Musil and the Crisis of European Culture* (Berkeley and Los Angeles, 1980), p. 279; H. G. Wells, *After Democracy: Addresses and Papers on the Present World Situation* (London, 1932), p. 24; and L. Volovici, *Nationalist Ideology and Anti-Semitism: The Case of Romanian Intellectuals in the 1930s* (Oxford, 1991). The principal objections to

representative democracy summarised here (in order) are from Heinrich von Treitschke, *Politik* (1898), 3rd edn (Berlin, 1913), vol. 1, p. 62; Edmund Burke, 'Reflections on the Revolution in France (1790)', in *The Works of Edmund Burke* (London, 1886), vol. 2, pp. 396–7, 365; G. W. F. Hegel, *Vorlesungen ueber die Philosophie der Weltgeschichte*, III, in *Philosophische Bibliothek*, edited by Georg Lassen (Leipzig, 1920), p. 604; Johann Gottlieb Fichte, *Grundlage des Naturrechts*, part 1 (1797), in *Fichtes Werke* (Leipzig, 1908), vol. 2, p. 163; Friedrich Daniel Ernst Schleiermacher, *Ueber die Begriffe der verschiedenen Staatsformen* (Berlin, 1818); Georges Sorel, *The Illusions of Progress* (London, 1969), p. 150; and Prince Kropotkin, *Paroles d'un Révolté* (Paris, 1885), p. 190, and *Anarchist Communism* [1887] (London, 1920), p. 6.

61 *The Times* (London), 10 August 1936.

62 From a 1908 letter to Robert Michels, in Max Weber, *Briefe 1906–1908*, in *Max Weber-Gesamtausgabe* (Tübingen, 1990), vol. II, 5, p. 615.

63 J. A. Hobson, *Democracy and a Changing Civilisation* (London, 1934), p. vii.

64 Cited in F. C. Egerton, *Salazar, Rebuilder of Portugal* (London, 1943), pp. 224–7.

65 V. I. Lenin, *A Contribution to the History of the Question of Dictatorship* (1920), in *Collected Works* (Moscow, 1966), vol. 31, pp. 340–61.

66 Benito Mussolini, *Le fascisme* (Paris, 1933), pp. 19ff.

67 This and all following quotations are drawn from *Parliamentary Debates, House of Commons, 1947–1948*, vol. 444 (10 November 1947), pp. 36–155, and ibid., 11 November 1947, pp. 203–318.

UNDER THE BANYAN TREE

1 Winston Churchill, *India. Speeches and an Introduction* (London, 1931), pp. 30, 136, 77; Hira Lal Seth, *Churchill on India* (Sant Nagar, Lahore, 1942), p. 16.

2 HMG, *Report of the Indian Statutory Commission*, 1 (London, 1930), pp. 299–300.

3 HMG, *Report of the Indian Statutory Commission*, 1 (London 1930), pp. 118–19.

4 'Foundation Stone Laid by the Duke', *The Statesman* (13 February 1921), p. 12.

5 Cited in Deyan Sudjic, *Architecture and Democracy* (London and Glasgow, 1999), p. 30.

6 'Message from the King. Brilliant Scene', *The Statesman* (19 January 1927), p. 7.

7 The following quotations are drawn from Shashi Tharoor, *Nehru. The Invention of India* (New Delhi and London, 2003), pp. 48, 167.

8 From the unfinished review 'Roads to Freedom (April 1919)', in *Selected Works of Jawaharlal Nehru* (New Delhi, 1972), vol. 1, p. 141.

9 The quotation from the Sapru Committee of the Constituent Assembly is drawn from Granville Austin, *The Indian Constitution: Cornerstone of a Nation* (New Delhi, 1966), p. 147.

10 Jawaharlal Nehru, *An Autobiography* (London, 1936), p. 503.

11 'The Rashtrapati (1937)', first published in *The Modern Review* (Calcutta),

and reprinted in *Selected Works of Jawaharlal Nehru* (New Delhi, 1976), vol. 8, pp. 520–23.

12 Max Weber, 'Politik als Beruf', in *Gesammelte Politische Schriften* (Tübingen, 1958), p. 523.

13 Ogden Nash, 'The Pandit' (1961), in *Everyone but Thee, Me and Thee* (Boston, 1962).

14 Compare Rajni Kothari, *Politics in India* (Delhi, 1970) and the different emphases in his *The State Against Democracy: In Search of Humane Governance* (Delhi, 1988).

15 B. R. Ambedkar, 'Speech on the Adoption of the Constitution', in B. Shiva Rao (ed.), *The Framing of India's Constitution: Select Documents* (New Delhi, 1968), vol. 4, p. 944.

16 According to a Centre for the Study of Developing Societies survey (reported in *India Today*, 31 August 1996, pp. 30–39) of those who voted in the 1996 elections, above average voting predominated among the 'very poor' (+2.9 points above the average turnout), the Scheduled Castes (+1.9 points), and the villagers (+1.1 points). Below average voting predominated among graduates and postgraduates (-4.5 points), urban residents (-3 points) and the upper castes (-1.6 points). More generally, see Yogendra Yadav, 'Understanding the Second Democratic Upsurge: Trends of Bahujan participation in electoral politics in the 1990s', in Francine Frankel et al. (eds), *Transforming India: Social and Political Dynamics of Democracy* (Delhi, 2000), pp. 122–34.

17 The implosion of parliamentary politics by rough-handed party manoeuvrings in Goa during the period 1990–2005 is traced in Peter Ronald deSouza, 'A Carnival of Greed', *Indian Express* (10 February 2005); the 'lathicharging' and use of water cannon by the Chandigarh police against black armband-wearing members of the Punjab Assembly is reported in *The Hindu* (27 February 2005), p. 5; the spread of lawlessness in the state of Bihar is well described by Vandita Mishra, 'We don't talk anymore', *The Indian Express* (11 February 2005).

18 A. B. Vajpayee, 'Challenges to Democracy in India', *Organiser*, 24 November 1996; and 'Vajpayee Advocates a Change in Our System of Governance', *Organiser*, 9 March 1997.

19 *Times of India* (28 December 1993), pp. 1, 11.

20 In the run-up to the 2004 general election, the prominent Indian writer and scholar Ashis Nandy captured this point about political crooks with the remark that some parts of the Indian new middle class were 'prepared to support politicians who defend them even if they are corrupt or have a criminal record. Their attitude of "Yes, we know he's a bastard, but at least he's our bastard" suggests a conclusion: the successful functioning of democracy in India has created an upper caste of modern, Westernised Indians, a section of whom have become ambivalent about democracy itself' (from the author's interview with Ashis Nandy, Delhi, 26 February 2004).

21 See Sri Aurobindo, 'Bande Mataram' (20 March 1908), in *Collected Works* (Pondicherry, 1970), pp. 767–9, and R. K. Mookerji, *Hindu Civilization: From the Earliest Time up to the Establishment of the Maurya Empire* (Bombay, 1950 [originally published in 1936]), especially pp. 99, 214, and p. 209: 'The Pali texts furnish interesting information on the working of

Buddhist Samghas in strict and minute conformity with genuine democratic principles. The essence of democracy is government by decision based on discussion in public meetings or assemblies. The Pali texts describe the meetings of religious assemblies or Samghas in all their stages.'

22 K. N. Govindacharya, 'Agenda', *The Pioneer*, 6 April 1997.

23 Compare the account of the beginning of the world, through the sacrifice of the primeval giant Purusha, in the Rig Veda, 10.90: 'When they divided the Man, into how many parts did they apportion him? What do they call his mouth, his two arms and thighs and feet? / His mouth became the Brahmin; his arms were made into the Warrior [*kshatriya*], his thighs the People [*vaishiya*], and from his feet the servants [*shudra*] were born.'

24 Quoted in William Dalrymple, 'Trapped in the Ruins', *Independent on Sunday* (20 March 2004), p. 4.

25 Cited in Edward Luce, 'Master of Ambiguity', *Financial Times Magazine* (London), 3 April 2004, pp. 17–21.

SEA CHANGES

1 Kader Asmal et al. (eds), *Nelson Mandela In His Own Words* (London, 2003), p. 62.

2 Barrington Moore, Jr, *Social Origins of Dictatorship and Democracy. Lord and Peasant in the Making of the Modern World* (Boston, 1967), p. 418.

3 The full audio text of the speech delivered in West Berlin on 26 June 1963 can be found at www.americanrhetoric.com/speeches/jfkichbineinberliner.html

4 Sidney Verba, 'Problems of Democracy in the Developing Countries', unpublished remarks (Harvard-MIT Joint Seminar on Political Development, October 1976); S. E. Finer, *The Man on Horseback: The Role of the Military in Politics* (Harmondsworth, 1976), p. 223.

5 Cited in John Keane, *Violence and Democracy* (Cambridge and New York, 2004), p. 1.

6 Stan Sesser, 'A Rich Country Gone Wrong', *New Yorker*, 9 October 1989, pp. 80–81.

7 Cited in Francisco Weffort, 'Why Democracy?', in Alfred Stepan (ed.), *Democratizing Brazil. Problems of Transition and Consolidation* (New York and Oxford, 1989), pp. 327–50.

8 Details of the 'smile revolution' (*la manifestación de las sonrisas*) are drawn from my interview with Ana Frega, Ana Maria Rodríguez, Carlos Demasi and Inés Cuadro, Montevideo, 15 November 2005. The events are well captured in the documentary film *Y el pueblo dijo ¡no¡* (Montevideo, 1994).

9 *Svobodné Slovo* (Prague), 18 November 1989. A longer account of the Prague events is to be found in John Keane, *Václav Havel: A Political Tragedy in Six Acts* (London and New York, 1999), pp. 338–59.

10 Cited in Bernard Gwertzman and Michael T. Kaufman (eds), *The Collapse of Communism by the Correspondents of 'The New York Times'* (New York, 1990), p. vii.

11 Henry Adams, *Democracy. An American Novel* (New York, 1961 [1880]), p. 189.

12 Francis Fukuyama, 'The End of History?', *The National Interest* (Summer

1989); and my interview with him, 'On the Road to Utopia?', *Independent* (London), 19 June 1999.

13 See the Freedom House report *Democracy's Century. A Survey of Global Political Change in the 20th Century* (New York, 1999).

14 All following quotations are drawn from Samuel P. Huntington, *The Third Wave. Democratization in the Late Twentieth Century* (Norman, OK, and London, 1991), especially chapters 1 and 6.

15 Joseph Schumpeter, *Capitalism, Socialism, and Democracy* (New York and London, 1942), p. 269.

16 Samuel P. Huntington, *The Third Wave. Democratization in the Late Twentieth Century* (Norman, OK, and London, 1991), p. 39.

17 The following quotations are from Julius Nyerere, 'Misingi ya Demokrasi', in *Sauti ya TANU*, number 47, reprinted in E. B. M. Barongo, *MkikiMkikiwa Siasa Tanganyika* (Dar es Salaam, 1966), pp. 220–23; Julius K. Nyerere, *Freedom and Unity; Uhuru na Umoja: A Selection of Writings and Speeches, 1952–1965* (London, 1967), p. 104; Julius K. Nyerere, 'Hotuba ya Rais' (10 December 1962), in Tanganyika, *Parliamentary Debates*, National Assembly (Dar es Salaam, 1962); and the pamphlet, *Democracy and the Party System* (Dar es Salaam, 1967).

18 The following description is drawn from the *Tanganyika Sunday News* (Dar es Salaam), 16 December 1962, p. 7.

19 The birth of monitory democracy calls radically into question the bitter attacks on majority-rule, representative democracy by market liberals, notably Friedrich von Hayek. In his well-known and influential *Law, Legislation and Liberty: The Political Order of a Free People* (London and Henley, 1979), von Hayek, a self-proclaimed lover of 'liberty', declared: 'I must frankly admit that *if* democracy is taken to mean government by the unrestricted will of the majority I am not a democrat, and even regard such government as pernicious and in the long run unworkable' (p. 39). The basic purpose of government, he reasoned, is the creation of 'a framework within which individuals and groups can successfully pursue their respective aims, and sometimes to use its coercive powers of raising revenue to provide services which for one reason or other the market cannot supply' (p. 139). That being so, the most urgent task of the age was to defend free markets and limited constitutional government – von Hayek called it 'demarchy' – against the corrupting effects of the party-driven process of buying votes during elections, a process that leads inevitably to the triumph of bloated government ('totalitarian democracy' and 'plebiscitary dictatorship' he variously called it) that crushes individual freedom and the respect for constitutional laws designed to restrain the exercise of governmental power. Von Hayek's insistence that representative democracy must be restrained so that democracy can be protected from its own worst tendencies arguably placed much too much faith in the spontaneous freedoms allegedly generated by markets; its recognition of market failures was poor. It supposed rather too readily that constitutional mechanisms could be relied upon to have self-restraining effects upon the power and scope of government. There is as well the suspicion that 'demarchy' would in practice quickly degenerate into a species of state authoritarianism. Von Hayek was fond of proposing (see ibid., p. 113) a bicameral system of government regulated principally by an assembly charged with the task of defining and

protecting the constitutional framework. The assembly members would comprise men and women aged between forty-five and sixty, elected as representatives for a fifteen-year term by voters who cast their ballots for a representative of their choice only once in their lives, in the calendar year in which they reached the age of forty-five. Quite apart from numerous technical objections to the whole proposal for an assembly that resembled a senate of the wise, von Hayek never made clear exactly how public support could freely be won for constitutional rule by an elite based on such a restricted franchise. There is another fundamental objection to von Hayek's reasoning which is more elementary. It is an empirical objection: that von Hayek failed to spot the growth of monitory democracy, with its scores of new *non-market* and *extra-constitutional* mechanisms designed to monitor and make publicly accountable exercises of power, not only in the field of domestic and cross-border government but also in the local, regional and global fields of markets and other civil society institutions.

20 A Green Paper for the Council of Europe, *The Future of Democracy in Europe. Trends, Analyses and Reforms* (Strasbourg, 2004).

21 George Eliot, *Felix Holt: The Radical* (Edinburgh and London, 1866), chapter 5, p. 127; Walt Whitman, 'Election Day, November 1884'.

22 Archon Fung and Erik Olin Wright, 'Thinking about Empowered Participatory Governance', in Archon Fung and Erik Olin Wright, *Deepening Democracy. Institutional Innovations in Empowered Participatory Governance* (London and New York, 2003), p. 5.

23 For those who are interested: the proposed electoral system was a local variant of the Single Transferable Vote, or STV, a system whose origins are shrouded in controversy. At the time of the Citizens' Assembly, the STV method was being used in elections in the Republic of Ireland, Australia, Malta, local government elections in New Zealand, and Northern Ireland (except in the case of elections to the British House of Commons). The STV principle – known in Australia as the Hare-Clark Proportional Method, and in the United States as choice voting – was more complex than that of the existing first-past-the-post system. Designed to provide proportional representation, to minimise wasted votes and to ensure that votes are explicitly for candidates rather than party lists, the STV system relies on multi-seat constituencies (electoral districts) in which, put simply, each candidate can only be elected if she or he receives a certain minimum number of votes – a threshold or quota most commonly known as the Droop quota. (For those who are really interested: the quota is determined by the formula: total number of unspoiled votes ÷ (the number of seats + 1) +1. Under the STV system, voters rank the list of candidates in order of preference. They place a '1' beside their most preferred candidate, a '2' beside their second most preferred candidate, and so on. As soon as a candidate has votes above the quota they are declared elected. Their excess or 'surplus' votes are transferred to other candidates, according to the voters' allocated preferences. Meanwhile, the candidate with the fewest votes is eliminated, and her or his votes are transferred to the other candidates who remain in the count. The whole process is repeated until all seats have been filled. In the event that no candidate reaches the quota at the outset, candidates with the lowest number of votes are first eliminated, and their voters' preferences are transferred, until sufficient candidates reach the

quota. It is worth noting here that the STV method – like all other voting methods – is not without problems. In some circumstances, STV eliminates, at an early stage in the count, a candidate who might have gone on to be elected, had they not been eliminated earlier in the contest – an effect that violates the 'one vote, same value' rule (for which computerised counting systems using the so-called Meek's method can provide considerable relief, as happens in New Zealand). There is also the problem, sometimes called the 'donkey vote' problem, that when candidates are listed alphabetically there is some advantaging of candidates whose surnames begin with an early letter in the alphabet (one remedy for which is the variable ordering of candidates from one ballot paper to another, called the Robson rotation, named after Neil Robson, a Tasmanian parliamentarian who championed the method). There is, finally, the tricky question of how to fill vacancies caused by the death or removal of sitting members in a multi-member constituency. Vacancies can be filled by re-examining the ballot papers from the previous election – the so-called 'countback method' used in the Australian Capital Territory, Malta and elsewhere. Another option is to have an official or elected representatives of the same political party as the departed member appoint a new member to fill the vacancy, as happens in the Republic of Ireland, where vacancies at the local authority level are filled by the co-option of a candidate who is nominated by the departed councillor's party colleagues. Vacancies can be filled by holding a 'single-winner' by-election, or by the most straightforward method: that used in the European Parliament by the Republic of Ireland members, each of whom, upon election, is required to provide a replacement list of candidates in the event that she or he can no longer hold their seat. On the history of the single transferable vote, see Clarence Hoag and George Hallett, *Proportional Representation* (New York, 1926), especially chapter 9. The conventional view is that the first recorded defence of a system of proportional representation with a single transferable vote was provided by the London barrister Thomas Hare in an 1857 pamphlet entitled *The Machinery of Representation*. A second edition of the pamphlet appeared the same year, and during the next fifteen years Hare published successive editions of a more refined set of proposals entitled *The Election of Representatives*. In 1861, Hare's proposed system was lauded by John Stuart Mill as 'among the very greatest improvements yet made in the theory and practice of government'; see his *Considerations on Representative Government* (London, 1861), p. 142. While Mill's handsome puff bolstered the reputation of Thomas Hare, other minds and hands had long been at work on the same principle. The general idea of STV appears to have been dreamed up independently by several figures, including the French mathematician and logician Joseph Diaz Gergonne (1771–1859), whose essay 'Arithmétique politique. Sur les élections et le système représentatif', *Annales de Mathématiques*, vol. 10 (1820), pp. 281–8, provided an abstract sketch of a method of election that protected voters from the danger that their votes would be wasted: 'At the elections', wrote Gergonne, 'the voters would group themselves freely, according to their opinions, their interests, or their desires, and any citizen from a department who bore a mandate from two hundred voters would become a Deputy in the elective chamber' (p. 286). At about the same time, quite by coincidence, the invisible hand of electoral invention prompted an English schoolmaster from Kidderminster and Birmingham, Thomas Wright Hill (1763–1851), to experiment with a system of proportional representation, with a single transferable vote, in the local Society for Literary and Scientific Improvement; as we have seen, his son Rowland Hill, founder of the modern postal system and Secretary of the Colonization Commissioners for South Australia, subsequently made world history by introducing the same scheme (in 1840) into the Municipal Corporation of Adelaide. A third figure, a Danish professor of mathematics and later Finance Minister and Council President, Carl Christoffer Georg Andræ (1812–93), was unaware of the experiments associated with Gergonne and Rowland Hill. Yet Andræ was the prime mover in the introduction and use of an early form of restricted-franchise STV in the 1856 election of two-thirds of the members of the Rigsraad, or Supreme Legislative Council, of the federated realm of Denmark, including Schleswig and Holstein; see the account of his contribution to STV, written by his son Poul Georg Andræ, *Andræ og hans Opfindelse Forholdstals Valgmaaden* (Copenhagen, 1905), translated into English as *Andræ and His Invention: The Proportional Representation Method* (Copenhagen and Philadelphia, 1926).

24　An example can here be drawn from the United States, where electronic voting systems, pioneered by companies such as Election Systems and Software, were first used more extensively than in any other monitory democracy. During the November 2006 mid-term elections, Florida's 13th Congressional District ballot results showed that nearly 15 per cent of those who cast ballots using touch-screen voting machines – 18,000 voters altogether – supposedly failed to vote for either candidate in a hotly contested congressional race. That figure compared with undervote rates ranging from 2.2 to 5.3 per cent in neighbouring counties. More than a few of the unlucky 13th Congressional District voters complained to reporters that they could not even find the congressional race on their screens. Possibly this was caused by poor ballot design, although many interviewees insisted that they had looked hard for on-screen election details. Some 60 per cent of those interviewed reported that after casting their vote they had tried to confirm that their choice had been registered, but in vain; their vote simply did not appear on the ballot summary page they were shown at the end of the voting process. Evidence from other districts showed that if there were indeed bugs in the software then these disproportionately worked against the Democratic challenger, Christine Jennings, and instead favoured the Republican candidate, Vern Buchanan, who won by a mere 369 votes. The fact that Buchanan won a recount – a recount of the votes the machines happened to have recorded – meant little or nothing to the disappointed losers. It served only to deepen their disappointment.

25　Ernest Bevin, *Parliamentary Debates (Hansard)*. *House of Commons Debates* (London, 1946), vol. 427, 22 October 1946.

26　See documents 1–3 in Martin Martiny and Hans-Jürgen Schneider (eds), *Deutsche Energiepolitik seit 1945. Vorrang für die Kohle. Dokumente und Materialen zur Energiepolitik der Industriegewerkschaft Bergbau und Energie* (Cologne, 1981), pp. 21–36.

27　The strength of the belief of representative democrats in the efficacy of top-down government regulation was underscored by the first American ambassador to Argentina, Frederic Jesup Stimson, *The Western Way. The Accomplishment and Future of Modern Democracy* (New York and London, 1929), pp. 86–7: 'The portentous increase of such governmental agencies, all of which, in their ultimate analysis, depend on the will or prejudice of an individual official uncontrolled by precedent other than his own, may be vividly shown by enumerating the number and the purposes of such boards, commissions, commissioners, or censors created throughout the United States in the last few years. In one year (1907) they numbered 262; their functions in that year included the execution, regulation, or control of railroads, steamship companies, all common carriers, transportation companies, terminal companies; telephone and telegraph, gas, water, heating, lighting, power companies, or public service generally; city building and health and poor commissions; education and the public schools; jails, asylums, and almshouses; fish and game; immigration (into a State); corporations in general; all special kinds of plumbers; blacksmiths; building and loan associations; hotels; sweatshops; epileptic colonies; horseracing.'

28　James Madison, *The Federalist Papers*, no. 51.

29　*Newsweek* (12 June 1961) and Evan Thomas, 'Bluster Before the Fall', *Newsweek* (15 September 2003).

30　Robert Putnam and Nicholas Bayne, *Hanging Together. Co-operation and Conflict in the Seven-Power Summits* (London, 1987), p. 29.

31　Rosa Parks and James Haskins, *Rosa Parks: My Story* (London, 1992); see also 'Parks Recalls Bus Boycott. Excerpts from an interview with Lynn Neary', http://www.npr.org/templates/story/story.php?storyId=4973548 (National Public Radio, 1992).

32　President Roosevelt, Address to the White House Correspondents' Association, Washington (15 March 1941).

33　The early years after World War Two witnessed many new lines of thinking about the future of democracy within a global context. See, for instance, Thomas Mann, *Goethe and Democracy* (Washington, DC, 1949); Jacques Maritain, 'Christianity and Democracy', a typewritten manuscript prepared as an address at the annual meeting of the American Political Science Association (New York, 29 December 1949); Harold Laski et al., *The Future of Democracy* (London, 1946); Albert Camus, *Neither Victims nor Executioners* (Chicago, 1972 [first published in the autumn 1946 issues of *Combat*]); Reinhold Niebuhr, *The Children of Light and the Children of Darkness. A Vindication of Democracy and a Critique of its Traditional Defenders* (London, 1945); Pope Pius XII, *Democracy and Peace* (London, 1945); Sidney Hook, 'What Exactly Do We Mean By "Democracy"?', *New York Times*, 16 March 1947, pp. 10ff; and A. D. Lindsay, *Democracy in the World Today* (London, 1945), which mentions the claim (first made by E. H. Carr) that it was Stalin of all people who placed 'democracy' in the forefront of Allied war aims by describing (in a radio broadcast of 3 July 1941) the Soviet war against Hitler as 'merged with the struggle of the peoples of Europe and America for independence and democratic liberties'. Carr's claim is misleading, if only because President Roosevelt's widely publicised address to the White House Correspondents' Association (15 March 1941) happened earlier.

34　Niebuhr, *The Children of Light and the Children of Darkness. A*

Vindication of Democracy and a Critique of its Traditional Defenders, p. vi.

35 Charles Malik, 'What Are Human Rights?', *The Rotarian* (August 1948); and the speech 'Required: National Moral Leadership [26 February 1948], reprinted in Habib C. Malik (ed.), *The Challenge of Human Rights. Charles Malik and the Universal Declaration* (London, 2000), pp. 87–95.

36 Interview with Mustafa Ercan, director of Mazlumder (Istanbul, 24 September 2005).

37 John Perry Barlow, 'A Declaration of the Independence of Cyberspace', Electronic Frontier Foundation, 8 February 1996, http://www.eff.org/~barlow/Declaration-Final.html

38 Harry G. Frankfurt, *On Bullshit* (Princeton and Oxford, 2005).

MEMORIES FROM THE FUTURE

1 From a lecture delivered by Sheikh Rashid al-Ghannouchi, exiled leader of the Tunisian An-Nahda Party, Centre for the Study of Democracy (London), 3 November 2006.

2 To link our imaginary muse with Mnemosyne, as a story-telling device, as a method of looking imaginatively at the deep-seated trends of the present 'from the outside', by anticipating their probable long-term effects, is to recall the strong relationship that existed between memory and assembly democracy. The personification of memory, Mnemosyne was described (for instance, in Hesiod's history of the origins of earth and the gods in *Theogony*, verses 131–6) as a Titaness, as the daughter of Gaia and Uranus. Zeus slept with her for nine consecutive nights, and she later gave birth to the Nine Muses. Pausanias and others recalled that there was a spring or stream dedicated to her at the Oracle of Trophonius at Lebadea, in Boeotia, on the north shore of the Gulf of Corinth (Pausanias, *Guide to Greece*, 9.39.3: 'After this you are escorted by the priests, not to the oracle [of Trophonius] straight away, but to two streams which flow very close to each other. First you have to drink the water of Lethe, so you will forget all your current preoccupations. Then you drink the water of Mnemosyne, which makes you remember what you see after you go down.'). References to Mnemosyne persisted well into the era of *dēmokratia*. Funerary inscriptions on gold leaves found in graves from Thurii, Hipponium, Thessaly and Crete, dating from the fourth century BCE, show that the dead were provided with instructions, when they arrived in Hades, to avoid drinking from the stream of Lethe, lest they forget their pasts; and that instead they should slake their thirst from the fountain and stream of Mnemosyne, from whom their memories would be preserved.

3 Italo Calvino, 'The Watcher [1963]', in *The Watcher and Other Stories* (New York, 1971), pp. 1–74. In the course of the day at the polling station set up inside the vast 'Cottolengo Hospital for Incurables', the poll watcher, a communist named Amerigo Ormea, observes with remarkable dispassion the nuns and priests herding their victims into the polling booths. The situation is grotesque, yet Amerigo notes the matter-of-factness of the voting, for 'in Italy, which had always bowed and scraped before every form of pomp, display, sumptuousness, ornament, this seemed to him finally the lesson of an honest, austere morality, and a perpetual, silent revenge on the

Fascists . . .; now they had fallen into dust with all their gold fringe and their ribbons, while democracy, with its stark ceremony of pieces of paper folded over like telegrams, of pencils given to callused or shaky hands, went ahead.'

4 Thomas Carlyle, *Latter-Day Pamphlets* (1850), in *The Works of Thomas Carlyle* (London, 1899), vol. 10, 5; Oscar Wilde, 'The Soul of Man Under Socialism', *The Fortnightly Review*, 290 (February 1891), pp. 292–319.

5 Richard S. Katz and Peter Mair et al., 'The Membership of Political Parties in European Democracies, 1960–1990', *European Journal of Political Research*, 22 (1992), pp. 329–45; and Peter Mair and Ingrid van Biezen, 'Party Membership in Twenty European Democracies, 1980–2000', *Party Politics*, 7, 1 (2001), pp. 5–21.

6 Peter Ronald deSouza et al. (eds), *State of Democracy in South Asia. A Report* (New Delhi, 2008), pp. 92, 253, 266–7; and Murray Goot, 'Distrustful, Disenchanted and Disengaged?', in David Burchell and Andrew Leigh (eds), *The Prince's New Clothes: Why Do Australians Dislike Their Politicians?* (Sydney, 2002), p. 13.

7 Max Weber, *Badische Landeszeitung* (16 December 1897), p. 1, cited in Wolfgang J. Mommsen, *Max Weber and German Politics 1890–1920* (Chicago and London, 1984), p. 77.

8 Van Vollenhoven showed how the historical development of modern forms of supranational law had deep roots in the medieval world; how, after about 1500, the break-up of the medieval Christian world and the rise of territorial states priding themselves on unrestrained sovereignty fostered talk of the laws of war (*ius belli*); and how, after three centuries, the rebirth of what Jeremy Bentham first called 'international law' led initially to talk of a *ius belli ac pacis* (the right of any 'sovereign' state to decide whether it should be at war or peace), then to talk of a *ius pacis ac belli* (the right of a state to live in peace with other states, using war sparingly, for that purpose). Van Vollenhoven was adamant that a new era of peace – an age of *ius pacis* – was thinkable, but he was equally clear that it would be possible only if a global police force could be invented and deployed. He favoured keeping separate the right of military intervention from legal judgements and punishments of the crimes of the violent. What were peoples of the world to do in the event of an eruption of fighting? No need for a long dispute to find out who was right, or who was ready to come to the assistance of those who needed protection, he thought. That should come at a later stage, van Vollenhoven recommended. The first priority was for the police to issue a warning: stop fighting. If this order was not obeyed, the police force must intervene, to separate the opponents, to put an end to the fighting. Then would come the trial and punishment of the guilty, the attempted righting of wrongs, the provision of compensation of suffered losses.

9 From a press conference featuring Donald Rumsfeld, United States Defense Secretary, CNN (7 October 2001).

10 The following quotations are from Dobrica Ćosić, *Srpsko pitanje – demokratsko pitanje* (Belgrade, 1992), p. 129; *Piščevi zapisi (1981–91)* (Belgrade, 2002), pp. 393, 402; and *Piščevi zapisi (1992–3)* (Belgrade, 2004), pp. 24–5, 56, 135–6.

11 George Orwell, 'You and the Atom bomb', *Tribune*, 19 October 1945,

reprinted in *Selections from Essays and Journalism: 1931–1949* (London 1981), p. 715.

12 President Bill Clinton, 27 September 1993, cited in Tony Smith, *America's Mission. The United States and the Worldwide Struggle for Democracy in the Twentieth Century* (Princeton, NJ, 1994), p. 311. The same point was repeated in President Clinton's 1994 State of the Union address: 'Ultimately, the best strategy to ensure our security and to build a durable peace is to support the advance of democracy elsewhere. Democracies don't attack each other, they make better trading partners and partners in diplomacy' (www.pub.whitehouse.gov/urires/12R?urn:pdi://oma.eop.gov.us/1994/1/26/1.text.1)

13 Dan Reiter and Allan C. Stam, *Democracies at War* (Princeton, NJ, and Oxford, 2002), p. 2.

14 From an interview with Henry A. Kissinger, CNN International, 26 November 2006.

15 Mark Peceny, *Democracy at the Point of Bayonets* (University Park, Penn., 1999); John A. Tures, 'Operation Exporting Freedom: The Quest for Democratization via United States Military Operations', *Whitehead Journal of Diplomacy and International Relations*, 6 (2005), pp. 97–111.

16 During the 1920 presidential election campaign that produced a landslide victory for the Republicans, the winning candidate, Warren Harding, used the phrase 'at the point of bayonets' to attack Woodrow Wilson's unpopular Haitian policies. The Democrats' vice-presidential candidate, Franklin Delano Roosevelt, had boasted during the campaign that while serving as Assistant Secretary of the Navy he had written the new constitution of Haiti. Harding scoffed that 'he would not empower an Assistant Secretary of the Navy to draft a Constitution for helpless neighbours in the West Indies and jam it down their throats at the point of bayonets borne by U.S. Marines' (cited in H. Schmidt, *The United States' Occupation of Haiti, 1915–1934* (New Brunswick, NJ, 1971), p. 118). It should be remembered that Harding's calculated remark resonated with the deep prejudice of white American policy makers that black Haitians were genetically incapable of self-government. 'Dearie me, think of it. Niggers speaking French' was the remark of William Jennings Bryan after receiving a one-hour briefing on Haitian culture at the start of American military intervention in Haiti in 1915 (cited in Schmidt, op. cit.). Bryan was the three-times Democratic Party presidential candidate whose nickname was 'The Great Commoner' because of his stated faith in the goodness of the common people.

17 Amnesty International, *United States of America: Guantánamo and beyond: The continuing pursuit of unchecked executive power*, 13 May 2005, AI Index: AMR 51/063/205, pp. 83–109. Human Rights Watch, *United States: Ghost Prisoner. Two Years in Secret CIA Detention*, vol. 19, no. 1(G), February 2007, pp. 37–42.

18 President George W. Bush, at a press conference given at the White House, 13 April 2004.

19 From the 414 BCE play by Aristophanes, *The Birds*, verses 1570–71; and Joseph de Maistre, 'On the Nature of Sovereignty', in Richard Lebrun (ed.), *Against Rousseau* (Montreal, 1996), p. 152.

20 'Sweet Neo Con', from the Rolling Stones' album *A Bigger Bang* (2005), was recorded May–June 2005.

21 From Ellen Knickmeyer and Naseer Mehdawi, 'In Syria, Iraq's Fate Silences Rights Activists', *Washington Post*, 26 October 2006, A 18.

22 José Luis Velasco, 'Democratización y Conflictos Distributivos en América Latina', in Waldo Ansaldi (ed.), *La Democracia en América Latina, un barco a la deriva* (Buenos Aires, 2007), pp. 131–54; and Leonardo Curzio, 'La Transición a la Democracia y la Construcción de Ciudadanía en México', in ibid., pp. 313–31.

23 From the speech by Prime Minister Ariel Sharon, Jerusalem (28 January 2002); and the remarks by President George W. Bush to the 20th Anniversary of the National Endowment for Democracy, Washington, DC (6 November 2003).

24 Quotations are from 'An Open Mind for Win-Win Cooperation', speech by H. E. Hu Jintao, President of the People's Republic of China, at the APEC CEO Summit (Busan, South Korea), 17 November 2005; and the reported speech by President Hu Jintao at the APEC CEO (Hanoi, North Vietnam), 17 November 2006, in Sun Shangwu, 'Hu: China to pursue peace, prosperity', posted at www.chinadaily.com.cn/china

25 State Council Information Office, *Building of Political Democracy in China* (Beijing, 19 October 2005). Earlier quotations and references are drawn from Liang Qichao, 'Xin zhongguo weilai ji [An Account of the Future of New China]', in his *Yinbingshi zhuanji [Monographs from the Ice-Drinker's Studio]* (Shanghai, 1902); the weekly Canton lectures delivered by Sun Yat-sen during the first months of 1924 were published as *San Min Chu I. The Three Principles of the People* (Shanghai, 1927), pp. 149–360; and Mao Tse-tung, *On New Democracy* (January 1940) (Peking, 1966).

26 On 5 November 2006, the Beijing Summit of Forum on China–Africa Cooperation adopted a declaration read out in the Great Hall of the People by Chinese President Hu Jintao, Ethiopian Prime Minister Meles Zenawi and Egyptian President Mohammed Hosni Mubarak. 'We hold that the establishment of a new type of strategic partnership is both the shared desire and independent choice of China and Africa, serves our common interests, and will help enhance solidarity, mutual support and assistance and unity of the developing countries and contribute to durable peace and harmonious development in the world', the declaration said. To promote this 'new type of strategic partnership', the leaders pledged to use a variety of measures, including high-level visits, two-way trade and investment cooperation, and public health and personnel training and cultural exchanges. The leaders called on 'the international community' to honour its commitments to debt relief and the opening of markets, and promised to 'properly handle issues and challenges that may arise in the course of cooperation through friendly consultation in keeping with China–Africa friendship and the long-term interests of the two sides'. At the two-day Summit, the African leaders reiterated their countries' firm commitment to 'the one-China policy' and 'China's peaceful reunification'.

WHY DEMOCRACY?

1 'Afghans take first awkward steps towards democracy', *Financial Times* (London), 9/10 October 2004.

2 Amartya Sen, 'Democracy as a Universal Value', *Journal of Democracy*, 10, 3 (1999), pp. 3–17.

3 George F. Kennan, *The Cloud of Danger* (Boston and Toronto, 1977), pp. 41–2, 45.

4 An exchange along these lines is reported by the English journalist Jonathan Dimbleby, '. . . and we don't care', *Sunday Times* (London), 27 April 2008, p. 3.

5 From an interview with Mathias Greffrath and others, 'Den Planeten verwestlichen!', *Süddeutsche Zeitung* (München), 20 November 2001 (translation mine); my interview with Richard Rorty (Paris, 10 May 2002); and Richard Rorty, 'The priority of democracy to philosophy', *Objectivity, relativism, and truth. Philosophical Papers*, vol. 1 (Cambridge and New York, 1991), p. 193.

6 Cited in *Daily Star* (Beirut), 3 February 2003.

7 Thucydides, *History of the Peloponnesian War*, Book 2, 64.3; compare the remarks of Kurt A. Raaflaub, 'Democracy, Power, Imperialism', in J. Peter Euben et al. (eds), *Athenian Political Thought and the Reconstruction of American Democracy* (Ithaca, NY, and London, 1994), pp. 103–46.

8 Josiah Ober, 'Learning from Athens', *Boston Review*, March/April 2006; and *Democracy and Knowledge: Innovation and Learning in Classical Athens* (Princeton, NJ, 2008).

9 James Mill, 'Government', *Encyclopaedia Britannica* (Edinburgh, 1820), reprinted as *An Essay on Government* (Cambridge, 1937).

10 Giuseppe Mazzini, *Thoughts Upon Democracy in Europe*, first published in the *People's Journal* (1847) and reprinted in *Joseph Mazzini. A Memoir by E.A.V. with Two Essays by Mazzini* (London, 1887), pp. 171–257.

11 Theodore Parker, 'The American Idea', in *Additional Speeches, Addresses, and Occasional Sermons* (Boston, 1855), vol. I, p. 33; and 'The Nebraska Question', in ibid., vol. I, p. 327.

12 Nahum Capen, *The History of Democracy: or, Political Progress, Historically Illustrated, From the Earliest to the Latest Periods* (Hartford, Conn., 1874), p. v.

13 From 'Christianity and Democracy', a typewritten manuscript prepared as an address at the annual meeting of the American Political Science Association in New York on 29 December 1949, and again at Gettysburg College on 19 February 1950, for the Adams County Round Table of the National Conference of Christians and Jews. The manuscript is preserved in the University of Notre Dame Archives, Notre Dame, Indiana, Jacques Maritain Papers, 6/04 F. The following quotations are drawn from pp. 2–5.

14 Njabulo Ndebele, *The Cry of Winnie Mandela* (Claremont, 2004), pp. 82, 84.

15 The vital importance of the imagined space between the mundane and transmundane worlds was emphasised in conversation and subsequent correspondence (in June 2006) with the Iranian clerical scholar, Mohsen Kadivar (b. 1959). 'From the point of view of Islam', he told me in Tehran, 'human beings are endowed with magnanimity [the word he used was *keramat*]. They are the carriers of the spirit of God . . . and are therefore entitled to act as God's viceroy or Caliph on earth.' In the eyes of God, he continued, human beings are both trustworthy and saddled with the God-given duty to decide on earth how to live, and to live well. Core religious precepts play (for believers) an important role in fulfilling this duty, said Kadivar, but

these precepts come in two types: they are immutable or variable. The unity of God, the prophecies of Muhammed and the certainty of the Hereafter are unquestionable gifts to humanity. But God has left for human beings great scope for the exercise of human judgement: it is not only that the interpretation (*ijtihad*) of scriptural texts and traditions is contingent, subject to freshly decided edicts by human beings themselves. The religious texts are either silent about worldly affairs, or they just don't apply to a wide variety of matters, such as operating an air traffic control system, or deciding how best to secure the welfare of children within marriages that fall apart. Hence the inescapability of *politics*: the collective definition and handling by human beings of their collective affairs. Kadivar went on to say that theocracy is not a type of government, and that Muslims are therefore faced with a choice among three different types of politics – democracy, autocracy and aristocracy. Only democracy can satisfy the formal requirements of Islam. Kadivar said he once called this type of government peculiarly suited to Muslim societies a 'religious democracy'. He now preferred to speak of a 'democracy in Islamic society or democracy for Muslims'. He had in mind democratic institutions – civil society organisations, free and fair elections, the rotation of office holders, equal respect for Muslims and non-Muslims, public supervision of governmental power – that are infused with the religious conscience of citizens who regard their polity as legitimate because it is ultimately authorised by God. Since God had entrusted *all* people with the responsibility of living well on earth, and since living well depends upon the learned capacity to contribute as equals to the common ordering of collective affairs, democracy – not the system of appointive, absolute guardianship known as *velayat-e faqih* – is a requirement of serving God and living in dignity as a Muslim in today's world.

16 This section draws upon John Keane, 'Humble Democracy: New Thinking about an Aging Ideal', *Think India Quarterly*, vol. 10, 2 (April–June 2007), pp. 1–34 (originally delivered as the B. N. Ganguli Memorial Lecture, CSDS, Delhi, 25 February 2005).

17 Benedetto Croce, 'Liberalism and Democracy', in *My Philosophy and Other Essays on the Moral and Political Problems of Our Time* (London, 1951), p. 94.

18 Montesquieu, *De l'esprit des lois*, book 11, chapter 6 and book 19, chapter 27.

19 Cited in Kathleen Freeman, *The Pre-Socratic Philosophers* (Oxford, 1949), p. 399.

20 Walt Whitman, 'Democratic Vistas', in *Complete Prose Works* (Philadelphia, 1892), paragraph 55.

21 From an interview with Gough Whitlam, 'Good life's work for Labor titan', *Weekend Australian* (Sydney), 8–9 July 2006, p. 26.

22 Alexis de Tocqueville, *Democracy in America*, edited by J. P. Mayer (New York, 1969), volume 1, p. 12.

23 C. S. Lewis, 'Equality [1943]', in Walter Hooper (ed.), *Present Concerns: Essays by C. S. Lewis* (New York, 1986), p. 17, paragraph 1.

24 From my interview with Martin Lee QC, Legislative Council Building, Hong Kong, 25 May 2005.

25 E. M. Forster, 'What I believe [1936]', in *Two Cheers for Democracy* (London, 1951).

PHOTO AND ILLUSTRATION CREDITS

Figure 49: Keystone-Mast Collection, UCR/California Museum of Photography, University of California, Riverside
Figure 50: The Oregon Historical Society, Portland
Figure 51: Wisconsin Historical Society (WHi-5586)
Figure 56: Biblioteca Nacional, Madrid
Figure 70: Staatliche Graphische Sammlung, Munich
Figure 77: The National Archives, Richmond
Figure 79: Library and Archives Canada
Figure 80: Dixson Library, State Library of NSW
Figure 82: Old Bell Museum, Montgomery, Powys
Figure 83: Australian Centre for Ancient Numismatic Studies, Macquarie University (W.L.Gale Collection), Sydney
Figure 84: Print Collection, Miriam and Ira D. Wallach Division of Art, Prints and Photographs, The New York Public Library, Astor, Lenox and Tilden Foundations
Figures 85 and 88: Mitchell Library, State Library of NSW
Figure 89: John Murray Publishers, London
Figure 92: Pictures Collection, State Library of Victoria
Figure 94: Städtischen Galerie im Lenbachhaus und Kunstbau, Munich
Figure 95: Popperfoto/ Getty Images
Figures 97 and 98: Henri Cartier-Bresson/ Magnum Photos
Figures 102, 103, 105, 108, 109, 114, 118, 123, 134, divider 3: Associated Press
Figures 106 and 131: AFP/ Getty Images
Figure 111: Mark Chilvers/ The Independent, London
Figure 112: Freedom House
Figure 113: Fairfax Photos
Figure 117: Action on Disability and Development, Somerset
Figure 119: B. Davidson/ Magnum Photos
Figure 120: UN Photos Library
Figure 121: Getty Images
Figure 122: CAIDA/ Science Photo Library
Figure 124: Zita Sodeika
Figure 125: L'Unità
Figure 130: Global Instant Objects
Figure 133: IISH Stefan R. Landsberger Collection, http://www.iisg.nl/landsberger
Divider 4: Professor Wu Hung

INDEX